The Routledge Reader in Christian–Muslim Relations

The theological interest in Christian–Muslim dialogue has grown considerably in recent years. How Isla[illegible] d Christianity have approached each other through doctrinal debate is one of the mos[illegible] rbing ways of understanding the challenge of interreligious relations or Christian–M[illegible] olemics. This volume provides an indispensable reading and reference tool, showin[illegible] uslim and Christian scholars have shaped the discourse on the varying interfaces b[illegible] ristianity and Islam. The Reader contains a substantial introduction and prese[illegible] of scholarly approaches to Christian–Muslim relations. Included are selections [illegible] polemical material, focusing on critical and appreciative approaches to the Je[illegible] d, Bible/Qur'an and God question for Muslims and Christians.

Mona [illegible] is Professor of Islamic and Interreligious Studies at the University of Edinbu[illegible]

The Routledge Reader in Christian–Muslim Relations

Edited by
Mona Siddiqui

Routledge
Taylor & Francis Group
LONDON AND NEW YORK

For Ashar and Bina

First published in 2013
by Routledge
2 Park Square, Milton Park, Abingdon, Oxon OX14 4RN

Simultaneously published in the USA and Canada
by Routledge
711 Third Avenue, New York, NY 10017

Routledge is an imprint of the Taylor & Francis Group, an informa business

British Library Cataloguing in Publication Data
A catalogue record for this book is available from the British Library

Library of Congress Cataloging in Publication Data
A catalog record for this book has been requested

ISBN: 978-0-415-68554-2 (hbk)
ISBN: 978-0-415-68556-6 (pbk)

Typeset in Baskerville
by Taylor & Francis Books

MIX
Paper from responsible sources
FSC www.fsc.org FSC® C004839

Printed and bound by CPI Group (UK) Ltd, Croydon, CR0 4YY

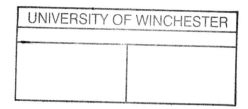

Contents

Acknowledgements

Every effort has been made to trace copyright holders and obtain permission to reproduce material. Any errors or omissions brought to the attention of the publisher will be remedied in future editions.

1. in Roggema, Poorthuis and Valkenberg (eds), *The Three Rings: Textual Studies in the Historical Trialogue of Judaism, Christianity and Islam*. Leuven: Peeters, 2005, pp. 71–90.
2. © *Jerusalem Studies in Arabic and Islam*, 20 (1996), pp. 200–29.
3. in Beaumont, *Christology in Dialogue with Muslims: A Critical Analysis of Christian Presentations of Christ for Muslims from the Ninth and Twentieth Centuries*. Oxford: Regnum, 2005, pp. 93–112.
4. in Thomas, *Early Muslim Polemic against Christianity: Abū ʿĪsā al-Warrāq's 'Against the Incarnation'*. Cambridge: Cambridge University Press, 2002, pp. 87–97.
5. in Grypeou, Swanson and Thomas (eds), *The Encounter of Eastern Christianity with Early Islam*. Leiden: Brill, 2006, pp. 237–56.
6. in Al-Tabari, *The Book of Religion and Empire*, trans. A. Minghana. Manchester: Manchester University Press, 1922, pp. 140–61.
7. in Roggema, Poorthuis and Valkenberg (eds), *The Three Rings: Textual Studies in the Historical Trialogue of Judaism, Christianity and Islam*. Leuven: Peeters, 2005, pp. 183–201.
8. © *The Muslim World*, 66(2) (April 1976), pp. 81–95.
9. © *The Muslim World*, 55(3) (July 1965), pp. 195–202.
10. in Francisco, *Martin Luther and Islam: A Study in Sixteenth-Century Polemics and Apologetics*. Leiden: Brill, 2007, pp. 97–128.
11. in Zwemer, *The Disintegration of Islam*. New York: Fleming H. Revell, 1916, pp. 7–10, 49–59, 181–90.
12. in Kraemer, *The Christian Message in a Non-Christian World*. Grand Rapids: Kregel, 1956, pp. 215–26, 353–65.
13. © *The Muslim World*, 70(2) (April 1980), pp. 91–121.
14. © *Journal of Ecumenical Studies*, 5(1) (1968), pp. 45–77.
15. in Nettler and Taji-Farouki (eds), *Muslim–Jewish Encounters: Intellectual Traditions and Modern Politics*. Abingdon: Taylor & Francis, 1998, pp. 171–99.
16. © *The Muslim World*, 77(2) (1987), pp. 80–95.
17. © *International Journal of Middle-Eastern Studies*, 23 (1991), pp. 291–315.
18. in Haddad and Haddad (eds), *Christian–Muslim Encounters*. Gainesville: University Press of Florida, 1995, pp. 143–57.
19. in Khalidi, *The Muslim Jesus: Sayings and Stories in Islamic Literature*. Cambridge, MA: Harvard University Press, 2001, pp. 110–21.

20. in McAuliffe, *Qur'ānic Christians: An Analysis of Classical and Modern Exegesis*. Cambridge: Cambridge University Press, 1991, pp. 204–39.
21. © *Cultural Anthropology*, 6(2) (1991), pp. 131–46.
22. © *Review of Religious Research*, 47(2) (2005), pp. 162–74.
23. © *Islam and Christian–Muslim Relations*, 21(4) (October 2010), pp. 357–72.

Introduction

Mona Siddiqui

There is no one dominant account of the Christian–Muslim encounter nor is there one authoritative voice. Both these religions are lived religions with complex histories of conflict and coexistence which have influenced mutual perceptions and understandings over the centuries. Furthermore, cultural differences aside, Christianity and Islam are religions which experienced internal schisms brought about by theological and political conflicts. In Christianity this became manifest mainly through Eastern Orthodox, Roman Catholic and Protestant traditions, and in Islam, principally through the Sunnī and Shīʿi sectarian divide although many other groups followed. Outside institutional structures, some claim that mystical dimensions retained a distinct approach to the search for God, and in Islam, Sūfism coloured both groups with its spiritual perspectives on this world as a reflection of a hidden God.

As the youngest of the three monotheistic faiths, Islam from its beginnings developed in both confrontation and conversation with Christians. While it would be difficult to emphasise any one political or theological type of encounter which is dominant between the two faiths and their diverse civilisations, certain themes have continued to recur as prevailing points of debate and polemic over the centuries. Theological discussions cannot be taken out of their political and sociological contexts but such encounters do have an inner life inspired and shaped by the questions posed *by* the faithful *to* the faithful. Christians and Muslims have approached each other throughout history in multiple ways, often without meeting one another but in written responses to the polemics against their faith. In more recent times, the focus on commonalities between the monotheistic religions not just in face to face conversations but in the attempts to reconcile common themes and aspirations needed, for 'living together', have somewhat shifted the focus from the doctrinal to the sociological. Whereas once the issues of the Trinity, Incarnation, scripture and prophecy challenged the scholars to write sophisticated doctrinal defences, apologies or accusations, today there has been a concerted movement on the part of many, though not all, away from doctrine to devotion. By this I mean that the relatively modern notion that Judaism, Christianity and Islam belong to the Abrahamic family has resulted in a stress on the values and principles which unite the faithful as opposed to those beliefs which divide. Such ventures are usually defined as approaches to 'dialogue', but dialogue itself is a contested term. While there can be huge differences in popular and more irenic approaches as opposed to more critical and scholarly methodologies, for many an interest in another's faith is more an interest in the history of ideas, in theological reflection and in more nuanced understandings of how the faithful have defended their understanding of God, meanings of revelation and human destiny.

The purpose of this book is to provide the reader with a glimpse into different kinds of conversations and writings between Christians and Muslims and about Christianity and

Islam from the earliest encounters to the present day. While it is impossible to bring together all the influential reflections in just one reader, the present reader is weighted more towards theological writings on both sides; it is theology rather than history or politics which is the main focus. In other words I have focused more on text than context although, in this introduction, I have given very brief background comments on each article. Like any selection, there is a certain inevitable subjectivity but the material in this area is vast and the primary aim here is to give the reader a variety of perspectives and contexts. This range covers Qur'anic and biblical themes as well as the depiction of religious figures in poetry and folklore. The sheer volume of theological reflection from the eighth to ninth centuries onwards however cannot be exhausted and the reader may find that key names and discourses ideas are absent from this volume. Furthermore, owing to limited space and copyright issues, certain articles could not be included. Nevertheless, the collection gives a taste of the historical richness of conversations, polemics and encounters between the world's two largest faiths. So that the reader acquires a more comprehensive view of how the debates have shifted in more recent times, there is also material of a more dialogical nature where scholars reflect on current themes and tensions.

The book contains published articles and select chapters about notable contributors and their writings and also extracts from primary sources. Although no one person speaks for either faith, it would be true to say that at least in Christianity, figures such as Martin Luther and Thomas Aquinas are regarded as authoritative. I would argue that there is no such equivalent from the Islamic side although Islam seems to be represented by a wide range of political, poetical as well as theological voices.

This combination of authorities will help the reader acquire a deeper understanding of the language and mode of discussion and debate between Christians and Muslims. Many of the names and critical concepts will be familiar to scholars interested in the field of Christian–Muslim relations but the volume also includes articles which are not too easily accessible and a few which are quite dense in their inquiry. The overriding aim of this collection is to provide an insight into what the scholars/theologians actually said rather than what is said about them. Furthermore, the book brings together writings from Eastern as well as Western Christianity to reflect the wider response to Islam. Eastern Christianity and its engagement with Islam is often overlooked in current scholarly dialogical settings partly because many people are unaware of its profound contribution. In the concluding remarks to his book, *The Church in the Shadow of the Mosque*, Sidney Griffith laments that 'Western Christian thinkers engaged in interreligious dialogue with Muslims in the modern world, and those who in recent times have been concerned with comparative theology in the study of Christianity and Islam, have seldom if ever taken useful cognizance of the intellectual history of the Christians who lived for centuries in the world of Islam and who wrote Christian philosophy and theology in Syriac and Arabic.'[1]

It is hoped that this collection of articles will act as a useful resource for students of Muslim and Christian theology and those interested in interreligious encounter and comparative religion. The material is arranged as chronologically as possible in terms of the lives of the individuals concerned, although secondary sources in the latter part of the book reflect on earlier historical writings. The articles have been chosen to reflect a variety of exchanges, acrimonious and irenic, exegetical and poetical, allowing some historical insight and acting as individual pieces each telling its own story. However, some prior knowledge of theological concepts in both religions will undoubtedly enhance the reader's appreciation of the ebb and flow of ideas and influences.

Finally a brief note on presentation of material and introduction. The material in this collection has been extracted from the original sources and not edited in any way. This means that all spellings and diacritics have been left unchanged in the texts from their original publication. I am grateful to all the authors and publishers who have allowed for the entries to be republished here.

* * *

> The rapid rise of Islam in the seventh and eighth centuries placed Christian thinkers in an unaccustomed position. From its earliest days Christianity had defined itself against classical paganism on the one hand and Judaism on the other, but the religion of Muhammad demanded a different response, for it proclaimed itself the very culmination of Christianity.[2]

In his work on Christian writers of the East and their theological engagement with Islam, John Moorhead writes that the earliest Christian discussion of Islam is that contained in the *History of Heraclius*, the classical Armenian text, attributed to the Armenian bishop Sebeos and probably completed in 661. The text reflects a mixed image of Islam. Sebeos may have called the leader of the Ishmaelites 'the great ally of Antichrist' but he also asserts that Muḥammad 'taught his people to know God and to turn to the living God'.[3] A common theme for many Christians of the time was an attempt to understand why Muḥammad had been able to draw people to him with his teachings on God. Pseudo Dionysius of Tell Mahre, a Monophysite author writing in about 775, explains why the Arabs called Muḥammad 'the prophet':

> He had turned them away from different cults, had taught them the existence of one God, the creator of the Universe and had given them laws when they had been given over to the cult of demons and the adoration of idols, especially trees. Because he taught them the unity of God, because they triumphed over the Romans under his guidance, and because he gave them laws according to their desires, they called him Prophet and Messenger of God.[4]

Politics and theology affected much of the Christian assessment of Islam. While there were irenic as well as hostile attitudes to Islam within the Christians of the East, much of the doctrinal debate wrestled with the positive aspect of Islam which was the affirmation of one God and its negative doctrine which denied the divinity of Christ. Many of the Christian writers of the East placed Islam in the broad context of a monotheistic belief but critiqued the religion for its misunderstanding or denial of Christ's salvific status. One of the first and most significant Christians of the East to address the Muslim faith and its particular doctrines relating to Christianity was John of Damascus, also known as John Damascene. As a major figure of the Eastern Church, John of Damascus (*c.* 675–749), a Christian priest and monk of the eighth century, left two important theological legacies. The first was his defence of iconography in religious worship in conjunction with other monastic circles during the iconoclastic controversies.

The second of his theological legacies was the masterpiece which he wrote in the later years of his life known as *The Fount of Knowledge* or *Pēgē Gnoseōs*. Although John of Damascus or Mansūr ibn Sarjūn, as he was known in the Arabic-speaking world of Islam, lived all his life amongst Muslims, his surviving works are in Greek, 'the theological and liturgical language of the burgeoning Melkite Christian community, whose chief spokesman he was to become'.[5] Greek had remained the official language of the Umayyad administration in Syria although Syriac and Arabic were widely spoken. *The Fount of Knowledge* was divided into three parts and compiled with the purpose of providing a compendium of the 'teachings of the fathers' of Christian orthodoxy on the articles of Christian faith. He states in *The Fount of Knowledge* that his aim was not to say anything new but to display what the 'saintly and wise men have taught at different times'.[6] The three parts consist of a philosophical introduction (*Dialectics*), a refutation of heresies (*Concerning Heresies*) and a scholastic survey of faith (*Exposition of the Orthodox Faith*).

The Fount of Knowledge contains one section on 100 heresies, *De Haeresibus*. The relatively longer 101st heresy is the 'Heresy of the Ishmaelites'. While *De Haeresibus* is written principally for a Christian audience to contrast what is heretical from what is orthodox, this tractate is regarded by many as one of the first polemical Christian writings against Islam, discussing many of the themes which became the defining issues raised in later Christian–Muslim encounters. As Davids and Valkenberg show, in using a Christological criterion, John calls Islam a heresy because he does not distinguish between heresies and other religions since in his view 'they are equally to be judged as deviations from Christological truth.' However, John also introduces Islam as the prevailing 'superstition of the Ishmaelites' and the 'forerunner of the Antichrist'. Scholars disagree over whether John had detailed knowledge of Muslim sources and Arabic, but John was fully aware of the idolatrous character of much of pre-Islamic Arabia. Against this knowledge, he also recognised that Islam was a new and powerful threat to the region, albeit a proclaimed monotheistic threat. It was in this pre-Islamic idolatrous society of Mecca that Muḥammad had, according to John of Damascus, appeared as a false prophet.

By providing extracts in translation, the writers show that the biggest contention for John is the question of monotheism between Christians and Muslims. John was well aware that Muslims saw Christian monotheism in a very different light but he was not prepared to accept the Muslim accusation that Christians were themselves actually 'Associators' (*mushrikūn*) because they saw Christ as the 'Son of God'. In a fierce theological attack he accuses the Muslims of being 'Mutilators' by having disassociated God from His word and Spirit.

P.S. van Koningsveld shows how Paul was a contested and maligned figure among many Muslim scholars including the Andalusian Ibn Hazm (d. 1064). Drawing upon a recent discovery of a manuscript attributed to the early historian Sayf 'Umar al-Tamīmī (d. 797), van Koningsveld analyses the images of Paul by classical Muslim exegetes.[7] Paul is depicted in various ways including that of being a cunning Jew who faked his conversion. For Tamīmī, Paul did not just destroy the religious law but he was also responsible for attributing divinity to Christ, thus corrupting the essential teachings of Christianity. The article also looks at the image of Paul in the pseudepigraphical *Gospel of Barnabas*, the origins of which form part of the author's concluding remarks. Barnabas is taken as the chief opponent to Paul and his teaching of a Hellenistic Christianity.[8]

The ninth century has been indentified by scholars as the most creative period of Christian–Muslim dialogue. Mark Beaumont's chapter on 'The Christologies of Abū Qurra, Abū Rā'ita and 'Ammār al-Baṣrī and Muslim Response' is taken from his book, *Christology in Dialogue with Muslims*. Beaumont presents a detailed examination of how three different theologians representing three different views, Melkite, Jacobite and Nestorian, explained to their Muslim contemporaries how it was possible for God and man to be united in the person of Jesus Christ. There were of course differences of views between the three in how to explain human and divine natures. But Beaumont also considers what impact these Christological arguments regarding the Incarnation and sonship had on Muslims and looks briefly at a number of Muslim responses including that of al-Bāqillānī from the tenth century.

Although the language of substance and hypostasis was used to argue for the two natures of Christ, Beaumont states that some of these doctrines were argued on Islamic grounds using images which were familiar to Muslims. But he writes that the Muslim response was not convinced by Christian elaboration of the Incarnation because 'nothing in Islam allows for the union of the divine with a human body, and the use of divine anthropomorphisms in Islam to make room for Incarnation is not admissible'. Furthermore, Muslims also thought that in the formation of these Christological doctrines, Christians had forsaken the truth of the Bible.

David Thomas's contribution deals with one of the Muslim responses to Christological themes. Thomas has done extensive work on early Christian–Muslim polemics and in this extract by Abū 'Īsā al-Warrāq, translated from the original Arabic, he gives a sense of how one of the foremost Muslim intellectuals and theologians of ninth-century Baghdad wrote his refutation against Christian doctrines. Abū 'Īsā's *Refutation against the Incarnation* is the second part of the author's ambitious work *Refutation of the Three Christian Sects* (*Kitāb al-Radd 'alā al-thalāth firaq min al-Nasārā*). The work as a whole is a polemic against the main Christian doctrines of Trinity and Incarnation and the crucifixion and death of Christ. The polemic is levelled against the views held at the time by the major Christian sects, the Jacobites, Melkites and Nestorians. The Trinity and the Incarnation were consistent points of debate between Muslims and Christians. Muslims could not accept that God who is one and eternal could be incarnate in time and that he could have a human birth from Mary but also die on the cross. Resorting to metaphors was one way of explaining the nature and substance of Christ and how the Word and the Spirit were not separable from God.

Mark Swanson's ingeniously titled 'Folly to the *Hunafā*': The Crucifixion in Early Christian–Muslim Controversy' draws on an early manuscript containing the letters of St Paul in Arabic. Swanson notes that an early Arabic translation of the Gospel uses *hunafā*, from the Syriac *hanpé*, meaning 'pagans' or 'Gentiles' or 'Greeks'. According to St Paul, the majority of the *hunafā*' found the 'word of the cross', that is the Crucifixion, to be foolish. In the Islamic context the Arabic word *ḥanīf* refers to a distinctive monotheism in the Qur'an. Thus Christians living under Islamic rule in the seventh century found that the 'word of the cross' was not only a folly to the Greek *ḥunafā*' but also to the Muslim *hunafā*' who denied the death of Christ on the cross as understood from Q4:157. However, Christian interpreters throughout fourteen centuries have tried to construe this Qur'anic verse through readings which would allow for the reality of Christ's death on the cross, so central to Christian faith. With this introduction Swanson proceeds to analyse the defence of Christian doctrine on the Crucifixion in three texts, one Coptic (*History of the Patriarchs*), one Arabic (*On the Triune Nature of God*) and one Syriac (*The Debate of the Patriarch Timothy and the Caliph al-Mahdi*).

The rise of Muslim writing on Christianity flourished in the intellectual context of speculative theology of *kalām*, which began in the late eighth and early ninth centuries. A leading authority on early Muslim theology, Joseph Van Ess remarked that the history of Islamic theology during the second and third centuries (eighth and ninth centuries AD) is essentially a history of Mu'tazilism.[9] There has been a tendency among researchers to restrict the religious and political ascendancy of the Mu'tazilites to the early years of 'Abbāsid rule (AD 750–850). However, more recently, Daniel Gimaret has shown that the movement's influence was chronologically more widespread.[10]

Van Ess was also convinced that Christian influences had exercised a key role in the inception of *kalām* and that converts from Christianity had served as conduits for the transmission of dialectical methods. The Mu'tazila were a theological school which relied on rational arguments and logic as their central principles. They focused on five main principles in which the most prominent were the unity and justice of God. They engaged with a variety of Muslim and non-Muslim schools, sects and philosophies and, according to Monnot, were the 'pioneers of polemical religious literature'.[11]

One of the most famous scholars of this school was 'Alī Rabbān al-Ṭabarī (d. 855 or 861), a Persian physician of Nestorian Christian background who produced one of the first encyclopaedias of medicine. He converted to Islam very late in his life and writes that until that time he was neglectful and unaware of the right direction. He wrote his famous *Kitāb al-din wa-l-dawla* (*Book of Religion and Empire*) at the invitation of the caliph al-Mutawakkil (822–61) whom he thanks several times in the book for this honour. The text used here is the translation by A. Mingana published in 1922, *The Book of Religion and Empire*. Al-Ṭabarī explains in his prologue that the reason for writing the book is to show those to whom revelation was previously given how they have denied Muhammad's prophecy as foretold by previous prophets:

> They have hidden his name and changed his portrait found in the Books of their prophets-peace be with them. I shall demonstrate this, disclose its secret, and withdraw the veil from it, in order that the reader may see it clearly and increase his conviction and his joy in the religion of Islam.[12]

Al-Ṭabarī's major defence is levelled at the Christians though a small section at the end of the book depicts his arguments against the Jews. He writes that he has 'set forth one hundred and thirty arguments against them [Christians] from the Books of the prophets, apart from rational demonstrations, illustrative examples, and illuminating analogies'. Underlying many of the discussions in this book is the Christian refutation of Muhammad's prophecy on the basis that it was not prophesied by anyone or in any scripture. Al-Ṭabarī argues at some length that prophets have been acknowledged and accepted throughout history for various reasons and many neither performed miracles nor was their prophecy prophesied beforehand. Al-Ṭabarī's main task through his exegesis of the biblical prophets and biblical verses is to show that Muhammad's prophecy was already foretold in these books; the second is to argue that people have accepted earlier prophets even though their prophecies were neither prophesied nor did many perform miracles. There is no difference therefore between these earlier prophets and Muhammad.

Margaretha Heemskerk's article looks at the writings of the rationalist Muslim scholar Qāḍī Abū 'l-Hasan 'Abd al-Jabbār b. Aḥmad al-Hamadhānī al-Asadābādī (932–1025) who was born in Hamadhān in Iran. He is considered to be the leading and the last of the great Mu'tazilite thinkers of his time, and wrote on a variety of Islamic sciences. Before his appointment as chief judge, 'Abd al-Jabbār began to dictate to his students a serious work on Mu'tazilite doctrine. This eventually became his biggest theological work stretching over some twenty volumes and completed around 990. Its title is *Al-Mughnī fi abwāb al-tawhīd wa'l-'adl* (*Summa on the Topics of Unity and Justice*). 'Abd al-Jabbār included in this book a refutation of Christian and Jewish doctrines in the style of the *mutakallimūn* (rational theologians). Emphasising the unity of God and the truth of Muhammad's prophecy, 'Abd al-Jabbār refutes both the Christian doctrines of Trinity and Incarnation as well as the Jewish refusal to abrogate the Mosaic law with the prophecy and laws of Muhammad.

The twelfth century was a time of warfare between Christians and Muslims. The First Crusade ended when Jerusalem was seized on behalf of the Pope in 1099. Less than fifty years later, Turkish/Muslim forces regrouped, and the Turks took Edessa, in 1144. There then followed the Second Crusade (1147–9) and the Third Crusade (1189–92). All had papal approval. Christian support was marshalled against a Muslim adversary. Throughout the twelfth and into the thirteenth century European Christendom had a double mission: to kill Muslims and to retake Christian lands occupied by infidel Moors. Thomas Aquinas (1225–74) was an Italian Dominican priest of the Roman Catholic Church who ranks among the most influential philosophers and theologians in the West. In commenting on Thomas's vast theological and philosophical output, Henk Schoot writes:

> Aquinas would employ and reinterpret Aristotle in undertaking his most important task: explaining the Bible, disputing theological questions, and preaching. One can hardly pinpoint any area of theology where Aristotle is not employed: whether it is the doctrine of God, the question of the eternity of the world, the discussion of human moral life, natural law, politics, anthropology.
>
> His influence is everywhere. One could call this 'Greek' influence but because of the way Aristotle was transmitted to the West, it is Islamic as well. For it is through a number of Islamic scholars that the West received most of the teaching of Aristotle: their Arabic translations as well as their commentaries were translated into Latin and studied in the West. In fact, whenever one tries to describe Aquinas' relation to Islam, one should make a distinction between Islam as a religion and Islam as the religion of a number of very great philosophers.[13]

His two largest theological treatises are *Summa contra Gentiles* and the *Summa Theologiae.* He is also considered the foremost thinker of the medieval period to bridge the divide between Christian thought and Muslim philosophy. In his analysis of Thomas Aquinas's views on Islam, James Waltz questions the sources Thomas may have used which informed his knowledge of Islam and subsequently influenced his line of argument against Muslims. He posits the view that what Thomas needed was a concise summary of Muslim beliefs and ideas with some Christian interaction. This summary he found in the *Summa totius haeresis Saracenorum* or *The Summary of the Entire Heresy of the Saracens,* prepared by Peter the Venerable, abbot of Cluny, in the mid-twelfth century (1092–1156). Drawing on a range of Thomas's theological works, Waltz says that his main task was to argue for Christian truth. For Thomas seduction to Islam was relatively easy because the truth of Islam did not require any supernatural manifestation but could be understood by anyone with 'modest wisdom'. Muḥammad had enticed followers through the promise of carnal pleasures in paradise whereas Christianity offered eternal bliss. In short Islam contained no spiritualism comparable to Christianity. Waltz argues that Thomas did not give a sympathetic account of Islam and remained largely ignorant of its teachings.

Nicholas Rescher's article on Nicholas of Cusa brings us into the beginnings of the early modern period of Christian approaches to Islam. During the first half of the fifteenth century, European Christians looked towards Constantinople, which was a city besieged and which eventually fell to the Turks, the troops of Mehmet II, in 1453. The fall of the city saw a revival in the Christian polemic against Islam. Inigo Bocken describes what the loss of Constantinople to the troops of Mehmet II actually meant to many Christians:

> Until 1453, Islam was seen more as an exterior reflection, a reminder of the unfinished character of the earthly realisation of the City of God. In the traditional notion of a

> teleologically oriented order (*ordo*) the otherness of Islam had its place as a kind of obstinate obstacle, which sharpened the intellectual weapons for the realisation of a Christian life to be overcome at the end of history (or earlier, if possible). The year 1453 marks a turning point of this model and it is in fact the symbolic end of the reign of metaphysics or order as an interpretative framework of culture and society.[14]

It was in this climate that the philosopher, theologian and cardinal Nicholas of Cusa (1401–64) rose to prominence. Nicholas studied Latin, Greek, Hebrew and later Arabic and began his public life in 1421 at the Council of Basel. Here he became a passionate advocate for the religious and political unity of Christendom and in 1437 travelled to Constantinople to meet the patriarch of the Greek Orthodox Church in order to negotiate the reunification of the two branches of Christianity. Though his efforts were not successful, this was an important step in the history of ecumenical dialogue. Nicholas wrote his famous dialogue *De Pace Fidei* (*On the Peace of Faith*) and later his commentary on the Qur'an, the *Cribratio Alkorani* (*Sifting of the Qur'ān*) (1461). The latter was written under the aegis of his friend Pope Pius II, and while it is not a blanket rejection of the Qur'an, it is still a work of Christian polemics against Islam. For Nicholas the Qur'an is of genuine religious merit but heavily influenced by the Old and New Testaments. Muḥammad hid the secrets of the Gospels from the Arabs, and Muḥammad also went against God's commands in trying to impose Islam on the Arabs.[15] The Qur'an is 'a mixture in which the sound grains of truth are intermingled with the chaff of falsity'. Muḥammad's basic impulse was good but he went astray (because of heretical Christians and corrupting Jews) despite having caught glimpses of Christian truth. Nicholas covers a variety of material in the Qur'an and places them in his own Christian understanding.

Around a century later, the Ottoman Empire reached the height of its military power in the reign of Suleiman the Magnificent (r. 1520–66). The Ottoman advance was especially disturbing to people in Germany. However, when the military power of Hungary (the 'bulwark of Christendom') was destroyed at the battle of Mohacs in 1526, even opponents of the Habsburgs were convinced that central Europe was in grave danger. A Turkish presence in neighbouring Hungary was simply too close for comfort.[16] By the time of Martin Luther's rise to prominence (1483–1546), European leaders were accustomed to thinking of Muslims as their main military enemies. Turks, wars and the Ottoman Empire shaped the political background to Luther's time. However, as Robert Smith writes, 'Luther moved beyond constructions of the Turk as a mere military threat to a consideration of Islam itself.' He adds that 'Given their place in the center of European consciousness, it is unsurprising to find references to the "Turks" in writings from almost all of the major Reformers. Among them, however, only Luther substantively engaged the matter, producing theological perspectives both on the possibility of Christian war against the Turk and on the religion of the Turk, Islam.'[17] Adam Francisco's contribution, 'Luther's Knowledge of and Attitude Towards Islam', is taken from his excellent monograph *Martin Luther and Islam: A Study in Sixteenth Century Polemics and Apologetics*. While Luther was amazed at Muslim belief in the 'shameful' things in the Qur'an, he had an ambiguous attitude towards Islam, reflected largely in his conviction that the function of Islam and the expansion of the Muslim world was to act as both a poison and a cure for Christians. Islam was fundamentally a divine punishment for Christians for their transgressions. Francisco lays out the sources which Luther used for his observations on Islam, though it is doubtful as to whether Luther actually met any Muslims. Luther demonstrates some knowledge, even appreciation, of certain Muslim cultural practices but it is Muslim doctrine which Luther critiques. The

Muslim rejection of the Incarnation, the salvific role of Christ and the particular insistence on divine unity, were all problematic for Luther. Islam negated what Luther thought God had done for the salvation of humanity.

Contemporary voices and methods

The early part of the twentieth century saw Christian missionaries travel to Muslim lands where they formulated their own rather ambivalent opinions on the Muslim faith and Muslim life; there was both contempt and admiration for Islam and Muslim piety. For Samuel Zwemer (1867–1952), the American missionary and Princeton Theological Seminary professor, the need to evangelise amongst Muslims was paramount. In the extracts from his influential work, *The Disintegration of Islam*, he viewed 'the dead weight of formality called tradition' as 'Islam's intolerable burden'. It was what had led to the decline of Islam but, as Islam lost political power, this became 'a divine preparation for the evangelization of Moslem lands and the winning of Moslem hearts to a new allegiance. Jesus Christ is sufficient for them as He is for us.' But Zwemer saw that Islam was unwilling to compromise with Christian theology and lamented the fact that Christ's life had been eclipsed by the life of Muḥammad for Muslims. Whatever differences there were between the various schools and sects in Islam, their position towards Christ is essentially the same. Muslims could not accept the cross or the Crucifixion as the foundation of the Christian religion. Zwemer asserted that the central concern for Muslims was not Western Civilisation but the 'anti-Christian' character of this 'greatest of all the non-Christian religions'. He could not understand how Muslims saw Jesus only as a prophet in the long history of God's prophets:

> The Moslem doctrine of God and their denial of Jesus Christ, His incarnation, His atonement, His deity, are the very issues of the conflict. The Koran denies all that which is the supreme glory of the Saviour and which makes Him a Saviour at all.

Hendrik Kraemer (1888–1965) was a Dutch reformed missiologist and lay theologian who wanted to articulate new ways for missionaries. His writings suggest that he was prepared to understand the religions and cultures of non-Christians, partly brought about by his long stay in Indonesia. The extracts in this volume are taken from Kraemer's most significant work, *The Christian Message in a Non-Christian World*. Kramer's main thesis in this book is that God has revealed himself in Jesus Christ and that truth based on biblical realism means there is no continuity between Christianity and the non-Christian faiths. Non-Christian religions cannot bring people to the true knowledge of God because non-Christian religions are human achievements only. Kraemer was influenced by the Swiss theological giant Karl Barth (1886–1968), but, unlike Barth, Kraemer accepted that God reveals himself outside Jesus even though this has no soteriological significance.

Kraemer saw Islam as a superficial, shallow religion with no real concern for the essential problems of religious life. But Kraemer was puzzled by the strong allegiance Muslims had to their faith even if they were not always observant. He was impressed by the 'impressive ceremony' of Muslim prayer but saw the Islamic conception of God as 'hyperbolic theocentricity'. In many ways Kraemer saw Islam as the biggest challenge to the missionary goal, a challenge which demanded a renewed and stronger commitment, but Kraemer encouraged his fellow Christians to act with faith, hope, love and endurance while performing their missionary obligation to proclaim the Gospel.

Despite the long history of the Christian–Muslim encounter, the number of Muslims in the West writing on Christianity or with any deep knowledge of the faith is low. Spurred on by the Christian missionary zeal in the twentieth century, many Muslims took to refuting Christianity as part of refuting Western colonialism. But few took Christian theology seriously in the manner in which the scholars of the eighth and ninth centuries had engaged with doctrinal differences. In the modern period, Mahmoud Ayoub's contribution in the field of Christian–Muslim dialogue, however, is prolific. Ayoub was born in 1935 to a Muslim family in Lebanon but had a Christian schooling and grew up as a Christian. He returned to Shi'ī Islam as a university student and has lived and worked in the USA for much of his life. Ayoub has always argued that Islam has recognised Christianity much more than Christianity has recognised Islam. Nevertheless, there is an imbalance in the field of dialogue precisely because Muslims have generally not studied other religions seriously or understood Christianity largely from a Qur'anic perspective.

The article 'Towards an Islamic Christology II: The Death of Jesus, Reality or Delusion', is his survey of how Jesus' death has been explored in the classical and contemporary Qur'an commentaries. Ayoub states that the Qur'an contains an Islamic Christology which Christians should also take seriously even if it is not analogous to the Christologies of the early Church. He concentrates on Q4:157, stating that they plotted to kill him, but God saved him and it [or he] was only to appear so to them. This verse has been translated in many ways and Muslims have generally rejected the death of Jesus on the cross. But writing from a Muslim perspective, Ayoub argues that 'the denial of the killing of Jesus is a denial of the power of men to vanquish and destroy the divine Word, which is forever victorious'. There is no divine deception here, only an accusation against the 'human sin of pride and ignorance'.

Ismā'īl Rājī al-Farūqī (1921–86) was born in Palestine but the occupation of Palestine brought him to the United States. Ataullah Siddiqui writes that Farūqī's intellectual life was deeply influenced by Arab nationalism, a nationalism that was not just confined to the Arab race or Arab Muslims but included non-Arabic-speaking people living in territories near the Arab lands. Farūqī was a man of faith and one who recognised the political and intellectual powers of the West.[18]

In this article, 'Islam and Christianity: Diatribe or Dialogue', Farūqī criticises the Western missionary who preaches to Muslims the 'Western figurization of the religion of Jesus when the missionary himself has stopped finding meaning in that very figurisation because of the eroding forces of secularism.' He held that Islam and Christianity could not be impervious to the claims of one another but that dialogue should be about conversion to the truth. However, there cannot be two divergent claims to the truth, thus one must be false. Still, dialogue is education at its best and the 'altruistic arm of Islam and Christianity'. Dialogue needed to be a conversation between equals but Farūqī also gave primacy to the ethical rather than the theological questions in dialogue today. He explores the themes on which Christianity and Islam can converge to continue discussion. He ends with comments on the German American systematic theologian and Christian philosopher Paul Tillich. Quoting from Tillich that theology should remain 'rooted in its experiential basis', Farūqī nevertheless accuses Tillich of remaining 'straight-jacketed by his own self-imposed limitation'. For Farūqī, the Christian theologian cannot in such constraints understand other faiths or produce a fruitful dialogue with others. Comparing Farūqī with Hendrik Kraemer, Hugh Goddard writes, 'For all his undoubted knowledge about Christianity, therefore rather like Kraemer with all his knowledge of Islam, Farūqī somehow lacked that inner sympathy which would have enabled him to gain a deeper appreciation of Christianity. Perhaps, on the other hand, like Kraemer, he moved on during the course of his life to a more open set of opinions but fundamentally he seems to have remained an exclusivist.'[19]

The Tunisian-born Mohamed Talbi (b. 1921), who studied in Paris, has been another significant name in interfaith dialogue and the study of Islam's relationship with other religions. Ronald Nettler's article looks at an extract from Talbi's book, *Families of God* (*'Iyal Allah*) in which he discusses Talbi's ideas on religions and civilisations and provides some biographical context to Talbi. The book is based on interviews Talbi gave on these themes. Talbi's childhood was spent in Tunisia but in the 1940s he went to Paris which at that time was a 'city of intellectual ferment'. He was influenced by Communism, Existentialism and Freudianism but he preserved his Islamic traditions within this new climate of learning. Talbi was deeply influenced by the Catholic mystical scholar Louis Massignon, who opened his mind to a spiritual and philosophical Sūfism. He was also influenced by Regis Blachère, who taught him the spirit of self-critical inquiry through his own historical-critical approach to scholarship.

Nettler states that Talbi combines traditional learning with the challenges of modernity to understand Islam's position regarding other faiths. He adopts a 'liberal' understanding of the internal pluralism to be found in Islam which is that '*all* religious ideas and *all* faiths are paths to God *on the same spiritual level*'. This is a far cry from a common, traditional perspective. For Talbi, all human beings are unique and different and it is in this difference wherein lies glory. Ideational variety is a divinely ordained feature of human life and Islam should be predicated on change, not frozen in time. Talbi argues that 'man is by nature a pluralist' and that difference of opinion (*ikhtilāf*) has been part of Islam since its inception. This taken to its natural conclusion means that, in Talbi's theory, there is no way round various approaches to the Qur'an, but Talbi does not see this as a problem. People can hold all kinds of theoretical positions but, on the social and intellectual plane, the Muslim world has to go from tolerance to mutual respect of one another. Individual reasoning (*ijtihād*) has to be done in a non-dogmatic way with the universal and moral precepts of the Qur'an serving as a framework. Brotherly love must permeate the relations between Muslims and between Muslims and others. One example here is that the medieval concept of *dhimmī* has no place in a liberal democracy today. Islam cannot relegate Judaism and Christianity to a position of 'corrupted predecessor'. Rather the Qur'anic idea of confirmation of these two faiths obliges Muslims to conduct a continuous living dialogue with Jews and Christians by virtue of their monotheism. On this point Nettler argues that Talbi believed in the possibility of spiritual equality between all three religions 'while at the same time believers would also somehow reserve the right to attribute to their own faith a certain level of superiority'.

From the Catholic side, one of the biggest but controversial names of the twentieth century is the Swiss priest and theologian Hans Küng (b. 1928). In the late 1960s, he publicly rejected the doctrine of papal infallibility and was consequently stripped of his *missio canonica*, his licence to teach as a Roman Catholic theologian. He did however carry on teaching as a professor of ecumenical theology at the University of Tübingen until his retirement in 1996. Küng's article here poses the question, 'How can Christians today come to terms with the claims made by the Muslim faith about itself?' Küng states that Christianity can no longer demonise Islam nor ignore it politically or theologically. Küng asks that if grace can be found outside the Church, what about prophecy (*charismata*). Drawing on the teachings of Vatican II (1964), Küng states that Islam too can be a way of salvation but not in the 'ordinary' way, that is, the Christian way, but rather in an 'extraordinary' way, that is, non-Christian faiths.

Küng discusses whether Muḥammad can be accepted as a prophet by the Catholic Church as his name is absent from the dialogical statements of Vatican II. Küng calls for a self-critical questioning of an exclusively Christian understanding of revelation. He states that 'countless people in the distant past and in the present have experienced, and are experiencing, the mystery of God on the basis of the revelation of God in creation, and that all this also involves the grace of God and the faith of human beings'. For Küng, Judaism, Christianity and Islam 'represent faith in the one God; all share in the one great monotheistic world movement'. He extends this theme to the political dimension and writes that 'Politically, this faith in the one God ought not to be underestimated; it should be brought to people's attention. For instance, just as this faith played a part in the Camp David agreement, it could also be important in further peace efforts in the Middle East.'

Küng ends on the image of Jesus in Islam and how Muslims can understand Jesus in a broader way in the light of the Gospels. He states, 'In this way a new and deeper understanding could also be gained of a God who loves and suffers with people.' But even if Jesus remains the deciding factor regulating all Christian faith, can Christians accept prophecy after Christ?

Staying with the focus on Muḥammad, F.E. Peters uses Albert Schweitzer's pursuit of the 'quest of the historical Jesus' in nineteenth-century biblical studies to explore whether anything comparable can be done in the 'quest of the historical Muḥammad.' Peters, a notable scholar of Judaism, Christianity and Islam, sets out the main differences in approach:

> The most abiding and forbidding obstacle to approaching the historical Jesus is undoubtedly the fact that our principal sources, the documents included in the New Testament, were all written on the hither side of Easter; that is, their authors viewed their subject across the absolute conviction that Jesus was the Christ and the Son of God, a conviction later rendered explicit in Christian dogma. There is, however, no Resurrection in the career of Muḥammad, no Paschal sunrise to cast its divinizing light on the Prophet of Islam. Muḥammad is thus a perfectly appropriate subject of history: a man born of woman (and a man), who lived in a known place in a roughly calculable time, who in the end died the death that is the lot of all mortals, and whose career was reported by authorities who share the contemporary historian's own conviction that the Prophet was nothing more than a man. What is at stake in Islam, then, is not dogma as it is in Christianity, but rather piety.

Peter's argument is that there is no sectarian milieu in Islam like the Jewish and Hellenic movement from which Jesus and his movement came forth. There may be masses of poetry forming a pre-Islamic context but the 'Qur'an, in fact, stands isolated like an immense rock jutting forth from a desolate sea'. The surviving evidence for both Jesus and Muḥammad lies in literary rather than material evidence. But here Peters ask why there is so much scepticism about retrieving the actual words of Jesus and yet no similar debate about the Qur'an, the words of which were still spoken by Muḥammad in time. This is a very rich article throwing up all kinds of questions of the historian of early Islam and comparing the issue of redaction and the reliability or unreliability of sources.

While the doctrines of the Incarnation and the Trinity occupied the polemical space between Muslims and Christians, Ṣūfī poetry in the Islamic world invariably took a slightly different approach to the place and image of Jesus in Islam. Drawing upon Qur'anic verses and stories from the Apocrypha, the mystic imagination could easily create a different story and a different focus. This elaboration often included Mary, as Jesus is frequently mentioned in the Qur'an as 'Son of Mary'. Annemarie Schimmel, one of the most important Western scholars of Sūfī literature, examines the way Jesus and Mary are depicted in the poetry of the thirteenth-century poet mystic, Jalāl al-Dīn Rūmī. Jesus often appears as the ideal ascetic but one who is full of hope and of a smiling nature. Jesus' smiling nature is emphasised in contrast to the appearance of his cousin John and that 'The smiling was from confidence, and the frowning was from fear.' The linking of Jesus with spirit also features in Rūmī's verse. Jesus' quality of breathing life into the dead is for Rūmī the equivalent of a kiss:

> When someone asks you: "How did Christ quicken the dead?"
> Then give me a kiss in his presence: "Thus!"[20]

This life-giving breath (*dam-i ʿĪsā*) became the quality most associated with Jesus so that Jesus' breath brings life when it brings new concepts or possibilities to human imagination. Rūmī compares man's spirit to Jesus and his body to Mary, that one must endure the pains of the body to develop the spirit of Jesus. As Muslims recognise Mary's purity and virginal conception, she is a supreme image of the pure soul, 'made pregnant by the Divine spirit'. But Rūmī also saw the differences between the Muslim and Christian Jesus, 'That idea the Christian carried abroad, the Muslim has not that idea, that He is slaying this Messiah upon the cross.'[21]

That Jesus lives in a vast variety of Muslim literature and poetry has been well documented in recent scholarly studies of a 'Muslim Jesus'. This is a Jesus who lives an ascetic and pious life, shunning all worldly fortunes, living an ethical and saintly life by devoting himself to God. This Jesus is reflected also in the Prophetic sayings (*hadīth*). In his introduction to *The Muslim Jesus*, Tarif Khalidi calls the collective sayings attributed to Jesus by various Muslim scholars and mystics as the 'Muslim gospel'. While the Islamic Jesus of the Gospel may be a fabrication, he writes:

> Here is a Jesus who on the one hand is shorn of Christology, but who on the other is endowed with attributes which render him meta-historical and even, so to speak, meta-religious. In his Muslim habitat, Jesus becomes an object of intense devotion, reverence and love. He bears the stamp of Qur'ānic *nubuwwah*, or prophecy, but as he advances inside the Islamic tradition he ceases to be an argument and becomes a living and vital moral voice, demanding to be heard by all who seek a unity of profession and witness.[22]

The extracts in this collection are from Khalidi's book, a selection of sayings attributed to Jesus from the late ninth century. The main themes covered in his sayings are largely love of God, asceticism and renunciation of this world. These themes are woven into pithy, moral tales where Jesus speaks as a Muslim prophet. For example, 'The heart of a believer cannot really support the love of both this world and the next, just as a single vessel cannot really support both water and fire.' Such sayings illustrate how the Jesus of the Gospels was over time embraced by the Muslim Sūfīs to become the Jesus of Islamic Ṣūfism. Whether or not these images of Jesus can in any way be meaningful to Christians, it is certainly true that they reflect a particular kind of ascetic piety for which Jesus has been known throughout Muslim history.

The interest from Western scholars in the Qur'an and the images of Jesus and Christians in scripture and post-scriptural commentaries has increased steadily in recent times. This kind of scholarship has been invaluable for dialogical engagement as well as theological and historical scholarship. The chapter 'The Praiseworthy Amity of Christians' has been taken from Jane McAuliffe's ambitious work, *Qur'ānic Christians: An Analysis of Classical and Modern Exegesis*. The Qur'an speaks of Christians under various designations, as a particular religious group; it also makes references to Christianity through its focus on figures such as Mary and Jesus. While some verses accuse the Christians of being unfaithful to the message of Jesus, for trying to lead Muslims astray, there are also several verses which make more positive allusions to Christians and Jews, the 'People of the Book'. McAuliffe has taken certain of the more 'positive' Qur'anic verses and shown how the exegetes have interpreted them over the centuries. Beneath these concerns, the fundamental question she poses is whether the Muslim understanding of the term 'Christian' is consonant with the self-understanding of those who so define themselves.

McAuliffe has taken Q5:82–3, which extols praise on Christians as those who are 'closest in friendship' (to the Muslims). The classical exegetical perspectives demonstrate a variety of opinions on exactly which Christians are being referred to here and how broadly one can accept this sympathetic view of Christians. There are differences between the modern and classical commentators as well as between the Sunnī and the Shīʿī. The other focus of these particular verses is the castigation of the Jews in sharp contrast to the Qur'anic attitude towards the Christians. Nevertheless, commentators were divided on this issue as many saw in Judaism a religion much closer to Islam in its conception of monotheism.

One of the most curious aspects of Christian–Muslim scholarship is the gendered nature of Christian–Muslim encounter. There may be many reasons for this but the paucity of women who have been engaged in this area from earliest times to the present day is a little puzzling. While women are engaged at grassroots level of interfaith work, there are very few significant names in the history of Christian or Muslim encounter as well as in the contemporary academic world. Of the ones who have shown interest, a good number have focused on the role of Mary or Miriam (in Arabic) in Christian and Muslim piety. In the Qur'an Mary is often mentioned in the phrase, 'Jesus, son of Mary', to emphasise his human birth and her virginal conception. Mary is seen as a virtuous and chaste woman in the Islamic tradition and often regarded as a meeting point, a bridge between Islam and Christianity. R.J. McCarthy wrote of Mary in the two faiths that though Mary may not be a touchstone, she may well be a stepping stone. He wrote that the phrase 'chosen by God' meant that she was chosen in the same way the prophets were chosen.[23] And in 1988, Cardinal Arinze of the Vatican's secretariat for non-Christians addressed a greeting to Muslims whom he called brothers and sisters in God. He quoted Mary, 'the mother of Jesus whom both Christians and Muslims – without according her the same role and title-honour as a model for believers'. The portrait of Mary was a surprising feature for even the earliest Christian respondents to Islam. Bartholomew of Edessa (ninth century) declared, 'In the entire Qur'ān there do not occur any praises of Muhammad or of his mother Aminah, such as are found about our Lord Jesus Christ and about the holy Virgin Mary, the Theotokos.'[24]

In her analysis of Rachel, Mary and Fatima as 'female saints whose cults are located within monotheistic, male-dominated religious traditions', Susan Sered writes:

> Mary, as the Virgin Mother of God, is essentially inimitable, whereas Rachel and Fatima are more realistic models. While women can strive to be faithful, modest,

> generous, or wise, to be a virgin mother is an impossible goal for mortal women. In a different sense, though, Mary is the most positive model of the three. Fatima and Rachel suffered in life, died young, and weep in eternity; Mary is rarely portrayed as a victim. Especially during the past two decades … the Church has made some effort to describe Mary not only 'as a mother exclusively concerned with her own Divine son, but rather as a woman whose action helped to strengthen the apostolic community's faith in Christ'.[25]

Sered's contribution is a thoughtful piece comparing female figures in religious traditions and how they shape their own traditions but also say something about the issue of gender in religion.

Perhaps the most tragic event of recent years to cause a major shift in Western consciousness about Islam has been the attacks on the Twin Towers of September 11th 2001, referred to as 9/11. These attacks provoked all kinds of reactions and responses, political, sociological and theological. Many argued that 9/11 had brought religion back in the most violent way. While this may be a contested point, what 9/11 did do was convince many onlookers that religious expression could quite easily be equated with religious fanaticism, and religious fanaticism could have its roots in the interpretation of those very scriptures held sacred by millions.

Dialogue, interfaith worship, prayer and all kinds of reconciliation activities flourished amongst religious groups in the aftermath of 9/11 as a means of showing that militant Islamism was not the same as the Islamic faith practised by millions of peaceful Muslims all over the world. However, for some 9/11 was proof that there were irreconcilable theological differences between Islam and Christianity and that, in short, Islam was fundamentally a religion of violence. Richard Cimino's article, 'No God in Common', explores how American Christian evangelicals reasserted their differences with Islam through apologetics to show the truth of Christianity. Soon after 9/11, certain evangelicals rose to global fame for their polemical stance against Islam such as Franklin Graham, Pat Robertson and Jerry Falwell. However, the article also explores how the greater and more visible pluralism in American society challenges evangelical identity. The literature that attacks Islamic doctrine places it within the critique of pluralism and syncretism in American religion and society.

American evangelicals are more likely than other Americans to be opposed to Islam, and central to their negativity is that Islam encourages violence and terrorism. Cimino explains that after 9/11 much of the polemical literature against Muslims was propagated by ex-Muslims, many of whom had converted to Christianity to expose the 'real' Islam. Another area where evangelical anti-Islamic polemics have flourished in recent years is in the biblical prophecy movement. This movement gathers together pre-millennial evangelicals who interpret the Bible as providing a blueprint of the end times and the return of Christ. Israel plays an important role in 'gathering together the Jews of the world and rebuilding the temple, thereby hastening the return of Christ to earth'. This kind of thinking has resulted in considerable political support for Israel among the fundamentalist and evangelical groups.

As said above, interfaith initiatives have grown considerably in recent years with many organisations attempting to mobilise global and not just local recognition.The final contribution comes from the Lutheran Norwegian academic Oddbjørn Leirvik on the issue of brotherly and neighbourly love in Islam. Leirvik has written much on the interpretation of Jesus in Muslim history and is also heavily involved in Christian–Muslim relations. Leirvik sets out the framework for his discussion which is the open letter sent to the world's

Christian leaders in 2007 by 136 Muslim leaders and intellectuals. This letter, 'A Common Word between Us and You', was a follow-up to a shorter letter, sent in 2006 by 38 Muslims in response to Pope Benedict XVI's lecture at the University of Regensburg. In this lecture, on the subject of faith and reason, Pope Benedict spoke of the tendency in the modern world to 'exclude the question of God' from reason. In this lecture the Pope quoted a Byzantine emperor's strong criticism of Muhammad's teaching.

The 2007 letter proposed the double commandment of love as a common frame of reference for future dialogue and cooperation between Muslims and Christians. As for neighbourly love, the biblical reference was the commandment to love your neighbour as yourself. Regarding love of the neighbour in Islam, the primary reference was to two particular versions of a prophetic saying, 'None of you has faith until you love for your brother what you love for yourself.' And also, 'None of you has faith until you love for your neighbour what you love for yourself.' Leirvik states that these two *hadīths* were confused in the document with little attempt to explore the tensions between 'brother', implying group solidarity, and 'neighbour', implying universal obligations.

Leirvik draws upon classical and modern commentators to analyse these two prophetic sayings and the Qur'anic notion of *jār* (neighbour) and *akh* (brother). He looks at whether the commandment to love your brother is about intra-Muslim solidarity and the commandment to love your neighbour as yourself has more universal implications. He finds that the authors of 'A Common Word' read both versions of the *hadīth* from a universalistic perspective. He also explores the inclusivist concepts of brotherhood in interreligious settings and what that means for solidarity of faiths. Leirvik concludes that notions of brotherhood in both Islam and Christianity initially implied a radical breach with established family ties and kinships but that the 'notions of kinship, brotherhood and neighborhood – and the implicit tension between them – thus capture some of the most pressing issues in modern ethics and moral identity formation today: the relation between family values, religious brotherhood and faith-transcending solidarity'.

Notes

1 Sidney H. Griffith, *The Church in the Shadow of the Mosque: Christians and Muslims in the World of Islam*, Princeton: Princeton University Press, 2008, p. 176.
2 John Moorhead, 'The Earliest Christian Theological Response to Islam', *Religion*, 11, 1981, 265–74.
3 Moorhead, 'Earliest Christian', 266.
4 Pseudo-Dionysius of Tell Mahre, *Chronique de Denys de Tell Mahre*, quatrieme part, ed. and trans. J.B. Chabot, Paris, 1895, p. 4 and quoted in Moorhead, 'Earliest Christian', 267.
5 Griffith, *The Church*, pp. 40–1.
6 Daniel J. Sahas, *John of Damascus on Islam: The Heresy of the Ishmaelites*, Leiden: E.J. Brill, 1972, p. 52.
7 This article has two appendices in Arabic.
8 The Gospel of Barnabas, which is a mixture of 'biblical Gospels, apocryphal Jesus material, peculiar readings of the Old Testament and Islamic teachings', received much attention in the twentieth century as a primary point of reference in Muslim polemical writings aimed at the refutation of Christianity. A useful summary of its main points and influences can be found in Oddbjorn Leirvik, *Images of Jesus Christ in Islam*, 2nd edn, London: Continuum, 2010.
9 Joseph Van Ess, 'Wrongdoing and Divine Omnipotence in the Theology of Abū Ishāq al-Nazzām', in T. Rudavsky (ed.), *Divine Omniscience and Omnipotence in Medieval Philosophy*, Dordrecht: D-Reidel, 1985, pp. 53–67.
10 See his entry in Daniel Gimaret, 'Mu'tazila', in the *Encyclopaedia of Islam*, 2nd edn, Leiden: E.J. Brill, pp. 783–93.

11 Guy Monnot, *Penseurs musulmans et religions iraniennes: Abd al-Jabbār et ses devanciers*, Paris: J. Vrin, 1974, p. 101. See also D. Gimaret, 'Mu'tazila', in H.A.R. Gibb *et al.* (eds), *The Encyclopaedia of Islam, New Edition*, Leiden: E.J. Brill, 1960–2002, V11, pp. 783–93.
12 *Kitāb al-dīn wa-l-dawla, The Book of Religion and Empire*, trans. A. Mingana, Manchester: Manchester University Press, 1922, p. 3.
13 Henk Schoot, 'Christ Crucified Contested: Thomas Aquinas', in Barbara Roggema, Marcel Poorthuis and Pim Valkenberg (eds), *The Three Rings*, Utrecht: Thomas Instituut, XI, 2005, pp. 142–3.
14 Inigo Bocken, 'Nicholas of Cusa and the Plurality of Religions', in Barbara Roggema, Marcel Poorthuis and Pim Valkenberg (eds), *The Three Rings*, Utrecht: Thomas Instituut, XI, 2005, p. 163.
15 http://jasper-hopkins.info/CAII-12-2000.pdf *Cribratio Alkorani II, 19.*
16 Gregory J. Miller, 'Luther on the Turks and Islam', *Lutheran Quarterly*, 14:1, 2000, 79–97.
17 Robert O. Smith, 'Luther, the Turks and Islam', *Currents in Theology and Mission*, 34:5, 2007, 351–64.
18 Ataullah Siddiqui, *Christian–Muslim Dialogue in the Twentieth Century*, London: Macmillan, 1997, pp. 85–6.
19 Hugh Goddard, *A History of Christian–Muslim Relations*, Edinburgh: Edinburgh University Press, 2000, p. 162.
20 Annemarie Schimmel, 'Jesus and Mary as Poetical Images in Rumi's Verse', in Yvonne Y. Haddad and Wadi Z. Haddad (eds), *Christian–Muslim Encounters*, Florida: University Press of Florida, 1995, pp. 144 and 147.
21 A.J. Arberry, *Mystical Poems of Rumi*, Chicago: University of Chicago Press, 1968, p. 78.
22 Tarif Khalidi, *The Muslim Jesus*, Cambridge, MA: Harvard University Press, 2003, p. 45.
23 R.J. McCarthy, 'Mary in Islam', in Alberic Stacpoole (ed.), *Mary's Place in Christian Dialogue*, Wilton, CT: Moorhouse-Barlow, 1982, pp. 205–8.
24 Bartholomew of Edessa, *Refutation of the Hagarene*, in Jaroslav Pelikan, *Mary Through the Centuries*, New Haven: Yale University Press, 1996, p. 77.
25 Susan Sered, 'Rachel, Mary, and Fatima', *Cultural Anthropology*, 6:2, 1991, pp. 137–8.

1 John of Damascus

The Heresy of the Ishmaelites

Adelbert Davids and Pim Valkenberg

Introduction

Even in his lifetime John of Damascus was highly esteemed in the Greek church; soon after his death he was actually surnamed *Chrusorruas* ('streaming with gold'). He owed this esteem not so much to his refutations of Judaism and Islam, but to the liturgical hymns and homilies he composed and his opposition to iconoclasm. In the Latin West he became an authoritative dogmatic author when the systematic part of his massive theological work *The Fountain of Knowledge* was translated into Latin in the twelfth century. John was often called the 'systematiser' of Greek theology. Others saw him merely as a compiler of early Greek patristic writings. John's refutation of Islam deserves special attention, since it was the first serious Greek response to the new religion.

The dates of John's life[1] are uncertain, but not his descent. Born in 650 or perhaps much later in the seventh century, he was of noble birth and a member of the rich Melkite family, the Manṣūrs of Damascus. His grandfather had been prefect of the town and had been disloyal to the Byzantine emperor by surrendering the keys of Damascus to the invading Arabs in 635. John's father was secretary of the treasury during the reign of the Umayyad caliph Mu'awiya I (660–80). Because of the anti-Christian politics of caliph 'Abd al-Malik, John left Damascus and retired to the monastery of Mar Saba, a centre of theological learning and liturgical tradition in the Judaean desert near the Dead Sea. Soon after 706 he was ordained priest by patriarch John V of Jerusalem (706–35). The see of Jerusalem had been vacant for six decades; now the new patriarch could rely on John's collaboration, his thorough literary education, his theological zeal and his prolific writing.[2] The exact year of his death (around 750) is not certain. According to tradition he lived to a ripe old age.

The iconoclastic policy of the Byzantine emperor Leo III (717–41) shook Greek Orthodoxy profoundly when Leo banned the veneration of icons in 726.[3] The heaviest opposition to this prohibition came from monastic circles. John's three orations in defence of holy images are considered among the most distinguished witnesses to the liturgical and theological meaning of icons. In Greek liturgical services many hymns that he composed for special feast days and seasons are still in use.

John's dogmatic works include mainly treatises about the right faith in christology. He defended orthodoxy against 'Nestorianism' (condemned at the Council of Ephesus in 431), 'monophysitism' (condemned at the Council of Chalcedon in 451), and 'monotheletism' (condemned at the Council of Constantinople in 681). Besides these treatises he compiled a large trilogy, commonly known as *Pege gnōseōs* ('Fountain of Knowledge'). The three parts are: a philosophical introduction (*Dialectics*), a refutation of all heresies (*On Heresies*) and an ample dogmatic survey of the *Exposition of the Orthodox Faith.* As John lived in an exclusively Christian-Islamic environment at Damascus and in the Greek community of Mar Saba and Jerusalem, there are no indications of any direct contacts with Jews.[4]

When John refers to Judaism it is not due to direct contact with contemporary Jewish believers. In one chapter of his *Exposition,*[5] 'Against the Jews on the question of the sabbath', he follows the traditional patristic pattern of anti-Jewish polemics.[6] The sabbath has mystical and spiritual meaning; its observance was imposed on Jews under Mosaic law because of their carnal and materialistic way of life. Under the spiritual law of Christ service of the Lord is not just partial – all of life is dedicated to him.

The refutation of Islam, a religion John had known at Damascus since childhood, is an important text, as there was no earlier Greek tradition on the subject that John could fall back on. This refutation, part of which is presented below,[7] is the hundredth – and last – heresy in his treatise *On Heresies.* In the course of literary tradition this treatise, originally written by John as the second of the three parts of *Fountain of Knowledge,* has seen further editions (with supplements)[8] and circulated as an independent work.

The chapters/heresies 1–80 of John's *On Heresies* are copied verbatim from a summary of an earlier heresiological work. Epiphanius of Salamis (ca 315–403), who grew up in a monastic environment in Palestine and Egypt to become a bishop and an admired leader of a monastic community in Cyprus, had written a lengthy refutation of all heresies under the title *Panarion* ('Medicine Chest'). In this book he reveals himself as vehemently anti-Jewish; a fervent adherent of the Orthodox faith of the Council of Nicaea (325), which had condemned Arius; and a passionate opponent of the speculative theology of the Alexandrian Origen (d. 254). He deals with all heresies from Adam to his own lifetime, eighty in total (corresponding with the eighty concubines of Song of Songs 6:8). Each of the seven sections into which the book is divided is introduced by a summary, not written by him but reflecting his treatment of the various heresies.[9] Section I concentrates mainly on Judaism, which – along with barbarism, Scythianism and Hellenism – is a mother of heresies.

The heresies that John of Damascus's *On Heresies* adds to Epiphanius's eighty are mainly christological, but his final chapter – chapter 100, on the new religion of Islam – is totally different from the foregoing 99 chapters. Whereas the other 99 heresies are merely catalogued succinctly,[10] Islam is a focus of special attention, as it is a 'heresy' with its own 'Holy Book'.[11]

The first half of this refutation, which deals with fundamental topics, has been translated below[12] and provided with a commentary. The second part of John's refutation – not translated and commented on in this article – deals with more specific aspects of the new religion. The translation below is based on that of Chase,[13] but with emendations according to B. Kotter's critical edition. Major corrections are given in the footnotes; minor ones (e.g. terminological and orthographic adjustments) are not mentioned. The arrangement of the text is the work of the authors of this article.

Translation of John of Damascus, *On Heresies,* 100: On Islam (Part One)

I. Historical Introduction

There is also the superstition of the Ishmaelites, which to this day prevails and deceives the people,[14] being a forerunner of the Antichrist. It derives from Ishmael, who was born to

Abraham of Agar, and for this reason they are called 'Agarenes' and 'Ishmaelites'. They are also called 'Saracenes', which is derived from 'destitute by Sara',[15] because of what Agar said to the angel: 'Sara hath sent me away destitute'.

These used to be idolaters and worshiped the morning star and Aphrodite, whom in their own language they called Khabar, which means 'great'.

And so down to the time of Heraclius they were very great idolaters. From that time to the present a false prophet named Muḥammad has appeared in their midst. This man, after having chanced upon the Old and New Testaments and likewise, it seems, having conversed with an Arian monk, devised his own heresy.

Then, having insinuated himself into the good graces of the people by a show of seeming piety, he proclaimed that a certain scripture[16] had been sent down to him from heaven. Having written some ridiculous compositions in this book of his, he teaches them to worship in the following way.[17]

II. Tradition from the Qur'an

He says that there is one God, creator of all things, who has neither been begotten nor has begotten.

He says that Christ is the Word of God and His Spirit, but a creature and a servant, and that He was begotten, without seed, of Mary the sister of Moses and Aaron. For, he says, the Word of God and the Spirit entered into Mary and they begot Jesus,[18] who was a prophet and servant of God.

And he says that the Jews wanted to crucify Him in violation of the Law, and that they seized Him and crucified His shadow.[19] But Christ Himself was not crucified, he says, nor did He die, for God out of His love for Him took Him to Himself into heaven.

And he says this, that when Christ had ascended into heaven God asked Him: 'O Jesus, didst thou say: "I am the Son of God and God"?' And Jesus, he says, answered: 'Be merciful to me. Lord. Thou knowest that I did not say this and that I do[20] not scorn to be thy servant. But sinful men have written that I made this statement, and they have lied about me and have fallen into error.' And, he says, God answered Him:[21] 'I know that thou didst not make this statement.'[22]

There are many other extraordinary and quite ridiculous things in this writing, which he boasts came down[23] to him from God.

III. Refutation of This Tradition

But when we ask, 'And who is there to testify that God gave him a scripture? Or which of the prophets foretold that such a prophet would rise up?', they are at a loss. And we tell them[24] that Moses received the Law on Mount Sinai, with God appearing in the sight of all the people in cloud, and fire, and darkness, and storm; and that all the prophets from Moses onwards foretold the coming of Christ and how Christ, God and incarnate Son of God, was to come and be crucified and die and rise again, and how He was to be the judge of the living and dead.

Then, when we say: 'How is it that this prophet of yours did not come in the same way, with others bearing witness to him? And how is it that God did not in your presence present this man with the scripture to which you refer, just as He gave the Law to Moses, with all the people looking on and the mountain smoking, so that you, too, might have certainty?', they answer that God does as He pleases.

'This,' we say, 'we also know, but we are asking how the scripture came down to your prophet.' Then they reply that the scripture came down to him while he was asleep. Then we jokingly say to them that as long as he received the scripture in his sleep and did not actually experience the operation, then the popular adage applies to him.

When we ask again: 'How is it that when he enjoined you[25] in this scripture of yours not to do anything or receive anything without witnesses, you did not ask him: "First do you show us by witnesses that you are a prophet and that you have come from God, and show us just which scripture testifies about you"',[26] they are ashamed and remain silent.

With good reason we say to them:[27] 'Although you may not marry a wife without witnesses or buy or acquire property; even although you neither receive an ass nor possess a beast of burden unwitnessed; and although you do possess both wives and property and asses and so on through witnesses, yet it is only your faith and your scripture that you hold unsubstantiated by witnesses.'

For he who handed this down to you has no warranty from any source, nor is there anyone known who testified about him before he came. On the contrary, he received it while he was asleep.

IV. Mutual Accusations: 'Associators' versus 'Mutilators'

Moreover, they call us 'Associators',[28] because, they say, we introduce an associate alongside God by declaring Christ to be the Son of God and God. We say to them in rejoinder: 'The prophets and the scripture have delivered this to us, and you, as you persistently maintain, accept the prophets. So if we wrongly declare Christ to be the Son of God, it is they who taught this and handed it down to us.' Some of them say that we have added such things, by allegorising the prophets,[29] while others say that the Hebrews deceived us out of hatred[30] by writing in the name of the Prophets so that we might be lost.

And again we say to them: 'As long as you say that Christ is the Word of God and Spirit, why do you accuse us of being "Associators"?' For the Word and the Spirit are inseparable from that in which they naturally have existence.[31] If, therefore, He [Christ] is in God as His Word, then it is obvious that He, too, is God.[32] If, however, He is outside of God, then, according to you, God is without word and without spirit. Consequently, by avoiding the introduction of an associate with God you have mutilated Him. For it would be far better for you to say that He has an associate than to mutilate Him and introduce [Him] as a stone or a piece of wood or some other inanimate object.[33] Thus, you speak untruthfully when you call us 'Associators'; we call you 'Mutilators' of God.[34]

A Theological Commentary

In this short commentary on John of Damascus's text we want to highlight the main theological implications of the manner in which he deals with Islam in the four parts of the text from the *Fount of Knowledge*. We show how the heresiological context in which he refers to Islam entails some references to Judaism as well. To put it briefly, John of Damascus uses a christological criterion in his approach to religious phenomena; consequently he does not distinguish between heresies and other religions, since in his view they are equally to be judged as deviations from christological truth. This construction of orthodox Christian identity determines his approach to Islam, which has been the standard for Christian theologians' judgment of Islam over the centuries.[35]

I. Historical Introduction

The first part introduces Islam as a new religious phenomenon. Its origin is of 'recent' times, namely the reign of emperor Heraclius (610–41). In 636 the Arabs crashed the Byzantine army on the banks of the Yarmuk, a tributary of the Jordan, whereupon the way into Syria and Palestine lay open before them. Because John of Damascus was one of the first Christian authors to write about this new religion, the information he gives is quite useful from a historical point of view. But the way in which he gives it reveals his own point of view: that of a theologian who wants to underline the differences between orthodox faith in Christ and heretical conceptions. Three issues are important: first, the way in which John of Damascus identifies this new religious phenomenon; secondly, the idolatrous nature of the ancient religion of the Arabs; and finally, the deceptive nature of Muḥammad's prophethood.

In the very first sentence, 'There is also the superstition/religion of the Ishmaelites which to this day prevails and deceives the people, being a forerunner of the Antichrist', John of Damascus tells his readers what his approach to this new religion is. The word he uses for this phenomenon, *thrēskeia,* is in itself quite neutral, since it may mean 'religion' or 'cult'.[36] But the context in which John uses it makes it questionable. Consequently most translators choose a word with a negative connotation, such as 'superstition'. This derogatory slant is understandable, since the author does not intend to recognise Islam as a religion in its own right. His intention is to highlight the differences between orthodox Christian faith and traditions that deviate from the orthodox way of confessing Christ as the Son of God. All religious phenomena are weighed against this norm and found wanting, be they what modern historians of religion would regard as heresies within the ambit of Christianity or different religions.

As a result he considers the new religion a threat: it has become the most powerful religion in the region; moreover, it leads the people astray and must therefore be considered an instrument directed against Christ and his followers. John of Damascus's text differs in tone from the apocalyptic texts in which Christians expressed their first reactions to this new challenge,[37] but he does take over some of their apocalyptic imagery: Islam is an instrument of the Antichrist and, more specifically, one of the great signs used by false prophets to deceive even the faithful (Matt. 24:24). John of Damascus interprets the prominent position of Islam in his time as a sign that ushers in the end time. Thus he anticipates the theme of Muḥammad's deceptive prophethood: it is contrasted with that of John the Baptist (surnamed *prodromos* or 'forerunner' in Greek), who was venerated especially in Damascus. John of Damascus offers theological objections to the fact that the John the Baptist's church has been turned into a mosque, even though Christians and Muslims could venerate *Yaḥyā* there together.

In the same sentence, John gives the new religion a name that shows the 'need to fit Islam into a Judaeo-Christian frame of reference, rather than considering it in itself'.[38] The word *Ishmaelites* refers to the story of Abraham, as John of Damascus tells his readers in the next sentence. Again, the word itself may have a positive meaning, since it refers to an important tradition in the Qur'an and Muslim tradition, according to which *Ibrāhīm,* together with his son *Ismāʿīl,* is the father of true monotheistic faith (*hanīfiyya*).[39] Moreover, the Qur'an relates how Abraham, together with his eldest son Ishmael, introduced the cult of the one true God in Mecca at the place of the Ka'ba (Q 2:124–29). From the Christian and Jewish points of view, however, the reference is less positive, since Ishmael was the son of Hagar, an Egyptian female slave, and therefore not as important as Isaac, the son of Sarah,

Abraham's first wife. The Hebrew scriptures relate how Sarah induced Abraham to send Hagar away out of envy, because she was pregnant (Gen. 16). This Judeo-Christian frame of reference also explains the two other names that John of Damascus uses in this first part: *Hagarenes,* after the mother of Ishmael, and Saracenes because she was humiliated by Sarah. Of this last name, John of Damascus gives an etymology ('destitute by Sara')[40] that indicates how the Judaeo-Christian framework determines the negative approach to the new religious phenomenon. Again, the names in themselves are neutral and can even be seen as positive designations of Muslims' religious identity; *Saracenes,* for instance, may be interpreted as 'people coming from the East' or 'Arabian nomads living in tents'.[41] The name *Hagarenes* may be one of the earliest identifications of the new religion, since we find it in Greek and Syriac texts of about 640. It may mean 'the children of Abraham through Hagar', but for Muslims the Arabic word *muhājirūn* refers primarily to those who took part in the *hijra* from Mecca to Medina.[42]

The second issue in the introductory part of the text is the ancient religion of the Arabs. John of Damascus is quite clear in his general estimation: they were idolaters. This negative judgement has two functions. In the first place, it stresses that the Arabs did not have the right faith in God. In this respect John aligns himself with the argument of defenders of monotheism against those who venerate idols. In this debate Jews, Christians and Muslims construct their identity over against polytheism on similar lines. But at the same time John establishes continuity between this ancient idolatry and Islam: they venerate material objects, whereas Christians worship their God in a spiritual way.[43] This theme recurs at the end of the text.

Two of these material objects are specified: the morning star and Aphrodite, whom the Arabs used to call *khabar,* meaning 'great', as John of Damascus correctly points out. Although this could possibly refer to some of the idols venerated at the place of the Ka'ba in Mecca, the name '*khabar*' poses problems. It might be a rendering of *kubra* ('the great one') as an epithet for Aphrodite, or a misreading of the phrase *Allāhu akbar* ('God is most great') as 'God and the great one'.[44]

Finally, the figure of Muḥammad is presented as a false prophet and an impostor. On the one hand John of Damascus acknowledges the similarities between his proclamations and the Jewish and Christian faiths, hence that Muḥammad must somehow have consulted the Old and New Testaments. Moreover, he showed a kind of piety and produced a kind of scripture. But these similarities crumble under the weight of the overriding criterion of the right faith in Christ. In the first place, Muḥammad's words do not honour Christ adequately as the Son of God, and therefore he must have taken them from some heterodox source. The Arian monk mentioned by John of Damascus in this context might reflect an early version of the story that Muḥammad had obtained his christological knowledge from a heterodox Christian. Meanwhile the Baḥīrā legend was developed in Muslim circles for apologetic purposes as well, since it could indicate that Christians recognised Muḥammad as a prophet.[45] Interestingly, John constructs the identity of this monk as an Arian, as if to demonstrate that in highlighting the human nature of Christ as the prophet of God, Muslims are both unorthodox and unoriginal.[46] The relation between Arianism and Islam is a reconstruction by John of Damascus and accords with his defence of Greek Orthodoxy and his emphasis on the first ecumenical Council of Nicaea (325), which was convened to condemn the heresy of the Alexandrian theologian Arius (d. 336). Besides, 'new heresies' were always derivations from older ones – such had been the rule that governed heresiology since long before John. In Muḥammad's time there would have been no direct traces of fourth century Arianism in Arabia. In the second place, the fact that Muḥammad claims to have received a revelation from God detracts from Christ's uniqueness to such an extent that no Christian can accept him as a real prophet of God. His piety is feigned and his scripture is a fraud. Hence John of Damascus contrasts Muḥammad's worship (*sebas*) and its tradition (*paradosis*) with orthodox faith in Christ and its tradition.

II. Tradition from the Qur'an

In this part John of Damascus maintains the informative tone of his text. This time it is not about the religion of the Ishmaelites but about the text from which this religion is said to have originated. He does not accept the claim that the Qur'an was sent down by God but tells his readers that Muḥammad fabricated 'some ridiculous compositions in this book of his'. In other words, the stories about God, pious though they may be, cannot be a form of orthodox faith, because they were not received from God in a genuine revelation but were forged in a crypto-tradition. The real author is not God, as Muslims claim, but an impostor.

John of Damascus elaborates on this point by selecting some of the 'extraordinary and quite ridiculous things' from this writing. But this is not the whole truth: if the texts were merely ridiculous, they would not be so threatening to his Christian faith. The point John of Damascus wants to drive home by quoting these texts is that they seem to echo the orthodox faith on many points while in fact distorting it. To this end he concentrates on what the Qur'an has to say about God and Christ.

The first sentence by Muḥammad that John of Damascus quotes refers to one of the most famous tenets in Islamic tradition: 'there is but one God, creator of all things, who has neither been begotten nor has begotten'. While the first part clearly suggests the beginning of the *shahāda* or Muslim creed 'There is no god but God', the end points to *sūrat al-ikhlāṣ* (Q 112), which describes the Muslim conception of true religion. It is a kind of credal formula that underlines true monotheistic faith: 'He begets not, nor has He been begotten' (*lam yalid wa-lam yūlad,* Qur'an 112:3). That there is but one God, creator of all things, is also stated at the beginning of the creed of the Council of Nicaea (325)[47] and that God has not been created is also accentuated elsewhere by John.[48] But the words 'He begets not' may be considered to contradict the wording of the Nicaean creed, which says about Jesus Christ that he was 'begotten of the Father'.[49] In the original context of Muḥammad's life, though, these words were almost certainly not aimed at Christianity, since it is quite probable that in Mecca they were directed against a form of polytheism that spoke about the gods as if they constituted a family.[50] According to this hypothesis, these references to a family of gods (father, mother and child) might have influenced the Qur'anic interpretation of the triune God as a kind of 'divine family', in which Jesus would be the son of God and Mary.[51]

If the first sentence outlines the theology of the Qur'an, the second summarises its christology: 'Christ is the Word of God and His Spirit, but a creature and a servant.' At first glance the beginning of this quotation suggests a close parallel with orthodox Christian faith.[52] But the words 'Word' (*kalima*) and 'Spirit' (*rūḥ*) in the Qur'an highlight Christ as God's prophet, not as his Son.[53] The full quotation, therefore, underscores the differences between the two religions: 'O you people of the Book, do not go beyond the bounds of your religion, and do not say of God but the truth. The messiah, Jesus, son of Mary, was only a messenger of God, and His word which he emitted to Mary, and a spirit from Him. So believe in God and His messenger and say not "Three". Refrain; better it is for you. God is indeed only one God. Glory be to Him; far be it that He should have a son, for to

Him belongs all that is in the heavens and all that is in the earth. And God suffices for a Guardian.'[54]

In the quotation as rendered by John of Damascus, Mary, the sister of Moses and Aaron, is mistaken for Mary the mother of Christ.[55] This might be one of the subtle ways in which John shows that the tradition of the Qur'an cannot be correct, but in fact the Qur'an does sometimes seem to confuse these two women.[56] Another possible source of confusion in the Greek text as rendered by John of Damascus is the plural pronoun in 'they begot Jesus': is it Word and Spirit that begot Jesus, or the two of them together with Mary? In any case, the Qur'an wants to preserve Mary's virginity, while underlining that Jesus was not physically generated by God. He is but a human being, although he is a prophet and messenger of God. This brings the message of the Qur'an close to the belief of Arius, who denied the full divinity of the Logos by subordinating it to the creator God. The Council of Nicaea condemned Arius's refusal to accept that God was never without his Logos, because in his view the Logos was not from eternity, not pre-existent, and not consubstantial with the Father, but was created by the Father out of nothing.[57]

The next paragraph broaches a topic that has been a major bone of contention between Christianity and Islam: was Jesus crucified by the Jews or not? John here refers to the Qur'an, where it is said that the Jews uttered 'a great calumny against Mary (...) saying, "We slew the Messiah, Jesus son of Mary, the messenger of God". Yet they slew him not nor crucified him, but it only appeared so to them. Those who disagree concerning him are in doubt about it, for they have no knowledge of him, but the following of surmise; they did not slay him for a certainty. But God exalted him to His presence, for God is Mighty and Wise. There is none of the people of the Book but will believe in him before his death, and on the Day of Resurrection he will be a witness against them.'[58] As the full quotation from the Qur'an makes clear, this text is not directed against Christians but against Jews who boast of having crucified a person whom they consider to be an impostor, while the Qur'an takes the side of this prophet of God. The people of the book, here especially the Jews, will believe in him before their death, and he will testify against them on the day of judgment. Thus a text that seems to underscore the similarities between Christians and Muslims in their assessment of Christ as the prophet of God in Islam's original polemics against Judaism, is used by John of Damascus in his polemics against Islam to demonstrate the differences between the two religions. The theme of prophethood connects the three religions, but the question of who is God's greatest prophet and of how God deals with his prophets divides them. Is the prophet of God ultimately a suffering servant, as most Jews and Christians seem to think? Or is he a triumphant witness to God, as other Christians and most Muslims think?

The final excerpt from the Qur'an reports an imaginary discussion between God and Christ after his ascension to heaven. It elaborates on the idea that Christ will witness against those who misconstrued him, but this time, according to the teaching of the Qur'an, his witness is directed against orthodox Christians. Those who say that he is the son of God and God self speak erroneously; they are the liars and heretics. In the words of the Qur'an: 'And when God said: "O Jesus, son of Mary, did you say to the people: 'Take me and my mother for gods apart from God'?", he will say: "Glory be to You. It behoves me not to say what I have no right to. Had I said it, You would surely have known it. You know what is in myself, and I know not what is in Yourself, for You are Cognizant of the unknown. I said only to them what You commanded me with: 'Serve God, my Lord and your Lord'. And I was watching over them as long as I stayed amongst them. But when You caused me to die, You were Yourself the Watcher over them, for You are witness of everything".'[59]

From this series of quotations from the Qur'an it is quite clear that there are many parallels between the new religion and orthodox faith, so that they sometimes seem to be two different traditions within the same religion. But the main issue between them, the human or divine nature of Christ, divides them, so that each considers the other heterodox. The fact, however, that the Islamic tradition claims to originate from a new scripture revealed by God shows that the differences go deeper than just heresy. Accordingly John of Damascus launches his attack on this new prophet and his new scripture at this point.

III. Refutation of This Tradition

The style of the third part of our text differs greatly from that of the previous parts. The historical approach, apparently aimed at giving information, changes dramatically into a debate that resembles a dialogue because of the exchange of viewpoints between the *dramatis personae* in the text: 'we say … they reply … they call us … we say to them in rejoinder'.[60] In fact, however, the text represents an apologia in which John of Damascus defends his own faith by disqualifying the credentials of the prophet who introduced the new tradition.[61]

In the first place, Muḥammad is not a trustworthy prophet, because his coming was not foretold by the Old Testament prophets. Here John of Damascus applies a traditional argument from the debate between Jews and Christians. From their side Christians claim that several texts in the Old Testament contain references to Jesus Christ as the promised Messiah. They even claim that the reference to Christ is the true sense of those texts in the prophets and Psalms, so that the only true interpretation would have to be christological. Jews, on the other hand, argue that these texts either refer to past events or to a future kingdom of God that has not been established yet, since there are no signs that the Messiah has come. Here John of Damascus adapts the Jewish argumentation to undergird his Christian opposition to the newly declared prophet. In his eyes, the Muslims did not know what to say since they were unable to provide the same kind of interpretation of Jewish and Christian scriptures as Christians could in the case of the Jewish scriptures.[62]

The Jewish character of John of Damascus's argumentation grows more pronounced when he compares Moses and Muḥammad: Moses received the law on Mount Sinai while the entire people looked on, but Muḥammad received his book without any witnesses at all. The same line of reasoning was used later by Jews like Judah Halevi[63] to show that Judaism is based on more credible foundations than Islam. John of Damascus, for his part, pursues his argument relentlessly, like a lawyer who has silenced his adversary in cross-examination: if you, according to your Muslim law, need witnesses when purchasing property, how come that you have no witnesses for something as important as the foundation of this law?

When the Muslim interlocutors admit that Muḥammad received God's message in his sleep, John of Damascus cannot resist the temptation to ridicule this prophet by using a popular saying that has been lost from the text.[64] His point is, of course, that even Muḥammad himself could not testify to the circumstances in which he received God's message. A sleeping recipient is the exact opposite of a trustworthy witness. But at this point John of Damascus seems to forget the theological nature of his point. Not only is the fact that Muḥammad was asleep during the *Laylat al-Qadr* used by Muslims to ensure that he could not have contributed anything of his own to this revelation; but the idea that God reveals God-self to people when they are asleep is well documented in both the Old and the New Testament as well.[65]

IV. Mutual Accusations: 'Associators' versus 'Mutilators'

After this imaginary debate on the credibility of Muḥammad as a prophet, the final part of the text raises the most famous controversial issue between Muslims and Christians: proper worship of God. The Muslims' accusation is fairly well known and can be found in the Qur'an as well; 'Unbelievers are they who say "Surely God is the Messiah, son of Mary." But the Messiah said: "O children of Israel, worship God, my Lord and your Lord." For surely whoever ascribes partners to God, God shall surely forbid him the garden, and their abode shall be the fire. And the iniquitous shall have no helpers. Unbelievers are they who say: "God is the third of three." Yet no god is there but one God. And unless they refrain from what they say, a painful torment shall afflict those of them who disbelieve.'[66] John of Damascus summarises this accusation with the Greek word *hetairiastai,* 'those who take other gods beside the true God', or in one word: 'associators'. This is a faithful rendering of the Arabic *mushrikūn*: 'those who let others share in being God', or 'those who ascribe partners to God'.[67] In short, Muslims charge Christians with polytheism, which is against the Muslim tenet of *tawḥīd* the oneness of God.

John of Damascus replies with a reference to the Christian tradition of revelation: this is what we have learnt from the scriptures and the prophets. The counter-attack follows immediately: you tell us that you accept all the prophets, so if they taught us this, it is on their authority that we believe that Christ is the Son of God and God. This leads to the issue of the interpretation of scripture, in which John of Damascus shows some awareness of Muslim ideas on scriptural interpretation that would lead to the doctrine of *taḥrīf,* which holds that the Jewish and Christian scriptures are no longer trustworthy revelations of God, since they have been deliberately corrupted.[68] Some Muslims accuse Christians of adding things to the scriptures by allegorising the prophets, while others accuse the Hebrews of deceiving 'us' (Christians, but Muslims as well?) by ascribing their own texts to the prophets.[69] These accusations, probably referring to christological interpretation of the Old Testament and to the pseudepigrapha, do not entirely concur with the later doctrine of *taḥrīf,* since this is usually connected with the idea of deliberately deleting references to Muḥammad as the future prophet of God. The reference to the Hebrews in the text shows that Jews are once again drawn into this debate between Muslims and Christians.

In a second reply, John of Damascus refers to the fact that Muslims also speak about Christ as Word and Spirit of God. While it is true that the Qur'an refers to Jesus the son of Mary as Word and Spirit of God, these words feature in a polemical context: 'O you people of the Book, do not go beyond the bounds of your religion, and do not say of God but the truth. The Messiah, Jesus, son of Mary, was only a messenger of God, and His word which he emitted to Mary, and a spirit from Him. So believe in God and His messenger and say not "Three".'[70] Because of this every modern scholar writing about the dialogue between Christians and Muslims immediately remarks that the words 'word' and 'spirit' in the Qur'an cannot have the same meaning as they have in orthodox Christian faith. John of Damascus, however, takes the opportunity to draw his orthodox conclusion: if Christ is a Word and a Spirit coming from God, he must be in God and thus he must be God. If the Muslims deny this, they separate and place outside God what is part of God, hence John's retort: 'You call us "Associators"; we call you "Mutilators".' If one takes Word and Spirit away from God, God becomes an inanimate object, like a stone or a piece of wood.

These words introduce another debate in the part of the text that is not included in our analysis: when Muslims accuse Christians of idolatry because they venerate the cross, John of Damascus replies that Muslims themselves venerate the stone of the Ka'ba. An allusion to this discussion may be found in the words 'to introduce Him as a stone or a piece of wood'. But these words probably also refer to *sūrat al-ikhlāṣ* once again: 'Say: "He is God, One God, the Eternal Refuge. He begets not, nor has He been begotten, and neither is there any equal to Him".'[71] The word *'ṣamad'*, translated here as 'eternal', seems to connote everlastingness, immobility and impenetrability. It was, however, rendered in Greek (maybe by Theodore Abū Qurra, one of John's pupils) with *holosphairos* ('spherical') or *holosphuros* ('solid round'), which prompts the association between this God and the stone of the Ka'ba. This 'monolithic' Christian conception of the God of Islam greatly influenced Byzantine polemics against Islam.[72]

Conclusion

There are a number of reasons for including John of Damascus's text on the heresy of the Ishmaelites in this volume on religious interactions between Jews, Christians and Muslims in the Middle Ages. First of all, John of Damascus was the very first theologian in the Greek tradition to react to this new phenomenon, and in so doing he created a picture of Islam that would be influential for ages to come. Secondly, although he did not pay much attention to the Jews of his time and rather adopted, in an oblique manner, the form of anti-Judaism that he inherited from his sources, his defence of Christianity against Islam betrays some Jewish lines of reasoning. Not only does John of Damascus deny that the Old and New Testaments contain some hidden references to Muḥammad as a future prophet, like the Jews denied such references to Christ as the Messiah in their scriptures, but he also harks back to the example of Moses as a prophet with a trustworthy tradition. This shows how two traditions that are at loggerheads suddenly appear to have a lot in common when confronted with a new religious tradition which claims to have received a new and more authoritative revelation from the same God.

Notes

1 There are several Greek biographies of John of Damascus, but they are all of the hagiographical genre and of a later date. When they do give details about John's life they go back to an Arab *Vita* of the ninth century; see R. Le Coz, *Jean Damascène, Écrits sur l'Islam. Présentation, commentaires et traduction,* Sources Chrétiennes, 383 (Paris, 1992), pp. 41–58 (with literature). For John's life and works, see H-G. Beck, *Kirche und theologische Literatur im byzantinischen Reich* (Munich, 1959; repr. 1977), pp. 476–86; B. Kotter, 'Johannes von Damaskus', *Theologische Realenzyklopädie,* 17 (Berlin – New York, 1988), pp. 127–32; A. Louth, *St John Damascene. Tradition and Originality in Byzantine Theology,* Oxford Early Christian Studies (Oxford, 2002), pp. 3–28.

2 The *editio princeps* of John's works is by M. Lequien (Paris, 1712) and is reproduced in *Patrologia Graeca,* pp. 94–96. B. Kotter started the critical edition *Die Schriften des Johannes von Damaskos* in the series *Patristische Texte und Studien* (Berlin, 1969 – …); since 1969 five volumes have appeared.

3 See esp. P. Schreiner, 'Der byzantinische Bilderstreit: kritische Analyse der zeit genössischen Meinungen und das Urteil der Nachwelt bis heute', *Settimane di Studio del Centro Italiano di Studi sull'Alto Medioevo,* 34, 1 (1988), pp. 319–407.

4 At least according to John's edited works. For still unedited anti-Jewish texts, see H. Schreckenberg, *Die christlichen Adversus-Judaeos-Texte und ihr literarisches und historisches Umfeld* (*1.-11. Jh.*) (Frankfurt am Main, 3d enl. ed., 1995), pp. 473–74.

5 *Expositio fidei,* 96 (IV 23), Kotter, *Die Schriften,* II, pp. 224–27; ET: F.H. Chase, *Saint John of Damascus: Writings,* The Fathers of the Church, 37 (New York, 1958), pp. 389–93.

6 Schreckenberg, *Die christlichen Adversus-Judaeos-Texte*, p. 473.
7 According to Kotter's critical edition, *Die Schriften*, IV: *Liber de haeresibus. Opera polemica*, PTS, 22 (1981), pp. 60–67; and Le Coz, *Jean Damascène*, pp. 210–27, with French translation. The Greek text also appears in R. Glei – A.T. Khoury, *Johannes Damaskenos und Theodor Abū Qurra. Schriften zum Islam*, Corpus Islamo-Christianum, 3 (Würzburg, 1995), pp. 73–84 (with German translation). There are two English translations of the refutation, based on the older editions of Lequien and Patr. Gr.: Chase, *Saint John of Damascus*, pp. 153–60, and D.J. Sahas, *John of Damascus on Islam: The "Heresy of the Ishmaelites"* (Leiden, 1972), pp. 132–41 (with the Greek text of Parr. Gr. 94).
8 As a result the chapter on Islam features in the older editions (Lequien; Patr. Gr.) as ch. 101. For the manuscript tradition of *On Heresies*, see B. Kotter, *Die Überlieferung der Pege Gnoseos des hl. Johannes von Damaskos* (Ettal, 1959), pp. 197–214; Kotter, *Die Schriften*, IV, pp. 2–17; and for *On Heresies* as part of *Pege gnōseōs*, see H.G. Thümmel, 'Zur Entstehungsgeschichte der sogenannten Pege gnoseos des Ioannes von Damaskos', *Byzantinoslavica*, 42 (1981), pp. 20–30, here pp. 27–29.
9 These summaries are incorporated in the editions as introductions to sections of the *Panarion*. The *Panarion* is edited in the series Die griechischen christlichen Schriftsteller: *Epiphanius*, I, ed. K. Holl (Leipzig, 1915); II, ed. K. Holl sec. rev. ed. J. Dummer (Berlin, 1980); III, same eds (1985); ET by F. Williams, *The Panarion of Epiphanius of Salamis, Book I (Sects 1–46)*, Nag Hammadi Studies, 35 (Leiden, 1987), and *The Panarion of Epiphanius of Salamis, Books II and III (Sects 47–80, De Fide)*, Nag Hammadi and Manichaean Studies, 36, ibid., 1994.
10 With the exception of chapter 80 on the heresy of the Messalians; here John augments Epiphanius's text from later sources.
11 There is also a *Disputatio Christiani et Saraceni*, allegedly composed by John of Damascus, but more probably by John's 'pupil' Theodore Abū Qurra (ca. 755-ca. 830). For the authorship, see Glei-Khoury, *Johannes Damaskenos*, pp. 59–62; Louth, *St John Damascene*, pp. 77; 81. For the Greek text of the *Disputatio Christiani et Saraceni*, see Kotter, *Die Schriften*, IV, pp. 427–38; Le Coz, *Jean Damascène*, pp. 238–51 (with French translation); Glei-Khoury, *Johannes Damaskenos*, pp. 168–83 (with German translation). Sahas, *John of Damascus*, pp. 142–55 (with English translation), has the Greek text from Parr. Gr. 96. For Theodore Abū Qurra, see Glei-Khoury, *Johannes Damaskenos*, pp. 47–58; and: *A Treatise on the Veneration of the Holy Icons written in Arabic by Theodore Abū Qurrah, Bishop of Harrān (C. 755-C.830)*, transl. into Engl. by S.H. Griffith, with intr. and notes (Louvain, 1997), pp. 1–20 (with lit.).
12 From the critical edition: Kotter, *Die Schriften*, IV, pp. 60–63. See also the Greek text in Le Coz, *Jean Damascène*, pp. 210–19.
13 Chase, *Saint John of Damascus*, pp. 153–56.
14 Chase: 'keeps people in error'.
15 Chase: 'which is derived from *Sarras kenoi*, or *destitute of Sara*'.
16 John of Damascus uses the word *graphē*. In the translation above the word is systematically rendered by 'scripture', even though in his translation Chase uses other terms such as 'book' (for the Koran), 'Scriptures' (for the Bible).
17 Chase's translation has been changed according to the critical edition; Le Coz, *Jean Damascène*, p. 213 translates this as 'il leur transmet cette façon d'adorer Dieu'; Glei-Khoury, *Johannes Damaskenos*, p. 75: 'lehrte er sie auf diese Weise die Ehrfurcht <vor Gott>'.
18 See also the translation by Le Coz, *Jean Damascène*, p. 213: 'le Verbe et l'Esprit de Dieu sont entrés en Marie et ont engendré Jésus'. Chase had: '(…) entered into Mary and she brought forth Jesus'; also Glei-Khoury, *Johannes Damaskenos*, p. 75: 'und sie gebar Jesus'.
19 Chase: 'that they seized His shadow and crucified this'; Glei-Khoury, *Johannes Damaskenos*, p. 75: 'dass sie <aber nur> ein Schattenbild von ihm zu fassen bekamen und kreuzigten'.
20 Chase: 'did'; Glei-Khoury, *Johannes Damaskenos*, p. 77: 'Du weisst, dass ich (…) mich auch nicht überheblich gezeigt habe'.
21 Chase: 'And God answered and said to Him'.
22 Chase: 'did not say this word'.
23 Chase: 'was sent down'.
24 Chase: 'we remark'.
25 Chase: 'us'.
26 Chase: 'what scripture there is that testifies about you'.

27 Translation according to the critical text. The older editions were defective; therefore Chase inserted: '[Then we continue]'.

28 Chase has *'Hetaeriasts, or Associators'*. In the following lines Chase has only: 'Hetaeriasts' for John's *hetairiastai.*

29 'by having allegorized the prophets': translation of Sahas, *John of Damascus,* p. 137; Chase translates: 'that it is by misinterpretation that we have represented the Prophets as saying such things'; Glei-Khoury: 'bei der Auslegung der Propheten'.

30 'out of hatred, deceived us': translation of Sahas, *John of Damascus,* p. 137; Chase translates: 'that the Hebrews hated us and deceived us'.

31 Chase: 'For the word, and the spirit, is inseparable from that in which it naturally has existence'.

32 'as His Word' according to the critical edition. The older editions had omitted 'as' and Chase's translation is therefore: 'Therefore, if the Word of God is in God, then it is obvious that He is God'.

33 Chase: 'to mutilate Him, as if you were dealing with a stone (…)'.

34 In Greek: *hetairiastai* ('Associators') and *koptai* ('Mutilators').

35 See A.-Th. Khoury, *Les théologiens byzantins et l'Islam: textes et auteurs (VIIIe-XIIIe S.)* (Louvain – Paris, 1969), pp. 47–67; N. Daniel, *Islam and the West: the Making of an Image* (Edinburgh, 1960; rev. ed., Oxford 1993), p. 13.

36 See Sanas, *John of Damascus,* p. 68 ('superstition') and Le Coz, *Jean Damascène,* p. 89 ('religion'). R.G. Hoyland, *Seeing Islam as Others saw it: a Survey and Evaluation of Christian, Jewish and Zoroastrian Writings on Early Islam* (Princeton, 1997), p. 485 renders it with 'cult'.

37 Hoyland, *Seeing Islam as Others saw it,* pp. 257 ff.

38 J.-M. Gaudeul, *Encounters & Clashes: Islam and Christianity in History,* vol. I: *A Survey* (Rome, 1984), p. 29. Though not an official publication, this widely distributed, photocopied summary of a course at the *Pontificio Istituto di Studi Arabi e Islamici* gives a very useful survey of the history of interaction between Christians and Muslims, including a collection of texts in vol. II.

39 For Abraham's role in the history of Judaism, Christianity and Islam, see K.-J. Kuschel, *Streit um Abraham* (München, 1994).

40 Cf. Gen. 16:8 (on Sarah in the desert) and Deut. 15:13 (Hebrew slaves should not be freed 'empty-handed' [LXX: *kenos*]).

41 Le Coz, *Jean Damascène,* p. 92, mentions as a possible etymology: Saracenes/*sharqiyyūn* ('Orientals'); another explication traces Saracenes to the Greek *Arabes skēnitai* ('Arabs living in tents').

42 See P. Crone and M. Cook, *Hagarism: the Making of the Islamic World* (Cambridge, 1977), pp. 8–9.

43 Cf. B. Roggema, 'Muslims as crypto-idolaters – a theme in the Christian portrayal of Islam in the Near East', in *Christians at the Heart of Islamic Rule. Church Life and Scholarship in 'Abbasid Iraq,* ed. D. Thomas (Leiden, 2003), pp. 1–18. Cf. Van der Heide on Maimonides' portrayal of Islam in this volume.

44 See Hoyland, *Seeing Islam as Others saw it,* p. 106.

45 See Daniel, *Islam and the West,* p. 15; B. Roggema, 'The Legend of Sergius-Baḥīrā: some remarks on its origin in the East and its traces in the West', in *East and West in the Crusader States,* eds. K. Ciggaar and H. Teule (Leuven, 1999), pp. 107–23.

46 Le Coz, *Jean Damascène,* p. 98.

47 *Decrees of the Ecumenical Councils,* ed. by N.P. Tanner, I (London – Washington DC, 1990), p. 4. To John the ecumenical councils are of paramount importance and serve as guidelines in his theology; see B. Studer, *Die theologische Arbeitsweise des Johannes von Damaskos* (Ettal, 1956), pp. 65–68; K. Rozemond, *La christologie de saint Jean Dam ascène* (Ettal, 1959), p. 48ff.

48 John usually speaks of God-creator who is not created (*aktistos*), instead of 'not having been begotten'; see *Expositio fidei,* 3 (I, 3), Kotter, *Die Schriften,* II, p. 11; cf. 5 (I, 5), Kotter, *Die Schriften,* II, p. 13: about the one God.

49 *Decrees of the Ecumenical Councils,* p. 4: *gennēthenta ek tou patros.*

50 Cf. W. M. Watt, *Companion to the Qur'ān* (Oxford, 1967; repr. 1994), p. 332.

51 See Qur'an 5:116; LeCoz, *Jean Damascène,* p. 104.

52 Cf. *Disputatio* (n. 11), 5, Kotter, *Die Schriften,* V, p. 433; Le Coz, *Jean Damascène,* p. 238, where the Muslim says: 'In my Scripture Christ is called Spirit and Word of God', whereupon the Christian asks: 'In your Scripture are the Spirit of God and the Word said to be uncreated or created?' (transl. by Sahas, *John of Damascus,* p. 149).

53 See G. Parrinder, *Jesus in the Qur'ān* (Oxford, 1965; repr. 1995), p. 136; R. Arnaldez, *Jésus fils de Marie, prophète de l'Islam* (Paris, 1980).

54 Qur'an 4:171; translation *The Bounteous Koran.* A Translation of Meaning and Commentary by Dr. M.M. Khatib. Printed alongside the Arabic text of The Royal Cairo Edition, Authorised by Al-Azhar 1984 (London, 1986), p. 132.

55 For Mary the sister of Moses and Aaron, see esp. Num. 16; for the birth of Christ from Mary, *Disputatio* (n. 11), 8, Kotter, *Die Schriften,* IV, pp. 435–36; Le Coz, *Jean Damascène,* p. 244: the eternal Logos of God 'created' (*ektisen*) a perfect man from the flesh of the holy virgin Mary. The word *ektisen* was omitted in the older editions (Patr. Gr. 96, 1345A).

56 Qur'an 3:36; 19:28; see Watt, *Companion to the Qur'ān,* p. 143.

57 John of Damascus follows the Council of Nicaea strictly (see n. 46). He devotes ch. 6 (I, 6) of his *Expositio fidei,* Kotter, *Die Schriften,* II, p. 15, to the Logos (God was never without his Logos), and ch. 78 (IV, 5), Kotter, *Die Schriften,* II, p. 177, to the question whether the hypostasis of Christ is created or uncreated. For Arius's phraseology, which is not always unequivocal, see É. Boularand, *L'hérésie d'Arius et la "foi" de Nicée,* I: *L'hérésie d'Arius* (Paris, 1972), pp. 71–79, and for the underlying Greek philosophical concepts, R. Williams, *Arius: Heresy and Tradition* (London, sec. ed., 2001), pp. 181–98. For the Muslim discussions on the status (created or uncreated) of the Word of God, see Le Coz, *Jean Damascène,* pp. 158–62. As L. Gardet and M.-M. Anawati make clear in their *Introduction à la théologie musulmane: essai de théologie comparée* (Paris, 1948), there is an interesting analogy between the Christian and the Muslim discussions on the (un)createdness of the Word in the period of *kalām* and scholastic theology. See also H.A. Wolfson, *The Philosophy of the Kalam* (Cambridge MA – London, 1976).

58 Qur'an 4, 156–59; translation Khatib, pp. 129–30. The quotation by John of Damascus avers that it was not Christ who was crucified but his shadow. This is often seen as a reference to docetism as known from many, esp. Syriac and Gnostic sources; cf. Le Coz, *Jean Damascène,* p. 108, n. 4 and Parrinder, *Jesus in the Qur'ān,* p. 110. The same can be said about the text from the Qur'an; see Watt, *Companion to the Qur'ān,* p. 72. See also *Disputatio* (n. 11), 8, Kotter, *Die Schriften,* IV, p. 436; Le Coz, *Jean Damascène,* p. 244: 'the Logos of God did not eat or drink or sleep, was not crucified *and did not die, but crucified was his holy flesh which he had received from the Holy Virgin*'; the italicised passage does not appear in older editions (Patr. Gr. 96, 1345A).

59 Qur'an 5, 116–17; translation Khatib, p. 161.

60 Sahas, *John of Damascus,* p. 79, notes that 'this discussion reveals that the author is reproducing here some of the most important points which emerged in actual conversations between himself, or other Christians, and Muslims'.

61 Hoyland, *Seeing Islam as Others saw it,* p. 486.

62 According to Sahas, *John of Damascus,* p. 81, this could be one of the indications of the authenticity of the text, since Muslims started to prove the prophethood of Muḥammad by interpreting certain texts from the Jewish and Christian scriptures from the ninth century onwards. In fact, however, Muslims developed such an interpretation of Jewish and Christian scriptures at an earlier stage; see M. Accad's contribution to this volume.

63 See W. van Bekkum's contribution to this volume.

64 Lequien (Patr. Gr. 94, 767) suggested as the text of the popular saying the expression '*oneirata moi legeis*' ('You're spinning me dreams') from Plato (without further reference); Lequien possibly had in mind Plato, *Republic* 563 d: 'you are telling me my dream' (cf. J. Adam, *The Republic of Plato,* Cambridge, sec. ed. by D.A. Rees, II, 1963, p. 249: 'manifestly proverbial'). The phrase '*oneirata moi legeis*' in fact comes from Lucian, *Dialogues of the Dead,* 30 (25), 2 (Lucían, VII, Loeb, 1961, p. 172). – Euthymius Zigabenus (ca. 1100), who in the chapter on Islam in his *Panoplia* made use of John of Damascus's *De haer.*, has: 'who sleeps speaks odd things and sees often strange dreams' (Patr. Gr. 130, 1336D; cf. Le Coz, *Jean Damascène,* p. 214, n. 1), but he does not mention a popular saying. John of Damascus could have had in mind Homer, *Odyssey* 19, 560–61: 'Stranger, know that dreams are baffling and unclear of meaning, and that they do not at all find fulfillment for mankind in every case' (Loeb, 1995, p. 275).

65 See Le Coz, *Jean Damascène,* p. 112 for some examples.

66 Qur'an 5, 72–73; translation Khatib, p. 152.

67 See Hoyland, *Seeing Islam as Others saw it,* p. 486.

68 See Le Coz, *Jean Damascène,* p. 114 and Sanas, *John of Damascus,* p. 82.

69 J-M. Gaudeul, *Encounters and Clashes: Islam and Christianity in History*, II: *Texts* (Rome, 1984), p. 11, refers to two forms of *taḥrīf* in the footnotes he added to Sahas's translation of this text: falsification through interpretation, and textual falsification respectively.

70 Qur'an 4, 171; translation Khatib, p. 132.

71 Qur'an 112; translation Khatib, p. 826.

72 See Sahas, *John of Damascus*, p. 77; idem, '"Holosphyros"? A Byzantine Perception of "The God of Muḥammad"', in *Christian-Muslim Encounters*, eds. Y. and W. Haddad (Gainesville, 1995), pp. 109–25, and B. Roggema, 'Muslims as crypto-idolaters', p. 12.

2 The Islamic Image of Paul and the Origin of the Gospel of Barnabas

P.S. van Koningsveld

To Qāsim al-Sāmarrā'ī, in friendship and grateful acknowledgment.

The Islamic image of Paul and its sources were the subject of a lively discussion between Stern and Pines in the 1960s. The sources of Qāḍī 'Abd al-Jabbār's treatment of the early history of Christianity in his book *Tathbīt dalā'il al-nubuwwa,* were the key-issue of the dispute. The outspokenly anti-Pauline view found in the work of 'Abd al-Jabbār was ascribed by Pines to a Judaeo-Christian source. Without totally dismissing the possibility of an original Judaeo-Christian inspiration, Stern, on the other hand, stressed the purely Islamic character of many of the details in the work of 'Abd al-Jabbār, while rejecting the existence of a Judaeo-Christian source. At the same time he drew attention to a few striking parallels between the Jewish *Life of Jesus* (*Toledoth Yeshu*) and some aspects of the Islamic image of Paul, not only in the work of 'Abd al-Jabbār but also in several other Islamic sources.[1]

A similar controversy has developed around the *Gospel of Barnabas,* an Islamic pseudepigraphical piece of anti-Christian polemic, preserved in one Italian and one Spanish manuscript only, which greatly influenced the inter-religious debate of the present century by way of printed translations into various languages, including English, French, Arabic, Turkish, Urdu and Indonesian. Cirillo, to whom we are obliged for a critical study of the composition and origin of the Italian version, attempted to prove that this text must be interpreted as an elaboration of a lost Judaeo-Christian source as well.[2] This theory has been challenged by various hypotheses concerning the author of the book and its origin. Prominent among these is the thesis that the work is an early seventeenth-century product of the literary culture of the Moriscos, probably after their expulsion from Spain.[3]

The aim of this contribution is not to reopen the debate concerning the possible existence of Judaeo-Christian sources or influences. I believe that it is necessary to deal with the existing Islamic material first, before starting the research for a connection between the Islamic material and its pre-Islamic sources, whether they be Jewish, Christian or Judaeo-Christian. What I want to do is, first of all, to present some fresh material, derived from manuscripts and printed sources, which casts additional light on the Islamic Paul. My second aim is to discuss the relevance of these, as well as the other Islamic material, for our understanding of the historical growth and spread of these legendary traditions, both in the eastern and western parts of the Islamic world. Finally, the results of this investigation will serve as a starting point for a fresh discussion of the origin of the *Gospel of Barnabas.*

I. A report by Sayf ibn 'Umar and the image of Paul in Eastern Islam

The image of Paul in Islamic sources from al-Andalus and Christian Spain is closely linked to a report of the historian Sayf 'Umar al-Tamīmī (d. 796 or 797). This report appears in folios 127a–129b of a manuscript of 175 folios which was recently discovered by Qāsim al-Sāmarrā'ī in the library of the Islamic University of Imam Muḥammad ibn Sa'ūd in Riyāḍ. According to al-Sāmarrā'ī, this manuscript contains substantial fragments of Sayf's *Kitāb masīr 'Alī wa-'Ā'isha* and his *Kitāb al-Ridda wa-'l-futūḥ*.[4] The full text of this report is given in Appendix I of this article. At this point we shall confine ourselves to a short summary.

Sayf b. 'Umar discusses Paul's adverse influence on early Christianity in a discussion on the factors which led to the assassination of Caliph 'Uthmān. He adduces the story of Paul as a parallel to that of 'Abd Allah b. Saba', a Jew from San'ā' who was called Ibn al-Sawdā' because he had a black mother. His role in early Islam was similar to that of Paul in early Christianity. Ibn Saba' is said to have converted to Islam in the time of 'Uthmān and traveled through various countries in order to lead the people astray. He started in the Hijāz, then went to Buṣra and Kūfa. He then continued to preach in al-Shām, but was unable to mislead any of its inhabitants. Subsequently he was expelled to Egypt, where he taught that Muḥammad was more worthy to return (at the end of time) than Jesus, thus laying down the doctrine of the Return.[5] After this he taught that there were a thousand prophets, that every prophet had a regent and that 'Alī was the regent of Muḥammad. The next step in his teaching was the doctrine that Muḥammad was the Seal of the prophets, while 'Alī was the Seal of the regents.[6] In short, Ibn Saba' developed the doctrines which became the basis of the great discord between Shi'ite and Sunnite Islam, just as Paul had laid down the basis for the discord between the different Christian sects.

The story of Paul is presented by Sayf on the authority of 'Aṭiyya, from Yazīd al-Faq'asī, from Ibn 'Abbās. In the Riyāḍ manuscript, Sayf's name is preceded by the same *riwāya* as that given by al-Ṭabarī when quoting Sayf's work, viz. al-Sārī—Shu'ayb. He relates that after the assumption of Jesus, his followers numbered seven hundred families. Paul, the King of the Jews, whose *kunya* was Abū Shā'ul, urged that the Christians be killed, but they succeeded in escaping. Paul warned them (apparently the Jews) that the followers of Jesus would gain their enemies' favor and then come back to wage battle against them. They accepted his suggestion of using a trick to prevent this disaster. Paul left his royal position, put on clothes of the followers of Jesus and went to their army to deceive them. The Christians praised the Lord for the miracle of his capture. At his request, they brought him to their chiefs. He told them that on his way back from them he had met Jesus, who had taken his hearing, sight and reason. When Jesus returned these faculties to him, he promised the Lord to serve the cause of His followers and to teach them the *Tawrāt* and its rules. They believed him.

On his orders, they built a house for him where he devoted himself to a religious life. At a certain moment, after he had locked himself in, he informed them that he had had a vision in which he was instructed that the only correct direction for prayer was towards the east. They believed him and left their *qibla*. Then he convinced them, on the basis of another vision, that all food was permissible in the eyes of God. After having a third vision, he convinced them that it was their duty to abolish any form of violence and revenge. They accepted this and abolished warfare. Finally, during a longer period of seclusion he had a vision that he wanted to reveal only to a small group of four. For this reason he sent away everyone except Ya'qūb, Nasṭūr and Malkūn, together with a fourth person called "the Believer." He tried to convince them that God in fact had made Himself manifest to them in the person of Jesus, but had then withdrawn from their sight. This statement caused discussions and dissension, and various trinitarian doctrines arose. The "Believer" stressed that all this was contradictory to the true teachings of Jesus. Consequently, he left them and urged his followers to remain faithful to the only true teaching, that of Jesus. Each of the four taken into Paul's confidence gathered a group of followers. The "Believer" had the smallest group. Thereupon, Paul urged the other three to fight the Believer and his followers. However, they fled to Palestine, where they were taken captive by the Jews. They asked the Jews to leave them alone, since they only wanted to live in caves, in hermitages and on mountain tops, and to wander about through the countryside. Their offspring introduced heresies into their religion, except for a small remnant of followers of the "Believer," who survived among them and stayed loyal to their original doctrine. Some of them escaped to the Arabian Peninsula, where thirty of them lived as monks, and saw the Prophet and believed in him. In short, the role of Paul in the corruption of Christianity, according to this story, was twofold: he corrupted some important sacred rules of the religious law, and he spoiled the kernel of the faith itself.

Among the Islamic stories about Paul and those directly related to them, we can isolate a group of four which exclusively deal with the second element of Paul's action, viz. his corruption of the faith. The protagonists of the various versions of this group differ widely. Even Paul himself, in some cases, is completely absent, as are the founding fathers of the Jacobite, Nestorian and Melkite churches, as well as the fourth, anonymous characters, gnostically referred to in Sayf's version as the "Believer." It is helpful to adduce these parallels in an attempt to make some sense of the growth and original meaning of the Islamic legends concerning Paul.

The first two stories are found in the historical work of Ibn al-Jawzī (d. 1200). According to the first of these, quoted on the authority of Abū Ma'shar, to whom it was transmitted by Muḥammad ibn Ka'b al-Quraẓī, a hundred Jewish scholars gathered after the assumption of Jesus. The four most learned among them hold a discussion whose subject is, of course, Jesus. One of them, using almost precisely the same arguments as Paul did in Sayf's story, said that Jesus was God, and had manifested Himself on earth to mankind and subsequently returned to heaven. Another concluded that Jesus was only God's son, and not Mary's. A third claimed that Mary was a sinner, and no virgin. The fourth man present, however, stressed, in Qur'ānic terms, "that Jesus used to inform you that he was the servant of God and the spirit of God and His word which He had cast into Mary." Later, each of them attracted followers to his doctrine on Jesus.[7]

In this version Paul is totally absent, and the role of the Church fathers is played by three anonymous Jewish scholars. The fourth scholar, the counterpart of the true "Believer" of Sayf's version, again represents the Islamic view. Assuming that the third scholar in fact represents the Jewish point of view, which seems plausible,[8] the other two can be said to represent the confused and contradictory Christians views. Thus the truth of Islam is contrasted with the confused and perverted dogmatic doctrines, not only of the Christians, but of the Jews as well.

According to Ibn al-Jawzī's second version (quoted by him on the authority of Shaybān, to whom it had been transmitted by Qatāda), after the assumption of Jesus the Jews elected four scholars to be questioned about him. The story is shorter than the previous one, and the answers differ in a few important respects. First of all, the groups of believers in each of the doctrines are identified. Secondly, the doctrine that the birth of Jesus resulted from his mother's sinful deed is omitted and is replaced by another, trinitarian creed. Those who believe that Jesus was God Himself are identified as the Jacobite Christians. Those who believe that he was the son of God are called the Nestorian Christians. Then follows the view of the third scholar, who stressed, according to this version, that Jesus was God, and so were both his mother and God Himself. His followers are identified as the "Israelite Christians," and their religion is called the "religion of the Emperor" (the Melkites). The fourth man, who is straightforwardly called "the Muslim man," takes upon himself the defense of the Qur'ānic doctrine and goes on to refute the other three. However, no details are provided about the vicissitudes of his followers.[9] We observe that in this form of the legend, on the dogmatical level, the polemic is directed exclusively against Christianity. The Jews have indeed caused the perverted and confused Christian teachings, but their own view is absent.

In the other two stories of this group, which were adduced by Stern,[10] Paul is the protagonist. The first is a piece of commentary on the Qur'ānic verse: "And the Christians say Christ is the son of God, that is what they say with their mouths," etc. (9:3), found in al-Damīrī's *Ḥayāt al-ḥayawān* and quoted by him on the authority of al-Kalbī (d. 763).[11] The story relates that the Christians followed Islam for eighty-one years after the assumption of Jesus. Then a war broke out between them and the Jews. As a subterfuge Paul, who had killed many followers of Jesus, presented himself to the Christians as a repentant coreligionist. After having studied the Gospel in their church for a whole year, he departed for Jerusalem. Having taught Nasṭūr that Jesus, Mary and God were the three members of the Trinity, he left him as his lieutenant. Then he went to the land of the Romans, where he taught a man called Jacob that Jesus was not a man, but had become a man, that he had no body, but became a body, and that he was the son of God. After this he converted a man called Malkān, whom he taught that Jesus was and is God. After he had killed himself as a sacrifice, each of the three disciples began to call upon their fellow men to adopt their doctrine. This was the origin of the three Christian sects.

Similar to this version is that quoted by al-Qarāfī (d. 1285) in his polemical work *al-Ajwiba al-fākhira:* Paul, before committing suicide in an act he declared to be a sacrifice to Christ, revealed the contradictory doctrines concerning Jesus to three Christian kings who used to come on pilgrimage to him every year while he was living in a hermitage, together with a monk whom he had been able to convince of his sincerity and holiness. After his death, the kings and their followers started to fight each other, which was, of course, exactly what Paul had wanted them to do.[12] Paul acted in this way "because he was a Jew and he used to fight and kill many Christians."[13]

First of all, like the second version preserved by Ibn al-Jawzī, these versions do not contain any reference to a specifically Jewish point of view. Secondly, the three confused views are not described as the personal views of three individual Jewish scholars but as the perverted teachings, maliciously conveyed by Paul to three Christian disciples or kings. Finally, the fourth person, representing the view of Islam, is completely omitted, and so are his followers. However, the element common to all four versions discussed is the idea that the contradictory and perverted beliefs concerning Jesus are ultimately of Jewish origin. In two versions, where the Jewish scholars figure prominently and without Paul present, this motive occupies a central place and is brought out in a straightforward manner. In al-Kalbī's version, where Paul has become the chief actor, the Jews as a people are still present, although only in the background. One should keep in mind, however, that Paul, even when he seems to act totally on his own, always remains first and foremost a Jew, who uses his conversion to Christianity as a mere stratagem in order to lead the Christians astray. This conviction is expressed explicitly by al-Qarāfī, in whose version the Jews are not mentioned but Paul's Jewishness is.[14]

If we assume that the story was originally meant to be an Islamic polemic against both Jewish and deviant Christian views on Jesus, then the conclusion is that the first version preserved by Ibn al-Jawzī, where the contradictory opinions include both Christian and Jewish views, is the one closest to the original. If this is the case, we should consider the possibility that Paul was only introduced at a later stage of the development of the story and that the Christian sects belong to this later stage as well. When Paul is included the polemic became more outspokenly anti-Christian, though the Jews remained the ones to be blamed.

This raises the question of how the apostle Paul came to be associated with a theory on the origin of heretical doctrines on the status of Jesus. As a possible explanation I would suggest that there was a confusion, at some point between the apostle and his namesake, Paul of Samosata (known in Arabic as Būlus al-Shimshāṭī). This led to the eventual fusion of these two different legendary traditions. Paul of Samosata served as the patriarch of Antiochia from the year 260 A.D. He was dismissed by a synod in 269 for his heretical doctrines. According to the 19th Canon of the Council of Nicea, his followers could remain members of the Church, but had to be rebaptized. According to some Islamic polemical sources, Būlus al-Shimshāṭī was the first to state that Jesus combined manhood and divinity. Before his time, the Christians were united on the view that he was created human. This is precisely the role attributed to the apostle Paul by Sayf's report. Like the apostle Paul in Sayf's story, Paul of Samosata is accused of having been "the first to have spoiled the religion of the Christians." He held the view that "our lord Christ had been created as a human being from the divinity as one of us in his substance. The beginning of the son was from Mary. He had been chosen [by God] to become the savior of the human substance which was accompanied by the divine grace and which fused with it through [divine] love and will. For that reason he was called the son of God. He also said: God is one substance and one hypostasis."[15]

Whatever the case, the main aspects of the apostle Paul and his actions, as mentioned in the two versions of the tradition described above, are as follows. First, Paul is not only by origin but also by religious conviction a Jew who sides with the Jews against Jesus' followers. Consequently, his conversion to Christianity was not genuine, but rather out of guile and cunning. Secondly, Paul's pernicious actions are restricted to the corruption of the Christian faith.[16]

The other main Islamic tradition concerning Paul gives a different picture of his personality and actions. It also describes Paul as a "cunning and roguish Jew, out for mischief and assisting mischief-doers, a trouble-maker and power-seeker who employed all kind of tricks to this end."[17] However, his conversion to Christianity is not portrayed as a trick. The ensuing conflict with the Jews about his conversion motivated Paul to look for the protection of the Romans. He approached their governor with the claim that he followed the religion of Caesar, king of the Romans, and had broken away from the Jewish religion. By doing so he betrayed the true religion of Jesus (namely Islam). He did not do this out of loyalty to the Jews, but in order to gain prominence among the Romans and to incite them, out of revenge, against the Jews. Paul's corruption of Christianity by the introduction of pagan (namely Roman) customs is part of his pro-Roman and anti-Jewish strategy. It involved, for instance, the abolition of circumcision, of rules of ritual purity and food prohibitions, as well as changing the prayer direction. Qāḍī 'Abd al-Jabbār's version, discussed by Pines and Stern, presents a detailed elaboration of this tradition. It does not, however, contain any references to Paul's influence on the emergence of the Trinitarian heresies.[18]

Sayf's story is then a result of a fusion of elements from both traditions described. On the one hand, there was the legend focused on the contradictory views of Islam and Christianity regarding the status of Jesus. Paul was presented as an outspoken Jew who converted to Christianity as a subterfuge in order to combat Christianity. This version seems to be the basis of Sayf's report. Only a few elements of the other tradition, such as Paul's change of the *qibla* and his abolition of the food prohibitions, were interpolated into it. (Paul's abolition of the *jihād* has no parallel in the traditions we have discussed and seems to be specific to Sayf's story).[19] Paul's conflict with the Jews and his connections with the Romans were completely left out in Sayf's report. This is quite logical, since it would have implied two contradictory views of Paul.

From the above analysis it would also follow that the fourth person (the "Believer") is an integral part of the story, even in the more original form in which Paul is not mentioned. (The "Believer" does not figure in the tradition of 'Abd al-Jabbār at all). The "Believer" and his followers represent Islam and illustrate above all the belief in the continuity and the essential uniformity of the theological preaching of all the prophets, including Moses, Jesus and Muḥammad, a fundamental Islamic doctrine proclaimed in the Qur'ān. He may be compared with the "Believer" of the people of Fir'awn (Sūrat Ghāfir: 28), who stood up in defense of Moses, saying: "Would you kill a man because he says: my Lord is God?" For instance, the "Believer" according to Ibn al-Jawzī kept his belief secret, but when they tried to kill Moses he defended him. Various authorities have speculated about his identity.[20] A similar believer, whose identity was also discussed by scholars, is found in Sūrat Yāsīn.[21] In line with the teaching of the Qur'ān, the idea of continuity between the prophets, including Jesus and Muḥammad (notwithstanding the increasing heresy and dissension), is also expressed by many historians. Al-Mas'ūdī, for instance, deals with "the people of the intermediate period between Christ and Muḥammad … who were monotheists and professed the resurrection."[22] Ibn Kathīr identifies the followers of 'Abd Allāh ibn Addiyūs (?) as those who believed that Jesus was no more than a servant and messenger of God.[23] This group, according to him, settled in deserts and wastelands, where they built hermitages, monasteries and cells and lived an ascetic life and did not mix with the other sects who believed in the heretical Trinitarian doctrines and introduced innovations, e.g., changing the direction of their *miḥrābs*.[24] Therefore, to make sense of the vicissitudes of the true "Believer" and his followers, there seems to be no cogent reason to look for Judaeo-Christian or other sects living on mountaintops or in deserts and caves: we are simply dealing here with a literary embroidery upon a genuinely Islamic *theologoumenon*.

The apologetic nature of the story may have met with some skepticism on the part of historians. Al-Ṭabarī (d. 923), though relating, on Sayf's authority, the story of 'Abd Allāh ibn Saba' as the founder of the Shī'a, does not present the parallel report on Paul, also found in this source.[25] Perhaps he was just not interested in including such a long-winded digression while dealing with the caliphate of 'Uthmān. But he did not include this passage in his discussion of the early history of Christianity either. In fact, the only data concerning Paul found in his work relative to his arrival and crucifixion in Rome, together with Peter, by the order of Emperor Nero.[26] The omission of Sayf's report on Paul in al-Ṭabarī's work may account for the more or less neutral or even positive attitude towards Paul in many other historical works from the Mashriq.[27]

Al-Mas'ūdī (d. 956), for instance, places the crucifixion of Peter and Paul in the days of the Emperor Claudius and identifies them with the two messengers sent to Antiochia mentioned in Sūrat Yāsīn. According to him, the bodies of Peter and Paul had been put into crystal glass cases in which they were preserved in various churches in Rome "until this day." "But most of those who occupy themselves with the history of the world," al-Mas'ūdī adds, "think that they were killed during the reign of fifth emperor [Nero]."[28] In another passage al-Mas'ūdī identified Paul with the third messenger sent by God to Antiochia.[29] Ibn al-Jawzī (d. 1200), to whom I have already referred, identifies Paul as one of the two messengers described in Sūrat Yāsīn.[30] The crucifixion of Peter and Paul in Rome is also mentioned, without any additional negative views, by other historians, including Ibn al-Athīr (d. 1232).[31]

II. Transmission in al-Andalus and Christian Spain

The influence of Sayf's story on Paul can be traced in Islamic sources from al-Andalus and Christian Spain. All of these are outspokenly polemical. First of all, Ibn Ḥazm (d. 1064) shows knowledge of it in his famous *Kitāb al-Fiṣal.* "One of the things we have heard related by their [the Jews'] scholars, without anyone denying it boils down to the following: their rabbis on whose authority they have adopted their religion—the Tawrāt as well as the Books of the Prophets (peace be upon them!)—agreed to bribe Paul the Benjaminite (may God curse him!). They ordered him to profess outwardly the religion of Jesus (peace be upon him) and to deceive his followers and to induce them to follow the doctrine of his divinity. They told him: we shall take upon ourselves your sin. He was extremely successful, as is generally known." Ibn Ḥazm condemns this practice vehemently as an immoral act. He adds that this is a thing which "we do not consider unlikely to have been committed by them, because they have indeed intended to do the same with us and with our religion, even though it was impossible for them to reach their goal [in this case]. This happened when 'Abd Allāh ibn Saba', known as Ibn al-Sawdā' the Jew, the Ḥimyarite (may God curse him!), converted to Islam with the purpose of deceiving as many Muslims as he could. In fact, he induced a contemptible group of partisans of 'Alī to profess his divinity, just like Paul had suggested the idea of the divinity of Christ to the Christians. These partisans of 'Alī are the *Bāṭiniyya* and the *Ghāliya* to this day; the least unbelieving of them are the *Imāmiyya*—may God curse them all!"[32]

Elsewhere in his book Ibn Ḥazm remarks that according to the Christians Paul had prohibited circumcision, "one of the firmest legal prescriptions of the *Tawrāt.*"[33] He also discusses the various Epistles of Paul, which he apparently had in Arabic translation. He ridicules Paul's views, for example, on circumcision which he quotes from his Epistle to the Galatians: "The cursed Paul says in one of his Epistles, viz. the one to the Galatians, in the sixth chapter, 'We testify to every man who has been circumcised that he is obliged to keep the laws of the *Tawrāt* completely.' However, somewhat earlier he writes: 'If you are circumcised, Christ will profit you nothing.' How strange that he apparently prescribed two [different] religions to them! The person who is circumcised is obliged to keep the laws of the *Tawrāt,* but Christ will profit him nothing. However, Christ will indeed profit the uncircumcised, although he is not obliged to keep the religious laws of the *Tawrāt*! Nevertheless, Paul and the other disciples were circumcised according to the unanimous Christian view. It follows that Christ did not profit them, while they were bound to keep all the laws of the Jews. Since most Christians now living among the Muslims are circumcised,[34] it follows that, if he was speaking the truth, Christ does not profit them either, while they are obliged to keep all the laws of the *Tawrāt.* But if Paul lied concerning this matter, how could they then accept the teaching of their religion from a liar? Yet one of these two possibilities must be true." Referring to the second chapter of the Epistle of the Galatians, Ibn Ḥazm remarks: "He also says that John, the son of Zebedee, and James, the son of the carpenter, together with Peter, ordered people to abandon circumcision, while they would do the contrary. But this is not the way to establish the truth in preaching religion! It is rather a guileful instruction and a form of deceit." Ibn Ḥazm portrays Paul, based on his epistles, as a hypocrite and a liar. Some passages in Paul's *Epistles* remind him of the immoral role played by Paul at the initiative of the Jewish rabbis as he quoted earlier from Sayf's report. He considers the odiousness of these passages as proof of the veracity of that story.[35] However, Ibn Ḥazm's work does not contain any trace of the other main Islamic tradition of the image of the apostle, namely the person who abolished genuine Christian customs under Roman influence, as found in 'Abd al-Jabbār's book.

Ibn Ḥazm does not quote Sayf's book explicitly, neither does an anonymous author from al-Andalus usually called "al-Imām al-Qurṭubī," of the early thirteenth century. He included Sayf's complete story in the second introduction to the third chapter of his anti-Christian polemic devoted to the establishment of the Muhammad's prophethood. The author simply states that the story is found in historical books "preserved by us and by them." Apart from minor textual deviations which might be helpful to future editors of Sayf's work, there are three differences that deserve our attention. First of all, the third vision of Paul, leading to the abolition of the *jihād* by his followers, is omitted. I would suggest that during the Reconquista, with continuous battles between Muslim and Christian Spain, this vision had lost much of its credibility. The second difference are some glosses on the followers of Paul's three disciples explaining the origins of the Jacobites, Nestorians and Melkites. Finally, the author has added a small elaboration about the further vicissitudes of the "Believer's" spiritual offspring. After explaining that they fled to the Arabian Peninsula, where thirty of their monks met the Prophet and died as Muslims, the author says, referring to the story of Paul: "This took place, but God knows best, about forty years after Christ. Consequently, the whereabouts of the 'Believer' and his followers continued to be concealed, whereas the followers of the other sects remained divided but intermingled. Their situation was not consolidated until the time of the Emperor Constantine."[36] Apparently, the author was unable to provide more specific data concerning the "Muslim" group as an historical entity in the period between Paul and Muḥammad.

In the last chapter of his book, al-Qurṭubī pays special attention to the practical and ritual side of Christianity. He explains why the religion of the Christians is contradictory in many aspects to the teaching of Jesus himself. He reminds his readers of the story quoted previously concerning Paul, who changed their *qibla* and abolished their dietary laws.[37] The abolition of circumcision is ascribed by him to Constantine.[38] In his discussion of the many changes and corruptions made by the Christians in Jesus' religion, he mainly relies upon Christian sources from al-Andalus. He does not refer to Paul's romanizing activities, as described by 'Abd al-Jabbār.

As I have stressed elsewhere, the Egyptian Mālikī author (of Maghribī extraction), quoted above, incorporated many sections of the work of al-Qurṭubī into his own polemical work, without acknowledging his source.[39] This also holds true for the story of Paul derived from Sayf ibn 'Umar.[40] This passage is preceded in al-Qarāfī's work by another legend on Paul as an impostor and cheat who spread Trinitarian beliefs and sowed discord among the Christians, to which we referred above.[41] Both reports are mentioned in a section on circumcision. Al-Qarāfī introduces the first passage, derived from an unknown source, with the remark that all Christians used to be circumcised until the time of Paul, who forbade this practice and was like the Devil to them.[42] Elsewhere, al-Qarāfī states that "this cursed Paul was the first to corrupt the religion of the Christians after they had professed the Unity of God. He changed the foundations of their laws and altered the system of their rules concerning circumcision, among others. He was the originator of the confession of Trinity [which arose] from his evil view."[43] There is clearly some influence from the other main Islamic tradition concerning Paul. Al-Qarāfī does not adopt the view of his Andalusian source that the Emperor Constantine was responsible for the abolition of circumcision. He had access to other ideas about Paul as well.

Another author, of Tunisian extraction, who lived as a captive in Christian Spain at the beginning of the fourteenth century, showed much greater inventiveness in describing Sayf ibn 'Umar's story than all his Andalusian predecessors. I am referring to Muḥammad al-Qaysī, who is the author of an as yet unpublished piece of anti-Christian polemic, preserved in a single Arabic manuscript in the National Library of Algiers. Several manuscripts of the Aljamiado translation of this work are preserved in Spanish libraries. Both the Arabic original and its Aljamiado translation were circulated among the Muslim communities of Christian Spain during the fourteenth and fifteenth centuries.[44] A few relevant extracts from the Arabic original are presented in Appendix II. I shall confine myself here to a short summary.

The author presents Sayf's story at the beginning of his work as an illustration of the historical causes of the division among the Christians. He explicitly states that this story was derived from the "fifth volume" of the *Dīwān* of Sayf ibn 'Umar al-Tamīmī on the authority of Ibn 'Abbās. As in al-Qurṭubī, the third vision of Paul concerning the *jihād* is omitted, but al-Qaysī did not quote the passage from "al-Qurṭubī," who does not mention his source, as pointed out above. It seems reasonable to conclude that one or more links in the Andalusian/ Spanish transmission of Sayf's story are still missing. Following Sayf's story on Paul, the author deals with the many inconsistencies and improbabilities of the Gospels. He relates that among the Christians there was a group of friars called "the Temple," who were a remnant of the "Believer's" followers. They were supported by and served the Temple, preserved clerical rule and took the remnant of the donations. They were very wealthy, considered themselves monotheistic, and doubted Muḥammad's message. They taught that the true religion was the Unity of God, that Jesus was the Messenger and Servant of God and that the beliefs of the Christians were sheer heresy.

In 709 H., all the priests and clerics became suspicious of them. They started to investigate and spy on them, and finally discovered that one of them, their leader and representative, had converted to Islam. After a religious dispute, this leader handed over a letter to his opponents in which he defended the friars and explained their pure monotheistic belief, which was in conformity with Islam. They passed this letter on to the Pope in Rome, who opened it secretly. The letter started with the Islamic *basmala* formula and the usual eulogy on the Prophet. It accused the Christians of following the mendacious teachings of Paul the Jew, and abandoning the teachings of the imams and Jesus. The Pope informed his inner circle about the contents of the letter and hid it in his ark. When the Pope died, shortly afterwards, the ruler of France discovered the letter and was outraged that no one had informed him about it. He summoned the priests and informed them of the letter. "By God," he said, "this is what Jesus has promised us! The Muslims will inevitably appear from the Arabian Peninsula and from the whole of al-Andalus. They have discovered [the truth of] our religion and are well informed about our secret. Since these letters testify that no one but God should be worshipped, so expel these friars, because I fear they will let in the Muslims who will find out that these [friars] are monotheists and will then destroy our country. I will send for the ruler of Portugal, the knights, the [common] men, and the rulers of Castile and Aragon in order to form a coalition against this people and expel the friars, Jews and Muslims and send them to the land of the Muslims to seize it and their land will become ours." Thereupon, he expelled the Jews from his land, and confiscated the friars' wealth and possessions. They took a solemn oath to expel the Muslims and to baptize the Mudejars. An army recruited from Europe gathered on the coast of Barcelona. Don Jaime, their leader, also asked for assistance from the ruler of Majorca. All the Catalonian noblemen joined the troops, and set out to fight the Muslims.

The author identifies the Templars[45] as the remnant of the "Believer" in Sayf's story. The dramatic events he refers to can be verified. The expulsion of the Jews from France took place on July 22, 1306.[46] The initiative for the persecution and dissolution of the Templars was taken by the French King in 1307. Clement V (1305–14) overcame his initial opposition and agreed to cooperate in an investigation, after rumors about the Templars' heretical views began to spread. Clement V dissolved the Order during the Council of Vienna in 1312. Rumors spread in Aragon about the Templars linking them with the Muslims. After the Templars' arrest it seems that several of them entered the service of the Sultan of Granada.[47] During their interrogation, a few indications of some form of "crypto-Islam" came to light in the organization of the Templars. Many witnesses reported a secret ceremony in which Christ was abjured. One of the members of the order interrogated denied his belief in Christ saying he had asked "In whom should I believe, then?" The answer was "In the one great God whom the Muslims worship."[48] This phenomenon in the order of the Templars can be explained hypothetically by assuming that they were Muslim captives (slaves) in the order, who were freed after having been baptized. Many Muslim captives served in the order.[49] Perhaps, al-Qaysī, the author of this source, was associated with the order of the Templars during his long captivity in Christian Spain. This would explain his interest in the vicissitudes of the Templars and his sympathy towards them.

III. Origin of the "Gospel of Barnabas"

What is the relation, if any, between these Islamic traditions and the image of Paul in the pseudepigraphical *Gospel of Barnabas*? In this text, Paul is explicitly mentioned twice. In the prologue, Barnabas, who introduces himself as an apostle of Jesus, says:[50] "Très chers, le grand et admirable Dieu nous a visités, ces jours passés, par son prophète Jésus Christ, en grande miséricorde de doctrine et miracles. C'est pourquoi beaucoup, trompés par Satan, sous couvert de piété, prēchent une doctrine fort impie: ils appellent Jésus fils de Dieu, rejettent la circoncision, alliance de Dieu à jamais, et autorisent toutes sortes d'aliments impurs. Parmi eux, Paul lui-même est dans l'erreur, et je n'en parle pas sans douleur." In the last chapter, Paul is again said to be in error because he taught that Jesus was the son of God.

The three accusations proposed here *could* have been derived from the Eastern Islamic tradition concerning Paul, which is discussed above. It is much more difficult to assume that these accusations are an offshoot of the Andalusian-Spanish tradition, because the rejection or prohibition of circumcision was not clearly attributed to Paul by Muslim writers in that tradition. As we saw, Ibn Ḥazm only quotes the Christian view, claiming that Paul prohibited circumcision. He himself ridiculed Paul for his inconsistent views concerning this matter, making reference to his *Epistles*. The early twelfth-century author, al-Qurṭubī, attributes the abolition of circumcision to Constantine. Al-Qaysī, who lived in Christian Spain at the beginning of the fourteenth century, does not mention it at all.

At the same time, however, one observes a radically different sentiment in the Islamic traditions and the *Gospel of Barnabas*. In the latter, Paul is "in error," he is "deceived," but he is not the ruthless and rancorous deceiver working on behalf of or against the Jews, as portrayed in the Islamic sources. The errors of Paul are reluctantly admitted. Notwithstanding the parallels, the general atmosphere is very different.

Chapter 91 of the *Gospel of Barnabas* mentions an uprising in Judaea. The Roman army, at the instigation of Satan, pushed the Hebrews into saying that "Jesus was God who had come to visit them." "Some said that Jesus was God who had come to this world; others denied this but said that he was God's son; others denied this [as well], because God did not resemble a human being in any way. He did not beget children, but Jesus of Nazareth was a [only] prophet of God." The uprising is followed by the gathering of three armies of 200,000 soldiers each, led by the High Priest (on horseback, with the "tetragrammaton" on his forehead), Pilate the Governor and King Herod. Jesus denies all claims to divinity (Chapter 93 ff.) and announces the coming of the Messiah in the person of Muḥammad (Chapter 96). Tranquility only returns after the Senate of Rome, at the request of the three leaders, issued an order prohibiting people from calling Jesus God or Son of God. Transgressors faced the penalty of death (Chapter 98). It is tempting to recognize in this story some traces and elaborations of the legends discussed above, concerning the origin of the heresies about Jesus. However, there are no direct connections between the two traditions.

Though the *Gospel of Barnabas* contains many Islamic motifs analyzed in detail by numerous writers, the precise origin of these elements and how the author combined them with Biblical and other material still remains far from clear.[51] In order to get onto the right track, in my view, one has to study the earliest existing evidence, namely the two surviving manuscripts, in Italian and Spanish. As for the Italian manuscript, Cirillo has convincingly dated the water-mark of the paper on which it is written to the second half of the sixteenth century. The earliest dated specimens of this type of paper are known to be from Mantua (1588) and Verona (1591).[52] The binding of this manuscript was made of Turkish leather, decorated in the Ottoman style with a double gilt-edged frame and a central floral medallion on both covers.[53] Although the main text is in Italian, the lay-out of the text shows that this manuscript was executed in accordance with the Ottoman tradition. The folio numbers are given in Arabic numerals, as in Ottoman manuscripts (both in Arabic and Turkish) of the same period. The punctuation marks in the form of conspicuous red dots, as in Arabic and Turkish religious manuscripts, are found throughout the book.[54] The main text is written within frames so as to separate it from the marginal glosses and other material, a practice which is also common in Islamic manuscripts. Red lines were added over numerous passages of the text in order to highlight them. Precisely the same method is often found in Arabic and Turkish manuscripts, in which, for instance, passages of a text may be separated in this way from the commentary in the body of the text or the margins. Special frames were left for the titles of the chapters, which were completed in Italian for the first 29 chapters only. Arabic numerals were added to indicate the chapter numbers in the margins of these chapters. Although the main text is in Italian, all these technical aspects would accustomed [*sic*] to Islamic book techniques.

The accessibility of the text to non-Italian readers familiar with Ottoman book techniques was further enhanced by a series of marginal (and, in a few cases, interlinear) glosses in Arabic, some of which are comments. These glosses can be divided into various categories. Many of them simply translate or summarize passages of the main text. Others, however, give some comments. The author of these glosses shows familiarity with the Islamic and Christian traditions on Biblical writings and with the Islamic teachings on Jews and Christians. On fol. 9a, there is reference to the Psalms, as a commentary on the following passage in the text: "Que soit béni le saint nom de Dieu qui créa le splendeur de tous les saints et prophètes avant toute chose pour l'envoyer pour le salut du monde comme il l'a dit par David son serviteur: 'Avant Lucifer, en splendeur des saints, je t'ai créé!'"[55] The gloss states: "He relates in the Psalms that God first created the Light of Muḥammad. All the prophets and saints are lights. (This is part [of the text])."[56] Another example is found on fol. 14b, where Jesus remarks: "Je vous le dis en vérité: les scribes et les docteurs ont rendu vaine la loi de Dieu avec leurs fausses prophéties contraires aux vrais prophètes de Dieu. Aussi Dieu est-il irrité contre la maison d'Israël et contre cette génération incrédule!" There is the following gloss there: "The Jews falsify [or twist] the words in some places. (This is part [of the text]). Moreover, the Christians falsify words in the Gospel. To this I am a witness, as well as this book."[57] Elsewhere the glossator gives an explanatory remark about some rare expressions in the text. For example, when Jesus, before performing a miracle, addresses God with the name "Elohim Sebaoth," the glossator explains that this is a Hebrew name.[58] When Jesus says to the Jewish scribes: "Pour quelle raison avez-vous supprimé le précepte de Dieu pour observer vos traditions?" the glossator adds: "Jesus says to the Jewish scholars: 'Why do you falsify the rules of God and follow a heresy which you invent of your own accord?' (This is part [of the text])." The Arabic has: *Qāla 'Īsā li-'ulamā' Banī Isrā'īl: li-mā tuḥarrifūna aḥkām Allāh wa-tattabi'ūnakum (sic) bid'a tuḥdithūnakum (sic) min 'indikum? Minhu.* The suffix *kum* in the two verbal forms quoted above, I think, indicates that the glossator came from a Romance country, probably Italy. On the other hand, Cirillo noted many linguistic aspects of the Arabic which point to the influence of Turkish. Not only are there occasional Turkish words (such as *tinbal*, lazy), but also the grammar and syntax reflect the Turkish milieu of the glossator.[59]

Another important category of marginal notes in Arabic are an almost complete series of chapter-titles. As already noted, the frames for the chapter-titles were left blank after Chapter 26. This gives the impression that, at some point, the person who prepared the manuscript decided to replace the rather long-winded Italian titles with the more concise Arabic ones. He decided to call the chapters *Sūras*. A few examples are: Chapters 9: *Sūrat al-ḥajj;* 13: *Sūrat al-amn;* 14: *Sūrat al-mā'ida;* 16: *Sūrat tark al-dunyā;* 17: *Sūrat ikhlāṣ;* 32: *Sūrat al-bid'a;* and 33: *Sūrat al-mushrikīn.* This creates the impression that this gospel should be seen as a worthy precursor of the Qur'ān. The original Italian text has 222 frames for chapter titles, but the glossator apparently intended to reduce as the same Arabic title is designated in the margins to several chapters with blank frames, thereby indicating that these "chapters" would be combined in copies and translations of the work. Thus, for instance, the same Arabic title appears in the margins of Chapters [52] through [56], which would combine five originally independent textual entries into a single "Sūra of the Resurrection" *(Sūrat al-qiyāma).*

Cirillo correctly remarked that the whole manuscript, both the Italian and Arabic parts, is by a single author. As a proof of this, he points out that on fol. 33a a marginal Arabic gloss is linked to a related textual passage line, which is usually only found within the body of the text, thereby confirming the unity of the text and glosses. The Oriental techniques followed in the Italian text, pointed out above, lead to the same conclusion, as does the fact that the glossator "edits" the text by adding an almost complete series of Arabic chapter-titles.

Was the person who prepared the Italian manuscript in this way merely a scribe, as assumed by Cirillo, or was he the actual author of the *Gospel of Barnabas*? At this point it is pertinent to look at the Spanish text. The Italian manuscript has 34 blank pages before it starts with the prologue of Barnabas. It omits an introduction, found in the Spanish version. Here the curious story of the "discovery" of the *Gospel of Barnabas* is related by the "discoverer" himself, who uses the pseudonym Fray Marin.[60] He used to work with Pope Sixtus V (1585–90) in the Papal library. One day while the Pope had fallen asleep, and Fray Marin took the *Gospel of Barnabas,* the first book he found upon [*sic*], from the library. This was a book he had been looking for a long time. After reading it, he converted to Islam. This plot is only revealed after a description of Fray Marin's long quest for religious truth. Asking himself how the Jewish people had successfully based their faith on the Bible alone, while this was such a difficult book on which the Christians (the "unbelievers") had many commentaries, he concluded that the glosses could only have disappeared as a result of human malice. He incidentally got to know the glosses on the Bible written by prophets, such as Isaiah and Ezekiel, which, of course, differed from those "of [his] days," and concluded that there were probably many more than the four canonical gospels. The discord between Paul and Barnabas was a clear indication that other apostles might also have written gospels. Incidentally, Fray Marin got hold of another three rare books, all of which "spoke evil of Paul." Among these was the work of Irenaeus, who, among others, based himself on the *Gospel of Barnabas.* It was the discovery of this book which finally set him on the right path.

This, however, is not the end of the story. Following Fray Marin's instruction, there is a note that the Spanish text was translated from the Italian in Istanbul, by one Mustafa de Aranda from the village of Ambel who was Aragonese by origin. There is no reason to doubt this information. He could have been one of the Moriscos who stayed in the Ottoman capital after their expulsion from Spain in the early seventeenth century. One understands that this Spanish version was circulated in Morisco circles, outside Turkey as well, and became known to a Morisco author in Tunis, Ibrahim Taybili. He is in fact the only seventeenth century Muslim author known to have explicitly mentioned it in a work he wrote around 1634.[61]

The most obvious conclusion that can be drawn from the above mentioned data is that the *Gospel of Barnabas* was originally written in Italian, by an ex-Christian, Muslim author who combined Christian theological erudition with an admirable familiarity with Islamic sources and a fair knowledge of Arabic. The most probable place of composition is Istanbul, where the work would have been written after the author had become deeply involved in Islamic learning, which would hardly have been the case in Rome.[62] The "discovery" of the "original" in the Pope's library is, of course, a mere literary device, which is familiar from numerous other pseudepigraphical texts.

Notes

1 S. Pines, *The Jewish Christians of the Early Centuries of Christianity According to a New Source* (Jerusalem, 1966). (Proceedings of the Israel Academy of Sciences and Humanities, vol. II no. 13, 74 pp.); idem, "Notes on Islam and on Arabic Christianity and Judaeo-Christianity," *JSAI* 4 (1984), 135–52; idem, "Studies in Christianity and in Judaeo-Christianity based on Arabic sources," *JSAI* 6 (1985), 107–61, especially pp. 107–44; S.M. Stern, "'Abd al-Jabbār's Account of how Christ's Religion was Falsified by the Adoption of Roman Customs," *The Journal of Theological Studies,* New series, vol. 19 (1968), 128–85; see also Stern's article, "Quotations from apocryphal gospels in 'Abd al-Jabbār," ibid., 18 (1967), pp. 34–57. See also C. Adang, "Muslim Writers on Judaism and the Hebrew Bible from Ibn Rabban to Ibn Ḥazm" (Nijmegen, 1993, Ph.D. diss.), p. 71, with reference to L. Nemoy, "The Attitude of the Early Karaites towards Christianity," *Salo Wittmayer Baron Jubilee Volume on the Occasion of his Eightieth Birthday* (Jerusalem, 1974), English section, II, 697–715.

2 L. Cirillo and M. Frémaux, *Evangile de Barnabé. Recherche sur la composition et l'origine par L. Cirillo.* Text and trans., L. Cirillo and M. Frémaux (Paris, 1977), esp. pp. 247–50, "La formation de l'Evangile de Barnabé." Cf. Pines (1966), pp. 70–73.

3 L.F. Bernabé Pons, "Edición y estudio del manuscrito español del Evangelio de Bernabé. Evangelio hispano-islámico de autor morisco (siglos XVI–XVII)" (Ph.D. thesis, Alicante, 1992) 5 vols., esp. pp. 545–621. Thanks to my Dutch colleague, the Rev. J. Slomp, I have been able to see the first 2 vols. of this thesis, containing the study. Cf. M. de Epalza, "Le milieu Hispano-Moresque de l'Evangile islamisant de Barnabé (XVIe–XVIIe siècles)." *Islamochristiana* 8 (1982), pp. 159–83.

4 I thank my friend Qāsim al-Sāmarrā'ī, who is preparing a study and a printed edition of the MS, for photocopies of the relevant pages of the MS as well as for his permission to reproduce this source here. I also thank him for his kind help in tracing other relevant sources. See now also the edition of al-Sāmarrā'ī, entitled Kitāb *al-Ridda wa-'l-futūḥ wa-Kitāb al-jamal wa-masīr 'Ā'isha wa-'Alī, ta'līf Sayf ibn 'Umar* (Leiden, 1995), vol. 1, pp. 132–35 and vol. 2 (facsimile of the manuscript) pp. 62a–64b.

5 *Kāna Ibn Saba' yahūdiyyan min ahl Ṣan'ā' ummuhu sawdā' fa-aslama zamāna 'Uthmān b. 'Affān thumma tanaqqala fī buldān al-muslimīn, yuḥāwilu dalālatahum fa-bada'a bi-'l-Ḥijāz thumma 'l-Baṣra thumma 'l-Kūfa thumma al-Shām fa-lam yaqdir 'alā mā yurīdu 'inda aḥadin min ahl al-Shām fa-akhrajūhu hattā atā Misr wa-'ghtamara fīhim fa-qāla lahum fīmā kāna yaqūlu: al-'ajab mimman yaqūlu inna 'Īsā yarji'u wa-yukadhdhibu bi-anna Muḥammadan yarji'u wa-qad qāla 'llāh 'azza wa-jalla: inna 'lladhī farada 'alayka 'l-qur'ān larādduka ilā ma'ād fa-Muḥammad (s) aḥaqq bi-'l-rujū' min 'Īsā. Qāla: fa-qīla dhālika 'anhu wa-wada'a lahum al-raj'a fatakallamū fīhā* (MS Riyāḍ, fol. 129b).

6 *Thumma qāla ba'da dhālika innahu kāna alf nabī wa-li-kulli nabī waṣī wa-kāna 'Alī waṣiyya Muhammad. Thumma qāla: Muḥammad khātim al-nabiyyīn wa-'Alī khātim al-awṣiyā'* (MS Riyāḍ, fol. 129b).

7 Ibn al-Jawzī, *al-Muntaẓam fī ta'rīkh al-mulūk wa-'l-umam,* ed. Muḥammad 'Aṭā' and Muṣṭafā 'Aṭā' (Beirut, 1992), vol. 2, p. 40.

8 Plausible, because it was indeed ascribed to the Jews in Islamic sources such as Ibn Qayyim al-Jawziyya (d. 1350): *Hidāyat al-ḥayārā fī ajwibat al-yahūd wa-'l-naṣārā* (Riyāḍ n.d.). Published in a *majmū'a* entitled *Al-Jāmi' al-farīd,* pp. 477–682; this passage is on p. 638. Cf. also *Encyclopaedia Judaica,* s.v. "Jesus" (last section) and Stern 1967, p. 49.

9 Ibn al-Jawzī, op. cit. p. 41.

10 Stern, "'Abd al-Jabbār," pp. 178 and 181.

11 As Stern pointed out, it is also quoted, though anonymously, by the eleventh-century writer al-Isfarā'inī, in his *Kitāb al-Ṭabṣīr fī'l-dīn.*

12 Al-Qarāfī, Aḥmad ibn Idrīs, *Al-Ajwiba al-fākhira 'an al-as' ila al-fājira* (Beirut, n.d.), pp. 120–21. The same story is also found in Jalāl al-Dīn Rūmī's and in al-Tustarī's Persian version of Ibn al-Haytham's *Stories of the Prophets*; cf. Stern, op. cit., p. 181.

13 *Bi-sabab annahu kāna yahūdiyyan wa-kāna shadīd al-qitāl wa-'l-qatl li-'l-naṣārā* (al-Qarāfī, op. cit., p. 120).

14 The problem of the ultimate origin of these stories does not concern us here. It might be useful to study this problem in connection with the story of the ten Jewish scholars who converted to Islam in order to combat it from within. Cf. J. Leveen, "Mohammed and his Jewish Companions," *Jewish Quarterly Review* 16 (1925–26), 399–406; cf. M. Schwabe in *Tarbiz* (1930) pp. 74–89.

15 *Fa-qāla Būlus hādhā-wa-huwa awwalu man afsada dīn al-naṣārā: inna sayyi-danā al-Masīḥ khuliqa min al-lāhūt insānan ka-wāḥid minnā fī jawharihi wa-inna ibtidā'a 'l-ibn min Maryam wa-innahu 'ṣṭufiya li-yakūna mukhalliṣan li-'l-jawhar al-insī saḥibathu al-ni'ma al-ilāhiyya fa-ḥallat fīhi bi-'l-maḥabba wa-'l-mashī'a wa-li-dhālika summiya 'bna 'llāh* (Ibn Qayyim al-Jawziyya, op. cit., p. 646). Ibn Qayyim quotes the church history of Sa'īd ibn al-Biṭrīq (d. 940) on whom cf. Graf, *GCAL* vol. 2, p. 32 ff.

16 The view of al-Shahrastānī (d. 1153) in his *Kitāb al-milal wa-'l-niḥal* also seems to be based on this main line of the legendary tradition about Paul. He accuses Paul of having made himself a partner of Simon Peter and "changed the bases (*awdā'*) of his knowledge and to have mixed these with the arguments of the philosophers and his own confused ideas." Al-Shahrastānī seems to accuse Paul here of a certain "corruption of the Scriptures," and provides an example of this. He mentions certain points from the passage on Melchizedek in the Epistle to the Hebrews (6:20–27:17), claims which he calls the "Epistle of Paul to the Greeks," and which he claims to have seen. See W.M. Watt, "al-Shahrastani over *de triniteitsleer,*" in *Historische betrekkingen tussen moslims en christenen,* ed. P.S. van Koningsveld (Nijmegen, 1981) (=Midden Oosten en Islampublicatie 9), pp. 1–19, esp. p. 9.

17 Stern (1968), p. 137.

18 A summary of the views of 'Abd al-Jabbār on Paul is also given by A.M. al-Sharfī, *Al-fikr at-islāmī fī 'l-radd 'alā 'l-naṣārā ilā nihāyat al-qarn al-rābi' /al-'āshir* (Tunis, 1986), pp. 427–30. Sharfī draws

attention to 'Abd al-Jabbār's remark that the materials he presented concerning Paul and the contradictions between historical Christianity and the religion preached by Jesus were hardly mentioned elsewhere: *fa-ḥtafiẓ bi-dhālika fa-innaka lā takādu tajiduhu fī kitāb*; elsewhere he expressed the same idea: *wa-in kāna qad ittafaqa min ḥikāyāt aqwālihim wa-'l-radd 'alayhim mā lā yakādu yūjadu fī kitāb* (al-Sharfī, p. 427 n. 4).

19 In al-Andalus and Christian Spain this element of Sayf's story was omitted, as we shall see below.

20 *Al-Muntaẓam,* vol. 1, pp. 345–46.

21 See, for instance, Ibn al-Jawzī, *al-Muntaẓam,* vol. 2, pp. 31–32, where he is identified with Habīb al-Najjār.

22 Al-Mas'ūdī (d. 956) *Maçoudi. Les prairies d'or,* trans. C. Barbier de Meynard and Pavet de Courbeille (Paris, 1863), 9 vols; vol. 1, 128–29. Some considered them to be prophets, others did not. The men dealt with in this section are: Ḥanẓala ibn Ṣafwān (in connection with the *aṣḥāb al-rass;* cf. Qur'ān 25:40; 21:12–15); Dhū 'l-Qarnayn; the *ahl al-kahf;* Jirjīs; Habib al-Najjār, who was in Antiochia. Two disciples of Jesus were sent to him, together with a third one to help. There is a difference of opinion about this third person: many claim he was Peter, but others, including the Christian sects who believe that the other two were Thomas and Peter, say that he was in fact Paul. By a trick, Paul apparently succeeded in rescuing his two companions. Habīb al-Najjār believed in their message. According to al-Mas'ūdī, the Qur'ān refers to these events in Sūrat Yāsīn. Cf. also Pellat's article "Futra" in *EI*[2], s.v.

23 Stern, *op. cit.,* p. 181 n. 1 remarks that he has read somewhere, without quoting the passage, about a man called 'Abd Allāh ibn 'Adhūq ("or something like this") who followed Jesus's uncorrupted religion and lived to see and convert to Islam.

24 Ibn Kathīr, *al-Bidāya wa-'l-nihāya* (Cairo, 1932–39), 14 vols; vol. 2, p. 101.

25 Muḥammad ibn Jarīr al-Ṭabarī: *Ta'rīkh al-rusul wa-'l-mulūk,* ed. de Goeje et alii, vol. 2, 2941 ff; cf. *EI*[2] s.v. 'Abd Allāh b. Saba' (M.G.S. Hodgson).

26 Vol. I, pp. 741 and 737.

27 Also al-Jāḥiẓ (d. 868) does not show any influence of the above-mentioned Islamic legends concerning Paul. He merely criticizes the superstitious belief of Christians in the "miracles and signs" Paul would have brought. This may be a mere reflection of the Biblical story of Paul's conversion and the miracles connected with it. See *Rasā'il Jāḥiẓ,* ed. 'A.S. Hārūn, vol. 1, pp. 251–52 (*Ḥujaj al-nubuwwa*) (Cairo, 1979).

28 *Murūj al-dhahab,* ed. M. Muḥyī al-Dīn 'Abd al-Ḥamīd (Cairo, 1948), 2nd edition, vol. 2, pp. 299 ff.

29 Vol. 1, pp. 128–29.

30 *Al-Muntaẓam,* vol. 2, p. 32 (on the authority of Muqātil [b. Sulaymān]).

31 *Al-Kāmil,* ed. Tornberg (Leiden, vol. 1, 1867), pp. 228 and 231. According to the index, these are the only places where Paul is mentioned in this work.

32 Ibn Ḥazm al-Andalusī, Kitāb *al-fiṣal fī 'l-milal wa-'l-ahwā' wa-'l-niḥal* (Cairo, 1317–21) (5 vols.), vol. 2, pp. 221–22; M. Asín Palacios, *Abenházam de Córdoba y su historia crítica de las ideas religiosas* (Madrid, 1927–32) (5 vols.), vol. 2, pp. 386–88. The Arabic text has Ibn al-Sū' as the surname of Ibn Saba' which, I presume, should be corrected in accordance with Sayf's original version. Adang (1993) p. 71, unaware of Sayf b. 'Umar's report, suggested that Ibn Ḥazm's most likely source for this story would have been a Karaite informant who wished to discredit the Rabbanites.

33 Asín, *Abenházam,* vol. 3, p. 37 (possibly a reference to Acts 21:21); cf. A. Bouamama, *La littérature polémique musulmane contre le christianisme depuis ses origines jusq'au XIII*[e] *siècle* (Alger, 1988), p. 95.

34 Ibn Ḥazm may be referring here to the Christians of Muslim Spain; cf. Asín Palacios, *Abenházam,* vol. 3, p. 109 n. 188. The Christian inhabitants of Northern Spain were, however, envisaged as uncircumcised; cf. A. al-Azmeh, "Mortal Enemies, Invisible Neighbours: Northerners in Andalusī Eyes," in *The Legacy of Muslim Spain,* ed. Jayyusī (Leiden, 1992), pp. 259–72, esp. p. 264: "Thus, in a general ethnological sense, critics of Ibn García (fifth/eleventh c.) charged Northerners in general with being swineherds, descendants of uncircumcised drunkards and insatiable women. … "

35 Ibid., vol. 2, pp. 70–73, trans. vol. 3, pp. 108–15.

36 Qurṭubī, *al-I'lām bi-mā fī dīn al-naṣārā min al-fasād wa-'l-awhām wa-iẓhār maḥāsin dīn al-islām wa-ithbāt nubuwwat nabiyyinā Muḥammad 'alayhi al-ṣalāt wa-'l-s'salām,* ed. A.H. al-Saqqā (Cairo, 1980), pp. 241–44.

37 Al-Qurṭubī, *I'lām,* p. 393; cf. pp. 398 and 423.

38 Ibid., p. 394.

39 In my article "La Apología de al-Kindī en la España del siglo XII: Huellas toledanas de un 'animal disputax'," in: *Estudios sobre Alfonso VI y la Reconquista de Toledo,* vol. 3 (Toledo, 1989), pp. 107–29.

40 In his work *al-Jawāb al-saḥīḥ li-mā laffaqahu ʿAbd al-Masīḥ,* written in 1306 A.H., al-Alūsī quotes Sayf's report through al-Qarāfī (ed. Cairo, vol. 2, 331 ff; I owe this reference to my friend Prof. J. Sadan). However, the modern Islamic image of Paul falls outside the scope of this article.

41 Al-Qarāfī, *Al-Ajwiba,* pp. 120–22.

42 *Wa-lam tazal al-naṣārā kulluhā takhtatinu ilā zamān Būlus fa-nahāhum Būlus wa-huwa Iblīs ʿalā 'l-naṣārā; akhrajahu hādhā Būlus min al-dīn* (ibid., p. 120).

43 Ibid., p. 124.

44 On the Arabic and Aljamiado versions of this text see G.A. Wiegers and van Koningsveld, "The Polemical Works by Muḥammad ibn Sirāj al-Qaysī and Their Circulation in Arabic and Aljamiado Among the Mudejars of the Fourteenth Century," *Al-Qantara,* (1994), pp. 163–99.

45 On the Templars, see: H. Finke, *Papsttum und Untergang des Tempelordens* (Munich, 1907); A.J. Forey, *The Templars in the Corona de Aragón* (London, 1973).

46 See Y. Baer, *Historia de los judíos en la España cristiana,* trans. José Luis Lacave (Madrid, 1981), I, p. 313.

47 Forey, *Templars,* pp. 357–58, 277.

48 ... *dixit et deposuit quod postquam dictus frater Albertus fecit eum Christum abnegare et dixit sibi quod in eum non crederet, ipse frater Gualterius interrogavit eum: "In quem ergo credam?" et ipse frater Albertus respondit: "In unum deum magnum quem adorant Sarraceni"; nec enim credendum est esse Deum Patrem, Filium et Spiritum Sanctum, quia essent tres dii et non unus in cuius figuram illius dei magni*; A. Gilmour-Bryson, *The Trial of the Templars in the Papal State and the Abruzzi* (Città del Vaticano, 1982 [=Studi e Testi 303], p. 255).

49 Cf. e.g., Forey, op. cit., pp. 239–41; 285–87; 398–99 (document no. 26).

50 In these quotations I follow the French translation of Cirillo and Frémaux.

51 The Christian substructure was analyzed by Cirillo (1977) and the Islamic context was dealt with very ably by Bernabé (1992). Both works have elaborate bibliographies.

52 Cirillo (1977), pp. 41–42.

53 Ibid., pp. 40–41.

54 In addition to these one finds various punctuation marks of the usual Western type, cf. Cirillo, op. cit., pp. 44–45.

55 French translation, Cirillo and Frémaux.

56 *Dhakara fī 'l-Zabūr: awwalu (sic) khalqi 'llāh nūr Muḥammad; kullu 'l-anbiyā' wa-awliyā' (sic) nūr. (minhu).* The remark *minhu* is a technical term in Arabic manuscripts to denote that an appended marginal note is not a gloss but a part of the main text, especially when preceded by the remark *ṣaḥḥa* ("correct"). In this case this expression indicates that the gloss concerned presents a translation, summary or further explanation of the contents of the main text. Cirillo and Frémaux have translated this frequently occurring expression erroneously with the words: "Grâces à Dieu!"

57 *Al-yahūd yuḥarrifūna al-kalim min baʿd mawāḍiʿihi (minhu). Wa-baʿdahu al-naṣārā yuḥarrifūna al-kalim fī 'l-Injīl. Hādhā anā shahīd (sic) wa-hādhā 'l-kitāb.*

58 *Allāhu Shabāwut Allāhu ʿAluhin: hadhā ism lisān ʿimrān[ī]. Minhu* (fol. 17b). Cf. Cirillo and Frémaux: "Ce nom est de la langue d'Amran. Grâces à Dieu!" It seems more logical to assume that *ʿimrān* is a vulgar spelling of *ʿibrānī*. The final long ī is frequently omitted in these glosses. E.g.: *Lā ilāha min ghayri ilāhi Ban[ī] Isrāʾīl* (fol. 19b); *Sūrat al-laḥm al-insānī* (fol. 20a).

59 Op. cit., p. 48.

60 "Que tenía 'por mal nombre Pray Marin'." Bernabé, op. cit., p. 196. Use Bernabé for the following short summary, pp. 196 ff.

61 M. de Epalza 1982; Bernabé, op. cit., pp. 51–52.

62 In his article "Muḥammad as the Messiah: A Comparison of the Polemical Works of Juan Alonso with the Gospel of Barnabas," *Bibliotheca Orientalis* (1995), pp. 245–91, G.A. Wiegers has shed important new light on the origins of the Gospel of Barnabas.

3 The Christologies of Abū Qurra, Abū Rā'iṯa and 'Ammār al-Baṣrī and Muslim Response

Mark Beaumont

Two questions arising from the apologetics of Abū Qurra, Abū Rā'iṯa, and 'Ammār al-Baṣrī will be explored in this chapter. Firstly, what developments in Christology can be observed as a result of engagement with the Islamic context? Secondly, what impact did these presentations of Christology have on Muslims? In answer to the first question, Sydney Griffith has suggested that Islam forced Christian theologians in the Middle East to make an intelligible case for their beliefs.[1] He sums up Abū Rā'iṯa's Christological apologetics as an attempt to support "the reasonableness or the non-contradictory nature" of the Incarnation.[2] This is an apt judgment of Abū Rā'iṯa in particular among the three apologists, but it is a verdict that can also be applied to Abū Qurra and 'Ammār to a large extent. An examination of the arguments employed by the three men to demonstrate the reasonableness of the Incarnation will show to what extent this conclusion is true. If Griffith is right, then the development in the writing of Christology is to be seen especially in the justification of the notion of Incarnation as worthy of God given the prevailing conception of his nature.

The second question can be answered by studying the writing of Muslims on Christianity. Despite the fact that the refutations of Abū Qurra by 'Īsā ibn Sabīh al-Murdār (d. 840), and of 'Ammār by Abū l-Hudhayl (d. c. 840) are no longer extant, it is possible to discover the views of other Muslims about the Incarnation.[3] The criticisms by several ninth and tenth century Muslim authors of Christological affirmations made by Christians provide an indication of the impact of Christian apologetics in the period. These writers are al-Qāsim ibn Ibrāhīm al-Ḫasanī al-Rassī (d. 860), 'Ali ibn Rabbān al-Ṯabarī (d. 855), Abū 'Īsā al-Warrāq (d. 861), al-Nāshi' al-Akbar (d. 904), and Muḫammad ibn al-Ṯayyib al-Bāqillānī (d. 1014).[4]

The Christology of Abū Qurra

Developments in the Language of Christology

Abū Qurra's Christological summaries show similarities and differences between his Christology in dialogue with other Christians and his Christology in dialogue with Muslims. The Christological summary in his *Confession of the Orthodox Faith* written in the context of dialogue with other Christians may be compared with the one in his *Treatise on the Atonement* written in the context of dialogue with Muslims.[5] Two similarities are striking in the Muslim context. Firstly, Christ is called 'the eternal Son' in dialogue with Muslims as much as in debate with Christians. Use of the term 'son' would surely have been understood by a Muslim as a direct denial of the Qur'ānic assertion that God had no son, but Abū Qurra did not resort to calling Christ by the more Qur'ānic title 'word'. Secondly, Christ is 'begotten of God before time' in both summaries, but the term 'begotten' would probably be understood by Muslims as a challenge to the Qur'ānic denial that God begets. It appears then that Abū Qurra did not attempt to redesign the language of his Christology at these points in order to accommodate Qur'ānic conceptions of Christ. Three differences seem to be intentional changes for a Muslim context. Firstly, he drops the concept of 'hypostasis' when writing with Muslims in mind. In the *Confession,* he says that the eternal Son "formed for his hypostasis a living body", whereas in his *Treatise on the Atonement* he writes that the eternal Son "took a body, making it like himself". For Muslims he spells out the mechanics of the Incarnation in a way that he could take for granted in the Christian context. For Christians he writes of the eternal Son forming a body to accommodate both human and divine natures, but for Muslims he describes the entry of the eternal Son into Mary's womb to extract a human body from her in order to shape it into his own likeness. Abū Qurra then appears to be interpreting inherited theological language in the Muslim context so that technical terms do not impede understanding.

Secondly, Abū Qurra does not describe two natures in Christ when writing for Muslims, so setting aside the key element that defined the Christology of his own community in favour of terms that would communicate clearly to Muslims what all Christians believed about the Incarnation. Thirdly, in his search for language more understandable to Muslims, Abū Qurra appears to have used the expression 'took' in the light of the Qur'ānic denial that God took to himself a son. Here he asserts that it is the Son who took to himself a human body. The idea of the eternal Son 'taking' a human body was not a traditional way of describing the Incarnation in Christian theology. At the beginning of his *Treatise on the Incarnation* Abū Qurra has the Muslim use the verb in his very first question, "How can the Son who is divine want to take a body in which he will suffer?"[6] He represents the Muslim using the language of "taking a body" rather than the usual Christian language of "becoming human". Abū Qurra probably believed that such a shift in language facilitated dialogue with Muslims. Whether Muslims actually used this manner of speaking is debatable, but putting such a question on the lips of his fictitious Muslim enabled Abū Qurra to communicate the Incarnation in a way that Muslims might find more acceptable. These three changes in language are modest and leave most of the traditional Chalcedonian terminology in place. Abū Qurra's aim seems to have been to modify that tradition where he could without losing its essential elements when addressing a Muslim context. More important for him were arguments supporting that tradition based on Islamic patterns of thought.

Arguments for the Incarnation

Abū Qurra used three arguments to demonstrate the reasonableness of the Incarnation. The first of these is based on the Qur'ānic picture of God seated on his throne which allows Abū Qurra to show that there are situations where it is appropriate for the divine to interact with the created world. Discussion among Muslim scholars in the early 'Abbasid period about the anthropomorphisms of the Qur'ān provided Abū Qurra with an opportunity to engage in an Islamic debate as a Christian. If the Mu'tazila thought that nothing could be learned from the anthropomorphisms of the Qur'ān about the nature of God, and if the Traditionists held that it is not possible for us to know how God sits on a throne and is present elsewhere at the same time, then Abū Qurra offers a third interpretation which could be more satisfying.[8] If the Incarnation is true then it becomes a key to interpret God's relationship with the created world, because God restricted himself to a human body while at the same time leaving himself free to be elsewhere ruling the world. According to Abū Qurra, this Christian reading of God's session on a throne is ultimately more satisfactory than any interpretation offered by Muslims because it allows us to say that this is how God works in his world. There is a solution to the apparent paradox of God limiting himself to a particular place, and it is to believe that God is at one and the same time limited and unlimited. But only the Incarnation gives this solution. Only the fact that the divine becomes limited to the human body without becoming trapped there allows this third way of reading the throne texts. By engaging with Muslim forms of argumentation he forced intellectual Muslims to take him seriously as an equal, and offered an apologetic that worked as long as Muslims themselves debated the interpretation of anthropomorphisms.

The second argument defending the Incarnation is that the body indwelt by the divine nature was perfectly adapted for the purpose so that no imperfection could cross over from the human to the divine. Abū Qurra has the Muslim raise the issue of impurity. "It is undeniable that God sits on the throne but he does not take up residence in the body. The throne is pure but the human body is not suitable for God."[9] Here is the heart of the problem for Muslims. The purity of God must be preserved at all costs, but Incarnation automatically destroys purity. The logic of transcendence must be maintained in the face of Christian denial. Abū Qurra seeks to defend divine enfleshment by taking 'impurity' out of the discussion. He alludes to the Qur'ānic belief in the purity of Christ expressed in *sūra* 19:19 as a basis for his argument that in the case of Christ there is no suspicion of impurity in his nature. His own interpretation of that purity is that the Holy Spirit cleansed the human body taken from Mary before the eternal Son united himself with it, and so God himself guaranteed the purity of the human body by his own action. This is a very significant argument in the light of *sūra* 19:19, because it offers to Muslims a way of seeing human flesh as fitting for God's indwelling. If Gabriel announced to Mary that she was to bear a 'pure boy' then it follows that Christ was conceived without any defect. But then this purity is a perfect ground for the union of divine and human natures. Muslims cannot claim that indwelling this pure human body taints God's pure character. Therefore the Incarnation is not an unreasonable idea when it implies a union of divine and human natures. The appeal to purity could possibly have provoked Muslims to rethink their distaste for such a union, and despite their probable rejection of the Incarnation as undermining transcendence, they may have become aware of one reason why Christians believed in the Incarnation.

Thirdly, in his *Treatise on Sonship* Abū Qurra deploys another argument based on the anthropomorphisms of the Qur'ān. The treatise sets out to deal with the Muslim suspicion that Incarnation implies physical begetting on God's part. The opening question of the Muslim is, "how can God give birth in the light of the fact that a man only has offspring after intercourse with a woman?"[10] Abū Qurra's answer is a counter-question, "if you accept that God can be called the One who hears and the Wise, why can't you accept that he can be called the Father?"[11] He appeals to the Mu'tazilite interpretation of the divine attributes in this question, since if they are correct in supposing that God does not actually have ears with which to hear, then Christians are correct in holding that God does not actually have a child in the normal way. Christians are not guilty of attributing physical fatherhood to God. They speak of fatherhood and sonship in a non-physical sense because the relationship of father and son exists outside time and space. Therefore God cannot have given birth to a son in the sense that human fathers do, since the Son lives forever with the

Father. The logic of the Incarnation is dependent on the definition of God as Father of the Son from all eternity. Muslim acceptance of the validity of this argument would depend on a fresh reading of the Qur'ānic texts that denied that God begot a son, but this was probably unlikely given the outright rejection of the language of sonship in the Qur'ān.

These three defensive arguments support Griffith's view that Christian apologists in the early 'Abbasid period were concerned to uphold the non-contradictory nature of the Incarnation. Abū Qurra used debate among Muslims as a resource for Christian apologetics in order to draw attention to conceptual difficulties encountered by Muslims in their understanding of God's action in the world. A purely transcendent interpretation of the anthropomorphisms of the Qur'ān leads to the emptying of such expressions of their meaning. On the other hand, a willingness to accept that God acts in the world without a willingness to understand how he acts leads to an inability to make sense of God's character. However, Christian belief in the Incarnation provides us with a way to bring the transcendence of God into ordinary human life without sacrificing God's otherness, and it also shows how God works in his world without becoming restricted to it. Abū Qurra's three arguments are still useful for Christians who want to uphold the Incarnation in a Muslim context.

The Christology of Abū Rā'iṯa

Developments in the Language of Christology

The Christological summary in Abū Rā'iṯa's dialogue with Abū Qurra may be compared with the one in his *Treatise on Christianity* written with an Islamic context in mind.[12] Both summaries present the eternal Word as uniting with human flesh from Mary, with the result that there was one nature consisting of divine and human characteristics. Abū Rā'iṯa presents a Miaphysite Christology in both contexts. The divine and human aspects of Christ are not two natures because the human aspect cannot be equal to the divine without infringing the character of God. The divine hypostasis takes on human characteristics after the union with human personality. This divine hypostasis is equivalent to the divine nature, so Melkites like Abū Qurra are wrong to speak of nature and hypostasis as distinct.

Within the substantial agreement between the two summaries are four differences that show an adjustment to an Islamic audience. Firstly, Abū Rā'iṯa drops the expression 'the eternal Son' in the Muslim context, for unlike Abū Qurra, he seems to be more sensitive to Islamic rejection of sonship for Christ. Therefore, he uses the phrase 'the eternal Word' because he probably believes that it is less open to misunderstanding by Muslims. Secondly, there is no mention of God as 'Father' in the summary for Muslims, which further reduces the risk of misunderstanding by Muslims. Thirdly, he uses the verb 'take' in the apology for Muslims but not in the dialogue with Melkites, to refer to a divine 'taking' of a human body. Like Abū Qurra, Abū Rā'iṯa appears to be offering a reflection on the Qur'ānic teaching that God did not take to himself a son by suggesting that it was not God who took a son, but the eternal Word of God who took a human body. This sharing of the same linguistic innovation by Abū Rā'iṯa and Abū Qurra may be traceable to an earlier apologist whose work is not available today. Alternatively, one of them may have been the source of the innovation, but it would be difficult to know the direction of borrowing, given the facts that they debated with each other and that their writing cannot be dated with enough precision to judge who borrowed from whom. Fourthly, he uses the Islamic term *ṣifāt* to describe the divine and human aspects of Christ. Muslims used *ṣifāt* for the attributes of

God such as hearing, seeing, knowing and willing, but Abū Rā'iṯa applies the idea to Christ. This enables him to argue that in Christ there is one divine nature which has two attributes, just as in God there is one nature with several attributes. This is Jacobite one-nature Christology being interpreted in a way that Muslims might be able to understand through the use of the language of attributes. For if Muslims were able to hold that God was one even with many attributes, then Christians could point out that they believe that the divine nature in Christ is one even when it has human characteristics. This is a significant innovation by Abū Rā'iṯa which arises out of his Miaphysite tradition but is not determined by it. Rather the new context of engagement with Islamic language provides him with the linguistic resources to develop a novel description of the union of divine and human characteristics in Christ that would perhaps make sense of the union to Muslims.

These four linguistic innovations show that Abū Rā'iṯa was alert to the need for sensitivity to Islamic discourse in a more thorough fashion than Abū Qurra. They also challenge Sidney Griffith's claim that Abū Rā'iṯa had both Melkites and Muslims in view in his apologetic writing so that "we should not assume that his quarrel with these two groups, especially as it was conducted in Arabic, was aimed in two different directions."[13] This opinion is surprising in the light of his earlier statement that "the Arabic language became the catalyst for new thought models in Christian theology, especially in as much as Arabic was and is inextricably intertwined with an Islamic religious consciousness."[14] It would be more accurate to say that Abū Rā'iṯa wrote for two different audiences. In his argument with Melkites he used concepts translated into Arabic from Syriac, but in his apologetic work addressed to Muslims he removed some traditional Christological terminology that might be misunderstood and adopted some Islamic concepts that might make Christology more understandable.

Arguments for the Incarnation

In his Letter on the Incarnation Abū Rā'iṯa presents five arguments which attempt to show the reasonableness of the Incarnation to Muslims. Two of them are shared with Abū Qurra. The first of these shared arguments is the defence of Christ's sonship as being outside time, and the second is the defence of the human body as suitable for union with the divine nature by means of interpretation of the session of God on his throne.[15] The need to place the concept of 'sonship' outside time was obviously felt by all Christians in dialogue with Muslims, since the Nestorian Timothy I, the Melkite Abū Qurra, and the Jacobite, Abū Rā'iṯa used the same argument. These three Christian communities had a common understanding of the Father/Son analogy which gave them a theological unity in the face of the Islamic denial of 'son' as a true descriptive category for Christ. If the sonship of Christ was not from eternity then Muslims were right to reject it as demeaning to God's character. On the other hand, if Muslims could see that Christ's sonship is a non-physical notion, then they would have no grounds for rejecting the idea as unworthy of God.

The second argument shared with Abū Qurra is the use of the session of God on his throne to point out to Muslims that God can be in the world without ceasing to be transcendent over it. If Muslims reject any suggestion that God is confined to the throne then Christians can claim that the divine nature indwells the human body of Christ but is not confined to it. Whereas Abū Qurra alluded to contemporary debate among Muslims, Abū Rā'iṯa engages directly in debate with Islamic interpretation of the throne texts of the

Qur'ān. "God is in heaven and on the throne" must mean that he is Lord of heaven and Lord of the throne, and that God is in heaven and the throne and does not just appear in them.[16] His much more direct challenge to Muslim interpretation of the Qur'ān would no doubt have evoked a more immediate response than Abū Qurra's less direct argument, though the conclusion of the argument would probably have been unacceptable to Muslims whichever way it was presented.

There are three new arguments put forward by Abū Rā'iṯa. The first of these appeals to Muslim understanding of the attributes of God to support the Incarnation of the second person of the Trinity. If Muslims define God as knowing, willing and performing, they have to admit that these attributes do not always function together. If God allows evildoers to enter paradise then he knows and performs what he does not will, the entry of evil people into paradise. Yet Muslims claim that these apparently contradictory attributes do not affect the unity of God. On the same basis, Christians claim that when "one of the three hypostases became Incarnate without the other two" all three remained united. Diversity in attributes does not destroy unity in nature.[17] The second novel argument in support of the Incarnation makes use of the relationship between the human mind and body to explain the way the divine and human attributes work together in Christ. Abū Rā'iṯa has the Muslim ask whether the water of the womb is essential to the divine nature as a result of the Incarnation. The reply is negative since the physical body is no more essential to the divine nature of Christ than a human body is essential to a human personality.[18] If a Muslim grants that there is a kind of duality in human beings as a result of the union of non-material mind with material body then he might be prepared to entertain the possibility that non-material divine nature has united with material human nature. It is not nonsense for Christians to believe that divine and human characteristics have united in Christ.

The third innovative argument concerns the relationship between Christ and other messengers of God. The Muslim wonders why it is not more fitting for God to send a pure human to save humanity than to become human himself. Abū Rā'iṯa concedes that God did send human messengers such as Noah, Abraham and Moses but few listened to them. God could not save humanity merely by sending more of the same, so he decided to solve the problem through the Incarnation. There were two advantages to this decision; when people saw the divine nature in human flesh they were more able to respond to God's will, and in addition, God was able to show his goodness in a way that would not have been possible merely through messengers.[19] Here Abū Rā'iṯa appeals to the Qur'ānic sequence of prophetic messengers familiar to Muslims, but takes Christ out of the list into a separate category. This argument that Christ is superior to all other messengers flies in the face of the presentation of Christ in the Qur'ān where he is presented as one among several messengers who stand together as equals in God's sight. Abū Rā'iṯa directly challenges the clear teaching of the Qur'ān, a method he usually avoids. Acceptance of the initial premise that Christ was superior to other messengers because of his divinity would depend on a leap of faith by a Muslim that seems highly unlikely. Elsewhere, Abū Rā'iṯa tended to begin his arguments for the Incarnation with premises acceptable to Muslims before attempting to reach Christian conclusions. As a result this argument is not as useful in dialogue with Muslims as the four others surveyed.

Abū Rā'iṯa does not develop a fresh Christology in dialogue with Muslims. His apologetic strategy does nevertheless force him to argue for the reasonableness of his view of Christ in the light of Islamic convictions. Unlike Abū Qurra, he is explicit about the nature of Muslim thought, even to the point of relying on the teaching of the Qur'ān to support his own argument. The presupposition seems to be that, properly understood, a Christian view of Christ is not incompatible with Islamic conceptions of him.

The Christology of 'Ammār al-Baṣrī

A Defence of Nestorian Christology

'Ammār's known Christological writing is addressed to Muslims, and if he wrote for a Christian context only, his writing is not available. It is then not possible to compare his Christology for Muslims with a Christology for Christians. However, a comparison can be made between the apologetics of 'Ammār, Abū Qurra and Abū Rā'iṯa. 'Ammār's description of the Incarnation differs from Abū Qurra's and Abū Rā'iṯa's in his insistence on talking of a unity of two natures in two hypostases. He acknowledges this difference in his shorter apologetic work, *The Book of the Proof.*[20] In the answers to fifty-one questions he also affirms this two natures, two hypostases view. He finds it necessary in dialogue with Muslims to show why this view is more accurate than those of the Melkites and the Miaphysites. According to 'Ammār this view safeguards God from becoming embodied. Miaphysites have to concede that God is embodied because they claim that there is only a divine nature in the Messiah. Melkites are subject to the same difficulty, since God must be embodied if Mary is God's mother.[21] Clearly 'Ammār believes that a Nestorian Christology is less susceptible to Muslim objections than rival ones. 'Ammār then, in dialoguing with Muslims, is conducting another debate with Christian rivals, using the Islamic context to show that Nestorian Christology is truer than other types of Christology. It is almost as if the Nestorian is grateful to Islam for providing a platform for re-instating the anathematized Nestorian teaching to its rightful place as the truth.[22]

Arguments for the Incarnation

'Ammār uses three arguments found in other apologetic writing. Firstly, he shares with Timothy I, Abū Qurra, and Abū Rā'iṯa the argument that the begetting of the Son by the Father was outside time and therefore unlike human procreation. 'Ammār's version of the argument is different because he appeals to Islamic interpretation of the attributes of God to support a non-physical understanding of the Father/Son relationship. Since Muslims do not interpret the knowledge and wisdom of God according to human knowledge and wisdom, the fatherhood of God should not be interpreted according to the way humans understand fatherhood. If God's attributes are eternal and non-physical then the sonship of Christ must also be eternal and non-physical. This way of putting the argument is more sophisticated than his contemporaries' versions that simply state that Christians do not understand the sonship of Christ as bound by time, and therefore has greater usefulness in dialogue with Muslims.

Secondly, in common with his contemporary apologists he holds that the human characteristics of Christ do not adversely affect the divine nature, since the suffering of Christ was endured only by his human nature. If this is difficult to imagine then he suggests the analogy of coal that is heated by fire but does not impart blackness to it.[24] This analogy is particular to 'Ammār's presentation of the argument, again showing his desire to support the Christian case with ideas that might appeal to Muslims as reasonable. Thirdly, he shares with Abū Rā'iṯa the related argument that the divine nature is not limited by the humanity of Christ, but adds an analogy to help the Muslim to see the sense of the argument. The divine nature relates to the human nature in the same way that the sun lights up the earth without being limited to it.[25]

'Ammār has several arguments not found in other Christian apologetic writing in the period. They are of two kinds; arguments that are based on Islamic premises, and arguments that show the value of the Incarnation once the idea is granted as possible. He has two innovative arguments based on Islamic premises. Firstly, in order to deal with the denial that God begets in *sūra* 112:3, he refers to the divine attributes of mercy and anger which imply that God suffers. If Muslims hold that, in fact, God does not suffer despite the apparent meaning of 'anger' and 'mercy', then Christians are justified in believing that the Father can have a Son without 'begetting' imputing imperfection to God in any way.[26] Secondly, 'Ammār appeals to the manner of God's creative work to present the process of Incarnation. If Muslims do not know how God created the world then it is not a weakness for Christians to be ignorant about the way the divine nature united with the human nature in Christ. 'Ammār's reminder that agnosticism about the actions of God is a necessary position for both Muslims and Christians has a continuing validity, though there will always be a contention between Muslims and Christians concerning divine actions deemed admissible by one side or the other.[27]

'Ammār is especially interested in showing Muslims the value of the Incarnation for faith in God, despite the fact that Islam seems to reject the idea. He has six arguments commending the Incarnation as inherently true that do not depend on premises held by Muslims. Four of them come from *The Book of the Proof*. The first of these states that since human messengers cannot show God's character, only God Incarnate can enable people to see him. Christ did exactly this when he revealed to the people of his day his divine authority.[28] This appeal to the historical Jesus of the Gospels is unusual in ninth century apologetics, which are typically focused on the developed Christology of the Christian communities of the Middle East. Secondly, God chose to become visible to people as an act of mercy, in recognition of the fact that people make images of the divine in their search for him. This is sheer condescension by God who knows that the weakness of humans needs to be taken into consideration in the process of revelation and salvation.[29] Here 'Ammār probably has made too strong a connection between God's choice to become visible in Christ and the supposed need of humans to see God, because Christians normally affirm the former but not the latter. Moreover, in the context of dialogue with Muslims this argument is flawed, since it seems to suggest that the desire to visualize God is acceptable to him, an idea which the Qur'ān flatly opposes.

The third argument is related to the second in that 'Ammār again uses the notion of the desired visibility of God for human beings. This time the visibility comes at the Day of Judgment when humanity will appear before the divine judge, but since God cannot be seen directly on that day, he has chosen Christ as an appropriate means of being seen. However, the idea that the human Christ is God's veil in the judgment room is less than appropriate to the argument, because it follows that God is not seen as such, but only the veil of Christ's human nature. A Muslim would rightly infer that since veils hide rather than reveal, 'Ammār is actually arguing for the hiddenness rather than the revelation of the divine nature. The fourth argument has to do with the outcome of judgment for those being saved. If God gave humans authority over the rest of the created world, then he will surely give them similar authority in the eternal world. This is guaranteed by the Incarnation of the divine nature in the human. The idea of believers ruling with Christ in the afterlife is found in the New Testament but not as a result of the Incarnation as such.[32] ‘Ammār seems to be arguing that human beings can only rule as a result of the fact that the human Christ showed his divine authority, and that without the Incarnation there would be no rule for believers in the next life. However, the argument lacks coherence in the form in which ‘Ammār expresses it, and would therefore be hardly likely to commend the Incarnation to a Muslim.

Two further arguments for the value of the Incarnation come from *The Book of Questions and Answers*. Firstly, the Incarnation is supported by the purity of Christ from the beginning to the end of his life. While Abū Qurra and Abū Rā’iṯa both appealed to the purification of the human body taken from Mary before the union with the divine nature, only ‘Ammār argues that the maintenance of that purity is significant for the Incarnation to be verified. At least one other human being is said to have been pure at the point of conception, according to ‘Ammār, so it is not enough for Christ to be pure at the outset of his life. He quotes Jeremiah 1:4 as evidence that God purified the prophet Jeremiah in the womb, and goes on to argue that Christ could have lost his purity during his life, but, unlike the rest of humanity, he kept himself pure.[33] The implication of this testing of Christ throughout his life is that the human nature in Christ has a role to play alongside the work of the divine nature. The divine nature does not need to be tested for it is always perfect, but the human nature does need to be tested to prove its continuing suitability as an abode for the divine nature. Here ‘Ammār parts company from the emphases of Abū Qurra and Abū Rā’iṯa, for whom the fact that the eternal Word fashioned a body from the flesh derived from Mary ensures the continuing purity of that human nature. This is not adequate according to ‘Ammār, since the human nature taken from Mary may be susceptible to failure after the union with the divine. He believes that the human nature in Christ was active in responding to the will of God, which contrasts with Abū Rā’iṯa’s assumption that only the eternal Word responds to God’s will. ‘Ammār’s Christ has human struggles that Abū Rā’iṯa’s seems to know nothing of. This conviction arises from the fact that Christ can only save other humans if he has gone through the same experiences as they have. The continuing relevance of this argument can be seen in the way Karl Pfander in the nineteenth century and Kenneth Cragg in the twentieth century appealed to the obedience of Christ as essential to his value for humanity.[34]

The second innovative argument in *The Book of Questions and Answers* follows on from the establishment of Christ’s complete obedience to the will of the Father. The culmination of that obedience involved death on the cross to release humans from the judgment of God and to grant them eternal life. The value of Christ’s death and resurrection lies in the gift of resurrection life to humanity. ‘Ammār’s analogies of a prizefighter using up all his strength to defeat an opponent, and of a doctor swallowing poison before administering harmful medicine are interesting attempts to commend the idea to Muslims. It was not enough for Christ to promise the resurrected life to others without offering proof that it could happen, so he willingly submitted to death and resurrection to “place firmly in their hearts the promise of their resurrection”.[35] This is an argument for the Incarnation that looks to the end rather than the beginning of the action, thus Incarnation is not defined merely by the commencement of a union between the divine and human natures as Abū Qurra and Abū Rā’iṯa seem to argue. Without the willing submission of Christ to death there is no guarantee that death can be overcome, and without the resurrection of Christ there can be no certainty that humans will have a life beyond this one. ‘Ammār’s argument is based on the teaching of several New Testament texts,[36] and has often been repeated in modern apologetics for Muslims.[37]

Muslim Responses to Christian Views of Christ in the Ninth and Tenth Centuries

The Truth about Christ Comes from the Qur'ān

The first type of response was to appeal to the Qur'ān as the measure by which to judge Christian beliefs. This was the approach of al-Qāsim ibn Ibrāhīm al-Ḫasanī al-Rassī (d. 860) who wrote a *Reply to the Christians* possibly in the period from 815 to 826 during which he debated with Christians in Egypt. If this is the case his *Reply* is the earliest surviving Muslim writing against Christian beliefs.[38] Al-Qāsim documents the three main Christian presentations of the Incarnation by Melkites, Jacobites and Nestorians before concluding that all of them depart from the teaching of "the prophets and apostles of God".[39] He does not actually specify at what points Christian teaching on the Incarnation diverges from that of the Qur'ān, but he may have taken for granted that his Muslim audience did not need much assistance with such a critique. His intention seems to have been to provide Muslim readers with an accurate reference work of Christian thought, as can be seen in his description of the Incarnation. Melkites believe that the Messiah had two natures, divine and human, in one hypostasis; Jacobites hold that the divine nature and the human nature are one, "just as the human spirit and body are one;" and Nestorians claim that the Messiah had two natures and two hypostases.[40] These are good summaries of the three main Christian positions, even noting the distinctive mind/body analogy used only by Jacobites.

Alongside the presentation of separate Christologies, al-Qāsim notes that all three Christian communities hold a common view of the purpose of the Incarnation. "The reason for the descent of the divine Son from heaven was because of the sin of Adam, which included all of his descendents. He delivered them from the power of Satan by offering himself on the cross."[41] But this is a mistaken notion since the crucifixion did not take place as Christians believe. They may have a tradition in their scriptures that the Jews put Christ to death, but the Jews themselves did not claim to have crucified him. "The Christians gave their interpretation from their own opinions."[42] Only here does al-Qāsim refer to Qur'ānic teaching to refute Christian belief, but his underlying assumption is that Christians have developed their beliefs about Christ as a result of poor scriptural foundations. They are wrong about the facts of Christ's death and their concepts of Incarnation are a product of their imagination.

Christian Scriptures do not Support the Incarnation

A second type of critique made by 'Alī ibn Rabbān al-Ṯabarī (d. 855) and al-Nāshi al-Akbar (d. 904) was to separate developed Christology from that found in the Bible in order to show that Christian thought had forsaken its roots. 'Alī al-Ṯabarī claimed to have been a Christian for seventy years in his *Reply to the Christians,* which must have been written sometime around the middle of the ninth century.[43] The fact that he had been a Christian most of his life is seen in his familiarity with the Bible on which he bases his criticism of Christology. He has two particular points to make; the Bible presents a human rather than a divine Christ, and the father-son terminology found in the Gospels has been radically changed by developed Christological formulations into something it was not intended to mean. In support of his first point al-Ṯabarī quotes from the Messianic prophecies of the Old Testament, such as Psalm 8, where the Messiah is clearly expected to be a human being without any hint that he might be divine.[44]

His second point is that Christological writing has taken father-son language in the New Testament out of context. In the Gospels the term 'father' is used as a metaphor in the same way that clan leaders and aged people are called father by those who are not their children. Similarly, the term 'son' is figurative like the sons of leaders who are not their actual children. However, Christian tradition has corrupted this understanding of the father-son analogy, "because Christians hold the literal truth of these names."[45] They want to hold that the Father is a parent while being beyond the process of creation, and they claim that the Son is born before time. But these are self-contradictory positions that do not arise from the Gospel accounts from which the terminology is taken. Worse still, developed Christology has made the Son equal to the Father in a way that is both a false interpretation of the Gospels and logically incoherent.

> "To say on the one hand that the Son is like his Father in his eternity, and on the other that he is not like his Father because he is born, is to deprive the words [father and son] of any meaning … If the Father and Son are equal in power and eternity then what authority remains for the Father over the Son?"[46]

Al-Ṯabarī is able to make great play over the removal of the father-son analogy from typical figurative use by Christian doctrinal formulations. How could Christians have gone from a metaphor for the lordship of God over the submitted Christ as found in the Gospels to a divine paternity of a divine offspring occurring beyond space and time? Sadly for al-Ṯabarī, Christians have ended up being unable to separate the divine from the human in their thinking. The only solution for them is to go back to the human Christ in their scriptures.

Al-Nāshi' al-Akbar also contrasts the Christologies of the ninth century with the portrait of Christ in the Gospels in order to show how Christians have forsaken their roots. He blames Christians for superimposing Greek philosophical categories on the language of the Gospels.

> "Whoever looks at the evidence of the Gospel will come across the saying of the Messiah – 'Consecrate the people in the name of the Father and the Son and the Holy Spirit'. There is no evidence here as to whether the Messiah is eternal or contingent, or whether he has one essence or not. These Greek philosophical expressions which have been adopted by Christians would not occur to those who examine the Gospel where Jesus (*'Īsā*) says – 'I am going to my Father and your Father, my Lord and your Lord', and makes himself the same as them."[47]

In other words Christians are guilty of reading into the father-son analogy ideas that simply don't belong to the original image in the Gospels. A straightforward interpretation of these sayings of Jesus leads to the conclusion that he referred to God as his father and himself as God's son in deferential terms. The father is Lord, so the son is submitted to his father. The son turns out to be on the same level as those to whom he is speaking, rather than on the same level as God. Subsequently, Christians have reinterpreted the sonship as equality of status with the father via the alien concept of eternal sonship imported from Greek thought. Al-Nāshi' quotes Melkite and Jacobite Christological formulas to illustrate the distance between them and the Gospels. Melkites believe that the Messiah has two natures, eternal and temporal, in one hypostasis, whereas the Jacobites hold that the Son joined with the human and became one nature, "God the Word who is Jesus".[48] When compared with the figurative language of Jesus in the Gospels such formulae seem to bear no relation to the true intent of Jesus to be submitted to his Lord and to lead others in that submission. The simplicity of the Gospel accounts has been abandoned by Christians who have elaborated Jesus into a divine being through complex ideas borrowed from the wrong sources.[49]

Arguments for the Incarnation are Incoherent

A third type of response was to deny the validity of the apologetics put forward by Christians to defend the Incarnation as reasonable. Abū 'Īsā al-Warrāq (d. 861) and Abū Bakr Muhammad ibn al-Tayyib al-Bāqillānī (d. 1014) argued that the analogies used by Christians to explain the Incarnation were inadequate for the task because the notion of the union of the divine with the human was basically incoherent. Abū Īsā stands out among the Muslim authors of his time for his thoroughness in handling Christian material. In his *Refutation of the three Christian sects* he surveys in great detail the Christologies of the Melkites, Jacobites and Nestorians, pointing out inconsistencies in their use of language to show that Christians were incapable of making sense of their beliefs about Christ. His main criticism of the language used by Christians has to do with terminology for the humanity of Christ. He observes that Nestorians and most Jacobites claim that the eternal Son united with "a particular human being", but that Melkites hold that the eternal Son united with "the universal human" nature shared by all humans "in order to save everyone." The Melkites believe that if the Son "had united with one human being then he could only have intended to save this individual and not everyone."[50] However, he notes that despite this observation, Nestorians, Jacobites and Melkites are not consistent in the way they describe the humanity of Christ. "They all tend to apply the explanations loosely, interpreting the human nature as a human being and vice versa."[51] This lack of precision in the use of language is confirmed by the terminology for the Incarnation found in these Christologies. "Sometimes they say the Word became human (*ta'annasa*) and some of them say the Word became embodied (*tajassada*)."[52]

Abū 'Īsā lists seven metaphorical explanations given by Christians of the union of the divine Word with the human body; firstly, the Word united with the human body in the sense of mixing and mingling with it; secondly, the Word took the body as a temple; thirdly, the Word took the body as a garment; fourthly, the Word dwelt in the body; fifthly, the Word appeared in the body without indwelling it; sixthly, the Word appeared in the body like a seal in clay, without being transferred to the clay itself; seventhly, the Word appeared in the body as a face appears in a mirror without being part of it.[53] Of these seven analogies only the idea of indwelling is used by Abū Qurra and Abū Rā'ita. 'Ammār has indwelling as well as the temple and garment analogies. As far as Abū 'Īsā is concerned the amount of disagreement between Christians tells against the coherence of the idea of union between divine and human natures. Such internal inconsistency does not encourage Muslims to take Christology as a source of true information about Christ. Abū 'Īsā seems to list the variety of Christian perspectives in order to show how much more rational is the teaching of Islam. If Christian faith in Christ corresponds with a Muslim view then Christianity has little to teach that is not confirmed by Islam. Where Christian teaching about Christ differs from Islamic teaching it is likely to be faulty. This can be illustrated by his criticism of the death of Christ. If the divine nature died then Christians worship a dead god, and if only the human nature died then the Messiah did not actually die, "because the human alone was not the Messiah". Whichever argument is put forward by Christians "causes the collapse of the uniting".[54] The logic of transendence is transparent to any sane thinker, confirming the rational excellence of Islam.

Abū Bakr al-Bāqillānī provides a critique of two more analogies used by Christians to explain the Incarnation. The first of these appeals to the session of God on his throne. "There are those who say that the Word indwells the human nature without being confined to it, just as the Creator descends on his throne without being confined to it. This is irrational, because the Creator is not on his throne in the sense that he indwells it."[55] Al-Bāqillānī points out that any use of God's contact with his throne as an analogy for the contact of the Word with the human body is illegitimate because Christians claim an indwelling of the Word. The parallel is simply not there in the session on the throne, for God cannot be thought by any stretch of the imagination to be within his throne in the way that the Word is supposed to be in the human body. Both Abū Qurra and Abū Rā'iṯa had appealed to the session of God on his throne as a helpful analogy for the Incarnation, but al-Bāqillānī demonstrates the gap between the Christian affirmation of divine embodiment and the Islamic conviction that God transcends that which he has created.

The mind-body analogy is also criticized for failing to provide what Christians really argue for. "The idea that the mind is the essence of the person and yet is not affected by the body is futile."[56] When applied by Christians to the Incarnation the analogy does not work since they want to maintain that the Word was basically unaffected by the body. The mind-body analogy was used by Abū Rā'iṯa because he believed that in fact the human body did not influence the human mind, but this understanding of human psychology lacked cogency for Muslims like al-Bāqillānī.

Both of these analogies are inadequate for the task to which Christians put them because they attempt to support the union of the divine with the human, a notion which is completely impossible. Al-Bāqillānī dismisses these apologetic moves as incapable of achieving what Christians desire because the basic belief in the Incarnation is irrational in the first place.

Conclusion

The developments in Christology are mainly seen in the presentation of arguments to commend the rationality and value of the Incarnation as understood within the traditions of the three authors, Abū Qurra the Melkite, Abū Rā'iṯa the Jacobite, and 'Ammār the Nestorian. Abū Qurra and Abū Rā'iṯa shared a common concern to argue for the Incarnation on Islamic grounds, even to the extent of using the same Islamic conceptions as premises of their arguments. They both appealed to the session of God on his throne, familiar to Muslims from the Qur'ān, as a way of defending the reasonableness of divine union with a human body. 'Ammār was more inclined to present arguments that showed the value of the Incarnation as a means of the revelation of God, but he did also develop some distinctive arguments based on Islamic ideas. There were some developments in the language of Christology, especially in the writing of Abū Rā'iṯa, who used the concept of attributes to describe the divinity and humanity of Christ when addressing a Muslim audience. However, Abū Qurra and 'Ammār were less inclined to adopt Islamic terminology, preferring to explain the meaning of their Christological traditions in ways that might be intelligible to Muslims.

The response by Muslim authors illustrates the way such arguments were received. Ultimately the Christian case for the Incarnation is perceived to be a poor building on any Islamic foundations suggested. Nothing in Islam allows for the union of the divine with a human body, and the use of divine anthropomorphisms in Islam to make room for Incarnation is not admissible. However, the fact that al-Bāqillānī took the trouble to refute such arguments in the second half of the tenth century shows that Muslim intellectuals felt the force of the Christian case made over a century before. This may suggest that arguments based on Islamic premises can have a continuing usefulness to Christian apologists. Muslim reading of the Gospels to deny the divinity of Christ put Abū Rā'iṯa and 'Ammār on the defensive, but they were convinced that the divinity of Christ was clearly portrayed there. Perhaps these ninth century discussions of the Gospels have less relevance in modern times in the light of critical Gospel scholarship, but the issues surrounding scriptural roots for developed Christology raised by 'Ammār's presentation of a tested Christ have a continuing importance.

What does remain relevant to the twenty first century is the attempt to show the coherence of the Incarnation on Islamic terms. For modern Christians who continue to uphold the Incarnation, the models provided by these three ninth century apologists still have value. Their careful distinction between the transcendence of God and his immanence in Christ can be usefully employed today among Muslims who fear that God may be tarnished by too close an identification with humanity. If Christ was able to defeat sin throughout his life and conquer death through new life as 'Ammār argued, then no shame attaches to the divine nature that was in him. Muslims need not reject Incarnation if transcendent majesty is preserved.

Notes

1 S.H. Griffith, 'Ḫabīb ibn Hidmah Abū Rā'iṯah, a Christian *mutakallim* of the First Abbasid Century', *OC* 64 (1980), 161–201, 161.
2 *Ibid.*, 192.
3 These refutations by leading Mu'tazilite scholars are mentioned in B. Dodge, *The Fihrist of al-Nadīm, a Tenth Century Survey of Muslim Culture*, vol. 1, 388 & 394.
4 There are two other Muslim commentators on Christology who are not expounded here. Abū 'Alī al-Jubba'ī (850–914) gives a brief summary of the three main Christologies without offering a critique. The tenth century writer 'Abd al-Jabbār gives a fuller account of Christology, but seems to be dependent on Abū 'Īsā al-Warrāq for his information and provides no fresh evaluation of his own.
5 See chapter three.
6 Abū Qurra, 'Treatise on the Incarnation', in Bacha, 180.
7 His *Treatise on the Incarnation* is a sustained defense of the reasonableness of the incarnation based on the implications of God's session on his throne.
8 For a good summary of Islamic debate on Qur'ānic anthropomorphisms in the early ninth century see the introduction to B. Abrahamov, *Anthropomorphism and Interpretation of the Qur'ān in the Theology of Al-Qāsim ibn Ibrāhīm* (Leiden: 1996), 1–18.
9 Abū Qurra, 'Treatise on the Incarnation', in Bacha, 183.
10 Abū Qurra, 'Treatise on Sonship', in Bacha, 94. See chapter two: 22 for a similar question posed by al-Mahdī to Timothy.
11 Abū Qurra, 'Treatise on Sonship', in Bacha, 95.
12 See chapter four.
13 See S.H. Griffith, 'Ḫabīb ibn Hidmah Abū Rā'iṯa', 168.
14 *Ibid.*, 165.
15 Abū Rā'iṯa, 'Letter on the Incarnation', questions 32–34 and 26–29.
16 *Ibid.*, question 29.
17 *Ibid.*, question 6.
18 *Ibid.*, question 7.
19 *Ibid.*, questions 13–18, especially the answer to 18.
20 'Ammār al-Baṣrī, 'The Book of the Proof', 62.

21 'Ammār al-Baṣrī, 'The Book of Questions and Answers', question 12.
22 See P.K. Hitti, *History of the Arabs* (London: 1970), 354f, for the rivalry between Nestorians and other Christians to be accepted as 'true' representatives of Christianity to their Islamic rulers.
23 'The Book of the Proof', 59.
24 'The Book of Questions and Answers', questions 5 and 8.
25 *Ibid.*, question 11.
26 'The Book of the Proof', 62.
27 See the debate on such admissibility between Kenneth Cragg and Ismā'īl al-Farūqī in chapter eight: 136–38.
28 'The Book of the Proof', 65.
29 'The Book of the Proof', 67.
30 *Ibid.*, 69.
31 *Ibid.*, 72.
32 See for example Ephesians 2:6 and Revelation 20:6, 21:5.
33 'The Book of Questions and Answers', questions 33–36.
34 See chapter seven for Pfander and chapter eight for Cragg.
35 'The Book of Questions and Answers', questions 30–34.
36 See for instance John 11:25f; Acts 2:31f; and 1 Corinthians 15:21–23.
37 See the use made of the voluntary death of Christ by Pfander in chapter seven, Cragg in chapter eight and Küng in chapter nine.
38 See D. Thomas, 'The Bible in Early Muslim Anti-Christian Polemic', *ICMR* 7 (1996), 29–38.
39 Al-Qāsim, 'Radd 'alā al-naṣārā', (ed.) I. de Matteo, 'Confutazione contro I Christiani dello Zaydati al-Qāsim b. Ibrāhīm', *RSO 9* (1921–22), 301–64, 319.
40 *Ibid.*, 316f.
41 *Ibid.*, 317.
42 *Ibid.*, 319.
43 'Alī al-Ṭabarī, 'Radd 'alā al-naṣārā', (ed.) I.-A. Khalife and W. Kutsch, *MSJ* 36 (1959), 113–48, 119.
44 *Ibid.*, 146.
45 *Ibid.*, 147.
46 *Ibid.*, 148.
47 Al-Nāshi' al-Akbar, *Kitāb al-Awsāt fi-l-Maqālāt,* (ed.) J. van Ess (Beirut: 1971), 82.
48 *Ibid.*, 80.
49 See similar Muslim argumentation answered in the apologetics of Abū Rā'iṭa and 'Ammār, as well as the basic agreement of John Hick with such arguments in chapter nine, though with no awareness of these authors.
50 Abū 'Īsā al-Warrāq, 'Radd 'ala al-thalāth firāq min al-naṣārā: al-juz' al-thānī, al-radd 'alā al-ittiḫād', ed. D. Thomas, *Early Muslim Polemic against Christianity*, Cambridge, 2002, 87.
51 *Ibid.*
52 *Ibid.*
53 *Ibid.*, 88.
54 *Ibid.*, 119.
55 Al-Bāqillānī, *Kitāb al-Tamhīd,* (ed.) R.J. McCarthy (Beirut: 1957), 88.
56 *Ibid.*, 90.

Bibliography

Abrahamov, B., *Anthropomorphism and Interpretation of the Qur'ān in the Theology of Al-Qāsim ibn Ibrāhīm* (Leiden: E. J. Brill, 1996)

Al-Akbar, al-Nāshi', *Kitāb al-Awsāt fī-l-Maqālāt* (ed. J. van Ess, Beirut: Dar al-Nashar, 1971)

Bacha, C., *Les oeuvres arabes de Théodore Aboucara, Évêque d'Haran* (Beyrouth: 1904)

Al-Bāqillānī, Abū-Bakr, *Kitāb al-Tamhīd* (ed. R.J., McCarthy, Beirut: Librairie Orientale, 1957)

Dodge, B. (ed. and trans.) *The Fihrist of al-Nadīm* (Vols. 1 & 2, New York: Columbia University Press, 1970)

Griffith, S.H., 'Ḥabīb ibn Khidmah Abū Rā'iṭah, a Christian *mutakallim* of the First Abbasid Century', *Oriens Christianus* 64 (1980), 161–201

Hitti, P.K., *History of the Arabs* (tenth edition, London: Macmillan, 1970)
De Matteo, I., 'Confutazione contro i Christiani dello Zaydati al-Qāsim b. Ibrāhīm', *Revista degli Studi Orientali* 9 (1921–2), 301–64
Al-Ṯabarī, 'Ali, 'Radd 'alā al-naṣārā', (eds.) Khalife, I-A., and W. Kutsch, *Mélanges de L'université Saint Joseph* 36 (1959), 113–48
Thomas, D., 'The Bible in Early Muslim Anti-Christian Polemic', *Islam and Christian-Muslim Relations* 7 (1996), 29–38
—— *Early Muslim Polemic against Christianity*. Abū Īsā al-Warrāq's *'Against the Incarnation'* (Cambridge: Cambridge University Press, 2002)

4 Extracts from *Early Muslim Polemic against Christianity: Abū ʿĪsā al-Warrāq's "Against the Incarnation"*

David Thomas

1 Their Teachings About the Uniting

After giving praise to God for bestowing upon him knowledge of his oneness, imploring his help against those who have erred in their faith, and affirming that all his strength and power come from God, the enemy of the Christians said:[1]

The Nestorians and the majority of the Jacobites claim that the Son, the Word, united[2] with *a* temporal human being born of Mary, | and the Melkites claim that the Son united with *the* temporal human being. When they say "*a* human being" the Nestorians and the majority of the Jacobites mean one human being and one individual, because according to them the Son in fact united with a particular human being, and not the universal. And when the Melkites say "*the* human being" they mean the substance which is common to all human individuals. This is because, according to them, the Son in fact united with the universal human, and not a particular, in order to save everyone, as they claim. The Melkites say: If it had united with one human being then it could only have intended to save this individual and not everyone. Thus, their differences over the description of the action of uniting cause them to disagree over the terms "*a* human being" and "*the* human being", although according to those acquainted with their ideas they all tend to apply the explanations loosely, interpreting "*the* human being" as "*a* human being" and *vice versa.* The principle they seek to maintain is this definition which we have given from them above.

Sometimes they interpret "it united" as "it became one", and "uniting" as "oneness",[3] the meaning of the two words being the same for them, that one resulted from two. Sometimes they say "it became human", sometimes some of them say "it became flesh", and others "it became composite",[4] thinking it easy enough to substitute "composition" for "uniting" because of the familiar usage of the term. They all agree that the expression "uniting" is correct.

They all quite agree that the uniting was an action occurring at a particular time by which the Messiah became Messiah. Then they differ over this action, what it was, the way it happened, and how two could become one.[5] Some of them claim that the Word united with the human in the sense of mixing and mingling with him; others that it took him as a habitation and location; others that it put on the body as a garment;[6] others that it came to dwell in him and controlled its affairs through and by means of him. Some say it did not come to dwell in him but controlled affairs by means of him and appeared to mankind through him, though not by indwelling or intermingling; others that it appeared in him as the imprint of a seal appears in impressed clay, for the imprint is not transferred to inhere in the clay or mix with it, nor does it move from its place. Others say it has nothing to do with any of these at all, but means that the Word appeared in this particular body just as a man's form appears when his face is seen in a clean, polished mirror. They claim that the uniting occurred in this way and no other.

The majority of the Jacobites claim that the uniting did not occur in any of these ways, but in the sense that the two substances became one substance, and that the hypostasis[7] which was the Word and the hypostasis which was the temporal human being became one hypostasis.[8]

We say only "the majority of the Jacobites", and we shall not discuss all the Jacobites here because among the Jacobites there are other divisions which differ from these over the uniting and who the Messiah was. They have other titles, but we shall not state these or discuss their views in this book, nor the views of other Christian divisions such as the Maronites, the Julianists, the Sabellians, the Arians, the Paulicians, followers of Paul of Samosata, or any other of their sects.[9] For we have written this book specifically about the majority of these three sects and not others.[10] We have previously given descriptions of the Christian divisions, their titles and names, and reported some of the reasons for the distinctions between their beliefs and the proofs employed by each group, in the book in which we have described people's views and the differences between them.[11] So, everything I attribute to the Jacobites in this book I intend only as from the majority and not these divisions which are separate from the main body.

The letter in Sabellians written as "b" is a letter between "b" and "f", though it is closer to "b". And the letter written as "b" in Paulicians is a letter which is a shade like "b" and another sound not found in Arabic which lies somewhere between "b" and "f". Many of those who write the name write this letter as "f" though it is closer to "b". It is not the same kind of letter as that in Sabellians.[12]

The majority of Christians already possessed a view about the Trinity and the Uniting before the split into Jacobites, Melkites and Nestorians. They agreed upon it when Arius initiated a controversy about the Trinity and called people to follow him. Their bishops and leaders met together and published a repudiation of this man, setting down the views upon which they had agreed that day.[13] And the claims they set down and agreed upon are:

> The eternal Divinity is one substance comprehending three hypostases,
> the Father who is generating and not generated,
> the Son who is generated and not generating,
> and the Spirit which pours forth from them both.
> The Son came down from heaven
> and took a body from Mary of the seed of David,
> and clothed himself in it;
> he appeared to mankind, was crucified, killed and buried,
> and after three days he rose again and ascended into heaven.

They made copies of this book and sent them to the majority of their towns and cities. This comprised everything they held until the differences arose in later times.[14]

Concerning their views about the Messiah, the three sects differ between themselves.[15] The Nestorians claim that the Messiah was both Anointer and Anointed, divine and human, meaning by "Anointer" the Word, and by "Anointed" the human who was born of Mary. They claim that he was two substances and two hypostases with one will: an eternal substance, the Word, and a temporal substance, the human born of Mary; an eternal hypostasis, the Word, and a temporal hypostasis, the human who was born of Mary. Some of them may say, "two natures and two hypostases", though in this instance "nature" and "substance" are identical.

Some of the Melkites say that the Messiah was two substances and one hypostasis with two wills: an eternal substance, the Word, and a temporal substance, the universal human; an eternal hypostasis, the Word, and nothing more. They deny that he had a temporal hypostasis precisely because, according to them, the Word united with the universal human not a particular. They say: The universal human is not a hypostasis since it is not an individual. Hence they claim that the Messiah was one hypostasis. Many of them say: The Messiah was one hypostasis possessing two substances and two wills, having the same reason for saying that he was one hypostasis as those above, and employing the same argument.

The majority of the Jacobites claim that the Messiah was one substance from two substances and one hypostasis from two hypostases, meaning that the substance of the Word and the substance of the human taken from Mary became through the uniting one thing, one nature, one hypostasis and one will. For, they say, if the Messiah had been two hypostases or two substances then their number would not have been eliminated by the uniting. They compare this to a lump of coal which when placed in the fire becomes an ember. The ember, they say, is not fire alone and not a lump of coal alone, for it has become an ember, they claim, through the uniting of the fire with the lump of coal. They say that this particular human being became a Divinity, but do not say that the Divinity became a human being, just as the lump of coal can be said to have become fire by virtue of becoming an ember, but the fire cannot be said to have become a lump of coal. Likewise, they claim, if the brightness, heat, and flames of a fire take hold of a heated dinar then the dinar is said to become fire, but the fire is not said to become a dinar.[16]

The three sects claim that the Messiah was crucified and killed, but then they differ over the crucifixion and killing, concerning whom in reality these things affected and who in reality the crucified was. The Nestorians claim that the Messiah was crucified with respect to his human nature but not his divine nature, and that the crucifixion affected the human being born of Mary but not the Divinity, since the latter cannot be harmed by crucifixion, killing or suffering. By their expression "his human nature" they mean his humanity, and by "his divine nature" his divinity, the latter signifying the Word which united with the human in him.

Many of the Melkites claim that the crucifixion and killing affected the Messiah in his entirety in the body, "the Messiah in his entirety" being the divine nature and the human nature. Many of them say that the Messiah possessed two substances one of which was the divine and the other the human nature, unlike the Nestorians who say that he was crucified with respect to his human nature. The Melkites say that since the human nature of the Messiah was the universal human nature and not a hypostasis or an individual, its isolation during the crucifixion or anything else was not possible, and neither was its resurrection in isolation and alone. They say: This being the case, the killing and crucifixion must have affected the Messiah in his entirety. They say: If the divine nature had been isolated from the human nature and not united with it, then death and resurrection would not have been possible for it and neither could human hands have harmed it. Many of them claim that the crucifixion, killing and suffering all harmed the Divinity, may he be exalted, by control[17] not by any physical constraints.

The majority of the Jacobites claim that the crucifixion and killing affected the Messiah who was one substance from two. They say: If the crucifixion and killing had only affected one of the substances then the incarnation would have been ruined, the uniting dissolved, and the crucifixion and killing would have affected one who was not Messiah, since each of the two substances alone was not the Messiah. Hence they say: The Divinity was crucified for us, that is, to save us.[18] Their expression "the Divinity was crucified" is like their expression "the human became divine": they do not mean to suggest by it that the crucifixion and killing could have affected the divine nature if it were isolated and not united. For in their view this could only happen to it because it united with the human nature; if it had not done so then the killing, crucifixion and suffering could not have happened to it.

These, then, are the main views of the Nestorians, the Melkites, and those Jacobites I have specified. I shall now begin my refutation of them, if God the exalted one wills. To God, Lord of power and strength, I appeal for help.[19]

(In the name of God the Compassionate, the Merciful. To God I appeal for help.

The second part of Yahyā b. 'Adī b. Ḥumayd Ibn Zakariyya's demonstration of the error of Muḥammad b. Hārūn, known as Abū Īsā al-Warrāq, in the second part of his book on the refutation of the three Christian sects, the Jacobites, the Nestorians and the Melkites. It runs from the beginning of the argument about the uniting to the end of the book.)

151. The Argument Against Them About the Uniting and the Birth[20]

[The Trinity and the Uniting]

Say to them[21] all together: Tell us about the uniting of the Word with the human being with whom it united. Was this an action of the Word and not of the Father or the Spirit, or was it an action of the three hypostases?[22]

If they claim that the uniting was an action of the three hypostases, we say: Then why was it the uniting of the Word and not of the Father or the Spirit? | And why was it the Word that united and not either of the others, although it had no part in the action of uniting that they did not have?

And if they claim that the uniting was an action of the Word and not of the Father or the Spirit, they acknowledge an action of the Son which is other than the action of the Father or the Spirit. And they single him out in carrying out an act which the Father and Spirit did not. But if it is possible for one of them to act alone without the others, this is possible for each of the other two hypostases. And if this is possible, it is possible for each of them alone to control a world without its two companions, and to create a creature without its two companions. This is a departure from their teachings.[23]

Notes

1 In addition to the text and English translation of this Introduction in Thomas, *Polemic*, pp. 66–77, it is also published with a French translation by E. Piatti, "La doctrine des Chrétiens d'après Abū 'Īsā al-Warrāq dans sa traité sur la Trinité", *Mélanges de l'Institut Dominicain d'Etudes Orientales* 20, 1991, pp. 7–30.

Throughout the first part of the *Tabyīn*, on the Trinity, Yaḥyā employs the formula "Then the enemy of the Christians said", *thumma qāla khaṣm al-Naṣārā*, to introduce each quotation from Abū 'Īsā. In the second part, on the Uniting, he changes to the less charged "Then Abū 'Īsā said", *thumma qāla* Abū 'Īsā (though for no apparent reason, in MS V113 at para. 163 the first formula reappears).

In paras. 1–8 (Thomas, *Polemic, pp.* 66–9), Abū 'Īsā summarises the three sects' teachings about the Trinity.

2 The archaic forms in which this verb and its derivations appear in the MSS, *iytaḥada, iytiḥād* and *muwtaḥid,* have been modernised.

3 These forms appear in all MSS as *a.t.w.ḥ.d and a.t.w.ḥ.ā.d,* and in V113 and V114 with *tashdīd* as *a.t.w.ḥ.ḥ.d* and *a.t.w.ḥ.ḥ.ā.d.* Their morphological irregularity is difficult to explain satisfactorily, but given the context they may originally have been the fifth verbal forms *tawaḥḥada* and *tawaḥḥud,* which an early copyist who did not recognise them changed to resemble the more common eighth form. The form *tawaḥḥud* is also used in precisely this context by ʿAmmār al-Baṣrī (Hayek, *ʿAmmār,* p. 71.2 and see also 51.3, 70 ult. and note) and al-Shahrastānī (*Milal,* p. 172.3). On its occurrence in al-Shahrastānī see W. M. Watt, "Ash-Shahrastānī's *Account of* Christian Doctrine", *Islamochristiana* 9, 1983, p. 250, n. 2, and also D. Gimaret and G. Monnot, eds., *Livre des religions et des sectes* 1, Louvain, 1986, p. 613, n. 5. The latter suggest that the term is used to designate the reuniting of the incarnate Word with the Godhead, but this seems strained. The word is certainly odd in the context, but its form and position are best explained, as Watt suggests, by the need to find a suitable term to balance *tajassud* in the previous clause.

4 See ʿAbd al-Jabbār, *Mughnī,* vol. V, pp. 82.19–83.2. These synonyms were common among Arab Christian authors at this time.

5 Many of the metaphors that follow were used by Christians from early times to explain the Incarnation. Although some were favoured by particular denominations, most were employed with different interpretations of meaning by writers from all denominations.

ʿAbd al-Jabbār almost certainly makes use of this passage in *Mughnī,* vol. V, p. 83.7–13 (see G. Monnot, "Les doctrines des Chrétiens dans le 'Moghnī' de 'Abd al-Jabbār", *Mélanges de l'Institut Dominicain d'Etudes Orientales* 16, 1983, pp. 9–30), and it probably forms the basis of al-Bāqillānī's list in *Tamhīd,* pp. 87.4–88.10.

6 The metaphors of the habitation and clothing were particularly preferred by Nestorian theologians at this time. Both Timothy I (Mingana, "Apology", p. 163) and ʿAmmār al-Baṣrī (Hayek, *ʿAmmār,* pp. 194.6–16, 196.13–16) made use of them. See also Yaḥyā Ibn ʿAdī in his letter to the Nestorian Abū al-Ḥasan al-Qāsim Ibn Ḥabīb, ed. E. Platti, *La grande polémique antinestorienne de Yaḥyā b. ʿAdī* (*Corpus Scriptorum Christianorum Orientalium* 427, 428 text; 437.438 trans.), Louvain. 1981–2, text pp. 7.12f, 30.13ff.

7 Abū ʿĪsā employs the term *uqnūm,* transliterated from the Syriac *qnōmā,* which was commonly used at the time for an individual Person of the Godhead, and any identifiably individual being; see Hayek, *ʿAmmār,* pp. 50.1–4, 51.5–6 (in the variant form *qunūn*); al-Qāsim Ibn Ibrāhīm, *Radd,* p. 315.23–5 (identifying *uqnūm* as *shakhṣ).*

8 See Yaḥyā, *Polémique antinestorienne* text, pp. 6.9–7.7, giving a Jacobite account of the uniting that fully agrees with this statement.

9 This list of Christian sects corresponds closely to the one given at the end of the *Radd,* para. 352, where Abū ʿĪsā signals his intention to begin a refutation of these minority groups. The list he gives there contains these five groups together with six more.

10 An implication of this clear statement, coming after the reference to the minority groups, is that even as he began the *Radd* Abū ʿĪsā was aware that a full refutation of Christian doctrines would have to include these other groups. Hence his planned work against them, which he anticipates at the very end.

11 This is a reference to Abū ʿĪsā's major work on religions which is usually referred to by other authors as *Kitāb maqālāt al-nās* or simply *Kitāb al-maqālāt.* It contained descriptive accounts of the main beliefs prevalent in the Islamic world in the early ʿAbbasid period, and was clearly a source of information for the *Radd ʿalā al-Naṣārā;* see Thomas, "History of Religions", and pp. 30f. above.

12 E. Platti says that this explanation of phonetic distinctions is a later copyist's interpolation ("Doctrine des Chrétiens d'après Abū ʿĪsā al-Warrāq". p. 27, n. 1 to para. 13 of the Arabic text) though there seems no reason to agree. Abū ʿĪsā was as capable as anyone else of going into this degree of explanatory detail, and there are indications in the *Radd* that he personally heard Christians presenting their arguments (para. 256. p. 206 below, where he mentions that some Melkites sometimes offer a particular answer, and Thomas, *Polemic,* p. 96.16, where he refers to *ajwibathum al-masmūʿa minhum*). The two sounds he attempts to distinguish are apparently a quiescent "v" in the case of *Sabāliyya* (it has disappeared completely in the form given by al-Qaḥaṭbī in the list of sects from his work by ibn al-Nadīm. *Fihrist,* p. 402.15, where it appears as *Sāliyya*), and a "p" in the case of *Bawliyya* (see van Ess, *Häresiographie, p.* 83, n. 2).

13 This is a reference to the Council of Nicea, which met in 325 with the main purpose of condemning the Christological teachings of Arius.

14 This version of the Creed is unlike any known from other sources, its main distinguishing features being the detailed description of the triune Godhead, and the restriction to articles on the Godhead and person of Christ. Since these are the two subjects of the *Radd*, it might follow that Abū ʿĪsā himself composed it, especially since the first article resembles his general account in the Introduction of the relationship between the Persons (Thomas, Polemic, p. 66.13–15). But some of its features argue against this. Firstly, the reference to the Spirit proceeding from both the Father and the Son, *wa-rūḥan munbathiqan baynahumā,* disagrees with explicit statements elsewhere in the *Radd* that it proceeds from the Father alone (Thomas, *Polemic,* pp. 66.15, 174.21–176.2 though in a passage which corresponds almost *verbatim* with the first of these and is probably based upon it or its source, ʿAbd al-Jabbār, *Mughnī*, vol. V, p. 81.12, gives this statement as *wa-lam tazul al-rūḥ fāʾidan min al-ab wa-al-ibn* = Abū ʿĪsā, *Radd, wa-lam yazul al-rūḥ munbathiqan min al-ab, wa-rubbamā jaʿalū makān "munbathiq" "fāʾidan",* raising the possibility of textual alteration). And secondly, the reference to the Son clothing himself in the human body, *fa-tadarʿa bihi,* recalls a Nestorian metaphor of the Incarnation (see n. 6 above).

But there are also difficulties which prevent an easy attribution to a Christian source. Firstly, no informed Christian would have acknowledged this as the Creed of Nicea, as Abū ʿĪsā so clearly assumes. Secondly, its intriguing reference to the doctrine of the double procession of the Holy Spirit has always been rejected by the Eastern churches, so its inclusion in a compilation that would derive from an eastern source is surprising (though it was not unknown in Muslim circles; al-Bāqillāni, *Tamhīd,* p. 86.15, mentions it without comment). And thirdly, references to clothing metaphors are absent from known versions of the Creed including Nestorian (see Gaudeul, *Riposte aux Chrétiens par ʿAlī al-Ṭabarī,* pp. V–X, quoting the Creed of Theodore of Mopsuestia and the version given in Arabic by ʿAlī al-Ṭabarī himself).

There is no doubt that the Creed is compatible with Christian beliefs, and it seems to be incompatible with what Abū ʿĪsā says about the Spirit elsewhere. So it may have originated among some Nestorians who maintained their own credal principles. But what remains surprising (whatever its origins) is that, whereas he shows such care elsewhere, Abū ʿĪsā should accept this as the Nicene Creed.

15 Having summarised views about the mode of uniting in the Messiah, in this paragraph Abū ʿĪsā presents views about the divine and human elements in his composite make-up. These form the basis of the second major section of the refutation against the Incarnation, paras. 230ff.

16 The origin of the comparison with the coal and the fire goes back at least to the fifth-century reflections upon the glowing coal in the vision of the prophet Isaiah, Is. 6.6–7, in which it was employed to show how the humanity of Jesus was united so inextricably with the divine that it became incorruptible (A. Grillmeier, *Christ in Christian Tradition* 2/2, London, 1995, pp. 82–7). The reference to the *dinār* indicates that Monophysite Christians in the Islamic world had updated the image. Evidence that the coal metaphor was ecumenical in interpretation is shown in its use by both the Jacobite Abū Rāʾiṭa (Graf, Abū *Rāʾiṭa, text,* p. 33.13ff.), and the Nestorian ʿAmmār al-Baṣrī (Hayek, *ʿAmmār,* pp. 179 ult.–180.3), the latter following the precedent of Nestorius himself (Grillmeier, *Christ in Christian Tradition* 1, London, 1975, pp. 516f).

17 For a fuller discussion of Abū ʿĪsā's understanding of the term *tadbīr,* see para, 218 and n. 50 below.

18 This is one of the handful of references in the *Radd* which show that Abū ʿĪsā was aware of the Christian meaning of the crucifixion. He does not comment on it in his refutation.

19 He now continues with the first part of his attack, against the doctrine of the Trinity, paras. 16–150.

20 This is one of the few structural markers visible in the work. See also paras. 220, 230, 304, and further 161, 187, 242 and 274.

21 Abū ʿĪsā frequently employs passive forms to introduce the Muslim question or rejoinder; here the Arabic is *yuqālu lahum.* In order to avoid clumsy English constructions, these have nearly always been translated with active forms or imperatives.

22 As shown in the discussion above, pp 69–71, this was evidently a question which was familiar within Muslim–Christian debate in this period. It is clear from Abū ʿĪsā's formulation of it here that he, like other Muslims, understood the hypostases as separate entities capable of individual action. The word he employs, *uqnūn,* which is transliterated from the Syriac *qnōmā* (the variant *qunūm* also appears), was the most familiar Arabic term for the Greek *hypostasis* at this time.

23 Although Abū ʿĪsā does not acknowledge it, there is an echo here of Q 21.22, which was the origin of the proof of there being only one God based on the argument of mutual hindrance

between two or more deities; see R. J. McCarthy, *The Theology of al-Ash'arī*, Beirut, 1953, pp. 9f. and p. 10 n. 8.

24 In his Introduction, para. 2 (Thomas. *Polemic*, pp. 66f.), Abū 'Īsā summarises the Melkite teaching on the Trinity as follows: "The Eternal One is one substance which possesses three hypostases: the hypostases are the substance but the substance is other than the hypostases." Al-Nāshi' al-Akbar attributes this interpretation specifically to a sub-group of the Melkites; van Ess, *Häresiographie.* p. 80.1–8, and see his discussion on pp. 76f. (German). The word employed for substance, *jawhar*, was becoming the most usual translation of *ousia* at this time.

25 See Abū 'Īsā's description of the Melkite Christology in para. 14: "The Messiah was two substances and one hypostasis . . . an eternal hypostasis, the Word, and nothing more." This accurately summarises the Chalcedonian Definition which states that Christ was two distinct natures brought together "into one Person and one hypostasis . . . one and the same Son and only begotten God the Word".

26 Abū 'Īsā may be acknowledging here that he has some knowledge of the contents of Christian scripture. He also reveals his awareness of the dangers in arguing from scriptural texts, since what can be claimed from one can be refuted from another.

Bibliography

'Abd al-Jabbār, Abū al-Ḥasan b. Muḥammad, *Al-mughnī fi abwāb al-tawḥīd wa-al-'adl,* Cairo. 1958–65 *(Mughni) Tathbīt dalā'il al-nubuwwa,* ed. 'A.-K. 'Uthmān, Beirut, 1966 (*Tathbīt*)

al-Bāqillānī, Abū Bakr, *Kitāb al-tamhīd,* ed. R. J. McCarthy, Beirut, 1957 (*Tamhīd*)

Ess, J. van. *Frühe mu'tazilitische Häresiographie,* Beirut, 1971, ed. and trans. al-Nāshi'al-Akbar, *Kitāb al-awsaṭ fī al-maqālāt* (*Häresiographie*)

Gaudeul, J.-M., *Riposte aux Chrétiens par 'Alī af-Ṭabarī,* Rome, 1995, see 'Alī b. Rabban al-Ṭabarī *La correspondance de 'Umar et Léon (vers 900),* Rome, 1995

Gimaret, D., and Monnot, G., eds. *Livre des religions et des sectes,* vol. I. Louvain, 1986

Graf, G., *Die Schriften des Jacobiten Ḥabīb Ibn Ḫidma Abū Rā'iṭa* (*Corpus Scriptorum Christianorum Orientalium* 130 text, 131 trans.), Louvain, 1951 (*Abū Rā'iṭa*)

Grillmeier, A., *Christ in Christian Tradition, London,* 1975–95

Hayek, M., *'Ammār al-Baṣrī, théologie et controverses,* Beirut, 1977, ed. and trans., *Kitāb al-burhān, Kitāb masā'il wa-ajwiba* (*'Ammār*)

Ibn al-Nadīm, Abū al-Faraj, *Kitāb al-Fihrist,* ed. M. Riḍā-Tajaddud, Tehran, 1971 (*Fihrist*)

McCarthy, R. J., *The Theology of al-Ash'arī,* Beirut, 1953

Mingana, A., "The Apology of Timothy the Patriarch before the Caliph Mahdi, Woodbrooke Studies 3", *Bulletin of the John Rylands Library* 12. 1928, pp. 137–292 ("Apology")

Monnot, G., "Les doctrines des Chrétiens dans le 'Moghnī' de 'Abd al-Jabbār", *Mélanges de l'Institut Dominicain d'Etudes Orientales* 16, 1983, pp. 9–30

Platti, E., *La grande polémique antinestorienne de Yaḥyā b. 'Adī (Corpus Scriptorum Christianorum Orientalium* 427, 428 text; 437, 438 trans.), Louvain, 1981–2

—— "La doctrine des Chrétiens d'après Abū 'Īsā al-Warrāq dans sa traité sur la Trinité", *Mélanges de l'Institut Dominicain d'Etudes Orientales* 20, 1991, pp. 7–30

al-Qāsim b. Ibrāhīm al-Ḥasanī, *Al-radd 'alā al-Naṣārā,* ed. I. di Matteo. "Confutazione contro i Cristiani dello Zaydita al-Qāsim b. Ibrāhīm", *Rivista degli Studi Orientali* 9, 1921–2, pp. 301–64 (*Radd*)

al-Shahrastānī, Abū al-Fath. *Kitāb al-milal wa-al-niḥal,* ed. W. Cureton, London, 1846

Thomas, D., *Anti-Christian Polemic in Early Islam,* Abū 'Īsā *al-Warrāq's "Against the Trinity"* (University of Cambridge Oriental Publications 45), Cambridge, 1992

——, "Abū 'Īsā al-Warrāq and the History of Religions", *Journal of Semitic Studies* 41, 1996, pp. 275–90

Watt, W. M., "Ash-Shahrastānī's Account of Christian Doctrine", *Islamochristiana* 9, 1983, pp. 249–59

Yahyā Ibn 'Adī, see Platti

5 Folly to the *Ḥunafā'*

The Crucifixion in Early Christian–Muslim Controversy[1]

Mark N. Swanson

Introduction

One of the oldest known Arabic versions of the letters of St. Paul is found in a manuscript of the ninth century AD preserved in the library of St. Catherine's Monastery at Mount Sinai and catalogued as Arabic MS 155.[2] In it, we find a rendering of I Corinthians 1.22–25 that we might translate as follows:

> [T] he Jews demand signs, and the *ḥunafā'* seek wisdom.
> As for us, we proclaim the crucified Christ, for the Jews a thing of doubt, and for the nations folly, but for those who are chosen, from among the Jews and from the *ḥunafā'*,
> Christ is the power of God and the wisdom of God; because the folly of God is wiser than the people, and the weakness of God is stronger than the people.[3]

The word left untranslated, *ḥunafā'* (singular *ḥanīf*), comes from the Syriac *ḥanpē,* meaning 'pagans' or 'Gentiles' or 'Greeks'. According to St. Paul in his early Arabic dress, the generality of the *ḥunafā'* found the 'word of the cross' (1 Cor. 1.18) to be 'folly' (*ḥumq*), the precise opposite of the wisdom (*ḥikma*) that they were seeking.

As is well known, the loan word *ḥanīf/ḥunafā'* is not only to be found in the Arabic writings of Christians of Syriac background, but occurs several times in the Arabic sacred scripture of the Muslims, the Qur'an. There it has a distinctive meaning, referring not to Greek pagans but rather to persons with a monotheistic faith such as that of Abraham, who was 'not a Jew, neither a Christian; but he was a *ḥanīf* and a *muslim*'.[4] In Islamic usage, *ḥanīf* very quickly came to be a synonym of 'Muslim' and *al-ḥanīfiyya* a synonym of 'Islam'.[5]

Christians who found themselves under Islamic rule as a result of the conquests of the seventh century AD quickly discovered that the New Testament 'word of the cross' had not only been folly to the Greek *ḥunafā'* of whom St. Paul had spoken, but was also a puzzle, at the very least, to the Muslim *ḥunafā'*. In particular, they learned that the Muslims' sacred scripture appeared to deny the simple *fact* of the crucifixion of Christ—to say nothing of its meaning and redemptive significance. The critical verse *al-Nisā'* (4) 157 is part of a polemic against the Jews, who are rebuked for a variety of offenses—*including their claim to have crucified Christ.* To this claim the Qur'an responds:

> … mā qatalūhu wa-mā ṣalabūhu, wa-lākin shubbiha lahum …
> … they did not kill him, nor did they crucify him, but it was made to appear so to them …

Christian interpreters throughout fourteen centuries have sought ways of construing this verse to allow for the reality of Christ's death on the cross, so central to Christian faith. In the Christian version of the legend of Baḥīrā the monk, which may date to the ninth century AD, the claim is made that the original Christian meaning (!) of the verse is that 'Christ did not die in the substance of his divine nature'.[6] Much more recently, Louis Massignon[7] and scholars from his extended circle (including Giulio Basetti-Sani[8] and François Jourdan[9]) have suggested that the verse need not deny the fact that Jesus was crucified, and have offered ingenious interpretations in support.

Yet, in spite of a rather intense Christian desire to find readings of *al-Nisā'* (4) 157 that would allow for the fact of Christ's crucifixion, the main trajectory of Islamic commentary on the verse[10] affirms that Jesus was *saved* from crucifixion and raised alive into heaven, leaving as the principal issue for scholarly speculation the question: what or who was crucified in Jesus' place? (When identifications are hazarded—and agnosticism on the question is a respectable option—they range from a volunteer among the disciples, to one of those coming to arrest Jesus, to Judas Iscariot).[11] Furthermore, Christian texts from early in the Islamic period show that Christians were aware that (most) Muslims did not believe that Christ was crucified. For example, the Arabic *Life of Shenoute* preserves a little historical apocalypse that may well date back to the 690s AD[12] and that refers to the 'children of Ishmael' as 'those who deny my sufferings, which I accepted upon the cross'.[13] More familiar is the statement of St. John of Damascus in his chapter on Islam in *On Heresies*. Writing in the second quarter of the eighth century (if the attribution to John is correct),[14] the Damascene reports the Qur'an as saying

> that the Jews, having themselves transgressed the Law, wanted to crucify him, and having arrested him they crucified his shadow; but Christ himself was not crucified (they say), nor did he die, for God took him unto Himself in heaven, because He loved him.[15]

In this chapter I will present three Christian texts from the second half of the eighth century that give something of the flavor of the Christian responses to the Qur'anic denial of the crucifixion. The three texts are different in literary genre, original language and community of origin. Taken together, however, they give us a range of Christian responses that will set the apologetic tone and agenda for centuries to follow.

The History of the Patriarchs of Alexandria

The historical, apocalyptic and apologetic literature of the Christian communities in the early Islamic period is full of allusions to the power of the cross and to the miracles done by it. For examples one may well turn to *The History of the Patriarchs of Alexandria. Life* number 46 in this famous Arabic compilation, that of Patriarch Michael I (744–68), was originally written in Coptic by a contemporary, one Yūḥannā or John, spiritual son of Mūsā, bishop of Awsīm in Giza.[16] John's chronicle, written around 770, is punctuated by stories about and allusions to the cross. Miracles are performed with the sign of the cross, as, for example, when Bishop Mūsā heals a paralytic boy.[17] In other stories, Muslim individuals deride the cross—with startling consequences. For example, John tells the following story:

> On a certain day the governor in Alexandria wanted to launch the ships of the fleet into the sea. There was a crowd of the Orthodox in the Church of St. Mary, about ten

thousand people. A young man of the Muslims saw an image pictured on the wall [of the church], of the Lord Christ on the cross and the one with the spear who was piercing him.

He said to the Christians, to test them, 'What is he, this one who is on the cross?' They said to him, 'It is the sign of our God Christ on the cross for the salvation of the world'. At this he took a rod, ascended to the upper gallery, and stabbed the picture [of Christ] in his other side, the left one, while mocking in his speech and blaspheming. Suddenly the form of the young man was extended as if he were crucified, like the image that he had stabbed, and he felt great pain, as if he had been stabbed in his side like the image. His hand stuck to the rod that he had used to stab, and no one was able to remove it from his hand. And he was suspended in the midst of the people, between heaven and earth. He remained that way the entire day, crying out and saying, 'O people, I have been stabbed in my side'.

Then the Muslims cried out to the Christians in a loud voice, glorifying God, the doer of wonders, and asked them to pray to God for his deliverance. So the Christians prayed, saying '*Kyrie eleison*' many times. But he did not descend from his place until one of the Muslims said to him, 'Unless you confess the creed of the Christians and say that this image is the image of Christ the son of God, and say what the Christians say and believe like them, he will never let you down'.

The Muslim accepted that word [of advice], confessed that it was an image of Christ, and said, 'I am a Christian, and I will die in the religion of Christ'. Then he descended into the midst of the crowd. And he went to the monasteries and was baptized there.[18]

This story is immediately followed by the Coptic historian's account of the Abbasid revolt—which resulted in much devastation in Egypt and great hardship for Pope Michael. Remarkably, John makes the claim that it was *through the sign of the cross* that the Abbasid rebels achieved victory. As John tells the story, God called a certain 'Abd Allāh and his father Abū Muslim to fight against the Umayyad caliph Marwān II by means of dreams in which God promised them victory. In their first military encounter, the rebels' ill-equipped army of twenty thousand triumphed over the caliph's hundred thousand fighting men, including forty thousand horsemen, 'with God's help' (as John puts it).[19] We read:

Abū Muslim saw the angel of the Lord, in his hand a golden staff surmounted by a cross. So he defeated his enemies; [Abū Muslim] observed that wherever the cross drew near, [his enemies] fell down dead before it. And the followers of 'Abd Allāh and Abū Muslim took their horses and weapons.[20]

Soon afterwards, we read,

The *shaykh* Abū Muslim ordered his soldiers to make crosses of every kind and to make them go before them, saying to them: 'This is that by which God has given us the victory, and which has taken the empire for us'.[21]

Earlier in his history, John had mentioned the Nubian King Mercurius of Dongola, who was called 'the New Constantine'.[22] Ironically, however, it is Abū Muslim, the leader of the Abbasid revolt, who most fully inhabits the role of a 'new Constantine', receiving a vision from God and conquering in the sign of the cross! In this startling way the power of the cross is vindicated—even though John is constrained to report that, not long after their triumph, the Abbasids 'forgot ... that it was God who had given them the kingship; and they abandoned the holy cross that had given them the victory'.[23]

Such stories about the power of the cross can be found in all the literatures of Christians who found themselves under Muslim rule or in conflict with the Muslims. They do not lack an apologetic edge. As Johannes den Heijer has pointed out, with reference to *The History of the Patriarchs,*

> [t]hese texts are actually a complicated mixture of history and legend, of fact and fiction. To be sure, their intrinsic value lies, not in their reference to actual historical events, but in their reflections of attitudes and mentalities. In quite a few cases, their real message is interconfessional polemics, or, at least, an assessment of the relations between their own religious community and the others, translated, so to speak, into the language of narrative.[24]

John makes the apologetic aspect of his narrative explicit in a story about a contest between rival religious communities to see whose prayers will be answered during a time of inadequate Nile flooding. According to John, 'this withholding of the water took place according to God's will, in order to show forth His wonders ... *and the truth of the Christian religion*'.[25] As he relates the story, it is only the Christians, praying with great display of crosses on the Feast of the Glorious Cross (17 Tūt = September 14), to whom God responds by causing the level of the Nile water to rise.[26]

Such stories may be understood, in part, as an *indirect* defense of Christian claims about the crucifixion of Christ in the face of Islamic denial: were the Christian claims not true, the cross would have no power. The fact that the cross *does have* power—whether the healing sign of the cross made by a Christian bishop, or the crosses that accompany prayer for a provision-miracle, or a wall-painting that resists mockery, or a military standard that scatters the enemy—vindicates the rudely paradoxical Christian claim that the one crucified is none other than (in the words of the Christians in John's story about the wall-painting) 'our God Christ', who is 'on the cross for the salvation of the world'.[27]

On the Triune Nature of God

Another way of defending Christian claims about the crucifixion of Christ without directly taking on Sūrat *al-Nisā'* (4) 157 and its body of interpretation is the argument from prophecy. In a missionary and apologetic enterprise that can be traced back to the New Testament itself, Christians had sought to convince Jews that Jesus of Nazareth was the promised Messiah of Israel's scriptures and that his career was foretold in those scriptures in considerable detail. Collections of scriptural *testimonia* to the Incarnation, ministry, passion, resurrection and ascension of Christ were made, probably appearing in book form as early as the second Christian century.[28]

As Christian apologists became aware of the Islamic challenges to Christian belief, it was natural that they should 'redeploy' available apologetic resources—a move that seemed all the more natural because of the similarities that these apologists discerned between beliefs of the Jews and those of the Muslims, sometimes called the 'new Jews'.[29] John of Damascus stated the logic of this case well when, in response to Muslims' claim that Muḥammad is a prophet, he said:

> We say: ' … Which of the prophets foretold that such a prophet would arise?' And they being at a loss, [we say] … that all the prophets in succession, beginning from Moses, prophesied Christ's advent, that Christ is God, that the Son of God would come in the flesh, be crucified, die and be raised, and will be the Judge of the living and the dead.[30]

A few lines further on, John makes a comment with respect to the divinity of Christ that could equally well apply to the reality of his crucifixion: 'This is what the prophets and the scripture have handed down; and you, as you strongly insist, accept the prophets!'[31]

We find Old Testament prophecies of the crucifixion in the oldest dated Arabic Christian apologetic text in our possession, that found in Sinai Arabic MS 154 and called by its first editor *Fī tathlīth Allāh al-wāḥid* or *On the Triune Nature of God*.[32] The date given in the text is 746 years since God had 'raised up and fashioned' the Christian religion,[33] which converts to AD 755 if we measure these years from the Incarnation[34] or AD 788 if we measure from the crucifixion and resurrection.[35] In any event, we are dealing with an original Arabic apology for the Christian faith dating back to the second half of the eighth century.

The unnamed Melkite author opens his work with a beautiful prayer full of Qur'anic echoes,[36] and then proceeds to treat issues at the heart of Christian-Muslim controversy: Chapter One is a defense of the doctrine of the Trinity, while Chapter Two explains the necessity for the Incarnation of the Word of God. This apology for the Incarnation is a remarkable attempt to take a traditional Christian redemption narrative, that of the incarnate Word's cunning defeat of the Devil in order to save humankind, and to reshape it so that its presentation of salvation history has clear parallels with Qur'anic sequences of stories about the messengers of God such as those found in Sūrat *al-A'rāf* (7) or Sūrat *Hūd* (11).[37] In an unforced and natural way, the author weaves Qur'anic expressions and narrative details into his narrative. Just so, Chapter Two of *On the Triune Nature of God* is an important milestone in the history of Arabic Christian soteriological discourse.

This chapter is less significant, however, for the history of Christian apologetic specifically with respect to the *crucifixion*. The author, of course, does affirm that Christ's crucifixion is central to the story of human redemption. At the climax of the chapter we read: 'He crucified sin by his crucifixion, killed death (which Adam inherited through trespass) by his death, and showed forth the resurrection'.[38] However, the author does not explain *how* he can make such claims, or *how* it is that Christ's ignominious death by crucifixion defeats sin, death and the devil. While Chapter Two of *On the Triune Nature of God* exploits Qur'anic sequences of messenger-stories in order to offer an explanation for the necessity of the Incarnation of the Word, with regard to the *crucifixion* of the incarnate one it simply reasserts traditional liturgical language, without *apologia*.

We do find something approaching an apology for Christian claims about the cross, however, in the final chapter of the treatise (at least, in the shape in which we now have it).[39] That chapter begins as follows:

> And this is what the prophets of God prophesied concerning the crucifixion of Christ, through which he redeemed us from the misguidance of the Devil and his works:
>
> Moses prophesied, to whom God spoke and caused his face to blaze [so that] none of the Children of Israel were then able to look at his face. He prophesied concerning

the crucifixion of Christ and said to the children of Israel in the *Tawrāt,* which God sent down to him: 'You shall see your life hanging before your eyes, and you shall not believe' [Deut. 28.66, LXX]. What life was hanging before the eyes of the children of Israel, in which they did not believe, other than the Light of God?

So understand what the prophets have prophesied by the Holy Spirit concerning Christ, who was crucified, and who by his crucifixion crucified sin and destroyed the Devil.[40]

The author then goes on to discuss another passage from the Pentateuch which Christians have traditionally understood as a prophecy of Christ's crucifixion, the story of the bronze serpent in the wilderness (Numbers 21.6–9).[41]

There is nothing surprising about the quotations found here. The Septuagint version of Deuteronomy 28.66, while unfamiliar to most contemporary Western Christians, is first attested as a prophecy of the crucifixion in Melito of Sardis and is used frequently thereafter.[42] What might be surprising, however, is the way the author limits himself to passages from the Pentateuch—when the Gospels themselves offer prophecies from so many other parts of scripture.[43] We may be reminded here of the Syriac account of an early religious discussion between a Christian patriarch and Muslim official, the *Letter of Mar Yoḥannan the Patriarch,* which purports to date to a time shortly after the Islamic conquest of Syria, but which may well be a composition of the early eighth century.[44] Responding to the Patriarch's claims that the divinity of Christ is announced not only in Moses but in all the prophets, the Muslim official insists that the Christian confine himself to quotations *from Moses.*[45] The author of *On the Triune Nature of God* does just that in his chapter on the cross. He stresses that the prophecies are those of the prophet to whom God spoke directly[46] and to whom God sent down (*anzala*) the *Tawrāt.*[47] According to him, the Muslim reader should be prepared to accept Moses' prophecies, and hence the reality of Christ's crucifixion: 'So understand what the prophets have prophesied by the Holy Spirit concerning Christ, *who was crucified.*'[48] For this eighth-century Christian apologist, Moses' prophecies of the crucifixion should settle the matter of its historicity once and for all.

The Discussion between the Caliph al-Mahdī and the Catholicos Timothy

The religious discussion between the Abbasid caliph al-Mahdī (775–85) and Timothy the Great, Catholicos of the ('Nestorian') Church of the East (780–823), has been justly described as 'the most famous of the early exchanges between the two great religions'.[49] The discussion itself is usually dated to 781; the Syriac report of the encounter which Timothy sent to his friend, the priest Sargīs, dates to sometime between 786 and 795.[50] Various recensions of the report were made in both Syriac and Arabic, manuscript evidence for the latter extending back to the tenth century.[51]

The text is of great significance for the history of Christian-Muslim encounter, not least because we find, perhaps for the first time, a direct and sophisticated Christian response to *al-Nisā'* (4) 157. The Caliph had asked about the Christian practice of venerating the cross, and Timothy, in his response, quite naturally spoke of the redemptive significance of the death of the Son of God in the flesh.[52] The Caliph first asks whether this meant that God could die, then, after hearing out Timothy's careful distinctions between Christ's divinity and humanity, he quotes *al-Nisā'* (4) 157: 'they did not kill him, nor did they crucify him, but he made a likeness for them'.[53]

The first argument that Timothy offers in response may be summarized as follows: the Qur'an itself bears witness to the *fact* of Jesus' death, while the *manner* of this death was foretold by the prophets. To show that the Qur'an itself bears witness to the fact of Jesus' death, he quotes two verses: *Maryam* (19) 33, where Jesus says, 'Peace be upon me the day I was born, and the day I die, and the day I am raised up alive!' and *Āl 'Imrān* (3) 55, 'When God said, "Jesus, I will cause thee to die and will raise thee to me"'. The Caliph is ready with a response: Jesus had not *yet* died, but would die in the future. To this, Timothy responds something as follows:

> And likewise he has not yet ascended into heaven, and has not yet been raised up alive, but will ascend and be raised later! But you have it that he ascended into heaven alive. He did not ascend until he died and was raised, as we saw earlier. So if he ascended, then he had previously died … .[54]

To understand the argument, we must keep in mind the order of the verbs in the quoted verses: *amūtu* ('I die') is followed by *ub'athu ḥayyan* ('I am raised up alive') in the verse from Sūrat *Maryam*, while *mutawaffīka* ('I will cause thee to die'—if this is the correct interpretation) is followed by *rāfi'uka ilayyā* ('I will raise thee to myself) in the verse from Sūrat *Āl 'Imrān.* Timothy assumes that the sequence of the verbs reflects the order of their occurrence, so that the two verses taken together establish the logical and temporal sequence: death, resurrection, ascension. It is therefore on Qur'anic grounds, Timothy argues, that one cannot affirm that the ascension of Jesus into heaven has already occurred without also affirming that his death has already occurred. Then, having to his satisfaction demonstrated that the Qur'an affirms the past *fact* of Jesus' death, Timothy turns to the Old Testament for confirmation of the *manner* of that death, offering prophecies of the crucifixion from David,[55] Isaiah,[56] Jeremiah,[57] Daniel[58] and Zechariah.[59]

Timothy's argument is not unimportant, as Christian arguments of this sort may have played a role in the developing Islamic exegetical tradition of *Āl 'Imrān* (3) 55 and other verses referring to Jesus. Two features in the exegesis of *Āl 'Imrān* (3) 55 might be mentioned. First, there is a tendency to interpret *mutawaffīka,* most naturally translated as 'will cause thee to die', in some way that does not refer to death.[60] Al-Ṭabarī reports the interpretation 'I will cause thee to *sleep*',[61] as well as the interpretation that became standard for much of the tradition, *mutawaffīka* = *qābiḍuka,* 'I will *take* thee'.[62] A second strategy for dealing with the verse, also reported by al-Ṭabarī,[63] is to take it as a case of *al-taqdīm wa-al-ta'khīr,* a phenomenon in Arabic syntax in which words appear in the reverse of their logical or temporal order. For example, Sūrat *al-Qamar* (54) 18 reads: 'How then were My chastisement and My warnings', even though the warnings (*nuẓur*) logically precede the chastisement (*'adhāb*).[64] As applied to *Āl 'Imrān* (3) 55, this means that in the phrase 'I will cause thee to die and raise thee to me', 'the "and" does not impose the temporal order', as al-Ṭabarsī puts it.[65] If this is the case, then the verse can well mean: 'I will raise thee to me, and *afterwards* will cause thee to die'.

This was not the last word in the discussion, and a slowly developing Christian-Muslim conversation on these matters may be traced.[66] The main lines of the conversation are already set, however, in the report of the Catholicos Timothy.

The *second* argument developed by Timothy has to do with the mysterious words *shubbiha lahum.* According to the Syriac debate-report, the Caliph al-Mahdī responds to Timothy's recital of Old Testament predictions of the crucifixion by saying, 'He made a likeness for them in this way'.[67] It appears that, according to the report, the Caliph understands the

Qur'anic *shubbiha lahum* as implying that *any* evidence which Christians might advance to support their claim that Christ was crucified is but an instance of *tashbīh,* and therefore an appearance with no basis in reality.

Timothy responds to this with a dilemma-question. If the prophetic and apostolic claims about Christ's crucifixion are but *tashbīh,* who then is the author of this *tashbīh*: God or Satan? For Timothy, it is obvious that the answer cannot be God: 'It is entirely unfitting for God that He deceitfully show one thing in the place of another'. Can the *tashbīh,* then, be ascribed to Satan? Timothy thinks not, for one would then have to be prepared to admit not only that Satan played a role in the divine economy, but was also able to deceive the disciples—who, according to the New Testament, had the power to cast out demons.

Timothy's argument was developed further by later apologists. An Arabic tract entitled *The Refutation of the One Who Denies the Crucifixion* expands Timothy's (two-fold) dilemma into a four-fold exclusive disjunction: those who claim *tashbīh* must admit that its author be either God, Christ, Satan or the Jewish leaders—but none of these possibilities is admissible.[68] There is little that is new here, however. The main lines of the conversation are set with Timothy.

There is much more that can be said about Timothy's discourse on the crucifixion. Among the Caliph's interventions is a dilemma-question that has appeared over and over again in Islamic controversial texts. According to the Syriac report, al-Mahdī asks:

> Which of the two do you say: was Christ willing to be crucified, or not?
>
> If he was willing to be crucified, why then are the Jews who fulfilled his will cursed and despised?
>
> But if he was not willing to be crucified, and he was crucified [all the same], he was weak whereas the Jews were strong. How can he be called 'God' who was unable to deliver himself from the hands of his crucifiers, whose will appeared much stronger than his?[69]

Timothy responds with a number of examples that illustrate the mystery of creaturely disobedience and divine-sovereignty,[70] or that distinguish between intention and result, since good results can result from that which is intended for ill. For example, the Muslim who dies while fighting *fi sabīl Allāh* is prepared to die and expects to be rewarded with Paradise; but this does not mean that his killer is blameless.[71] This response and others like it were repeated by other Christian apologists.[72] Indeed, on this issue there is very little evidence of any development of ideas: Muslim controversialists thought that the dilemma-question was powerful and regularly repeated it; Christian apologists had what they considered a convincing set of answers, which they regularly repeated.[73] Once positions were drawn up, conversation stopped.

There is, however, one part of Timothy's response to the Caliph's dilemma-question that *was* open to further development. Timothy is constrained to stress the *freedom* with which Christ went to his crucifixion. Christ was, of course, capable of escaping from his captors. But:

> If he had delivered himself from the Jews, then he would not have been crucified. If he had not been crucified, neither would he have died. If he had not died, neither would he have risen to everlasting life. And if he had not risen to everlasting life, then people would have remained without a sign of or arguments for [the reality of] everlasting life.

> Today, because of the resurrection of Jesus Christ from the dead, the eyes of all people are looking towards everlasting life. So that this expectation of everlasting life and of the world to come be firmly impressed upon the people, therefore, it was fitting that Jesus Christ rise from the dead; and so that he rise from the dead, it was fitting and right that he first die; and so that he die it was right first that his death—as also his resurrection—be witnessed by all. [Therefore] it was fitting that he die the death of the cross.[74]

Here Timothy has moved from an argument about the *fact* of the crucifixion to one about its *fittingness*: Christ's public crucifixion followed by his glorious resurrection is the appropriate way in which God grants the witnesses 'expectation of everlasting life and of the world to come'.

Timothy here is working with a 'narrative redescription' of the story of Jesus[75] that is markedly different from that which we have found in *On the Triune Nature of God*: rather than a narrative about Christ's turning the tables on Satan, Timothy assumes a narrative that describes Christ's life, death and resurrection in large part as *a divine demonstration of the reality of the general resurrection,* a demonstration that affords hope and confidence to his faithful people. This soteriological narrative has deep roots in the Antiochene Christological tradition, as may be seen, for example, from the *Catechetical Homilies* of Theodore of Mopsuestia preserved in Syriac by the Church of the East.[76] While it is no great surprise to find this narrative in Timothy, it seems that he senses its potential for making sense of the crucifixion of Jesus in an Islamic environment: Christians *and* Muslims claim to believe in the resurrection of the dead, though it is only the believers in Christ who have a sure 'sign of or arguments for' its reality.

Many of the great arabophone Christian apologists of the generation after Timothy would contribute to the development of this redemption-narrative in Arabic. One of the most sensitive analyses of the character of Christ's death and resurrection as divine demonstration is found in the work of another 'Nestorian' apologist, 'Ammār al-Baṣrī.[77] This train of apologetic thought was not restricted to East Syrian circles, however, for we find contributions to it in the work of the 'Jacobite' Ḥabīb Abū Rā'iṭa[78] and of the 'Melkites' Ibrāhīm al-Ṭabarānī[79] and the anonymous author of the eighteenth chapter of the compendium *al-Jāmiʿ wujūh al-īmān.*[80] To the best of our present knowledge, Timothy stands at the head of this series. He emerges, therefore, as a significant Christian apologist for the reality of Christ's death on the cross. While his apology includes several elements of a *direct* response to the Qur'anic denial of Christ's crucifixion in *al-Nisā'* (4) 157, it may be that his greatest contribution to a Christian 'theology-with-a-mind-for-Islam'[81] was an *indirect* response, a way of narrating the salvation worked by Christ that placed Christ's crucifixion at the very center of the story and made a plausible case that—in his words—'it was fitting that he die the death of the cross'.

Conclusion

By some time early in the eighth century AD, Christians in the *Dār al-Islām* had come to know that the dominant Islamic interpretation of important Qur'anic verses—*al-Nisā'* (4) 157 in particular—was that Jesus the Messiah did *not* die on the cross, but rather was saved by God from those who willed his crucifixion. Some Christian teachers tackled the texts and their interpretation head on, as when the catholicos Timothy questioned the dominant interpretation of *al-Nisā'* (4) 157 both from the point of view of its coherence with the plain sense of other Qur'anic verses (Q 3.55 and 19.33) *and* from the point of view of internal coherence (i.e., the meaning of *shubbiha lahum*). But in addition to this new skill of arguing for Christian truth on the basis of Qur'anic texts, Christian apologists, like the scribe 'trained for the kingdom of heaven' in St. Matthew's Gospel (Matt. 13.52), brought the old as well as the new out of their apologetic storehouses.

The old, of course, did not remain unchanged. Christian teachers reached deep into the tradition and 'redeployed' traditional apologetic and catechetical motifs and strategies, often in very striking ways, so as to be effective within the Islamic environment. The examples that have been presented in this paper may communicate something of the range and boldness of this redeployment. In a startling instance of the continuing liveliness of Byzantine imperial ideology in Egypt more than a century after the Islamic conquest, the Coptic scribe John recalled the story of the emperor Constantine's military victories in the sign of the cross—and used it to explain the success of the Abbasid rebels against the Umayyads. An unknown Melkite, perhaps a monk of Mt. Sinai, remembered Old Testament prophecies of the crucifixion that had been collected in ancient controversy with Jews—and redirected them to the attention of Muslims who honored Moses, the prophet to whom God spoke directly. Timothy the Great, Catholicos of the Church of the East, drew on a venerable soteriological tradition in which Jesus Christ, through his death and resurrection, becomes an 'earnest' of the believers' 'participation in the event'[82]—and brought it into direct contact with the central Qur'anic proclamation of the reality of the general resurrection.

The churches that found themselves in the *Dār al-Islām* possessed a centuries-old repertoire of means to speak the 'word of the cross'; their eighth-century teachers used and supplemented these means in new and sometimes surprising ways as they attempted to offer an *apologia* for their Christian hope (1 Peter 3.15) in a religious environment dominated by the Muslim *ḥunafā'*. In doing so, they developed lines of argument that many of their successors would follow.

Notes

1 This article draws heavily on my unpublished dissertation: M.N. Swanson, 'Folly to the *Ḥunafā'*: The Cross of Christ in Arabic Christian-Muslim Controversy in the Eighth and Ninth Centuries A.D.', doctoral dissertation, Pontifical Institute for Arabic and Islamic Studies, Rome, 1992.

2 The manuscript was published by M.D. Gibson, ed. and trans., *An Arabic Version of the Epistles of St. Paul to the Romans, Corinthians, Galatians, with Part of the Epistle to the Ephesians, from a Ninth Century MS in the Convent of St. Katharine on Mount Sinai* (*Studia Sinaitica* 2), London, 1894.

3 My translation of the text in ibid., p. 39 (Arabic).

4 *Āl 'Imrān* (3) 67. The English rendering here and throughout this chapter leans on that of A.J. Arberry, *The Koran Interpreted,* London, 1955.

5 See W.M. Watt, 'Ḥanīf, *EI*[2], vol. III, pp. 165–66; S.H. Griffith, 'The Prophet Muḥammad, his Scripture and his Message, according to the Christian Apologies in Arabic and Syriac from the First Abbasid Century', in Toufic Fahd, ed., *La vie du prophète Mahomet* (*Colloque de Strasbourg, 1980*), Paris, 1983, pp. 118–21.

6 See B. Roggema, 'A Christian Reading of the Qur'an: The Legend of Sergius-Baḥīrā and its Use of Qur'an and Sīra', in D. Thomas, ed., *Syrian Christians under Islam: The First Thousand Years,* Leiden, 2001, pp. 57–73, here p. 61.

7 L. Massignon, 'Le Christ dans les Évangiles, selon Ghazali', *Revue des Études Islamiques* 6, 1932, pp. 533–36.

8 G. Basetti-Sani, *The Koran in the Light of Christ: A Christian Interpretation of the Sacred Book of Islam,* Chicago, 1977, pp. 163–74.

9 F. Jourdan, 'La mort du Messie en Croix dans les églises araméennes et sa relation à l'Islam jusqu'à l'arrivée des Mongols en 1258', doctoral dissertation, Université de Paris Sorbonne and Institut Catholique de Paris, 1988, pp. 273, 299–300, 315–16, 380.

10 There did exist dissent from this main trajectory in the early Islamic centuries, notably from Ibn al-Rāwandī, Rhazes, and certain Ismā'īlīs. See Swanson, 'Folly', ch. 3, II.D.

11 N. Robinson, *Christ in Islam and Christianity,* Albany, NY, 1991, pp. 127–41; Swanson, 'Folly', ch.3, I.B.

12 For the text, see E. Amélineau, *Monuments pour server à l'histoire de l'Egypte chrétienne aux IVe et Ve siècles,* Paris, 1888, pp. 338–46 (with French translation and comment at pp. lii–lviii). See also R.G. Hoyland, *Seeing Islam as Others Saw It: a Survey and Evaluation of Christian, Jewish and Zoroastrian Writings on Early Islam* (*Studies in Late Antiquity and Early Islam* 13), Princeton, 1997, pp. 279–82. Hoyland dates the text earlier in the seventh century than I do; the issue is the Muslim building project which the apocalypse describes as 'rebuilding the Temple that is in Jerusalem'. I take this to be a reference to the Dome of the Rock (completion usually dated to AD 692); see the report of Anastasius of Sinai published by B. Flusin, 'L'Esplanade du Temple à l'arrivée des Arabes, d'après deux récits byzantins', in J. Raby and J. Johns, eds, *Bayt al-Maqdis,* Part 1: *'Abd al-Malik's Jerusalem* (*Oxford Studies in Islamic Art* 9), Oxford, 1992, pp. 17–31.

13 Amélineau, *Monuments,* p. 341.

14 For a recent discussion of matters of authenticity and date, see A. Louth, *St. John Damascene: Tradition and Originality in Byzantine Theology* (*Oxford Early Christian Studies*), Oxford, 2002, pp. 33–34 (on the date of the *Pēgē Gnōsēos*), 76–83 (on the chapter on Islam).

15 *Die Schriften des Johannes von Damaskos herausgegeben vom Byzantinischen Institut der Abtei Scheyern,* IV. *Liber de haeresibus. Opera polemica,* ed. B. Kotter (*Patristische Texte und Studien* 29), Berlin, 1981, p. 61, lines 18, 22–25; see also D.J. Sahas, *John of Damascus on Islam: The 'Heresy of the Ishmaelites'*, Leiden, 1972, pp. 132–33.

16 *History of the Patriarchs of the Coptic Church of Alexandria,* III. *Agathon to Michael I* (*766*), ed. and trans. B. Evetts, in *Patrologia Orientalis* 5, 1910, pp. 88–215. On the sources and redaction of the *History of the Patriarchs,* see J. den Heijer, *Mawhūb ibn Manṣūr ibn Mufarriğ et l'historiographie copto-arabe: Étude sur la composition de l'Histoire des Patriarches d'Alexandrie* (*Corpus Scriptorum Christianorum Orientalium* 513 = subs. 83), Louvain, 1989.

17 *History of the Patriarch,* p. 134. Later in the narrative, Bishop Stephen of Shutb made the sign of the cross to return a newborn baby to normal after calling it to bear witness that he was the legitimate son of his deceased father; ibid., pp. 204–5.

18 Ibid., pp. 149–50. Here and later, my translation of Evetts' Arabic text. For another story of this sort, see ibid., pp. 102–3.

19 Ibid., p. 152.

20 Ibid.

21 Ibid., p. 153.

22 Ibid., p. 140.

23 Ibid., p. 189.

24 J. Den Heijer, 'Apologetic Elements in Coptic-Arabic Historiography: the Life of Afrahām ibn Zur'ah, 62nd Patriarch of Alexandria', in S.K. Samir and J. Nielson, eds, *Christian Arabic Apologetics during the Abbasid Period* (*750–1258*), Leiden, 1994, pp. 193–94.

25 *History of the Patriarchs,* p. 194. Emphasis added.

26 Ibid., pp. 193–97.

27 See above, p. 241.

28 See J. Daniélou, *Études d'exégèse judéo-chrétienne* (*Les Testimonia*) (*Théologie Historique* 5), Paris, 1966, esp. pp. 5–11. While Melito of Sardis probably composed a book of *testimonia,* the oldest such works in our possession are those of Cyprian (written AD 246–48) and one attributed to Gregory of Nyssa (from c. AD 400). On these, see A.L. Williams, *Adversus Judaeos: A Bird's-Eye View of Christian* Apologiae *until the Renaissance,* Cambridge, 1935, pp. 56–64 and 124–31.

29 So the catholicos Timothy in his (Syriac) Letter 40 to Sergius; *Dialectique du langage sur Dieu de Timothée I* (*728–823*) *à Serge,* ed. and trans. H. Cheikho, Rome, 1983, p. 275, no. 7 (French translation, p. 186). See S.H. Griffith, 'Jews and Muslims in Christian Syriac and Arabic Texts of the Ninth Century', *Jewish History* 3, 1988, pp. 65–94.

30 John of Damascus, *Liber de haeresibus,* ed. Kotter, pp. 61–62, lines 33–41.

31 Ibid., p. 63, lines 63–64.

32 M.D. Gibson, *An Arabic Version of the Acts of the Apostles ... with a Treatise on the Triune Nature of God* (*Studia Sinaitica* 7), Cambridge, 1899.
33 Sinai Arabic MS 154, f. 110v. This date was first pointed out in a scholarly publication by K. Samir, 'Une apologie arabe du christianisme d'époque umayyade?', *Parole de l'Orient* 16, 1990–91, pp. 89–90.
34 Sidney H. Griffith has maintained this position, e.g. in his 'The View of Islam from the Monasteries of Palestine in the Early 'Abbāsid Period: Theodore Abū Qurrah and the *Summa Theologiae Arabica*', *Islam and Christian-Muslim Relations* 7, 1996, p. 11 and p. 25 n. 20.
35 I have argued for this position in M.N. Swanson, 'Some Considerations for the Dating of *Fī Tatlīt Allāh al-Wāḥid* (Sinai Ar. 154) and *al-Ǧāmiʿ Wuǧūh al-Īmān* (London, British Library or. 4950)', *Parole de l'Orient* 18, 1993, pp. 115–41. See also Hoyland, *Seeing Islam*, p. 503.
36 See M.N. Swanson, 'Beyond Prooftexting: Approaches to the Qur'an in some Early Arabic Christian Apologies', *The Muslim World* 88, 1998, pp. 305–8.
37 Ibid., pp. 308–11.
38 Sinai Arabic MS 154, ff. 107v–108r.
39 Ibid., ff. 137v–139v, where the text breaks off. One has the impression that one is close to the end of the chapter, and perhaps to the end of the treatise as a whole. Note that this chapter on the cross was not edited by Gibson.
40 Ibid., f. 137r–v. The Arabic text is published in M.N. Swanson, 'The Cross of Christ in the Earliest Arabic Melkite Apologies', in Samir and Nielsen, *Christian Arabic Apologetics during the Abbasid Period (750–1258)*, p. 129.
41 Sinai Arabic MS 154, ff. 137v–139r.
42 See J. Daniélou, 'Das Leben, das am Holze hängt: Dt 28, 66 in der altchrist-lichen Katechese', in J. Betz and H. Fries, eds, *Kirche und Überlieferung: Festschrift für Joseph Rupert Geiselmann*, Freiburg/Br, 1960, pp. 22–34.
43 See, for example, the Old Testament passages quoted by the Catholicos Timothy, notes 55–59 below.
44 The text was published by M.F. Nau, 'Un colloque du patriarche Jean avec l'émir des Agaréens', *Journal Asiatique* ser. 11, 5, 1915, pp. 225–79 (Syriac text and French translation). For a thorough discussion of the text and its date, see G.J. Reinink, 'The Beginnings of Syriac Apologetic Literature in Response to Islam', *Oriens Christianus* 77, 1993, pp. 165–87.
45 Nau, 'Un colloque du patriarche Jean', pp. 250–51 (Syriac text), 260 (French translation).
46 In Chapter Two, the author echoes *al-Nisā'* (4) 164, *wa-kallama-llāhu Mūsā taklīman* ('and God spoke to Moses directly') as he tells the story of Moses.
47 Note how precisely the apologist uses the Islamic vocabulary of revelation.
48 See the text above, p. 246.
49 Hoyland, *Seeing Islam*, pp. 472–73.
50 The Syriac text is reproduced and translated in A. Mingana, 'The Apology of Timothy the Patriarch before the Caliph Mahdi', in *Woodbrooke Studies: Christian Documents in Syriac, Arabic, and Garshūni*, vol. 2, Cambridge, 1928, pp. 91–162 (reproduction of Syriac text), 15–90 (English translation). For the dates, see H. Putman, *L'Église et l'Islam sous Timothée I (780–823)* (*Recherches ILOB, Nouvelle Série, B. Orient Chrétien* 3), Beirut, 1975, pp. 184–85; R. Caspar, 'Les versions arabes du dialogue entre le catholicos Timothée I et le calife al-Mahdî (IIe/VIIIe siècle): "Mohammed a suivi la voie des prophètes"', *Islamochristiana* 3 (1977), pp. 116–17.
51 For the recensions, see the works listed in the previous note and the literature cited there. There are quotations from Timothy's report in the recension of the Ibrāhīm al-Ṭabarānī debate translated by Vollers from a tenth-century manuscript: K. Vollers, 'Das Religionsgespräch von Jerusalem (um 800 D) aus dem Arabischen übersetzt', *Zeitschrift für Kirchengeschichte* 29, 1908, pp. 29–71, 197–221.
52 The passage under consideration here is found in Mingana, 'The Apology of Timothy', p. 114, col. 1 (Syriac text), pp. 40–41 (English translation).
53 The Syriac text renders the Qur'anic passive *shubbiha* with an active form.
54 Caspar, 'Les versions arabes', p. 141 (no. 30). While I normally follow the Syriac text, the redactor of the Arabic recension edited by Caspar has skillfully cleared up some confusion in the Syriac, notably the misunderstanding of *ub'athu* as 'I was sent'.
55 Psalm 22.16b–18: 'They pierced my hands and feet, all my bones cried out, they gazed at me and watched me. They divided my garments among them, and for my raiment they cast lots'.

56 Isaiah 53.5: 'He was killed for our sins and abased for our iniquity'.

57 Jeremiah 11.19: 'Wood shall ravage his flesh and shall cast him out from the land of the living', to which Timothy adds Isaiah 50.6: 'I gave my body to blows and cheeks to slaps. I did not turn my face away from shame and spitting'. The Jeremiah passage, while unfamiliar today, is attested as a prophecy of the crucifixion as early as Justin Martyr; see G.T. Armstrong, 'The Cross in the Old Testament according to Athanasius, Cyril of Jerusalem and the Cappadocian Fathers', in C. Andresen and G. Klein, eds, *Theologia Crucis—Signum Crucis: Festschrift fur Erich Dinkler zum 70. Geburtstag,* Tūbingen, 1979, pp. 17–38, here pp. 23, 33, 38.

58 Daniel 9.26a: 'The anointed one shall be killed, and shall have nothing'.

59 Zechariah 13.7: 'Smite the shepherd of Israel upon his cheeks' and 'Awake, O sword, against my shepherd'.

60 See N. Robinson, *Christ in Islam and Christianity,* Albany, NY, 1991, ch. 12.

61 Abū Ja'far Muḥammad al-Ṭabarī, *Tafsīr al-Ṭabarī: Jāmiʿ al-bayān 'an ta'wīl āy al-Qur'ān,* ed. Maḥmūd Muḥammad Shākir and Aḥmad Muḥammad Shākir, Cairo, 1955–69 (incomplete), vol. VI, p. 455 (no. 7133); cf. *al-An'ām* (6)60 and *al-Zumar* (39)42.

62 Ibid., pp. 455–57 (nos 7134–40).

63 Ibid., p. 458.

64 This example is given by al-Ṭabarsī as coming from al-Daḥḥāk (d. 723); Abū 'Alī al-Faḍl al-Ṭabarsī, *Majmaʿ al-bayān fi tafsīr al-Qur'ān,* Beirut, n.d., vol. II, p. 95. Another example of Qur'anic *taqdīm wa-ta'khīr* that receives early mention is *Āl 'Imrān* (3)43, 'prostrate yourself and bow', even though in actual prayer the bowing precedes the prostration.

65 al-Ṭabarsī, *Majma' al-bayān,* vol. II, p. 95.

66 A few more details may be found in Swanson, 'Folly', ch. 3, II.A.

67 For this entire discussion see Mingana, 'The Apology of Timothy', p. 114, col. 2 (Syriac text), pp. 41–42 (English translation).

68 See Swanson, 'Folly', Appendix II (edition of the text) and ch. 3, II.C.2 (discussion). The text may be found in Vatican Arabic MS 107, ff. 106r–107v.

69 Mingana, 'The Apology of Timothy', p. 116, col. 2 (Syriac text), p. 43 (English translation). The translation given here is my own. The same dilemma-question is posed by:

a. 'Alī al-Ṭabarī in his *Refutation of the Christians,* in the fragments preserved in the refutation by al-Ṣafī Ibn al-'Assāl; Marqus Jirjis, ed., *Kitāb al-ṣaḥā'iḥ fi jawāb al-naṣā'iḥ, taṣnīf al-Safi, … Ibn al-'Assāl,* Cairo, 1927–28, pp. 119–20.
b. Abū 'Īsā al-Warrāq in his *Against the Incarnation,* ed. and trans. D. Thomas, *Early Muslim Polemic against Christianity: Abū 'Īsā al-Warrāq's 'Against the Incarnation'*, Cambridge, 2002, pp. 160–63.
c. The hero of *The Story of Wāṣil,* edition and translation in S.H. Griffith, 'Bashīr/Bēsér: Boon Companion of the Byzantine Emperor Leo III: The Islamic Recension of his Story in *Leiden Oriental MS* 951 (2)', *Le Muséon* 103, 1990, pp. 318–19.

70 Timothy mentions the fall of Satan and of Adam: their sin does not imply divine weakness; Mingana, 'The Apology of Timothy', pp. 116, col. 2–117, col. 2 (Syriac text), pp. 43–44 (English translation).

71 Ibid., pp. 117, col. 2–118, col. 1 (Syriac text), pp. 44–45 (English translation). Timomy also gives the examples of Joseph and his brothers (ibid., p. 119, col. 2 / p. 46), and of the enemy who razed and burned a palace that happened to be slated for demolition (ibid., pp. 119, col. 2–120, col. 1 / pp. 46–47).

72 Early arabophone Christian apologists who responded to the dilemma-question include:

a. Theodore Abū Qurra; see S.H. Griffith, 'Some Unpublished Arabic Sayings attributed to Theodore Abū Qurrah', *Le Muséon* 92, 1979, pp. 29–35; or Samir Khalil, '*Kitāb "Jāmiʿ wujūh al-īmān" wa-mujādalat Abī Qurra 'an ṣalb al-Masīḥ', Al-Masarra* 70, 1984, pp. 417–19.
b. Habib Abū Rā'iṭa, in *On the Incarnation,* ed. G. Graf, *Die Schriften des Jacobiten Ḥabīb ibn Ḥidma Abū Rā'iṭa* (*Corpus Scriptorum Christianorum Orientalium* 130=ar. 14), Louvain, 1951, pp. 60–63;
c. 'Ammār al-Baṣrī, in *Kitāb al-masā'il wa-al-ajwiba,* ed. M. Hayek, *'Ammār al-Baṣrī: Apologie et controverses* (*Recherches ILOB, Nouvelle Série B. Orient Chrétien* 5), Beirut, 197–7, pp. 242–43 (*maqāla* 4, *mas'āla* 40).

d. Eustathius the Monk, in *Kitāb Ustāth,* Mingana chr. ar. MS 52, ff. 49v–51r.
e. An unknown Melkite in *al-Jāmi' wujūh al-īmān,* ch. 18, Question 5; British Library or. MS 4950, f. 119r-v, published in Samir Khalil, '*Ṣalb*' (see a. above), pp. 414–17.

73 All this material is summarized in Swanson, 'Folly', ch. 4, III. 'Excursus'. This excursus is reproduced in an *estratto* from the dissertation: M.N. Swanson, *Folly to the* Ḥunafā': *The Cross of Christ in Arabic Christian-Muslim Controversy in the Eighth and Ninth Centuries A.D., excerpta ex dissertatione ad doctoratum apud Pontificium Institutum Studiorum Arabicorum et Islamologiae,* Cairo, 1995, pp. 61–73.
74 Mingana, 'The Apology of Timothy', pp. 118, col. 2–119, col. 1 (Syriac text), pp. 45–46 (English translation). The translation given here is my own.
75 The phrase is that of M. Root, 'The Narrative Structure of Soteriology', in S. Hauerwas and L.G. Jones, eds., *Why Narrative? Readings in Narrative Theology,* Grand Rapids, MI, 1989, pp. 263–78, here p. 267.
76 See A. Mingana, ed. and trans., 'Commentary of Theodore of Mopsuestia on the Nicene Creed', in *Woodbrooke Studies,* vol. 5, Cambridge, 1932 (esp. chs 6–7, pp. 62–82) and idem, 'Commentary of Theodore of Mopsuestia on the Lord's Prayer and on the Sacraments of Baptism and the Eucharist', in *Woodbrooke Studies,* vol. 6, Cambridge, 1933. Note the commentary in R.A. Greer, *Theodore of Mopsuestia: Exegete and Theologian,* Westminster, 1961, ch. 4, esp. pp. 74–75. I thank Prof. Gerrit Reininck for directing my attention to Theodore.
77 See his *Kitāb al-masā'il wa-al-ajwiba,* in Hayek, *'Ammār al-Basrī,* pp. 228–42 (*maqāla* 4, *mas'āla* 32–39).
78 See, for example, passages from his *On the Incarnation* in K. Samir, 'Création et incarnation chez Abū Rā'iṭah: Étude de vocabulaire', in *Mélanges en hommage au professeur et au penseur libanais Farid Jabre* (*Publications de l'Université Libanaise, Section des études philosophiques et sociales* 20), Beirut, 1989, pp. 187–236, here pp. 206–9 (nos 199–215).
79 Ibrāhīm explicitly makes the claim that it is the Christians alone who have sure knowledge of the reality of the resurrection: G. Marcuzzo, ed. and trans., *Le dialogue d'Abraham de Tibériade avec 'Abd al-Raḥmān al-Hāšimī à Jérusalem vers 820* (*Textes et études sur l'orient chrétien* 3), Rome, 1986, pp. 512–15 (nos 535–45).
80 See Chapter 17, Question 25, 'On the death of Christ our Lord by means of public crucifixion', in British Library or. MS 4950, ff. 109v-110r.
81 The expression is that of K. Cragg, *The Arab Christian: A History in the Middle East,* Louisville, 1991, p. 291.
82 Mingana, 'Commentary of Theodore of Mopsuestia on the Lord's Prayer and on the Sacraments of Baptism and the Eucharist', pp. 19–20, with comment in Greer, *Theodore of Mopsuestia,* p. 74.

6 Extracts from *The Book of Religion and Empire*

Al-Tabari

XXVIII The Prophecy of the Christ about the Prophet—May God Bless and Save Both of Them

On this subject the Christ—peace be with Him—uttered a sentence recorded and perpetuated in the Book of the Apostle John, in the fifteenth chapter of his Gospel: "The Paraclet, the Spirit of truth, whom my father will send in my name, He shall teach you everything."[1] The Paraclet, then, whom God would send after the Christ, and who would testify to the name of the Christ—peace be with Him—is the One who would teach mankind everything that they did not know before; now among the disciples of the Christ there has not been, down to our time, a single one who taught mankind anything besides what the Christ had already taught; the Paraclet, therefore, who taught mankind what they did not know before, is the Prophet—may God bless and save him—and the Kur'ān is the knowledge that the Christ has called "everything."

And John said about Him in the sixteenth chapter: "If I go not away, the Paraclet will not come unto you. And when He is come, He will reprove the world of sin. He shall not speak anything of himself, but will direct you in all truth, and will announce to you events and hidden things."[2] John said, too, about Him: "I will pray my Father to give you another Paraclet who will be with you for ever."[3]

The interpretation of the saying "He will send in my name," is this: as the Christ was called Paraclet, and Muḥammad also was called by the same name,[4] it was not strange on the part of Christ to have said "He will send in my name," that is to say He will be "my namesake" (or: "my equal," *sami*). Indeed, it seldom happens that the Christ—peace be with Him—is mentioned in a chapter of the Books of the prophets—peace be with them—without a simultaneous mention of the Prophet—may God bless and save him—as adhering to Him and making one pair with Him, because he came after Him.

When I examined carefully the word "Paraclet," and searched deeply for the meaning of the saying of the Christ, I found another wonderful mystery in it; it is that if somebody counts the total of the numerical value of its letters, it will be equivalent to the same total as that of the letters of the words: *Muḥammad bin 'Abdallāh, an-Nabbīyul-Hādi.*[5] If somebody says that one number is missing, because the word is *Paracleta,*[6] we will answer that the letter *Alif* is a paragogical addition to the Syriac nouns. The words which would exactly be equivalent to the numerical value of the word, without any addition and diminution, are *Muḥammad Rasūlun Ḥabibun Ṭayyibun.*[7] If someone says that the same number is obtainable from other names, this will not be possible for him until he brings forth, from a scriptural evidence, the man who would answer to the description given by the Christ in His saying: "The Paraclet whom He will send, the Spirit of truth whom my Father will send in my name, He shall teach you everything;" and he will not be able to find a way for that.

And the disciple John said in his Epistle found in the Book of the Acts which is the history of the Apostles:[8] "My beloved, believe not every spirit, but discern the spirits that are of God. Every spirit that confesseth that Jesus Christ hath come and was in flesh is of God, and every spirit that confesseth not that the Christ was in flesh, is not of God."[9] The Prophet—may God bless and save him—has believed that the Christ has come, that He was in flesh, and that He was the "Spirit of God and His word which He cast into Mary."[10] His spirit, therefore, is, on the testimony of John and of others, a true and just spirit, coming from the Most High God, and the spirit of those who pretend that the Christ is neither in flesh nor a man is from somebody outside God.

And Simon Cephas, the head of the Apostles, said in the Book of the Acts: "The time hath come that judgment must begin at the house of God."[11] The interpretation of this is that the meaning of the house of God mentioned by the Apostle is Maccah, and it is there and not at another place that the new judgment began. If somebody says that he meant the judgment of the Jews, the answer is that the Christ had already told them that "There shall not be left in the temple one stone upon another that shall not be thrown down, and remain in destruction till the day of the Resurrection."[12]

It has become evident that the new judgment mentioned by the Apostle is the religion of Islām and its judgment. This is similar to the saying of the prophet Zephaniah—peace be with him—who said on behalf of God: "I will renew to the people a chosen language;"[13] Arabic was the new and the chosen language for the new judgment and religion. Daniel, too—peace be with him—said in this sense what we have already mentioned. There was not in that time a house related to God to which the adversary might cling and say that the judgment began there, except Maccah. If somebody says that the Apostle meant the Christian religion, how could he say about a religion and a judgment which had already appeared for some time: "The time hath come that it must begin"? This is an impossible hypothesis.

And the evangelist Luke reports in the eleventh chapter of his Gospel that the Christ said to His disciples: "When I sent you without purse, and scrip, and shoes, were ye harmed and lacked ye in anything? And they said: No. Then He said: But now he that hath no purse let him buy one, and likewise a scrip; and he that hath no sword, let him sell his garment, and buy a sword with it for himself."[14] The laws and prescriptions that the Christ had promulgated and preached were only submission, resignation, and obedience; when, then, at the end of His life He ordered His disciples and the standard-bearers of His religion to sell their garments in order to buy swords, men of discernment and intelligence know that He referred to another Dispensation, viz. to that of the Prophet—may God bless and save him—in pointing to his swords and his arrows which the prophets had described prior to His coming.

Simon Cephas unsheathed his sword and drew it out of its scabbard, in the night in which the Jews seized the Christ, and struck with it one of the soldiers, and cut off his ear; but the Christ—peace be with Him—took it with His hand and returned it back to its place in the soldier's head, and it became immediately as sound as it was before; and then He said to Simon: "Put up the sword into the sheath. He who draws the sword shall be killed with the sword."[15] In this He referred to the sword-drawers of His nation and His followers, but He referred to the Muslim Dispensation when He ordered His disciples to sell their garments in order to buy swords; and swords are not bought except for the sake of unsheathing them and striking with them.

And Paul, the foremost among the Christians, whom they call an apostle, said in his Epistle to the Galatians: "Abraham had two sons, the one by a bond-maid, the other by a free-woman. But he who was of the bondwoman was like other people, but he of the free-woman was by promise from God. Both are an allegory for the two laws and covenants. Hagar is compared with Mount Sinai, which is in Arabia, and answereth to Jerusalem which now is. But Jerusalem, which is in heaven, answereth to his free wife."[16] Paul has settled many points by this saying. The *first* is that Ishmael and Hagar had inhabited the country of the Arabs, which he called the countries of Arabia; the *second* is that Mount Sinai, which is in Syria, extends and links up with the desert countries, since he says that Hagar is compared with Mount Sinai, which is in the countries of Arabia; and Sinai is the mountain mentioned in the Torah at the beginning of these prophecies: "The Lord came from Sinai, and rose up from Seir, and appeared from Mount Paran."[17] In this Paul testified that the Lord, who according to the saying of the Torah, came from Sinai, was the Prophet—may God bless and save him—and that it was he who appeared in the countries of Arabia. We have demonstrated above that the meaning of the word "Lord" refers to "prophets" and to "lords." What would be clearer and more distinct than the mention by name of the countries of Arabia? He meant by this vocable the country of the Arabs, but he wrote it in a foreign and unnatural manner, *Arab* instead of *'Arab.*[18]

The *third* meaning is that Jerusalem answers to Maccah; and the *fourth* is that this second law and this second covenant are, without any doubt, from heaven. Paul called both of them by one name, and did not distinguish between them in any way. As to the supremacy that he gave to the free-woman, and to his saying that the son of the bond-woman was not born by promise, it is one-sidedness and prejudice on his part, because in the convincing passages of the Torah about Ishmael, which I have quoted above, there is sufficient evidence to show that he also was born, not only by one promise, but by several promises.

These are clear prophecies and established facts, perpetuated throughout the ages, which, if somebody apart from the Muslims claims, his only gain will be the deadliest arrow and the greatest lie; this will only be done by a wretched Jew or a babbling Christian, excusing with it themselves, and deceiving themselves and others. It is indeed evident to the Christians especially, and to the Jews generally, that God has intensified His wrath against the Children of Israel, has cursed them, forsaken them and their religion, and told them that He will burn the stem from which they multiplied, destroy the mass of them, and plant others in the desert and in the waste and dry land. On this subject, how great is my amazement at the Jews, who avow all these things and do not go beyond contemplating them, and burden themselves with claims through which they become full of illusion and deception. To this the Christians bear witness by their evidence against the Jews, morning and evening, that God has completely destroyed them, erased their traces from the register of the earth, and annihilated the image of their nation.

As to the community of the Christ—peace be with Him—they have no right to claim all the prophecies that I have succinctly quoted about the Prophet—may God bless and save him. They cannot claim to have made kings captives, to have enslaved princes and conducted them linked together with bonds and fetters, to have inherited desert and waste lands, to have beheaded people, to have multiplied killing and havoc in the earth, and other peculiarities which are fitting and due only to Ishmael and Hagar and their descendants, and to Maccah and its pilgrims.

Moreover, many prophets have distinctly mentioned by name the Prophet—may God bless and save him—have described him with his sword-bearers and archers, and told that death and rapacious birds shall go before his armies, and that his country shall be overcrowded with numerous caravans of camels and files of animals, and that he shall destroy the nations and the kings opposing him. All these confirm his religion, enhance his rank, and testify to the veracity of what his messengers have told about him. This is especially the case with Daniel, who closed all the prophecies with something that expels every doubt, and this is that the God of heaven will set up an everlasting kingdom which shall not change and perish. He who does not submit to him that God has chosen and raised is to be scorned and despised.

Notes

1 Joh. xiv. 26 (Syr. "The Holy Spirit").
2 Joh. xvi. 7, 8, 13.
3 Joh. xiv. 16.
4 In the *Shifā* of Yaḥṣubi "Paraclet" is given as a name of Muḥammad. (In the chapter of the Prophet's names.)
5 I.e. "Muḥammad, the rightly guiding Prophet, son of 'Abdallah."
6 According to the Syriac pronunciation.
7 I.e. "Muḥammad is a beloved and good apostle."
8 The Bible used by the author incorporated the Acts and the Catholic Epistles under one title *Praxis,* as it is in the Syrian Churches.
9 I Joh. iv. 1–3.
10 Ḳur. iv. 169.
11 I Pet. iv. 17.
12 Matth. xxiv. 2, etc.
13 Zeph. iii. 9 (cf. supra, p. 121).
14 Luk. xxii. 35–36.
15 Matth. xxvi. 51–52; Joh. xviii. 10–11; Luk. xxii. 50–51.
16 Gal. iv. 23–26.
17 Deut. xxxiii. 2. Cf. supra p. 86.
18 The author refers to the Syriac version where, curiously enough, the word is written in the Greek way without the strong guttural at the beginning.

XXIX The Answer to Those Who Have Said that the "Refugees" and the "Helpers" Embraced the Faith Without Any Sign

Somebody might say something similar to what was used as an argument by an uncle of mine renowned for his ability in discussion and for the superiority of his intelligence, and known in the regions of 'Irāḳ and Khurāsān by the name of Abu Zakkār Yaḥya ibn-Nu'mān. In one of the books that he wrote: *Answer to Adherents to Religions,*[1] he declared that he examined the reasons why many *Refugees* and first disciples, both men and women, embraced Islām, and he did not find anyone who adhered to it by reason of a sign that he had seen or a miracle that he could report. This was a strong objection against Islām for me also, and I did not cease to be deceived and fascinated by it, until I seceded from his faith; I found then that the answer to it was easy, and the outlet from it broad. Indeed, if we retort with the same argument against them, a statement will be credited to us, which if they were to destroy, the prophecies of many of their prophets would also be destroyed. The entry of some people into the religion of a prophet without having seen a miracle from him is not something which would make vain all the other miracles of that prophet, nor is the abstention of a prophet from showing a sign on a given occasion something which would give him the lie.

The prophet Ezekiel—peace be with him—says in the tenth chapter that a company from the children of Israel came to him to test him, and to ask him some questions. The answer that Ezekiel gave them was: "God has told me, and has ordered me to tell you, that the Lord of Lords says: I swear by My name that I am the living one, and that I shall not give any answer to what you are asking."[2]

As to the Christ—peace be with Him—a great crowd followed Him and believed in Him without having seen any sign from Him. About this there is the saying of the evangelist Matthew, found in the fourth chapter of his Gospel, to the effect that when the Christ—peace be with Him—"was walking by the shore of the sea of Galilee, He saw two brethren, one of them was Simon whom He called Cephas—to whom He gave the direction of the affairs of His nation, and whom He constituted the foundation of His religion—and Andrew, his brother, fishing in the sea. He made a sign to them and said to them: Follow Me, and I will make you after this day fishers of men; and they forthwith left their nets and followed Him."[3] And Matthew said in this chapter that the Christ "going on from thence, saw other two brethren, James the son of Zebedee, and John, fishing with their father; He called them to His faith, and they left their father and followed Him."[4] And Matthew said in this chapter that when the Christ "passed forth from thence, He saw a publican called Matthew, and said unto him: Follow Me; and he went with Him."[5] He means his own self, because he is the evangelist Matthew, one of the four who wrote the Gospel.

These are five from the heads, the foremost, and the earliest of the twelve Apostles, and the Gospel declares that they followed the Christ without having seen any sign and heard any convincing word from Him, apart from a mere call. Would that I knew what harm has come to the Christ from that, or what has shocked my uncle Abu Zakkār and those who subscribe to his opinion, from the fact that those who followed the Prophet—may God bless and save him—did so without having seen a sign from him. If what we have mentioned necessarily annuls the remaining miracles of the Christ—peace be with Him—it is then that the signs of the Prophet—may God bless and save him—will necessarily be annulled, on the ground that those who embraced his religion did so without having seen a sign from him.

Some people came to the Christ—peace be with Him—asking Him for a sign; and He not only did not show them any sign, but rebuked them strongly and reproved them with their generations. The evangelist Matthew bears witness to that, in the twelfth chapter, and tells that a company of the Jews came to the Christ and asked Him for a sign, but He answered them and said: "The evil and adulterous generation seeketh after a sign; and there shall be no sign given to it, but the sign of the prophet Jonas."[6] He told them that He would not show them a sign at all, because they were from the evil generation, meaning by that all the race of the Jews. As to the sign of Jonas which He mentioned, it is his three-days stay in the whale's belly; further, this is not one of the prophecies of the Christ, but it is one of the signs of Jonas; and Jonas was a long period of time before Him. A sign consists in wonders that a prophet shows to onlookers, which nobody besides him is able to perform; or in his prophesying about things hidden from him, which are realised in his time.

If somebody says: "My sign is that Moses rent the sea, and the Christ quickened a dead man," it will not be accepted from him, because this is an argument in favour of another one, and not of himself; however, no one can think of the Christ that He was short of answers, nor that He contradicted Himself, nor that He promised something from which He afterwards desisted, nor that He said that He would not do something which He did. His saying, therefore, to those of the Children of Israel who had asked Him for a sign, that there would be no answer to their demand, emanates either from God or from Himself; if it emanates from God, God then did the contrary of what He said to them, because He showed them signs at the hands of the Christ, after this event; and if it emanates from

Himself, then the Christ also did the contrary of what He said, and disagreed with His first saying; and this does not suit Him, and is inconceivable of somebody like Him. As to me, I count this also as an alteration and corruption in the text of the Gospel, by translators and copyists.

And Matthew said in the sixteenth chapter that when the Jews saw the Christ calling people and turning them away from Judaism, they gathered to Him and said: "By what authority doest thou what we see, and who gave thee this authority?" In answer to them Jesus said: "I also will ask you one thing, which if ye tell Me, I in like wise will tell you about your question. Tell Me about the baptism of John, son of Zacharias, whence was it? From heaven, or from earth?" The crowd abstained from answering, and said "We do not know;" and the Christ said "Neither tell I you by what authority I work."[7] We do not see that He answered the crowd about what they had asked Him, but He simply competed with them by propounding another question to them; and no one was able to find fault with Him on this account.

And Matthew said in the sixth[8] chapter that Pilate, the representative of the King of the Romans, said to the Christ, when the Jews brought Him to him: "I adjure thee by the truth of God to tell me: art thou the Christ, son of God, or not?" And the Christ—peace be with Him—did not say to him more than "Thou hast said."[9] There is neither affirmation nor negation in this saying, and one is allowed to say that He meant to dispel and discard this attribution from Himself, and to rebuke those who ascribed it to Him; if not, why did He not say "I am the son of God," when He was asked? And why did He not show a sign to clear up the question, and put the Jews to shame and confusion? This also is a question to which the Christ gave no answer, and it has not prejudiced the dignity of His rank nor His previous signs.

And it is said in the Gospel which is in the hands of the Christians that the Jews said to the Christ: "If thou be the son of God, come down from the cross, that we may believe in Thee;"[10] and He did not do it, nor did He show any sign; and we do not say, because of this, that He had no previous sign; indeed He foresaw more than anybody else the issues of this question, and what God wanted from Him, or had determined for Him.

More forceful is what Matthew said in the second chapter, that Satan said to the Christ when he was tempting Him: "If thou be the son of God, direct these stones to become bread;" and the Christ did not say to him more than: "It is written in the Books of Revelation that man shall not live by bread alone, but by every word that proceedeth out of the mouth of God."[11]

Do you not see—may God guide you—that the Christ—peace be with Him—and other prophets were asked questions to which they gave no answers, and were requested to perform miracles which they did not perform, because God had not permitted them to act otherwise and had not opened to them at the moment the doors of miracles? And the disciples asked the Christ—peace be with Him—about the Hour; and He said: "This is a secret and a hidden thing from Me, which God alone knoweth."[12] Since this has not been a cause of blame and reprobation to the Christ, it likewise must not be for the Prophet—may God bless and save him.

These are convincing and fair replies and answers, and cogent arguments, to that proposition and contention to which the disciples of my uncle Abu Zakkār and those who subscribe to his opinion, cling. I did not find a single Christian scholar, either in ancient or in modern times, who argued with this point against the Muslims, except my uncle; but God has refuted and explained it by His grace and favour, and by the wisdom, the replies, and the good suggestions of the Commander of the Faithful—may God strengthen him—and by what I profited by them.

Now exercise your mind—may God guide you—and let not your intelligence be idle; know that you have been created for a great task, and that you are standing at the brink of heaven or of Fire; he with whom this brink crumbles away into Fire[13] shall be in the abyss of everlasting shame, eternal regret and torment, which the Christ—peace be with Him—has described as a fire which is not quenched, and as worms which do not die;[14] but he whom truth takes up to the courts of heaven and to the altitudes of the heavenly Gardens, shall be happy and a winner of a great victory, and shall possess eternal peace and happiness, which no eye has seen and of which no ear has heard. Give, therefore, good advice to your souls, and do not deceive them; be true to them, and do not beguile them. Truth has become clear, the hiding veil has been withdrawn, and evidence has become manifest.

Notes

1 This book seems to be lost.
2 Ezek. xx. 1–3.
3 Matth. iv. 18–20.
4 Matth. iv. 21–22.
5 Matth. ix. 9.
6 Matth. xii. 39.
7 Matth. xxi. 23–28.
8 *Sic* Cod.
9 Matth. xxvi. 63–64.
10 Matth. xxvii. 40, etc.
11 Matth. iv. 3–4.
12 Matth. xxiv. 36, etc.
13 Ḳur. ix. 110.
14 Mark, ix. 44, etc.

XXX The Answer to those Who Have Blamed Islām in One of its Practices or in One of its Prescriptions

If a man from the *People of the Book* reviles one of the rules of the faith, and one of the practices of the Muslims, he will be grossly unjust to us, will repudiate and blame all the prophets, and will expose himself to sin and punishment. If they blame sacrifices, they are inherited from Abraham and from all the prophets of his posterity—peace be with them. If they reprobate circumcision, it was practised by the Christ and by those who preceded Him. If they condemn divorce, their own Books will render their endeavour fruitless; and if they condemn swearing by God, it is the saying of the Most High to His prophets;[1] the prophet Isaiah—peace be with him—declared on behalf of God: "I drew the permanent word out of My mouth, that unto Me every knee shall bow, and by Me every tongue shall swear."[2] And Paul, whom the Christians call an apostle, said that God made His promises to Abraham, in his seed, and swore to him by Himself.[3] And Daniel said that the angel who appeared to him lifted his hand to heaven and swore by the Eternal Merciful that all that he had said would surely take place.[4]

If they blame the Holy War, Abraham fought the four kings who had made inroads into the country of Jazīrah to invade its inhabitants; he protected his neighbours and the people with whom he was living, destroyed the armies of the enemy with his servants and men born in his house, and won from this fact honour, credit, eternal remembrance, and perpetual praise; he gave back to their respective kings all the booty and the men he saved, and did not hold back anything from the spoils, not even a bead or a utensil, after these kings had abandoned their countries and surrendered them.[5]

And Joshua, son of Nun, killed thirty-one kings from the kings of Syria,[6] and did not leave in one of their towns called 'Āni[7] a single dweller, nor a man to blow the fire; and he did not call them to religion, nor did he require tribute and capitation from them, nor did he receive ransom from them, as the Muslims do.

And the prophet Samuel—peace be with him—said in the twelfth chapter that the prophet David—peace be with him—raided a Syrian country called Philistia, and did not leave there a single man nor a single woman without killing them. He then took sheep, cattle, asses, and camels, and swept away with him goods, treasures, and furniture, without calling the inhabitants either to religion, or to pay tribute, or to submit.[8] And the Book of Samuel relates that David was hungry one day, and sent his retainers to a certain man in search of food, and they did not bring him anything. He then went with his men to attack this man and the inhabitants of his village; but behold, he saw the man's wife coming to meet him, bringing him food and wine, for fear that he should punish her husband.[9] He accepted that from her, and was satisfied; and his wrath cooled down and left him. This and similar deeds of prophets are neither reprobated nor blamed.

As to the Prophet—may God bless and save him—he ordered, with persuasion and dissuasion, to worship One, Eternal, and Omnipotent God, in order that religion might be One and the Supreme Being One. He who responds to that has the prerogatives and the obligations of the Muslims; and he who does not respond but gives tribute on his hand in an humble condition,[10] he spares his blood with this tribute and upon his submission has a right to the compact of protection. This point constitutes a fine subject of meditation for the unbelievers; indeed, it lowers their amour-propre and their pride, and calls the people of honour and self-esteem among them to change their state of lowliness, and their compact of protection by means of tribute, for the glory of dignity and freedom. If they are averse to tribute and submission, war shall be behind them.

And Moses—peace be with him—did more than that. When he ordered the Children of Israel to leave Egypt and go away, he told them that the Most High God had ordered that every one of them should borrow the garments of his neighbour and acquaintance and the jewels of their wives and daughters, and that they should inform them that it was for the occasion of one of their feasts. The Egyptian people yielded to this, adorned the Israelites with what they had, and lent them both their useful and necessary things. The Children of Israel numbered then about six hundred thousand combatants. When all was gathered to them and was in their possession, they journeyed all the night and departed one and all. And God rent the sea for them, and they crossed it; Pharaoh sought after them, and they dreaded him, but God drowned Pharaoh, and set the heart of the Israelites at rest from him.[11] The owners of those borrowed objects, and their wives and daughters were deprived of their loaned articles; and their treasures, a griffin carried them away;[12] and they bit their fingers out of regret.

All this was not unlawful and illicit, but was simply the right of booty and spoils; for the world belongs to the Most High God, and its Kingdom and ornaments belong to those of His servants upon whom He bestows them, as He said in His Book: "Thou givest the Kingdom to whomsoever Thou pleasest, and strippest the Kingdom from whomsoever Thou pleasest."[13] And inasmuch as what was done by the prophets whom we have mentioned is not shameful and sinful, but as something done by Way of tacit authorisation and good-will of God,[14] so also are to be considered the holy war against the polytheists and the attacks against the unbelievers, the injunction of which God laid upon the Prophet—may

God bless and save him. Without holy war no religion could stand, no inviolable thing could be safe, no gap could be filled, and the Muslims would become the prey and possession of their enemies. Men would scarcely remain in a religion with such standing without passing to what is higher and safer.

The Christ—peace be with Him—had forbidden war and given warning against its causes in saying: "Whosoever shall compel thee to go a mile, go with him twain; whosoever taketh away thy coat, give him thy cloak also; whosoever shall smite thee on thy cheek, turn to him the other also."[15] By this order the Christ—peace be with Him—left but little spiritual and temporal power to His followers, and transferred their heritage to the members of another nation who stirred war in East and West, and kindled it with spears and swords as far as the countries of the Greeks, of the Franks, of the tent-dwelling Turanians,[16] and of the Armenians. Outside these countries what Christians are to be found in the country of the Turks except a small and despicable quantity of Nestorians scattered among the nations? or what are those found among the Arabs except a sprinkling of Jacobites and Melchites?

Then we have seen that the Christ—peace be with Him—gave permission ultimately to take swords; and in that he abrogated the first order. He said, indeed, to His disciples: "Let each one of you sell his garment and buy a sword with it for himself."[17] And He said: "Think not I am come to sow peace on earth, but war."[18] He who slurs Islām in what has been considered good, and put in practice, by the prophets whom we have mentioned, deviates from the path of justice.

If somebody reprobates the saying of the Prophet—may God bless and save him,—that in the world to come there is food, and drink, the answer would be that the Christ—peace be with Him—declared also such a thing to His disciples when He drank with them and said to them: "I will not drink of this fruit of the vine, until I drink it another time with you in the kingdom of heaven."[19] In this He declared that in heaven there is wine and drink; and where drink is found, food and pleasures are not blamed. And Luke declares in his Gospel that the Christ—peace be with Him—said: "You shall eat and drink at the table of my Father:"[20] And John declares that the Christ—peace be with Him—said: "There are many mansions and dwellings at my Father's."[21]

All these confirm the existence of food and drink in the world to come, and of mansions and pleasures, according to what the Most High God said in His Book: "And gardens shall they have therein and lasting pleasure."[22]

Notes

1 One line of the text is much damaged here, and some words have only been conjectured.
2 Isa. xlv. 23.
3 Cf. Galat. iii. 16.
4 Cf. Dan. xii. 7.
5 Cf. Gen. xiv. 5 seq.
6 Josh. xii. 24.
7 Probably '*Ai* (cf. Josh. viii. I seq.)
8 Cf. I Sam. xxvii. 8 seq.
9 Cf. I Sam. xxv. 2–36.
10 Ḳur. ix. 29.
11 Cf. Exod. xi. 2; xii. 35–37, etc.
12 A proverb meaning "that they would not see them again."
13 Ḳur. iii. 25.
14 Ḳur. lvii. 20.

15 Matth. v. 39–40; Luk. vi. 29.
16 This is probably the earliest mention made of the Turanians in any Christian or Islamic work. See *A Manual on the Turanians and Turanianism,* London, 1918, pp. 12–14. The author appears to believe that at least a great number of the Turanian Turks were Christian in his time, and seems to imply that *Turanian* is not absolutely identical with *Turk.* The habitat of the Turanians was probably not very far from Mongolia.
17 Luk. xxii. 36 (cf. supra, p. 143).
18 Matth. x. 34.
19 Matth. xxvi. 29.
20 Luk. xxii. 30.
21 Joh. xiv. 2.
22 Ḳur. ix. 21.

XXXI The Answer to Those Who Reprobate the Fact that the Prophet—May God Bless and Save Him—Contradicted Moses and Christ—Peace Be With Both of Them—in Changing the Rules of the Torah and the Gospel

If one of those adversaries who penetrate deeply into science contends that the Prophet—may God bless and save him—believed in the Torah and the Gospel in his words, but disagreed with them in his actions, and that in the fact of his confirming them once and contradicting them another time there are in him indications of inconsistency, we will reply that God—may He be blessed and exalted—is Wise, Knower, Compassionate, Merciful; creatures are for Him, guidance is from Him, power and strength are by Him; and His servants are not to object to what He does, nor to interfere with His prescience and the secrets of His Providence, but they should submit and obey.

The most High God said through Moses—peace be with him—"God will raise you up a prophet from amongst your brethren, like unto me; hearken unto him; and he who does not hearken unto him, I will avenge myself on him."[1] The Prophet—peace be with him—appeared from amongst the brethren of the Jews, followed the prescriptions of God, and believed in Moses, of whom he said that "he conversed with God,"[2] and believed also in Jesus, of whom he said that He was "The Spirit of God and His Word, whom He has chosen, honoured, and taken to heaven; and He is with Him;"[3] and he did not contradict Moses in the article of the unity of God, nor did he utter on this subject ambiguities and equivocations as the Christians did, but he openly and clearly proclaimed it, and rendered faith pure and his saying precise. Moreover, all the prophets agreed with him with regard to the *Ḳiblah,* divorce, circumcision, fight against the unbelievers, protection of children by forcible means, and retaliation. And he multiplied sacrifices to the Most High God alone, and renewed to his nation rules and prescriptions which tally with the order of God; and the servants of God have nothing left to them but to obey God through him.

If people were permitted to slight and reprobate divine orders and economy of this kind, one would be allowed to say about the Christ that He once believed in the Torah and said: "I am not come to destroy it, but to fulfil it; verily, I say unto you, Till heaven and earth pass, one letter shall not pass from it,"[4] and then He openly contradicted Moses, and flung the Torah aside, to such an extent that the learned men of His community have reason to say openly and publicly: "The Old Testament has passed and gone, and the New Testament has come and appeared;"[5] they mean by Old Testament the Torah and its laws and the other Books of the prophets, and by New Testament the Gospel and the Books of the Apostles. As to the pillar of the Torah—the prop of Judaism—its rites, its circumcision, its sacrifices, its feasts, its law of retaliation, its decisions, its priesthood, and its altars, the

Christ—peace be with Him—has abrogated and annulled all of them. He did not leave the Jews a feast, without abolishing it; a Sabbath, without infringing it; a circumcision, without gently rejecting it; a sacrifice, without forbidding it; an altar, without despoiling it; and a priest, without calling him adulterous and profligate.

Matthew said in the thirteenth chapter that the Christ—peace be with Him—"went on the Sabbath day through the cornfields, and His disciples were anhungred, and began to pluck the ears of corn and to eat;"[6] and He did not blame their action, nor did He reprobate it. And Matthew said in this chapter[7] that the Christ, pointing to the Children of Israel who were present with Him, said: "You have heard the Torah say, Whosoever shall put away his wife, let him give her a writing of divorcement; but I say unto you that whosoever shall put away his wife, saving for the cause of fornication, causeth her to commit adultery, and whosoever shall marry a divorced woman shall commit adultery."[8] One might say, in disapprobation of this saying: What has a husband to do with a wife who committed sorcery, or became infidel, or poisoned her parents, or killed her child, or had intercourse with him? Can he not divorce her for all these? But how? That would be impossible for him, because the Christ has permitted divorce only in case of adultery.

And He said in this chapter: "You have heard that it has been said in the Books of Revelation: A tooth for a tooth, and an eye for an eye; but I say unto you: Whosoever shall smite thee on thy cheek, turn to him the other cheek also, and whosoever shall ask thee, refuse him not."[9] And Paul, who has the precedence among them, and whom they obey, said: "Circumcision is nothing, and uncircumcision is nothing."[10] In this he openly abolished circumcision. This and similar things are not considered blameable and reprehensible on the part of Christ—may God bless and save Him—; similarly, the new rules, the additions to, and the subtractions from, the rules of the Torah and the Gospel, which the Prophet—may God bless and save him—has innovated, are not to be reprobated and blamed.

Notes

1 Deut. xviii. 18–19 (cf. supra, p. 85).
2 Ḳur. iv. 164, etc.
3 Ḳur. iv. 156, 169, etc.
4 Matth. v. 17–18.
5 This thought is frequently found in the East Syrian or Nestorian Breviary.
6 Matth. xii. I.
7 *Sic* Cod.
8 Matth. v. 31–32.
9 Matth. v. 39–40, 42
10 I Cor. vii. 19.

XXXII The Answer to Those Who Have Pretended that No One but the Christ—Peace Be With Him—Mentioned the Resurrection

The Christians have said that nobody but the Christ has made known the Resurrection, and proclaimed the Last Day and the Revivification. By my life, He has proclaimed it and announced it in clear words, and God has honoured Him with an honour greater than that of His predecessors; but the prophets who preceded Him knew it and mentioned it. The prophet Moses said on behalf of God: "I am alone, and there is no God besides Me; I kill and I make alive."[1] And the prophet David said in the Psalter: "The giants shall be resuscitated and revivified, and they shall glorify Thee, O Lord, and they shall declare that Thy grace is in the graves."[2] And God—may He be blessed and exalted—said also through him: "I will revivify them and resuscitate them from the teeth of the lions and from the depths of the sea."[3] And the prophet Daniel—peace be with Him—said: "A great multitude shall be resuscitated from the graves, some to everlasting life, and some to perdition and to the contempt of their companions for ever."[4] And Hannah the prophetess—peace be with her—said in the Book of the prophet Samuel—peace be with him—"The Lord killeth and maketh alive; He bringeth down to the grave, and bringeth up from it."[5] And the Most High God said to Daniel—peace be with him—"Go and lie down (in conformity with) the decreed order; and thou shalt rise, at the appointed moment, at the end of the world."[6]

Notes

1 Deut. xxxii. 39.
2 Ps. lxxxviii. 10.
3 Ps. lxviii. 22
4 Dan. xii. 2.
5 I. Sam. ii. 6.
6 Dan. xii. 13.

7 A Mu'tazilite refutation of Christianity and Judaism

Two fragments from 'Abd al-Jabbār's *al-Mughnī fī abwāb al-tawḥīd wa-'l-'adl*

Margaretha Heemskerk

The Mu'tazila

The Mu'tazila was a Muslim theological school that defended its doctrine by the use of rational arguments. According to a standard account, the school originated as the result of a difference of opinion between the famous Muslim theologian al-Ḥasan al-Baṣrī (d. 728) and some of his disciples. At issue was whether a Muslim, after having committed grave sins, is still a Muslim or whether he is an unbeliever. In al-Ḥasan's opinion, he is neither a Muslim nor an unbeliever, but a hypocrite (*munāfiq*). Wāṣil b. 'Aṭā' (d. 748) and 'Amr b. 'Ubayd (d. 761) disagreed with him and declared that a Muslim who has committed grave sins is not a hypocrite but a malefactor (*fāsiq*). Thereupon they dissociated themselves (*i'tazala*) from his study-circle.[1]

The Mu'tazilites distinguished themselves from other Muslim theological schools by their adherence to five principles (*al-uṣūl al-khamsa*).[2] The first principle concerns the oneness of God (*al-tawḥīd*). The Mu'tazilites asserted that God has several essential attributes, such as His being eternal, living, all-knowing and almighty, but they denied that He is corporeal and rejected anthropomorphism.[3] Their second principle concerns God's justice (*'adl*), which, according to them, implies that all His acts are good.[4] On the basis of this principle, they denied that human acts are predestined by God. They asserted that God has given humans freedom of choice because it would not be just if He punished them for committing sins that had been predetermined by Him and that they had not committed of their own free will.

The third principle is the so-called 'intermediate position' (*al-manzila bayn al-manzilatayn*). This refers to Wāṣil's and 'Amr's judgment about the status of a Muslim who has committed grave sins. The fourth principle, which is referred to as 'the promise and the threat' (*al-wa'd wa-'l-wa'īd*), concerns God's reward for those who have been obedient to Him and His punishment of the disobedient. The fifth principle is commanding the right and forbidding the wrong (*al-amr bi-'l-ma'rūf wa-'l-nahy 'an al-munkar*), which concerns the obligation of Muslims to admonish other people to be obedient to God, and to warn them about being disobedient to Him.

Although all Mu'tazilites adhered to these five principles, they differed about several details. In fact, the Mu'tazila consisted of various groups that each followed the teachings of a specific Mu'tazilite master. The Basra Mu'tazilite school can, for example, be distinguished from the Baghdad school. 'Abd al-Jabbār belonged to the Basra school and specifically to the Bahshamiyya (or Bahāshima), the group that adhered to the teachings of Abū Hāshim al-Jubbā'ī (d. 933).[5]

'Abd al-Jabbār's Life and Works

Abū 'l-Ḥasan 'Abd al-Jabbār b. Aḥmad b. 'Abd al-Jabbār al-Hamadhānī al-Asadābādī was born around the year 932 in Iran, in a town near Hamadhān called Asadābād.[6] He became a Mu'tazilite when he was a young student and traveled around in order to fulfill his religious studies, which included Shāfi'ite law. When he was in Basra, a centre of Mu'tazilite learning, he decided to study Mu'tazilism there and later traveled to Baghdad to continue these studies there. After some years he himself became a teacher of this theological school. He taught the Mu'tazilite doctrine in Baghdad and in other places. In 977 the Būyid vizier al-Ṣāḥib b. 'Abbād in Rayy[7], who favored Mu'tazilism, invited him to come to Rayy as his chief judge. 'Abd al-Jabbār accepted and held this important post until the death of al-Sāḥib in 995. From then on, until the time of his death in Rayy in 1024,[8] he devoted all his time to dictating his books and teaching Mu'tazilism to his many students.

In 970, before his appointment as chief judge, 'Abd al-Jabbār started to dictate a voluminous work to his students. This work, which was to contain all subjects of the Mu'tazilite doctrine, is called *al-Mughnī fī abwāb al-tawḥīd wa-'l-'adl* ('The Satisfying [Book] on the Topics of Unity and Justice'). The writing of this twenty-volume work took twenty years. It was completed in Rayy in 990 and presented to al-Ṣāḥib b. 'Abbād. Apart from this work, 'Abd al-Jabbār dictated more than sixty other works during his long life, but most of them have been lost. One of the works that has been preserved is *Tathbīt dalā'il al-nubuwwa* ('The Establishment of the Proofs of the Prophethood').[9] In the book itself, 'Abd al-Jabbār says that he completed it in 995, which is the year in which he lost his position as chief judge.[10] This means that the book was completed later than the *Mughnī*.

On the first page of *Tathbīt dalā'il al-nubuwwa,* 'Abd al-Jabbār announces: 'This is the book of the establishment of the proofs of the prophethood of our prophet Muḥammad, the messenger of God—prayers and the peace of God be on him—and the evidences of his miracles and the manifestation of his signs, and the refutation of those who deny them'. The *Tathbīt* is a refutation of Christian and Jewish doctrines, and in it 'Abd al-Jabbār has included new sources that he did not use in the *Mughnī*. Shlomo Pines, who made an extensive study of the *Tathbīt,* concluded that these new materials were written by Jewish Christians. Later he identified these Jewish Christians as the 'Īsāwiyya.[11] The 'Īsāwiyya was a Jewish sect that believed that Jesus and Muḥammad were true prophets, but denied that this implied that they should follow Muslim law. They continued to obey the Mosaic law.[12] Their founder is said to have been Abū 'Īsā Isḥāq b. Ya'qūb al-Iṣfahānī (eighth century). They spread over the Muslim world and still existed in the sixteenth century. There was probably a community of 'Īsāwites in Rayy,[13] so it is possible that 'Abd al-Jabbār was personally acquainted with them.[14]

Jews and Christians in 'Abd al-Jabbār's Period

During 'Abd al-Jabbār's lifetime, the dynasty of the Būyids (or Buwayhids, 932–1062) ruled Iran and later Iraq as well. Power was usually divided over several princes who controlled the different parts of the empire. The Būyids had a preference for Shiism and favored the Shiites. In this period there was great interest in philosophy and rational thought. Jews and Christians enjoyed great freedom and several Christians held important posts as high-ranking officials or secretaries to the Būyids and their viziers.[15] Some Christians were philosophers, such as Yaḥyā b. 'Adī (d. 975). He and his school enjoyed the respect of many Muslim intellectuals. The famous Muslim philosopher al-Fārābī (d. 950) studied in Baghdad with the Nestorian philosopher Abū Bishr Mattā b. Yūnus (d. 940), who was also the teacher of Yaḥyā b. ʿAdī.[16] The Muʿtazilite Abū ʾl-Ḥusayn al-Baṣrī, a pupil of ʿAbd al-Jabbār, studied philosophy with the Christian philosopher Abū ʿAlī b. al-Samḥ (d. 1027), a pupil of Yaḥyā b. ʿAdī.[17] The Melkite Naẓīf al-Rūmī (tenth century) was a physician of the Būyid ʿAḍud al-Dawla (ruled 949–83). He translated Greek philosophical works into Arabic and, at the request of ʿAḍud al-Dawla, he wrote a treatise in Arabic on the doctrines of the Melkites, the Jacobites and the Nestorians.[18]

Several Jews participated in the intellectual life of the Būyid period and some of them were physicians or court financiers.[19] Iraq was an important centre of Judaism: the so-called exilarch, head of the Jews, had his residence in Baghdad, and there were two Talmudic academies (*yeshivot*) in Iraq, one of them in Sura and the other in Baghdad. The latter had first been in Pumbeditha, but it had moved to Baghdad at the end of the ninth century.[20] In the Būyid period, the Jews of Baghdad sympathized with the Shiites, who lived in the district of Karkh. At first they were favored, together with the Shiites, but after the year 1000, when the power of the Būyids diminished and ʿAbbasid caliphs became stronger, they suffered together with the Shiites from oppressive measures and mob attacks.[21]

In the Būyid period, Jews, Christians and Muslims were not only in contact with each other while fulfilling their professional obligations as physicians, secretaries, bankers or traders, but they also saw each other at meetings (*majlis*, plural *majālis*) organized by the Būyids, their viziers, or other important persons. The Būyids made their courts into centers of learning, just as the ʿAbbasid caliphs had done before them. They invited poets, philosophers, scholars and theologians to their courts, where they met and discussed all kinds of subjects. It was their pride to have well-known scholars in their palaces. Some viziers, such as al-Ṣāḥib b. ʿAbbād in Rayy, held the same sort of meetings set by the example of their Būyid masters. Less formal meetings and classes were held in mosques, private houses and other places. It is reported that some owners of bookstores organized scholarly discussions in their shops.[22]

Christians and Jews participated in these meetings. The Christian philosopher and trader Abū ʿAlī ʿĪsā b. Zurʿa (d. 1008), for example, took part in meetings held by the vizier Ibn Saʿdān.[23] Ibn Zurʿa himself held sessions which were attended by the Muslim secretary and courtier Abū Ḥayyān al-Tawḥīdī (d. 1023), who himself also participated in the meetings held by the viziers Ibn Saʿdān and al-Ṣāḥib b. ʿAbbād, ʿAbd al-Jabbār's patron.[24] Ibn Zurʿa is reported to have held discussions with his Jewish friend Ibn Mūsaj and other Jews.[25] Al-Ṣāḥib b. ʿAbbād held discussions with the Jewish exilarch. There is a report of a debate between them on the inimitability of the Qur'an.[26] Another, somewhat earlier, example of personal contact between a Muʿtazilite and a Jew is a meeting (*majlis*) that was attended by the famous Muʿtazilite Abū ʾl-Qāsim ʿAbdallāh b. Aḥmad al-Balkhī al-Kaʿbī (d. 931). It is reported that at this meeting, attended by all Baghdad's important theologians (*mutakallimūn*), a Jew discussed the abrogation of laws with some of them. At one point in the dispute they asked al-Kaʿbī to judge between them. When the Jew questioned al-Kaʿbī's authority, al-Kaʿbī pointed to the respect shown to him by all who were present at this meeting.[27]

Muʿtazilite Polemics against Christians and Jews

Muʿtazilite books in which Christianity or Judaism are refuted were often given the title ʿRefutation of the Christians' (*al-Radd ʿalā ʾl-Naṣārā*) and ʿRefutation of the Jews' (*al-Radd 'alā 'l-Yahūd*). Ibn al-Nadīm (d. 995), who made a bibliography of the books known in his time, called the *Fihrist*, mentions several Mu'tazilite books with such titles.[28] Among them are *al-Radd 'alā 'l-Naṣārā* and *al-Radd 'alā 'l-Yahūd* by al-Jāḥiẓ (d. 869),[29] three versions of *al-Radd 'alā 'l-Naṣārā* (short, medium and extensive) by Abū 'Īsā al-Warrāq (d. 861 or later), as well as his *Radd 'alā 'l-Yahūd*.[30] Polemics against Jews and Christians can also be found in heresiographies such as the *Kitāb al-awsaṭ*, attributed to al-Nāshi' al-Akbar (d. 906).[31]

A. Anti-Christian Polemics

The main subject of Muslim polemics against the Christians is the divine trinity and especially its implications with respect to the divine nature and sonship of Jesus. In the Qur'an, the divinity of Jesus is denied. It is expressly said that Jesus was a prophet, a servant of God, who said: 'God is my Lord and your Lord. Worship Him' (Q 3:51 and 19:36; see also Q 5:117). The divine trinity is rejected (Q 4:171 and 5:73) and the idea that God can have a son is strongly denied (Q 10:68, 17:111, 19:88–93, 21:26–29 and several other verses). However, it is self-evident that Muslims cannot use Qur'anic verses as an argument in their polemics against Christians because Christians do not accept the authority of the Qur'an. They deny Muḥammad's prophethood and consequently deny that the Qur'an is a revelation from God. Because of this, Muslims have to resort to rational arguments that are acceptable to both Christians and Muslims.

B. Anti-Jewish Polemics

The abrogation (*naskh*) of the Mosaic law and the inimitability (*i'jāz*) of the Qur'an were the main subjects in the disputes between Jews and Muslims. We have seen before that at the meeting attended by al-Balkhī al-Ka'bī, a Jew discussed the abrogation of laws. The inimitability of the Qur'an was the subject of the debate between al-Ṣāḥib b. 'Abbād and the Jewish exilarch. We shall see that there is a close relationship between these two subjects.

The Muslim principle of abrogation relates to Qur'anic verses that have been rendered inoperative by verses that were revealed later.[32] Because of this, Muslims are no longer bound to observe what is decreed in the earlier verses, but only what is decreed in verses that were revealed later. The application of this principle to holy books that were revealed before the Qur'an means that the divine prescriptions in the Torah and the Gospel have been abrogated by the prescriptions in the Qur'an because the Qur'an was revealed later. Jews and Christians reject the abrogation of their laws, arguing that abrogation of their laws is not possible and that Muḥammad is not a true prophet.

In Islam, an important criterion for the authenticity of a prophet is that his mission is confirmed by God by means of a miracle. Examples of such miracles are Abraham's not being burned by a fire (Q 21:69), the rod of Moses becoming a serpent (Q 7:107), and Jesus bringing the dead to life (Q 3:49 and 5:110). Consequently, Muḥammad's prophethood must also be confirmed by a miracle, but the Qur'an makes no clear mention of him performing any, unless one regards the reference to the Prophet's night journey to Jerusalem (Q 17:1) as a miracle. There are miracle stories about Muḥammad that are not found in the Qur'an but that are known from reports about him, although these reports are open to criticism regarding their authenticity because of the way in which they were transmitted.[33] However, in the Qur'an it is suggested that the Qur'an itself is a miracle that establishes Muḥammad's prophethood (Q 29:50–51). According to Muslims, the miraculous nature of the Qur'an is proven by its inimitability (*i'jāz*), which is to say that no human being is able to produce an equally wise and eloquent book.[34] Because this proves Muḥammad's prophethood, the abrogation of earlier revelations is often discussed in relation to the inimitability of the Qur'an.

Jewish theologians refuted Muslim polemics by referring to an account about Moses, who is reported to have said that his law is imposed on the Jews forever.[35] They also argued that abrogation implied that God had changed his mind and pointed out that this contradicted God's omniscience, since changing one's mind (*badā'*) is a sign of ignorance.[36]

Christianity and Judaism in the *Mughnī*

Al-Mughnī fī abwāb al-tawḥīd wa-'l-'adl, in short *al-Mughnī,* is a twenty-volume work that comprises all subjects of the Mu'tazilite doctrine. It consists of two main parts, based on two of the main Mu'tazilite principles: divine unity and justice. 'Abd al-Jabbār explains that the other three principles are included in the second principle. The first part of the *Mughnī* consists of five volumes, whereas the second part consists of fifteen.[37] In the first four volumes 'Abd al-Jabbār discusses the qualities of God and erroneous opinions about Him that have to be rejected. In the fifth volume, which is called 'the non-Muslim sects' (*al-Firaq ghayr al-Islāmiyya*),[38] he describes and rejects the doctrines of other religions about God. The main discussion of Christian doctrines is to be found in this volume on pages 80–151. 'Abd al-Jabbār lists the things that all Christians agree on concerning God and Jesus and describes the doctrinal differences between thé Nestorians, the Jacobites and the Melkites.[39] This volume does not contain a chapter on Judaism.

Judaism is extensively dealt with on pages 97–142 of the sixteenth volume of the *Mughnī,* which is called 'The Inimitability of the Qur'an' (*I'jāz al-Qur'ān*).[40] The subject of this volume is closely connected to those of the preceding volume, entitled *Prophethood and Miracles* (*Al-tanabbu'āt wa-'l-mu'jizāt*). The sixteenth volume first discusses the authenticity of historical reports, and secondly the abrogation of laws in general. Then the abrogation of the Mosaic law is dealt with, followed by a section on the prophethood of Muḥammad, the inimitability of the Qur'an and the other miracles of Muḥammad. The inimitability of the Qur'an is the foremost subject of this volume, and relatively little attention is given to the other miracles.

It is clear that in the *Mughnī* 'Abd al-Jabbār discusses Christian and Jewish doctrines within the totality of his exposition of Mu'tazilite doctrine. This is coherent with his method of working. He not only discusses the Mu'tazilite opinion on a subject but also deals with divergent opinions. Typically he first describes the Mu'tazilite, and in particular the Bahshamite opinion on the subject to be discussed, together with the method that is to be followed in the discussion (see, for instance, the beginning of the second fragment). He introduces this by the words: 'Know that ... ' (*I'lam anna* ...). Next he describes several divergent opinions on the subject under discussion, such as those held by other Mu'tazilites, non-Mu'tazilite theologians, philosophers or non-Muslims. Thereupon he refutes these opinions one by one. Usually he introduces the opinion that is to be refuted by the words: 'If he says: ... ' (*Fa-in qāla:* ...). Then he introduces the refutation of this opinion with the words 'He is told: ... ' (*Qīla la-hū:* ...). 'Abd al-Jabbār may use slightly different wordings, as can be seen in the two selected fragments.

It is evident that the renderings of the statements of opponents and 'Abd al-Jabbār's refutations are not reports of actual discussions that he had with them. Rather, they were meant to instruct Mu'tazilites on how to refute these opinions. The method of first mentioning an opponent's opinion and then refuting it by arguments was consistently applied by the Mu'tazilites and other rational theologians (*mutakallimūn*). Without doubt this was closely related to the practice of the meetings described above. Those who intended to participate in these meetings could prepare themselves by studying the books. They could learn which statements they could expect from opponents and which arguments they could use to refute them.

Another indication that the descriptions of statements and their refutations are not reports of actual discussions is that 'Abd al-Jabbār often mentions the sources in which he found them. In his refutation of Christian doctrines, he frequently refers to arguments given by Abū 'Alī al-Jubbā'ī and al-Jāḥiẓ, both Mu'tazilites. In fact, he includes complete paragraphs from al-Jāḥiẓ's refutation of the Christians. We know this because al-Jāḥiẓ work has survived, which means that his text can be compared with 'Abd al-Jabbār's text. This is not possible with respect to Abū 'Alī al-Jubbā'ī's book, because it has been lost.[41] As a result, we do not exactly know when 'Abd al-Jabbār stops citing al-Jubbā'ī and starts giving his own comments.

1. Fragment from 'Abd al-Jabbār's *Refutation of Christianity* (*al-Mughnī*, V, pages 105–7)

[Jesus cannot have the title 'son of God']

As for those of them [the Christians] who say: 'He [God] is the father of the Messiah in the sense of adoption (*tabannī*) and generosity (*karāma*)', this, first of all, makes it untenable for them to say that He has always been a father. It makes it necessary that He was a father when He created Jesus. Apart from this, adoption in its true meaning is only possible for those who can have a son in reality or for those that can produce their equal and belong to the same kind of animal. For that reason, a dead [person] cannot adopt a living [person]; as he is dead, he cannot have a son in reality. Neither can a young man adopt an adult person or a calf (*'ijl*) or a young camel (*faṣīl*). What we say about Zayd adopting someone else is not disproved by what we say about him glorifying and honouring him. Accordingly, we can glorify someone whom we cannot adopt. What is meant by it is that he treats him in the same way as his son, with respect to education and the distinction and qualifications that are connected to [the relationship between] son and father, and this is impossible for the Eternal and Sublime. So, how can it be said that He adopted him?

Besides, this statement makes it necessary that each prophet is His adoptive son by the way of adoption. In this respect 'Īsā (Jesus) has no special distinction that the others do not have. Apart from this, human beings may fraternize with someone else, in the same way as they adopt someone else, in the manner of bestowing honors [upon him] and treating him in reality in the same way as brothers [do]. So there is no difference between those who say: 'He [God]—He be praised—adopts [a son] in this sense', and those who say: 'He fraternizes with someone else'. If this is wrong, it is established that their statement that He—He is exalted and powerful—is a father and that He has a son in this way, is not right.

With respect to those who say: 'If it is right that Ibrāhīm (Abraham) is a friend (*khalīl*) [of God], should it then not be right that 'Īsā is a son of His, not in [the sense of] real sonship, but in the sense of generosity?' Our master Abū 'Alī [al-Jubbā'ī],—may God have mercy upon him—said: 'Friend in the real [sense] is right with respect to Ibrāhīm and Him [God]—He is exalted—, because friendship (*khulla*) is derived from preference (*iṣṭifā'*) and favor (*ikhtiṣāṣ*). A human being is said to be a friend of someone if he [the last mentioned] favors him with matters that he does not favor others with. Since He—He is exalted and powerful—favored Ibrāhīm—peace be upon him—with His inspiration (*waḥy*) and His honor, which He did not favor someone else with in his period, it is allowed to say that he was the friend of God (*khalīl Allāh*), and so he called himself a friend of God. This analogy makes it necessary that each of the prophets is described as being a friend of His, because He has favored each one of them with inspiration and honor which distinguish him from others. Because of this, our prophet [Muḥammad]—may God's blessing be upon him—said: 'If I took a friend (*khalīl*), I would take Abū Bakr as a friend, but your master is the friend of God—He is exalted and powerful'.[42] He called himself a friend of God—He is exalted and powerful—and refrained from taking one from his people (*umma*) as a friend, because his information and explanation are meant for them all. It is not allowed that he should favor [only] one of them with that, in accordance with the special honors that God—He is exalted—bestowed on him, when He assigned the mission (*risāla*) to him and not to the other people of his period.

After He had favored Ibrāhim with this, it became a title (*laqab*) for him. This is not impossible for a name. Do you not see that the Qur'an has been distinguished by this appellation [i.e. *al-qur'ān*], although its meaning may also apply to something else, and Moses was distinguished as being 'the person addressed by God' (*kalīm Allāh*),[43] although God—He is exalted—[also] has spoken to the angels.

(Next, 'Abd al-Jabbār discusses other meanings of friendship, which he himself thinks are less adequate. This part is left out of the translation. The translation continues at page 107, line 13):

Then the name [i.e. *khalīl*] became like a distinction for him [Ibrāhīm]. The same is not possible with respect to sonship,[44] because the strict meaning (*ḥaqīqa*) of son (*ibn*) is that he is born from a father, being from his water, and this is impossible with respect to God—He is exalted. It is therefore not right that 'Īsā is described as the son of God in the same way as Ibrāhīm is described as a friend of His.

(Next, 'Abd al-Jabbār cites from al-Jāḥiẓ's *al-Radd 'alā 'l-Naṣārā*.)

1.1 Explanation of This Fragment

'Abd al-Jabbār discusses in this fragment a question that has also been discussed by al-Jāḥiẓ, who said: 'I asked them [the Christians] about their statement: "If God has taken one of His servants as a friend (*khalīl*), is it then possible that He takes one of his servants as a son (*walad*)?"'.[45] Al-Jāḥiẓ says that some theologians considered this possible, if it was meant as adoption. He himself rejects it: 'But we—may God have mercy upon you—do not consider it acceptable that God should have a son, not in the manner of procreation, nor in the manner of adoption'.[46]

'Abd al-Jabbār starts off by pointing out that when Christians claim that Jesus was adopted by God, they cannot maintain that God was always his father. This touches on the dogma of the trinity. According to 'Abd al-Jabbār, Christians say about the three hypostases (*aqānīm*) that 'the son is always being generated by the father and the father is always generating the son'.[47] 'Abd al-Jabbār points out that if Jesus was adopted by God, it implies that he was first created by Him. In the Qur'an it is said that each human being is created by God (Q 22:5 and 40:67).

In order to make it clear that adoption cannot apply to God, 'Abd al-Jabbār refers to the meaning and usage of the term adoption (*tabannī*). The Arabic word is derived from the root b-n-(w/y), from which the Arabic word *ibn* (son) is also derived. The literal meaning of the Arabic verb *tabannā* is 'to take as a son'. 'Abd al-Jabbār explains that adoption (taking as a son) is only possible for living beings who are of the same kind and who could, in reality, be father and son. Therefore, it is not possible for a dead person to adopt a living person or for a man to take a camel as his son. 'Abd al-Jabbār declares that one should not refute this by equating adoption with conferring honor. In making this statement, he refers to a hypothetical person with the name of Zayd, a standard practice for giving examples. He admits that honor is part of the relationship between a father and his son, but he denies that each person conferring honor can adopt the person being honored. There are cases in which conferring honor is possible but adoption is impossible. From all this, 'Abd al-Jabbār concludes that it is not possible to say Jesus was adopted by God.

Another argument produced by 'Abd al-Jabbār is that if it were possible for God to take someone as his son, it would also be possible for Him to take someone as His brother. Both relations are family relations. This means that someone could be referred to as 'the brother of God'. Those who admit that this is impossible should also admit that it is impossible for someone to be the son of God.

'Abd al-Jabbār also points out that if it were right to refer to Jesus as 'son of God', this would necessarily hold for all other prophets. It would mean that each prophet could be referred to as 'son of God'. This would probably be denied by the Christians.

Next 'Abd al-Jabbār discusses the question of whether the title 'son of God' is comparable to the title 'friend (*khalīl*) of God'. This title was given to Abraham, because in the Qur'an it is said: 'God took Ibrāhīm as his friend' (Q 4:125). 'Abd al-Jabbār asserts that this means that by making him a prophet, God honored Abraham and preferred him above other people. In fact, the title 'friend of God' can be applied to all prophets, because they were all preferred by God above other human beings. Muḥammad called himself a friend of God. 'Abd al-Jabbār then explains that it is possible for a name that could refer to more than one person or thing to refer to one specific person. As examples he mentions the word *qur'ān,* which means 'what is read/recited'. It could be used for other books but has become the name of the scripture of Islam. Another example is the title 'addressed by God', which is a special title given to Moses, even though it could also have been used in reference to the angels because they, too, are addressed by God.

'Abd al-Jabbār takes into account the true meanings of words. The true meaning of 'friend' is a person who is specially favored by someone else. It is indeed possible that God especially favors a human being and Abraham can therefore be referred to as 'friend of God'. However, the true meaning of 'son' is that this person is procreated by another person, his father, by means of the ejection of the latter's sperm. 'Abd al-Jabbār affirms that this way of procreation is not applicable to God. Because of the true meaning of the word 'son', Jesus cannot be referred to as 'son of God'.

2. Fragment from 'Abd al-Jabbār's *Refutation of Judaism* (*al-Mughnī*, XVI, pages 138–39)

Chapter on [the explanation] that the abrogation (*naskh*) of the law (*sharī'a*) of Moses by the law of our prophet—peace be on them both—is right and indisputable.

Know that the reliable [method] for this is to establish the prophethood (*nubuwwa*) of Muḥammad—may God bless him and give him peace—by means of the miracles that give evidence for this, because from his religion (*dīn*) and law it is necessarily (*bi-iḍṭirār*) known that he has brought what abrogates the law[48] of those who came earlier, concerning the observance of the Sabbath, the nature of the prayers and their stipulations, the fasting and its peculiarities, and other rules. However, some laws are in conformity with the law of those who came earlier, although they were introduced by him [Muḥammad]—peace be with him—, because the welfare (*maṣlaḥa*) [of humankind] required this conformity, just as it required the divergence from what was earlier.

If he says: 'So you say that his law abrogates all that precedes it. That is not right if a part of it is in conformity to it',

Then he is answered: 'What we mean by this is that it is obligatory to obey this new [literally: initiated] law and to renounce that [i.e. the preceding] law. Even if a person on whom God's obligations are imposed (*mukallaf*) performed an action that is similar in both [laws], [but he did this] in obedience to the first [law], he would make a mistake, although it is right if he performs it in obedience to the second [law], because [in that case] his knowledge is from him [Muḥammad]—may God bless him—and because he derives its pecularities, regulations and aspects from the law [brought by Muḥammad]. From this point of view, it is right to say that all preceding laws are abolished by his law—peace be with him. Because of all this, what some of the jurisprudents (*fuqahā'*) say is untenable: [i.e.] that he—may God bless him—and his people (*umma*) devoted themselves to the law of those who preceded [them], as we already have explained, with respect to the principles of law (*uṣūl al-fiqh*). [You may understand it in this way:] when, after his [Muḥammad's] appearance—may God bless him—, all persons on whom God's obligations are imposed (*mukallaf*) had to renounce every preceding law and the knowledge they had about it from the time before him [Muḥammad], it was as if they all were told: "It is abrogated by his law—may God bless him—and what is in conformity to it becomes equal to what is different in this respect".'

We have explained that, when his prophethood—may God bless him—has been established, the Jews cannot refute that he has brought the abrogation of the law of those who came before him, because we have explained that there is no objection to this, neither from the point of view of reason nor from the point of view of revelation. We have [also] explained that nothing, in any way, thwarts the establishing of the abrogation of the law of Moses—peace be with him. This holds for all Jews, except for a small group belonging to the 'Ānāniyya (Karaites), because they deem it possible that the law of Moses is abrogated, both from the point of view of reason and from the point of view of revelation, although they refute the prophethood of Muḥammad—may God bless him. They maintain that his prophethood is not established, because the Qur'an cannot be a miracle (*mu'jiz*). We will speak about them later. However, they have resorted to this after they had noticed how our masters disclosed the incoherence (*tahāfut*) Of their discourse (*kalām*) with respect to the impossibility of the abrogation of the laws. So they turned to this [declaring the abrogation of laws possible], because they thought it left more room [for refutation], after the many questions that our masters disclosed with respect to the inimitability (*i'jāz*) of the Qur'an. Except for this, their [the Jews'] foremost scholars follow the same method, [which is] that the prophethood of someone who maintains that the law of Moses is abrogated cannot be right. [They are] the 'Ānāniyya (Karaites) among them, the Ashma'iyya (Rabbanites), the Samāra (Samaritans) and the other sects.[49] We will explain what is to be said about their sticking to the rejection of the prophethood of our prophet Muḥammad—may God bless him—on the account that his miracles are not transmitted in such a way that they are evidence (*ḥujja*).

2.1 Explanation of This Fragment

Moses (Mūsā) is an important prophet in Islam. His life is extensively described in the Qur'an, including the episode in which God gave him the Tables of Law (Q 7:142–45 and 7:154). In several verses in the Qur'an, it is said that God has revealed a book to Moses, the Torah (see, for instance, Q 11:17, 40:53–54, and 28:43). Even though Muslims acknowledge Moses' prophethood, they do not observe the Sabbath and several other rules, which are observed by the Jews. The Muslims claim that they are not bound to keep these observances because the Mosaic law has been abrogated by the new law brought by Muḥammad.

Nevertheless, several rules in the Mosaic law and in Muḥammad's law are the same. 'Abd al-Jabbār does not give examples, but we may think of the prohibition against eating pork. Does this mean that only a part of the Mosaic law has been abrogated? 'Abd al-Jabbār rejects this. He declares that a preceding law is abrogated in its totality. The new law must be followed, because this law has been brought by Muḥammad. 'Abd al-Jabbār declares that a Muslim who performs something in the conviction that he is following an earlier law makes a mistake, even if it concerns a rule that conforms with a rule of Muḥammad's law. It is wrong, not because of the act itself, but because of his conviction that he is obeying an earlier law.

'Abd al-Jabbār explains that the similarities and differences between the earlier laws and Muḥammad's law depend on the welfare of the people in both periods. We should bear in mind that he refers to divinely made laws, which God has made known to the people by means of a prophet. According to the Mu'tazilite doctrine, God imposes duties on those who are able to understand and perform them. These persons are referred to as *mukallaf.* Children, the insane and animals are exempted from these duties because their minds are incomplete.[50] God helps the *mukallaf* to fulfill their duties in several ways. One way is His sending a prophet, who informs the people about the duties God has imposed on them.[51] According to the Mu'tazilite doctrine, God knows what is best for the people, and He acts in accordance with this.[52] If He knows that some new duties will be better for them, He will impose these and send a prophet to inform the people about these duties. This information is found in the law brought by the prophet.

'Abd al-Jabbār declares that the Jews must first be convinced that Muḥammad is a true prophet and then they must admit that the Mosaic law has been abrogated by Muḥammad's law. Most Jewish theologians reject both the prophethood of Muḥammad and the possibility that a divine law can be abrogated. 'Abd al-Jabbār reports that these theologians even declare that someone who maintains that the Mosaic law has been abrogated can a priori not be a prophet. So alongside their claim that there are no miracles that affirm his prophethood, they use this as an argument to reject Muḥammad's prophethood. In order to convince them and other non-Muslims that Muḥammad did indeed perform a miracle, 'Abd al-Jabbār defends the inimitability of the Qur'an. This topic follows the discussion about the abrogation of the Mosaic law.

According to 'Abd al-Jabbār a group of Karaites admitted that, in principle, the abrogation of laws is possible. Of course, as long as they rejected the prophethood of the prophets who came after Moses, they could still maintain that the Mosaic law has not been abrogated.[53] These Karaites were probably in contact with Mu'tazilites, because 'Abd al-Jabbār says they knew that the Mu'tazilite masters had demonstrated the weakness of the Karaites' reasoning with respect to the refutation of abrogation. It is conceivable that some of these Karaites participated in the meetings described above.

Conclusion

In the two fragments presented above, ʿAbd al-Jabbār does not address the Jews and the Christians directly, but he talks about them and their opinions. It is evident that the *Mughnī* is a book for Muʿtazilites. It is a detailed explanation of the Muʿtazilite doctrine, meant to be studied by theologians and advanced students. In this book, ʿAbd al-Jabbār's main object when refuting the Jews and the Christians is to establish the correctness of the Bahshamiyya Muʿtazilite doctrine. This does not imply that the Muʿtazila was not interested in the conversion of adversaries. Quite the contrary, the Muʿtazila engaged in missionary activities from their very beginning.[54] Wāṣil b. ʿAṭa', who, as we have seen, is considered to have founded the Muʿtazila, organized meetings with adversaries, including adherents to other religions. He sent out emissaries in order to win Muslims over to his doctrine and to convert infidels.[55] In their discussions with adherents to other religions, the Muʿtazilites preferred rational arguments to arguments based on revelation, as the participants would not recognize each other's religious books, whereas rational arguments were acceptable to all. This may be seen as the origin of the Muʿtazilites' rational method of argumentation.[56]

The Muʿtazilites tried to convince their adversaries of the truth of their doctrine by refuting those opinions that were at variance with it. As a matter of course, the subjects of these refutations varied according to the doctrines of the adversaries. Consequently, the main theme of the refutation of the Jews was the abrogation of the Mosaic law. This is a subject that is at the centre of the Jewish religion and the Jews could not be indifferent to it. However, this subject had little appeal to the Christians, as they admitted that the New Testament implied the abrogation of the Mosaic law.

It is obvious that in their refutation of Christianity, the Muʿtazilites focused on the trinity and the incarnation, as these are the principal elements of Christian doctrine. Besides, the Muʿtazilites themselves had a great interest in precisely these subjects, as the oneness of God is a central doctrinal point in Islam. It was important for them, and for other Muslim theologians, to establish the absolute oneness of God by showing the inadequacy of all doctrines that are at variance with it. For this reason, ʿAbd al-Jabbār not only refutes the Christian doctrines of trinity and incarnation but also the doctrines of the dualist religions, including Manichaeism and Mazdakism.[57]

The refutations of adversaries were included in the totality of the Muʿtazilite theology. For this reason, ʿAbd al-Jabbār refutes the trinity and the incarnation as part of his discussion of the divine oneness in the *Mughnī*, whereas he refutes the Jews' denial to abrogate the Mosaic law as part of his discussion of prophethood. Apart from these subjects, ʿAbd al-Jabbār makes relatively few references to the Jews and the Christians in the *Mughnī*, at least as far as I was able to notice. ʿAbd al-Jabbār's main object in composing the *Mughnī* was not to refute the Jews and the Christians but to expose the totality of the Muʿtazilite doctrine. He therefore refutes the Jews and Christians on separate occasions, in different volumes of the *Mughnī* and with respect to different subjects.

Notes

1 W. Montgomery Watt, *The Formative Period of Islamic Thought* (Edinburgh: Edinburgh University Press, 1973), pp. 209–11. Watt, however, comes to the conclusion that this story must be a late invention that does not reflect the historical course of events.
2 On the five principles of Muʿtazilism, see Watt, *The Formative Period*, pp. 228–49.
3 D. Gimaret, 'Muʿtazila', in *The Encyclopaedia of Islam, New Edition*, ed. by H.A.R. Gibb and others (Leiden: Brill, 1960–2002), VII, pp. 783–93 (pp. 787–89), and J.R.T.M. Peters, *God's Created Speech* (Leiden: Brill, 1976), pp. 255–58.

4 Gimaret, 'Mu'tazila', pp. 789–91, and Watt, *Formative Period,* pp. 238–42.
5 On Abū Hāshim al-Jubbā'ī and the Bahshamiyya, see Margaretha T. Heemskerk, *Suffering in the Mu'tazilite Theology* (Leiden, 2000), pp. 20–35.
6 On his life and works, see 'Abd al-Karīm 'Uthmān, *Qāḍī 'l-quḍāt 'Abd al-Jabbār b. Aḥmad al-Hamadhānī* (Beirut, 1968), Peters, *God's Created Speech,* pp. 6–16, and Heemskerk, *Suffering,* pp. 36–53.
7 Rayy was situated not far from present-day Teheran.
8 Some of 'Abd al-Jabbār's biographers mention the year 1023 or 1025 as the year of his death. See 'Uthmān, *Qāḍī 'l-quḍāt,* pp. 26–27.
9 Edited by 'Abd al-Karīm 'Uthmān (Beirut, 1386/1966, 2 vols). See about this work: Gabriel Said Reynolds, 'A Medieval Islamic Polemic Against Certain Practices and Doctrines of the East Syrian Church: Introduction, Excerpts and Commentary', in *Christians at the Heart of Islamic Rule: Church Life and Scholarship in 'Abbasid Iraq,* ed. by David Thomas (Leiden, 2003), pp. 215–30; S. Pines, *The Jewish Christians of the Early Centuries of Christianity According to a New Source* (Jerusalem: *Proceedings of the Israel Academy of Sciences and Humanities,* 1966); S. Pines, '"Israel, My Firstborn" and the Son-ship of Jesus, a Theme of Moslem Anti-Christian Polemics', in *Studies in Mysticism and Religion, Presented to Gershom G. Scholem on his 70th Birthday,* ed. by E.E. Urbach and others (Jerusalem, 1967), pp. 177–90; S. Pines, 'La collusion entre les Byzantins et la subversion islamique et la lettre injurieuse d'un 'roi' de Byzance (Deux extraits d''Abd al-Jabbār), in *Studies in Memory of Gaston Wiet,* ed. by M. Rosen-Ayalon (Jerusalem, 1977), pp. 101–27; S. Pines, 'Studies in Christianity and in Judaeo-Christianity Based on Arabic sources', *Jerusalem Studies in Arabic and Islam,* 6 (1985), 107–61; S. Pines, 'Gospel Quotations and Cognate Topics in 'Abd al-Jabbār's *Tathbīt* in Relation to Early Christian and Judaeo-Christian Readings and Traditions', *Jerusalem Studies of Arabic and Islam,* 9 (1987), 195–278. This article and Pines' other articles on 'Abd al-Jabbār's *Tathbīt* have been reprinted in Shlomo Pines, *Studies in the History of Religion* (Jerusalem, 1996).
10 Elsewhere in the manuscript the date 400 (1009 AD) is given. See S. Pines, *The Jewish Christians,* p. 237, n. 1.
11 S. Pines, 'Gospel Quotations', pp. 274–75.
12 For the 'Īsāwiyya, see Steven M. Wasserstrom, *Between Muslim and Jew: the Problem of Symbiosis under Early Islam* (Princeton, 1995), pp. 71–89, S. Pines, 'al-'Īsāwiyya' in *The Encyclopaedia of Islam, New Edition,* IV, p. 96, Camilla Adang, *Muslim Writers on Judaism and the Hebrew Bible* (Leiden, 1996), pp. 96–97 and 202; Shahrastani, *Livre des religions et des sectes,* trad. avec introd. et notes par Daniel Gimaret et Guy Monnot, 2 vols (Leuven, 1986), I, pp. 604–5.
13 Wasserstrom, *Between Muslim and Jew,* pp. 41 and 88.
14 Reynolds concludes from the text of the *Tathbīt* that 'Abd al-Jabbār was primarily addressing the Nestorian Christians. He points out that at the time that 'Abd al-Jabbār wrote the *Tathbīt,* Rayy was an important centre for the East Syrian Church. See Reynolds, 'A Medieval Islamic Polemic', pp. 219–21.
15 Heribert Busse, *Chalif und Grosskönig: die Buyiden im Iraq (945–1055)* (Wiesbaden, 1969), pp. 451–79.
16 Joel L. Kraemer, *Humanism in the Renaissance of Islam: the Cultural Revival during the Buyid Age* (Leiden, 1986), p. 77.
17 Kraemer, *Humanism,* pp. 130–31.
18 Kraemer, *Humanism,* pp. 132–34.
19 Kraemer, *Humanism,* pp. 78–84.
20 Busse, *Chalif und Grosskönig,* pp. 485–86, and David Sklare, 'Responses to Islamic Polemics by Jewish Mutakallimūn in the Tenth Century', in *The Majlis: Interreligious Encounters in Medieval Islam,* ed. by Hava Lazarus-Yafeh and others (Wiesbaden, 1999), pp. 137–61 (p. 144).
21 Busse, *Chalif und Grosskönig,* pp. 489–91.
22 Kraemer, *Humanism,* pp. 56–58.
23 Kraemer, *Humanism,* pp. 121–22, and Busse, *Chalif und Grosskönig,* pp. 509–10.
24 Kraemer, *Humanism,* pp. 122 and 212–22.
25 Sklare, 'Responses to Islamic Polemics', p. 143.
26 Kraemer, *Humanism,* p. 82.
27 Aḥmad b. Yaḥyā Ibn al-Murtaḍā, *Kitāb Tabaqāt al-Mu'tazila* (*Die Klassen der Mu'taziliten*), hrsg. von Susanna Diwald-Wilzer (Beirut and Wiesbaden, 1961), pp. 88–89.

28 Abū 'l-Faraj Muḥammad b. Abī Ya'qūb Isḥāq [Ibn] al-Nadīm, al-ma'rūf bi-'l-Warrāq, *Kitāb al-Fihrist,* ed. by Riḍā Tajaddud al-Ḥā'irī al-Māzandarānī (Beirut, 1988, 3e pr.), pp. 207, 210–11 and 214–16.

29 The Arabic text of al-Jāḥiẓ's *Radd 'alā 'l-Naṣārā* has been published in Abū 'Uthmān 'Amr b. Baḥr al-Jāḥiẓ, *Three essays of Abū 'Othman 'Amr ibn Baḥr al-Jāḥiẓ,* ed. by J. Finkel (Cairo, 1926), pp. 10–38. For an English translation of part of the text (pp. 13–22), see Joshua Finkel, 'A Risala of al-Jahiz: A Reply to Christians', in *The Early Christian-Muslim Dialogue: a Collection of Documents from the First Three Islamic Centuries (632–900 A.D.)*, ed. by N.A. Newman (Hatfield, Pennsylvania, 1993), pp. 685–717. Originally published in *Journal of the American Oriental Society,* 47 (1927), 311–34.

30 [Ibn] al-Nadīm, *Kitāb al-Fihrist,* p. 216. The text of Abū 'Īsā's *Answer to the Three Sects of the Christians* (*al-Radd 'alā al-thalāth firaq min al-Naṣārā*) has been preserved together with the text of its refutation by the Christian philosopher Yaḥyā b. 'Adī. It has two main parts: the incarnation and the trinity. For the part on the incarnation, see Abū 'Īsā al-Warrāq, *De l'incarnation,* ed. et trad. par E. Piatti (Leuven, 1987) and David Thomas, *Early Muslim Polemic against Christianity: Abū 'Īsā al-Warrāq's "Against the Incarnation"* (Cambridge, 2002). For the part on the trinity, see David Thomas, *Anti-Christian Polemic in Early Islam: Abū 'Īsā al-Warrāq's "Against the Trinity"* (Cambridge, 1992). See also Emilio Piatti, 'La doctrine des Chrétiens d'après Abū 'Īsā al-Warrāq dans son traité sur la trinité', *Mélanges: Institut Dominicain d'Études Orientales du Caire,* 20 (1991), 7–30.

31 Josef van Ess, *Frühe Mu'tazilitische Häresiographie: zwei Werke des Nāsi' al-Akbar (gest. 293 H.)* (Beirut, 1971). This work contains the Arabic text and a summarizing comment to the text.

32 David S. Powers, 'The Exegetical Genre *nāsikh al-Qur'ān wa-mansūkhuhu*' in *Approaches to the History of the Interpretation of the Qur'ān,* ed. by Andrew Rippin (Oxford, 1988), pp. 117–38, and Hava Lazarus-Yafeh, *Intertwined Worlds: Medieval Islam and Bible Criticism* (Princeton, 1992), pp. 35–41.

33 For these miracle stories about Muḥammad, see Camilla Adang, *Muslim Writers on Judaism,* pp. 162–67.

34 Yusuf Rahman, 'The Miraculous Nature of Muslim Scripture: a Study of 'Abd al-Jabbār's *I'jāz al-Qur'ān*', *Islamic Studies,* 35 (1996), 409–24, Issa J. Boullata, 'The Rhetorical Interpretation of the Qur'ān: *i'jāz* and Related Topics', in *Approaches to the History of the Interpretation of the Qur'an,* pp. 139–57, and Lazarus-Yafeh, *Intertwined Worlds,* pp. 14–17.

35 John Wansbrough, *The Sectarian Milieu: Content and Composition of Islamic Salvation History* (Oxford, 1978), pp. 109–13. Wansbrough has included the translation of a dispute between al-Naẓẓām (d. circa 845) and a Jew about abrogation. The Arabic text of this debate has been edited and translated by A.S. Tritton in his article '"Debate" between a Muslim and a Jew', *Islamic Studies,* 1/2 (1962), 60–64.

36 Adang, *Muslim Writers on Judaism,* pp. 208–10.

37 For the outline of the *Mughnī*, see Peters, *God's Created Speech,* pp. 34–35.

38 Edited by Maḥmūd Muḥammad al-Khuḍayrī (Cairo, 1958).

39 Monnot gives an outline of the chapter on Christianity and a French translation of its first pages in his article 'Les doctrines des chrétiens dans le *Moghnī* de 'Abd al-Jabbār', *Mélanges de l'Institut Dominicain d'Études Orientales du Caire,* 16 (1983), 9–30 (reprint in Guy Monnot, *Islam et religions* (Paris, 1986), pp. 239–59). See also Thomas, *Anti-Christian Polemic,* pp. 46–50. Jan Peters describes and compares 'Abd al-Jabbār's, Mānkdīm's and Ibn Mattawayh's refutations of the trinity and the incarnation in his article 'Triniteit en incarnatie in de kalam van de Mu'tazila' in *Historische betrekkingen tussen moslims en christenen,* red. Sjoerd van Koningsveld (Nijmegen, 1982), pp. 81–91.

40 Edited by Amīn al-Khūlī (Cairo, 1380/1960).

41 Abū 'Alī al-Jubbā'ī (d. 915) was a famous theologian who belonged to the Basra school of the Mu'tazila. His refutation of Christian doctrines may have been called *al-Radd 'alā 'l-Naṣārā.* See Daniel Gimaret, 'Matériaux pour une bibliographie des Gubbā'ī', *Journal Asiatique,* 264 (1976), 277–332 (p. 288).

42 Abū Bakr (d. 634) was one of the first converts to Islam. He was a close companion to Muḥammad and the first caliph (*khalifa*).

43 This refers to Q 4: 164, where it is said that God really spoke to Moses (*wa-kallama 'llāhu Mūsā taklīman*). See also Q 7: 143.

44 Reading *bunuwwa,* instead of *nubuwwa.*

45 al-Jāḥiẓ, *Three essays*, p. 25. On this question, see also David Thomas, *Early Muslim Polemic*, pp. 14 and 42. Thomas refers to his article 'The Question better not Asked', in *Islam in the Contemporary World*, ed. by T. Gabriel (New Delhi, 2000), pp. 20–41, to which I have not had access.
46 al-Jāḥiẓ, *Three essays*, ed. by Finkel, p. 26.
47 ʿAbd al-Jabbār, *al-Mughnī*, V, p. 81, line 11.
48 Reading *sharīʿata*, instead of *sharīʿatahu*.
49 For the identification of the ʿAnāniyya and the Ashmaʿiyya, see Adang, *Muslim Writers*, pp. 81–82. On the Karaites, see van Bekkum on Judah Halevi in this volume.
50 Heemskerk, *Suffering*, pp. 146–48.
51 Heemskerk, *Suffering*, pp. 150–51.
52 Martin J. McDermott, *The Theology of al-Shaikh al-Mufīd (d. 413/1022)* (Beirut, 1978), pp. 71–76.
53 ʿAbd al-Jabbār does not mention the opinion of the ʿĪsāwiyya, who acknowledged Muḥammad's prophethood but rejected the abrogation of the Mosaic law. Perhaps he did not know them yet, or he did not consider them a Jewish sect.
54 Josef Van Ess, 'Disputionspraxis in der islamischen Theologie: eine vorläufige Skizze', *Revue des Études Islamiques*, 44 (1976), 23–60 (pp. 50–51).
55 Sarah Stroumsa, 'The Beginnings of the Muʿtazila Reconsidered', *Jerusalem Studies in Arabic and Islam*, 13 (1990), 265–93 (pp. 269 and 291–92).
56 Van Ess, 'Disputionspraxis', p. 36.
57 See *Mughnī*, V, pp. 9–79, and Guy Monnot, *Penseurs musulmans et religions iraniennes: ʿAbd al-Jabbār et ses devanciers* (Paris, 1974).

8 Muḥammad and the Muslims in St. Thomas Aquinas

James Waltz

Although M.-D. Chenu proposed, twenty-five years ago, research on "Islam and Christendom" based on the *Summa contra Gentiles* (hereafter *SCG*), the vast literature devoted to St. Thomas Aquinas contains very few works concerning him and Muslims, and most of these consider the impact of Islamic philosophy upon his thought.[1] The present paper is unconcerned with Thomas' philosophical debt to Muslim thinkers; instead, it seeks to follow Chenu's suggestion, and to stimulate further investigation of the topic, by examining Thomas' attitudes toward, sources of his knowledge of, and the significance of his works concerning Islam and Muslims.

Some may object that Thomas was not concerned with Islam and concur with Norman Daniel, the leading authority on the medieval Christian "image" of Islam, that Thomas "can scarcely be counted among writers on the religion of Islam," but the evidence cited on the following pages should dispel those objections.[2] Moreover, most scholars agree Thomas wrote the *SCG* in response to Ramón of Peñafort's request for a "work against the errors of unbelievers," particularly Muslims, and a lesser work (ignored by Daniel), *De rationibus fidei contra Saracenos, Graecos et Armenos,* at the request of a cantor of Antioch, probably writing on behalf of his Dominican bishop, Elias.[3] Those works, and comments in the *Summa theologica,* provide ample testimony for our purposes.

Thomas' purpose in the *SCG* was the twofold task of a "wise man": "to meditate and speak forth of the divine truth … and to refute the opposing error" (I, 1; cf. I, 2); hence he explained that some divine truth is accessible to human reason and some surpasses it, that the latter type is confirmed by supernatural works (I, 6) and that humans must believe both (I, 4–5). He then proceeded to contrast Christianity and Islam. He claimed Christianity, like the philosophers who sought to "lead men from the pleasure of sensible things to virtue," promises spiritual and eternal goods, and unlike the "Old Law" preaches many truths that transcend human reason, thereby admitting divine inspiration and curbing "presumption, which is the mother of error" (I, 5). Miracles "and not the violent assault of arms or the promise of pleasures" attested the truth of divinely inspired spokesmen; "truths are preached that surpass every human intellect; the pleasures of the flesh are curbed; it is taught that the things of this world should be spurned," exactly as God had foretold "through many pronouncements of the ancient prophets," whose books Christians venerate. Thomas then presented the following account of Muḥammad and his teaching:

> On the other hand, those who founded sects committed to erroneous doctrines proceeded in a way that is opposite to this. The point is clear in the case of Mohammed. He seduced the people by promises of carnal pleasure to which the concupiscence of the flesh goads us. His teaching also contained precepts that were in conformity with

> his promises, and he gave free rein to carnal pleasure. In all this, as is not unexpected, he was obeyed by carnal men. As for proofs of the truth of his doctrine, he brought forward only such as could be grasped by the natural ability of anyone with a very modest wisdom. Indeed, the truths that he taught he mingled with many fables and with doctrines of the greatest falsity. He did not bring forth any signs produced in a supernatural way, which alone fittingly gives witness to divine inspiration; for a visible action that can be only divine reveals an invisibly inspired teacher of truth. On the contrary, Mohammed said that he was sent in the power of his arms—which are signs not lacking even to robbers and tyrants. What is more, no wise men, men trained in things divine and human, believed in him from the beginning. Those who believed in him were brutal men and desert wanderers, utterly ignorant of all divine teaching, through whose numbers Mohammed forced others to become his followers by the violence of his arms. Nor do divine pronouncements on the part of preceding prophets offer him any witness. On the contrary, he perverts almost all the testimonies of the Old and New Testaments by making them into fabrications of his own, as can be seen by anyone who examines his law. It was, therefore, a shrewd decision on his part to forbid his followers to read the Old and New Testaments, lest these books convict him of falsity. It is thus clear that those who place any faith in his words believe foolishly (I, 6).

It is apparent that Thomas did not seek to give an objective or sympathetic account of Muḥammad and his teaching; indeed, he said nothing about its content but focused instead upon its hearers, its forms and its proofs, all of which served to discredit it. Many of Muḥammad's hearers were indeed nomads, and the ferocious intertribal warfare of pre-Islamic Arabia was often brutal; but many other Arabs were city dwellers, more or less distinctly removed from nomadic life, and Arabs had no monopoly on seventh-century brutality. However, the brutality which concerned Thomas was the animal-like addiction to "carnal pleasure," abhorrent to those vowed to celibacy yet redolent of the lust and sensuality of pre-Islamic Arabic poetry.[4] The alleged ignorance and stupidity of his hearers further discredited Muḥammad: "no wise men … believed in him"; instead his hearers were "utterly ignorant of all divine teaching," demonstrated his falsity by their stupidity, and showed their foolishness by believing in him. Clearly, "wise" Christians who shunned sensual pleasures were vastly superior to such Muslims.

In discussing the form of Muḥammad's teaching, Thomas allowed that Muḥammad taught some truths, apparently very simple ones accessible to the natural reason (such as monotheism, which he knew Muslims believed). But he focused on Muḥammad's mingling false and fabulous doctrines with those few truths, his perversion of the Old and New Testaments and his prohibition of the reading of them, which suggests that Thomas knew something of the Muslim claim that the Qur'ān perfects and supersedes the earlier revelations. He emphasized, however, that Muḥammad "seduced" (note the sexual imagery again) his hearers by giving "free rein" to carnal pleasure here on earth and promising similar pleasure eternally in paradise, a possible allusion to Islam's permission of polygamy and a certain indication of his knowledge that Muslims "hold that in the resurrection men will have use for food and sexual pleasure as they do now" (IV, 83). Sorely troubled by that hedonistic teaching, Thomas attacked it several times: objecting that such a "fable" attracted only brutes and nomads, complaining that the felicity which is virtue's reward does not consist in pleasures of the flesh as Jews and Muslims taught (III, 27), and lamenting that the emphasis on fleshly pleasures impeded contemplation—man's closest approach to God.

But most serious for Thomas was the lack of proofs supporting Muḥammad's teachings. His assertion that previous prophets had not foretold Muḥammad's coming may be directed against the Muslim claim that Jesus had predicted Muḥammad's prophetic mission.[5] More importantly, unlike a "true" prophet, Muḥammad performed no miracles; instead, he relied on military might, used also by "robbers and tyrants," to force others to become his followers, and gave only natural reasons to attest the truth of his teaching. Similar shortcomings characterized earlier "false" prophets and Daniel notes that in Thomas' extended treatment of prophecy (III, 154) "all the points we have seen applied to Muhammad are to be found, although he does not explicitly admit that the thought of Muhammad was in his mind at all."[6]

Although Aldobrandino Malvezzi rightly noted the importance of this *SCG* chapter for showing such a great man's knowledge of and opinion regarding Islam, it is difficult to agree with Daniel's judgment that "sexuality and violence ... was the sum of the impression of Islam that St. Thomas Aquinas received."[7] Thomas knew more than that. He knew Muslims believed in one god, in a prophet, in a scripture which resembled the Old and New Testaments, and in a physical paradise. He also knew they rejected the authority of the Old and New Testaments and that Muḥammad claimed no miracles to "prove" his prophetic mission. And as already noted, it is possible to infer that he knew even more details of Islamic belief when he wrote the *SCG*. In the opening chapter of *De rationibus fidei,* he displayed acquaintance with other Islamic ideas and some Muslim objections to Christianity:

> Truly the Saracens deride us because we say Christ is the Son of God, when God had no wife; and they consider us madmen because we confess three persons in God, yet do not profess three gods. Also they deride our saying that Christ, the Son of God, was crucified for the salvation of humankind, because if God is omnipotent, He could save humankind without the passion of His Son, and He could fashion man so he could not sin. Again they blame the Christians because they eat their God on the altar, and because the body of Christ, even if it were so large as a mountain, ought by now to be consumed. ... About the true merit which depends on free will, you assert both the Saracens and other nations attribute the necessity of human acts to divine foreknowledge or foreordination saying that man cannot die, nor even sin, unless God so ordained for man; and that every individual has his outcome written upon his brow.

The last sentence accurately presents orthodox Islamic predestination doctrine as well as the more popular belief in fate (*kismet*). And the first three fairly state Muslim views on the Christian doctrines of the Trinity, Incarnation, Crucifixion, Atonement and Transubstantiation—issues in Christian-Muslim disputations and disagreements from the early years of Islamic advance. It appears unlikely that Thomas knew the disputation literature directly, although John of Damascus, whom he often cites, gave guidelines for disputations and composed a tract, "On the Heresy of the Ishmaelites," which Thomas may have read and used.[8] But he certainly knew the basic issues in Christian-Muslim relations.

However, Thomas' knowledge, although more extensive than Daniel suggests, was yet severely limited. He himself confessed his inadequate knowledge of "the sacrilegious remarks of individual men who have erred" (I, 2). He could not consult the sharīʿa or ḥadīth which embody Islamic law, he certainly manifests no knowledge of Islamic history, and, despite his claim that Muḥammad's perversions and fabrications "can be seen by anyone who examines his law," there is no evidence that he ever read the Qur'ān, although Latin translations were available.[9] Whence, then, did he obtain his knowledge?

The circumstances of his life and times offered several possibilities. He grew up in the lands of, and in a family noted for its outstanding service to, the Emperor Frederick II, whose army boasted Muslim soldiers and whose court supported Muslim scholars. Next he studied at the University of Naples, an imperial foundation enriched by products of Islamic scholarship. At Paris he encountered and closely followed al-Farābī's theological formulations, critically reinterpreted Ibn Rushd's (Averroës) Aristotelianism and gained knowledge of other Muslim philosophers either directly or through his teachers; he apparently considered such thinkers neither brutes and nomads nor ordinary, devout Muslims.[10] He might have tapped a growing knowledge of Islamic literature and legend which benefited Dante Alighieri and a growing dissatisfaction with crusades as a means of dealing with Muslims. And his missionary correspondents may also have supplied Thomas with much information about the Muslims and their errors.[11]

None of the aforementioned possibilities, however, really appears decisive, especially for a scholar who habitually relied on the written word as an authoritative source. What Thomas needed was a concise summary of Muslim beliefs and ideas, preferably with some Christian reaction to them. And exactly such a summary was available to him in the *Summa totius haeresis Saracenorum,* prepared by Peter the Venerable, abbot of Cluny, in the mid-twelfth century. Peter had initiated a large-scale translation project to make the Qur'ān and other Arabic-language works useful for understanding and opposing Islam available in Latin. He relied heavily upon them, particularly the *Apology* of al-Kindi, a ninth-century work, in composing the *Summa.* His work marked a considerable advance in Latin Christian knowledge of Islam and Muslims, and by using it Thomas incorporated the most accurate information available in his own writings.[12]

Although verbatim parallels between the *Summa* and *SCG* I, 6 are rare, the identity of themes and treatment is striking and persuasive. Peter depicted a paradise of eating and drinking and sensual satisfaction mirrored in Thomas' references to it and remarked that Muḥammad, to "more easily attract to himself the carnal minds of men … loosed the reins on gluttony and impurity"—a close parallel to Thomas' "he gave free rein to carnal pleasure." He termed the Arabs "barbarians," "simple and uninstructed" and "ignorant of both the divine and the human law"; hence Muḥammad's preaching which "accorded with their reason" easily led them astray and mingled "good things, mixing truth in with falsity." Taught the scriptures by a Nestorian monk and some Jews, Muḥammad, said Peter, "wove together … a diabolical scripture," at the same time taking over and rejecting the Old and New Testaments and preventing his followers from consulting them by "the iron barrier of impiety." Peter believed that Muḥammad sought to become a king and pretended prophethood as a means to that end; thus he saw Muḥammad's prophetic claims following rather than preceding his first battles, and believed that Muḥammad and later Islam gained success, territory and subjects by force of arms. That kingship via prophecy argument is, for Kritzeck, "the most serious misconstruction in the *Summa,*" and Peter's "essential error" is "regarding Mohammed's prophethood as postdating his first battles"; yet Thomas' claim that Muḥammad "was sent in the power of his arms," and "forced others to become his followers by the violence of his arms," seems to echo Peter though avoiding the grossness of his misstep.[13] It appears certain, then, that Thomas relied upon Peter's *Summa* in composing *SCG* I, 6.

The evidence is similarly good for the *Summa*'s role in Thomas' arguments in *De rationibus fidei.* Peter noted that Muslims worshiped God but denied the Trinity of persons in the unity of the Godhead, and Kritzeck rightly observes that that was an immense advance over the common European view of Islam as a form of polytheism. He also knew that since the Muslims held that sexual intercourse was essential for fatherhood, Christ could not be the son of God. Moreover, he established the Muslim denial of the incarnation, atonement, crucifixion, and resurrection of Christ.[14] Thomas made the same points in chapter one of *De rationibus fidei,* as noted earlier, but also went beyond Peter's account; however, he explicitly attributed at least some of those added objections to information supplied by his correspondent.

In addition to those specific resemblances, Thomas, like Peter, seemed to regard Islam as a summation of Christian heresies. Peter wrote of Muḥammad "vomiting ... almost all the dregs of the ancient heresies" and asserted he denied the trinity with Sabellius, Christ's divinity with Nestorius, and Christ's death with Mani. Thomas, in both *SCG* and *De rationibus fidei,* presented extensive summaries of orthodox arguments against earlier heretics, apparently in the belief that he was thereby providing relevant and practical help for his missionary correspondents.[15] Moreover, Thomas, again like Peter, sought in "the natural reason, to which all men are forced to give their assent" (I, 2) a common ground for discussion with Muslims, and with his Antiochene correspondent sought "moral and philosophical reasons which the Saracene accept" (c. 1). Through demonstrative arguments, Thomas believed, adversaries could be won to that natural truth "which faith professes and reason investigates" (I, 9). That willingness to consider Muslims amenable to reason made him, for Daniel, "the great but lonely exception" among his contemporaries; but Peter had adumbrated the same approach a century earlier.[16]

However, Thomas' use of reason was much more thoroughgoing. Starting from the premise that God is an intellect, he reasoned that the ultimate end of the universe must be the good of an intellect, namely truth. Therefore, he stated, the office and work of a wise man, which he was undertaking, was to meditate upon divine truth, teach it to others, and "refute the opposing falsehood," which is also impiety (I, 1).[17] Divine truth, however, had both a natural component amenable to human reason and a revealed component surpassing the power of human reason; hence, "if our opponent believes nothing of divine revelation, there is no longer any means of proving the articles of faith by reasoning, but only of answering his objections—if he has any—against faith" (I, 9). And both those difficulties confronted Thomas:

> The sacrilegious remarks of individual men who have erred are not so well known to us so that we may use what they say as the basis of proceeding to a refutation of their errors, [and] some of them, such as the Mohammedans and the pagans, do not agree with us in accepting the authority of any Scripture, by which they may be convinced of their error (I, 2).

Thus, while it was possible to argue against the Jews from the Old Testament and against heretics from the New, "the Mohammedans and the pagans accept neither the one nor the other." Adversaries of revealed truth could be overcome by the authority of Scripture confirmed by miracles, but because Muslims did not accept the authority of Scripture, it would be useless to multiply scriptural quotations, as earlier Christian anti-Muslim writers did, and "vain to introduce authorities against those who do not accept authorities." "Likely arguments," however, could be used to train and console the faithful

> and not with an idea of refuting those who are adversaries. For the very inadequacy of the arguments would rather strengthen them in their error, since they would imagine that our acceptance of the truth of faith was based on such weak arguments (I, 9).

He repeated this explanation to his Antiochene correspondent, noting that "as it is not possible to prove our faith by necessary reasons because it surpasses the human mind, so to disprove it by necessary reason is impossible because of its truth," and taught that a Christian disputant should be ready not to prove, but to defend, the faith (c. 2).

In Thomas' day defense of the faith was not merely verbal. Scholars, churchmen and political leaders debated the propriety of the use of force against unbelievers. Crusades and crusading ideas still flourished, and conversion of Muslims to Christianity proceeded best where Christians held political control. Both the *SCG* and *De rationibus fidei* were intended primarily for use in lands where Christians exercised political authority over significant numbers of Muslims. That accorded with a position explained by Thomas in the *Summa theologica*:

> Among unbelievers there are some who have never received the faith, such as the heathens and the Jews: and these are by no means to be compelled to the faith, in order that they may believe, because to believe depends on the will: nevertheless they should be compelled by the faithful, if it be possible to do so, so that they do not hinder the faith by their blasphemies, or by their evil persuasions, or even by their open persecutions. It is for this reason Christ's faithful often wage war with unbelievers, not indeed for the purpose of forcing them to believe, because even if they were to conquer them, and take them prisoners, they should still leave them free to believe, if they will, but in order to prevent them from hindering the faith of Christ.
>
> On the other hand, there are unbelievers who at some time have accepted the faith, and professed it, such as heretics and all apostates: such should be submitted even to bodily compulsion, that they may fulfill what they have promised, and hold what they at one time received.[18]

Although permitting bodily compulsion against heretics and apostates, Thomas forbade its use against those who had never received the faith, holding they were not to be compelled to the faith or forced to believe. But war, if necessary, could be used to defend the faith against their blasphemies, lies and persecutions. Like the founder of his order, Thomas saw educated Christian leadership as the best defense against error and the best offense for missionary purposes.

In keeping with his position that reason can defend, but not prove, the faith, Thomas devoted the bulk of both the *SCG* and *De rationibus fidei* to exposition of Christian faith with no explicit reference to Muslim objections. His task was to argue for Christian truth without relying upon faith or appealing to the dogmas of the church, but rather using philosophical truth as a common ground from which to proceed. He performed that task remarkably well, for within forty years of his death Peter Marsilio claimed the *SCG* was "without equal in its field"; and although his contemporary, the Parisian Lullist Thomas le Myésier, criticized Thomas' refusal to use rational arguments to prove the Christian faith, Ramón Lull himself, the greatest medieval Christian missionary to Muslims, agreed with Thomas in permitting crusades to secure a free hearing for missionaries, emphasizing disproof of Islam, and seeking to present Christianity nationally. And Demetrios Kydones, a Greek convert to Roman Catholicism, translated both the *SCG* and *De rationibus fidei* into Greek during the fourteenth century.[19]

Despite that testimony, some recent scholars dispute the purpose of the *SCG*. M. M. Gorce held that the Gentiles were Greek and Arab philosophers who studied at Paris and concluded that "it is not very easy to see what profit any but a few doctors or rabbis would gain from a work so scholarly and so difficult in its philosophy," while Fernand Van Steenberghen found it "clear that what St. Thomas wrote was a treatise of apologetical theology, for the use of men preparing to preach Christian doctrine among pagans, principally those in Moslem countries." M. D. Chenu concluded that the *SCG* was pertinent both to the apologetic requirements of missionary activity and the intellectual crisis produced by Muslim-transmitted Greek science and philosophy, and he thought that study of the *SCG* should stimulate research on Islam and Christendom and contribute to the development of dialogue.[20]

Thomas Ohm contended nearly forty years ago that Thomas' contributions are even more valuable for modern times than for his own. Thomas' works were then being widely used to train both missionaries and indigenous clergy in mission lands, and heartily recommended to confront contemporary philosophical "gentiles."[21] Today increasing knowledge of one faith by the other's followers and greater awareness of the history of Christian-Muslim relations are producing meaningful dialogue in which persons of both faiths, in the words of Vatican II's statement on non-Christian religions, "strive sincerely for mutual understanding."[22] Since the points at issue and the arguments about them remain similar if not identical to those of Thomas' day, his rational presentation of Christian faith still merits study. And both Christians and Muslims in contemporary dialogue could fruitfully use as their motto these words of Hilary which guided Thomas' life and work: "I am aware that I owe this to God as the chief duty of my life, that my every word and sense may speak of him."[23]

Notes

1 Marie-Dominique Chenu, *Introduction à l'étude de Saint Thomas d'Aquin* (Montréal: Institut d'études médiévales de l'université de Montréal, 1950), tr. A.-M. Landry and D. Hughes, *Toward Understanding Saint Thomas* (Chicago: H. Regnery, 1064), p. 295. P. Mandonnet and J. Destrez, *Bibliographie Thomiste,* 2d ed. rev. by M.-D. Chenu (Paris: J. Vrin, 1960), has but two entries under the heading "Les Arabes et S. Thomas"; Vernon J. Bourke, *Thomistic Bibliography* (St. Louis: The Modem Schoolman [supplement to Vol. XXI], 1945) has eighteen. Almost all treat the philosophical impact, as do other items under the heading "Averroism." No count has been made of items listed in *Bulletin Thomiste* since 1940. *SCG* citations are from Anton C. Pegis, tr., *On the Truth of the Catholic Faith (Summa Contra Gentiles),* I (Garden City: Hanover House, 1955).

2 M. M. Gorce, "La lutte 'contra Gentiles' à Paris au XIIIe siècle," in *Mélanges Mandonnet* (Paris: J. Vrin, 1930), I, 223–43, held the *SCG* was not at all concerned with Muslims. Norman Daniel, *Islam and the West: The Making of an Image* (Edinburgh: Edinburgh University Press, 1960, 1962), p. 336, n. 25.

3 The *locus classicus* for the occasion of the *SCG* is the early fourteenth-century chronicle of Peter Marsilio, *De gestis Jacobi I, regis Aragonum*; translated by Pegis in *On the Truth of the Catholic Faith,* I, 20–21.

> Furthermore, strongly desiring the conversion of unbelievers, Raymond [of Peñafort] asked an outstanding Doctor of Sacred Scripture, a Master in Theology, Brother Thomas of Aquino of the same Order, who among all the clerics of the world was considered in philosophy to be, next to Brother Albert, the greatest, to compose a work against the errors of unbelievers, by which both the cloud of darkness might be dispelled and the teaching of the true Sun might be made manifest to those who refuse to believe. The renowned Master accomplished what the humility of so great a Father asked, and composed a work called the Summa Contra Gentiles, held to be without equal in its field.

De rationibus fidei is listed by I. T. Eschmann, "A Catalogue of St. Thomas's Works," in Étienne Gilson, *The Christian Philosophy of St. Thomas Aquinas*, tr. L. K. Shook (New York: Random House, 1956), p. 419; but not by Daniel, *Islam and the West*, p. 398, where it should appear. I have used S. E. Fretté and P. Maré, *D. Thomae Aquinatis Opera Omnia* (Paris: L. Vivès, 1872–88), XXVII, 128–42; translations which follow are mine. A lengthy, and little-known, examination of the work's thought is Martin Grabmann, "Die Schrift: *De rationibus fidei contra Saracenos, Graecos et Armenos ad cantorem Antiochenum*, des Heiligen Thomas von Aquin," *Scholastik, Vierteljahrsschrift für Theologie und Philosophie*, XVII (1942), 187–216.

4 Discussions of pre-Islamic poetry, with representative selections, appear in Reynold A. Nicholson, *A Literary History of the Arabs*, 2d ed. (Cambridge, England: Cambridge University Press, 1930), chapters 2 and 3, and Arthur J. Arberry, *Aspects of Islamic Civilization* (London: Allen & Unwin, 1964), chapter 1. Seventh-century Arab social structure is enlighteningly examined by William Montgomery Watt, *Islam and the Integration of Society* (London: Routledge & Kegan Paul; Evanston: Northwestern University Press, 1961).

5 S. 61:6 says Jesus promised a messenger to come after him, whose name is the praised one (Aḥmad, which equals Muḥammad), the parallel with the Christian Gospel according to John 14.16, 26 is obvious; Daniel, *Islam and the West*, p. 53 and notes p. 335.

6 Daniel, *Islam and the West*, p. 72; his chapter II is entitled "Revelation: The Christian Attack upon 'Pseudoprophecy.'" The moral qualities of the prophet—love of metaphysical and religious truths; separation of conscience and heart from satisfaction of the senses, voluptuousness and brutal instincts; and complete renunciation of all ambitions and worldly glories—which inform Thomas' judgments were earlier expounded by Moses Maimonides, *The Guide of the Perplexed*, tr. Shlomo Pines, 2 vols. (Chicago: University of Chicago Press, 1963), part II, chapter 36. For Maimonides, the second criterion was most important for determining a prophet's authenticity. A thorough examination of how Thomas incorporated and transcended the works of Maimonides, Ibn Sīnā, al-Ghazālī and Ibn Rushd in formulating his presentations of prophecy in *De veritate* 12; *Summa theologiae* II, ii, quaestiones 172–76; and *SCG* III, 154, is José María Casciaro Ramírez, *El dialogo teológico de Santo Tomás con musulmanes y judios: el tema de la profecía y la revelación* (Madrid: Consejo Superior de Investigaciones Científicas, Instituto "Francisco Suárez," 1969) (Bibliotheca Hispana Biblica, 2).

7 Daniel, *Islam and the West*, p. 145; Aldobrandino Malvezzi, *L'islamismo e la cultura europea* (Florence: Sansoni, 1956), p. 107.

8 On Islamic fatalism see William Montgomery Watt, *Free Will and Predestination in Early Islam* (London: Luzac, 1948). The standard authority on Byzantine theological controversy with Islam is now Adel-Théodore Khoury, *Les théologiens byzantins et l'Islam: Textes et Auteurs* (*VIIIe–XIIIe s.*), 2d ed. (Louvain and Paris: Nauwelaerts, 1969); and *Polémique byzantine contre l'Islam* (*VIIIe-XIIIe* S.), 2d ed. (Leiden: E. J. Brill, 1972); a brief overview of those detailed studies is his *Der theologische Streit der Byzantiner mit dem Islam* (Paderborn: Schöningh, 1969), also available in French. The arguments of Armand Abel, "Le chapitre CI du *Livre des Hérésies* de Jean Damascène: son inauthenticité," *Studia Islamica*, XIX (1963), 5–25, are convincingly refuted by Daniel Sahas, *John of Damascus on Islam: The "Heresy of the Ishmaelites"* (Leiden: E. J. Brill, 1972), who presents John as very knowledgeable about Islam.

9 For medieval European knowledge of Islam see, in addition to Daniel, *Islam and the West*; Ugo Monneret de Villard, *Lo studio dell'Islam in Europa nel XII e nel XIII secolo* (Vatican City: Biblioteca Apostolica Vaticana, 1944) (Studi e Testi, 110); Marie-Thérèse d'Alverny, "Deux traductions latines du Coran au Moyen Age," *Archives d'histoire doctrinale et littéraire du Moyen Age* 22–23 années (1947–48), 69–131; R. W. Southern, *Western Views of Islam in the Middle Ages* (Cambridge, Mass.: Harvard University Press, 1962); and the Spoleto symposium on *L'Occidente* e *l'Islam nell'alto medioevo*, 2 vols. (Spoleto: Centro italiano di studi sull'alto medioevo, 1965) (Settimane di Studio XII).

10 Thomas' early years are presented in unusual fulness in James A. Weisheipl, *Friar Thomas d'Aquino* (New York: Doubleday, 1974), pp. 5–20; one of Thomas' brothers accompanied Emperor Frederick II on the "crusade" of 1228–29. On the Muslim soldiers see I. Egidi, "La colonia saracena di Lucera e la sua distruzione," *Archivio storico per le provincie napoletane*, XXXVI (1911), and for Muslim scholars Charles H. Haskins, *Studies in the History of Medieval Science* (Cambridge, Mass.: Harvard University Press, 1924), pp. 242–71; and Martin Grabmann, "Kaiser Frederick II und

sein Verhältnis zur aristotelischen und arabischen Philosophie," in his *Mittelalterliches Geistesleben: Abhandlungen zur Geschichte der Scholastik und Mystik,* II (Munich: M. Hueber, 1936), 103–37. Robert Hammond, *The Philosophy of Al Farabi and its Influence on Medieval Thought* (New York: Hobson Book Press, 1947) gives extensive citations in parallel columns from al-Fārābī and Thomas showing the letter's almost verbatim dependence on the former; those citations are reproduced more accessibly in Eugene A. Myers, *Arabic Thought and the Western World in the Golden Age of Islam* (New York: Ungar, 1964). Casciaro, *El dialogo teológico,* also offers many parallel-columned comparisons of Thomas' and an Islamicate philosopher's (or Maimonides') treatment of a prophecy topic; he sees Thomas progressing from a close dependence on them in *De veritate* to a relatively independent position going well beyond them in *Summa theologiae,* but says little about Thomas' presentation in *SCG.* Ernest Renan, *Averroes et l'Averroisme* (Paris: A. Durand, 1852) turned Western attention toward the Muslim philosopher; J. Guttmann later considered *Der Einfluss der maimonidischen Philosophie auf das christliche Abendland* (Leipzig: Fock, 1908). Recent summaries of a century's scholarship are Fernand van Steenberghen, *Aristotle in the West: The Origins of Latin Aristotelianism* (French original Louvain: Éditions de l'Institut supérieur de philosophie, Université de Louvain, 1946; English translation Louvain: Nauwelaerts, 1955) and Francis E. Peters, *Aristotle and the Arabs: the Aristotelian Tradition in Islam* (New York and London: New York University Press, 1968), who (p. 222) notes the contrast between Thomas' harsh judgments on Islam and openness to Islamicate philosophers.

11 Key works on the thorny problem of Islamic influences on Dante are Miguel Asín Palacios, *La escatologia musulmana en la Divina Comedia* (Madrid: E. Maestre, 1919), Eng. tr. Harold Sunderland, *Islam and the Divine Comedy* (London: J. Murray, 1926), and Enrico Cerulli, *Il 'Libro della Scala' e la questione delle fonti arabo-spagnole della Divina Commedia* (Vatican City: Biblioteca apostolica vaticana, 1949) (Studi e Testi, 150). Dissatisfaction with crusades is amply documented in Palmer A. Throop, *Criticism of the Crusade: A Study of Public Opinion and Crusade Propaganda* (Amsterdam: Swets & Zeitlinger, 1940). Although we do not know what Ramón of Peñafort wrote to Thomas, some account of major points in Christian-Muslim confrontation probably accompanied his request; it certainly formed part of the Antiochene cantor's missive, for Thomas, in listing the points at issue, twice uses the expression "you assert." Perhaps Ramón Martí shared insights from his Semitic studies and knowledge of things Islamic with Thomas; a letter of Ivo Pinsard, prior of the convent of Santiago in Paris, to Joseph de Voisin, editor of Martí's *Pugio fidei adversus Mauros et Judaeos* (Paris: Henault, 1651; 2d ed., Leipzig: F. Lanckis, 1687) and printed therein, asserts both were friends and fellow students of Albert the Great. And possibly personal relationships and correspondence rather than formal writings conveyed the influence of Martí on Thomas hypothesized by Miguel Asín Palacios, "El averroismo teológico de Santo Tomás de Aquino," *Homenaje a Don Francisco Codera* (Zaragoza: M. Escar, 1904), pp. 271–331, and contested by Luis G. Alonso Getino, *La "Summa contra Gentes" y el "Pugio fidei" (Carta sin sobre a Don Miguel Asín Palacios)* (Vergara, Tip. de "El Santísimo Rosario," 1905), and José Maria Llovera in an address on Martí delivered to the 1929 Congreso de la Asociación para el Progreso de las Ciencias and summarized in Tomás y Joaquín Carreras Artau, *Historia de la filosofía española: Filosofía cristiana de los siglos XIII al XV* (Madrid: Real Academia de Ciencias Exactas, Físicas y Naturales, 1939), I, 147–70.

12 James Kritzeck, *Petar the Venerable and Islam* (Princeton: Princeton University Press, 1964) provides ample information and copious bibliography on all these topics; in addition, there is a newly edited text of the *Summa* on pp. 204–11 and most of it is either translated or paraphrased in Kritzeck's discussion of the work.

13 Kritzeck, *Peter the Venerable and Islam,* pp. 126–40, *passim.*

14 Kritzeck, *Peter the Venerable and Islam,* pp. 117–19.

15 Kritzeck, *Peter the Venerable and Islam,* p. 136. The first thirty-six chapters of *SCG* IV refute the errors of eleven early heretics, including Arius and Theodore of Mopsuestia whose views resemble those held by Muslims.

16 Daniel, *Islam and the West,* p. 55.

17 Kritzeck, *Peter the Venerable and Islam,* p. 141.

18 *Summa theologica,* II, 1, q. 10, art. 8; tr. Fathers of the English Dominican Province (London: Burns, Oates & Washbourne, 1917), IX, 134–36.

19 For Peter Marsilio see n. 3 above. Thomas le Myésier was a student at Paris in the 1280s, shortly after Thomas' death; he died in 1336. His remarks and those of Lull are given in J. N. Hillgarth, *Ramon Lull and Lullism in Fourteenth-Century France* (Oxford: Oxford University Press, 1971), p. 260,

n. 378, and p. 25, respectively. Lull's views are well known; it is Hillgarth's linking them with those of Thomas which is significant. Moreover Hillgarth considers the influence of Ramón of Peñafort on Lull decisive; he was

> the stimulus to three leaders in the thirteenth century mission to Muslims—Thomas, Lull and Ramón Martini [Martí], whose *Explanatio symboli* (1257) and *Pugio fidei* (1278) attempted to provide a rational apologetic for Christianity, as did *SCG*—and the impetus for a new direction in medieval Christian efforts away from crusading to missionary activity (p. 5).

20 Gorce, "La lutte," (n. 2 above) held the *SCG* was not inspired by Ramón of Peñafort but rather by Pope Alexander IV and that it was not at all concerned with Muslims. He was decisively opposed by D. Salman, "Sur la lutte 'contra Gentiles' de S. Thomas," *Divus Thomas,* XL (1937), 488–509. Van Steenberghen, *Aristotle in the West.* pp. 193–96, briefly recounts the controversy and offers his own judgment. Chenu, *Introduction à l'étude de Saint Thomas,* pp. 289–92, 295–96; his entire chapter X is devoted to *SCG.*

21 Thomas Ohm, "Thomas von Aquin und die Heiden- und Mohammedaner-missionen," in Albert Lang, *et al.*, eds., *Aus der Geisteswelt des Mittelalters: Studien und Texte Martin Grabmann zur Vollendung des 60 Lebensjahres von Freunden und Schülern gewidmet* (*Beiträge zur Geschichte der Philosophie und Theologie des Mittelalters: Texte und Untersuchungen,* Supplementband III) (Münster i.W., Aschendorff, 1935), 735–48; the statements occur on pp. 739–41. Grabmann thought *De rationibus fidei* showed Thomas a man for all times; "Die Schrift ... ," 216. The application to contemporary "gentiles" was made in the 1938 Aquinas lecture at Marquette University by Mortimer J. Adler, *St. Thomas and the Gentiles* (Milwaukee: Marquette University Press, 1943).

22 "Declaration on the Relationship of the Church to Non-Christian Religions" given at Rome on October 28, 1965, and translated by Joseph Gallagher in Walter M. Abbott, ed., *The Documents of Vatican II* (New York: Association Press, 1966). Attention to the declaration's position on Jews has so overshadowed its statement on Muslims (section 3) that its full citation may be useful here, as a measure of how far understanding has improved since Thomas' day:

> Upon the Moslems, too, the Church looks with esteem. They adore one God, living and enduring, merciful and all-powerful, Maker of heaven and earth and Speaker to men. They strive to submit wholeheartedly even to His inscrutable decrees, just as did Abraham, with whom the Islamic faith is pleased to associate itself. Though they do not acknowledge Jesus as God, they revere Him as a prophet. They also honor Mary, His virgin mother; at times they call on her, too, with devotion. In addition they await the day of judgment when God will give each man his due after raising him up. Consequently, they prize the moral life, and give worship to God especially through prayer, almsgiving, and fasting.
>
> Although in the course of the centuries many quarrels and hostilities have arisen between Christians and Moslems, this most sacred Synod urges all to forget the past and to strive sincerely for mutual understanding. On behalf of all mankind, let them make common cause of safeguarding and fostering social justice, moral values, peace, and freedom (Abbott, ed., p. 663).
>
> [Ed. note: Father Julius Basetti-Sani discussed the statement of Vatican II with regard to Islam in *M.W.,* LVII (1967), 126–37, 186–96.]

23 Hilary of Poitiers, *De Trinitate,* I, 37; cited in Pegis, tr., *SCG,* 1, 2.

9 Nicholas of Cusa on the Qur'ān

A fifteenth-century encounter with Islam

Nicholas Rescher

This fall[1], the 500th anniversary of the death of Nicholas of Cusa—equally well known under the Latinized name of Cusanus—is being commemorated throughout centers of learning in the West. The attention of many minds is focused once more upon the work of this great Catholic thinker who stood on the threshold of that crucial juncture of the Renaissance, separating the medievals from the moderns. Scholar, philosopher, theologian, cardinal, church official and personal friend to a pope, Nicholas embodied a truly remarkable versatility of capabilities and achievements. On the sky-map of philosophy, his star has gleamed brightly century after century.

It is a sensible view that perhaps the best way to commemorate an important thinker lies in taking serious account of his work, rather than in simply praising it. And since one cannot, within the limits of a single lecture, take into serious account the vast output of a multifaceted and productive scholar, it becomes necessary to confine oneself to some particular part of his work. I have chosen here to deal with Nicholas of Cusa's treatise on the Qur'ān because to me this treatise seems both to be of considerable interest in itself and to throw some light upon Nicholas' tenor of thought.

I Background

To appreciate the significance of Nicholas of Cusa's work on the Qur'ān, one should begin by looking briefly at the historical background of the thinking about Islam in the realm of Latin Christianity. This historical course of development may be divided into three (somewhat overlapping) phases.

(I) First Period (1100–1250+)

The first period runs from around 1100 to somewhat after 1250. This period saw a great deal of interest in Islam within Latin Christendom. Many scholars occupied themselves with Arabic works, in science and philosophy, and the period was one of active translation of philosophical, scientific, and even theological works from Arabic.

It was during this period that Peter the Venerable, Abbot of Cluny (d. 1156), an able and farsighted scholar and friend of the eminent philosopher Bernard of Clairvaux, sponsored a Latin translation of the Qur'ān. This translation was prepared around 1141–43 by collaboration between a Spaniard, Hermannus Dalmata, and an Englishman, Robertus Angligena, "Robert the Englishman"—also known as Robertus Retenensis. This version, which "abounds in inaccuracies and misunderstandings, and was inspired by hostile intention,"[2] was destined to become the form in which the Qur'ān was known in Latin Christendom.

Numerous manuscript copies were made in medieval times, and four centuries later it was published by Theodor Bibliander of Zürich.

During this first period, then, an active and intelligent interest in matters relating to Islam was manifest among European men of learning.

(2) Second Period (1250–1400)

The second period runs from roughly 1250 to around 1400. During this period, with the gradual collapse of the Crusades—and the increasing stridency of the Church in keeping crusading fervor aglow in the face of mounting difficulties—a shrill, almost hysterical tone comes into the discussion. One instance, among many, is the *Gesta imperatorum et pontificium* by Thomas of Tuscany (d. 1278). According to Thomas, Muhammad is a thief, a murderer, a beast in human form, a magician, the first-born and emissary of Satan himself.[3]

(3) Third Period (1400–1500)

The third period runs from about 1400 to around 1500. With the ending of the Crusades and the erosion of the crusading spirit—and the concomitant concentration upon local issues and difficulties—European interest in Islam went into a state of suspension. It was well on the way to atrophy when a development of political history occurred which is of great significance as background for Nicholas' treatise. During the first half of the fifteenth century, the eyes of thinking European Christians turned once again to the East, focusing upon Constantinople. That great city had slipped by gradual stages into the state of an isolated enclave existing as a beleaguered Christian island within the hostile surrounding sea of the Ottoman Turks. This situation led, on the one hand, to an interest in a possible reconciliation between the Church of Rome and that of the East—a circumstance which took Nicholas himself on a mission to Constantinople in the late 1440's. On the other hand, the Turkish threat to Constantinople rearoused the European interest in Islam which had become dormant since the fervor of the Crusades. The fall of the city in 1453 saw a revival in the Christian polemic against Islam.

Thus, Nicholas of Cusa's treatise on the Qur'ān was part of the reawakening of European concern about Islam which arose in the face of the imminent and ultimately actual fall of Constantinople to the Turks. So much for the historical background.

II Sources

What were Nicholas of Cusa's sources of information about Islam? We are in the fortunate position of being able to answer this question with great accuracy and detailed exactness. For not only did Nicholas, as a good scholar, cite the sources for his work, but, also, he left his books to the library of the hospital that was endowed by him at Cusa. Here the very books used by him are preserved and his annotations of them can be inspected by interested students.

As to the Qur'ān itself, Nicholas used, as he himself tells us in the preface of his book, the already-mentioned translation sponsored by Peter the Venerable in the twelfth century. This translation was unquestionably a mixed asset, for although it did make it possible to have at least *some* first-hand contact with the Qur'ān, its errors and inaccuracies were so numerous and so significant that they rendered the original quite unrecognizable.

Apart from this deficient translation of the Qur'ān itself, Nicholas' most important—and actually more helpful—source, was the treatise entitled *Propugnaculum fidei* by the Florentine Dominican, Ricoldus of Monte Crucis (ca. 1310; printed Venice, 1609).[4] Ricoldus had traveled extensively in the East, and had lived for some years in Baghdad. He knew Arabic and in his book cites the Qur'ān in accurate translations of his own. He is reasonably well informed about Islam, and evinces more factually accurate understanding of Islam than virtually all other medieval writers on the topic. It was in large part from this distinctly superior source that Nicholas' understanding of the nature and teachings of Islam were derived. His own work draws upon that of Ricoldus at virtually every important point.

Enough has now been said about the background and the sources of Nicholas' treatise on the Qur'ān. Let us turn to the work itself.

III The Leading Idea

In 1461–62, a period during which he held important offices in Rome under the aegis of his friend Pope Pius II, Nicholas of Cusa wrote his *Cribratio Alchorani* ("Sifting of the Qur'ān").[5] He had been equipped for this task by some personal experience of Islam derived from a visit in Constantinople in 1437–38, in connection with a mission working in the interests of unity between the Eastern and Western churches. (We might note parenthetically that, in consequence of this, Nicholas himself participated in the negotiations at the Council of Florence in 1438 which resulted in an abortive agreement for such a union.)

Over and above this brief occasion for first-hand contact, Nicholas was widely read in the ramified literature on Islamic matters available in Latin. No contemporary European thinker could match his knowledge of the Latin literature relating to Islamic philosophy and religion.

The guiding idea of Nicholas' *Cribratio Alchorani* is a shrewd and an interesting one. It is definitely not, as the majority of its medieval predecessors were, a blanket denunciation, but a careful attempt to sift out the Christian and the non-Christian elements of the Qur'ān. (This objective is made explicit in the very title of the treatise itself: *cribrare* = to sift out.) Rather than reject the Qur'ān *en bloc,* Nicholas wants to distinguish between a Muhammad who has listened to the voice of the God who enters into the hearts of all men, and a Muhammad who advances ideas and objectives of his own.

Notwithstanding its greater discrimination, Nicholas' *Sifting of the Qur'ān* is avowedly a work of Christian polemic against Islam. Conforming to the tradition derived from St. John of Damascus in the eighth century, who classes Islam as a Christian heresy, Nicholas regards Muhammad as having started from a Christian position under the influence of Christian (Nestorian) teachers, departing from it at first partly under the corrupting influence of Jews, partly to render the message more readily audible to the heathen Arabs. Then, ultimately, Muhammad made increasingly radical departures in order to exploit his growing following as an instrument of personal power.

Inherent in this view is a possibility that greatly intrigued Nicholas and some of his friends. If Islam is a corrupted version of Christianity, if Christianity is the starting point of Islam—the purified proto-Islam of a corrupted Qur'anic Islam—then a Muslim "return" to the Church becomes a thing conceivable. This train of thought provides the background for that very curious document of church history, the letter of 1461/2 of Pope Pius II to Sultan Muhammad II calling upon the Sultan to accept Christianity and to become the successor of the byzantine emperors as temporal head of the Christian Orient.[6] This letter, to which the Sultan did not even deign to make a reply, for a brief time aroused the imagination of Europe by the dazzling prospect of a religious triumph as climax to a long course of military catastrophe in the East.

IV Nicholas' View of the Qur'ān

Nicholas of Cusa's conception of the Qur'ān is, as we have indicated, unique in its radical departure from the standard strain of Christian polemic against Islam. His view is as follows:

Muhammad's basic impulse was good—his eye was upon the path to God revealed to men imperfectly by Moses and fully by Christ, and he sought to guide the heathen Arabs to this path and make it easy for them. The Muslim well arose from a sound spring, even though heretical Christians and corrupting Jews poisoned it, and the self-interest which made Muhammad into a tool of the devil ultimately perverted it.

Not only was Muhammad's starting intention valid, but the work he produced, the Qur'ān, is of genuine religious merit. It contains much that is sound and incorporates a great deal of truth. It is a work heavily influenced by the Old and New Testaments, whose reflected light illuminates it at many points. (The extent to which this view requires sympathetic interpretation is evidenced by the fact that the Qur'ān contains but one direct quotation from the Scriptures—Qur'ān 21:105; Ps. 37:29). Of course it goes amiss at numerous and crucial junctures, and of course it contains nothing of merit over and above what is to be found in the Gospels. *Si quid pulchri, veri et clari in Alcoran reperitur, necesse est, quod sit radius lucidissimi Evangelii* (*Cribratio,* I, 6).

How did Nicholas explain his view that Muhammad, having caught many glimpses of Christian truths, went fundamentally astray? How did he account for the departures of the Qur'ān from the New Testament? Here Nicholas has ready a threefold answer: (1) misunderstandings due to the impeding machinations of Nestorians and of Jews who influenced Muhammad, (2) deliberate didactic departures to adapt the message to the primitive and pagan Arabs, and (3) deliberate falsifications to serve the self-interest of the Prophet and/or the political advantage of his following.

The greater part of Nicholas of Cusa's discussion is thus devoted to a detailed critique of the departures of the Qur'ān from Christian teachings and the deployment of a Christian polemic—in its fundamentals along the usual lines—against the teachings of Islam, dwelling largely upon an apology of those Christian teachings which, like the doctrine of the trinity, had formed the foci of Islamic attacks on Christianity.

On Nicholas' view of the matter, the Qur'ān is thus a mixture in which the sound grains of truth are intermingled with the chaff of falsity. The correct Christian approach to the Bible of Islam cannot be a complete condemnation, but should be a carefully discriminative sifting (*cribratio*) of truth from error.

This attitude infuses and shapes the whole strategy of Nicholas' polemic against Islam. It is entirely *internal,* taking its stand upon the Qur'ān itself: upon its own recognition of the truth of the Gospels. As Nicholas sees the matter, the Qur'ān, in its recognition of the Bible and in the acceptance of the Biblical view of Jesus' message and role, condemns itself out of its own mouth at all points at which it departs from Biblical teachings. This line of thought determined Nicholas' concept of the basis for a sound and effective Christian polemic against Islam, and led him to dwell at some length upon matters in respect to which the declarations of the Qur'ān appeared to him as self-contradictory. (One example is chapter 9 of book III, devoted to the thesis "that Muhammad wrote of Christ sometimes as god and man both, sometimes only as man, and sometimes as god in the singular, sometimes in the plural.")

This point of view also provides the rationale which brought Nicholas to that favorite concept of our day: the idea of a dialogue. Writing to his friend John of Segovia, he welcomed the idea of a conference with the Muslims: *Non est dubium medio principium temporalium, quos Teucri sacerdotibus praeferunt, ad colloquia posse perveniri, et ex illis furor mitigabitur, et veritas se ipsam ostendet cum profectu fidei nostrae.* In this hopeful view of the constructive value of a "dialogue" (colloquium)—that this would mitigate the furor of disputation and prove useful for religion—Nicholas of Cusa is perhaps more a child of our time than of his own.

V Some Blind Spots of Nicholas' View of the Qur'ān

It is, however, only just to say that—despite the fact that his judgment of the Qur'ān was unusually favorable for his place and time—Nicholas' view of the Bible of Islam was subject to certain sharp limitations, perhaps even deserving the name of blind spots.

Of these, the first and most obvious relates to the literary quality of the Qur'ān. The Bible of Islam is a work whose beauty of language was from the first accepted by Muslims as a proof of divine inspiration. This element was, of course, wholly lost on Nicholas, for whom the Qur'ān (seen only in dry-as-dust translations) might as well have been a dissertation of scholastic theology.

A more crucial point is bound up with this first blind spot. Nicholas is able to see merit in the Qur'ān only at those points at which it agrees with the Gospels. He is flatly unwilling to grant that there may be some special merit of insight or inspiration in the Scripturally nonredundant parts of the Qur'ān—not, to be sure, as regards its declarations on matters of faith and doctrine, but in its essentially secular ordinances, for example, those regarding the reformation of the social or communal affairs of the Arabs.

In his eagerness to use the Qur'ān itself as an instrument of his cause, Nicholas is occasionally led to do (no doubt unwittingly) violence to the text in order to bend it to his objectives. Consider, for example, the following Qur'ān passage, cited in the translation of A. J. Arberry: (Sūrah 4, "Women," verses 167–70):

> People of the Book, go not beyond the bounds in your religion, and say not as to God but the truth. The Messiah, Jesus son of Mary, was only the Messenger of God, and His Word that He committed to Mary, and a Spirit from Him. So believe in God and His Messengers, and say not, 'Three.' Refrain; better is it for you. God is only One God. Glory be to Him—that He should have a son! To Him belongs all that is in the heavens and in the earth; God suffices for a guardian. The Messiah will not disdain to be a servant of God, neither the angels who are near stationed to Him.[7]

This is an obvious piece of anti-Christian, anti-trinitarian polemic. But Nicholas cites only a part of the text in isolation from its context: "Jesus son of Mary is God's messenger (*sic,* there is no 'only') and His spirit (*sic,* and not 'a spirit from Him') and His word sent unto Mary" (*Cribratio,* I, 12). Taken thus, out of context and in deceptive translation, Nicholas (*loc. cit.*) uses this passage as a proof text to show that the Qur'ān itself countenances a trinitarian position and recognizes the divinity of Jesus.

Needless to say, however, there should be no astonishment over the fact that the merits which Nicholas can find in the Qur'ān extend over a limited area. The noteworthy thing is that there is any such area at all.

VI The Rationale of Nicholas' Treatise

The unique character of Nicholas' treatise, as a Christian evaluation of the Qur'ān that is prepared to find in it good points as well as bad, derives not from his sources—how could it?—but from his own brain. It developed against the backdrop of his thinking about the nature of religion as such.

Nicholas' attitude toward the nature and diversity of religions is set forth in his important treatise "On Peace or Concord in Religion" (*De pace seu concordantia fidei*):[8] Here Nicholas expounds a view of religions which—while not (of course) overtly relativistic—emanates a certain aura of relativism. The basic concept developed here may be indicated by the analogy of mountain climbing. The mountaintop represents the summit of genuine religious knowledge, and the different paths leading up to the same summit—some rendering its attainment easy of access, others rocky, difficult, and full of pitfalls—represent various diverse religions. The analogy—which I use only for explanatory purposes: it is nowhere explicit in Nicholas' writings—illustrates graphically the tenor of his thought about religious diversity, a diversity he regards as perfectly legitimate—if not as regards the fundamentals of doctrine, then at any rate as regards rite. *Una religio in rituum varietate.* The positivity of Nicholas' approach to the Qur'ān must be judged—and can only be understood—within this background context of the basic rationale of his religious philosophy. The comprehensive philosophical perspective he brought to the particular case made it possible for Nicholas to see gleams of the light of Truth where eyes of narrower vision saw only the unmixed handwork of the devil.

VII Conclusion

We live in an era which, whatever may be its shortcomings in other respects, is a time of increased mutual sympathy and understanding between diverse religious groups. In a domain once ruled by bitter theological warfare, we can hear the beating of the wings of the dove of peace. The idea of a reconciliation between Christianity and Islam may even nowadays seem remote, but it cannot today be dismissed as an utter absurdity. The thesis of St. John of Damascus that Islam is but a Christian heresy provides the continuing basis for a possible reconciliation, at any rate on the Christian side of the divide. Nicholas of Cusa realized, more clearly than any other theologian of his day, the implications, both theological and practical, of such a position. Ours is a generation preoccupied almost to obsession with the concept of communication. The phrase "lack of communication" has become one of the hallmark clichés of the day. In his stress upon the need for Christian-Islamic interchange, Nicholas struck a note that evokes resonance in our thoughts. As Christianity and Islam draw increasingly into peaceful contact with one another in our own time, Nicholas de Cusa deserves more and more clearly to be numbered as a member of the small band of men of prophetic insight. And come what may, one cannot but honor him not only as a mind of great penetration, but as a man of good will, whose sympathetic vision was able to discern the light of truth where his compatriots saw nothing except the unmixed blackness of error.

Notes

1 Public lecture delivered at the Cusanus Commemoration Conference held at the University of Rochester, November 6, 1964.

2 A. J. Arberry, *The Koran Interpreted* (New York, 1955), p. 7.

3 Nikolaus von Cues, *Sichtung des Alkorans,* tr. by Paul Naumann, 2 vols., Leipzig, 1943 (Schriften, des Nikolaus von Cues, ed. E. Hoffman, vols. 6, 7), p. 26 of Preface.
4 See further J. W. Sweetman, *Islam and Christian Theology,* Part II, Vol. 1, pp. 116, 160.
5 Nicholas of Cusa's *Cribratio Alchorani* is now readily accessible in a German translation by Paul Naumann, *op. cit.* Our discussion owes much to Naumann's informative introduction.
6 See P. Naumann, *op. cit.,* pp. 11–12; cf. Sweetman, *op. cit.,* p. 161, note 3.
7 The best English translation of the Qur'ān is that of A. J. Arberry, *The Koran Interpreted,* 2 vols., London, 1955. Arberry's preface provides interesting information about the transmission of the Qur'ān to Europe.
8 See further R. Klibansky and H. Bascour, *Nicolai de Cusa de Pace Fidei,* Supp. III of *Mediaeval and Renaissance Studies,* the Warburg Institute, University of London, 1956.

10 Luther's Knowledge of and Attitude Towards Islam

Adam S. Francisco

The previous chapter described the context for Luther's interest in Islam. It demonstrated that, in addition to all the wartime propaganda and apocalyptic allusions, he was concerned on a very practical level with Christian perceptions of Islam. Moreover, he was eager to provide enough information to his readers so that they would be able to stand firm and defend the truthfulness of Christianity. To demonstrate the veracity of the Christian faith before a seemingly monolithic and imposing religion like Islam, however, requires knowledge of its ideology. While Luther was never personally exposed to Muslims or Muslim apologetic literature—and thus could not anticipate some of its overwhelming critiques of Christianity—he did attempt to obtain a solid grounding in its teachings before critiquing it. Thus, before analysing the particular arguments he put forward, Luther's knowledge of the Muslim world and his attitude towards Islam need to be addressed.

Luther's Source Material

Luther's knowledge of the Muslim world was derived primarily from medieval literature on Islam. While he did not list his sources in any one work, he made mention of them throughout his writings. For example, in 1530 he noted how he had not been able to acquire a copy of the Qur'ān yet so his study of Islam had been limited to two medieval polemics. 'Although I have eagerly desired for some time to learn about the religion and customs of the Muḥammadans, nothing has been available to me except a certain *Refutation of the Alcoran* [*Confutatio Alcorani*] and the *Critique of the Alcoran* [*Cribratio Alkorani*] by Nicholas of Cusa. I have tried in vain to read the Qur'ān itself.'[1] This statement appears in his preface to Georgius de Hungaria's *Tractatus de moribus, condictionibus et nequicia Turcorum,* which also included a host of information on the Muslim Turks, and in the Wittenberg and Nürnberg editions of 1530 was entitled *Libellus de ritu et moribus Turcorum.*[2] For the next decade he tried to obtain a copy of the Qur'ān, but it was not until 1542, on Shrove Tuesday, that he received a copy of it in Latin translation.[3]

These four resources constitute the main body of Luther's source material.[4] There are, however, several places where he mentioned having at least an acquaintance with other works. For example, in a letter from 1542 he noted how he had seen several excerpts of the Qur'ān contained in polemical material published in 'Köln and elsewhere.'[5] The work from Köln to which he referred is undoubtedly the 1533 edition of Dionysius the Carthusian's large *Contra Alchoranum & sectam Machometicam.*[6] The identity of the other work (or works) published 'elsewhere' is less certain. In light of the literature available, however, this could simply be a reference to Riccoldo's *Confutatio,* Nicholas' *Cribratio,* or, perhaps, the recently published paraphrased translation of Dionysius' *Contra Alchoranum,* entitled *Alchoran.*

Das ist des Mahometischen Gesatzbüchs und Türckischen Aberglaubens ynnhalt und ablänung (1540).[7] It could also refer to the Spanish Franciscan Alfonso de Espina's *Fortalitium fidei in universos Christianae religionis inimicos,* which he referred to elsewhere in his discussions on the Qur'ān.[8]

Luther was also acquainted with contemporary reports of Turkish culture. Although the exact identity and contents of these are not known for certain, except for Georgius' *Tractatus,* how widely he read in order to obtain information can be gleaned from a comment in one of his three appeals for prayers to be raised against the Turks wherein he noted how he had read numerous *neue zeitung* and other literary descriptions of the Turks.[9] These could refer to any number of works, but he must have at least read the Italian Bishop Paolo Giovio's *Commentario delle cose de' Turchi* after it was translated and published in both Latin (1537) and German (1538) from a press in Wittenberg.[10]

A few other miscellaneous sources also need to be mentioned in order to give as complete of a picture as possible of Luther's reading or at least acquaintance with works on Islam. First, a recorded conversation at the table of the Luther household indicates that he read Guillame Postel's *De orbis terrae concordia* (1544), which contained a lengthy summary of Qur'ānic teachings. Judging by Luther's response to questions from his students regarding its worth, however, it is clear that he did not value it too highly.[11] Another work from the previous year (1543) and the most important source on Islam in the sixteenth century, Theodor Bibliander's massive anthology of Islamic texts in Latin translation, anti-Qur'ānic polemics, and historiographical accounts of the Turks, was probably at least viewed by Luther. After all, he was responsible for ensuring its publication and also contributed two prefaces to the volume.[12] The Wittenberg library register contains several other important sources for information on Islam ranging from a few of Raymond Llull's works to Bernard von Breydenbach's popular volume describing his pilgrimage to Jerusalem.[13] However, there is no direct evidence that he consulted these as source material.

An interesting aspect of Luther's reading with regard to Islam, which has not been pursued by scholars, is his knowledge of Latin translations of Arabic works.[14] In addition to Averroes (Ibn Rushd, 1120–98), who he mentioned quite a few times throughout his biblical commentaries and other places, he seems to have been acquainted with other 'Arab' authors as well. In his addendum to the *Verlegung des Alcoran* he mentioned Avicenna (Ibn Sīnā, 980–1037), the physicians Ibn Māsawayh (d. 857), a Nestorian Christian, and 'Alī ibn al-'Abbās (fl. 949–82), and the astronomers Abū Ma'shar Ja'far ibn Muḥammad (787–886) and al-Farghānī (fl. 860) as 'Saracens' who 'did not believe the Qur'ān but were led by reason.'[15] While Luther's comment on their alleged disregard for the Qur'ān may be unwarranted, on the basis of this passage it is tempting to include Luther in the long list of western admirers of Arab and Persian philosophy and science.[16] However, without further analysis into his acquaintance with their works this seems to be premature.

Regardless, Luther's main sources undoubtedly consisted of Riccoldo's *Confutatio,* Nicholas' *Cribratio,* Georgius' *Tractatus,* and a Latin translation of the Qur'ān. His attitude towards these sources is particularly interesting and will elucidate his approach towards studying the religion and culture of the Turkish Muslims.

Luther's most important polemical source was the slightly corrupt version of Riccoldo da Monte di Croce's *Contra legem Sarracenorum.* The manuscript that he used, as the tide *Confutatio Alcorani seu legis Saracenorum, ex graeco nuper in latinum traducta* indicates, was twice removed from its original autograph. Demetrios Kydones (c. 1324–97), a notable Byzantine scholar, translated it into Greek during the mid-fourteenth century, and an Italian named Bartholomy Picenus de Montearduo, after an unsuccessful attempt to find the original, rendered it back into Latin (c. 1506). Editions of this translation were printed in Rome (1506) and Paris (1509, 1511, and 1514), but it was a manuscript copy, which is now located at the Sächsische Landesbibliothek in Dresden, that Luther read and annotated.[17] His second earliest source was, as indicated above, the *Cribratio* of Nicholas of Cusa. Unlike the *Confutatio,* however, it cannot be ascertained how much he studied it for he does not mention it, at least specifically, anywhere else in his writings. Presumably, he read it through at least once, but, as Hartmut Bobzin argues, it was probably only on a superficial level.[18]

What is interesting with regard to Luther's attitude towards these sources is that he originally criticised them as straw-man arguments. In 1530 he wrote, before gaining access to the Qur'ān,

> The authors of the *Confutatio* and the *Cribratio* seem to have intended through pious examination to frighten sincere Christians away from Muḥammad and hold them secure in their faith in Christ. Still, while they eagerly take pains to excerpt from the Qur'ān all the most base and absurd things that arouse hatred and can move people to ill-will, at the same time they either pass over without rebuttal or cover over the good things it contains.[19]

Over a decade later, only a few days after Luther read a complete text of the Qur'ān, he reversed this judgement (on the *Confutatio*).

> I have often read the book of Brother Richard entitled *Confutatio Alcoran,* but I could not believe that there are, on this earth, reasonable men, whom the Devil has talked into believing such shameful things. ... In any case [my reading of the Qur'ān] demonstrates that this brother Richard did not make up the material in his book, but it correctly compares with [it]. And there can be no suspicion of fabrication here. ... This I therefore say: that I must believe this brother Richard, who so long ago refuted the Qur'ān.[20]

Upon reversing his opinion and because there was no better work (*weil man kein bessers hat*) Luther rendered the *Confutatio* into his own German in 1542.[21]

After reading both of the works for the first time Luther gained access to the *Tractatus*. In contrast to these he initially thought that Georgius was a more reliable source on the religion and culture of the Muslim Turks. 'Whoever this man was', he wrote,

> The author of this book seems to present his case with the highest degree of credibility. Accordingly, he has achieved a high level of authority with me, so that I trust him to be narrating the truth with as much sincerity as power. Although the things he details are moderate and few, and I would wish for more and greater things, nevertheless, even such moderate and small matters are presented credibly. He relates details so as not only to recount the evils of the Turks but also to exhibit alongside them the best things, and he presents them in such a way that through comparison with those people he might reprove and censure our own. Nevertheless, he does not approve of such things, however piously they are done, but refutes them with as much vigour and strength as had been done up to that time. His writing certainly bears the clear signs of a forthright and sincere heart that writes nothing from hatred, but sets forth everything out of love of the truth.[22]

Although 'indulgence must be granted to this author', he continued, 'he is truly to be praised for the noble zeal, candour, and diligence by which, to the extent he was able, he distinguished himself faithfully.'[23] On account of this Luther decided to edit and publish it in 1530.[24]

As mentioned above it took Luther over a decade to acquire a copy of the Qur'ān in spite of the fact that there were, by 1542, four complete Latin translations of it available.[25] Unfortunately, the manuscript that Luther read has been lost, so ascertaining which of the four available translations he was acquainted with is a bit difficult.[26] The only comment that Luther made with regard to the nature of the manuscript was that it was a 'very poor translation' (*seer ubel verdolmetscht*) and that he wished to see a 'clearer' (*klerern*) one. Now, Luther did not know Arabic, although it has been suggested,[27] consequently his comment that he read a 'poor translation', especially when he wrote that he wanted to see a 'clearer' and not 'better' version, should be taken as a reference to the state of the manuscript and the style of the Latin.[28] This only brings us slightly closer to identifying what translation Luther actually read, but based on its turgid Latin and wide dissemination in comparison to the others we must assume that it was the first western translation of the Qur'ān completed by Robert of Ketton in the mid-twelfth century.[29]

In spite of the fact that Luther found the translation 'poor' or, rather, difficult, there are some features to Robert's Qur'ān that make it a more accessible read in comparison to the others. Thomas Burman has recently argued compellingly that this translation of the Qur'ān, although it was a paraphrase, was not necessarily corrupt. Not without its blunders, it was 'able to impart to [its] reader the Muslim interpretations of ambiguous or unclear passages', and is 'disinterestedly faithful at many points to both the literal meaning and the received interpretation of the Islamic Scriptures.' So, although it is certainly a 'freewheeling paraphrase', it 'nevertheless reflected what Muslims themselves thought to be the meaning of the Qur'ān.'[30] Thus, by extension, when Luther read it he was reading a fairly reliable representation of the text (as far as translated texts of the Qur'ān go).

Luther on the Study of Islam and the Qur'ān

With Luther's reliance upon the aforementioned texts, which were composed in the context of debate where for the most part the 'Muslim interlocutor was absent',[31] along with his theological convictions, it should come as no surprise that he was extremely hostile towards Islam. Nonetheless, in spite of his enduring and impetuous description of the Turks as the Devil incarnate (*der leibhafftige Teuffel*) or one among many of the Devil's minions (*diaboli agminibus*), he also criticised the transmission of false images of the Islamic Turks. He could, in one paragraph, describe the life and nature of the Turks as depraved and yet, in the following sentence, protest against any deliberate misrepresentations of them.[32]

The concern for truthfully depicting the life of the Turks carried over into Luther's study of their religion. Although he was convinced that the mission of Islam was to bring about the total destruction of Christianity, he advocated and strove to represent Islamic teachings as accurately and completely as he could. This also meant that elements of Muslim piety, which were on the surface noble and praiseworthy, should be brought to light. For example, in *Vom kriege widder die Türcken,* he mentioned that he had heard of admirable qualities amongst the Turks such as that they 'are faithful, friendly, and careful to tell the truth.' Not only did he believe this, but, he added, 'I think that they probably have more fine virtues in them than that.'[33] A year later, in his preface to the *Tractatus,* he repeatedly praised the outward appearances of Islam, and noted that compared to the state of European

Christendom 'the religion of the Turks or Muḥammad is far more splendid in ceremonies and, I might almost say, in customs than ours, even including that of the religious or all the clerics. ... Our religious are mere shadows when compared to them, and our people clearly profane when compared to theirs. Not even true Christians, not Christ himself, not the apostles or prophets ever exhibited so great a display.'[34] At about the same time that he wrote these things, noting the apparent consistency of Islam, he wrote the following striking, and certainly hyperbolic words, 'The abominable Muḥammad almost became my prophet'![35]

Luther believed that irrespective of whether it could be perceived as positive or not everything needed to be revealed about Ottoman Islamic culture. The whole truth needed to be told for only then could an accurate and legitimate evaluation take place. 'Indeed, those who only censure and condemn the base and absurd characteristics of the enemy but remain silent about matters that are honest and worthy of praise do more harm than good to their cause. What is easier than to condemn things that are manifestly base and dishonest (which in fact refute themselves)?' Rather, if one could show that even the apparent 'good things' in the Muslim religion were based on a faulty foundation then, and only then, could one begin to do real damage to the credibility of Islam. 'But to refute good and honest things that are hidden from sight, that is to further the cause, that is to lift up and remove the scandal, to despoil the messengers of their counterfeit image of the light and to render them appropriately hateful because of their base plundering of the light.'[36]

Luther's concern that the Turks and their religion be thoroughly represented was expressed throughout the course of his writings. Already in *Vom kriege,* wherein he addressed the Ottoman religion specifically for the first time, he stated how he was 'disgusted ... that neither our great lords nor our scholars have taken any pains to give us any certain knowledge about the [religious or political] life of the Turks.'[37] Then, noting how he had some parts of the Qur'ān and would someday like to translate it into German,[38] he explained that he would base his summary and criticism only on what he knew to be true, that is, he was sure of it because it was derived 'from the Qur'ān of the Turks' (meaning citations from the Qur'ān found in, for example, Riccoldo's *Confutatio*). Anything else that he heard, he stated, he would not bring up because he could not 'be sure about it.'[39] Echoing this early sentiment over the lack of Islamic and Ottoman studies in his own day, he was equally surprised at how little had also been done in the past. He wrote,

> It amazes me ... that long ago no one rendered the Qur'ān into the Latin language, even though Muḥammad has ruled and caused great harm more than nine hundred years ago. Yet no one has taken it upon themselves to investigate what Muḥammad's faith was. They were merely satisfied knowing that Muḥammad was an enemy of the Christian faith. But the where and how from point to point has not become publicised, which nevertheless is necessary to know.[40]

Luther placed a high priority on reading and studying the Qur'ān as a means to properly understand Islam. This can be seen most clearly in his involvement with its publication in 1543.[41] When he had received word that the Council of Basel was in a deadlock over whether or not it could be published, he sent a letter arguing on behalf of its production. He wrote, 'Therefore, because the Turks are coming near, this is still our opinion: that pastors have reliable evidence for preaching the abomination of Muḥammad to the people. ... In order to honour Christ, to do good for Christians, to harm the Turks, to vex the Devil, set this book free and do not withhold it.'[42] He then appealed to the apologetic legacy of the church fathers. 'And if the holy fathers had not freely received the books of heretics how would they have encountered its secret poison … and warned and protected the church?'[43] As it turned out, Kenneth Hagenback has demonstrated, the support from a host of humanists in Strassburg notwithstanding, Luther's letter was the primary cause behind the council's overturn of the ban.[44] And shortly afterwards Luther sent his preface for inclusion in the project in which he reiterated his concern for basing judgements on legitimate information. 'But what can we say about matters that are still outside our knowledge?' One must read the Qur'ān for 'it is of value for the learned to read the writings of the enemy.'[45]

Luther's interest in the reading and study of the Qur'ān was obviously not motivated by disinterested inquiry. It served pedagogical purposes with an apologetic and polemical goal. This is especially clear, again, in his letter to Basel. First, he argued, if people were truly informed about the religion of the Turks, particularly by reading the Qur'ān, this would militate against apostasy rather than cause it. 'I am of the mind that one causes nothing more annoying nor can render more damage (more than with any weapons) than if one brings their Qur'ān to the light of day.' Once its contents were made public he was convinced that everyone would be able to see 'what a cursed, shameful, and dreadful book it is, full of lies, fables, and every abomination.' The Turks themselves 'conceal and gloss over' it. 'As evidence', he continued, 'they are unwilling to see the Qur'ān translated into different languages. Because they probably feel that it would bring a great apostasy in all sensible hearts among them.'[46]

An acquaintance with the Qur'ān would not only ensure and protect Christians from being enticed by the Turks; also, Luther naively suggested, if the Turks themselves really knew what it said, or at least those who were reasonable, they too would see its errors. Only a thorough acquaintance with the Qur'ān could aid in the reinforcement of the truth of the Christian faith against error. This, he wrote, was why he supported its publication. 'We have desired to use your publisher to help against such apostles of the Devil and teachings of the shameful Muḥammad … that the blasphemous seduction might arm and protect the least of us against such poisonous teaching and not only us Christians but also that some Turks might themselves be converted.'[47]

Luther's Knowledge of Islam

There is little scholarly consensus concerning the nature and extent of Luther's knowledge and comprehension of Islam. In the first attempt to outline the Reformer's familiarity with Muslim religious beliefs, C. Umhau Wolf gave the following assessment: 'A fair amount of knowledge can be gleaned by the student reading the works of Luther. In most of his material, Luther's knowledge was unusually accurate. … The most impressive characteristic about Luther's knowledge of the Turks and of their religion is the almost total absence of important gaps.'[48] Other scholars have posited the opposite. For example, Stephen Fischer-Galati wrote, 'Luther's views on the Turks and Islam … were simplistic.'[49] Ludwig Hagemann even notes that he 'did not concern himself with Islam as a religious factor.' His critique of Islam resulted not from his evaluation of Muslim doctrine but rather from his identification of the Turks as an 'eschatological anti-Christian power.'[50] Oddly enough, no one has outlined in detail or undertaken a thorough analysis of the breadth and depth of Luther's understanding of the Muslim world. This gap in scholarship will be filled in so that a proper assessment of his knowledge and attitude towards Islam might be reached. Before moving into a survey of Luther's knowledge of Islam, however, a brief note on the methodology employed here is necessary.

There are a few locations in Luther's vast literary corpus that offer short, partial summaries of Islamic teachings and practices, but in each case they do not constitute everything he knew about the Turk's religion. In other words, Luther never wrote a treatise devoted to outlining everything he had learned about the faith of Muslims. Rather, there are several descriptions of various aspects relating to Islam in his writings on the Turks and, of course, the *Tischreden.* In addition to this, there are also relatively lengthy anecdotes contained in works that would otherwise seem to have nothing to do with the Turks or their religion such as his lectures and sermons on the Bible. Moreover, he also studied one of the most influential medieval polemical works against Islam several times (Riccoldo's *Confutatio*), edited the *Tractatus* for publication, and also read the Qur'ān, presumably, attentively. So, paying heed to Wolf's reasonable assumption that Luther did not write down everything that he knew about Islam,[51] in addition to investigating Luther's actual writings, his two primary sources (besides the Qur'ān) have been examined in order to gain insight into the breadth of his knowledge on Islam. Furthermore, Luther could barely say anything about Islam without making some sort of scathing remark. Thus, in sifting through the various relevant sources it has been necessary, on several occasions, to deduce the information on Islam he had obtained to which his criticism referred.

To begin with, Luther used several terms in reference to Islam and Muslims. Although one of his most preferred sources noted that Saracens called their religion al-Islam (*Elesalem*),[52] he favoured terms such as 'Turkish faith', 'religion of Muḥammad', 'Muḥammad's sect', or 'Muḥammadanism.' When he did translate Riccoldo's transliteration of al-Islam he mistakenly rendered it *Elesam,*[53] and when he referred to Turkish Muslims he simply called them Turks, although he was aware that not all Turks were Muslims. Alluding to Muslims in general, he used either the term 'Saracen' or 'Muḥammadan' even though he knew, from Riccoldo, that they called themselves 'not Saracens but Muslims' (*nicht Sarraceni, Sondern Maselamin*).[54]

The extent of Luther's knowledge of Islamic history is not completely discernible. In several places, while mentioning an historical anecdote regarding Muḥammad, Saracens, or Turks, he referred to having read of it in 'the histories', although not once does he identify his source(s).[55] Regarding the Turks, however, he at least drew upon two histories published in Wittenberg: Giovio's *Commentario* and Georgius' *Tractatus.* And from these he occasionally referred to the activities of various Ottoman sultans.[56] Nevertheless, drawing from the scattered allusions to Islamic history, a skeleton of his relatively broad knowledge of the rise of Islam can be constructed. The first chapter of the *Tractatus* placed the origins of the 'law of Muḥammad' and 'sect of the Saracens' during the pontificate of Pope Boniface V (619–25) and the reign of the Byzantine Emperor Heraclius (610–41).[57] It was during this time, 'already 900 years ago', Luther noted in the margin of the *Verlegung,*[58] that Muḥammad appeared, following the notorious heretics of earlier Christian centuries such as Marcion, Ebion, Novatus, Manes, Arius, and Pelagius.[59] Translating Riccoldo, Luther wrote,

> Heraclius defeated the Persian King Khosrau [II] and brought the holy cross back to Jerusalem with great triumph 620 years after Christ's birth. And in Heraclius' fifteenth year Muḥammad, an Arab, appeared who had become rich through a widow that he had married. Thereafter he became a leading figure among highway robbers and came to aspire with such hope to become the king in Arabia. However, because he was viewed as one of unimportant origins, they did not accept him. Then he passed himself off as a prophet. And after he had contracted epilepsy or, fell to an epidemic, and

> continually fell down ... he said that an angel had spoken to him. And he said that several words which he heard (as he said) were like a bell that rang in his ears.[60]

From this point on, he explained, Muḥammad attracted an increasing number of followers.

Although this passage and several paragraphs on the history of Muḥammad's early followers up until the codification of the Qur'ān under caliph 'Uthmān clearly served to indict Muḥammad and prove his revelations fraudulent, they do indicate, hitherto unreported by modern scholars, that Luther had some insight into the early years of Islam.[61] The subsequent history of the Muslim world after the death of Muḥammad and the first three rightly-guided caliphs, on the other hand, were only known piecemeal to Luther. The *Tractatus* mentioned the so-called Arab conquests of the Holy Land and North Africa and early invasions of Sicily and Rome (846).[62] And the *Verlegung* noted the divisions in the Muslim world between those who 'follow Muḥammad', the orthodox Sunnīs, and those who 'follow 'Alī', the Shī'i, and alluded briefly to sub-sects such as the Assassins of Lebanon and the sevener Ismā'īlīs.[63] Details of Sufi dervish groups found amongst the Turks, such as the *Mevlevi* or whirling dervishes, whose practices described in this fifteenth-century document can still be witnessed today, are found aplenty in the *Tractatus*.[64]

While his knowledge of general Arab Muslim history was slight, Luther read several important accounts of Ottoman history. The most complete reports were contained in the Latin and German translations of Giovio's *Commentario*. This early chronicle recorded the primary activities of the Turks under the sultans all the way back to *gazi* Osman himself. In Luther's works, he referred to Ottoman history in passing several times, especially in relation to the Fall of Constantinople to Sultan Mehmet and the conquest of the Mamlūks under Sultan Süleyman's father Selim.[65] In summary, he saw the history of Islam—the Saracens and then the Turks after them—as nothing short of phenomenal for its progressive and steady growth.[66]

Also, along with their history, Luther had a fairly good knowledge of Ottoman culture. On the surface he admired the Turks for their discipline and modesty. He noted he had heard that they were friendly and honest.[67] And on account of their devotion to the law brought by Muḥammad they led 'very pious' and 'abstemious' lives.[68] The virtues of Muslim culture were, however, only admired insofar as they served to extol discipline amongst unruly, licentious Germans and, moreover, when they provided a convenient apologetic weapon for his doctrine of justification against what he perceived as Rome's legalism.[69]

The elements of Turkish culture that Luther discussed in particular were quite broad. With reference to Muslim women, he mentioned that it was 'customary among the Turks for women to veil both the head and the whole body.'[70] The prohibition of alcohol, or at least wine, was also mentioned repeatedly by the German who was himself quite fond of drinking in moderation. In a passage from the *Verlegung*, he noted that Muḥammad forbade the consumption of wine because it could potentially lead to drunkenness. He continued noting that wine is *ein gute Creatur Gottes*, but stated that its misuse should rightly be condemned. So, altering the *Confutatio*'s concluding accusation that the Arabs of Muḥammad's day were all intemperate lightweights, Luther simply noted that 'perhaps' Muḥammad had to condemn it because they could not hold their alcohol.[71]

Several other aspects of Turkish Muslim culture were discussed by Luther such as circumcision, domestic practices, the respect children had for elders, education, etc., but none received as much attention as marriage. The issue of marriage in the Qur'ān and amongst the Turks, as Luther perceived it, will take up a significant portion in chapter 5 so the discussion here will be limited. In general, however, Luther was under the impression that Muslim men were permitted to take as many wives as they pleased and were allowed to divorce them just as freely. Although he noted that there were those who chose not to take advantage of this, 'this is the law', he wrote, 'and anyone who wants to can follow it.'[72] In a brief passage he explained the Qur'ān's marriage and divorce laws.

> A Saracen is apparently allowed to put away his wife and take her back as often as he wishes. Yet, strangely, after a wife has been sent away for the third time, she may not be retrieved. When former husbands want their wives back, they offer money to the person who received the discarded woman. He lets it be publicly known that he wishes a divorce. When this happens, she can return to her former husband. It sometimes happens that the woman is so pleasing to the second man that he makes the statement that he will not separate from her. Thus the original couple lose money, marriage, and hope. Such regulations ought not be applied to dumb animals, let alone people.[73]

Human beings, regardless of national or religious identity, he wrote elsewhere, had 'no right to make marriage a free thing as though it were in our power to do with as we pleased, changing and exchanging.'[74]

Apart from the perceived marital practices of the Turks, Luther did not seem too interested in other cultural aspects of Islam. Instead, he was much more enthused about learning and especially critiquing the doctrine of the Turks. He expressed this at a table conversation. 'Personal anecdotes which they narrate about Muḥammad do not move me for we must attack the doctrine of the Turks.'[75] In fact, he was most concerned about doctrine with all his opponents. His intense preoccupation with it was succinctly stated in his lectures on Galatians where he wrote, just as 'in philosophy a tiny error in the beginning is very great at the end, in theology a tiny error overthrows the whole teaching.'[76] Diverging from the popular medieval approach of discrediting the prophet in order to discard his teaching, Luther thought that if he could show the teachings of Islam to be erroneous wavering Christians would automatically reject the 'law of Muḥammad' and, though improbable, some Turks might be moved to embrace the Christian Gospel. Due to his polemical, apologetic, and missiological focus, the elements of Muslim religious beliefs that he acquired were primarily the contentious elements between Christianity and Islam.

The *point de départ* and bedrock of Luther's theology as well as his religious epistemology was the incarnation of God in Christ. In his own words, *In Christo crucifixo est vera Theologia et cognitio Dei.*[77] It should not surprise one, then, to see that he was fixated on the Qur'ānic teachings about Jesus, for, as he wrote in *Heerpredigt,* christological doctrines are what distinguished Christianity from 'all other faiths on earth.'[78] His first summary of 'Islamic christology' was located in *Vom kriege* where he noted that the Turks regarded Christ as a sinless and holy prophet whose prophetic mission was limited 'to his own time', just like any other prophet. His sonship and co-equality with God the Father and the Holy Spirit in the one divine *ousia,* he continued, was rejected and consequently Muslims did not believe him to be 'the Saviour of the world who died for our sins.' On account of this, even though Muslims praised Jesus (*'Īsā*) as a messenger of God, according to Luther, Muḥammad shows himself to be 'a destroyer of our Lord Christ and his kingdom.' Without the divine personage and redemptive work of Christ, he concluded that 'all Christian doctrine and life are gone' for 'it leaves almost nothing of Christian truth remaining.'[79]

The Qur'ānic rejection of the deity of Christ, although 'extraordinarily pleasing to reason', Luther suggested, was the product of a *mélange* of beliefs from heretics, Jews, and heathens.[80] These various alleged heretic-sources, particularly in reference to the nature of Christ, were repeated frequently in Luther's writings. For example, the claim that Christ never asserted that he was God, Muḥammad obtained from the Arians. That Christ will be revealed again at the end of the world to kill the anti-Christ was thought to be from the Jews.[81] And that Christ was not crucified but rather 'another, who was similar to him' (*einen andern, der jm ehnlich gewest*)[82] was killed instead was derived partly from the Manicheans and, in the margin Luther noted, Muḥammad himself.[83]

In addition to these, Luther grew more familiar with several aspects of Islamic christology over time, especially after he read the Qur'ān. For example, he commented repeatedly on Qur'ān 6:101: 'How can [God] have a son when He has no female companion.'[84] When he first encountered this passage he sarcastically remarked, 'O klugheit!'[85] Later on in the *Verlegung*, removing a significantly less abrasive comment of Riccoldo, Luther wrote,

> He thoughtlessly lies about God against the Gospel … that it is not possible for God to have a son because he does not have a woman. And he continually repeats this as if it is a solid, excellent reason. However, such wisdom is just like when I say: 'God cannot be living for He does not eat or drink, does not crap or piss, does not have a runny nose or cough.' Christians know full well how God can have a son and it is not necessary that Muḥammad teach us how God must first become a man and have a woman to produce a son or a bull must have a cow to produce a calf. Oh how over-powered in the flesh of women Muḥammad is. In all his thoughts, words, deeds, he cannot speak nor do anything apart from this lust. It must always be flesh, flesh, flesh.[86]

Although not in terminology, Luther knew that the denial of Christ's divinity was based on the admonition to avoid *shirk* or associating partners to God.[87] He of course considered this charge to be erroneous. The Qur'ān 'lies about Christians', he wrote, when it says 'that they give a partner to God. That is an open lie, for Christians in the entire world say that God is one and is indivisible. Certainly nothing is more united than the Godhead or Divine Essence.'[88] Yet, in spite of all these attacks on traditional Christian christology Luther often admitted that, among the many things that the Qur'ān had to say about Christ, insofar as his humanity was concerned, it spoke of him highly.[89]

Although Luther never admitted and probably never did completely see the underlying rationale of Islamic theology, particularly *vis-à-vis* Christianity, he knew the basic framework of Islamic thought. Whereas the point of departure of Luther's theology was the person and work of Christ (alongside the Scriptures), for Muslims, arguably, it is the uncreated, eternal speech of God recorded in the Qur'ān.[90] Early on he knew its centrality in both religious doctrine and jurisprudence for already in 1520 he noted that the Turks did not distinguish between spiritual and temporal laws but rather saw the two as a unified whole, which were guided, ordered, and ruled by 'their Qur'ān.'[91]

Before delving deeper into Luther's understanding of the Qur'ān's message, it is necessary to discuss his views on the messenger for the two are closely linked. Muḥammad is not conceived of as just a prophet (*nabī*) in Islamic thought; he is also regarded as a messenger (*rasūl*) who, like Moses (*Mūsā*) and Jesus (*ʿĪsā*), received a revelation (recorded in Scripture) from God. The difference with Muḥammad was that he brought the revelational lineage of all *nabiyyūn* and *rusul* to a close.[92] The message that he brought (embodied in the Qur'ān) was the pinnacle of God's revelation and distinguisher (*al-Furqān*) of all correct doctrine of both past and present. This Islamic conception of the history of God's special revelation to man through messengers and Scripture was best described to Luther in Georgius' *Tractatus*.

> The general opinion of nearly all Turks concerning their law is as follows: They say the first great prophet, to whom for the first time the law was given by God, was *Mūsā*, that is Moses, the book *Tawrāt* was given to him, which we call the pentateuch; And every human, who adhered at that time to this law, was saved. When, however, in the course of time human vice and carelessness broke this law, after this transgression the second great prophet *Dāwud* was chosen, who we call David, to whom the book *Zabūr* was given, which we call the Psalms. This was first kept like the previous and then, after it was broken, the third great prophet *'Īsā* followed, that is Jesus, to whom the third law was sent in the book of the *Injīl*, which we call the gospel and which was at its time for all the cause of salvation. It finally, like the preceding ones, was abandoned, and the fourth elected [messenger] was Muḥammad, who received from God the book with the law, which is called the Qur'ān.[93]

Riccoldo also explained the abrogation of the 'law' brought by Jesus. In a chapter where it seems he artificially placed words into the mouths of Muslims, he wrote,

> Saracens try to reply [to Christian interrogation] saying, 'We do not say that the Gospel is not from God, since the Qur'ān clearly bears witness to this. Neither do we say that it is imperfect, since it is from God. But the Gospel involves such difficult and excellent things that we cannot do them. For who can love God with his whole heart and love his neighbour as himself? Who can pray for his persecutors and accusers? … [T]he Gospel commands certain other excellent things. Therefore, since it was not a law that was capable of being kept, God made provision for the world through a law of salvation. He made lighter commands and gave the world the Qur'ān, which does not contain these difficult things at all, but exists to save men through itself in an easy way.'[94]

Luther apparently considered Georgius' explanation to be more representative of Islamic teaching for he repeats it several times throughout his writings. His first mention of it is in *Vom kriege* where he explained how the Qur'ān described Jesus' prophetic ministry as being limited 'to his own time' and brought to completion 'before his death, just like any other prophet.' The prophethood of Muḥammad was, on the other hand, regarded as universal, he wrote. 'Since Christ's office of prophet is now complete he [Muḥammad] has been commanded to bring the world to his faith.'[95]

Luther was fully aware that Muḥammad is regarded by Muslims to be 'the universal prophet of the entire world' (*der gemein Prophet aller welt*) who was also 'the end, sign, and seal (or completion) of all the prophets' (*das Ende, Sigel und Schweigen [oder auffhören] aller Propheten*).[96] He was also cognizant that the Qur'ān and Muslim apologists claimed that the coming of Muḥammad had been foretold in the previous books sent down by God. Rendering Qur'ān 61:6 into his German, he wrote, 'Christ prophesied much in the Gospel concerning him [Muḥammad] to the children of Israel. There he said, "I announce to you an apostle of God who will come after me, who will be named Muḥammad".'[97] In response, he initially mustered a simple 'O Teuffel' in a marginal comment, and, as will be seen below, offered a significant rebuttal in a later chapter of the *Verlegung*.

The issue of Christ's restricted or limited prophetic vocation and the universality of Muḥammad's is discussed extensively in other works. For example, in his sermons on the Gospel of John he explained the abrogation of Christ's 'law' by Muḥammad in contrast with the former's abrogation of the Law of Moses. 'Just as we Christians say that Moses and Abraham were circumcised but believe that circumcision is a thing of the past today, so the Turk declares that Christ's word and mission no longer have validity.'[98] In another passage where he acknowledged that 'Muḥammad … speaks of Christ in a laudatory way' further insight is gained into his understanding of Muḥammad's role in the history of God's revelation. 'It is a very wicked error when the monks and sophists portray Christ as a new lawgiver after Moses', he began and then added,

> Not unlike the error of the Turks, who proclaim that their Muḥammad is the new lawgiver after Christ. Those who portray Christ this way do Him a supreme injury. He did not come to abrogate the old Law with the purpose of establishing a new one; but, as Paul says here, He was sent into the world by the Father to redeem those who were being held captive under the Law. These words portray Christ truly and accurately. They do not ascribe to Him the work of establishing a new Law; they ascribe to Him the work of redeeming those who were under the Law.[99]

Luther clearly understood how Islam posits that Jesus, like prophets before him, brought a law or *sharīʿa* to the community over which they guided as a prophet. What he did not mention and probably never really grasped was that Islam does not posit an abrogation of the religion of Moses or Jesus.[100] Rather, the Qur'ān's own image is that the religion Muḥammad proclaimed was both equivalent to the religion of Adam and all the prophets afterward. To the claim that Christianity (and Judaism) is older and therefore superior it asserts that they were at one time legitimate and *ipso facto,* in a sense, Islamic, but the Jews and Christians created innovative teachings and were led astray. Muḥammad and the Qur'ān thus restored the monotheistic orthodoxy (*ḥanīfiyya*) of primitive Judaism and Christianity while bringing a new improved *sharīʿa* not just for the Arabs but the entire world. Whether Luther grasped this completely is doubtful.

Luther did, however, manage to acquire a fairly broad understanding of the particular teachings of Islam. By the sixteenth century, allegations that Muslims worshipped a multiplicity of gods were rare. Luther could on a few occasions accuse the Turks of worshipping the Devil or holding Muḥammad as a deity.[101] However, such exaggerations were rhetorical devices or large, involved theological inferences. He was completely aware of Islam's monotheism, and in several places he referred to the Turks' belief in one God. 'Turks … feign great religious zeal and boast against us Christians of their belief in the one God, the Creator of heaven and earth.'[102] In another place he wrote that a Muslim 'names and has in mind the true God who created heaven and earth.'[103] He even informed his readers that the Muslims call God *Alla.*[104] 'In the Arabic language Allah means God', he wrote and speculated that, etymologically, it was 'a corruption from the Hebrew *Eloha.*'[105]

One enduring and controversial passage concerning Luther's understanding of the Muslim God is contained in the *Großer Katechismus.*[106] In the explanation of the third article of the Apostles' Creed, he wrote, 'All who are outside the Christian church, whether heathen, Turks, Jews, or false Christians and hypocrites, even though they believe in and worship only one, true God [*ob sie gleich nur einen wahrhaftigen Gott glauben und anbetten*] nevertheless do not know what his attitude is toward them. They cannot be confident of his love and blessing.'[107] Although this passage seems clear[108]—that Muslims believe in one God but that even this misses the mark by solely relying on the hidden God instead of the revealed God in Christ—it has been obfuscated by problematic translations. For example, two of the most recent English translations render the clause *ob sie gleich nur einen wahrhaftigen Gott glauben und anbetten* as 'even though they believe in and worship only *the* one true God.'[109] However, the original German does not contain the definite article. Furthermore, the grammar and the context do not demand it.[110] So this passage should be translated as it has been above.

Islam's monotheism is, of course, built upon the fundamental doctrine of the unicity of God or *tawḥīd*. Luther was acquainted with this teaching especially in connection to the Qur'ānic denial of the Trinity.

> For if you were to ask such a very saintly Jew, Turk, or heretic whether he believes that this one God, Creator of heaven and earth (whose name they exalt so piously and whom they call Father—although all this falsely), really is a Father and has a son in the Godhead outside of creation, he would be horrified in his great holiness and would regard this as frightful blasphemy. And if you would ask further whether the same, one God, Creator, Father (as they call Him with their lying mouths) is also a son, who has a Father in the Godhead, he would stuff up his ears in his great zeal, gnash his teeth, and worry that the earth might swallow you and him. And if you continue to ask whether the same, one God, Creator, and Father (as they boastfully call Him) is also a Holy Spirit, who has the Father and the Son, from whom He derives His divine essence, this super holy man would run away from you as though you were the vilest Devil just come from hell.[111]

Rejection of the Trinity was, according to Luther, tantamount to idolatry. Therefore, he alleged that Muslims 'invent a god such as they wish to have, not as God has revealed Himself.'[112] Moreover, the allegation of *shirk*, prompted by the doctrine of *tawḥīd*, was a false allegation when directed at Christians. 'Although the Qur'ān says: "You should not take three Gods for there is one God" this does not counter us and proves nothing. For we say ourselves, yes even the heathen, that there is only one God, in addition, he is also singular and indivisible, nothing could be more singular.'[113]

While he recognised that one of the fundamental concerns of Islamic thought was maintaining *tawḥīd*, Luther, perhaps unsurprisingly, showed no sympathy towards it. This is especially clear in his ruminations over the first clause of the *shahāda* or Muslim profession of faith. He sarcastically remarked, in his first mention of it, 'For they have been taught in the Qur'ān that they shall boast constantly with these words, "There is no God but God." All that is really a device of the Devil. For what does it mean to say, "There is no God but God," without distinguishing one God from another?'[114] Even Georgius de Hungaria's explanation that the entire *lex Turcorum*—that is, Islam—was grounded (*fundata*) upon this confession did not cause any further investigation into its deep theo-logic.[115] Rather, he continued to disparage it especially in the *Verlegung*. Muslims say that it is necessary that 'one should repeat these words everywhere: "There is no God but God and Muḥammad is God's apostle", and God is great.' But, he asked,

> What is this particularly great thing, as if here we are informed of a dubious or odd new teaching? Who does not know that God is God and that he is great? Who has ever heard that God is not God or that he is impotent? … It sounds like as if one was saying: 'There is no ass but an ass', 'there is no cow but a cow', 'there is no man but a

> man.' Everyone certainly knows that an ox or a dog is not an ass, also that man or angels are not God. Fools and senseless people like to speak like this.[116]

Rather than a mere tautology, the first clause of the Arabic rendering of the *shahāda*—*lā ilāha illa Allāh*—is indicative of a strong theocentric theology. In confessing 'there is no God' (*lā ilāha*), at the very level of grammar, there is an absolute negation of anything worthy of divinity and therefore worship. The conjunction (*illa*) denotes the only exception, God (*Allāh*). Luther had neither the tools nor the teacher to gain a better understanding of this.[117]

Likewise, he was only somewhat aware of the way the theocentrism of Islam worked out in relation to human agency. In a passage from *Vermahnung,* he explained that on account of the Turks' strong doctrine of determinism they were thus extremely courageous, to the point of fanaticism, during battle, for they were convinced that 'no one may die unless his fated hour has come.' This reckless abandonment, which, according to Luther, was akin to 'Epicurean philosophy', was one of the primary causes of the success of the Turks.[118]

In comparison to his brief comments on the determinism of Islam, Luther was acutely aware of Muslim theological anthropology. He noted that one of the most fundamental differences between the Christian and Islamic teachings on human nature was the rejection of the doctrine of original and hereditary sin. 'The doctrine concerning the cause of human infirmity, calamity, and death, especially the propagation of sin after the fall of the first parents has always existed in the church. This, Muḥammad, like an Epicurean, considers an absurd fable.'[119] He had in mind Qur'ānic passages on the absolution of Adam's sin shortly after creation and the preservation of his original righteousness before God as well as his elevated status over the angels (for example, 2:30–37, 7:19–25).[120] If all this were true then, Luther wrote, the Turks' 'strongest argument' was that, logically speaking, universal guilt and condemnation was inconceivable and only probable if God were terribly unjust.[121] Furthermore, without sin as a universal condition of humankind there would be no need for a Saviour. If all this were true, then perhaps he would have, by necessity, embraced Muḥammad as his prophet, but he was, of course, convinced that the Qur'ān was wrong on this point and alleged that it was the result of 'the Devil speaking through Muḥammad.'[122]

The opinion that Satan spoke through Muḥammad who in turn recorded or was later recalled to have said these demonically inspired words naturally coloured Luther's impression of the Qur'ān.[123] Nevertheless, he was still able to grasp, mainly from Riccoldo, the significance of the Qur'ān in the life of Muslims. He knew that they firmly and unswervingly maintained that it is the word of God (*Gottes wort*) and that they derived religious, ethical, and legal teachings from it.[124] And although he mentioned that some of the Turkish interpreters of the Qur'ān 'make it their one aim to interpret [it] allegorically',[125] he was well aware of the general high regard for the literal Arabic text. The Qur'ān itself, noted Luther in reference to sūrah 42:7, was revealed in Arabic and Arabic alone, and therefore the Muslims would not translate it into another language.[126] Although he did not know it from experience, but rather from Riccoldo, he explained how the poetical and rhythmic nature of the Arabic text testified that it was 'the law of God revealed to Muḥammad' and that it 'proves that Muḥammad was a true prophet.'[127]

In response, Luther had an enormous amount to say about the law of God and the receptor (Muḥammad) of this law, but since the proceeding chapters will be devoted to Luther's engagement with the Qur'ān and its teachings, a short excursus on his impression of it will suffice for now. Generally, Luther regarded the Qur'ān as a spurious text. While he did occasionally note that it contained some good things (that is, its parallels to the Bible),[128] he was convinced and instructed his readers that it was the product of human imagination,[129] plagiarism from the Bible,[130] and, ultimately, demonic influence.[131] He described its contents, like Riccoldo, as a collection of 'sermons or doctrines' thought to be of divine origin, 'as if they were spoken out of the mouth of God.'[132]

While Luther read a very short description of the Mu'tazilite controversy,[133] he was not aware of the significance of the doctrine of the uncreated character of the Qur'ānic text. He was, however, for the most part correct in his view that the Arabic root of Qur'ān meant, like the Hebrew *qara'a,* to call out, recite, preach, or read.[134] He also knew that the message that was believed to have been sent down (*hinab gesand*)[135] was not only meant to be recited but also to replace former books or to restore the message that had been corrupted or altered (*gefelscht*) by Jews and Christians.[136]

As indicated above, there is mention in several places of Luther's works that Muḥammad and the Qur'ān abrogated previous books sent down by God.[137] He was also aware of the claim that the actual biblical texts had been corrupted (*taḥrīf al-lafẓ*), especially by the expunging of prophecies of Muḥammad from both the Old and New Testaments and the misinterpretation of the biblical text (*taḥrīf bi al-ma'nā*) such as the passages where Christ is purported to claim equality with God.[138] His understanding of this was, like so many others before him, limited, though, for he was only exposed to Christian responses to the charge of *taḥrīf.*[139] In any case, Luther was convinced that this lacked merit, not only because of his unwillingness to believe that the Bible was corrupt but also because the reliability of text of the Qur'ān itself was questionable. After reading and translating Riccoldo's rendering of the history of the collection of the text, he noted in the margin, 'The Turks do not know where the Qur'ān came from.'[140]

Apart from that which is in the Qur'ān Luther also knew of a few Islamic traditions. The most notable of these and the ones he dwelled on most were Muḥammad's night journey (*al-isrā'*) and ascent into heaven (*mi'rāj*), which are recounted in chapter 14 of the *Verlegung.*[141] And from what he read in Georgius' *Tractatus* he also mentioned several references to Sufi legends of miracles in association with graves of holy men and women.

Also from Georgius he knew of the basic duties or five pillars of a Muslim's religious life. He first read of these in chapter 13 of the *Tractatus* where they are described in some detail. The *shahāda* is quoted in Turkish—*Layllaha hillallach mehemmet erczullach*—and, according to Georgius, citing the *communem opinionem* of the Turks for support, simply meant that 'God is one, and Muḥammad is his great prophet.'[142] Luther, translating Riccoldo (instead of Georgius), rendered it (accurately) into German: 'There is no God but God and Muḥammad is the messenger of God.'[143] In addition to the criticism mentioned earlier, he wrote in the margin that repeating this was as useless as saying the Ave Maria. The daily canonical prayers (*Salāt*), fasting during Ramadan (*Sawm*), taxes (*Zakāt*), and the *Hajj* were also known to Luther. A slight amount of admiration can be sensed from him as he learned of the piety of the Turks when he mentioned, 'the fasts, prayers, and common gatherings of the people that [the *Tractatus*] reveals are nowhere seen among us.' One should, however, make no mistake, for he often remarked that true faith in the true God 'has absolutely nothing to do with discerning what ceremonies, customs, or laws are better or worse, but declares that all of them squeezed together … are not enough for justification.'[144] And here is one of the chief errors of Islam, according to Luther, which rendered it a false religion. It taught that man was able to, by his own merit, achieve righteousness before God. Although a Muslim's display of righteousness surpassed, by far, any papist, it was still a religion that, in addition to rejecting formal articles of the Christian faith such as the divinity of Christ, Trinity, and the sufficiency of the Bible, was fundamentally flawed by its espousal of a righteousness that comes by works.

From the above analysis it is clear that Luther had a fair knowledge of Islam—both in terms of breadth and comprehensiveness. While Wolf's claim that his 'knowledge was unusually accurate' devoid of 'important gaps' is untenable, Fischer-Galati's and Hagemann's counter claims are equally unjustified when the overall context of the first half of the sixteenth century is taken into consideration. With the exception of a few of his younger contemporaries, for example, Theodor Bibliander and Guillame Postel, Luther's understanding was as broad and perceptive as anyone's knowledge was during his time and, according to contemporary research, surpassed most.[145] In addition to the historical context, his sources and obvious polemical and apologetic intent for his study of Islam enabled him to grasp several key points of contention between the Muslim and Christian religions.

It was the key points of contention between Islam and Christianity that made all the difference to Luther. While he could at times admire the prudence and discipline of the Turks, the theological doctrines of the Qur'ān were simply irreconcilable with the exclusive claims of Christianity. Moreover, and more seriously, the teachings and many of the practices of Muslim Turks, such as the *shahāda,* posed serious problems with identifying and worshipping the one, true God. Still furthermore, formal theological questions aside, ultimately Islam threatened and, in fact, severed the gift of salvation offered to human beings through the gospel of Christ. By rendering Christ a mere human and, still worse, not crucified, Islam negated what Luther thought God had done for the salvation of humanity by rendering the gospel obsolete. Islam, in Luther's mind, simply reintroduced a new, albeit superior to Rome's, religion of works righteousness. It was from this, as he informed Philip Melanchthon in 1530, that he began to grow agitated with the Turks and Muḥammad,[146] and propelled him to begin formulating arguments against the religion of the Turks. The proceeding chapters analyse these attacks on Islam in two successive, distinct stages in order to elucidate Luther's approach to Islam.

Notes

1 *Vorwort,* WA 30/2:205.2–8 (H-B, 258).

2 There are a few erroneous remarks about this work in relation to Luther in the secondary literature. Following a lead from the Weimarer Ausgabe (WA 30/2:198), Gordon Rupp attributed its authorship to Vincentius Ferrar (see 'Luther against "the Turk"', 259–60), and, on a different note, Gregory Miller dates Luther's preface to it as 1543 not 1530 ('Luther and the Turks', 80).

3 *Verlegung,* WA 53:272.16: 'Aber itzt diese Fastnacht hab ich den Alcoran gesehen Latinisch.' Shrove Tuesday in 1542 was 21 February.

4 Most scholars have maintained that these were his only sources. See Henry Preserved Smith, 'Luther and Islam', *AJSLL* 39:3 (1923), 218, 219; Hermann Barge, 'Luthers Stellung zum Islam und Seine Übersetzung der Confutatio des Ricoldus', *AM* 43:2/3 (1916), 113–14; G. Simon, 'Luther's Attitude toward Islam', *MW* 21 (1931), 258–59; C. Umhau Wolf, 'Luther and Mohammedanism', *MW* 31 (1941), 177; Grislis, 'Luther and the Turks', 180, 188n1; Walter Beltz, 'Luthers Verständnis von Islam und Koran', *WZGSR* 32:5 (1983), 88; Rajashekar, 'Luther and Islam', 182; Hagemann, *Luther und der Islam,* 29–31; Dean Apel, 'Luther's Approach to Islam: Ingemar Oberg's Search for Mission Praxis in the Weimar Edition of Luther's Works', *CT& M* 26:6 (1999), 441; Choi, 'Martin Luther's Response', 33.

5 WA Br 10:162.65–163.67: 'Das auch bereit an zu Collen und anderswo der Alcoran das mehrer teil mit statlichen confutation sind ausgangen.'

6 Cf. Bobzin, *Der Koran,* 70–76.
7 See Bobzin, *Der Koran,* 72n221, 75. The translator of this work is still unknown, but the cataloguer for the British Library suggests that it was the catholic humanist Heinrich von Eppendorff (1496–1551).
8 See *Enarratio capitis noni Esaiae,* WA 40/3:670.12–13. According to the editors of the Weimarer Ausgabe, he first read Alfonso de Espina's work in 1518 (see 670n3 and 669n1).
9 *Eine Vermahnung an alle Pfarrherrn,* WA 50:485.4–5: 'Es haben uns bis daher so mancherley neue zeitung und geschrey von der Tuercken anzug endlich jrre gemacht.' Cf. Miller, 'Luther and the Turks', 79–80.
10 WA 30/2:200, 204; cf. Rupp, 'Luther against "the Turk"', 260.
11 WA TR 5:472.20–25: 'D.M. Luther ward ein gross Buch bracht, welches ein Franzos, Wilhelmus Postellus genannt, von Einigkeit in der Welt geschrieben hatte, in welchem er sich heftig bemühete, die Artikel des Glaubens aus der Vernunft und Natur zu beweisen, auf daß er die Türken und Jüden möchte bekehren, und alle Menschen ... zu einem Glauben bringen.'
12 Both Luther's preface to the Qur'ān and to the *Tractatus* were included in one edition of the *Machumetis* of 1543. See Bobzin, 'Zur Anzahl', 213–19; *Der Koran,* 209–21.
13 See Sachiko Kusukawa, *A Wittenberg University Library Catalogue of 1536* (Cambridge: LP Publications, 1995), 17, 37, 39, 84.
14 They have been mentioned in passing, however, by Simon, 'Luther's Attitude', 261.
15 *Verlegung des Alcoran,* WA 53:389.33–390.2: 'Denn auch unser Medici und Astronomi viel der Sarracenen bücher haben, als Avicennam, Mesue, Hali, Albumasar, Alfraganus etc., die freilich Menschen gewest und dem Alcoran nichts gegleubt, sondern der vernunfft gefolget haben.' For specific works by these and other authors contained in the University of Wittenberg library, see Kusukawa, *Wittenberg Library,* 109, 114, 122–24, 130, 132, 134–36, 142–45.
16 See Edward Grant, *God and Reason in the Middle Ages* (Cambridge: Cambridge University Press, 2001), 70.
17 On this manuscript, see WA 53:265; Mérigoux, 'L'ouvrage', 38; and Antoine Dondaine, 'Ricoldiana: Notes sur les oeuvres de Ricoldo da Montecroce', *AFP* 37 (1967), 135. The Latin text, along with Luther's marginalia and editorial marks (for his German translation), is printed on odd-numbered pages in WA 53:273–387. The card catalogue from the Wittenberg library indicates that the manuscript was brought from Strassburg (Kusukawa, *Wittenberg Library,* 165).
18 Bobzin, *Der Koran,* 34.
19 *Vorwort,* WA 30/2:205.8–15 (H-B, 258).
20 *Verlegung,* WA 53:272.16–19, 26–27: 'Das Buch Burder Richards, prediger Ordens, Confutatio Alcoran genant, hab ich vormals mehr gelesen, Aber nicht gleuben können, das vernünfftige Menschen auff erden weren, die der Teufel solte bereden, solch schendlich ding zugleuben ... Aber itzt diese Fastnacht hab ich den Alcoran gesehen Latinisch. ... So viel aber daraus gemarckt, das dieser Bruder Richard sein Buch nicht ertichtet, Sondern gleich mit stimmet. Und das kein falscher wohn hie sein kan ... Das rede ich darumb, das ich diesem bruder Richard gleuben must, der so lange zuvor den Alcoran verlegt.' Already in the Kydone's Greek translation, Riccoldo's name was rendered 'Ρικάρδος' (Mérigoux, 'L'ouvrage', 52) hence Luther's designation, following his Latin manuscript, 'bruder Richard.'
21 *Verlegung,* WA 53:272.31. Evidence suggests that Luther read this work at least three times. He mentioned having consulted it, as already indicated, in the 1530 preface to the *Tractatus.* In a marginal note regarding when Muḥammad lived he noted that the year he made the remark was 1540 (WA 53:276). And he had to read it at least one more time when he began his translation of it in 1542. On Luther's dependence upon Riccoldo, also see E.I.M. Boyd, 'Ricoldus: A Dominican Missionary to Moslems in the Thirteenth Century', *MW* 8 (1918), 47.
22 *Vorwort,* WA 30/2:205.16–25 (H-B, 258–59).
23 *Vorwort,* WA 30/2:208.11–14 (H-B, 262).
24 See WA Br 215.14–15. This work is still heralded as the most important source for information pertaining to fifteenth-century Ottoman culture (see Klockow, ed., *Tractatus,* 3; Palmer, 'Fr. Georgius', 54).
25 Bobzin, 'Latin Translations', 201; Burman, 'Polemic', 187–88.
26 Bobzin, 'Latin Translations', 195.

27 Harfiyah Haleem et al. (eds.), *The Crescent and the Cross: Muslim and Christian Approaches to War and Peace* (London: Macmillan Press, 1998), 4.
28 Bobzin notes, 'Da Luther kein Arabisch verstand, kann sich diese Bermerkung nur auf den Stil der Übersetzung beziehen, und dieser ist schon sehr früh—und auch später noch—immer wieder kritisiert worden' (*Der Koran*, 38).
29 Bobzin, *Der Koran*, 38. On Robert's Qur'ān being the 'standard version' for European readers up until the eighteenth century, see pages 11–12.
30 Burman, *'Tafsīr'*, 707, 731.
31 Lewis, *Islam*, 13.
32 *Vom kriege*, WA 30/2:121.18–26 (LW 46:175–76). Cf. *Verlegung*, WA 53:392.35–37. 'Bleibt manches von dem, was Luther im Hinblick auf den Islam tat und schrieb, gleichwohl von Bedeutung. Wichtig ist hier vor allem Luthers Bemühen um authentische Kenntnisse über die islamische Lehre' (Bobzin, 'Gedanken Martin Luthers', 275).
33 *Vom kriege*, WA 30/2:127.19–21 (LW 46:182).
34 *Vorwort*, WA 30/2:206.3–5, 11–15 (H-B, 259).
35 *Der Cxvij. Psalm*, WA 31/1:256.6–7: 'Auch were mir bey hanent der schendliche Mahometh zum Propheten' (LW 14:38).
36 *Vorwort*, WA 30/2:205.25–28, 29–206.2 (H-B, 259).
37 *Vom kriege*, WA 30/2:121.19–23 (LW 46:175–76).
38 This has led to an erroneous note in the American Edition of *Luther's Works*, which states that he did eventually translate it into German (LW 43:235n24).
39 *Vom kriege*, WA 30/2:127.3–5 (LW 46:182).
40 *Verlegung*, WA 53:272.9–15: 'Und wunderte mich … das man den Alcoran nicht lengst hette in die Latinische sprache bracht, So doch der Mahmet nu lenger denn neun hundert jar regirt und so grossen schaden gethan hat, doch niemand sich drümb angenomen, zuerfaren, was Mahmet ein Feind Christlichs Glaubens were, Aber wo und wie von stück zu stück, ist nicht laut worden, Welchs doch von nöten ist zu wissen.'
41 See pages 59, 91.
42 WA Br 10:162.39–41: 'Darumb ist unser meinüng diese gewest, weil der Turcke herzu graset, das doch die pfarrher hetten ein gewis zeugnis dem volck fur zu predigen den grewel des Mahmets. … Christo zu ehren, den Christen zu gut, den Turcken zu schaden, dem teuffel zu verdries, bis buch lassen frey gehen und nicht hindern.'
43 WA Br 10:163.75–78: 'Und wenn die heiligen veter der ketzer bucher nicht hetten offentlich zu lesen bekomen, wie wolten sie yhrer heymlichen gisst … begegnet haben und die kirchen da fur gewarnet und geschutzt haben?'
44 Hagenbach, 'Rathe zu Basel', 291–326.
45 *Vorrede*, WA 53:572.13–14 (H-B, 263).
46 WA Br 10:162.32–39: 'Mich hat das bewogen, das man dem Mahmet oder Turcken nichts verdrieslichers thun, noch mehr schaden zu fugen kan (mehr denn mit alien wassen), denn das man yhren alcoran bey den Christen an den tag bringe, darinnen sie sehen mugen, wie gar ein verflucht, schendlich, verzweivelt buch es sey, voller lugen, fabeln und aller grewel, welche die Turcken bergen und schmucken und zu warzeichen ungern sehen, das man den alcoran ynn andere sprache verdolmetscht. Denn sie fulen wol, das yhnen grossen abfal bringet bey alien vernunfftigen hertzen.'
47 WA Br 10:162.54–59: 'Wir haben aber ewr drucker wollen hierin zu helffen brauchen wider solchen teuffels apostol und lere des schendlichen Mahmets, ob Gott wolt zu letzt gnade geben, das die lesterliche verfurung mocht gemindert und nicht allein wir Christen wider solche gisstige lere gewapent und verwaret, sondern auch ettliche Turcken selbs bekeret werden mochten.'
48 Wolf, 'Luther and Mohammedanism', 165.
49 Fischer-Galati, 'Reformation and Islam', 55.
50 Hagemann, *Luther und der Islam*, 16.
51 Wolf, 'Luther and Mohammedanism', 165.
52 *CA*, WA 53:341.10: 'Ipsi autem Saraceni vocant eam denominatiue Elesalem.' Originally, Riccoldo used the term 'din ellessalem' or *dīn al-Islām* (*CIS*, 10.12).
53 *Verlegung*, WA 53:342.2.
54 *Verlegung*, WA 53:310.10–11; This is a verbatim transcription from *CA*, WA 53:307–33 (cf. *CIS*, 7.47).

55 For example, *Der Achte Psalm Davids,* WA 40/2:227.8–12 (LW 12:115); *Von den Juden und ihren Lügen,* WA 53:485.7–9 (LW 47:220).

56 For example, see his brief comments on Mehmet and Selim in *Verlegung,* WA 53:272.24–26; *In Genesin Enarrationum,* WA 44:656.23–25 (LW 8:106).

57 *Tractatus,* 156.

58 *Verlegung,* WA 53:276.

59 *Auslegung des ersten und zweiten Kapitels Johannis,* WA 46:593.38–594.1 (LW 22:67).

60 *Verlegung,* WA 53:354.5–16: 'Heraclius der Persen könig Cosroe geschlagen und das heilige Creutz gen Jerusalem bracht hatte, mit grossem Triumph, anno sechs hundert und zwentzig nach Christi geburt, Und anno funffzehen Heraclij etc, Da brach herfur Mahmet ein Araber, der nu reich worden war, durch eine Widwen, die er gefreiet hatte, Darnach ward er ein Heubtman unter den strassen reubern und kam in solche hoffart, das er König in Arabia zu werden gedacht. Aber weil er eins geringen herkomens und ansehens war, namen sie jn nicht an. Da gab er sich fur einen Propheten aus, Und nach dem er das Falubel, oder die fallende seuche hatte, und stets darnider siel ... sprach er, Ein Engel hette mit jm geredt. Und sagt darnach etliche Sprüche, welche er hette gehort (wie er sagt) wie eine Glocke, die umb seine ohren geklungen hette.'

61 See especially *Verlegung,* WA 53:354.17–360.2.

62 *Tractatus,* 156; *Vom Mißbrauch der Messen,* WA 8:561.36–562.10 (LW 36:228).

63 *Verlegung,* WA 53:360.7–10, 346.1–15.

64 *Tractatus,* 274–84, 356; cf. Palmer, 'Fr. Georgius', 57.

65 *Von den Konziliis und Kirchen,* WA 50:579.1–3 (LW 41:91); *Verlegung,* WA 53:272.21–26.

66 *An Kurfürsten zu Sachen,* WA 54:404.10–12 (LW 43:278).

67 *Vom kriege,* WA 30/2:127.19–21 (LW 46:182).

68 *Reihenpredigten über Johannes,* WA 46:58.18–22, 60.34 (LW 22:330, 333).

69 See, for example, *Vorwort,* WA 30/2:207.3–4.

70 *In Genesin Enarrationum,* WA 44:320.37–321.1 (LW 7:26).

71 *Verlegung,* WA 53:325.30–34. For the base text see *CA,* WA 53:327.18–23.

72 *Vom kriege,* WA 30/2:126.26–28 (LW 46:181).

73 *Verlegung,* WA 53:320.26–322.6: 'Ein Sarracen mag sein Weib verstoffen und wider an nemen, so offt es jm geliebet, doch so fern, das er die, zum dritten mal verstoffen, nicht mus wider an nemen. Es were denn, das sie der ander Man nicht recht oder volkomen beschlaffen hette. Darumb wenn sie jre Weiber gern wider hetten, so geben sie geld dem, der die verstossen zu sich genomen hat (der zu weilen ein Blinder oder sonst geringe person ist), das er sole öffentlich sich lassen hören, Er wölle sich von jr scheiden. Wenn das geschehen ist, so kan sie der erste wider zu sich nemen. Es geschicht aber auch wol, das der selb ander man der frawen so wol gefelt, das er darnach spricht, Er könne sich nicht von jr scheiden. So hat denn jener beide, geld, Braut und hoffnung verloren. Aber solch Gesetze solt man nich Menschen, sondern unvernünfftigen thieren stellen.'

74 *Das fünffte, Sechste und Siebend Capitel S. Matthei,* WA 32:378.7–9 (LW 21:94–95).

75 WA TR 5:221.4–5: 'Personalia, quae dicunt de Mahomet, me non movent, aber die lehre der Turcken mussen wir angreiffen.' This was Luther's chief concern with all his theological opponents. In fact, he considered it his calling. For example, he told his colleagues and students, 'Doctrine and life must be distinguished. ... This is my calling. Others have censured only life, but to treat doctrine is to strike at the most sensitive point. ... When the Word remains pure, then the life (even if there is something lacking in it) can be molded properly. Everything depends on the Word' (WA TR 1:294.19–295–3, [LW 54:110]).

76 *Commentarius in Epistolam ad Gaiatas,* WA 40/2:46.17–19 (LW 27:37). Continuing, he added, 'Doctrine belongs to God, not to us; and we are called only as its ministers. Therefore we cannot give up or change even one dot of it (Matt. 5:18). ... For doctrine is like a mathematical point. Therefore it cannot be divided; that is, it cannot stand either subtraction or addition' (46.19–27).

77 *Disputado Heidelbergae habita,* WA 1:362.18–19. Thus, Otto Zöckler's thesis on the basis of Luther's apologetics, 'Die beste materielie Basis für alle Apologie des Christentums ist in diesem Satze zum Ausdruck gebracht: Jesus Christus allein befriedigt das Heilsbedürfnis und zugleich auch das Wahrheitsbedürfnis des Menschen' (*Geschichte der Apologie des Christentums* [Gütersloh: G. Bertelsmann, 1907], 309–10).

78 *Heerpredigt*, WA 30/2:186.15–16.
79 A year later he summarised what Islam expressly rejected of basic orthodox Christianity. 'Mahometh enim negat Christum esse filium Dei, Negat ipsum mortuum pro nostris peccatis, Negat ipsum resurrexisse ad vitam nostram, negat Fide in ilium remitti peccata et nos iustificari, Negat ipsum iudicem venturum super vivos et mortuos, licet resurrectionem mortuorum et diem iudicij credat, Negat Spiritum sanctum, Negat eius dona' (*Vorwort*, WA 30/2:207.40–208.2).
80 *Vom kriege*, WA 30/2:122.26–28 (LW 46:176–77, 181).
81 This is from Q 43:61 and two *ḥadīths*. See Al-Bukhārī, *Saḥiḥ al-Bukhārī*, trans. Muḥammad Khan (Chicago: Kazi Publications, 1979), 3:233–34 (no. 425), 4:436–37 (no. 657).
82 *Verlegung*, WA 53:280.27. Cf. Q 4:157.
83 See *Verlegung*, WA 53:280. 'Mahometus hanc victimam et placationem ridet', he wrote in his preface to the Qur'ān (*Vorrede*, WA 53:572.3–4).
84 Translation modified.
85 *Verlegung*, WA 53:280.
86 *Verlegung*, WA 53:334.24–35: 'Von Gott leuget er sicher daher wider das Euangelium ... Das ummüglich sey Gott, einen Son zu haben, denn er hat kern Weib, Und solchs zeucht er jmer an, als sey es ein fester köstlicher grund. Aber solche klugheit ist eben, als wenn ich spreche: "Gott kan nicht leben, denn er isst und trincket nicht, kacket und pisset nicht, rotzet und hustet nicht." Die Christen wissen wol, wie Gott einen Son haben kan, und ist nicht not, das Mahmet uns lere, wie Gott müste zuvor ein Man sein, der ein Weib hette, einen Son zu zeugen, oder ein Farre, der eine Kue hette, ein Kalb zu zeugen, Wie ist der Mahmet in dem Frawen fleisch ersoffen, in alien seinen gedancken, worten, werken, kan fur solcher brunst nichts reden noch thun, es mus alies fleisch, fleisch, fleisch sein.' The charge that Muḥammad was infatuated with sex was based on a *ḥadīth* (Al-Bukhārī, *Saḥiḥ al-Bukhari*, 1:165 [no. 268]), which Riccoldo reproduced in the *CA* (WA 53:313.20–22; cf. *Verlegung*, WA 53:316.20–24). Luther added in the margin, initialising it 'M.L.' as if to somehow say that he really believed it, 'Weib ist Mahmets Got, Hertz und ewiges Leben.' He reiterated this charge, insulting the prophet further, in *Von den letzten worten Davids*, WA 54:91.32–92.5 (LW 15:342–43). 'Neither did Muḥammad find it in his Bible, that is, in his bed of harlotry', he wrote, 'for that is where he did most of his studying. Thus this contemptible, filthy fellow boasts that God, that is, the Devil, had endowed him with so much physical strength that he could be with as many as 40 women and yet remain unsatisfied. Indeed, his choice book, the Qur'ān, smells and savours of his studies in that Bible, the carnality of harlots. He looked for and found the spirit of his prophecy in the right spot, that is, in the mons Veneris.'
87 For example, see Q 9:31.
88 *Verlegung*, WA 53:328.3–6: 'Von den Christen leuget er, das sie Gotte einen gesellen geben, Das ist eine offenberliche Lügen, Denn die Christen in der gantzen welt sagen, das Gott einig und unzerteilet sey, ja das nichts einigers ist, denn die Gotmeit oder Göttlich wesen.'
89 See, for example, *Verlegung*, WA 53:374.22–23.
90 See Q 85:22. Also see W. Montgomery Watt, *Bell's Introduction to the Qur'ān* (Edinburgh: Edinburgh University Press, 1970), 170–72.
91 *An den Christlichen Adel deutscher Nation*, WA 6:459.26 (LW 44:203).
92 Q 33:40.
93 *Tractatus*, 256.14–259.26: 'Communis opinio omnium fere Turcorum talis est de lege eorum: Dicunt enim primum prophetam magnum, cui data fuit lex primitus a deo, fuisse Missa, id est Moyses, cui datus est liber "tefrit", quem nos "penthateucum" uocamus; et omnem hominem, qui eo tempore ipsam legem obseruasset, saluatum esse. Cum autem per successum temporis humana malicia et negligentia hanc legem corrupisset, in huius preuaricationis remedium electus est secundus propheta magnus Daut, quem nos Dauid dicimus, cui datus est liber "czabur", quem nos "psalterium" uocamus. Quo prioris modo seruato et corrupto tercius quoque propheta magnus subiunctus est Yesse, id est, Ihesus, cui tercia lex cum libro "inglis", quem nos "euangelium" dicimus, missa est; que suis temporibus omnibus causa salutis fuit. Ea tandem precedentium modo euacuata quartus electus est Mechometus, qui legem cum libro, qui "alcoranus" dictus est.'
94 *CA*, WA 53:385.7–16: 'aD [*sic*] haec autem conantur respondere quidam superstitiosi et contentiosi saraceni dicentes: Non dicimus, quod euangelium non sit a deo, cum Alcoranum hoc manifeste testetur. Neque dicimus imperfectum esse, cum a deo sit: sed tam ardua et perfecta continet euangelium, ut non sufficiat mundus ea perficere. Quis enim deum ex toto corde et

proximum sicut seipsum potest diligere? Quis potest pro persequentibus et calumniantibus orare? ... Et alia quaedam perfectissima mandat euangelium. Quoniam igitur non erat lex, quae potuisset seruari, prouidit mundo deus per legem salutis et leuia fecit mandata et dedit mundo Alcoranum, quod minime continet difficilia haec, sed facile est ad saluandum homines per ipsum.'

95 *Vom kriege,* WA 30/2:122.8–9 (LW 46:176–77).

96 *Verlegung,* WA 53:302.13 (cf. 286.24), 326.18–19.

97 *Verlegung,* WA 53:284.7–9 (cf 286.30–31): 'Christus hab im Euangelio viel von jm geweissagt den Kindern Israel, da er spricht: "Ich verkündige euch einen Apostel Gottes, der nach mir kornen wird, der heisst Mahmet."'

98 *Reihenpredigten über Johannes,* WA 47:186.38–41 (LW 22:476).

99 *Commentarius in Epistolam ad Galatas,* WA 40/1:82.20–21, 562.13–20 (LW 26:32, 367–68).

100 On the distinction between the perpetual religion (*al-dīn*) of Islam from Adam forward and the abrogation of previous law (*sharī'a*), see Sayyid Maududi, *Towards Understanding Islam,* 22nd edn., trans. Khurshid Ahmad (Lahore: Idara Tarjuman-Ul-Quran, 1995), 142–43; Kenneth Cragg, *Jesus and the Muslim: An Exploration* (London: George Allen and Unwin, 1985), 17–74.

101 For example, 'The Turk swears by the Devil or Mohammed, whom he regards and worships as his god, the way we worship our Lord Christ and swear by Him' (*Das fünffte, Sechste und Siebend Capitel S. Matthei,* WA 32:384.38–385.2 [LW 21:102]).

102 *Von den letzten worten Davids,* WA 54:68.8–13 (LW 15:314).

103 *Vorrede auf die Propheten,* WA DB 11/1:3.15 (LW 35:271).

104 *Vom kriege,* WA 30/2:128.128.10–11 (LW 46:183).

105 *Vom kriege,* WA 30/2:128.8–11 (LW 46:183). Luther suggested Hebrew origins for several other Arabic terms as well. For example, in his exegesis of Genesis 42:6, where Joseph became governor over all of Egypt subject only to the Pharaoh, he noted a consonantal parallel between the Hebrew root for governor (שלט) and the term 'sultan' (*In Genesin Enarrationum,* WA 44:464.29–38 [LW 7:223]; cf. *Von den Juden und ihren Lügen,* WA 53:452.8–16 [LW 47:180]). For his conjecture on the invention of the term Turk by the Jews, see WA TR 2:533.25–26.

106 At least five articles have been written on the subject: E. Christian Kopff, 'Who Believes in and Worships the One True God in Luther's Large Catechism', *Logia* 13 (2003), 55–57; Charles Arand and James Voelz, 'Large Catechism, III, 66', *CJ* 29:3 (2003), 232–34; Thomas Manteufel, 'What Luther Meant', *CJ* 29:4 (2003), 366–69; and, most recently, Edward Engelbrecht, *One True God: Understanding Large Catechism II 66* (St. Louis: CPH, 2007).

107 *Der Großer Katechismus,* BELK, 661.66.5–18: 'Denn was außer der Christenheit ist, es seien Heiden, Türken, Jüden, oder falsche Christen und Heuchler, ob sie gleich nur einen wahrhaftigen Gott gläuben und anbeten, so wissen sie doch nicht, was er gegen ihn gesinnet ist, können sich auch keiner Liebe noch Guts zu ihm versehen.'

108 Especially in light of his conclusion: 'Therefore they remain in eternal wrath and damnation, for they do not have the Lord Christ, and, besides, they are not illuminated and blessed by the gifts of the Holy Spirit.'

109 Theodore Tappert (ed.), *The Book of Concord* (Philadelphia: Fortress, 1959), 419; Robert Kolb and Timothy Wengert (eds.), *The Book of Concord* (Philadelphia: Fortress, 2000), 440. Emphasis added.

110 *A fortiori,* Vincent Obsopoeus, a humanist scholar, immediately translated Luther's German into Latin rendering the disputed clause: 'quamquam unum tantum et verum Deum esse credant et invocent' (*Der Großer Katechismus,* BELK, 661.66.5–20).

111 *Von den letzten worten Davids,* WA 54:68.7–20 (LW 15:315).

112 *Enarratio Psalmi II,* WA 40/2:301.13–19 (LW 12:84).

113 *Verlegung,* WA 53:286.5–8: 'Und ob wol der Alkoran sagt: "Jr. solt nicht drey Götter nennen, Ursach: Es ist ein Gott", das ist nicht wider uns und beweiset nichts. Denn wir sagen selbs, ja die Heiden auch, das allein ein Gott sey, dazu also einig und unzerteilich, das nichts einigers sein könne.'

114 *Vom kriege,* WA 30/2:128.13–15 (LW 46:183).

115 *Tractatus,* 254.27–28, 29–30.

116 *Verlegung,* WA 53:318.11–20: 'Man sprechen solle allenthalben diese wort: "Es ist kein Gott, denn Gott, Und Mahmet ist Gottes Apostel", Und das Gott gros ist. Was ist das fur sonderlich gros ding, als were hierin etwa ein zweivel oder seltzam new lere? Wer weis nicht, das Gott

Gott ist, und das er gros ist, Wer hat je gehort, das Gott nicht Gott ist, oder das er Mein sey. … Es laut eben, als wenn einer spreche: "Es ist kein Esel, den ein Esel", "Est ist kein kue [*sic*], denn eine Kue", "Es ist kein Mensch, denn ein Mensch." Man weis wol, das ein Ochs oder Hund kein Esel ist, auch Mensch oder Engel nicht Gott ist. Narren und Wansinnige mügen so reden.'

117 Interestingly, there are parallels between Luther's theological theocentrism and Islam's. Cf. Jan Slomp, 'Christianity and Lutheranism from the Perspective of Modern Islam', in Hans Medick and Peer Schmidt (eds.), *Luther Zwischen den Kulturen* (Göttingen: Vandernhoeck and Ruprecht, 2004), 293; Philip Watson, *Let God Be God: An Interpretation of the Theology of Martin Luther* (Philadelphia: Fortress Press, 1966).

118 *Vermahnung,* WA 51:614.34–615.31 (LW 43:235–36).

119 *Vorrede,* WA 53:572.4–7 (H–B, 266).

120 See *In Genesin Enarrationum,* WA 43:581.28–35; *Predigt am Weihnachtstag, nachmittags,* WA 49:632.33–633.37.

121 *Das fünffte, Sechste und Siebend Capitel S. Matthei,* WA 32:500.25–37 (LW 21:242).

122 *Predigt am Weihnachtstag,* WA 49:63213.33–35: 'Jch gleubs, das der Teuffel uber dem Artickel den fall gethan, wie im Alckoran geschrieben, Das der Teuffel bekent durch den Mahometh.'

123 Luther is very inconsistent on this point. In some places he suggests that Muḥammad *wrote* the Qur'ān even though he knew that it was recorded after Muḥammad's death.

124 *Verlegung,* WA 53:284.27–28.

125 *In Genesin Enarrationum,* WA 43:668.1–3 (LW 5:347).

126 *Verlegung,* WA 53:340.19–20, 380.11–12.

127 *Verlegung,* WA 53:292.32–33: 'Gesetz von Gott dem Mahmet offenbart'; 348.4–5: 'Und das sol beweisen, das Mahmet ein rechter Prophet sey.' It is not clear whether Luther knew Muḥammad was illiterate (or, really, unlettered), which, in Islamic thought, strengthens the grounds for the argument of Muḥammad's legitimate prophethood on the basis of the beauty and inimitability of the Qur'ānic text.

128 *Vorwort,* WA 30/2:205.12–13; *Verlegung,* WA 53:326.10–11.

129 *In Genesin Enarrationum,* WA WA 44:743.24–26 (8:225); *Reihenpredigten über Johannes,* WA 45:524.1–5 (LW 24:69).

130 *Verlegung,* WA 53:354.25–26: 'Stellet Mahmet etwas, als ein Gesetze, durch seine gesellen, Nam etwas aus dem alten, etwas aus dem newen Testament' Even though it borrowed from the Bible, Luther wrote, 'it leaves almost nothing of the Christian truth remaining' (*Vom kriege,* WA 30/2:126.10–12 [LW 46:181]).

131 *Verlegung,* WA 53:352.15–16: 'Der erst Meister des Alcoran sey nicht ein Mensch, sondern der Teufel.' Cf. *Vom kriege,* WA 30/2:121.26–29 (LW 46:179).

132 *Verlegung,* WA 53:276.34–278.1: 'Ein Gesetz lassen ausgehen … als were es aus dem Munde Gottes gesprochen, dasselbe hat er genennet Alcoran, das ist ein Summa oder versamlung, nemlich der Göttlichen Gebot' (cf. 358.23–360.2).

133 *Verlegung,* WA 53:360.3–20.

134 'Strictly speaking, קרא means *ruffen, nennen,* "to call," "to name," "to read from a book," "to preach." Sometimes it also means "to meet." Moreover, I believe that this is why Muḥammad titled his book the Alcoran; for it is a compilation, or a textbook or his Bible, as the pope calls his decretals. Here, therefore, we take this word to mean "to teach," or "to read in a public assembly"' (*Lectures on Genesis,* LW 5:79). EI^2 5:400 notes that *qara'a* is probably derived from the Syriac word (*qeryana*) used in early Christian liturgies to denote a 'Scripture reading, lesson.'

135 *Verlegung,* WA 53:358.12.

136 *Verlegung,* WA 53:286.27. This will be dealt with in chapter 7.

137 On the Qur'ān's abrogation of former books, see Farid Esack, *The Qur'ān: A Short Introduction* (Oxford: Oneworld, 2002), 49–50; Hava Lazarus-Yafeh, *Intertwined Worlds: Medieval Islam and Bible Criticism* (Princeton: Princeton University Press, 1992), 37–41.

138 *Verlegung,* WA 53:286.25–26, 30–31; 334–3–5; 372; 12–374.12.

139 Muslim thought itself is diverse on this. See Abdullah Saeed, 'The Charge of Distortion of Jewish and Christian Scriptures', *MW* 92 (2002), 419–36.

140 *Verlegung,* WA 53:358: 'Die Türcken wissen nicht, wo der Alcoran herkome.'

141 *Verlegung,* WA 53:360.23–364.3. Merigoux notes that these were taken almost verbatim from *Liber denudationis* (*CIS,* 122n1).

142 *Tractatus*, 254.27–30: 'Deus est unus, et Mechometus est propheta eius maior.'
143 *Verlegung*, WA 53:300.1–2: 'Es ist kein Gott denn Gott, und Mahmet ist Gottes Apostel.' Cf. *CA*, WA 53:299.24; *CIS*, 81.28–29.
144 *Vorwort*, WA 30/2:206.6–8, 207.28–30 (H-B, 259).
145 See Miller, 'Luther on the Turks', 79. Cf. Michael Heath, 'Erasmus and War against the Turk', in Jean-Claude Margolin (ed.), *Acta Conventus Neo-latini Turonensis*, vol. 2 (Paris: Vrin, 1980), 994; Katya Vehlow, 'The Swiss Reformers Zwingli, Bullinger, and Bibliander and their Attitude to Islam (1520–60)', *ICMR* 6:2 (1995), 236; Jan Slomp, 'Calvin and the Turks', in Yvonne Haddad and Wadi Haddad (eds.), *Christian-Muslim Encounters* (Florida: University Press of Florida, 1995), 132; Fischer-Galati, 'Reformation and Islam', 56–58; Williams, *'Salus extra Ecclesia'*, 351.
146 WA Br 5:285.7–10: 'Ego incipio totis animi affectibus in Turcam et Mahometum commoveri ...'

Bibliography

Primary Sources: Martin Luther

Die Bekenntnisschriften der evangelisch-lutherischen Kirchen, ed. Hans Lietzmann, Heinrich Bornkamm, Hans Volz, and Ernst Wolf (Göttingen: Vandenhoeck and Ruprecht, 1952). [BELK]

D. Martin Luthers Werke, 69 vols (Weimar: Böhlau, 1883–2001). [WA]

D. Martin Luthers Werke: Briefwechsel, 18 vols (Weimar: Böhlau, 1930–1985). [WA BC]

D. Martin Luthers Werke: Deutsche Bibel, 12 vols (Weimar: Böhlau, 1906–1961). [WA DB]

D. Martin Luthers Werke: Tischreden, 6 vols (Weimar: Böhlau, 1912–1921). [WA TR]

Luther's Works, 55 vols (St. Louis: Concordia Publishing House and Philadelphia: Fortress Press, 1955–1986). [LW]

Primary Sources: Medieval and Early Modern

Apel, Dean, 'Luther's Approach to Islam: Ingemar Oberg's Search for Mission Praxis in the Weimar Edition of Luther's Works', CT&M 26:6 (1999), 439–450.

Arand, Charles and James Voelz, 'Large Catechism, III, 66', *CJ* 29:3 (2003), 232–234.

Barge, Hermann, 'Luthers Stellung zum Islam und Seine Ubersetzung der Confutatio des Ricoldus', *AM* 43:2/3 (1916), 79–82, 108–121.

Beltz, Walter, 'Luthers Verständnis von Islam und Koran', *WZGSR* 32:5 (1983), 85–91.

Bobzin, Hartmut, *Der Koran im Zeitalter der Reformation: Studien zur Fruhgeschichte der Arabistik und Islamkunde in Europa* (Stuttgart: Steiner Verlag, 1995).

——, 'Latin Translations of the Koran: A Short Overview', *Is* 70 (1993), 193–206.

——, 'Zur Anzahl der Drucke von Biblianders Koranausgabe im Jahr 1543', *BZGA* 85 (1985), 213–219.

Boyd, E.I.M., 'Ricoldus: A Dominican Missionary to Moslems in the Thirteenth Century', *MW* 8 (1918), 45–51.

Georgius de Hungaria, *Tractatus de Moribus, Condictionibus et Nequicia Turcorum-Traktat über die Sitten, die Lebensverhältnisse und die Arglist der Türken (1481)*, ed. and trans. Reinhard Klockow (Köln: Böhlau, 1993).

Secondary Sources

Al-Bukhārī, Muḥammad ibn Ismā'il, *Soḥiḥ al-Bukhārī*, trans. Muḥammad Khan, 9 vols (Chicago: Kazi Publications, 1979).

Burman, Thomas, 'Tafsīr and Translation: Traditional Arabic Qur'ān Exegesis and the Latin Qur'āns of Robert of Ketton and Mark of Toledo', *Speculum 73 (1998), 703–732.*

Choi, David, 'Martin Luther's Response to the Turkish Threat: Continuity and Contrast with the Medieval Commentators Riccoldo da Monte Croce and Nicholas of Cusa' (PhD Dissertation: Princeton Theological Seminary, 2003).

Cragg, Kenneth, *Jesus and the Muslim: An Exploration* (London: George Allen and Unwin, 1985).

Dondaine, Antoine, 'Ricoldiana: Notes sur les oeuvres de Ricoldo da Montecroce', *AFP* 37 (1967), 119–179.

Encyclopaedia of Islam, 2nd edn (Leiden: E.J. Brill, 1960–). [EI^2]

Engelbrecht, Edward, *One True God: Understanding Large Catechism II 66* (St. Louis: Concordia Publishing House, 2007).

Esack, Farid, *The Qur'an: A Short Introduction* (Oxford: Oneworld, 2002).

Fischer-Galati, Stephen, 'The Protestant Reformation and Islam, in Abraham Ascher, Tibor Halasi-Kun, and Béla Kiraly (eds), *The Mutual Effects of the Islamic and Judeo-Christian Worlds: The East European Pattern* (New York: Brooklyn College Press, 1979), 53–64.

Grant, Edward, *God and Reason in the Middle Ages* (Cambridge: Cambridge University Press, 2001).

Grislis, Egil, 'Luther and the Turks', *MW* 64 (1974), 180–193, 275–291.

Hagemann, Ludwig, *Martin Luther und der Islam,* 2nd edn (Altenberge: Christliche Islamisches Schrifttum, 1998).

Hagenbach, Karl, 'Luther und der Koran vor dem Rathe zu Basel', *BVG* 9 (1870), 291–326.

Haleem, Harfiyah et al. (eds), *The Crescent and the Cross: Muslim and Christian Approaches to War und Peace* (London: Macmillan Press, 1998).

Heath, Michael, 'Erasmus and War against the Turk', in Jean-Claude Margolin (ed.), *Acta Conventus Neo-latini Turonensis,* vol. 2 (Paris: Vrin, 1980), 991–999.

Kopff, E. Christian, 'Who Believes in and Worships the One True God in Luther's Large Catechism', *Logia* 13 (2003), 55–57.

Kusukawa, Sachiko, *A Wittenberg University Library Catalogue of 1536* (Cambridge: LP Publications, 1995).

Lazarus-Yafeh, Hava, *Intertwined Worlds: Medieval Islam and Bible Criticism* (Princeton: Princeton University Press, 1992).

Lewis, Bernard, *Islam and the West* (Oxford: Oxford University Press, 1993).

Manteufel, Thomas, 'What Luther Meant', *CJ* 29:4 (2003), 366–369.

Maududi, Sayyid, *Towards Understanding Islam,* 22nd edn, trans. Khurshid Ahmad (Lahore: Idara Tarjuman-Ul-Quran Ltd, 1995).

Mérigoux, Jean-Marie, 'L'ouvrage d'un frère prêcheur florentin en Orient à la fin du XIIIe siècle. Le *Contra legem Sarracenorum* de Riccoldo da Monte di Croce', *MD* 15 (1986), 1–59.

Miller, Gregory, 'Luther on the Turks and Islam', *LQ* 14 (2000), 79–97.

Palmer, J.A.B., 'Fr. Georgius de Hungaria, O.P., and the *Tractatus de moribus, condictionibus et nequicia turcorum', BJRL* 34 (1951/52), 44–68.

Rajashekar, J. Paul, 'Luther and Islam: An Asian Perspective', *LuJ* 57 (1990), 174–191.

Rupp, Gordon, 'Luther against "The Pope, the Turk, and the Devil"', in Peter Brooks (ed.), *Seven-Headed Luther: Essays in Commemoration of a Quincentenary, 1483–1983* (Oxford: Clarendon Press, 1983), 256–273.

Saeed, Abdullah, 'The Charge of Distortion of Jewish and Christian Scriptures', *MW* 92 (2002), 419–436.

Simon, G. 'Luther's Attitude toward Islam', *MW* 21 (1931), 257–262.

Slomp, Jan, 'Christianity and Lutheranism from the Perspective of Modern Islam', in Hans Medick and Peer Schmidt (eds), *Luther Zwischen den Kulturen* (Göttingen: Vandernhoeck and Ruprecht, 2004), 277–296.

——, 'Calvin and the Turks', in Yvonne Haddad and Wadi Haddad (eds), *Christian-Muslim Encounters* (Florida: University Press of Florida, 1995), 126–142.

Smith, Henry Preserved, 'Luther and Islam', *AJSLL* 39:3 (1923), 218–220.

Vehlow, Katya, 'The Swiss Reformers Zwingli, Bullinger, and Bibliander and their Attitude to Islam (1520–1560)', *ICMR* 6:2 (1995), 229–254.

Watson, Philip, *Let God Be God: An Interpretation of the Theology of Martin Luther* (Philadelphia: Fortress Press, 1966).

Watt, W. Montgomery, *Bell's Introduction to the Qur'ān* (Edinburgh: Edinburgh University Press, 1970).

Williams, George, 'Erasmus and the Reformers on Non-Christian Religions and *Salus Extra Ecclesia'*, in Theodore Rabb and Jerrold Seigel (eds), *Action and Conviction in Early Modern Europe* (Princeton: Princeton University Press, 1969), 319–370.

Wolf, C. Umhau, 'Luther and Mohammedanism', *MW* 31 (1941), 161–177.

11 Extracts from *The Disintegration of Islam*

Samuel M. Zwemer

Preface

> From heaven fought the stars,
> From their courses they fought against Sisera.
> That river Kishon swept them away,
> The ancient river, the river Kishon.
> O my soul, march on with strength.
>
> —The Song of Deborah.—Judges 5:20–22

Like all other non-Christian systems and philosophies Islam is a dying religion; from the outset it had in it the germs of death—neither the character of the Koran nor of its Prophet have in them the promise or potency of life that will endure. Even Carlyle, whose "The Hero as Prophet" is often quoted as an apology for Islam, admitted this. In his lecture on "The Hero as Poet" he said: "It was intrinsically an error that notion of Mahomet's, of his supreme Prophethood; and has come down to us inextricably involved in error to this day; dragging along with it such a coil of fables, iniquities, intolerances, as makes it a questionable step for me here and now to say, as I have done, that Mahomet was a true Speaker at all, and not rather an ambitious charlatan, perversity and simulacrum; no Speaker, but a Babbler! Even in Arabia, as I compute, Mahomet will have exhausted himself and become obsolete, while this Shakspeare, this Dante may still be young. … His Koran has become a stupid piece of prolix absurdity; we do not believe, like him, that God wrote that!"

Moreover, at the present time there are in Islam many evidences of decay. In 1899, a company of delegates from the Moslem world assembled in Mecca and gave fourteen days to investigate the causes for the decay of Islam. Fifty-seven reasons were given, including fatalism, the opposition of science, the rejection of religious liberty, neglect of education and inactivity due to the hopelessness of the cause itself. A leading Moslem editor in India wrote in 1914:—"We see that neither wealth nor 'education' nor political power can enable the Muslims to achieve their national salvation. Where then lies the remedy? Before seeking the remedy we must ascertain the disease. But the Muslims are not diseased, they have reached a worse stage. A diseased man has still life in him."

We find the same note of despair in the recent volume of essays by an educated Indian Moslem, S. Khuda Bukhsh, M.A. He speaks of the "hideous deformity" of Moslem society and of "the vice and immorality, the selfishness, self-seeking, and hypocrisy which are corrupting it through and through." Those who live among Moslems and read Moslem newspapers and books are more and more surprised that Islam itself is not conscious of its strength but of its weakness and decay, and that everywhere Moslems are bemoaning a day of opportunity that is lost. The Moslem pulpit and the Moslem press in the great centres of Islam unite in a wail of despair. "O ye servants of God," said a Cairo preacher last year, "the time has come for Moslems to look after their affairs and to regard their religion and conduct as a sick man looks toward his remedy and the man who is drowning toward dry land."

Moslems have long realized that the dead weight of formality called tradition, the accumulation of many centuries, is an intolerable burden. Frantic efforts have been made in many quarters to save the ship by throwing overboard much of this cargo. Others in their despair have sought for a new pilot. Messiahs and Mahdis have arisen and founded new sects or started new movements. The progress of western civilization and its impact has been felt everywhere in the economic and social life of Islam. We must add to all this the utter collapse of Moslem political power in Africa, Europe, and Asia. The stars from their courses are fighting against Sisera, and the future is dark for those who believe that Islam is the hope of the world. We, however, believe that when the crescent wanes the Cross will prove dominant, and that the disintegration of Islam is a divine preparation for the evangelization of Moslem lands and the winning of Moslem hearts to a new allegiance. Jesus Christ is sufficient for them as He is for us. "When that which is perfect is come, that which is in part shall be done away."

The purpose of the lectures here given is distinctly missionary, and in setting forth the present-day conditions and needs of these millions, many of whom are groping toward the light, our prayer is that the message may lead to the surrender of life for the work of missions. From all the seminaries where these lectures were given a number of graduates have already gone to the forefront of the battle in the Moslem world, in Syria, Persia, India, Arabia, Egypt, North Africa, and China. Their unfinished task awaits fulfilment.

The Dead Weight of Tradition

This same description would apply to a dozen and more other leading schools at Fez and Kairwan, at Bagdad and Bokhara, and to Islam as it is taught in China. Intellectual stagnation is a natural consequence. Nothing so effectually destroys the spirit of criticism and prevents progress in education as traditionalism. Two of the leading papers in Egypt ascribed the backwardness of Islam and its political downfall solely to the abandonment of the Koran and tradition. *Al Moayyad* (September 7, 1911) had a long article under the heading, "Only by the Book and the Traditions of the Prophet can we be guided and can we secure Happiness and Development."—"The Moslems once were the highest of the nations and the most progressive of peoples when they held fast to the glorious Book and the traditions; but now when the devil has plunged them into ignorance they have abandoned the Koran and made themselves despised and rejected of men. *Islam will never progress except by following the traditions of the Prophet even as it has never retrograded except by abandoning them.*"

Not only does tradition lay its dead hand on education, but it fixes forever ethical standards for Islam: standards which are mediaeval, Arabian, and therefore local; and worst of all, standards which cannot rise higher than the character of Mohammed and his Companions. Mr. R. Bosworth Smith, who wrote the most able apology for Islam in his "Life of Mohammed," confesses that "The religion of Christ contains whole fields of morality and whole realms of thought which are all but outside the religion of Mohammed. It opens humility, purity of heart, forgiveness of injuries, sacrifice of self to man's moral nature; it gives scope for toleration, development, boundless progress to his mind; its motive power is stronger, even as a friend is better than a king and love higher than obedience. Its realized ideals in the various paths of human greatness have been more commanding, more many-sided, more holy, as Averroes is below Newton, Haroun below Alfred, and 'Ali below St. Paul. Finally, the ideal life of all is far more elevating, far more majestic, far more inspiring even as the life of the founder of Mohammedanism is below the life of the Founder of Christianity.

"And when I speak of the ideal life of Mohammedanism I must not be misunderstood. There is in Mohammedanism no ideal life in the true sense of the word, for Mohammed's character was admitted by himself to be a weak and erring one. It was disfigured by at least one huge moral blemish; and exactly in so far as his life has, in spite of his earnest and reiterated protestations, been made an example to be followed, has that vice been perpetuated."

Mohammed had more than one "huge moral blemish," and yet his transgression of the letter and spirit of the seventh commandment is a sufficient illustration of the subject before us. Now, it is passing strange that orthodox tradition lays stress even on this side of the Prophet's life as proof of his superiority over other mortals, with the result that Moslem ethics have steadily deteriorated. The proof is evident in their literature. A few portions of tradition that deal with this matter—and one could compile bulky volumes on the subject—have recently been reprinted in Paris under the title "Théologie Musulmane."[1] The publishers, however, were not Orientalists or students of comparative religion. These traditions appeared in a series of prurient literature for popular sale on the boulevards to the demi-monde!

Again, because of traditionalism and its authority there is no real distinction in popular Islam between the ceremonial and moral law; the former is always emphasized to the detriment of the latter. A hundred illustrations might be given at random from Bokhari, or even from the Moslem press of today. Islam of the orthodox type is Phariseeism translated into Arabic. Sheikh Jasim, my friend in Arabia, with whom I had dealings for many years, was so astounded when he first read the words of Christ in the Sermon on the Mount and in the 23rd chapter of Matthew that he said, "This book was gotten up and printed by the missionaries as an attack on the manners and morals of Moslem mullahs." Every Moslem recognizes the portrait of the Pharisee in the Gospel and knows many such who are walking the streets of his native town. Some of the questions asked in *Al Manar* today indicate how they still tithe anise and cummin and forget the weightier matters of the law. The following topics were seriously discussed during the past year:

Is it allowed to read Bokhari during war time in order to receive victory through its perusal?
If a child uses its grandmother as a wet nurse, must the mother be divorced?
Are the articles written in opposition to divorce not an indictment of Mohammed and his religion?
Is it permitted to use tinctures in hospitals, since they contain wine?
Is wine unclean in itself, that is, to the outer touch or smell, if one does not drink it?
Is it forbidden by our traditions to listen to concert singers?
Is it permitted that women should learn writing?
Was the law of Mohammed created before all things? (Answer: Yes.)
Is a woman forbidden to engage in prayer during her periods? (Answer: Yes, undoubtedly.)
Are the instructions given to a man in the grave as to what he should answer the two angels obligatory?

Mr. Goldsack in a recent article on "Popular Islam in Bengal," points out how the distinction between greater and lesser sins has opened the door for every kind of hypocrisy and deceit. As long as a Moslem avoids those sins which are considered great, namely, the rejection of the Divine Unity, wasting the substance of orphans, usury, etc., then, says Mr. Goldsack, "lust, deception, lying, etc., belong to the smaller faults which God is said to 'blot out.' Such an idea is repulsive. It is blasphemy. It misrepresents God. It degrades His character as holiness. Sin with the Moslem, then, cannot be very deep. We have all heard of things being only skin-deep. With most Moslems sin does not go even that far. I think I am correct in saying that most Moslems view sin as an external pollution which may be removed by ablutions of water or sand. Mohammed himself was not free from this idea, for he said, 'He sent down upon you water from heaven that He might thereby cleanse you and cause the pollution of Satan to pass from you.'"

Not only do Moslems, according to orthodox tradition, deny hereditary sin and make light of actual sin, but the fall of Adam is regarded not as a moral but as a physical fall from Paradise. To quote again from Mr. Goldsack:

> "The emphasis in the story of Eden is placed on the idea of a fall *from,* not *in* Paradise. That beautiful garden is supposed to have been situated above in heaven, and Adam is said to have fallen to earth and landed on Adam's peak in Ceylon, while Eve alighted at a place near Jiddah, where her tomb is still shown, 173 yards long by 12 feet broad. Adam is said to have been distressed, not because he had lost communion with his Maker, but because he could hear no more the sweet singing of the angels. In all this there is no sign of repentance as we know repentance; there is only regret. True, it is taught that Adam and Eve were the original parents of all men, and that they ate of the forbidden fruit, but that we all have derived from them a tendency to evil, Islam has no teaching. In fact, Adam's act of disobedience was a mere error and nothing more, although he is represented as having cried over his offence for two hundred years."

Finally, it is in Moslem tradition even more than in the Koran that we find the cause of intolerance, hatred, and fanaticism. There is no universal brotherhood in Islam. Nowhere in Moslem law is the infidel put on the same platform with the believer. His testimony in a Court of Justice is not equal to that of a Moslem. The penalty for personal violence on a Christian or infidel is lower than in the case of a believer, and according to Moslem law there is no death penalty for the murder of a Christian! This was illustrated in the trial at the famous case of Wardani, who murdered the Prime Minister of Egypt, Butras Pasha. We read in "Minhaj et Talibin," a Manual of Mohammedan Law according to the school of Shafii, pp. 398 and 399:

> "When one kills a Moslem in an enemy's country, under the belief that he is an infidel not subject to Moslem authority, one is liable neither to a penalty under the law of talion nor to payment of the price of blood."
>
> "To render applicable the law of talion it is legally necessary—
>
> "1. That the deceased was a Moslem, or an infidel enjoying our protection, on some ground or other. An infidel not subject to a Moslem ruler, and an apostate, are proscribed, and may be killed with impunity."
>
> "A Moslem cannot be put to death for killing an infidel, even though the latter may be the subject of a Moslem prince; but an infidel who kills a Moslem or an infidel is liable to the law of talion, even though the two infidels are not of the same religion, or the criminal embraces the faith after committing the crime."

One may judge of the legal position of apostates and of the character of Moslem law in general by this paragraph:

> "Apostasy consists in the abjuration of Islam, either mentally, or by words, or by acts incompatible with faith. As to oral abjuration, it matters little whether the words are said in joke, or through a spirit of contradiction, or in good faith ... an attempt should be made to induce the apostate to return from his or her errors; though, according to one authority, this is only a commendable proceeding. The exhortation should take place immediately, or according to one jurist, in the first three days; and if it is of no effect, the guilty man or woman should be put to death. Where, on the contrary, the guilty party returns from his or her errors, this conversion must be accepted as sincere, and the converted person left alone; unless, according to some authorities, he has embraced an occult religion, such as the Zend, whose adherents, while professing Islam, are none the less infidels in their heart, or some doctrine admitting of a mystic or allegorical interpretation of the Koran."

The hatred toward Christians and Jews is ready to show itself, as did the hatred of Mohammed the Prophet, on the least provocation. The present Armenian massacres, the attempts at holy war or *jihad,* in recent years are examples. A paper published at Bagdad called *Mesopotamia* openly incited Moslems to kill all Christians solely because they were Christians and Italy had made aggressive warfare upon Turkey in Tripoli. (22nd *Dhu'l-Hajj,* A. H. 1329.) Even in India this spirit is often evident. Early in June, 1914, a cinematograph company at Karachi exhibited a film which depicted an imaginary episode in the life of an Oriental prophet, his intrigues and wars. The film was called *Azim* and undoubtedly represented only an Oriental story; but the Moslems were straightway offended and imagined it was an attack on their Prophet and a blasphemous exhibition. Before I quote from the *Comrade* of June 30th, we must remember how Moslem hearts were stirred at this time by the seizure of a washhouse pertaining to a mosque at Cawnpore, and the publication of Dr. Mingana's New Koran Text at Cambridge. In view of all these untoward happenings the editor of the *Comrade* unburdened his soul as follows:

> "This, as we have said, was a master-stroke of genius, for if neither Tripoli nor the Balkans, neither Persia nor Morocco, neither Cawnpore nor Calcutta would provoke the Mussalmans, this latest plot at Karachi was bound to do it. Dr. Mingana's Quran can only be read by the literate, but Mr. Greenfield's latest *'Hadees'* concerning the prophet of Islam can be seen as a moving picture by all alike. Really this Mussalman fanatic knows how to arouse the religious passions and fanaticism of his co-religionists in spite of all the antidotes provided by the creator of the 'Indian Peril.' The Deputy Commissioner who suggests merely deportation is a very milk-and-water sort of District Officer. The least which this friend deserves is being hanged, drawn, and quartered and then flung into a cauldron of boiling pitch. If this sort of namby-pamby disposition continues to show itself in our District Magistrates when dealing with such wicked and vile plotters, we are afraid we shall have to send them to the Balkans to learn something of the art and science of making the punishment fit the crime."

Such is the spirit of intolerance on the part of the editor of the leading Moslem paper in English in India; what may we expect in less favoured lands or from the illiterate classes? No one can live among them without daily experiencing the effects of this religion in producing fanaticism and contempt toward everything non-Moslem. After sixteen years' experience in Arabia among this class of Mohammedans I can only endorse the famous and sober though severe indictment of Islam given by Schlegel in his philosophy of history: *"A prophet without miracles, a religion without mysteries, and a morality without love—which has always encouraged a thirst for blood and which has begun and ended in the most unbounded sensuality,"—because on it there rested the dead-weight of Tradition.*

Note

1 By Paul De Kegla. Published by Albin Michel.

Present-Day Attitude Toward Christ and Christianity[1]

> *The Son of his love; in whom we have our redemption, the forgiveness of our sins: who is the image of the invisible God, the first born of all creation; for in him were all things created, in the heavens and upon the earth, things visible and things invisible, whether thrones or dominions or principalities or powers; all things have been created through him and unto him; and he is before all things, and in him all things consist. And he is the head of the body, the church: who is the beginning, the firstborn from the dead; that in all things he might have the pre-eminence.*—COLOSSIANS 1: 13–18.

AS in a total eclipse of the sun the glory and the beauty of the heavenly orb are hidden, and only the corona appears on the edge, so in the life and thought of Mohammedans their own Prophet has almost eclipsed Jesus Christ. Whatever place He may occupy in the Koran—and the portrait there given is a sad caricature; whatever favourable critics may say about Christ's honourable place among the Moslem prophets, it is nevertheless true that the large bulk of Mohammedans know extremely little, and think still less, about Jesus Christ. He has no place in their hearts nor in their lives. All the prophets have not only been succeeded, but supplanted by Mohammed; he is at once the sealer and concealer of all former revelations. Mohammed is always in the foreground, and Jesus Christ, in spite of his lofty titles and the honour given him in the Koran, is in the background. There is not a single biography of Jesus Christ, alone and unique, as a great prophet of God, to be found in the literature of Islam. Christ is grouped with the other prophets; with Lot, Alexander the Great, Ishmael, Moses, Abraham, Adam.

I have shown in my book, "The Moslem Christ," the significance of Christ's names in the Koran, the account of His life, death, and translation, and also the fuller account, although caricatured, of His life and ministry, according to Moslem tradition. In all missionary effort for Mohammedans the one question that decides both the destiny of men and of nations ever remains, what think ye of the Christ?

In treating of the present-day attitude among Moslems toward Christ and Christianity, we have emphasized modern movements and the new Islam rather than the traditional and historic attitude of the old Islam. Yet we must not forget that by its very nature this world faith joins issue with everything that is vital in the Christian religion, because it joins issue in its attitude toward the Christ. By this it must stand or fall. In this respect all schools of Moslem thought are practically the same. They differ in ritual and tradition; in interpretations, broad and narrow; in going back to the old Koran or in advocating the new Islam; but whether Shiahs or Sunnis, Wahabis or followers of Syed Amir Ali, their position as regards the Christ is practically the same.

"Islam," says Rev. G. Simon of Sumatra, "is not a preparation for Christianity; it is easier to build on a strange soil than first of all to tear down old buildings which are so firmly set together that they offer an unsurmountable obstacle to demolition."[2] The resolution passed by the Lucknow Conference, 1911, expressed this sentiment even more forcibly:

> "This Conference is persuaded that, in order to stem the tide of Moslem advance, it is important to strengthen the work among animistic tribes, pagan communities, and depressed classes affected by this advance; for we are clearly of opinion that adoption of the faith of Islam by the pagan people is in no sense whatever a stepping-stone towards, or a preparation for, Christianity, but exactly the reverse."

Christianity gladly admits the strength of theism as a basis of unity between Islam and Christianity. We assert as strongly as do all Moslems that there is only one God, *but because there is only one God there can be only one Gospel and one Christ. The words of Dr. James Denny are significant in this connection:*

> "As there is only one God, so there can be only one Gospel. If God has really done something in Christ on which the salvation of the world depends, and if He has made it known, then it is a Christian duty to be intolerant of everything which ignores, denies, or explains it away. The man who perverts it is the worst enemy of God and man; and it is not bad temper or narrow-mindedness in St. Paul which explains this vehement language [Galatians 1:9]; it is the jealousy of God which has kindled in a soul redeemed by the death of Christ a corresponding jealousy for the Saviour."

"It pleased the Father" that in *Jesus Christ* "all fulness should dwell"; *not* in Mohammed. "In *Him* dwelleth all the fulness of the Godhead bodily"; *not* in Mohammed. "In *Him* are hid all treasures of wisdom and knowledge"; *not* in Mohammed. "He is the way, the Truth, and the Life"; *not* Mohammed. This is the issue which cannot he avoided.

A belief in the deity of Jesus Christ our Saviour may be a mere matter of creed, the acceptance of a form of statement without personal investigation, the acceptance of a theological dogma based on logical proofs without personal experience; or it may be a conviction of the heart, an experience of the soul, a passion in one's life. In no part of the world's battlefield for righteousness and truth does belief in the deity of Jesus Christ so naturally and almost spontaneously turn this mere theological dogma into a spiritual experience, a logical necessity, and a great passion, as when face to face with Mohammedan denials of the claims of our Saviour, and their practical deification of Mohammed.

The utter helplessness and hopelessness of missionary work among Moslems on the part of any one who wavers or is uncertain regarding this belief in the deity of Christ is self-evident. The Moslem doctrine of God and their denial of Jesus Christ, His incarnation, His atonement, His deity, are the very issues of the conflict. The Koran denies all that which is the supreme glory of the Saviour and which makes Him a Saviour at all. Although both in the Koran and in tradition Jesus Christ has a high place among the prophets, and Moslems are willing to admit His sinlessness and power to work miracles, all this does not distinguish His person in any way, as to His nature, from other prophets who came before Him. Christ to them occupies no supreme place in heaven, nor does He in history. He has been at once succeeded and superseded by Mohammed in this respect. It is this anti-Christian character of the greatest of all the non-Christian religions which compels every worker among Moslems to look upon the doctrine of the Trinity or of the deity of Jesus Christ not as mere orthodox belief, but as the very life and heart of Christianity, without which we have no message, no motive power, and no hope of success.

The old Islam refuses compromise with Christianity and fully understands that the gulf in theological teaching cannot be bridged. Their attitude toward Christ is traditional, but toward Christianity, especially among those who hope that Islam will yet be victorious everywhere, is that of defiance and opposition. Although the political situation holds in check Moslem fanaticism and prevents freedom of speech through the censorship of the press, we must not be deceived by this outward calm. When circumstances are favourable and hearts are inflamed with passion, the Moslems of the old school, both Shiahs and Sunnis, have shown by their *jihads* and the massacre of Christians—their neighbours and outwardly their friends—what their real feeling is. The story of the Armenian massacres is still in our minds, and what took place at Urumia and Salmas and Van might have happened in Cairo or Calcutta at the outbreak of the European war had it not been for the strong hand of the British Government.

Not only is the symbol of the Cross a stumbling block to the Moslem of the old school, but the doctrine of the Cross is to him foolishness. The leading Moslem paper of Cairo characterized the belief in the Crucifixion as the foundation of the Christian religion, and then summarized the objections to it as follows:

1. It is opposed to reason.
2. It is opposed to theism. How can God, who is omnipresent and everlasting, degrade Himself by dwelling in a virgin's womb?
3. It is opposed to God's knowledge; for the plan of salvation—if such it is—was an afterthought.
4. It is opposed to both the mercy and justice of God; to His mercy because he allowed Christ to suffer, being innocent, without delivering Him; and to His justice in allowing those who crucified Him to do it unpunished.
5. It leads to impiety, because if this is the way of salvation, then no matter how wicked a man is he finds deliverance through the Cross, and will never be punished for his sins.
6. It is unnecessary. We have never heard it stated by any reasonable person, or those who are learned in law, that the attribute of justice is abrogated by the pardon of a criminal; on the contrary, it is considered a virtue to pardon an offender. Why should not God do so?

The old Islam, true to Koran teaching and the place always given to Jesus among the greater prophets, confesses Christ with their lips, but their heart is far from accepting His message. They do not attack the character of Jesus as do some of the Moslems of the new school. On the other hand, they exceed them in their violent opposition to Christian missions. The Egyptian press is typical in that respect. *Esh-Sha'ab,* once one of the leading papers, on March 1, 1914, had an editorial on the deceitful dealings of missionaries who, by mission boats on the Nile, hospitals, and schools, laid traps for the unwary. The same paper, publishing a missionary report of a girl's conversion, said, "Where are your wits, O ye who profess the religion of Islam? Why do you not oppose these bitterest enemies of your faith instead of leaving your daughters to be won over by their teaching." The public is warned against attending Christian meetings, and the preacher and his message are made the subject of scurrilous poems, as was the case in *Misr-al-Fitat,* 1913.

Al-'Alm the day after Christmas, 1910, spoke of the observance of Christmas Day as a holiday in the Government schools of Egypt as a dangerous heresy. "It is quite enough for us that we should see you rejoicing while we Moslems are roasting on the fire of unrest. It is quite enough that we see you opposing our political independence and raising your flags of joy in our country. Why should we longer show patience?"

Esh-Sha'ab spoke of the attendance at Christian meetings as follows: "The attendance at these meetings is one of the greatest evils a Moslem can commit. God will punish it more severely in the last day than adultery or drunkenness. Yea, it is the most terrible of crimes whether from the point of wisdom and prudence or from that of politics. Do you doubt the truth of your religion, O Moslems, that you seek advice from your enemies?"

The Egyptian press, like that of Turkey, often advocates the boycotting of all Christian institutions, including mission hospitals. In *Esh-Sha'ab,* June 23, 1914, a full page article appeared attacking Beirut College and characterizing its Bible teaching as subversive of Islam. "O fathers who have hearkened to the voice of the ignorant, why have you plunged your precious children into this fire of hell where devils are their guardians?"

Perhaps the greatest stir in the Moslem press was made by a conference of the Protestant Church in Egypt held a few years ago (1911), which had for its motto "Egypt for Christ." This challenge greatly aroused the ire of the old school. "Egypt," they said, "has been Moslem for thirteen centuries. We must not allow Protestants even to speak of Egypt belonging to Christ. How can they dream of Islam disappearing?"

We may sum up the situation as regards the vast majority of Mohammedans of the uneducated classes or those whose education still follows the old lines of thought, by saying that their attitude toward Christ and Christianity, although modified to some extent by contact with Christians, and especially through the influence of Christian hospitals and schools, still remains what it was throughout the past centuries. Afghanistan is a closed land for no other reason than because it is Moslem, and the chief danger to travel across the Arabian peninsula in any direction is the fact of being a Christian. Some years ago Sheikh Abd-ul-Haqq, of Bagdad, a Moslem of the old school, wrote an article on behalf of the Pan-Islamic league. It appeared in a French journal and was entitled "The Final Word of Islam to Europe."

Notes

1 The *middle* portion of this lecture has already appeared in print as Chapter XIV in the author's recent volume "Mohammed or Christ." London, 1915.—S. Z.

2 Edinburgh Conference Report, Vol. IV, p. 147.

12 Extracts from *The Christian Message in a Non-Christian World*

Hendrik Kraemer

Islam

Islam is a religion that is indeed a branch from the prophetic stock of Judaism and Christianity. In its entirety, however, it has become, like Roman Catholicism in Christendom, a great syncretistic body wherein are welded in one system theocratic and legalistic Islam, mysticism and various sorts of popular religion, in which the naturalistic vein of the primitive apprehension of existence shines through. Its genuine and original elements and structure are the result of the prophetic message of Muhammad, who proclaimed this message in the name of God the Compassionate, the Merciful, as the direct revelation of God. This distinguishes Islam clearly from the stock of naturalist religions; besides, this religion is unthinkable without the background of empirical Christianity and Judaism. To a great extent it is legitimate to understand Islam as a modified reflex of, and reaction upon, these two religions. Since its coming in the world till the present day different people have been inclined, therefore, to conceive it as a Christian heresy. There is much to be said in favour of this judgment; though in our opinion it misses the mark, because it ignores too much the independent self-consciousness which Islam has had from the outset.

In its main, genuine structure Islam is a simple religion. Its students are never weary of extolling its simplicity, pointing to the concise *lapidary shahada* (creed): There is no God but Allah, and Muhammad is His Apostle. Gibbon, the sceptic, in his *Decline and Fall of the Roman Empire,* describes Islam with subdued admiration, just because of this simplicity which contrasted so favourably with the intricate subtleties of the christological dogmas he had dealt with in previous sections of his work, and which seemed to agree admirably with the simplicity of the favourite religion of his age, natural religion. Gibbon calls the first "word" of the *shahada* about the uniqueness of God an eternal truth, and the second "word," as a good son of his century, he describes as a necessary fiction. His admiration bursts out in the sentence: "A philosophic atheist might subscribe to the popular creed of the Mahometans, a creed too sublime for our present faculties."

The truly remarkable and puzzling thing in Islam, however, is that it is, notwithstanding its undeniable simplicity, a manifold riddle. Why? Some reasons for this statement, which in our opinion is fundamental to a real understanding of Islam as a religion and to the missionary approach to it, may be mentioned.

Islam in its constituent elements and apprehensions must be called a superficial religion. The grand simplicity of its conception of God cannot efface this fact and retrieve its patent superficiality in regard to the most essential problems of religious life. Islam might be called a religion that has almost no questions and no answers. In a certain respect its greatness lies there, because this question-less and answer-less condition is a consistent exemplification of its deepest spirit, expressed in its name: Islam, that is, absolute surrender to God, the Almighty Lord.

On the other side, however, it is also the result of its superficiality. This superficiality appears from the deeply unsatisfactory way in which Islam deals with the crucial problems of religious and moral life, and this becomes the more evident because it arose in the shadow of Biblical realism.

In the most emphatic sense of the word Islam is a religion of revelation. *Wahj*, revelation, is the pivot on which it turns, and one of the central themes of its theological thinking. Muhammad, with true modesty, declared in the troublesome years of his courageous ministry in Mecca that the particularity of his person and his mission consisted exclusively in the fact of his being the conveyer of God's words made known to him, and in nothing else. The *Quran*, the collection of God's words made known to Muhammad, is thus the immutable word of God. Islam has rightly sensed and still senses that this book is the sole foundation for its claim to be an independent, to be *the* universal, God-given and ultimate, religion. The unassailable infallibility of this book has consequently been one of the deepest concerns in Islam, and has given rise to an enormous amount of stubborn, ingenious theological thinking. The Islamic idea of revelation is widely different from revelation in Biblical realism. The idea of revelation is there, even in a very rigid form, but in comparison with revelation in Biblical realism it has become externalized, fossilized as it were. Revelation in Biblical realism means, God constantly acting in holy sovereign freedom, conclusively embodied in the man Jesus Christ. In Islam it is a set of immutable divine words that take the place of God's movable acts and His speaking and doing through the living man Jesus Christ. The foundation of Islam is not, The Word became flesh. It is, The Word became book.[1] It is quite logical and intelligible that Islam should have developed its own species of Logos speculation in the well-known dogma of the uncreated, pre-existent and celestial *Quran*.

This externalization and fossilization of revelation in Islam seems to us to be one of the great marks of its religious superficiality. By its starting-point Islam·is condemned to feed on a mechanical idea of revelation. The religious advantage, however, of the idea of divine revelation as the basis of life in Islam is that it has fostered in its adherents a deep sense of the value and existence of absolute truth.

As a second instance of superficiality in crucial religious problems one might adduce the clumsy, external conception which Islam has of sin and salvation. Again, this is the more striking because Islam is of prophetic origin and has intimate relations with the sphere of Biblical realism. It satisfies itself with fragmentary and superficial opinions about these central problems in prophetic religion, speaking in an exceedingly facile and unconvincing way about the *tabula rasa* of the human mind at birth and about God's grace. It is significant to note that in Moslem theology there is hardly anything that could be reasonably called anthropology. There is hardly any surmise, either in the *Quran* or in its standard theologies, about the stirring problems of God and man that are involved in the terms sin and salvation. The whole drama of salvation between God and the world, so vivid in Biblical realism, from which Islam, historically speaking, is an offshoot, is entirely absent. Obedience in surrender to the God of Omnipotence is the core of Islam. This accounts for the strangely eventless relation between God and man that characterizes Islam. Obedience in fellowship with the God of Holy Love is the core of Biblical realism and accounts for the peculiarly eventful relation between God and man that characterizes Biblical revelation.

A third instance is the conflict about the relation of faith and works which has played a conspicuous part in the history of dogma in Islam. In the *Quran* the germs are present already of the two conceptions of faith that arise in every religion which has a set of central religious tenets. The first is the intellectualistic conception, which considers faith to be intellectual submission to authoritative tenets; and the second the deeper dynamic conception of faith as an inner conviction or, as it was formulated in Islam, to hold something as truth by the heart and confess it by the tongue. Ghazali, who reconciled orthodox Islam to mysticism, is, as so often, one of the deepest voices of Islam in this field. Yet in dogmatic controversy this important religious and moral problem of faith and works took the aspect of the relation between inward and outward conformity to Islam as a religious, social and political community, and lost its touch with the deeper religious question of which it is a part, namely, what is, respectively, the significance of faith and works in the problem of salvation?

Now we come to the riddle. This, religiously speaking, rather shallow and superficial religion has a grip on its adherents greater than any other religion has. Everyone who knows the Moslem world by personal experience will bear witness to the truly remarkable fact that a Moslem, whether he is a fervid and convinced or a lukewarm believer or even a secret disbeliever and agnostic, as a rule becomes beside himself with anger if a man turns Christian or changes his religious allegiance. All over the Moslem world we know the curious and disquieting (disquieting because it affects one so strangely) phenomenon that the average Moslem, though he may be extremely lax as to the observance of his religious duties and even dissolute in his behaviour, is ready to die for the sake of Islam, or to kill a man whom he considers to be a defiler of Islam. Europeans call this "Moslem fanaticism" and feel extraordinarily uneasy about this enigmatical enthusiasm for a faith whose rules are constantly neglected and transgressed. In Christianity one is accustomed to consider "martyrdom" for the faith only possible and reasonable in men who are devoted believers in word and deed. A very noteworthy fact in the Moslem world is that Islam as such, the religion of Islam apart from its content, is the object of fierce loyalty and absolute surrender. "The glory of Islam," "Islam in danger" are concepts able to evoke paroxysms of devotion.

The second reason why it appears legitimate to call Islam a riddle is that this religion, so lacking in depth, is also, when one considers its origin and material, an unoriginal religion, and yet notwithstanding that it excels all other religions in creating in its adherents a feeling of absolute religious superiority. From this superiority-feeling and from this fantastic self-consciousness of Islam is born that stubborn refusal to open the mind towards another spiritual world, as a result of which Islam is such an enigmatic missionary object.

Is there any explanation for solving this riddle of incompatibles? We might venture one by trying to find out where the core of Islam lies. Muhammad was possessed by two great religious aims—to proclaim God as the sole, almighty God, the Creator and the King of the Day of Judgment; to found a community, in Arabic called *umma,* ruled by the Law of God and His Apostle. These two objects constitute the core of Islam, its strength and its weakness.

Islam is radically theocentric, and thereby proclaims in the clearest possible way its prophetic origin. It takes God as God with awful seriousness. God's unity and soleness, His austere sovereignty and towering omnipotence, are burning in white heat within Islam. Whosoever has listened with his innermost being to the passionate awe that vibrates through the well-known sentences: *Allahu akbar* (God is great) and: *La sharika lahu* (He has no associate), knows that Islam has religious tones of elemental power and quality. The apprehension of the naked majesty of God in Islam is simply unsurpassed. Even in the dry books of *kalam* (the science of dogma) the theocentric character of Islam is overwhelmingly demonstrated by the fact that their main content is the doctrine of God, His Essence and His attributes. The Moslem who in sermons or in dogmatic controversies sincerely protests against *shirk*, that is the unpardonable sin of giving God an associate (in more arid terms, the sin of polytheism), is always a telling figure. This intense awe in the presence of God is the reason why the so-called Moslem prayer, the joint worship of the community, is always a deeply impressive ceremony, even when under the cloak of outward reverence and discipline the heart of the matter is gone. It is very significant to realize that in Islam the object of the meeting of believers for common worship is not to attend or participate in sacramental rites or in liturgical acts, dramatizing various relations between God and man, or to hear the Word, but simply to join in an act of reverent adoration and worship of God. In this light Moslem prayer is one of the most pertinent expressions of the religious spirit of Islam.

It is a very curious thing to note that in the really religious conceptions of Islam one can point to what might be called a process of super-heating. The conception of revelation in its ruthless consequence is super-heated. The same can be said about the conception of God. Islam is theocentric, but in a super-heated state. Allah in Islam becomes white-hot Majesty, white-hot Omnipotence, white-hot Uniqueness. His personality evaporates and vanishes in the burning heat of His aspects. These de-personalized aspects, although of course not devoid of the personal connotation connected with Allah, are the real objects of religious devotion. The surrender to Allah, the fundamental religious attitude in Islam, has that same quality of absolute ruthlessness. The ideal believer, the *abd* (or servant, as Islam says), is, so to speak, personified surrender and nothing else. God's Will becomes virtually august divine arbitrariness. To speak of a voluntarist conception of God in Islam is, properly speaking, inexact; one ought to call it a "potentist" conception, if such a word existed.

This hyperbolic theocentricity, which is accompanied by a hyperbolic over-intensification of all central religious apprehension in Islam, derives from the fact that man has no real place in the relation of God and man. One of the favourite expressions about God, which testifies to an intense religious feeling is, He whom everyone needs and who does not stand in need of anybody or anything. Man is entirely absorbed in the greatness and majesty of God and vanishes away. Fellowship does not exist between God and man. God is too exalted for that, and the relation of Father-child between God and man is not primarily abhorrent to the Moslem because of the association of parenthood and sexual life, but because it suggests a sacrilegious lack of reverence towards the Divine. The hyperbolic over-intensification of the purely religious element in the relation of God and man destroys that intrinsic unity of the religious and the ethical that is implied in a real relation between the divine and the human, for relation means fellowship and obligation. Man is so evanescent in the hyperbolically theocentric atmosphere of Islam that problems of theodicy, of the cry for a God of *righteousness*, etc., are entirely absent.

This hyperbolic religiousness may explain somewhat the intense grip that Islam has on the minds of its adherents.

The second element in the core of Islam, namely the conception of the Moslem community as an *'umma* ruled by the Law of God and His Apostle is, however, still more helpful to explain the tenacious grip of Islam on its adherents. Islam is a theocracy, a community, that is at the same time a religious, political and a social unit. In Medina this *'umma* and this conception were born, not in Mecca, because there the community was only a handful of believers, expecting God and His Day of Judgment. Because of this theocratic character the *shari'a* (religious law) is so absolutely central in Islam, and the theological discipline par excellence is the *fiqh* (religious jurisprudence); whilst the recognized religious leaders are the '*ulama*', that is, those who know the *shari'a*. The problem of modernizing Islam means therefore to come to terms with this *shari'a,* for the *shari'a* is virtually the regulation and sanctioning of a mediaeval society on the basis of the revelation.

The deepest, the most crucial problem of Islam is that its theocracy from the very first moment, when the '*umma* was born in Medina, has been a thoroughly secularized theocracy. By this expression we intend to suggest that the primary inspiration of this theocracy was not the vision of the Will of God as the sole valid law of life (although it is there too), but the necessity and desire in Muhammad to achieve by organization of his '*umma* a more powerful position. So Islam in its cradle was already a specimen of religious imperialism, which is another name for secularized theocracy. It has expressed this in theory (in its canonical public law) and in practice (in its history) by its claim to be the sole power divinely entitled to rule the world both in the religious and the secular spheres. The well-known division to be found in the *shari'a* of the world in a *dar-al islam* (the House of Islam) and a *dar-al-harb* (the House of War) expresses this in a very terse way. The fact that the only dogmatic differences that gave rise to real schism, such as the Kharijites and the Shi'a, were political[2] controversies, is very instructive.

It seems to us that a problem, still deeper than this deep problem, is that never in the whole history of Islam has this inherent and initial secularization of its conception of theocracy become a vexing religious problem for Moslem thinkers. Even Ghazali, unquestionably the man of the greatest religious and theological depth and sincerity that Islam has ever produced, does not touch it. Because the fact of its being a secularized theocracy from the outset is the backbone of theoretical and empirical Islam. Again and again one gets the impression that Islam is the religion of "natural man" notwithstanding its strong religious elements. In Pascal's short reflections on Islam in his *Pensées* he lays his finger with great religious intuition on the sore spot. He says: "*Mahomet a pris la voie de réussir humainement, Jésus Christ celle de périr humainement*" (Muhammad chose the way of human success, Jesus Christ that of human defeat).

The preceding picture is not at all complete in regard to empirical Islam as a whole, but it gives the whole *essence* of Islam. Islam being a civilization and being also, as every religion is, an historical growth, comprises many other elements. To mention two only, it comprises a system of ethics and especially a many-coloured body of mystical religion. As the last has such a great significance in nearly all Moslem countries, it is indispensable to say something more about it.

Original Islam has no connection whatever with mysticism. To discover in the *Quran* the first seeds of Moslem mysticism, from which the whole garden has supposedly grown up, is erroneous. The core of Islam is thoroughly anti-mystical and unmystical. The current method of construing developments in mysticism, beginning in the *Quran* and ending in Ghazali or Ibn-al-Arabi, demonstrates only the evolutionary passion that still animates thinking in the field of the history of religions, and nothing more. Islam as a civilization is the continuator of the Hellenic-Eastern civilization in its Christianized form. The Christian populations that were Moslemized naturally took their religious propensities and tendencies with them into the "House of Islam" and learned to express them in Muhammadan moulds, terms and outlooks. Margaret Smith's book, *Studies in Early Mysticism in the Near and Middle East,* and her books on al-Muhasibi and Rabi'a give an insight into this remarkable process. It is very interesting to note that the great and moving mystic literature of Islam, where the "way" of the "traveller" (*salik*) to God is described in its various stages, is born, like Eastern Christian mysticism, from the Terror of "the Day of the Lord." Just as in the Eastern Christian mysticism of those centuries, to abstain from the world, to conquer sensual desire, and to purify the heart are the stages on the way to God. The peculiar atmosphere of Christian mysticism betrays itself by its emphasis on joy and adoration; the peculiar atmosphere of Moslem mysticism by its emphasis on the awe of God. This pertains only to what may be called emotional mysticism. The so-called heterodox mysticism of Islam is a plant of a quite different soil; it belongs to the category of speculative developments of the ontological implications of naturalistic monism.

Ghazali has made mysticism in Islam from being a very important element in Moslem religious life into a recognized part of the great orthodox system. He did this by assigning to the *shari'a,* the *kalam* (dogmatical theology) and mysticism each its proper place. The religious law (*shari'a*) is the daily food; dogmatical theology provides with weapons necessary to defend the faith against unbelief and scepticism; mysticism is religion as an affair of the heart and vivifies the two other aspects of religious life with its warm breath. Since Ghazali no development of really decisive importance has taken place in the religious life of Islam. He saved Islam from petrification by his great synthesis, embodied in his famous work, *Ihya ulum al-din*; but at the same time he sanctioned the legalist and scholastic fetters in which Islam as a system was and is chained.

Ghazali is one of the deepest apologists of religion that have ever lived. He criticized, with amazing depth, Aristotelian rationalism and Neo-Platonic monism from the standpoint of real religious faith. He could do this because he was driven by two great, really religious urges, that so often create great religious men: the personal need of religious certitude, and his deep concern for the spiritual needs of the common man. His severe and fateful limitation was his conception of revelation. He remained bound to the conception inherent in Islam, namely, that revelation is constituted by the immutable words of God, contained in the *Quran.* This means actually that tradition (*naql*), not the living Reality of God, is the source and criterion of religious life. By virtue of this traditionalism and also by his patriarchal, emphatically non-prophetic vision of the masses, he justified and sanctioned, despite his "religion of the heart," the huge block of legalistic religion that is enshrined in the *shari'a.* Islam is still in this (religiously speaking) desolate condition. The process of conflict with and penetration by Western civilization in many respects plays havoc with Islam. This conflict has not yet released a really religious awakening, because the many modernist reactions to it are, on the whole, vindications of Islam in the face of modern life. The deeper issues of the essential nature of revelation and of its being a secularized theocracy are still evaded. Its defensive attitude rather strengthens than diminishes its (religiously speaking) unjustified feeling of superiority.

[…]

Through all the ages Islam has been, in relation to the missionary efforts of the Christian Church, the teacher of patience. Its great function has been, and will probably continue to be for the present and for the immediate future, to remind the Christian Church that Christian missions, if they will be really Christian, that is to say if they spring from the apostolic obligation towards a divine commission, are not primarily driven by motives of spiritual conquest or success, but by the urge towards faithful and grateful witness to Christ. The confrontation of the Christian Church with the difficult missionary problem that Islam embodies means in the first place for the Christian Church to remind itself of what obedient faith is.

The exceptional stubbornness of Islam towards the efforts of Christian missions has two reasons, and it is well to look them straight in the face when the Christian approach is being discussed. In the first place, the secret of the iron rigidity of Islam is that its real "holy" and its real "god" is group solidarity, conceived with passionate religious directness. The "religion of Islam" is a sanctity apart; the unbroken unity of Islam the sacred treasure of the Moslem community and the Moslem individual. We children of the present time, who behold the enormous forces of fanaticism and devotion that are inherent in the creed of group solidarity, are probably in a more favourable condition to understand Islam than ever before has been the case. A very pertinent way to define Islam would be to call it a mediaeval and radically religious form of that national-socialism which we know at present in Europe in its pseudo-religious form. As with all militant creeds of group solidarity Islam evinces therefore a bitter and stubborn resistance to any effort that might involve change of religion, or, to put it more adequately, to any break in the group solidarity.

In its relation to Christianity there enters, however, another factor of importance. The meeting of Christianity with the other great non-Christian religions is, properly speaking, a meeting of strangers, since they have been born in different geographical and spiritual hemispheres without any historical connection. With Islam the case is very different. Christianity and Islam are acquaintances from the very beginning. The first stood at the cradle of the latter and made no mean contribution to its birth. This might, however, be of slight significance, but there is another point that makes all the difference. In the years of its genesis Islam, having originally taken a friendly attitude towards Christianity as the valid religion of revelation for the "nation" of the Christians, became antagonistic towards it by the mouth of its prophet, that is virtually by the mouth of divine revelation. This antagonism to and indignant rejection of some cardinal elements of Christianity (Jesus' Sonship, His death on the Cross and consequently such doctrines as the Trinity and Reconciliation or Atonement) are incorporated in the *Quran,* the basis of the Moslem faith, and so belong to the system of Islam. To reject Christianity is with Islam not merely the natural and intelligible reaction of every religion or world conception that has sufficient vigour in it to want to maintain itself; with Islam it belongs to its religious creed. To accept Christianity implies the explicit recognition of the error of Islam. This creedal antagonism towards Christianity is strengthened and still more embittered by the kind of political relations which Moslem and Christian peoples have had in the course of history.

This whole background one must constantly have in mind when thinking about the Christian missionary approach to Islam. If we do this, it is at once clear why the prime condition of the approach to Islam is faith, hope, love and endurance that never wear out, and of which love is "the greatest of all" (I Cor. xiii.). By its stubborn rigidity and pride, implied in its being the deification of group solidarity, Islam is a trying religion to converse with. The missionary, however, who has fallen a victim to the attitude of fear or disgust or hatred of Islam, does better to go immediately home and never come back. Nobody has a right to throw a stone at him, but it is certain that he can only do harm. Only if faith, hope, love and endurance, however much tempted, ever and again break through triumphantly, will he perform his missionary obligation well. As this is the prime condition of all missionary approach to Islam, there follows from it the conclusion that the Christian Church must stand behind her ambassadors in this difficult field with prayer and loving remembrance to a degree quite different from what is practised now.

Those two elementary conditions in the Christian approach towards Islam are not mentioned here as mere pious, edifying talk, but as hard, matter-of-fact conditions. Whosoever nods impatiently, thinking, let us go on to more concrete and practical subjects, never has understood the root of the Moslem missionary problem and probably never will. Detailed proposals of avenues to Islam will not yield their full fruitage before these elementary conditions are fulfilled. The Christian Church and its missionary agencies should harbour no illusions about that. Whosoever has become bruised and bleeding in the struggle with Islam can testify to it.

Another important conclusion that in relation to the approach can be drawn from the general Moslem background is that the entrance to this impregnable religious citadel cannot be opened by presenting Christianity to the Moslem mind as the enrichment of its half-truths as to its belief in God, its veneration for Jesus, its logos speculation, its conception of fraternity, etc., or developing into full growth what is to be found, for instance, in the *Quran* about the Holy Spirit (*Ruh*) and the need for an intercessor. As the axis of Islam is wholly turning on the idea of group solidarity under the aegis of Allah and the Apostle, all the elements in the *Quran* or in the creedal evolution of Islam that have some connection with Christianity (and there are many because Islam is, culturally speaking, the continuation of the Hellenistic-Christian civilization of the Near and Middle East) have a wholly different character and tendency. Hence this fragmentary method[3] leads to nothing, for these elements are not half-truths in relation to Christianity; they simply belong to another plane of religious apprehension. The one thing that every missionary and Christian who preaches the Gospel in the "house of Islam" has to do with unwearying perseverance in regard to these elements borrowed from historical Christianity is to explain patiently what, according to Biblical realism, these elements really mean, and wait for the results. Generally speaking, the Moslem, however touchy he may be in religious matters, will listen attentively to a positive and restrained religious witness.

A significant item in the directly religious[4] approach to Islam is also that the best method undoubtedly is direct personal contact and study of the Bible in a spirit of human sympathy and openness, the Moslem being treated not as a non-Christian but as a fellow-man with the same fundamental needs, aspirations and frustrations, whose religious experience and insight are as worth while as the missionary's, simply because he is a living human being. The personal contact itself must show how one has to open the world of the Bible in every concrete instance, by beginning at the centre or at the periphery of Christian truth or somewhere between.

One point may probably be stated with great emphasis, namely, that especially in the world of Islam to present Christianity as a set of doctrines is the most awkward way conceivable. The following reasons may be mentioned to substantiate this dictum. Islam itself is creedal and doctrinal to the core. To present Christianity as a set of doctrines is to rouse the militantly intellectualist spirit of Islam (and of all creedalism), and to move entirely outside the religious sphere. Its wilful rejection of Christianity is directed against some definite Christian doctrines and is crystallized in some of its own doctrines. Moreover, even if the missionary avoids presenting Christianity in a doctrinal way, the Moslem will often force him by his attacks to pronounce upon doctrinal matters. Further, in the course of the ages Islam has lived together with the Eastern Churches, which are all the most appalling instances of petrified doctrinalism and ritualism. In consequence, the Moslem world has been robbed of any opportunity to get an idea of the dynamic forces of Christianity. A radical purging of the idea that doctrinalism is the genuine aspect of religion in the higher sense is badly needed in the Moslem world and in the Eastern Churches. The missionary approach, in so far as it is dependent on its own initiative, must abjure all doctrinal approach and invite the Moslem to penetrate into the living world of Biblical realism.

The presupposition on which these fundamental elements of the approach to Islam are built are, of course, a direct and vital contact with Biblical realism and a real knowledge of the Moslem ways of thinking and living and of the religious vocabulary of Islam. As long as the missionary societies accept such a low grade of this knowledge in most missionaries, even in countries where life is steeped in Islam and Arabic, it is self-deception to expect appreciable results.

In the discussion on the approach to Islam mysticism and the quality of religious life as found in the mystic orders (*tariqa*) have been very prominent. Very recently Dr Wilson Cash in his book, *Christendom and Islam,* devoted much attention to this side of Islam as one of the chief ways of finding new approaches and building bridges by personal contact with those Moslems who through mysticism search for God. This tendency is very intelligible, for it is undoubtedly true that amongst the mystically-minded in this religion the most sensitive spiritual people are to be found, with whom true human and religious contact is possible. Among these people one finds men and women of great spiritual beauty. C. F. Andrews in his picture of Zaka Ullah of Delhi has offered a very good model of this spiritual type in Islam. It is the more intelligible because, as was pointed out in our sketch of Islam,[5] for historical reasons Muslim and Christian Eastern mysticism of the emotional and contemplative type have much in common. Many missionaries whose own religious experience runs along the lines of the devotional life and whose religious emphasis falls on the communion of the soul with God and the inner drama that ensues from it, recognize this with great gratitude.

Taking the problem of mysticism as an approach to Islam in its completeness we must again, it seems, make a very important distinction between the practical and the theoretical. From the standpoint of human, evangelistic approach it is undoubtedly true that among mystically-minded people it is possible to find the greatest number of individuals with whom genuine religious intercourse is possible on the basis of common humanity. As always, this is from the missionary standpoint of very great value, and in Islam it is of specially great value because the well-known barrier of self-conscious pride is then absent. The mystics with their concentration on "God and the soul" have removed the axis of religious life from group-solidarity to communion with God in the purely religious sense of the word.

Theoretically speaking, the situation is entirely different. The idea or expectation that mysticism or the mystic orders are probably the domains of religious life in Islam whence the road to Christianity will be paved is founded on a double error. The first is that, however widespread mysticism in Islam may be, it is wholly an alien growth in this religion. It is true that in the mystic quarters of the Moslem world one can often find a delicious rest from the impregnable rigidity of the genuine Islamic system of faith and law, but the real missionary problem is just this system and not the exception that is embodied in mysticism. At the same time this situation suggests very vividly that one of the best ways to soften this rigid system is to encourage in all kinds of ways personal religious life in Islam, in which all emphasis falls on a life of religious and moral fellowship with God. The second error is contained in the fact that mysticism is a very complicated phenomenon. This appears immediately from the simple facts that can be observed in all the non-Christian religions, namely, that mysticism is not only the most lofty form of religious life in them, but the most degraded form as well, and that one can notice (at present this tendency is very marked) so often the curious amalgamation of mysticism and anti-religious scepticism in one and the same person.

Mysticism is one of the great universal forms of religious life that are essentially the same in all ages and environments. The mysticisms of all religions are clearly akin to each other. The explanation of this well-known fact is that mysticism is one of the most sublime and most dangerous products of naturalistic monism. Hence, the oneness of God and the soul is its fundamental theme, in ways and accents that vary extraordinarily; and the identity of the divine essence with the essence of man or the world is its fundamental pre-supposition. The grand theopanistic systems of India, of Far Eastern Buddhism, and of heterodox Moslem mysticism, in which man along the road of gnosis masters the rapturous certitude of his essential oneness with the Divine Essence and Ultimate Reality; the graded ways of contemplative mysticism striving for the beatific vision of God, which we encounter in all religions; the many variations of emotional mysticism, in which the soul pines and longs for the Eternal—these are all more or less offshoots from naturalistic monism. The first type of aristocratic theopanistic mysticism belongs wholly to it and is wholly antagonistic to the prophetic religion of Biblical realism. Contemplative mysticism has many affinities with naturalistic monism. It is easily prone, in its Christian forms, to live principally in a world of religious apprehension that is foreign to Biblical realism, but preserves the Christian colouring by Christian ideas and imagery. Emotional mysticism may be influenced by naturalistic monism, because hardly any form of mysticism escapes entirely the influence of this pull, but is often an independent growth in the positive religions of prophetic origin such as Islam, Judaism and Christianity. It is the need of the human soul for the imperishable and for the touch of fervour and immediate personal contact, entering upon a marriage with fundamental elements of, for example, Islam or Christianity. Mysticism in the typical sense of the word, either in its theopanistic, contemplative or emotional form, does not occur in the prophetic religion of Biblical realism. To call Paul or John mystics is to confound a tone of religious fervour and adoration with mysticism, which always has a tendency towards regarding *frui Deo* (to enjoy God) as the highest goal of the Christian life. To use other terms: the highest goal is to become absorbed in the contemplation and adoration of the pure Beauty of the Divine Essence, as, for example, can be learnt from Augustinian and mediaeval Christian mysticism. In Biblical realism, however, in this dispensation the irremovable centre of religious life is the Divine Will. The mystical attitude, in the sense of longing for the eternal and for adoration in the realm of religious life, is, however, a universal phenomenon in the religious life of mankind, and will always create in any positive religion, Christianity included, various forms of religious expression.

Two cardinal points must be kept constantly in mind in relation to this universal situation. First, the sole standard of reference being the prophetic theocentric religion of Biblical realism, the mystical tendencies of religious life are as real as every other tendency (the legalist, the moralist, the dogmatic, the ecclesiastical, etc.), and have to obtain authoritative guidance from this theocentric religion. Secondly, in the problem of the relation of Christianity to the non-Christian religions, one must never explain the similarity of the universal mystical attitude, which is to be found in all religions, by a similarity between the fundamental religious apprehensions of the different religions (for example, Christianity and Islam; Christianity and Hinduism or Buddhism). The first idea of similarity corresponds to a fact and hence can be a basis for universal religious contact; the second idea is a fallacy and leads to confusion.

The preceding, it seems, is applicable always and under all circumstances. What is there to be said, however, about the approach in the concrete situation of Islam as it is to-day?

The sketch of the present Moslem situation[6] has enlightened us as to the far-reaching effects of the cultural, political and economic revolution it is going through, and the typical differences between the politically dependent and independent Moslem countries. In surveying this whole scene it is very difficult to say whether, when compared with the past, the prospects of the Moslem missionary situation are at present brighter or gloomier. For both views substantial reasons can be adduced. In the past Christian missions had to do with a largely lethargic and stagnant Moslem world, in which missionary inroads were made along various lines. This work could, generally speaking, be done in the politically dependent as well as in the relatively independent countries by virtue of the protection of the great political powers. In the relatively independent countries (Turkey, Iran, for example) preaching to Moslems was practically forbidden and conversion to Christianity meant ostracism or death. A great and beneficent charitable and educational work was developed, and the evangelizing activity in the chief centres of Islam (Near and Middle East) was directed towards a revivification of the petrified Eastern Churches or (forced by the enmity of the bishops of these churches against the reformatory zeal kindled in their flock by the missionaries) the building up of Evangelical Churches composed of Eastern Christians. In the politically dependent countries, because this Christian legacy was absent and the principle of religious neutrality permitted a more direct witness to the Moslems, missionary activity had, according to the peculiar condition of Islam in these countries, a greater or less success in the gaining of converts. In India the results have been very meagre; in Java it has been possible to an appreciable degree to build up from converts from Islam Christian Churches, which are at present steadily growing and adding to their number.

To-day we have a deeply agitated Moslem world, confused, but also defensive, defiant and aggressive at the same time. In the politically dependent countries there is a growing irritation against foreign supremacy, especially strong in North Africa and the Near East, which results in the strengthening of Moslem group-solidarity and in a growing resentment against missionary activity, which is interpreted as a tool of Western imperialism. In others (India, the Dutch East Indies) there develops more and more, along the lines of literary, propagandist, educational and charitable activity, a counter-move, aiming at defending and strengthening Islam and attacking Christianity.

In the politically independent countries the substitute-religion of nationalism, with national consolidation as the *summum bonum*, has taken the place of the religion of Moslem group-solidarity and has opened up a startling chapter in the religious policy of states that have been Moslem during long centuries. Islam is disestablished and purposely starved (Turkey, Iran) or, as in Egypt, Islam is definitely used as an instrument in the working out of the new national destiny, with a consequent recrudescence of its social prestige, which results in an ever stronger pressure on the members of the Coptic Church to become Moslem. In both cases the result for Christian missions is a severe hampering of the scope of its activity. An indication of the paradoxical character of the situation, however, is that although in such countries as Turkey and Iran religious "propaganda" of any kind is forbidden, on the other hand the opportunity of witnessing to the Gospel in personal religious contact with Turks and Iranians (which was formerly forbidden) is greater than ever before and, at least legally, one is free to choose his own religion. Moreover, in the future it may become of great significance that the radically nationalist line of policy has demolished the age-old *millet-system*, which marked Christians and Moslems off from each other as different "nations" and did so much to create a thick wall of mutual suspicion between Islam and Christianity. At present not only Moslems but also Jews and Christians are considered Turks, because the Turks are no longer a religious Moslem unity, but a people bound together by unity in language, culture and national ideals.

If the present Moslem missionary situation is considered rather gloomy, it is apparently not because it is less favourable than in the past, for the present great stir has unmistakable advantages, but because it is so extremely complicated and utterly uncertain. The continuance or the destruction of organized missionary activity in many Moslem lands depends entirely on the favour or disfavour of the moment. It is impossible to discuss the many intricate problems that are connected with the various countries as to the concrete possibilities of approach, for example, the handling and the training of the convert, the condition of the Eastern Churches and the question as to how far they are fit for their apostolic obligation, because to discuss them satisfactorily would require more space and, above all, intimate practical acquaintance with the various fields. Only some main points can be touched upon.

A great stumbling-block to a right approach, especially in the present complicated situation with the severely restricted opportunities for evangelistic action, is the grievous lack of unity amongst the various missionary agencies and the rivalry between the quarrelling Eastern Churches. This discord undermines the forces that are already so pathetically exiguous over against the strong citadel of Islam, and, besides, evokes much justified criticism. It obscures to a lamentable extent the real character of Christianity. When one ponders on this situation one reminds oneself that especially in the Moslem mission field the aim of missions can only be the effort to unveil the content and meaning of Christianity in its purely religious aspects. It is utterly incomprehensible that the missionary agencies and Churches, always so eagerly on the look-out for new approaches to Islam, are so complacently inactive in relation to this situation. There is nothing in the conditions of the Moslem world that prevents them from setting to work at this matter. On the contrary, in view of the Moslem situation, literally everything urges towards the removal of this stumbling-block, which only waits for our determined will to be accomplished. In other words the practical demonstration of a deep and transforming ecumenical spirit in the missionary bodies and in the quarrelling Churches is one of the most needed and certainly most effective approaches to Islam.

A diligent cultivation of personal contacts on a high religious and moral plane of human openness and Christian humility, and the ministry to secular needs in a spirit of disinterested service are everywhere the roads that still lie open, although in view of the present situation these approaches will demand much ingenuity and tact.

The production of Christian literature, in periodicals or otherwise, aiming at the elucidation of what pure and undefiled religion is and wherein the essential religious and ethical character of Christianity consists, is in the present state of confused religious thinking and feeling not only a service to the cause of missions, but to the cause of humanity too. In this literary work one must also be always alive to the necessity of employing the religious terms and thought-forms of those to whom one appeals.

It seems that the time approaches more and more when the Christian Church will have to face a concrete meeting with Islam. Africa and the Dutch East Indies, the two great territories where Islam and Christianity are both spreading rapidly and where paganism as an established religion is on the brink of disappearing, will become in the near future the places where these two religions are the only official religions that occupy the field. Islam, especially in Africa, has many recommendations when the situation is viewed realistically. The Negro, by becoming Moslem, enters the religious, social, cultural and blood-community of Islam. Islam adapts itself very easily by its leniency to the current standard of Negro life. No long catechumenate is demanded; magical practices and ideas, so dear to the native mind, are easily incorporated; polygamy, that deep-rooted social institution in Africa, is even sanctioned and not at all combated as in Christianity. It is no self-complacency to say that Islam is in Africa at present stagnant and sterile, that it arrests real development because it does not afford such a real moral background as is to-day so badly needed in this continent, while on the other hand Christianity is progressive and does afford moral foundation. Yet there is no law that induces men to choose what is the best for them according to the thought of the best and most disinterested well-wishers of Africa. The way in which the white man handles the race problem subjects the Negro to revolting humiliation and teaches him daily the lesson that the godless "Christian" West does not know, as Islam does, about social, cultural and religious solidarity and unity with men of other races and cultures. This Christian-Moslem situation in Africa is for the missionary agencies and the Christian Churches a call to demonstrate real Christian unity and solidarity and to face race problems not as Europeans but as Christians who represent the community of Christ, in which everyone has his equal place irrespective of race.

How to educate the Churches in Africa and the Dutch East Indies to meet the Moslem problem in a way that does not fall far short of the spirit of Christ and the religious character of Christianity is a task that is looming up before us in the near future.

Notes

1 How near this conception is to the human mind appears from the fact that in Christianity it has always been the fatal inclination to interpret persistently the dynamic prophetic conception of revelation, as evident in Biblical realism, in the terms of this mechanical conception. The human mind, in Islam as well as in Christianity or elsewhere, expresses its desire for a sure guarantee of religious certitude in the clumsy form of the literal inerrancy of the document in which God's revelation is told. In Islam this mode of expression is in accordance with the basic conception of revelation in the *Quran*; in Christianity, however, it signifies a radical distortion of the basic conception in Biblical realism, because there the subject of revelation is not the Bible (as in Islam it is the *Quran*) but the living God of holy love as incarnated in Jesus Christ.
2 The question was, Who has the right to be the head (*Chalifa*) of the theocracy?
3 Compare Chapter IV.
4 For the moment the approach through schools, etc., is not discussed.
5 Chapter VI.
6 Chapter VII.

13 Towards an Islamic Christology II

The Death of Jesus, Reality or Delusion

Mahmoud M. Ayoub

Introduction

This is the second of a series of studies of the Islamic view of Jesus the Christ. We argued in our first essay, *M. W.*, LXVI (1976), 163–88, that Muslims have thought much and seriously about Christ and that there is an authentic Islamic understanding of Christ which deserves careful consideration as a legitimate Christology. The Christ of Islam, we wish to insist further, must not be dismissed as a distorted image of the true Christ of the Gospels, but must rather be seen as a living and dynamic personality, addressing humanity in many languages and across the barriers of dogma, creed and even scriptures.

The purpose of the present essay is to study some of the ways in which Muslim commentators (*mufassirūn*) of the Qur'ān have understood the Qur'anic verses dealing with Jesus. Our main concern is with one verse, and more specifically a single phrase, one which boldly denies the death of Jesus on the Cross at the hands of his opponents. They plotted to kill him, but God saved him and "it (or, he) was made only to appear so to them."[1] We shall endeavor in what follows to examine the meaning of this difficult and controversial phrase. The words *wa lākin shubbiha lahum* have generated much discussion, myth and legend throughout the long history of Islamic *tafsīr*. They have presented Muslims with a challenge, first, to understand God's ways with men, and, second, to answer convincingly the charge of history.

The Qur'ān offers itself as a Book of guidance to humankind.[2] For it to fulfill this purpose in human life, it must speak to the situation of the community of its receivers at every stage of its earthly existence. This the Qur'ān has done in large measure through tafsīr, or the science of Qur'anic exegesis. As one writing from within the community, my task will not be simply to present and analyze the opinions of the commentators on the subject. Rather, having done that, I wish to engage in the process of tafsīr myself by presenting my own understanding of this phrase, which is crucial to the Qur'anic view of Christ. In this I will be accepting the challenge of the divine Word, and that of history.

Three main stages in the history of the tafsīr of the verse with which we shall be concerned suggest themselves. The classical tradition is epitomized in the monumental commentary of Ṭabarī (d. 310/923) which has influenced subsequent commentators down to the present. Other works of the classical period differ little from that of Ṭabarī, which they take as their source and starting point. The second stage, which may be considered as the middle period, shows a greater interest in history as well as a greater awareness of Christian views. This stage is represented on the one hand by the polemical approach of the historian Ibn Kathīr (d. 774/1373), and by the brilliant, analytical and questioning mind of the theologian Fakhr al-Dīn al-Rāzī (606/1209) on the other. The irenic, spiritual and universal interpretation of the Sufis, of which examples will be considered in the essay, represents still another important trend. The third and final stage constitutes the modern period, beginning in the late nineteenth century with modernist reformers such as Muḥammad 'Abduh and his successors. Both the methodology and the concern of modern commentators are radically different from those of their predecessors. The views of some of the most important modern thinkers will be considered.

Shī'ī commentators, especially of the classical period, present a unique approach to the problems raised by the Qur'anic verse under consideration. It must be observed, moreover, that modern Shī'ī thinkers, such as 'Allāmah Ṭabāṭabā'ī, while employing the methodology of modern commentators, clearly continue the Shī'ī philosophical and theological tradition.

We shall follow a loose chronology, aiming not so much at a strict historical survey, but at a presentation of the major developments in tafsīr relevant to the subject at hand. Two texts of special importance will be translated in an appendix. The first presents an interesting parallel to the fourth Gospel of the Passion. The second is a selection from a Sufi tafsīr presenting what may be considered a "Sufi Christology." Finally, the ultimate aim of this study is to promote constructive and meaningful dialogue among the men and women of faith in the two communities.

I. Jesus, "The Word of Truth"[3]

Prophethood in Islam is the divine answer to human folly and false confidence, a source of guidance for men to God and the model of a fulfilled humanity. In every prophet, speaking on God's behalf to humankind, there is both a challenge and a judgment. The challenge is in the call to men and women of every age to return to their prophetic origins as exemplified in Adam, the first prophet, before whom the angels were commanded to prostrate themselves.[4] Human fulfillment must be achieved through human prophets; the Qur'ān therefore insists on the humanity of God's messengers.[5]

In the long drama of human prophets and a humanity challenged to seek prophetic fulfillment, Jesus plays a unique role. In him there is an originality of being that is akin to that of Adam.[6] In him, as in Adam, the divine power over and within creation is manifested. He represents a special creation; he is the Word of God injected into the human plane of existence.[7] Yet like other prophets, Jesus remains a human being created by God, His servant and messenger.[8]

Later Islamic tradition not only affirms the high status accorded to Jesus by the Qur'ān; it makes still greater claims of uniqueness for him. It is reported in a very early ḥadīth that the Prophet declared, "Every child born of the children of Adam Satan touched with his finger, except Mary and her son, peace be upon them both."[9] Jesus is therefore free from the taint of evil and impurity. That his mother shares in this great honor is only because she was accepted by God to be a pure vessel for His Word and messenger.[10] This purity, which Adam had till he was touched by Satan's finger and thus lost it, now remains exemplified in Jesus alone.

When the Qur'ān speaks of earlier prophets, it does so by way of example of God's dealings with faltering humanity. Jesus alone is presented as a challenge and a judgment. In the famous passage of the Qur'ān ending with the verse of the *mubāhala,* God confronts humanity with the challenge, "And whosoever disputes with you concerning him [Jesus], after the knowledge which has come unto you, say: 'Come! Let us summon our sons and your sons, our women and your women, ourselves and yourselves, then we will pray humbly and invoke the curse of God upon those who lie.'"[11] The knowledge which "came" to the Prophet concerning Jesus presents a rare instance of theology proper in the Qur'ān. The Christ of the Qur'ān is according to this theology fully human, in spite of his miraculous birth and special status. Like Adam, he is the creature of God not through the law of human generation, rather he is the object of the divine *amr* (Word of command).[12] Again, in spite of his humanity, and perhaps because of it, Jesus is made the agent of divine acts through his special miracles. To him alone among the prophets God gave the power to give health to the sick, life to the dead and even to crude matter. All this he did "by God's leave."[13]

The Qur'ān presents a Christology of the human Christ, empowered by God and "fortified with the Holy Spirit."[14] It is a fully Islamic Christology based not on borrowed distortions of early Christian heresies, but on the Islamic view of man and God. There are, no doubt, some resemblances between the Qur'anic story of Jesus and early Christian sources;[15] these are at best, however, similarities of framework and story, not of theology or essential view. Islam differs from Christianity on two crucial points. First, it denies the divinity of Christ, but without denying his special humanity. Second, it denies the expiatory sacrifice of Christ on the Cross as a ransom for sinful humanity, but again denies neither the actual death of Christ nor his general redemptive role in human history. Enough has been said about the first point. It is with the second that this essay is concerned.

II. Who died on the Cross?

In a series of verses directed against the children of Israel, to whom Jesus was sent as a messenger,[16] the Qur'ān first accuses them of killing prophets unjustly. It then reproaches them for uttering great calumnies against Mary, perhaps accusing her of adultery. Finally, the Qur'ān reproaches them for claiming to have killed Jesus the Christ:

> and for their saying: "We have surely killed the Christ, Jesus son of Mary, the messenger of God." They did not kill him, nor did they crucify him; rather it was made only to appear so to them. And those who have differed concerning him are in doubt regarding him (or it, the truth); they have no knowledge of him (or it), except the following of conjecture. They did not kill him (or it, their doubt) with certainty. Rather, God took him up to Himself, for God is Mighty and Wise.[17]

These two verses constitute the answer to a divine challenge, "They devised and God devised, and God is the best of devisers." (S. 3:54).

The important question here is, what do the words *wa lākin shubbiha lahum* mean? On the answer to this question, a number of different theories have been formulated and elaborated by Qur'anic exegetes throughout Islamic history. For the most part, their purpose has been to answer the question, "Who was killed and crucified if Jesus was saved by divine intervention?" In their eagerness to confirm the denial of the death and crucifixion of Christ at the hands of his enemies, commentators have generally interpreted the words *shubbiha lahum* to mean that another was made to bear his likeness (*shabah*) and die in his stead. Although later commentators questioned this reading on grammatical grounds, as will be seen below, they nonetheless continued to propound theories about who that substitute may have been.

Christian scholars, likewise, accepted this interpretation and propounded their own theories. Dr. Michel Hayek, a modern Lebanese theologian, comments as follows: "This opinion may be related to a Christian heresy which had many supporters in Najrān just before the rise of Islam. This was the heresy of the docetics who denied the sufferings of Christ. Some of them claimed that Simon the Cyrene was the man who bore the likeness of Christ (and died in his stead)."[18] Docetism, in whatever form it appeared, sought to preserve the divinity of Christ from the indignities of suffering and death. Islam, however, does not admit of docetism in any form. Its very human images of the life to come, as well as its insistence on the humanity of God's messengers, argues against such a view. Furthermore, neither the Qur'ān nor later Islamic tradition suggests a phantomlike appearance of Christ. He was, rather, a man, born in the usual way,[19] lived like other men, and like them must die and be resurrected for the final reckoning.[20]

It must therefore be argued that the Qur'ān only denies the death of Jesus on the Cross, and leaves open the question of his actual death. From the beginning the commentators had some knowledge of the Christian insistence on the crucifixion as an historical fact. They did not, however, grasp the implication of this fact for Christianity, and therefore tried to harmonize the Qur'anic denial with the Christian affirmation. They accepted a crucifixion as an historical fact, in agreement with Christians, but denied it of Jesus, in agreement with the Qur'ān. They adopted not a docetic position in interpretating the words *shubbiha lahum*, but a substitutionist one. Thus any parallels that this position may present with docetism can be only incidental.

The substitutionist solution to the problem raised two further questions. Why would God cause a man to suffer the trials of another, even if for the purpose of sparing His own messenger the ignominy of a shameful death? Second, what would the implications of this confusion of identities by God be for social norms and the credibility of historical testimony? The second of these two questions was eventually raised, and therefore deserves some attention later in this discussion. The first, however, underlies the choice of alternative solutions preferred by different commentators. To these, we shall now turn.

The traditions relating the story of Jesus are told on the authority of either Jewish converts like Wahb b. Munabbih, or of unnamed Christian converts as in the traditions of Ibn Isḥāq. Ṭabarī relates on the authority of Wahb the following story. When God revealed to Jesus that He would take him up to Him, Jesus and seventeen of his disciples went into a house (perhaps to celebrate the Passover). There, they were surprised by the Jews who were seeking Jesus. God, however, cast the likeness of Jesus on every one in the group so that he could not be distinguished from the rest. The Jews exclaimed, "You have bewitched us! Either bring forth Jesus or we shall kill you all."[21] They then took one of the group and killed him, believing him to be Jesus. Hence, "It was made only to appear so to them." After reviewing a number of traditions, Ṭabarī himself prefers the one just discussed. He bases his preference on two major considerations. The Jews, who denied the truth of what Jesus brought them from their Lord, deserved to be frustrated and to have their plan against Jesus, the prophet of God, thwarted. The disciples, *ḥawāriyyūn,* and the Christians who followed them were not telling a lie by asserting the crucifixion, as they did not see Jesus taken up to heaven. They thought, rather, that he was killed because he told them on the night before that his end was at hand. This interpretation, however, was not accepted by most commentators because it was related on the authority of only one traditionist, albeit the famous Wahb b. Munabbih.

Ṭabarī presents a possible alternative which, in his view, serves the same purpose. This is the story, again related on the authority of Wahb, which declares that Jesus was deserted by all his companions at the time of his arrest.[22] He was tied with a rope and dragged through the streets to the place where he was to be crucified. At that moment, he was taken up to heaven and his likeness cast on another whom the Jews killed, thinking him to be Jesus. Thus they were frustrated and the disciples were not telling a lie since they did not see him taken up. This solution, however, creates more problems than it solves. It makes historical Christianity based on a divine deception which was not disclosed until the Qur'ān was revealed centuries later. We shall return to this problem later.

Important to most of the substitutionist interpretations is the idea that whoever bore the likeness of Jesus, and consequently his suffering and death, did so voluntarily. It must have been felt by ḥadīth transmitters and commentators that for God to cause an innocent man to die unjustly to save another would be divine wrongdoing (*ẓulm*), which cannot be predicated of God. Thus the theory which eventually gained most popularity was that one of the disciples voluntarily accepted death as a ransom for his master.[23]

This theory in its simplest form was related by Ṭabarī on the authority of Qatāda (a well-known companion and ḥadīth transmittor). He said:

> It has been related to us that Jesus son of Mary, the prophet of God, said to his companions, "Who among you would consent to have my likeness (*shabahī*) cast upon him, and be killed?" One of them answered, "I would, O prophet of God." Thus that man was killed and God protected His prophet and took him up to Himself.[24]

In what appears to be the second stage in the development of this theory, the number of the disciples is set at nineteen. One of them consents to die in his master's place, then Jesus is taken up to heaven before their eyes. When the disciples came out of the besieged house, they declared that their master was taken up. The Jews verified this claim by counting the men several times; each time one was missing. Still, they took the man and killed him, thinking him to be Jesus.[25]

The next stage in the development of the theory presents a growing interest in historical accounts. The result is an interesting story composed of diverse elements, gospel materials and hagiography. It was related on the authority of Ibn Isḥāq (the famous biographer of the Prophet) that the king of the Jews who sought to kill Jesus was a man called David. When all the people had concurred, Jesus was greatly frightened by death. He prayed, "O God, if Thou wouldst take away this cup from any of Thine creatures, then take it away from me."[26] His skin was dripping with blood, from grief and fear.[27] Then he and his twelve disciples entered a house where he offered a place with him in Paradise to the one who would bear his likeness and die in his stead. The man who volunteered, according to this tradition, was not one of the twelve. His name was Sergus; he took the seat of Jesus and the Master was taken up to heaven.[28] It is of special interest that this story is supposed to have been related to Ibn Isḥāq by a Christian convert. Whether this reflects a local Christian tradition, or was an echo of docetic theology, albeit in a crude form, cannot be determined with certainty given the present state of our knowledge of Arabian Christianity of that period.

In time, however, we see a preference for what we may call punishment substitutionism. Here, God is completely absolved from the responsibility of injustice or wrongdoing. According to some versions of this theory, Jesus was sought by his enemies, who intended to kill him. God, or Gabriel, made him enter a house for refuge. His pursuers sent a man in to kill him. The man's name is variously given as Tiṭyānūs, Tiṭābūs, or Tiṭānūs. Jesus was taken up through an opening in the roof. Not finding him, the man came out to report to the people. But God had turned him into the likeness of Jesus, and he was killed in spite of his protests. God, however, cast the likeness of Jesus only on the man's face and not on his body.[29] Thus the people were confused as to the identity of the man they killed. This is added to explain the rest of the verse which declares that those who differed concerning him followed only their conjecture.

By the sixth Islamic century (twelfth century C.E.), we witness yet another development which seeks to interpret the entire passage in one complete story.[30] The Jews, the Qur'ān tells us, uttered great calumnies against Mary. A group of them reviled Jesus and his mother, calling him "sorcerer, son of a sorceress, reprobate, son of a loose woman." Jesus prayed, saying, O God, You are my Lord and I from Your spirit came into being and with Your Word You did create me. I did not come to them of my own accord. O God, curse those who reviled me and my mother.[31] God answered his prayer and turned the calumniators into apes and swine. The king and notables of the Jews, fearing a similar punishment, sought to kill Jesus. They besieged him and his disciples in a house, and one of them agreed to bear the likeness of his master and die in his place in order that the others may be saved. According to other versions of the same tale, the Jews sent the man Tiṭyānūs to kill Jesus who was alone hiding in a house. But he himself was killed, as we have already seen.

Judas Iscariot has had an interesting history in Christian piety and folklore. He appears in Muslim tafsīr very early, clearly introduced by Christian or Jewish reporters. Reporting on the authority of Wahb b. Munabbih, Ṭabarī tells the story of Judas selling his master for thirty pieces of silver; later he regrets his evil deed and hangs himself. At that early stage, however, Judas is not yet identified. Later, when Judas is specifically mentioned, his name is confused. In a tradition related on the authority of Ibn Isḥāq, who heard it from a Christian convert, Yudas Zechariah, Yutah or Butah (Judas Iscariot), led the Jews to Jesus and was himself made to bear the likeness of the master. Jesus was taken to heaven and Judas was siezed by the mobs who crucified him, thinking him to be Jesus. All the while, he cried out, "I am not the one you want! I am the one who led you to him."[32] This tradition has since been reported by most commentators.[33] Modern thinkers have generally preferred this alternative on special historical and psychological grounds, as will be discussed below.

Many commentators questioned the entire theory and sought to go beyond the literal meaning of the text. Others tried to present the whole episode in a credible historical account without rejecting the substitutionist interpretation. The account of the historian Ibn Kathīr (d. 747/1373) is one of the most interesting examples of this historical approach. It is a narrative account showing definite dependence on Gospel materials. We present it here in some detail.

The Jews envied Jesus for what God had given him, manifest revelations (*bayyināt*) and power to perform miracles (*mu'jizāt*), and sought to kill him. Jesus did not dwell with them; rather he roamed the earth, often with his mother. The Jews wrote to the king of Damascus, who was a worshipper of the stars, accusing Jesus of sedition and leading the people astray. The king then wrote to his governor in Jerusalem ordering him to arrest Jesus, place thorns[34] on his head and crucify him. Thus a group of the Jews went with soldiers to the house where Jesus lodged with his twelve, thirteen or seventeen disciples. They besieged them on a Friday past the midafternoon hour. Jesus asked his disciples, "Who among you would consent to bear my likeness and be my companion in Paradise?" A young man volunteered, but Jesus, thinking the youth too young for the task, repeated his request three times. Each time, however, only the youth indicated his readiness to ransom the master. Jesus then agreed and an opening appeared in the roof of the house through which he ascended to heaven. After this the companions of Jesus went out of the house and the youth was seized and killed.[35]

Thus the Jews and some Christian groups thought that it was Jesus, as did those of his companions who did not see him ascend to heaven. It is also said that his mother sat at the foot of the Cross and wept and that the man spoke to her.[36] The author, however, doubts this and adds, "... but God knows best." Then, commenting on the entire episode, he writes, "And all this is so that God may try His servants according to His infinite wisdom."[37]

The first to seriously question the substitutionist idea altogether was the famous commentator Abū 'l-Qāsim al-Zamakhsharī (d. 538/1143). His objections are based only on grammatical considerations. Nevertheless, he provides new arguments for many commentators after him. He begins by asking to what the verb *shubbiha* refers. If it is made to refer to Christ, Christ is the one to whom something else is likened, not the one likened to something else. The verb, on the other hand, cannot have as its subject the one killed, since he is never mentioned in the Qur'ān. Thus it must refer to the preposition, "to" (them), that is, "they were made to imagine it." It is possible also to make the verb *shubbiha* refer to the one slain, as in the phrase, "We have surely killed the Christ, Jesus," that is, the one who was made to appear to them like Jesus.[38] His famous disciple, Nāṣir al-Dīn al-Bayḍāwī (d. 685/1286) repeats the same objections, and then adds, "... or it may be that no one was killed; rather his being killed was falsely claimed and spread among men."[39] Bayḍāwī does not, unfortunately, develop the idea further.

The thinker who really faced the theological and philosophical issues which the substitutionist interpretation implies was Fakr al-Dīn al-Rāzī (d. 606/1209). Rāzī was not satisfied with repeating the views of his predecessors; rather he subjected every view to the careful scrutiny of his sharp analytical mind. He begins by raising two questions. The first is the one raised by Zamakhsharī, already discussed. The second and more important question concerns what would happen if it is supposed that the likeness of one man could be cast on another. Two problems would result. First, it would open the gate of sophistry so that no social norm such as marriage or ownership rights could be ascertained. Further, this would lead to doubt in historical testimony, that is, the ongoing transmission of historical reports (*tawātur*). This historical transmission provides a sure source of knowledge, provided that tawātur is based on concrete data. If however, we allow the possibility of the occurence of such confusion of identity, this would necessitate in the end doubt in all sacred laws (*sharā'i'*). Nor can it be argued that such an occurrence is possible only during the ages of prophets. This is because although the age of prophetic miracles (*mu'jizāt*) is ended, nonetheless the age of *karāmāt* (miracles as divine favors) is not, for miracles as divine favors are possible in every age. "In sum, the opening of such a gate necessitates doubt in tawātur, and this in turn necessitates doubt in fundamentals (*uṣūl*), and this in turn necessitates doubt in the prophethood of all prophets. This is a branch (*far'*) necessitating doubt in fundamentals and must therefore be rejected."[40] Rāzī then suggests that perhaps when Christ was taken up the Jews took a man whom they killed, claiming that he was Jesus, for Jesus was a man little given to social intercourse, and thus known only to a few chosen companions. "The Christian agreement in the transmission (of the crucifixion event) goes back to a few people whose agreement on a false report is not improbable."[41]

Having thus criticized the principle of the substitutionist theory, Rāzī reviews the various opinions without endorsing any of them. He saw these as only conjectures transmitted from one generation to the next; the acceptance or rejection of any of them would be in itself a matter of opinion. Rāzī was more concerned with the understanding of Christ, the spirit of God and His Word. But before we turn to this more important point, we should consider a few other examples of the substitutionist solution to complete our discussion.

The idea that no one actually bore the image of Christ and suffered in his stead may have had its origins in Mu'tazilī circles. To the Mu'tazilī, the notion that God could commit acts of injustice, for any reason, was most repugnant. Furthermore, for God to allow such confusion of identity, for whatever reason, would be too irrational and therefore inadmissible. Shī'ī authors, who had much in common with Mu'tazilī thought, report an interesting tradition to this effect on the authority of Abū 'Alī al-Jubbā'ī (d. 303/915), a well known Mu'tazilī theologian. Al-Shaykh al-Ṭūṣī (d. 459/1067) reports that the Jews sought to kill Jesus, but God took him up to Himself. They therefore took another whom they crucified on a high and isolated hill, allowing no one to come near him until his features had changed beyond recognition. They were thus able to conceal the fact of Jesus' ascension, which they witnessed, and to spread false reports of his death and crucifixion. This they did to prevent his ascension from becoming a reason for other Jews to believe in him. In this solution, the requirements of both justice and rationality are met. Moreover, those who later disagreed concerning Christ's end were not those who crucified him. Hence, the contention of both the Jews, who claimed to have crucified Jesus, and of the Christians, who asserted that he died on the Cross and was then taken up to heaven, are—from the point of view of Jewish and Christian reporters—historically true.[42]

Shī'ī popular piety presents Jesus from a definite Shī'ī perspective. According to Shī'ī piety, human beings are either in the wrong or in the right, depending on whether or not they follow the right authority or guidance of God's prophets and their true vicegerents, the imāms. We are told on the authority of the fifth imām, Imām al-Bāqir, that Jesus called his disciples together one evening to tell them of his coming ascension and asked who would consent to bear his image, be killed and be his companion in Paradise. A young man accepted and Jesus assented as well. He then told them that one of them would deny him twelve times before the morning, and one confessed his intention to be that person. Finally Jesus predicted, "You shall indeed be divided after me into three sects. Two of these will be calumnious towards God, and thus be destined for the fire; the third will follow Sham'ūn (Simon Peter), will be truthful towards God, and hence be destined for Paradise."[43] Jesus, as a true Shī'ī ascetic, then ascended to heaven wearing a woolen shirt, spun and sewed by Mary, his mother. As he reached the heavenly regions, he was addressed, "O Jesus, cast away from you the adornment of the world."[44]

Shī'ī authors in general report the usual traditions on the authority of the same traditionists cited by Sunnī commentators. Shī'ī traditions, however, and these are few, present, as we have seen, typically Shī'ī interpretations. To the element of human plotting (*makr*) and divine counterplotting, Shī'ī exegesis adds an element of divine mystery. Those who imagined that Jesus was killed and crucified did so in ignorance of the truth. Their conjecture (*ẓann*) was based on an incomplete knowledge of the facts. Thus the famous fourth Islamic century theologian and traditionist Ibn Bābawayh quotes the eighth imām, Imām al-Riḍā, as saying:

> The case of no one among the prophets of God and His Proofs (or Witnesses, *hujaj*) has been obscured (*shubbiha*) to men except that of Jesus alone. This is due to the fact that he was taken up from this world alive, and his spirit taken away from him between heaven and earth. He was taken up to heaven and there his spirit was returned to him.[45]

The word *shubbiha* in this context means not only "it was made to appear so," but also that the matter was made obscure. This interpretation is not at all implausible if we consider the rest of the verse, as we shall now do.

III. Did Jesus die?

The Qur'ān, we have argued, presents Jesus as a challenge not only to human folly and unbelief (*kufr*), but equally to human ignorance and the reliance on mere conjecture. Indeed, the Arabic word *ẓann* is the opposite not only of knowledge (*'ilm*), but also of absolute certainty or faith (*yaqīn*). The Qur'ān declares that, "Those who differed concerning him [Jesus] are in doubt regarding it [the truth]; they have no knowledge of it [the truth] save the following of conjecture (*ẓann*)."[46] In this reading, we may differ from some commentators, yet we have not forced the text to yield any meaning or idea not in consonance with the Qur'anic view of Christ. Nor were commentators from the earliest time unaware of this interpretation.

The famous scholar Ibn Qutayba (d. 276/889) comments on the passage, "They have no knowledge concerning it save the following of conjecture and they did not slay him (or, it) with certainty" (meaning, "they did not slay knowledge with certainty").[47] This interesting interpretation is based on a tradition attributed to the first actual commentator, Ibn 'Abbās, the cousin and companion of the Prophet. According to Ṭabarī, the disagreement (*ikhtilāf*) here concerns Jesus, whether he was the one who was killed by the Jews or someone else. Their having killed him was only a conjecture, the opposite of knowledge and certainty. "And this is like one man saying to another, 'You have not killed this matter with knowledge, nor have you killed it with certainty,'" Ṭabarī argues therefore that the *hu* ending of the word *qatalūhu,* "they slew him (or, it)," refers to *al-ẓann,* conjecture.[48]

If this interpretation is at all plausible, then the Qur'ān is addressing not only the Jewish contemporaries of Jesus, but all human beings of all times. The disagreement for which the Qur'ān reproaches the contemporaries of Jesus is not absent from Muslim thinking about Christ. In their earnest search for truth, many commentators obscured the essence of the Qur'anic view of Christ behind the veil of their own conjecture. The substitutionist theory will not do, regardless of its form or purpose. First, it makes a mockery of divine justice and the primordial covenant of God with humanity, to guide human history to its final fulfillment.[49] Would it be in consonance with God's covenant, his mercy and justice, to deceive humanity for so many centuries? Or, can it be said that the argument of the commentators would be really meaningful to Christians? Muslim commentators have generally assumed an attitude of overconfident superiority towards the Christians whom they were supposed to guide to the truth. This attitude has been generally a polemical one in that it assumes, as we have seen, that the Christian witness to the Cross of Christ is based on a divine deception, and is therefore false.

To be sure, there were those who sought to minimize or reject this attitude. In this they came nearer to the Qur'anic spirit of conciliation and search for meaning beyond the mere facts of history. This effort was made mainly by Sufi exegetes, although it was not limited to them. Rāzī, after reviewing and criticizing the various theories and notions of his predecessors, explains the Christian idea that only the human body of Christ suffered and died.

> For his [Jesus'] soul is of the substance of sanctity (*qudsiyya*) and exaltation (*'ulwiyya*). It is a celestial [soul] of intense luminosity, with the divine lights, and of great proximity to the angelic spirit. A soul such as this would not suffer because of the darkness of the body. For after its separation from the darkness of this body, it is liberated into the open courts of the heavenly realms and the lights of the world of majesty. There its exaltation and bliss are increased beyond measure.[50]

This statement goes a long way towards meeting the Qur'anic challenge of Jesus, the Christ. It also provides a good starting point for Muslim-Christian understanding.

Muslim commentators had some awareness, however imperfect, of the Christological issues in Eastern Christian theology. They therefore attributed this disagreement and conjecture to Christian errors concerning Jesus.[51] Yet even here, we see operating the Islamic view of the truth as transcending the flow of historical events. Islam, according to this view, is as old as history itself. It is the truth which all prophets have claimed, but which was forgotten or distorted until revealed with definite force and clarity in the Qur'ān. Thus Ibn Kathīr relates, in his interpretation of the verse in question, that the followers of Jesus were divided after him into three sects. One of them asserted that, "God was among us for as long as He willed, then went up to heaven." This was the Jacobite sect. The second said, "The son of God dwelt among us so long as he willed, then God took him up to Himself." These were the Nestorians. The third group declared, "The servant of God and His apostle sojourned among us for as long as God willed, then God took him up to Himself." These were the Muslims. "Since that time, Islam remained obscured until God sent Muḥammad."[52]

This view of the universality of the truth could be the basis of unity and dialogue within the diversity of humankind. If all human beings are seen as committed (*muslim*) to the divine will within the context of the spirit and cultural heritage of each human community, then the spirit of tolerance and understanding would prevail. If, on the other hand, the Islam of the Muslim community, with all its institutions as a reified religion, is to be used as the measure of religious truth, everywhere and in every age, then the divine wisdom in creating a world of religious and cultural plurality[53] has been in vain. The denial of this is possible, in our view, only on the most superficial level, where facts, not meaning, become the point of contention and polemics on both sides.

The Qur'ān, as we have already argued, does not deny the death of Christ. Rather, it challenges human beings who in their folly have deluded themselves into believing that they would vanquish the divine Word, Jesus Christ the Messenger of God. The death of Jesus is asserted several times and in various contexts.[54] Two of these are of special interest to the argument of this study. In Sūra 5 God questions Jesus directly, "O Jesus, son of Mary, did you say to mankind, 'Take me and my mother as two gods beside God?'" To this Jesus answers:

> I did not say to them save that which you commanded me (to say), "Worship God, my Lord and your Lord." I was a witness over them, as long as I was among them, but when You took me (or, caused me to die), You were the Watcher over them, and You are a witness over all things.[55]

Here the Oneness of God is contrasted with the humanity of Christ, which is stressed by the reference to the fact of his mortality.

The other verse we wish to discuss at some length is put in the context of confrontation, or struggle between Jesus and his opponents, where God intervenes directly on behalf of His messenger. The struggle begins when Jesus senses the denial or unbelief of his people. He asks his disciples, "Who shall be my supporters (*anṣār*) to God?" They pledged their support, in the words, "We shall be God's supporters; we believe in God, so bear witness that we are Muslims."[56] Then in answer to the plot of the people against Jesus, God assures him, saying, "O Jesus, I am surely taking you (or, causing you to die, *mutawaffika*) and lifting you up to me."[57] The verse goes on to promise Jesus salvation from the impurities of unbelief and to his followers authority over the people of unbelief until the day of resurrection, when all men shall return to God, who will judge among them. The verse clearly states an end to Jesus' earthly life followed by a celestial life with God.

Commentators went to great length in their attempts to harmonize this statement with what appears at first sight as its opposite. It is the declaration that Jesus did not actually die on the Cross, but was taken up to heaven. The solutions offered were, first, that the word *mutawaffika* means "receiving you."[58] The verb *tawaffa* literally means to reclaim a debt or a charge in its entirety from another person. In general usage, however, it means in its passive form, *tuwuffi*, to die, hence the verbal noun *wafāt*, death. Thus the dilemma is whether Jesus died and his soul was received by God, or his soul and body were both reclaimed and he went to heaven alive. The second solution implies that Jesus is still alive in heaven, having been taken up in his sleep so that he would not be frightened by the experience.[59] Ṭabarī cites Ka'b al-Aḥbār, the Jewish chief Rabbi, as saying:

> God, exalted be His Majesty, would not have caused Jesus, son of Mary, to die. … Thus, when Jesus saw the small number of those who accepted him and the multitude of those who rejected him, he complained to God. Then God revealed to him, "Surely I am receiving you (*mutawaffika*) and lifting you up to me. For the one whom I take up to Me is not dead, and I shall send you against the one-eyed liar (*al-A'war al-Dajjāl*) and you shall kill him. After this, you shall live for twenty-four years, then will I cause you to die the death of the living."[60]

It was early reported on the authority of Ibn 'Abbās that the word *mutawaffika* means "causing you to die," *mumītuka*.[61] Perhaps contemporary with this tradition was the alternative equating *tawaffi* (receiving or reclaiming) with *rafa'a* (to take up to heaven).[62] Still another tradition suggests that Jesus was taken to heaven and will die later, since the sequence of the action of receiving and taking up does not necessarily require the order given in the literal reading of the text.[63]

The traditions related on the authority of converts, such as Wahb b. Munabbih, retain a strong echo of Gospel accounts. Wahb declared that, "God caused Jesus, son of Mary, to die for three hours during the day, then took him up to Him." It is possible that the three hours here mentioned refer to the darkness that was supposed to have covered the earth at the time of Jesus' death.[64] Ibn Isḥāq reports on the authority of a Christian convert that God caused Jesus to die for seven hours, an idea which later commentators attribute to Christian reports.[65] There is no evidence of such a notion in Christian tradition. There were even suggestions that Jesus died for three days, then was resuscitated and taken up to heaven.[66]

Again, as usual, we find in Rāzī a genuine attempt to go beyond the literal reading of the text. He first interprets the word *mutawaffika* as possibly meaning "completing the term (*ajal*) of your life," and "protecting you from the evil schemes of your enemies." This also means that Jesus was taken up to heaven both in body and spirit, that is, as a complete person. Rāzī then argues that the word is to be understood metaphorically: "I [God] shall render you [Jesus] as though you are dead," because when Jesus was taken up to heaven and no news or trace was left of him on earth, he became as one dead.[67] The author takes the term *tawwafi* to include death, without being synonymous with it. It is rather a general term requiring specification of the kind intended, hence, "and 'taking you up to Me' is … a specification of the kind."[68] It could also mean that God accepted the deeds (*a'māl*) of Jesus, which He caused to be brought before Him.[69] Rāzī concludes:

> What is meant by this verse is that the Exalted One gave Jesus the glad tidings that his acts of obedience and good deeds were accepted. He informed him also that what troubles and hardships he had suffered at the hands of his enemies in the cause of manifesting his faith (*dīn*) and sacred law (*sharī'a*) would not be lost, nor would his reward be destroyed.[70]

In this interpretation, Rāzī may have been influenced by the Sufi view of Christ. He quotes the statement of the famous Sufi Abū Bakr al-Wāsiṭī that God said: "I am causing you to die to your desires and the limitations of your cardinal soul (*nafs*)."[71] Rāzī does not, however, carry this interpretation far enough for him to be a good representative of the Sufi view.

The Sufis, while not rejecting the traditional interpretation completely, have attempted to see Christ as the universal perfect man through whom all religions will be unified and humanity brought nearer to God. The significance of the death of Jesus is not in the how and when of history, but rather in its meaning to a humanity bound to this material plane of existence by lust, greed and anxiety. Nor is the significance of his heavenly subsistence with God dependent on whether his body, his spirit, or both were assumed to heaven. Rather, the significance of Christ's life in heaven is his example as a specially favored human being who has risen beyond this world of material existence to the divine presence. He was taken to the heaven which, according to al-Haṣan al-Baṣrī, "is the locus of the grace (*karāma*) of God and the dwelling place of His angels."[72] God wished him to be with the angels in order that "they may attain his grace (*baraka*), because he is the Word of God and His Spirit." Jesus may be taken as a concrete example of the spiritual journey of the man of faith from the plane of material existence to the celestial plane where God alone Is; there to Him alone belongs judgment and to no one of His creatures.

Jesus will return, to share in our human life, and more fully than he did during his first sojourn on earth. He shall then purify the earth from all falsehood and dissension. He shall kill the one-eyed liar, the symbol of all evil in the world. He shall remove the barriers which divide humanity spiritually. He shall marry and beget children. He shall die and be buried with Muḥammad in his grave and the two will be resurrected together.[73] In this final comingling of the bodies of the founders of two of the world's largest religious communities, we have perhaps the myth expressing hopes often drowned by the clamor of our empty words.

IV. The search for meaning: some modern attitudes

The Sufi approach had been unique in the long history of Muslim-Christian relations. It has not, unfortunately, received the attention it deserves as a possible basis for constructive dialogue. In fact, modern thinkers have generally ignored Sufi ideas along with much traditional literature dealing with interpretation of the life, death, and mission of Jesus.

The Shī'ī view of Christ resembles that of the Sufis in some important respects. First, it does not always insist on a literal understanding of the text. Second, it presents an ascetic image of Jesus, and finally, it does not generally favor a bodily ascension of Christ to heaven.

Modern Shī'ī thinkers have allowed the possibility that Jesus died and only his spirit was taken up to heaven. One modern commentator has argued that the Jews crucified not Jesus but another whom they mistook for him. Jesus, however, escaped and with his mother spent the rest of his life in hermetic seclusion. The author finds support for this view in the verse, "And we have made the son of Mary and his mother a sign, and led them for refuge to a hill of comfort and flowing water."[74] Jesus then died a natural death and his body was buried in that hill, while his spirit went up to heaven.

The well-known contemporary Shī'ī scholar, Sayyid Muḥammad Ḥusayn Ṭabāṭabā'ī, takes the same view, but on different grounds. He first argues that *wafāt* does not necessarily mean death, unless specified.[75] He argues further that although a literal reading of the words, "rather, God took him up to Himself," may suggest a bodily ascension, "God actually meant a spiritual (*ma'nawī*) and not a formal (*ṣuwarī*) assumption, because the Exalted One has no place of the kind occupied by bodies."[76] In this, the author follows a time-honored tradition in Mu'tazilī and Shī'ī thought which sought to explain metaphorically all anthropomorphic references to God in the Qur'ān. Even, he concludes, "if the text indicates literally bodily assumption, heaven means only the locus of proximity to Him and His blessings."[77]

Again, in agreement with the Mu'tazilī insistence on divine justice and the rationality of all things, Sayyid Ṭabāṭabā'ī interprets the words *shubbiha lahum* as "seizing someone else unknowingly."[78] For the Roman soldiers, who arrested Jesus and crucified him, did not know him. He bases this argument on the role of Judas, who identified Jesus for them. Thus *tashbīh,* seeming or appearing, could also mean "mistake" (*shubha*), and not the casting of the image (*ṣūra*) of one man on another. The author offers a final curious suggestion:

> Perhaps some historians have mentioned that the stories relating to Jesus, his mission and the historical events of the rulers and other preachers of his time refer to two men called Christ. The two may have lived five hundred years or more apart. The earlier was the true Messiah, neither killed nor crucified, and the later, the false Messiah, was crucified. Thus what the Qur'ān mentions concerning *tashbīh,* is that of Jesus, son of Mary, with the crucified Christ.

Perhaps aware of the historical problems which this suggestion raises, the author adds, "... and God knows best."[79]

In contrast with the Sufi and Shī'ī view of the death and assumption of Christ, contemporary Sunnī thinkers have shifted the emphasis of their arguments to a discussion of the meaning of the Cross in the Christian faith and to the question of the authenticity of the Gospel accounts regarding the death of Christ. In this, they have taken an important step towards facing the crucial issues involved in the Christian assertion of the Cross as an historical fact of cosmic dimensions, transforming and transcending history. Commentators of the classical and post-classical periods sought through an earnest and painstaking study of the Qur'ān to question the historicity of the Cross, without, however, grappling with the problems of its significance for Christianity. Modern thinkers, on the other hand, have turned to history, including the Gospel story, for support of their interpretations. They exhibit a fairly accurate knowledge of primary Christian sources, which they discuss not from a Christian, but from a strictly Islamic perspective. This approach can hardly serve as the basis for a fruitful encounter of the two faiths.

The modern approach is dialectic and personal, and while it takes traditional ideas into account, it is generally not bound by them. Hence, it is not to tradition that modern thinkers turn for their criticism of Christianity, but to the nineteenth century humanist attacks on religion. In this we see a kind of crystallization of a modern tradition. Early modernists in the Arab world, such as Muḥammad 'Abduh and his immediate successors, all belong to the nineteenth century. Their views have been adopted and in large measure repeated by later thinkers interested in Christianity in general.

Another important characteristic of the modern approach is a tendency to demythologize the Christ of the classical tradition, whether by rejecting tradition altogether, or by interpreting it metaphorically. Sayyid Quṭb, the famous leader of the Muslim Brothers, relies on the Gospel accounts for only the background of his interpretation of the verses under consideration. His purpose was to "remain in the shadow of the Qur'ān."[80] He accepts only what the sacred text states concerning the death and assumption of Jesus Christ, commenting that "as for the manner of his death and assumption, these are matters belonging to the unseen (*ghaybiyya*), and they fall in the category of obscure (*mutashabbihāt*) verses, whose exegetical meaning (*ta'wīl*) is known to God alone."[81]

Another modern thinker, Aḥmad Muṣṭafā al-Marāghī, offers a rationalistic view of Christ by interpreting tradition metaphorically. He argues from historical examples of identity confusion that it was possible for the Jews and the Roman soldiers to mistake another for Jesus.[82] Like Moses, who disappeared under the eyes of thousands of his people, Jesus disappeared and died a natural death. As for his ascension, it must be understood as the raising of status or degree with God; as we read of Idrīs (Enoch), "and We raised him into a high station."[83] Similarly, what is meant by Christ's return to the earth and his rule over it is, "the domination of his spirit and the mystery of his message over humanity in order that men may live by the inner meaning of the law (sharī'a) without being bound by its outer shell."[84] For Jesus did not bring a new law to the Jews. He was rather a reformer who sought to manifest the truth. Likewise, the liar (al-Dajjāl) whom Jesus is to kill at the end of time, is only a symbol of empty legends, falsehood and all the evils which would disappear were men and women to live by the spirit of the sacred law and fulfill its injunctions.[85]

It must be emphasized that Muslim thinkers do not reject the Gospels out of hand as complete distortions of the truth. They are regarded, on the contrary, as containing clear evidence of the essential truth of God's Oneness and the humanity of Jesus. It is interesting to observe further that throughout Islamic history, the fourth Gospel, with its Logos Christology, has been the one most often cited by Muslim thinkers in support of their arguments. Another document which provided the answer to many Christological questions for modern commentators is the Gospel of Barnabas. This is most probably a late work, written under Islamic influence and agreeing with Islam on many crucial points.[86] It was translated into Arabic in the early decades of this century by Antun Saadi, a Lebanese Christian. Since then, it has been regarded by Muslim scholars as coming nearest to the lost Gospel of Jesus (*Injīl 'Īsā*), and has therefore been the source of many of their arguments against Christianity.[87] The Gospel of Barnabas tells us that Judas Iscariot led the Jews and Roman soldiers to arrest Jesus at night in a house where Jesus and the disciples were sleeping. As he entered the house, Jesus was taken away by the angels, who carried him up to heaven. His likeness and his voice were cast upon Judas, who woke up the other disciples to ask where the master had gone. They, however, hailed him as the master and thought him distraught by the fear of death. This Judas was taken and crucified. He lost his mind so that his incoherent protests were considered as those of a madman. Jesus, on the other hand, appeared after three days to his mother and the rest of the disciples to comfort and reassure them, announcing the coming of the Prophet Muḥammad, who would fulfill all the things he had taught.[88]

The Gospel of Barnabas has provided modern commentators not only with a supposed first-hand report in support of the substitutionist theory, but also with what appears as a plausible justification. Thus we have come full circle back to the earliest interpretation of the words *shubbiha lahum* as meaning "another took his likeness and was substituted for him." Modern Muslim thinkers have been aware of the claim that Barnabas is a late document. Some have therefore used it only as partial evidence,[89] while others have argued that it is the true Gospel in full or in part, which Christians had hidden for many centuries until it was found in their most sacred institution, the Vatican Library. The question of the historicity of the event of the Cross remains open, nonetheless, and a more up-to-date study of the Gospel of Barnabas would help greatly in moving Christian-Muslim dialogue from scriptural polemics to the more important task of understanding and appreciating the significance of Christ for the two religious traditions. The critique of the Cross as the instrument of redemption by Sayyid Muḥammad Rashīd Riḍā in *Tafsīr al-Manār* typifies both the problem as well as the effort for greater Christian-Muslim understanding. We shall conclude our discussion of Muslim views of the death of Jesus with a brief analysis of this critique.

Rashīd Riḍā agrees with other contemporary commentators in taking the traditions regarding the ascension of Jesus and his return at the end of time metaphorically and with caution. He sees in the Qur'anic reference to Jesus as the apostle of God whom the Jews wrongly claimed to have killed an assertion of Christ's apostleship, not divinity. He argues further that the Gospels indicate that Jesus himself proclaimed the Oneness of God in the words, "and this is eternal life, that they know Thee, the only true God, and Jesus Christ whom Thou hast sent."[90] He likewise finds support in the same Gospel for the idea of doubt and conjecture concerning Jesus' identity even by the disciples: "You shall doubt me tonight."[91] These works are quoted by most modern commentators, all of whom miss their real significance, both for the evangelist and the Christian tradition in general. The author concludes from this that if the disciples, who know him most intimately, doubted him, then a mistake in identity would not be impossible. Therefore, this story is based on an historical account with an incomplete chain of transmission. Here again, the author of *al-Manār* echoes the usual demand that the only measure of true report is the model of ḥadīth transmission.

Having thus established his position regarding the problems of interpreting the Qur'anic text, the author adds: "The actual fact of the crucifixion is not itself a matter which the Book of God seeks to affirm or deny, except for the purpose of asserting the killing of prophets by the Jews unjustly, and reproaching them for that act."[92] The author then proceeds to the more important matter, namely, the Christian belief concerning Christ and the crucifixion. He begins with a detailed discussion of original sin, then the incarnation, and finally the work of redemption.

The author insists throughout on the necessity of reason in judging and accepting the truth of divine revelation. Thus he argues that the story of the crucifixion and redemption is unacceptable to anyone who believes in rational proof. The story implies that when Adam fell, God was for thousands of years seeking a way to reconcile His justice with His mercy. This imputes ignorance to God, and thus it is an act of unbelief (*kufr*). None in possession of an independent reason could accept the idea

> that the Creator of the universe could be incarnated in the womb of a woman in this earth which, in comparison to the rest of His creation, is like an atom, and then be a human being eating and drinking, experiencing fatigue and suffering other hardships

> like the rest of mankind. Then His enemies would level at Him insults and pain, and finally crucify Him with thieves and declare Him cursed according to the Book He revealed to one of His apostles, exalted be He over all this![93]

No one could believe in such a story on which, Christians claim, depends the salvation of humanity. "We say rather no one believes it because belief (*imān*) is the affirmation (*taṣdīq*) by reason of something that it can apprehend."[94]

The author goes on to ask how can we say that God had reconciled His justice with His mercy through the crucifixion of Christ when in reality this had nullified them both. For God allowed Jesus to suffer as a man without having committed any sin that merited this great punishment. God, therefore, cannot be both just and merciful if in attempting to reconcile the two, He loses them both. Perhaps referring to the doctrine of salvation by faith, the author protests that if the crucifixion would save the person believing in it, no matter how grave his sins and evil his deeds, where would the justice of God and His mercy be? "The claim of the people of the Cross, therefore, that clemency and forgiveness are opposed to justice, is unacceptable."[95] Sayyid Rashīd Riḍā then continues by contrasting this with the idea of salvation in Islam.

Obviously, these criticisms are not new, nor are they limited to Muslims. This study is not the place for us to argue for or against them. It must be observed, however, that reason has not been considered, even by Islam, as the final arbiter of faith. Indeed, the Qur'ān is replete with instances extolling the divine mystery in creation. Nor does the Qur'ān reject the nonrational conception of Jesus, outside the biological law of procreation. Christians have insisted from the start that the Cross is an obstacle to human wisdom and rationality. Faith is not logic, but the divine gift to man transcending and transforming human wisdom and rationality.

Rashīd Riḍā and Muḥammad 'Abduh were subject to missionary and secularist pressures. Thus their polemical arguments against Christianity must be seen in the context of Christian polemic against Islamic tradition, both in its religion and culture. Times have changed, and with the change of time there is a change of attitude. In his *Qarya Ẓālima,*[96] Dr. Kāmil Ḥusayn perhaps presents the first Muslim attempt to see the Cross in its true meaning. It is a judgment, not against any group of people, but against humanity, a repeatable act in any city, large or small, whose inhabitants choose to turn it into a "City of Wrong." In deciding to crucify Christ, the zealously religious men of Jerusalem agreed to crucify their conscience. Christianity would perhaps agree with this, but it would assert (and here the difference is vast and instructive) that in choosing to crucify their conscience, men and women everywhere and in every age crucify Christ anew.

Conclusion

It has been often argued by Christian scholars of Islam that because Islam was not forged in the face of persecution and martyrdom, it has no place for the mystery of suffering which in Christianity becomes the foundation for faith, hope and love. This view, we believe, is at best a simplistic one. The distraught Jacob, the patient Job, the persecuted Abraham and the martyred Zechariah and his son, John the Baptist, are but a few of the many examples of suffering in the way of God. Their stories, told and retold to the pious throughout Islamic history, have played an important, although little recognized role in Muslim piety. The Shī'ī ethos, which sees suffering as a dominant force in human history, has also played its important role in sensitizing Muslims to the power and profundity of human suffering.

Finally, the Prophet, in his moments of agony and depression, under the burden of the divine commision, and in his moments of fear and loneliness, had to be reassured by God with the words, "Have we not relieved your breast for you?"[97] Why then, it must be asked, does the Qur'ān deny the crucifixion of Christ in the face of apparently overwhelming evidence? Muslim commentators have not been able convincingly to disprove the crucifixion. Rather, they have compounded the problem by adding the conclusion of their substitutionist theories. The problem has been, we believe, one of understanding. Commentators have generally taken the verse to be an historical statement. This statement, like all the other statements concerning Jesus in the Qur'ān, belongs not to history but to theology in the broadest sense. It is similar to the Qur'anic assertion that Mary, the mother of Christ, was the sister of Aaron. In answer to the historian's protest, the Qur'ān declares that all the prophets are a continuous progeny,[98] not, of course, in the strict physical sense. Let us then, look at the verse again, this time from the point of view of theology, not of history.

The reproach of the Jews, "for their saying: 'We have surely killed Jesus the Christ, son of Mary, the apostle of God,'" with which the verse starts, is not directed at the telling of an historical lie, or at the making of a false report. It is rather, as is clear from the context, directed at human arrogance and folly, at an attitude towards God and His messenger. The words identifying Jesus are especially significant. They wished to kill Jesus, the innocent man, who is also the Christ, the Word, and God's representative among them. By identifying Christ in this context, the Qur'ān is addressing not only the people who could have killed yet another prophet, but all of humanity is told who Jesus is.

The Qur'ān is not speaking here about a man, righteous and wronged though he may be, but about the Word of God who was sent to earth and who returned to God. Thus the denial of the killing of Jesus is a denial of the power of men to vanquish and destroy the divine Word, which is forever victorious. Hence the words, "they did not kill him, nor did they crucify him," go far deeper than the events of ephemeral human history; they penetrate the heart and conscience of human beings. The claim of humanity (here exemplified in the Jewish society of Christ's earthly existence) to have this power against God can only be an illusion. "They did not slay him … but it seemed so to them." They only imagined doing so.

The words, *wa lākin shubbiha lahum* do not disclose, therefore, a long-hidden secret of divine deception; rather they constitute an accusation or judgment against the human sin of pride and ignorance. They are explained further in what follows: those who have disagreed about Christ are surely in doubt concerning the truth. They have no knowledge; they follow only conjecture, the foolish imaginings of their minds. What is this truth? It is, I think, the affirmation, once again, that God is greater than human powers and empty schemes: "They did not kill him, [that is, Jesus the Christ and God's Apostle] with certainty, rather God took him up to Himself, and God is mighty, and wise." Again, human ignorance, delusion and conjecture are all identified as a lack of certainty or firm faith. In the phrase, "and God is Mighty and Wise," these human limitations are contrasted with divine power and infinite wisdom.

The same verse presents Christ the Word as a challenge to human wisdom and power, and a judgment against human folly and pride. Men may "wish to extinguish the light of God with their mouths," that is, with their words of foolish wisdom, but God will perfect His light in spite of our foolishness and obstinacy.[99]

In their earnest striving for a true understanding of the sacred text, Muslim commentators did more than indulge in an exercise of textual analysis. The Qur'ān insists on "letting

God be God," and this the Muslim community has taken with uncompromising seriousness. The commentators expressed this insistence with eloquence and power, even at the risk of denying man the privilege of being man. On this privilege, with all its implications, the Qur'ān also insists, and with equal emphasis. Man, the crown of creation, "made in the best of forms,"[100] is also a "wrongdoing, foolish" creature.[101] Yet, in the end, the righteous men and women among God's servants will inherit the earth.[102] Humanity must be fulfilled and that is possible only through its exemplars, God's prophets and friends (*awliyā'*).

Christianity has insisted, and with equally uncompromising seriousness, on "letting God be man" in order for man to be divine. The gap between an extreme Islamic and an extreme Christian position on this point is admittedly vast. The difference is, I believe, one of theological terminology rather than intent. The final purpose for the two communities of faith is one: let God be God, not only in His vast creation, but in our little lives as well. Then and only then, could man be truly man, and the light of God would shine with perfect splendor in our mouths and hearts.

Appendix I: An early Muslim account of the Passion[103]

When God informed Jesus, son of Mary, that he would be soon departing this world, he was disheartened by death, and sorely grieved. He therefore called the disciples (*ḥawāriyyūn*) together for a meal which he had prepared for them. He said, "Come to me all of you tonight for I have a favor to ask of you." When they had all come together in the night, he served them himself, and when they had finished eating, he washed their hands and helped them to perform their ablutions with his own hands, and wiped their hands on his garments.[104]

The disciples regarded this as an act below the master's dignity and expressed their disapproval. But Jesus said, "Any one who opposes me in what I do tonight is not of me (that is, of my faith), nor I of him." Thus they concurred. When he had finished, he said, "As for what I have done for you tonight, serving you at table and washing your hands with my own hands, let that be an example for you. You regard me as the best of you, so let no one among you regard himself as better than the others, and let each one of you offer his life for the others as I have laid down my life for you.[105] As for the favor for which I have called you, it is that you pray God fervently that He may extend my term (*ajal*)."

But when they stood up in prayer, wishing to prolong their earnest supplications, they were overcome by sleep, so that they were unable to pray. He began to rouse them, saying, "To God be praise, could you not bear with me one night and render me help!" They answered, "We know not what had befallen us. We used to stay up the night in long fellowship (*samar*), but tonight we cannot keep ourselves from sleep, and whatever supplication we wish to make, we are being prevented from making." Then Jesus said, "The shepherd will be taken away and the sheep will be scattered."[106] With similar words he went on foretelling and lamenting his end. He continued, "In truth, I say to you, one of you will deny me three times before the cock crows. And another will sell me for a few pieces of silver and consume my price."[107]

After this, they went out, each his own way, and left him. The Jews then came seeking him, and they seized Sham'ūn (Simon Peter), exclaiming, "He is one of his companions," but he denied, saying, "I am not his companion." Others also seized him and he likewise denied. Then he heard the crowing of a cock, and he wept bitterly.[108]

The next morning, one of the disciples went to the Jews and said, "What will you give me if I lead you to Christ?" They gave him thirty pieces, which he took and led them to him. Prior to that, however, he (or: it) so appeared to them. [The phrase *wa kāna shubbiha ʿalayhim qabla dhālik* is inserted here without further explanation. It could mean that the disciple Judas bore his likeness or that they imagined something; no doubt the phrase is inserted to harmonize a Gospel account with Islamic exegesis. From here on, it is not clear who the actual object of the story is.] Thus they took him, after ascertaining that it was he, and tied him with a rope. They dragged him, saying, "You raised the dead and cast out Satan, and healed those who were possessed, can you not save yourself from this rope?" They also spat on him and placed thorns upon his head. Thus they brought him to the wood on which they wished to crucify him.[109] God, however, took him up to Himself and they crucified what seemed to them. [It is interesting to observe that the phrase, *faṣalabū ma shubbiha lahum* does not necessarily imply a person but a thing; otherwise, *man shubbiha lahum* would have been more appropriate.]

Then Jesus remained seven [days?]. [We are not told where, but perhaps in heaven.] Then his mother and the woman whom Jesus cured from madness [Mary Magdelene?] came to weep in the place where the crucified one was. Jesus came to them and said, "For whom do you weep?" They answered, "For you." He said, "God had taken me up to Himself and no harm befell me. For this is a thing which only appeared to them. Go now and tell the disciples to meet me at such and such a place." So they met him, eleven, but the one who sold him and led the Jews to him was missing. Jesus asked his companions about him and they said, "He regretted what he did, so he hanged and killed himself." Jesus said, "Had he repented, God surely would have turned towards him." [It is clear from this that Judas was not the one substituted for Jesus. At this early stage, the identity of the substitute was left unspecified.]

Jesus then enquired from them concerning a youth who followed them called John (Yuhannah). [The use of the Syriac "Yuhannah" rather than of "Yaḥyā", as well as the fact that John has no special place in this story, indicate that the source of the tradition was clearly the fourth Gospel.] He answered, "He is with you. Go now for everyone of you will speak the language of a different people. [This is perhaps a vague allusion to the descent of the Holy Spirit.[110]] Let him therefore warn them and leave them."

Appendix II: The Christ of Sufism[111]

Jesus was taken to heaven because his entrance into worldly existence was not through the gate of lust, therefore his departure from it was not through the gate of death. He rather entered through the gate of power (*qudra*), and departed through the gate of majesty (*ʿizza*). [In heaven] God gave him wings and clothed him with light and removed from him the desires for food and drink. Thus he flies with the angels, and is with them around the throne. For he is human and angelic, heavenly and earthly.

If, then, it is asked, why did God not return Jesus to the world after He had taken him up to heaven, the answer is that he shall return in the end to be a sign for the hour (*ʿilm li'l sāʿa*, that is, the Day of Resurrection) and the seal of general *walāya* (saintship). For after him, there is no *walī* (saint or friend of God) with whom God would close the Muḥammadan cycle (*al-dawra al-Muḥammadiyya*). [For in this] is its great ennoblement, in that it will be closed by a prophet-messenger who will be subject to the sharīʿa. Both Jews and Christians will believe in it [that is, Islam]. Through him [Jesus] God will renew the age of prophethood for the community (*umma*). He shall be served by the Mahdī and the men of the cave. He shall marry and beget children. He shall be one of the community of Muḥammad as the seal of his *awliyā'* and heirs with regard to *walāya*. [Sufi theology posits two concentric cycles of prophethood and *walāya*, beginning with Adam and ending with Muḥammad, the seal of the prophetic cycle. That of *walāya* will continue until the end of time. Jesus, however, will have the great privilege of culminating both cycles, being the perfect *walī* and perfect prophet.] For the spirit of Jesus is the manifestation of the Greatest Name, and an effulgence of divine power ...; he is the manifestation of the universal divine name, a primordial inheritance.

Notes

1 S. 4:157. The numbering is of the Egyptian edition and all Qur'anic translations are my own.
2 S. 2:1.
3 S. 19:34.
4 S. 7:11.
5 S. 6:8, 9, 50; 11:31; 17:94, 95; 25:7.
6 S. 3:59.
7 S. 3:45; 4:171.
8 S. 4:171–72; 5:17, 75.
9 Aḥmad b. Ḥanbal, *Musnad*, ed. Aḥmad Muḥammad Shākir (Cairo: Dār al-Ma'ārif, 1375/1955), XV, H. 7902 ff. See also Muslim b. al-Ḥajjāj al-Qushayrī al-Nīsabūrī, *Ṣaḥīḥ Muslim*, ed. Muḥammad Fu'ād 'Abd al-Bāqī (Cairo: Dār Iḥyā' al-Kutub al-'Arabiyya, 1375/1955), first edition, IV, H. 141–49.
10 S. 21:91; 66:12.
11 S. 3:61. See also Abū Ja'far Muḥammad b. Jarīr al-Ṭabarī, *Jāmi' al-Bayān 'an Ta'wīl āy al-Qur'ān*, ed. Maḥmūd Muḥammad Shākir and Aḥmad Muḥammad Shākir (Cairo: Dār al-Ma'ārif, n.d.), VI, 461.
12 S. 3:59.
13 S. 3:49.
14 S. 2:87, 253.
15 See, for example, the Infancy Gospel of Thomas and the Protevangelium of James in Edgar Hennecke, *New Testament Apocrypha*, trans. and ed. by R. McL. Wilson, I (Philadelphia: Westminster Press, 1963).
16 S. 3:49; 61:6.
17 S. 4:157–58.
18 Michel Hayek, *al-Masīḥ fī 'l-Islām* (Beirut: Catholic Press, 1961), p. 21.
19 S. 19:22, 23.
20 S. 19:33.
21 Ṭabarī, IX, 367, H. 10779.
22 See Appendix I for the complete text of this tradition.
23 See, for example, Abū 'l-Faraj Jamāl al-Dīn 'Abd al-Raḥmān b. 'Alī b. Muḥammad al-Jawzī al-Qarashī al-Baghdādī, *Zād at-Masīr fī 'Ilm al-Tafsīr* (Beirut: al-Maktab al-Islāmī, 1384/1964), first ed., II, 224; Abū 'Abdallāh Muḥammad b. Yūsuf b. 'Alī b. Yūsuf al-Ḥayyānī, commonly known as Abū Ḥayyān, *al-Bahr al-Muḥīṭ* (Riyāḍ: Maktabat al-Naṣr, n.d.), II, 373 and III, 389; and for a good review of the various ideas up to his time, 'Imād al-Dīn Abū 'I-Fidā' Ismā'īl b. Kathīr, *Tafsīr al-Qur'ān al-'Aẓīm* (Cairo: Dār Iḥyā' al-Kutub al-'Arabiyya, n.d.), I, 573 ff.
24 Ṭabarī, IX, 370, H. 10781.
25 *Ibid.*, 370.
26 *Ibid.*, 370–71; cf. Matt. 26:39; Mark 14; 36; Luke 22:42.
27 See Luke 22:44.
28 See Baghdādī, II, 244 ff.; Abū Ṭāhir b. Muḥammad al-Fayrūzabādī al-Shīrāzī, *Tanwīr al-Miqbās min Tafsīr Ibn 'Abbās* (Cairo: Muṣṭafā al-Babī al-Ḥalabī, 1370/1951), second ed., p. 68; for Shī'ī examples, see Abū 'Alī al-Faḍl b. Haṣan al-Tabarsī, *Majma' al-Bayān fī Tafsīr al-Qur'ān* (Tehran: Sharikat al-Ma'ārif al-Islāmiyya, 1373 A.H.), IH, 135.
29 See the previous footnote. See also Abū 'l-Barakāt 'Abdallāh b. Aḥmad b. Maḥmūd al-Nasafī, *Madārik al-Tanzīl wa Ḥaqā'iq al-Ta'wīl* (Cairo: Dār Iḥyā' al-Kutub al-'Arabiyya, n.d.), 1, 203, and Muḥīy al-Sunna b. Muḥammad b. al-Ḥusayn b. Mas'ūd al-Baghawī, *Ma'ālim al-Tanzīl* (N.p.: Maṭba'at al-Ṣāliḥī, 1249 A.H.), see the commentary on S. IV, 157–58, no pagination.

30 See the two previous footnotes, and Ibn Kathīr, I, 366 ff. and 573 ff.
31 Ismā'īl Ḥaqqī, *Tafsīr Rūḥ al-Bayān* (Istanbul: Al-Matba'a al-'Uthmānīyya, 1130 A.H.), II, 317. See also al-Qāḍī Sanā'allāh al-'Uthmānī al-Maẓharī, *Tafsīr al-Maẓharī* (Hyderabad, n.p., n.d.), II, 280.
32 Ṭabarī, IX, 370–71.
33 See, for example, Abū Ja'far Muḥammad b. al-Ḥasan al-Ṭūsī, *al-Tibyān,* ed. Aḥmad Shawqī al-Amīn and Muḥammad Ḥabīb Quṣayr (Najaf: Maktabat al-Amīnī, n.d.), III, 383 and Ibn Kathīr, I, 575, for his discussion of the various traditions.
34 Matt. 27:29, Mark 15:17, John 19:2.
35 Ibn Kathīr, I, 574.
36 *Ibid.,* 574; cf. John 20:26–27.
37 Ibn Kathīr, I, 574.
38 Abū 'l-Qāsim 'Abdallāh Maḥmūd b. 'Umar al-Zamakhsharī, *al-Kashshāf 'an Haqā'iq Ghawāmiḍ al-Tanzīl wa 'Uyūn al-Aqāwīl fī Wujūh al-Ta'wīl* (Beirut: Dār al-Kitāb al-'Arabī, n.d.), I, 587.
39 Al-Qāḍī Nāṣir al-Dīn al-Bayḍāwī, *Tafsīr al-Bayḍāwī* (Cairo: Muḥammad 'Alī Ṣabīḥ, 1951), p. 135.
40 Fakhr al-Dīn al-Rāzī, *Al-Tafsīr al-Kabīr* (Cairo: al-Maṭba'a al-Bahiyya, 1357/1938), first ed., XI, 100.
41 *Ibid.,* XI, 100.
42 *Ibid., XI,* 101.
43 al-Sayyid Hāshim b, Sulaymān b. Ismā'īl b. Sayyid 'Abd al-Jawwād al-Ḥusaynī al-Baḥrānī, *al-Burhān fī Tafsīr al-Qur'ān* (Tehran: Chapkhāneh Aftāb, n.d.), p. 285.
44 *Ibid.,* p. 285. See also 'Abd 'Alī Janqalarūsī al-Huwayzī, *Tafsīr Nūr al-Thaqalayn* (Qom: Maṭba'at al-Ḥikma, 1382 A.H.), I, 287.
45 Baḥrānī, p. 285.
46 S. 4:157.
47 Abū Muḥammad 'Abdallāh b. Muslim b. Qutayba, *Tafsīr Gharīb al-Qur'ān* ed. Aḥmad Ṣaqr (Cairo: Dār Iḥyā' al-Kutub al-'Arabiyya, 1348/1958), p. 136.
48 Ṭabarī, IX, 376.
49 S. 7:172; 2:38.
50 Rāzī, XI, 101. See also Ḥaqqī, II, 318.
51 See, for example, Rāzī, XI, 101; Ibn Kathīr, I, 573. For a different view, see Baghawī, commentary on S. 4:158 (no pagination).
52 Ibn Kathīr, I, 574–75.
53 S. 49:13.
54 See, for example, S. 3:55; 5:117; 19:33.
55 S. 5:117.
56 S. 3:52.
57 S. 3:55.
58 See Ṭabarī, VI, 455, for his detailed discussion. See especially Zamakhsharī, 1, 366.
59 Zamakhsharī, 1, 366.
60 Ṭabarī, VI, 456–57.
61 Most commentators mention this as an alternative. Modern thinkers generally insist on it. See, for early views, note 58, and below for modern ones.
62 Ṭabarī, VI, 457.
63 See Shīrāzī, p. 39.
64 See Hayek, *al-Masīḥ* p. 225; cf. Matt. 27:45; Mark 15:33; Luke 23:44.
65 See Ṭabarī, VI, 458 and Ibn Kathīr, 1, 366.
66 Muḥammad b. 'Alī b. Muḥammad al-Shawkānī, *Fatḥ al-Qadīr al-Jāmi' bayn Fannay al-Riwāya wa 'l-Dirāya min 'Ilm al-Tafsīr* (Cairo: Muṣṭafā al-Bābī al-Ḥalabī, n.d.), 1, 346, citing Ibn 'Asākir, who reports on the authority of Ibn Munabbih.
67 Rāzī, VII, 72.
68 *Ibid.*
69 *Ibid.*
70 *Ibid.*
71 *Ibid.* See also Shīrāzī, p. 39, "I shall cause your heart to die to the love of this world."
72 Haqqī, II, 318.
73 Maẓharī, II, 57.
74 S. 23:50. Muḥammad 'Alī Haṣan al-Ḥillī, *Al-Mutashābah min al-Qur'ān* (Beirut: Dār al-Fikr, 1965), first edition, 1, 204.

75 Seyyid Muḥammad Ḥusayn Ṭabāṭabā'ī, *Al-Mīzān fi Tafsīr al-Qur'ān* (Beirut: Mu'assasat al-A'lamī, 1970), III, 207.
76 *Ibid.*, III, 208. See also Ṭūsī, II, 478.
77 Ṭabāṭabā'ī, V, 132.
78 *Ibid.*, V, 133.
79 *Ibid.*, V, 133.
80 Sayyid Quṭb, *Fī Ẓilāl al-Qur'ān* (Beirut: Dār Iḥyā' al-Turāth al-'Arabī, 1386/1967), fifth edition, IV, 587.
81 *Ibid.*, I, 595–96.
82 Aḥmad Muṣṭafā al-Marāghī, *Tafsīr al-Marāghī* (Muṣṭafā al-Bābī al-Ḥalabī, 1373/1953), second edition, VI, 12–13.
83 S. 19:57.
84 al-Marāghī, III, 169.
85 *Ibid.*, III, 170.
86 *Gospel of Barnabas,* ed. and trsl. by Lonsdale and Laura Ragg (Oxford: Clarendon Press, 1907).
87 See, for example, Shaykh Muḥammad Abū Zahra, *Muḥāḍarāt fi 'l-Naṣrāniyya* (Cairo: Maṭba'at Yūsuf, 1385/1966), third edition, pp. 57 ff.
88 *Gospel of Barnabas,* pp. 481 ff.
89 See, for instance, al-Marāghī, III, 13, and Sayyid Quṭb, VI, 587.
90 Sayyid Muḥammad Rashīd Riḍā, *Tafsīr al-Manār* (Cairo: Dār al-Manār, 1367), second edition, VI, 18. *Oxford Annotated Bible,* Revised Standard Version, ed. by H.G. May and B.M. Metzger (New York: Oxford University Press, 1973), John 17:3. See also John 20:17.
91 Riḍā, VI, 19. This does not appear to be a direct quotation front the Gospels. Cf. Matt. 28:17 for a possible parallel.
92 Riḍā, VI, 23.
93 *Ibid.*, VI, 26.
94 *Ibid.*, VI, 26–27.
95 *Ibid.*, VI, 27.
96 Muḥammad Kāmil Ḥusayn, *Qarya Ẓālima* (Cairo: Maṭba'at Miṣr, 1958), pp. 1–3; translated by Kenneth Cragg under the title *City of Wrong* (Djambatan: Amsterdam, 1959).
97 S. 93:1.
98 S. 19:28; 3:34.
99 S. 9:32.
100 S. 95:4.
101 S. 33:72.
102 S. 21:105.
103 Ṭabarī, IX, 367 ff.
104 The author changes the washing of feet to that of the hands, cf. John 13.
105 I translate this word *nafs* as "life" in this context. This clearly theological statement has never been investigated by Muslim thinkers. Cf. John 15:12–14, for parallels.
106 Cf. Matt. 26:31.
107 Cf. John 13:38 and 13:21.
108 Matt. 26:75.
109 This is no doubt a telescoped account of the trial of Jesus, based essentially on John but echoing the Passion story of Matthew and Luke as well.
110 Cf. Acts 2:1–11.
111 Ḥaqqī, II, 318 ff.

14 Islam and Christianity

Diatribe or Dialogue

Ismā'il Rāgī A. al Farūqī

Precis

The Qur'ān set the doctrinal basis of Muslim-Christian relations which have varied in the past from very poor to excellent. The contemporary Christian missionaries fail to realize the strength of Jesus' influence upon the Muslims. Christian missionaries have been influenced by many unchristian ideas. Thus Western Christian missions to Muslims were not a mission of Jesus but only of a Western understanding of Jesus. The mission work has been a failure in most every respect and should be called off.

Isolation of the two faiths is impossible. Exclusivism, so often a mark of religion, is as bad as proselytism. Both religions assert that they have *the* truth, which is logically impossible. Christianity and Islam must be interested in each other's claims by means of dialogue, which is the altruistic extension of both religions. Only through dialogue will the two religions ever be united in the religion of God and truth. Conversion to *the* truth is the aim of dialogue. This dialogue will enable understanding of values and sets of meanings in both religions.

The dialogue must follow these ground-rules: (1) no religious pronouncement is beyond the reach of criticism, (2) internal coherence must exist, (3) proper historical perspective must be maintained, (4) correspondence with reality must exist, (5) freedom from absolutized scriptural figurization, and (6) dialogue should be carried on in areas where there is a greater possibility of success, e.g., the field of ethical duties.

Three themes for dialogue are discernible:

1. Contemporary Muslims and Christians are life-affirming in regard to God's creation and hold that man has a unique task to perfect this world. The theological usefulness of the notion of original, hereditary, collective, and vicarious sin are gone. Sin is personal and based on free will; it is primarily located in misperception and its solution is in education rather than forgiveness. Sin is not necessary nor is it predominant in human affairs. For modern Muslims and Christians the way out of the predicament of sin is in human rather than divine hands. Salvation is achieved by continuous education and each person must educate himself.
2. An awareness of the imperative of doing the will of God exists. Former notions of justification are insufficient. Justification is a continuous process which does not consist of confession to God, but of recognition of real values and the following of the long hard road in reaching these values. Knowledge is virtue. Neither great sin nor serious repentance is typical of most people, hence the confession of faith has but mediocre value. Justification is a psychic release which may enable a man with determination to reach his goal, but is not a value in itself.

3. Every man has an equal imperative to fulfill his moral mission which is yet unfulfilled on a world-wide basis. Redemption is only being accomplished by man rather than already having taken place. Justification and redemption are but a prelude to the perception and pursuit of value (God's will). This is possible to all people and has to take place all the time.

These reconstructions of religious thought are compatible with both Islam and Christianity but it is unlikely that the latter will be willing to accept these tenets. Roman Catholics through Vatican II have made too few advances in that respect and are still too condescending toward Muslims. Protestants, who may be represented by Paul Tillich, also consider the Christian figurization of God in Jesus as normative which prevents fruitful dialogue with Muslims. Protestant acceptance of the above ground-rules could lead to useful dialogue.

This is not the place to review the history of Christian-Muslim relations. This history may now be read in the erudite works of Norman Daniel.[1] The reading is sad and agonizing. The conclusion which may be safely drawn from this history is that Christianity's involvement with the Muslim World was so full of misunderstanding, prejudice, and hostility that it has warped the Western Christian's will and consciousness. "Would to God Christianity had never met Islam!" will reverberate in the mind of any student patient enough to peruse that history.[2] On the other side, Muslim-Christian relations have been determined by the Qur'ān.[3] Doctrinally, therefore, these relations have seen no change. Throughout their history, and despite the political hostilities, the Muslims revered Jesus as a great prophet and his faith as divine religion. As for the Christians, the Muslims argued with them in the manner of the Qur'ān. But when it came to political action, they gave them the benefit of the doubt as to whether they followed the Christianity of Jesus or of the Church. Muḥammad and 'Umar's wager for a Christian victory over the Zoroastrians, the Meccan Muslims' choice of, welcome and protection by Christian Abyssinia and Muḥammad's personal waiting upon the Christian Abyssinian delegates to Madīnah, the Prophet's covenant with the Christians of Najrān, 'Umar's covenant with the Archbishop of Jerusalem and his refusal to hold prayer on the premises of the Church of the Holy Sepulchre lest later Muslims might claim the place, the total cooperation of the Umawīs and 'Abbāsīs with their Christian subjects, and of the Umawīs of Cordova with Christians who were not their subjects—all these are landmarks in a record of cooperation and mutual esteem hardly paralleled in any other history. Some persecution, some conversion under influences of all sorts, some aggression, some doctrinal attacks going beyond the limits defined by the Qur'ān, there were, without a doubt. The Muslims in all places and times were not all angels! But such were scattered cases whose value falls to the ground when compared with the overwhelming spread of history which has remained true to this Qur'ānic position.

The Present Problem

Perhaps nothing is more anachronistic—indeed absurd—than the spectacle of the Western Christian missionary preaching to Muslims the Western figurization of the religion of Jesus. The absurdity is twofold: First, the West, whence the missionary comes and which sustains him in his effort, has for decades stopped finding meaning in that figurization which is the content of mission. Indeed, in the missionary himself, that figurization determines but one little portion of his consciousness, the remainder falling under the same corroding secularism, materialism and skeptical empiricism so common in Western thought and culture. Second, the missionary preaches this figurization to Muslims who, in North Africa and the Near East, were thrice Christians. They were Christians in the sense of preparing, through the spiritualization and interiorization of the Semitic religion, for the advent of Jesus. It was their consciousness and spirit which served God as human substrate and historical circumstance for that advent. Naturally, they were the first to "acknowledge" Jesus and to believe in him as crystallization of a reality which is themselves. They were Christians in the second sense of the Western figurization of Christianity when, having fallen under the dominion of Byzantium, they flirted with that figurization and in fact adopted all its doctrinal elements regardless of whether or not they officially joined the churches of Western Christianity. After living with this figurization a while, they welcomed and embraced Islām. But they remained, even as Muslims, Christians in the sense of holding the realization of the ethic of Jesus as the *conditio sine qua non* of Islāmicity and of realizing a fair part of the Jesus-ethic in their personal lives. The comedy in evidence today is that the missionary is utterly unaware of this long experience of the Muslim with Jesus Christ.

This Western missionary, whether *monastes* or other, has associated himself with, and often played the role of colonial governor, trader, settler, military, physician and educator. In the last two decades, after the Muslim countries achieved independence, he found for himself the role of development expert. Expertise in poultry-breeding, neurological surgery or industrial management, and the crying need of the Muslim as yet underdeveloped country were callously taken as God-sent occasions to evangelize, thus stirring within the Muslim a sense of being exploited and producing still more bitterness. Besides, such an expert-missionary is often sponsored by, if not the direct employee of, the aiding agency of the Western government; and a fair harmonization of his tactics and purposes with those of that government were safely presupposed. The Western World knows of no Christian who, moved by the Sermon on the Mount, came to live among Muslims as a native, who made their burden his burden, their hopes and yearnings his hopes and yearnings. Albert Schweitzer, the idol of the modern West in Christian self-giving to the natives of Africa, was as unchristian as to condemn all the Africans' search for liberty;[4] indeed publicly to request President Eisenhower to prevent a United Nations debate on Algeria. The Africans ought to be helped and their suffering relieved, this saint of the twentieth century commanded his fellow Christian whites—but as our colonial subjects! Moreover, where it dissociated itself from imperialism and was purely religious, Western Christian mission to the Muslim World was never a mission of Jesus, but a mission of the Western figurization of Christianity arrogantly asserted in words, hardly ever exemplified in deeds. Modern Christendom has produced a Mrs. Vester who really gave and, fortunately, is still giving of her life to the orphans of Jerusalem.[5] There probably were and still are other isolated individuals of this caliber. Nonetheless, the persistent effort needed to establish an ethically respectable relation with Muslim society has been neglected. Since it has brought hardly any significant conversions and aggravated the alienation of the two world communities, and since the Muslims, as well as Muslim World Christians, regard it as pouring ideological salt into political wounds inflicted by the Crusades and a century of colonization, the mission chapter of Christian history, as we have so far known it, had better be closed, the hunt called off, the missionaries withdrawn and the mission-arm of the Catholic Church and of the World Council of Churches liquidated.

To say all this is not to advocate isolation. In fact, isolation is impossible. The world is simply too small, and our lives are utterly interdependent. Not only our survival, but even our well-being and happiness depend on our cooperation. Mere diplomatic courtesy or casual coalescence of political interests will not suffice. No genuine and effective cooperation can proceed without mutual esteem and respect, without agreement on purposes, final objectives and standards. If it is to last through the generations and withstand the excruciating travails that it must and will face in the construction of a viable world-ecumene, cooperation must be firmly based on a communion of faith in ultimate principles, on communion in religion.

There is yet a more important and logically prior consideration why isolation is neither possible nor desirable. In Islām as well as in Christianity, and probably in all other religions, the man of religion does not, in his religious claim, assert a tentative hypothesis, nor *a* truth among other truths, or *a* version of the truth among other possible versions, but *the* truth. This is so much part of religious experience and of the claim resting on such experience that to deny it is to caricature the religion as a whole. Neither Islām nor Christianity can or will ever give it up. Certainly this is exclusivism; but *the* truth is exclusive. It cannot run counter to the laws of identity, of contradiction, of the excluded middle. Unlike science which works with probabilities, religion works with certainties. Religious diversity is not merely a religious problem. If the religion in question lays claim to *the* truth, contrary or diverse claims are intellectual problems which cannot be ignored. In the absence of evidence to the contrary, the exclusivist claim is as much *de jure* as it is *de facto*.

In our day and age, exclusivism casts a bad smell. Having worked with probabilities for three hundred years, as scientists or the audience of scientists, and—as philosophers or the audience of philosophers—with skeptical notions of the truth for over half a century, we contract our noses whenever an exclusive claim to the truth is made. As men of religion, I hope we all have the strength of our convictions, and feel neither offended nor shamed by what our faiths claim. On the other hand, there is something shameful about exclusivism, just as there is about mission. That is to lay one's claim with authority, to refuse to listen to or silence criticism, and to hold tenaciously to one's claim in face of evidence to the contrary. We regard the exclusivist in science stupid, and even insane, for running in the face of evidence. Such opprobrium equally belongs to the man of religion guilty of the same offence against the truth. Resistance to evidence, however, is not a necessary quality of religion, nor of the man of religion. It falls within the realm of ethics of knowledge. True, religious theses are not as easily demonstrable as those of science; and the man of religion appears often to flout the evidence when it would be more just to say that he is not yet convinced thereby. But where the evidence is significant or conclusive, to flout it is a deficiency of the man. Though its object is religious or moral, exclusivism is epistemological and hence not subject to moral considerations. On the other hand, although its object is epistemological, fanaticism is moral.

Islām and Christianity cannot therefore be impervious to each other's claims; for just as it is irrefutably true that each lays claim to *the* truth and does so candidly, it is irrefutably true that the truth is one, that unless the standpoint is one of skepticism, of two diverse claims to *the* truth, one or both must be false! In the awareness that the standpoint of religion is that of a claim to *the* truth, none but the most egotistic tribalism or cynicism would sit content with its grasp of *the* truth while diverse claims to *the* one and the same truth are being made just as candidly by others. The man of religion, however, is moral; and in Christianity and Islām, he is so *par excellence*. He must therefore go out into the world, teach *the* truth which his religious experience has taught him and in the process refute the contrary claims. In Islām as well as in Christianity, the man of religion is not a tribalist nor a cynic; and his personal relation to other men, if not the fate itself of other men, weighs heavily in the outcome of his own fate. Hence, both the Muslim and the Christian are intellectually and morally bound to concern themselves with the religious views of each other, indeed of all other men. To concern oneself with the convictions of another man is to understand and to learn these convictions, to analyze and criticize them and to share with their adherents one's own knowledge of the truth. If this is mission, then Islām and Christianity must missionize to the ends of the earth. I realize the equivocation of the term, and I suggest that the word itself "mission" be dropped from our vocabulary and the term "dialogue" be used to express the man of religion's concern for men's convictions.

"Dialogue" then is a dimension of human consciousness (as long as that consciousness is not skeptical), a category of the ethical sense (as long as that sense is not cynical). It is the altruistic arm of Islām and of Christianity, their reach beyond themselves. Dialogue is education at its widest and noblest. It is the fulfillment of the command of reality to become known, to be compared and contrasted with other claims, to be acquiesced in if true, amended if inadequate, and rejected if false. Dialogue is the removal of all barriers between men for a free intercourse of ideas where the categorical imperative is to let the sounder claim to the truth win. Dialogue disciplines our consciousnesses to recognize the truth inherent in realities and figurizations of realities beyond our usual ken and reach. If we are not fanatics, the consequence cannot be anything but enrichment to all concerned. Dialogue, in short, is the only kind of inter-human relationship worthy of man! Vouching for Islām and, unless my reading of Christianity has completely deceived me, for Christianity as well, dialogue is of the essence of the two faiths, the theater of their eventual unity as the religion of God, the religion of truth.[6]

We must say it boldly that the end of dialogue is conversion; not conversion to my, your or his religion, culture, mores or political regime, but to *the* truth. The conversion that is hateful to Islām or to Christianity is a conversion forced, bought or cheated out of its unconscious subject. Conversion as conviction of the truth is not only legitimate but obligatory—indeed, the only alternative consistent with sanity, seriousness and dignity. Moreover, the mutual understanding between Islām and Christianity which we yearn for is not merely the conceptual, descriptive knowledge of Islāmic texts and manuscripts achieved by the *Orientalistik* discipline, nor of the Christian tradition achieved by the Muslim and older discipline of *"Al Milal wa al Nihal"* where the elements constitutive of Christianity are simply listed as in a series. It is primarily an understanding of the religion in the sense of faith and ethos, of apprehending the moving appeal of its categories and values, of their determining power. Religious facts may be studied scientifically like any specimens of geology. But to understand them religiously is to apprehend them as life-facts whose content is this power to move, to stir and to disturb, to command and to determine. But to apprehend this power is to be determined by it, and to do so is precisely to attain religious conviction—in short, conversion, however limited or temporary. To win all mankind to *the* truth is the highest and noblest ideal man has ever entertained. That history has known many travesties of this ideal, that man has inflicted tremendous sufferings upon his fellowmen in the pursuit of it are arguments against man, not against the ideal. They are the reasons why dialogue must have rules. Dialogue according to rule is the only alternative becoming of man in an age where isolation—were it ever possible—implies being by-passed by history, and non-cooperation spells general disaster. Granted, the rules must be critical and their presuppositions the fewest and simplest.

Methodology of Dialogue

Granted then that dialogue is necessary and desirable, that its final effect should be the establishment of truth and its serious, free, candid and conscious acceptance by all men, we may now move on to the specific principles of methodology which guarantee its meaningfulness and guard against its degeneration into propaganda, brainwashing or soul-purchasing. These are the following:

1. No communication of any sort may be made *ex cathedra*, beyond critique. No man may speak with silencing authority. As for God, He may have spoken with silencing authority when man was an infant, and infant man may have accepted and submitted. To mature man, however, His command is not whimsical and peremptory. He argues for, explains and justifies His command, and is not offended if man asks for such justification. Divine revelation is authoritative, but not authoritarian; for God knows that the fulfillment of His command which issues from rational conviction of its intrinsic worth is superior to that which is blind. Fully aware of his moral freedom, modern man cannot be subjected; nor can he subject himself to any being without cause; nor can such cause be incomprehensible, irrational, esoteric or secret.[7]
2. No communication may violate the laws of internal coherence mentioned earlier. Paradox is legitimate only when it is not final, and the principle overarching thesis and antithesis is given. Otherwise, discourse will issue in unintelligible riddles.
3. No communication may violate the laws of external coherence; that is to say, man's religious history. The past may not be regarded as unknowable, and historiography assumed to stand on a par with either poetry or fiction. Historical reality is discoverable by empirical evidence, and it is man's duty and greatness to press ever forward towards the genuine understanding and reconstruction of his actual past. The limits of evidence are the only limits of historical knowledge.
4. No communication may violate the law of correspondence with reality, but should be open to corroboration or refutation by reality. If the laws of nature are not today what they were before Einstein or Copernicus, it is not because there are no laws to nature, nor because reality is unknowable, but because there is a knowable reality which corroborates the new insights. The psychic, ethical and religious sensitivities of the people, of the age, are part of this reality; and man's knowledge of them is most relevant for the Muslim-Christian dialogue we are about to begin.
5. Dialogue presupposes an attitude of freedom vis-à-vis the canonical figurization. Jesus is a point at which the Christian has contact with God. Through him, God has sent down a revelation. Just as this revelation had to have its carrier in Jesus, it had to have a space-time circumstance in the historical development of Israel. Equally, Muḥammad, the Prophet, is a point at which the Muslim has contact with God Who sent a revelation through him. Muḥammad was the carrier of that revelation, and Arab consciousness and history provided the space-time circumstance for its advent. Once the advent of these revelations was complete, and men began to put their faith there in numbers and confronted new problems calling for new solutions, there arose the need to put the revelation in concepts for the ready use of the understanding, in percepts for that of the intuitive faculties, and in legal notions and provisions for the guidance of behavior. The revelations were "figurized." Simultaneously, as is natural in such cases, different minds created different figurizations because they had different perceptions of the same reality. This latter pluralism is not a variety of the object of faith, the content revealed

an sich, but of that object or content *in percipi*, i.e., as it became the object of a perception that is intellectual, discursive, intuitive and emotional all at once. Within each religion, the object of faith which is also the content of the revelation was, in itself, all one and the same. Although the figurizations of the revelation were many, that of which they were the figurization was one. Jesus is one; the God who sent him, and the divine revelation with which he was sent, each and every one of these was one, not many. When, as objects of human knowledge, they were conceptualized and perceptualized, they became many. The same is of course true in the case of the figurization of Islām.

The pluralistic variety of men, of their endowments and talents, their needs and aspirations, and the peculiarities of their varying environments and historical circumstances produced a great array of figurizations in both religions. Undoubtedly, some of them were, some others were not, and still others were more or less inspired. There were differences in the accuracy of figurization, in the adequacy of conceptualization and perceptualization, and outrightly in the truthfulness and veracity of the representation. That is all too natural. Disputation and contention arose and lasted for many centuries; they continue to our present day. In the case of Christianity, it became evident that one of the figurizations surpassed in the mind of the majority all other figurizations. It must then be, the community concluded, an identical copy of the content revealed. Since this content is holy and is the truth, the thinkers of the community reasoned, all other figurizations are "heresies" inasmuch as any departure from the Holy is anathema, and any variance from the Truth is falsehood. Slowly but surely, the "other" figurizations were suppressed, and the chosen figurization stood as "the dogma," "the catholic Truth." In the case of Islām, the general religious and ethical principles revealed in the Qur'ān were subjected to varying interpretations, and a large array of schools produced differing figurizations of law and ethics. As in the case of Jesus, the life of the Prophet was the subject of numerous figurizations. In order to bolster its authority and add to its faith in its own genuineness, each school projected its own thought onto his own person. Consensus finally eliminated the radical figurizations and preserved those which, in the judgment of the community, contained all the essentials. Later Muslims sanctified this figurization of the fathers, solemnly closed the gates of any creative interpretation however orthodox, and practically, though not theoretically, hereticated every departure from what they had made canonical.

Being human conceptualizations and perceptualizations of reality, the figurizations of Islām and Christianity are necessarily tinged with the particularism of space-time. It is quite possible, therefore, that some later generation might find some aspect of the holy content in the old figurization dimmed by time or distance; that the said content might need to be rediscovered therein; that some other generation might find new figurizational items which express to them that content or some part thereof more vividly. Certainly this is what happened in the Reformation, which brought in its wake revivification of many an aspect of the divine revelation of Jesus and released new as well as dormant energies in the service of the holy. This is also what happened in the Taymiyan (fourteenth century) and Wahhābī (eighteenth century) reforms in Islām.

Would such a re-presentation or rediscovery necessitate the Christian's and the Muslim's going out, as it were, of their own figurizations? out of their "catholic" truths? Not *simpliciter*. For there is no *a priori* or wholesale condemnation of any figurization. But we should never forget that, as a piece of human work, every figurization is capable of growing dim in its conveyance of the holy, not because the holy has changed, but because man changes perspectives. Truth, goodness and value, God and the divine will for man as such, are always the same. But His will in the change and flux of individual situations, of the vicissitudes of history—and that is precisely what the figurization had been relational to—must be changing in order that the divine will for man be always the same. To question the figurization is identically to ask the popular question: What is God's will in the context of our generation? of our historical situation? indeed, in the context of our personal individuation? The dimness of the figurization must be removed at all costs; its meanings must be rediscovered and its relevance recaptured.

There are those who argue that the figurization can and should never be transcended. Some of these do not recognize the humanity of the figurization. Others insist that piety and morality are rediscoverable only in the figurization itself. To seek the ever-new relevance of the divine imperative is for them to relate the figurization of the fathers to the new situations of human life and existence. That that is not a barren alternative is proved for them by numerous movements within the Christian tradition, and by a number of juristic interpretations of the *sharīʿah,* in the Islāmic tradition. Whether or not the present needs can be met by such means cannot be decided beforehand, and must be answered only after the needs themselves have been elaborated and the relating attempted. We can say at this stage, however, that a considerable degree of freedom *vis-à-vis* the figurization is necessary to insure the greatest possible tolerance for the issues of the present to voice their claim.

6. In the circumstances in which Muslims and Christians find themselves today, primacy belongs to the ethical questions, not the theological. When one compares the canonical figurization of Christianity with that of Islām, one is struck by the wide disparateness of the two traditions. While Christianity regards the Bible as endowed with supreme authority, especially as it is interpreted with "right reason"—that is to say, in loyalty to the central tenets of the figurization according to the Protestant school, or in loyalty to the tradition of the Church as understood by its present authorities, according to the Catholic—Islām regards the Bible as a record of the divine word but a record with which the human hand had tampered, with holy as well as unholy designs. Secondly, while Christianity regards God as man's fellow, a person so moved by man's failure that He goes to the length of sacrifice for his redemption, Islām regards God primarily as the Just Being whose absolute justice—with all the reward and doom for man that it enjoins—is not only sufficient mercy, but the only mercy coherent with divine nature. Whereas the God of Christianity *acts* in man's salvation, the God of Islām *commands* him to do that which brings that salvation about. Thirdly, while Christianity regards Jesus as the second person of a triune God, Islām regards him as God's human prophet and messenger. Fourthly, while Christianity regards space-time and history as hopelessly incapable of embodying God's kingdom, Islām regards God's kingdom as truly realizable—indeed as meaningful at all—only within the contexts of space-time and history. Fifthly, while Christianity regards the Church as the body of Christ endowed with ontic significance for ever and ever, Islām regards the community of faith as an instrument mobilized for the realization of the divine pattern in the world, an instrument whose total value is dependent upon its fulfillment or otherwise of that task.

This list is far from complete. But it does show that the pursuit of dialogue on the level of theological doctrine is marred by such radical differences that no progress may be here expected without preliminary work in other areas. Since it is at any rate impossible for this generation of Muslims and Christians to confront one another regarding all facets of their ideologies at once, a choice of area for a meagre start such as this is imperative. Priority certainly belongs to those aspects which are directly concerned with our lives as we live them in a world that has grown very small and is growing smaller still. The Muslim-Christian dialogue should seek at first to establish a mutual understanding, if not a community of conviction, of the Muslim and Christian answers to the fundamental ethical question, What ought I to do? If Muslims and Christians may not reach ready appreciation of each other's ideas or figurizations of divine nature, they may yet attempt to do the will of that nature, which they both hold to be one. To seek "God's way," i.e., to understand, to know, to grasp its relevance for every occasion, to anticipate its judgment of every moral deed—that is the prerequisite whose satisfaction may put the parties to the dialogue closer to mutual self-understanding. Even if theories of God's nature, of His revelation, of His kingdom, and of His plans for man's destiny were to be regarded as objects of faith beyond critique, certainly the ethical duties of man are subject to a rational approach. Neither Christianity nor Islām precludes a critical investigation of the ethical issues confronting modern man in the world. The proximity of these issues to his life, his direct awareness of them as affecting his own life as well as that of mankind give immediacy to the investigation, and they assign the prerogatives of competence and jurisdiction to his personal and communal judgment in the matter. The relevance of the issues involved to world problems pressing him for an answer furnishes the investigation with a ready testing ground.

Moreover, ethical perceptions are different from the perceptions of theoretical consciousness where to miss is to perceive unreality. Difference in ethical perception is that of the brother who does not see as much, as far or as deep as the other. This is a situation which calls for the involved midwifery of ethical perception. Here, there is no question of error and falsehood, as every perception is one of value and difference consists in perceiving more or less of the same. Neither is the question one of an acquiescent profession of a propositional fact. It is rather one of determination of the perceiving subject by the value that is beheld; and for such perception to be itself, it must be the perception of the man, just as for his realization of the will of God to be itself, i.e., moral, that realization has to be his own free and deliberate act. On the purely theological level, when the impulse to make others heretical is at work, tolerance can mean either contemptuous condescension, conversion, or compromise with the truth. In ethical perception, on the other hand, disagreement is never banished or excommunicated; and heretication defeats its own purpose. Tolerance and midwifery—which are precisely what our small world needs—are the only answer. Their efforts are in the long run always successful; and, at any rate, they are in the Muslim's opinion the better as well as the "Christian" view.

Themes for Dialogue

Looking upon the contemporary ethical reality of Muslims and Christians, three dominant facts are discernible:

First, the modern Muslim and Christian regard themselves as standing in a state of innocence. Whatever their past ideas and attitudes may have been, both of them agree that man's individuation is good, that his life of person and in society is good, that nature and cosmos are good. Fortunately, modern Christian theologians too have been rejoicing in their rediscovery of God's judgment of creation "that it was good."[8] The ideological import of this re-discovery is tremendous. Man has rehabilitated himself in creation. He has found his place in it and re-presented his destiny to himself as one of engagement in its web of history. He is in God's image, the only creature with consciousness and spirit, unto whom the command of God has come, and upon whom the will of God on earth depends for realization as that will is, in itself, a will to a morally-perfected world. Certainly, God could have created the world already perfect, or necessarily-perfectible by the workings of natural law. But He created this world, "where rust and moth consume and where thieves break through and steal,"[9] i.e., a world where His will, or value, is not yet realized, that in the free realization of it by man, the moral values may be realized which could not be realized otherwise. Hence, this world is good, despite its imperfection; and man occupies therein the especially significant—indeed cosmic—station of the bridge through which the ethical elements of divine will enter the realm of creation. It is not surprising that a rediscovery of such momentum causes a great deal of joy, a feeling of self-confidence in the great task ahead. Gone are the sordid obsessions with the innate depravity, the intrinsic futility, the necessary fallenness and cynical vacuity of man and of the world. Modern man affirms his life and his world. Recognizing the imperativeness as well as the moving appeal of God's command, he accepts his destiny joyfully and presses forth upright into the thick of space-time where he is to make that will real and actual.

Secondly, the modern Muslim and Christian are acutely aware of the necessity and importance of recognizing God's will, of recognizing His command. This acknowledgment is the substance, the content or "meat" of their acknowledgment of God. "Recognition of God's command," "ethical perception" and "the act of faith" are mutually convertible and equivalent terms. Such acknowledgment is indubitably the first condition; for it is absurd to seek to realize the divine will in the world without a prior acknowledgment of its content, just as it is absurd to seek to realize what ought to be done without the prior recognition of what is valuable. How is one to recognize that which ought to be done in any given situation—which must be one among a number of possible alternatives—without the standard or norm with which the realizability in the alternatives of that which ought to be can be measured and ascertained? Indeed, if an axiology-free program of action could ever be envisaged, the agent thereof would not be a moral subject, but an automaton of duties. To be moral at all, the act must imply a free choice; and this is a choice in which consciousness of the value, or of its *matériel* as the spatio-temporal concretization thereof, plays the crucial part. All this notwithstanding, and however absolutely indispensable and necessary the acknowledgment of God's command and will may be, it is only a condition, a *conditio sine qua non* to be sure, but still a condition. Philosophically stated, this principle is that of the priority of the study of values to duties, of axiology to deontology. The act of faith, of acknowledgment, recognition and acquiescence, is the first condition of piety, of virtue and felicity. But woe to man if he mistakes the condition of a thing for the thing itself! The act of faith neither justifies nor makes just. It is only an entrance ticket into the realm of ethical striving and doing. It does no more than let us into the realm of the moral life. There, to realize the divine imperative in the value-short world, to transfigure and to fill it with value, is man's prerogative as well as duty.

Thirdly, the modern Muslim or Christian recognizes that the moral vocation or mission of man in this world has yet to be fulfilled, and by him; that the measure of his fulfillment thereof is the sole measure of his ethical worth; that in respect to this mission or vocation all men start out in this world with a carte blanche *on which nothing is entered except what each individual earns with his own doing or not-doing.* In the discharge of his mission in space-time, no man is privileged and every man is an equal conscript. For the command of the one God is also one, for all men without discrimination or election; and His justice is absolute.[10]

Dialectic of the Themes with the Figurizations

A. Modern Man and the State of Innocence

The notion of original sin, of the fallenness of man, appears from the perspective of contemporary ethical reality to have outlived its meaningfulness.

1. Sin is, above all, a moral category; it is not ontological. For modern man, there is no such a thing as sin of creation, of nature, of man as such, no sin as entry into existence or space-time. Physical death is perhaps the deepest mystery of the process of space-time; it is certainly a disvalue, but it is not moral, and therefore not sin, nor the consequence of sin.
2. Moral sin is not hereditary; neither is it vicarious, or communal, but always personal, always implying a free choice and a deliberate deed on the part of a moral agent in full possession and mastery of his powers. The actual involvement, or the "attraction," or "preparation," to which the free moral agent may be subject by merely being a member of his family, of his community, of his religio-cultural group, is not denied. Modern man is also aware that sin is an evil act the ontic consequences of which—whether material or psychological—diverge in space-time *ad infinitum,* affecting in some measure the being and lives of other people. He is equally aware that such consequences are not moral precisely because they are ontic, i.e., necessary, involving no choice on the part of the person whom they affect. Moreover, modernity has removed the hitherto necessary connection between existence and membership in the family, community or religio-cultural group. It was this strict necessity of the connection, characteristic of ancient societies, which, though partially, had induced the fathers to represent sin as a necessary and universal category. The modern Muslim and Christian no more hold a man as member of a group and as subject to the fixations operative in that group except as the result of a decision that man makes for himself. This is particularly true of those societies which have achieved a high degree of internal mobility, especially true of Western society. But the fact is that the whole world is moving in that direction and the day is not far when, from the perspective of the now-forming world community, the universalization of education and the termination of the age of societal isolation, it will be relatively easy to move from one culture to another.
3. Sin is not only a doing, whether introverted, as when the doing is strictly within the person's soul directly affecting neither his body nor anything else outside his soul, or extroverted, as when the doing is spatial involving his body, the souls and bodies of others, or nature. Such doing is only the spatio-temporal consequence of sin. Sin is primarily a perceiving. Here lies its locus and genesis, i.e., in perception. Its effect is in intent and doing. Accordingly, it can be counteracted only in the faculties of perception and its solution must therefore be in education. It is obvious that retaliation and retribution are by themselves inadequate to meet sin wherever it may take place. That forgiveness is equally inadequate becomes clear when we consider that by releasing the ethical energies of the sinner from frustration at his own misdeed, the spiritual power of forgiveness can cure only the sinner with strong ethical sensitivities. For it takes a sinner genuinely frustrated by his own moral failure to respond to its moving appeal. The rest—and the rest is surely the great majority—remain untouched by its power, if not encouraged and confirmed in their sinfulness. Education, on the other hand, ministers to everybody's need. It is universal in its application as all men stand to benefit from its

fruits. Admittedly, forgiveness does have an intrinsic power which acts on all perceiving subjects moving them to emulate the forgiver. Like love, courtesy and respect, it is "contagious." But it is forever personal, its activity and effect are always erratic; whereas education is always subject to deliberation, to critique and to planning.

4. It is within the realm of perception that the modern Muslim and Christian can make sense out of the Christian figurization's notion of sin. From this perspective, sin is man's propensity to ethical misperception. It is an empirical datum whose ubiquitousness is very grave and disturbing. Nonetheless, it is not necessary. The general propensity to ethical misperception is counterbalanced by the propensity to sound ethical perception which is at least as universal as its opposite. Indeed, there is far more value in the world than there is disvalue, far more virtue than sin. If by nature man falls in error in his cognition of the ethical, of value, it is equally by nature, if not by a stronger nature, that he is driven to keep on looking and trying despite the faltering. "Man by nature desires to know" the true, the good and the beautiful (said Aristotle); and "man is doomed to love the good" and pursue the true and the beautiful (said Plato). While his soul yearns for, seeks and pursues value, man's natural "will to live" keeps him on his feet, and his "will to do" propels him forward despite the setbacks of sin. True, man is by nature inclined to moral complacency, but he is equally inclined to the life of danger. And while modern man is certainly resolved in favor of the latter, our reason tells us that we should encourage him all the more because the life of danger holds the greater promise. Man may and certainly will err in ethical perception. But he is not hopeless; nor are his misperceptions—his sins—incorrigible. His fate, blest or unblest, devolves in the first place upon him alone.

If this is convincing to both, the dialogue must move on towards revivifying the figurization—recapturing whatever truth there is in it. We may hence expect it to bring out the following point. Ethical misperception, in all its varieties, is that which we ought to guard against, to avoid and to combat in ourselves, in the others and in all men. Indubitably, we must become fully aware of the enemy, of his tactics and defences, of his nature and constitution, if we are to fight him successfully. In the mind of the general, a very prominent place is occupied by "the enemy." It was such genuine awareness on the part of the fathers that induced them to put sin in man's flesh, in the passions for the lower values of pleasure and comfort, of life and power, in the overhasty realization of value, the surmounting of man's cosmic station, in the arrogant pride that the ethical job of man on earth has already been done and finished. In this sense everyone is susceptible to sin as every man has his temptations, his weak moments when his ethical perception is dimmed and his moral vigor is dull and slow to act. To be always conscious of this disposition, i.e., to keep it constantly in mind as the negative object of the moral struggle, is the peculiar merit of the fathers' emphasis on sin.

Unlike the fathers, therefore, the modern Christian and Muslim cannot think of sin as the predicament out of which there can be no hope of deliverance save by a non-human, divine act. Even if, in the interest of final victory in man's moral struggle, we overestimate the enemy, victory must certainly be possible if it is to be an objective and the struggle is to be sustained despite the eventual setbacks. Were we to grant that sin is necessary but keep in mind its meaning as ethical misperception, we would be contradicted by the fact that man has in fact perceived rightly when he perceived God's past revelations as genuine. This inconsequence may not be removed except by adding another fantastic assumption nihilating man's responsibility for genuine perception, *viz.*, predestination to right perception.

But that is a pure fabrication; that perception which is not the person's perception is not perception.

Finally, the dialogue must move towards a clear answer to the ethical question. If we keep our balance, we will recognize that the right mental and emotional attitude to sin is to keep it in consciousness in order to avoid and to surmount it. The road hitherto is and can be only education, the axiological *anamnesis* which causes the man to see for himself, to perceive value and expose his own ethos to determination by it. The teacher in general, whether mother, father or elder, teacher by concepts, or by example, is precisely the helper who helps man perceive rightly and thereby surmount the sinful misperceptions. Education is the unique processus of salvation. No ritual of water, therefore, or ablutions or baptism, of initiation or confirmation, no acknowledgment of symbols or authority, no confession or contrition, can by themselves do this job for man. Every person must do it for himself, though he may be assisted by the more experienced; and everybody can.

B. Justification as Declaring or Making Good

Looking at the figurization created by the fathers, the contemporary Muslim and Christian observe that its notion of justification as a declaring or making good the person who has acknowledged the figurization does not accord with contemporary reality. Here three considerations are in order. First, where ethical misperception has been the fact or the rule, no confession of any item in the figurization will transform misperception into perception. Even the confession of God as conceived of in the figurization does not constitute the "entrance ticket" we mentioned earlier, the *sine qua non* of salvation. What will do so is the confession of the content of divine will, of value itself. For it is the *materiale* values themselves, not the concepts and theories of "God" or "divine will" as enunciated or elaborated by the figurization, that move the human soul, that can be realized once they are known, and that must be known in order to be realized.

Second, education, as we have defined it, is a long and continuous growth which has no divisions admitting of the representation of its processes as a before and an after. Neither is the realm of values (the will of God) divided into two parts such that only the attainment of one, rather than the other, may be said to constitute, or begin, ethical living. Genuine perception, therefore, as well as genuine value-realization, is with the child as well as with the mature elder, though the objects (values and their relations) discerned may belong to different orders of rank. Salvation or, rather, an amount of it may be the work of the "faithful" of any religion as that of the "faithless"—the *goyim* or *barbaroi* of any faith without regard to the figurization to which they subscribe. The child must then be "justified" as much as the adult, the "sinner" as much as the "saved," provided he perceives that which his yet-undeveloped, or little developed, faculties enable him to perceive. Value-perception is a continuous growth-process. It does not admit of a moment of justification before which there was no growth at all and then, by divine fiat, it has come to be. Third, perception of genuine value is only the beginning of the process of felicitous achievement. Beyond it yet lies the longest and hardest part of the road, the realization in space-time of that which had been correctly perceived.

Another meaning of confession is conversion. It consists of a new openness of mind and heart to the determining power of the divine, of value. It is the state of fulfillment of the admirably-stated first command of Jesus, namely, to love God with all one's mind, all one's heart and all one's power.[11] This is certainly a radical transformation, for it entails a deliberate willingness to seek the good and to submit to its determination rather than to evil's. As the first step of faith, however, it must stand below the act of confession as perception of value at all. All it recognizes is the value of submission to value which is also a prerequisite but more fundamental, more elemental, than the first. It can also refer to an attitude that comes after perception of the whole, or a large part of the realm of value. In this case, it is of momentous significance if we regard the ethical phenomenon as necessarily broken into perception and action, as separate successive stages between which the devil and his temptations may intervene. This view rests upon the groundless assumption that ethical perception is formalistic and, hence, discursive and intellectual (Kant's "practical reason" trying to subdue and to discipline an erratic *"Willkur"*). The establishment of ethical perception as emotional *a priori* intuition (Scheler, Hartmann) has recaptured the unity of the ethical phenomenon as perception and action at the same time, and proved the Socratic formula "knowledge = virtue" once again true.

There is yet another sense, recognized and well-emphasized by the figurization of Christianity, in which faith and its confession can constitute a real achievement. This is the sense in which the confession of faith, i.e., the subject's conviction that he is now reconciled to God and accepted by the community, means the liberation of his ethical energies for self-exertion in God's cause. Since the state of sin is by definition the undesirable state of being, and faith is the consciousness of this undesirability at all levels, the solemn confession of faith becomes the resolution not to relapse into that which has so far been rightly perceived as undesirable. Psychologically speaking, assurance of the acceptance by God and the community of this resolution as something serious and significant, has the good effect of removing whatever fixity misperception may have developed in the moral subject and releasing his energies towards value-realization, *as if* a new page had been turned in his book-of-life. Though this must remain a mere "as-if," it is a powerful moment psychologically. In a person of ethically sensitive nature, the consciousness of sin may possess that person to the point of frustrating his determination by the good, his will to right perception and right action. In such a person, the phenomena of repentance, confession, reconciliation and acceptance can not only release pent up energies but create new ones and orient them towards the good to which they can then rush with a great surge. But, as we have said earlier in connection with the psychological effect of salvation upon the subject, we must remember that such responses and effects are the prerogative of the few, just as great sin equally belongs to the few. The majority, however, remains as little determined by the one as by the other. In the mediocre measure that the majority can have either the cause (sin) or the effect (justification), the advantage of the confession of faith must perforce be equally mediocre.

There is a sense, therefore, though a unique one indeed, in which the act of faith carries an ontic relation to man and cosmos, which is its capacity to infuse into the psychic threads of the subject new determinants and thus bring about a new momentum as it deflects the causal threads from the courses they would have taken had these new determinants not entered the scene. This "plus" of determination is as ontically real as any natural determination since both of them equally produce the same result, namely, the deflection of causal threads to ends other than those to which they would lead otherwise. But we should guard against ever confusing the nature of this "plus." It is certainly not a *justifacti,* a making just, for, ontologically speaking, the deflection of causal threads which constitutes the moral deeds have not yet taken place though it has become a real possibility. Nor is it a declaring just in the forensic sense that, whereas the same person remains the same, the scales of justice that pronounced him sinful have just been tipped in his favor by the fact of solemn confession. Such would be literally a case of "cheating." Nor, finally, is justification a considering of the sinful as innocent, ethically speaking. For it is neither a category of God's thought, nor one of the man's deeds which belong to history and can never be undone. It is only a psychic release in the justified sinner, whose real value is not intrinsic but derivative of that of the values which the newly-released energies may, or may not, realize.

C. Redemption as Ontic Fait Accompli

Thirdly, looking at the figurizations of the fathers, the modern Muslim and Christian recognize that redemption is not a *fait accompli* inasmuch as the filling of space-time with realized value is not yet, but has still to be done by man; that it is man's works, his actualization of divine will on earth as it is in heaven, that constitutes redemption. Were redemption a *fait accompli* in this sense, i.e., were the ethical job or duty of man towards God done and finished, his cosmic status, and hence his dignity, would be impaired. In that case, morality itself falls to the ground. Salvation must flow out of morality, not *vice versa*. The only morality that can flow out of accomplished salvation necessarily robs man's life and struggle in space-time of its gravity, its seriousness and significance. True, the already-saved man is not free to lead any life and must live like a person unto whom God had accomplished salvation. Such a man will therefore be under the obligation of gratitude for the salvation done. Far from underrating the order of rank of the ethical value of gratitude, the modern Muslim and Christian find any ethic in which gratitude is the determining cornerstone inadequate to confront space-time, to govern the plunging of oneself into the thick of tragedy-laden existence, to guide man's efforts for transformation of the universe into one fully realizing the will of God. Historically speaking, and in the figurizations of Christianity and Islām, the ethic of gratitude that emerged out of the notion of redemption as a *fait accompli* devaluated space-time as an unfortunate, insignificant interlude, the end of which was eagerly awaited. In the perspective of such an ethic, the fulcrum of life and existence is clearly shifted outside of space-time, which becomes no longer the "body" and theater in which the will of God is constantly prayed to be and should be done. That is all in addition to the superciliousness and complacency which the carrying around of one's title to paradise generates. If, on the other hand, redemption is remembered—and affirmed—to be the doing of man's cosmic vocation, the realization of value in space-time, then the assumption of redemption as accomplished salvation must be the greatest sin.

This consideration need not blind us to the fact, hinted at in the foregoing section, that redemption does achieve an ontically real accomplishment: namely, the release of energies and the infusion of determinants which would not have become real otherwise, and the actualization of ends other than those to which the un-increased determinants and energies would have led. But the "plus" of determination, the pent-up energies released by the redemptive act of faith are not bound to produce any given ends. As a rule, they will go to reinforce those applications of energies, or those causal *nexūs* at which the moral subject has already been working; and the act of faith presupposes that what has been discerned is the genuine truth, goodness and beauty. But the application of the new energy to the pursuit of what has been rightly discerned is not necessary. That is why sin is possible even after redemption—a fact which the figurization which understands redemption as a being-done of man's ethical vocation cannot recognize or affirm except through the inconsequence of paradox. Thus, it takes something more than redemption in the sense of forgiveness and release of ethical energies to achieve salvation in the sense of ethical felicity, of realizing value in space-time, of deflecting its threads towards value-realization, the bringing about of the *matériaux* of value and of filling the world therewith.

In giving us the notions of justification and redemption, therefore, the canonical figurizations gave us merely a prolegomenon to ethical salvation. These notions provide a cure for those who need it and these are of two kinds: the hypersensitive person, whose consciousness of his past ethical shortcomings and misperceptions has prevented him from trying again; and the hypochondriac, who dwells on his sad state of affairs so strongly and so long that he forgets that there is a task yet to be performed, however bad his past may have been, and that his complaining will not perform that task. Just like the man who has been so sick that he has lost the sense of life and can think only of death, and who will lead a superficial life if he were to come to a sudden cure, so the moral hypochondriac, upon redemption, would hardly exert himself morally, or know what to exert himself for, as his ethical vision has been warped by the long illness. Such a man will never recover from the event of his cure, of his redemption. He will never pass to the sanity, sobriety and gravity of facing space-time with its crying need for God, for value.

Both these types are rare; mankind is neither made of ethical geniuses and heroes, nor of hypochondriacs. For the majority of men, redemption remains an event of especial significance only inasmuch as it is the perception of that which ought to be and, in this capacity, it is an actual embarkation on the ethical road, a prolegomenon to real felicity. Valuable and necessary as it may be, it constitutes no salutary merit and those who have achieved it have achieved only the beginning. They are not the elect in any sense, and neither is their salvation guaranteed. What they achieve is not only possible, but actual for every man; all men must come to it sooner or later by nature as they begin consciously to live under the human predicaments of desiring knowledge and of loving the good. Far from furnishing ground for a new "election," a new particularism, and a new exclusivism, redemption in the only sense in which it makes sense, namely value-perception and value-realization, is truly universalist in that it expresses modalities of ethical living which are actual in all human beings. Ethical salvation, on the other hand, i.e., the actualization of divine will or moral value, is a progressive achievement open to all men by birth; and it is judged and measured on the scale of an absolute justice that knows no alternative to or attenuation of the principle "Better among you is the more righteous," for "whoso doeth good an atom's weight will see it then, and whoso doeth ill an atom's weight will see it then."[12]

Prospects

This has been a sample dialogue between Islām and Christianity. It has anchored itself in a common reality and paid the tribute due to the canonical figurizations. Beyond the latter, however, it has moved towards reconstructing religious thought consonantly with its own experience of reality and, without violating any of the necessary conditions of dialogue. However hard the results may have been on the Islamic and Christian figurizations, they can be claimed and asserted by the modern Christian as a continuation of that same loyalty to Jesus which produced the Christian figurization, and *mutatis mutandis* in the case of the modern Muslim. The novelty is that in asserting them the Christian is joined by the Muslim, and their communion will undoubtedly open limitless vistas of common religious and moral ideas for further exploration. As to whether the Christian is likely to enter into dialogue and follow this course in our generation, I am pessimistic.

A. The Catholic Church

On the Catholic side, we can safely take the record of Vatican II not only as representative, but as determining the future for at least this generation. As regards the issues taken up by the foregoing dialogue, Catholic Christianity is still to be heard from. As far as I know, Vatican II has not even attempted to discuss such issues, let alone re-present them as objects of a critical Christian-Muslim dialogue. It has stopped the calling of non-Christians by bad names. But that is too modest a contribution. Modern man takes the prerequisites of politeness, courtesy and mutual respect for granted, and he is not moved to admiring trance by an assertion or defence of them. As far as the Muslim is concerned, such defence is fourteen centuries late.[13]

As a matter of fact, Vatican II left much to be desired that is of far greater importance. Besides joining the Muslims to the devotees of most archaic religions, the statement—"the plan of salvation also includes those who acknowledge the Creator ... the Moslems ... [and] those who in shadows and images seek the unknown God"—merely subsumes them under the call of God.[14] The universality of the call is not an actual but an ought-universality, and hence it does not yield the desired universalism at all. If God called all men, it goes without saying that the Muslims are included. To exclude them is tantamount to counting them among the trees. If this is an advance over the former position where the Muslim was regarded as a subhuman, it is an advance which stinks by virtue of this relation. Moreover, the same document has stressed that of the pious among those who "do not know the gospel of Christ or His Church" only those may "attain to everlasting salvation" who do so "through no fault of their own."[15] The Muslim who has been thrice Christian is therefore excluded. The judgment—"whatever goodness or truth is found among them is looked upon by the Church as a preparation for the Gospel"[16]—may be as old and classical as Eusebius to which the text proudly refers. Condescending? Indeed! Do I see progressivism at the apex of which stands Christianity as the archetype of religion and the other religions as faltering approximations? Yes; but wait for the explanation of this religious diversity and imperfect approximations outside of Christianity! "Often men, deceived by the Evil One, have become caught up in futile reasoning and have exchanged the truth of God for a lie, serving the creature rather than the Creator"!!![17] The non-Christians do not even know God; neither do they serve Him! This is utterly out of tune with the twentieth century. Name-calling will not do. It is amazing that despite this low esteem of those who are not Christians, Vatican II agrees with my plea to seek mutual understanding and cooperation on the ethical level, "to make common cause ... on behalf of all mankind ... of safeguarding and fostering social justice, moral values, peace and freedom."[18] As a Muslim who has been thrice Christian, I applaud and stretch forth my hand in the hope that my Sermon-on-the-Mount ethic may prove contagious.

B. The Protestants

Unlike the case of Catholics, no pronouncement is vested with decisive authority for Protestants. Their position would have to be surmised from the writings of those who regard themselves as the spiritual thinkers of their community. I therefore propose to do no more than plumb one thinker on this matter who, many Protestants will probably agree, stands on the frontier of Christian theology. That is the late Paul Tillich.

In his *Christianity and the Encounter of the World Religions*, Tillich repudiated the neo-orthodox approach which refuses even to acknowledge the existence of such a problem as man's religions pose for Christianity.[19] He criticized the progressivist explanation of the religions of the world and refuted the circular arguments of those theologians who, assuming Christianity to be the *typos* of religion, measure man's religions with its rod.[20] He spoke of an original universalism of the early church meaning thereby Christianity's adoption of elements from other religions and their subjection to the particularist idea of Jesus as the Christ.

Though commendable, this idea is hardly adequate to meet the issue of inter-religious confrontation.[21] The problem is not one of approving of or adopting that which agrees or can be made to agree with us but of what to do with that which contradicts us, that which stands on the other side of us. On this issue Tillich suggests the possibility of self-criticism in light of the difference with other religions. Appropriately, he entitled his concluding lecture "Christianity Judging Itself in the Light of Its Encounters with the World Religions." No more promising title can be found than this. But before he let his audience rise to cheer, Tillich dissolved the whole promise as he defined the basis of any future self-judgment of Christianity. "There is only one point," he said, "from which the criteria can be derived and only one way to approach this point. The point is the event on which Christianity is based, and the way is the participation in the continuing spiritual power of this event, which is the appearance and reception of Jesus of Nazareth as the Christ, a symbol which stands for the decisive self-manifestation in human history of the source and aim of all being."[22] Evidently, the basis is not God, nor the will of God, but the Christian figurization of God. But loyalty to figurization produces footnotes and commentaries, not knowledge; and Christianity, if based upon such a principle, will learn nothing at all.

Here Tillich has failed in our fifth methodological principle, *viz.*, freedom *vis-à-vis* the canonical figurization. It seems as if Tillich, despite the depth and breadth of his vision, is telling the Muslim: Assuming the Council of Nicaea consisted of God as chairman, His angels and prophets as members, and that it did unanimously and under express divine command decide for all eternity what it did decide, what use can we make of what you or any other religion has to offer? The Muslim retort is that it is precisely here in the Nicene Council that the dialogue will have to start, if at all, assuming that the council is still on and deliberating. Consisting of men with holy as well as unholy motives and presided over by a pagan emperor interested in the political unity of the Empire more than in the truth, the council is either closed and hence only of didactic value to modern man, or open and modern man may participate therein as constituent member.[23] It was precisely at Nicaea that the split of Christianity into Eastern and Western formally began, not in the meaning usually attached to these terms as denoting the Roman Catholic Church and the Greek Orthodox Church, or the Churches of the West as distinguished from those of the East, but in the older sense of a Semitic Christianity of so-called "heretic" churches of the East and a Christianity figurized under terms supplied by Hellenistic consciousness. Only at "Nicaea" can the dialogue with Islām, the heir of that Eastern Christianity which was hereticated at Nicaea, be resumed.

In the last lecture of his career, "The Significance of the History of Religions for the Systematic Theologian,"[24] Tillich did not progress beyond the foregoing position. He called "Religion of the Concrete Spirit" the *"telos"* or the "inner aim" which the history of religions "is to become." This is composed of three elements: "the sacramental basis" which is "the universal … experience of the Holy within the finite"; the "critical movement against the demonization of the sacramental"; and the "ought-to-be … the ethical or prophetic element [which] becomes moralistic and finally secular" without the other two.[25] One can hardly miss the parochial representation of Western Christianity in this scheme where the first element is the Jesus-event, the second the Reformation, and the third, the secular moralistic humanism of modern times. And we must, in addition, overlook Tillich's lack of information, at least regarding Islām, evident in his generalization that "the universal religious basis is the experience of the Holy within the finite."[26]

Having defined these elements, Tillich then tells us that they always struggle against one another; but that when integrated within the Religion of the Concrete Spirit, they struggle as one organic whole against the domination of each.[27] "Kairoi" or "moments ... in which the Religion of the Concrete Spirit is actualized fragmentarily can happen here and there."[28] But "the whole history of religions" is "a fight for the Religion of the Concrete Spirit, a fight of God against religion within religion."[29] In this continuing world struggle of God against the demonic forces, "the decisive victory" was "the appearance of Jesus as the Christ."[30] "The criterion" of victory, or of the presence of the Religion of the Concrete Spirit is "the event of the cross. That which has happened there in a symbolic way, which gives us the criterion, also happens fragmentarily in other places, in other moments, has happened and will happen even though they are not historically or empirically connected with the cross."[31] Tillich even suggests the re-use of the symbol "Christus Victor" in this view of the history of religions.[32] How do we know that what happened in the *kairos* of Muḥammad or of the Reformation was "a fragmentary event of the cross" unless it is assumed that all religious moments are *kairoi* of the same? But if this is assumed beforehand, what novelty did the minor premise bring? Obviously, this is the same circular reasoning Tillich had criticized in Troeltsch and Otto, however disguised the terms.

Tillich's "last word" was his answer to the question of the meaning of the history of religions "to the religion of which one is the theologian." "Theology," he claimed, "remains rooted in its experiential basis. Without this, no theology at all is possible." Thus, in loyalty to the canonical figurization, Tillich persistently refused to recognize any sacrament-free consciousness as religious. Straight-jacketed by his own self-imposed limitation to the experience of the Christian figurization, the Christian theologian is to spend the rest of time "formulat[ing] the basic experiences which are universally valid [sic! the experience of the Holy in the finite is anything but universal] in universally valid statements."[33]

How can such an attempt see anything in the religions of man but fragmentary realizations of the Christian experience? Can it be said that such an attitude enables the Christian to understand the other faiths of other men, let alone produce a fruitful dialogue with the men of other faiths?

As for his systematic theology, its pages run counter to every one of the ethical insights we have attributed to modern man. One might conclude that if Tillich were still alive, he would not carry the dialogue a single step forward. Surprisingly, however, this conclusion is not true. For just before he died, he read the sections of this paper entitled "Methodology of Dialogue," "Themes for Dialogue" and "Dialectic of the Themes with the Figurizations" and wrote in a letter to the author: "I ... read your manuscript and thought it was an excellent basis for any discussion between Christianity and Islam. You bring out the points of difference with great clarity and sharpness. Not in order to let them stay where they are, but in order to show that behind the different figurizations there is, especially in the present moment, a common ground and a common emergency. I believe that with this presupposition in mind, a discussion could be very fruitful."

This was a surprise. It recaptures my lost optimism.

Notes

1 *Islam and the West: The Making of an Image* (Edinburgh: The University Press, 1960); *Islam, Europe and Empire* (Edinburgh: The University Press, 1966).

2 In considering that history one must take account of the following facts: The first missionaries which Islām sent to Christendom were met with swords drawn and were massacred at Dhāt al Ṭalḥ in 629 A.C. From that moment, however, a section of Christendom which might be called

"Semitic Christianity" welcomed the Muslims, gave them protection, listened to and were converted by, or simply tolerated them. These Christians were for the most part Arab or Semitic, though not necessarily Arabic speaking, and a fair number were Copts, whether Abyssinian or Egyptian. The Abyssinian state, Christian and theocratic, had previously welcomed and protected the Muslim refugees from Mecca and was regarded as a friend by the Muslims ever since. With the rise of the Islāmic state and the entry of Islām onto the stage of history, a much older division began to resume its shape: the division of Christianity itself into Eastern and Western, Semitic and Hellenic.

Though they had abandoned most of the so-called "heretical" doctrines of the ancestors, submitted themselves to the main pronouncements of the synods and councils and acquiesced to the theological, christological and ecclesiological tenets of catholic Christianity, the Semitic Christians cooperated with the Muslims. Despite the fact that the innate appeal of Islām, its exemplars in life and action, and the continuous exposure to its civilizing and cultural power had taken their toll of converts from their ranks, these Christians have survived in considerable numbers fourteen centuries of living under the political rule of Islām. Islāmically acculturated they certainly are; but not converted. They constitute a living monument of Christian-Muslim co-existence, of mutual tolerance and affection, of cooperation in civilization and culture building. Their inter-religious *modus-vivendi* is an achievement in which the whole human race may take rightful pride.

On the other hand, Western Christians, embittered by a military defeat initially brought about by their own intolerance to allow the Islāmic call to be heard, nursed their resentment and laid in wait. For three centuries, sporadic fighting erupted between the two camps without decisive advantage to either party. In the eleventh century, the Western Christians thought the time had come to turn the tables of history. The Crusades were launched with disastrous consequences to Christian-Muslim and Muslim-Christian relations. Christian executions, forced conversions or expulsion of the Muslims from Spain followed the political defeat of the Muslim state. For eight centuries, Islām had been the faith not only of immigrant Arabs and Berbers but of native Spaniards who were always the majority. The "Inquisition" made no differentiation; and it brought to an end one of the most glorious chapters in the history of inter-religious living and cooperation.

Modern times brought a story of continuous aggression and tragic suffering beginning with the pursuit and obliteration of Islām from Eastern Europe where the Ottomans had planted it, to the conquest, fragmentation, occupation and colonization of the whole Muslim World except the impenetrable interior of the Arabian Peninsula. Muslims remember with bitterness that this is the period when Christendom changed the script of Muslim languages in order to cut off their peoples from the Islāmic tradition and sever their contact with the heartland of Islām; when it cultivated and nursed Hindu and Buddhist reaction against the progress of Islām in the Indian sub-continent; when it invited the Chinese to dwell and to oppose Islām in Malaysia and Indonesia; when it encouraged the Greeks in Cyprus and the Nile Valley, the Zionists in Palestine and the French in Algeria; when, as the holder of political and economic power within the Muslim World, Christendom discouraged, retarded or impeded by every means possible the awakenings, renaissance and self-enlightenment processes of Muslim societies; when, controlling the education of Muslims, it prescribed for it little beyond the purpose of producing clerks for the colonialist administration.

Equally, modern times witnessed the strongest movement of Christian proseletization among Muslims. Public education, public health and welfare services were laid wide open to the missionary who was accorded the prestige of a colonial governor, and who entered the field with pockets full of "rice" for the greedy, of intercession with the colonialist governor for the enterprising, and of the necessities of survival for the sick and the needy.

Throughout this long history of some fourteen centuries of Christian-Muslim relations, the researcher can hardly find one good word written or spoken about Islām by Christians. One must admit that a number of Semitic Christians, of Western Christian Crusade-annalists or of merchants and travellers may and did say a few good words about Islām and its adherents. Samplings of this were given by Thomas Arnold in his *The Preaching of Islam* (reprinted by Sh. Muḥammad Ashraf, Lahore, 1961), especially the conclusion. Modern times have seen a number of scholars who conceded that Muḥammad's claims were candid, that Islāmic religious experience was genuine, and that underlying the phenomenon of Islām, the true and living God had been and still is active. But these are isolated statements even in the life of those who made them, not to speak of the deluge of vituperation and attack upon Islām, Muḥammad and the Muslims which fill practically all Christian writing about the world of Islām. Moreover, whatever little may be found belongs to Christians as individual persons. Christianity as such, i.e., the bodies which speak in its name, be they Catholic, Protestant or Greek Orthodox, has never recognized Islām as a genuine religious experience. The history of academic Western Christian writing on the subject of Islām is a history of service to the world of scholarship, though one of misunderstanding and falsification. As a librarian seeking to collate manuscripts, establish texts and analyze historical claims, the Christian scholar has done marvellous work which earned him the permanent gratitude of scholars everywhere. But as an interpreter of the religion, thought, culture and civilization of Islām, he has been—except in the rarest of cases—nothing less than a misinterpreter and his work, a misrepresentation of its object. (See the scathing analysis of A.L. Ṭībāwī, "English-Speaking Orientalists: A Critique of Their Approach to Islām and Arab Nationalism," *The Muslim World,* Vol. LIII, Nos. 3, 4 [July, October], 1963, pp. 185–204, 298–313.) Vatican II conceded that "the Moslems ... adore one God, living and enduring, merciful and all-powerful, Maker of heaven and earth and Speaker to men ... they prize the moral life and give worship to God ... " though it carefully equated these characteristics not with actual salvation but with the mere inclusion within "the plan of salvation." (*The Documents of Vatican II,* ed. Walter M. Abbott, S.J., New York, Guild Press [An Angelus Book], 1966, p. 663.) Little rewarding as this concession becomes when conjoined with the earlier statement that "whosoever ..., knowing that the Catholic Church was made necessary by God through Jesus Christ, would refuse to enter her or to remain in her could not be saved" (*ibid.,* pp. 32–33), anything similar to it has yet to come from the World Council of Churches—indeed from any Protestant church, synod or council of churches.

3 Before the Hijrah to Madinah and the establishment of the first Islāmic polity, the revelation of Muḥammad, i.e., the Qur'ān, defined the religious relation of Islām and Christianity. To the Jews, it asserted, God sent Jesus, a prophet and apostle born of Mary by divine command. He was given the Evangel, taught to relieve the hardships of Jewish legalism and to exemplify the ethic of love, humility and mercy. Those of his followers who remained true to his teaching are blessed. Those who associated him with God, invented trinitarianism and monkery and falsified the Evangel, are not. The former the Qur'ān described in terms reserved for the friends of God: "The Christians are upright; they recite the revelations of God during the night hours and prostrate themselves in worship. They believe in God and in the Day of Judgment. They enjoin the good, forbid evil and compete in the performance of good works. Those are certainly righteous" (Qur'ān, 3:113). "And you will find among the People of the Book the closer to you those who said that they were Christians; for many of them are priests and ascetics and are humble" (Qur'ān, 5:82). "In their hearts, We planned compassion and mercy" (Qur'ān, 57:27). Parallel to this lavish praise of some Christians, stands the Qur'ān's castigation of the others. "Some Christians said: The Messiah is the Son of God, thereby surpassing in unbelief the unbelievers of old. ... They have taken their priests and monks for gods, as well as the Messiah, son of Mary, whereas they were commanded never to worship but one God beside Whom there is none else" (Qur'ān, 9:30). "O People of the Book! Do not go to extremes in your religion and never say anything on behalf of God except the truth. Jesus, the Messiah, the son of Mary, is only a prophet of God, a fulfillment of His command addressed to Mary. ... So believe in God and in His prophets and do not hold the trinitarian view. ... God is the one God. May He be exalted above having a son. To Him belongs everything in heaven and earth" (Qur'ān, 4:171). As for what Muslim attitude towards Christians should be, the Qur'ān prescribed: "Say: O People of the Book! Let us now come to agreement upon a noble principle common to both of us, namely, that we shall not worship anyone but God, that we shall never associate aught with Him, and that we shall not take one another for lords beside God. And if they turn away, then say: Remember, as for us, we do submit to God. ... We believe in that which has been revealed to us and that which has been revealed to you and our God and your God is One. It is to Him that we submit" (Qur'ān, 3:64; 29:47). From this we may conclude that Islām does not condemn Christianity but reproaches some devotees of it whom it accused of deviating from the true path of Jesus. Every sect in Christianity has accused the other sects of the same. Yet, Christianity has never recognized Islām as a legitimate and salutary movement. It has never regarded Islām as part of its own tradition except to call Muḥammad a cardinal in rebellion against the Pope because of his jealousy for not being elected to the office, and Islām a "derelicta fide catholica" (*Islam and the West,* pp. 83–84).

4 Albert Schweitzer, *Out of My Life and Thought,* tr. C. T. Campion (New York: Mentor Books, 1955), pp. 147–48.

5 See Bertha Spafford Vester's article "Jerusalem, My Home" in *National Geographic Magazine* (December, 1964), pp. 826–47.

6 By their abuse, the Crusades and the last two centuries of Christian mission have spoilt the chances of the Muslim masses entering trustfully into such common endeavor. For the time being, the grand dialogue between Muslims and Christians will have to be limited to the intelligentsia where, in the main, propaganda does not convince and material influences produce no Quislings. This limitation is tolerable only so long as the Muslim World is underdeveloped and hence unable to match measure for measure—and thus neutralize—the kilowatts of broadcasters, the ink and paper of publishers and the material bribes of affluent Christendom.

7 The Qur'ān tells us that Abraham, the paragon of faith in the one true God, asked God to show him evidence of His power to resurrect the dead. When God asked, "Have you not believed?" Abraham retorted, "Indeed, but I still need to see evidence so as to put my heart at rest" (Qur'ān, 2:260). Likewise, the Qur'ānic discourse with the Meccans concerning their religion and Islam was a rational one, replete with "evidence" and with the retort, "Say, Bring forth your evidence [against God's] if you are truthful" (Qur'ān, 2:111; 21:24; 27:64; etc.). On a number of occasions, the Qur'ān speaks of "the evidence of God," "the proof of God" which it goes on to interpret in rational terms (see for example, Qur'ān, 4:173; 12:24; 23:118; 28:32).

8 Genesis 1:18, 21.

9 Matthew 6:19.

10 Certainly God may and does grant His grace to whomsoever He chooses; but such grace is never a category of the moral life, a credit which can be taken for granted or "counted upon" by any man. It remains a category of God's disposition of human destinies, never an attribute of men's lives. The gratuitous gift is not a tiling earned, by definition; and that which is not earned cannot figure on God's scale of justice—equally by definition.

There is yet another divine grace which is not quite gratuitous. It is called "grace" by equivocation; for it is a good thing which God grants freely but not whimsically, and which He does only in deserving cases. Such grace is really "a lift" on the road of ethical perceiving and living, accorded to those who are really persevering and hard-pressing forward towards the goal. Specifically, it is the gift of a sharper cognition of, or of a more total determination by the goal and no more. It is earned.

11 Matthew 22:37; Mark 12:30; Luke 10:27.

12 Qur'ān, 99:7–8.

13 "Call men unto the path of your Lord through wisdom and becoming preaching. Argue with men gently. ... Tell My worshippers to limit themselves to the comelier words. ... Do not contend with the People of the Book except with arguments yet more considerate and gentle. ... Those are the servants of God who ... when the ignorant dispute with them respond with 'Peace'" (Qur'ān, 16:125; 17:53; 29:46; 25:63).

14 *The Documents of Vatican II*, p. 35.

15 *Ibid.*

16 *Ibid.*

17 *Ibid.*

18 *Ibid.*, p. 663.

19 New York: Columbia University Press, 1963, p. 45.

20 Such as Ernst Troeltsch, Rudolph Otto, Adolph Harnack, etc. *Ibid.*, p. 43.

21 *Ibid.*, pp. 34–37. There is historical spuriousness in Tillich's claim that Christianity turned "radically exclusive and particularistic as the result of the first encounter ... with a new world religion," namely, Islām (*ibid*, pp. 38–39). In fact, Christianity was radically exclusive at Nicaea and at every other post-Nicene council. This characteristic was probably developed much earlier than Nicaea. Even if Tillich's claim were true, it constitutes a poor apology. The astounding novelty however is Tillich's claim that Christianity's self-consciousness with respect to the Jews and hence, Christian anti-Semitism, were the result of "the shock of the encounter with Islam."

22 *Ibid.*, p. 79.

23 The accounts of the tactics used in the Council or thereafter in order to implement or defeat its decision by the parties involved were far from inspiring any awe or silencing authority. "Intrigues and slanders of the lowest kind," wrote Harnack, "now began to come into play, and the conflict was carried on sometimes by means of moral charges of the worst kind, and sometimes by means

of political calumnies. The easily excited masses were made fanatical by the coarse abuse and execrations of the opponents, and the language of hate which hitherto had been bestowed on heathen, Jews and heretics, filled the churches. The catchwords of the doctrinal formulae, which were unintelligible to the laity and indeed even to most of the bishops themselves, were set up as standards, and the more successful they were in keeping up the agitation the more surely did the pious-minded turn away from them and sought satisfaction in asceticism and polytheism in Christian garb" etc. etc. (A. Harnack, *History of Dogma,* tr. by Neil Buchanan. New York: Dover Publications, Inc., 1961, Vol. IV, p. 61).

24 Published together with a number of other lectures by Tillich, and statements of friends at a memorial service dedicated to him, under the title, *The Future of Religions* (New York: Harper and Row, 1966), pp. 80–94.

25 *Ibid.*, p. 86.

26 *Ibid.*

27 *Ibid.*, pp. 86–88.

28 *Ibid.*, p. 89.

29 *Ibid.*, p. 88.

30 *Ibid.*

31 *Ibid.*, p. 89.

32 *Ibid.*, p. 88.

33 *Ibid.*, p. 94.

15 Mohamed Talbi

"For Dialogue Between All Religions"

Ronald L. Nettler

Mohamed Talbi is a twentieth-century Tunisian historian of North Africa and writer on Islamic religious thought and affairs. As a religious writer particularly concerned with Islam's views on and relations with other religions – especially the religions of the *Ahl al-Kitab* – Talbi has written extensively on the traditional Islamic foundations (as he sees them) for the theory and practice of inter-religious dialogue.[1] For Talbi this is itself part of a larger effort towards the construction of a modern Islamic thought which would reconsider, among other things, the nature of, and proper approaches to, traditional sources and ideas. There is an integration, then, of Talbi's ideas on inter-religious relations and his general Islamic religious thought.[2]

Talbi's outlook is, I believe, an important part of Islamic religious thought in the latter part of the twentieth century, particularly in his discussions of relations between religions, religion and politics, religion and history, and the interpretation of traditional religious texts. Still largely unstudied by students of modern Islam, Talbi's original work in Islamic thought requires analysis of his ideas and methods in historical and intellectual context.[3] I shall attempt to do this in small part in this chapter through discussion of a piece by Talbi on inter-religious dialogue. This piece is titled "For Dialogue Between All Religions". It is part of the third (final) chapter of a book of interviews with Mohamed Talbi on various questions concerning Islam in the modern world. Titled *Families of God* (*'Iyal Allah*), the book is a vehicle for Talbi to express his views and opinions on a number of (mainly Islamic) intellectual and religious issues. The possibilities and Islamic theoretical foundations of inter-religious dialogue and understanding are Talbi's main concerns here, in the context of his general Islamic thought. Although my interest is mainly in Talbi's theory of inter-religious relations, I shall first highlight certain aspects of his general thought in this book as background for an understanding of Talbi's specific arguments concerning the inter-religious issue. This may, one hopes, also help to elucidate that integral connection between Talbi's general thought and his ideas on the inter-religious affairs.[4]

The book *'Iyal Allah* is organized in an introduction, preface and three chapters (*abwab*), each chapter consisting of two subsections, and each one of these further subdivided in smaller sections. Chapter one is titled *Memories and Reflections*, chapter two, *Islam and Some Difficult Questions*, and chapter three, *Some Important Questions Concerning Civilisation.* Throughout, Talbi raises and elucidates issues of Islamic thought and religion, particularly as these pertain to Islam's modern situation, and especially with respect to the question of Islam's traditional conception of its own finality and superiority in a pluralistic modern world. Generally in his assessment of such issues Talbi takes a boldly "liberal" position, rooted in the traditional sources and constructively accepting the challenges with which modernity confronts Islam. I use the term "liberal" here in characterising Talbi's general position on religious issues, among other reasons because of his central conception of "religious pluralism" (*al-ta'addudiyya*) as both a desirable internal Islamic practice and as a mode of relationship between Islam and other faiths in the modern world. Pluralism for Talbi means *all* religious ideas and *all* faiths are paths to God *on the same spiritual level.* But if this is far-reaching from a certain common traditional Islamic perspective – and I believe it is – then on the other hand Talbi derives his support for his pluralism very much from traditional Islamic sources and in a way which is most impressive for its deep traditional learning. Further, Talbi's analysis and understanding of certain basic issues in religious thought and interpretation of sources, his particular type of opposition to *taqlid,* his support of *ijtihad* in a modern context and his historical contextual Qur'an interpretation, together also constitute elements of a "modernising" approach to religion interwoven with his theory of religious pluralism and inter-religious dialogue.[5]

In keeping with the emphases established above, I shall begin with discussion of certain parts of the *Introduction* and chapter one. Here, in answering a number of personal questions with autobiographical musings and wide-ranging thoughts, Talbi tells us of personal experiences which were clearly related to the development of his intellectual outlook, especially the central idea of pluralism. We shall also become aware here of a most interesting and extraordinary personality.

In the *Introduction* to the book, Talbi defines himself temporally and spiritually, thereby preparing the ground for his later exposition. Born in June, 1921, in Tunis, he describes his entrance in this world as a coming into "... *conditional existence* in the city of Tunis, from a mother whose origins may be found in the lands of the Ottoman Caliphate and a father whose roots are in Algeria."[6] Aside from the specific biographical information, Talbi's notion of "*conditional existence*" (*al-wujud al-zarfi*) is informative concerning his general Islamic worldview. For although perhaps not identical to aspects of the later *sufi* metaphysics initiated by the great mystical theoretician Ibn 'Arabi (1165–1240) and continued by his disciples, there is in Talbi's description of this world as "conditional existence" a strong similarity to that sort of sufi doctrine, particularly in his use of the term "being", "*wujud*". This phenomenal world of seeming transience and multiplicity, "conditional existence", is here implicitly contrasted with a presumed eternal existence of perfection. And indeed, in the next sentence Talbi expresses the full formulation: "I came into *partial existence* (*al-wujud al-juz'i*) in the realm of temporality and specificity of place, not knowing when I would ascend to *total existence* (*al-wujud al-kulli*), *i.e.,* moving from that life which is delimited by the boundaries of the physical body, of place and of time, to that absolute and complete life which is devoid of limitations (*al-haya al-mutlaqa al-kamila*)."[7] Although this formulation could simply be a reference to the earthly existence of *al-dunya* and the eternal, perfect existence of the next world, *al-akhira,* a pair of concepts basic to the conventional Qur'anic and Islamic theological worldviews, Talbi's use of the terms *wujud, kamil* and *mutlaq* make his formulation highly reminiscent of the *sufi* metaphysics identified with later theoretical sufism. The proper understanding of Talbi's particular formulation here, I think, is as a kind of mix of the more conventional Islamic notion of this world and the next with the *sufi* metaphysical conception. The *sufi* conception is not so much concerned with the distinction between *al-dunya* and *al-akhira,* although that may sometimes be involved, but rather with the distinction between perfect being (*al-wujud al-mutlaq*) and some sort of relative, imperfect, being (*juz'i,* partial, for example, as Talbi calls it). The imperfect is this phenomenal world which is characterised by diversity and multiplicity and is opposed to the realm of absolute being. Absolute being is unitive and incorporates all, including also the phenomenal world of multiplicity and flux. Indeed, for Ibn 'Arabi, the greatest exponent of this outlook, the absolute being and the world of multiplicity are as one, the latter simply being the "shadow" of the former.[8] For Talbi, the variety and multiplicity here in this world seems as a reflection and a hint of a greater unlimited world of harmony and oneness. The ultimate truth of all diverse ways, then, may be seen as the other side and even the progenitor of their diversity. This personal philosophical perspective on life seems to be of one fabric with Talbi's central notion of pluralism within the Muslim world and in relations between Islam and other traditions, as well as being related to Talbi's exegetical method and religious thought. But Talbi's later experiences in Paris as a student provide even more background to and understanding of his outlook, including his attitude towards Ibn 'Arabi's views. These we also learn about in chapter one, in the section titled *Memories*.

After a childhood and youth in Tunisia and a traditional Islamic upbringing, Mohamed Talbi went to Paris to study "... in the year 1947 on a derelict French ship ..."[9] which took thirty-six hours to travel from Tunis to Marseilles. This somewhat inauspicious seeming beginning in the event heralded a seminal period in Talbi's intellectual life. Paris in the post-war 1940s and 1950s was a city of intellectual ferment. In Talbi's words: "The intellectual life of Paris was variegated and profuse, and the cultural struggle intense."[10] Communism, Sartre's existentialism, Surrealism, all manner of literary trends and Freudian psychology were but some of the prominent intellectual styles. So diverse and rich was this intellectual life, says Talbi, that the Church established centres for students, in competition with the other trends, as the Church knew that the students were, more than any others, targeted by the existentialists and atheists.[11] Talbi says of himself that in such an environment "... it was possible I would be influenced by communism, Christianity, atheism or existentialism, as had happened to some of my friends, except that I preserved the (Islamic) tradition I had brought with me to France".[12] But Talbi says he did learn "many things"[13] in Paris. In particular, he learnt from Marxism, existentialism and Freudianism, while from his Islamicist teachers Louis Massignon and Regis Blachère he learnt about varieties of Islam which he had not previously been aware of and about new approaches to tradition. Thus: "Existentialism taught me, for example, that Idealism was not everything, and it is necessary to look at tangible reality ... and to open our eyes to it. Until today, I consider myself an 'idealist', but it is necessary to have an antidote with which to offset exaggerated Idealism; and this is what Sartre has given".[14] With respect to Marxism, although Talbi did not agree with its theory that dialectical materialism was the sole motivating force in history, he could believe that "... economic forces were without a doubt one of the basic agents influencing and determining history".[15] This gave another perspective on history, other than that of individuals as the sole determiners of events. On Freud and Freudianism, Talbi says the man has done us "an important service, (*khidma jalila*): For he revealed brilliantly the unconscious motivations which direct pens, dictate words and motivate man in ways of which he is unaware."[16] For Talbi this insight of Freud's was of value in particular because it pointed up the limitations of human knowledge and understanding. What could be more humbling than the realisation that we do not even always know our own motivations? This in Talbi's view highlights the Arabic saying, "God knows best ... with which our scholars ended their books".[17] But for Talbi there was another, related, meaning here as well: the deeply individual (even idiosyncratic) nature of human knowledge and perception, stemming as they do from these profound personal recesses, underscored again the natural foundation of intellectual and religious pluralism *in human nature itself.* We are all different and unique; this is our glory, and our unique and different ideas must be accorded respect. For "... God, glory be to Him, Most High, wanted us different, and this differentiation is a (divine) blessing, because it is the motivating force in history. ... "[18] Variety in human views for Talbi provided the "motor of history" which made history "continually changing",[19] rather than, as some claim, constantly "repeating itself"[20] and static. "Indeed", says Talbi, "I would say history is a dynamic process – there is no repetition in it".[21]

Talbi's conception of history as a dynamic process, underpinned as it is by his notion of ideational variety as a divinely-ordained feature of human life and nature, contains an implicit notion of Islam which later figures centrally in the development of his complete and explicit conception of Islam and of its relations with other religions. This conception of Islam is diametrically opposed to the view of Islam held by important "Islamist" thinkers representing "political Islam", such as Sayyid Qutb and certain traditional "conservative" trends. For Talbi's Islam is predicated on change and related historical/contextual ways of understanding sacred texts and traditions. The views of his "opponents" see Islam as eternal, frozen in time and unchanging.[22]

Talbi elaborates on the influences of Massignon and Blachère mainly in response to a question concerning the differences between the Islam he had lived in his home and that which he studied with these two prominent European scholars. Louis Massignon was for Talbi a mystical visionary who opened the young student's mind to a spiritual and philosophical sufism that he had not previously encountered. For although Talbi had grown up with a popular sufism at home, this was, he says, "practical",[23] consisting mainly of such rites as *dhikr* and *wird*.[24] But Massignon was a man who gravitated towards a more theoretical mysticism in his own "personal revival" as a Roman Catholic Christian, "… especially Islamic mysticism".[25] This was a mysticism of profound ideas and theories, challenging to the "dominating traditional Sunni Islam",[26] of Talbi's childhood and youth. Massignon spoke about Islam in general, not Sunni and not Shi'i: the spiritual Islam of thinkers "… from Suhrawardi, to ibn al-Farid, to al-Muhasibi, to al-Hallaj",[27] the greatest of mystics. And Massignon "… spoke about them in a language I had not known".[28] The combination of Massignon's personal mystical spirituality and the Islamic spirituality he taught clearly made an impact on Talbi, in revealing to him a universal mystical religiosity in which all religions and religious views come together, in spite of their exoteric doctrinal differences. The model Talbi proffers here he now explicitly formulates as the thought of Ibn 'Arabi: "… All the religions meet in mysticism to a certain extent. Let us mention, therefore, Ibn 'Arabi, where he says that his heart listens to the Torah, to the Injil and to all religions. And that his religion is the religion of love. It would be natural here for some to suspect of Ibn 'Arabi that he is not firmly within the Islamic orientation and that he deviates in some matters. But this is unimportant. For there is no doubt that Ibn 'Arabi was a firm believer. His books demonstrate this, as does his doctrine …"[29] The "religious pluralism" implicit here in Ibn 'Arabi's conception is a doctrine of respect for (even celebration of) scriptural and doctrinal differences, with the idea that they all come together in (or point towards) a universal spiritual truth. This makes more concrete and explicit the point raised above referring to Talbi's use of the "language of Ibn 'Arabi" in his *Introduction.* It must be considered as one important foundation of Talbi's conception of religious pluralism.[30]

Regis Blachère was a very different sort of man and scholar from Louis Massignon. For, says Talbi, Massignon was a believer and Blachère was not, although "… (Blachère) … did not himself acknowledge that he was an atheist, but only, putting it cautiously, 'an agnostic'"[31]. In any case, for Talbi, Blachère's classes "were extremely useful". Blachère epitomised in his approach the historical-critical orientation to Islam which was founded by the nineteenth-century German orientalist Theodore Nöldeke in his work *The History of the Qur'an.* Talbi found this approach useful in that it "… made me practice self-scrutiny and review my doctrinal beliefs. And this is a good thing, because it deepens faith ... Thus did Blachère teach me self-criticism and the understanding of others' views".[32] If Freud had taught Talbi that all one's views need a deep scrutiny for possible underlying psychic and personal motivations, Blachère, here representing the historical-critical approach of Nöldeke, has taught Talbi a corresponding *intellectual* self-criticism. For Talbi none of this was a danger to Islamic religious faith, but rather, as quoted above, "it deepens faith", for it helps one to attain truth concerning God's creation.

The section of *"Reflections"* in chapter one continues from the section *"Memories"*, explicating, in answer to questions, the same points, but in a more intellectual and less personal way. Two subjects stand out prominently here, the Muslim community, the *umma,* and knowledge, *'ilm.* I shall discuss these, however briefly, insofar as they contribute to understanding the issues of our main concern.

Talbi discusses the *umma* in response to questions concerning various modern usages of the term, in particular the issue of how the English term "nation" has been (and might be) rendered in Arabic. Talbi's comments on these matters are serious, but he reserves his (for us) most penetrating remarks for the various Qur'anic meanings of the term. Central here for Talbi are God's assertions in the Qur'an that all humanity are *one umma* (*umma wahida*). This is the Qur'anic spiritual meaning of *umma.* God is, in Talbi's view, here imparting the knowledge that the human *umma* is one, and that it (properly) gravitates towards Godliness (*rububiya*), worship (*'ibada*) and piety (*taqwa*).[33] Talbi's interlocutor then asks the question, "Are there not other meanings for *umma* in the Qur'an? e.g., Abraham was an *umma*?"[34] Talbi answers that there are indeed many other such meanings, focusing his response on "Abraham was an *umma*", and relating this to his Qur'anic comments on *umma* as the (three) spiritual virtues mentioned above which characterise the "one community of mankind".[35] Now using in addition to the Qur'an also Biblical references (Genesis 18, 18–19) Talbi argues "... it is clear that the allusion in the Qur'an and the Torah is to the 'community of the divine Unity' (*ummat al-tawhid*) which derives from Abraham, Peace be upon him".[36] Abraham is an *umma,* then "... because Abraham is the sign of Divine Oneness, and he is the link amongst the three monotheistic religions."[37] The *umma* "... in its Qur'anic meaning, is, therefore, a pure spiritual entity",[38] says Talbi, although "... on the historical level"[39] it is "partitioned in states and peoples ...".[40] The gap between the unitive Qur'anic conception of *umma* and the historical reality of human differentiation here again reflects the polarity of the one and the many which is so central to Talbi's vision of pluralism through a harmonisation of the many by invoking the common foundation in the one.

Talbi's reflections on knowledge (*'ilm*) are focused in two issues: first the need, as he sees it, for Third World (and particularly Muslim) nations to develop serious modern intellectual traditions. This, he says, would constitute a second independence from a colonialism of a different kind than the overwhelming political colonialism (*al-ist'imar al-julli*) from which his people had already freed themselves. This is "the hidden colonialism" of intellectual stagnation which must now be renounced, if the Muslim peoples are to have a successful future.[41] The second issue related to knowledge is Talbi's conception of knowledge being (at least in part) always subject to reconsideration, and the knower (*'alim*) being obliged continually to reconsider what he thinks he knows. Talbi addresses this from a first-person perspective in answer to the following question: "We want to consider, however briefly, the possibility of someone being characterised as authoritatively learned (*'alim*)".[42] Talbi says: "I reject categorically the concept of *'alim,* because we are seekers of knowledge (*tullab ma'rifa*) ... Possibly I might be called a professional historian, my profession being history. So I try to do well in this profession ... But I consequently reject the term *'alim,* because it promotes a lack of (intellectual) humility and this is what I reject … !!"[43] "Intellectual humility" is not simply a fine moral virtue for Talbi. It is much more. For it also reflects Talbi's main epistemological principle that knowledge, however compelling, is never absolutely certain, and that "… all (intellectual) progress (*taqaddum*) is only the sum of a series of (intellectual) ups and downs. Thus it is impossible for me to consider myself an *'alim,* and it is very difficult for me to consider any person an *'alim* in an absolute sense, although there were amongst the most learned of the *'ulama'* … distinguished figures who opened doors and developed many schools (of thought). But we know that all of them committed egregious errors. And who does not err? Every person is both knowledgeable and ignorant at the same time, knowledgeable about some things and ignorant of others; but his ignorance in all instances greatly outweighs his knowledge."[44]

If Talbi wants the Arab and Muslim peoples to enhance and develop their intellectual traditions, then it is this kind of knowledge and this particular approach to it which he would wish to inculcate. It is knowledge seen as provisional and the approach to it as critical. It is knowledge as a continuing quest for more perfect approximations of truth. No human seeker after truth in this way is exempt from error, even the most illustrious religious scholars. Every individual must strive to attain knowledge in this critical sense. Every individual must, therefore, be a *mujtahid,* says Talbi.[45] Using the term *mujtahid* in this context, especially after asserting that even the great religious authorities had erred, gives Talbi's argument a particular Islamic edge. For his conception of critical knowledge and his implied definition of it as *ijtihad* obviously points towards a religious epistemology which denies the authority of *taqlid.* But for Talbi this is not simply a doctrine of denial of *taqlid* in order to construct a modern Islamic theory of knowledge and its legitimation. It has also to do with a conception of knowledge which would provide a foundation for religious pluralism *within Islam* as well as between Islam and other religions.[46] Central in all this is Talbi's notion of interpreting the Qur'an and how the Qur'an fits in his general epistemology. For the absolute nature of the Qur'anic text must, one would have thought, be a principle upheld, even if in the context of Talbi's "conditional epistemology" knowledge is always provisional. In chapter two, *"Islam and Some Difficult Issues",* the discussion continues, with these matters taking a central position. I shall discuss some aspects of chapter two against the background of Talbi's thought as portrayed thus far, and in anticipation of looking closely at part two of chapter three, *"For Dialogue Between All Religions".*

Talbi treats two large themes in chapter two, *The Qur'an and the Necessities of the Age* and *Knowledge and Politics in Islam.* In these contexts, and here following his earlier line of thought, Talbi further develops his idea of religious pluralism, now in conjunction with a theory of Qur'anic exegesis. He then extends this thinking in the political sphere. The conception of knowledge, politics and religion in Islam which Talbi develops here has, not surprisingly, a distinctly "liberal" cast and an anti-Islamist tone. I shall discuss mainly the part on the Qur'an, the more relevant to my main purpose and to the preceding discussion, and refer to the part on politics only to draw out some additional examples.

Talbi's main argument concerning *The Qur'an and the Necessities of the Age* is based on his claim that differences of opinion, individual and sectarian, within Islam and between Islam and other religions, are part of a natural feature of human life. The "pluralism" which is so central to Talbi's thought is in his view a derivation of that truth of human nature. Thus, says Talbi, "Man is by nature a pluralist".[47] So even though religious pluralism is rejected by many in the Muslim camp, Islam today faces the challenge of pluralism which arises naturally. But, notwithstanding the resistance of many Muslim thinkers to such an idea, Talbi argues that difference in opinion, *al-ikhtilaf,* has in fact been part of Islam since its inception, and that this is in some sense the foundation of pluralism. He argues that *al-ikhtilaf,* in a sort of evolutionary way, seems at a certain point to become true pluralism. Thus: "(Different) trends (of thought) were numerous in the heart of the *umma* from the very inception of Islam".[48] Though *united* in its religious practices, the *umma* was *fragmented* in intellectual trends and social movements. This even at times caused mutual "excommunication" and "the notion that the shedding of blood was permitted".[49] "Pluralism" in its basic form of the variety of ideas which human beings by nature construct (*al-ikhtilaf*), and "pluralism" which goes beyond into some semblance of mutuality and toleration have, then, this sort of organic connection and overlap for Talbi.

Talbi says a prime example of the way in which this has worked in Islamic history is with respect to "... interpretations of the Qur'anic text – the text in which the *umma* all come together".[50] Here, says Talbi, the different interpretations (*ta'wilat*) of the Qur'an have "... reached the extreme limit of blatant mutual exclusion between the various Islamic intellectual trends ...".[51] But this was – and is – "natural" to man, as Talbi sees it, and positive.[52] The large implicit question here is, I believe, does anything go? That is, are all Muslim interpretations of the Qur'an (and, by extension, other Islamic texts) equal, and, if so, what happens when the proponents of the various claims begin to act politically (and in other ways) on behalf of their claims? Talbi explicitly addresses this issue in response to the interviewer's comment that, given all of what Talbi has said, might we not, then, have to conclude that "... each of us would (in that case) be appealing to his own Islam in making (religious) decisions, whether for good or for bad ... !"[53] Talbi's answer to this is twofold: he clarifies and expands his theoretical position, giving a theoretical solution to the problem, and he discusses his own particular approach to understanding the Qur'an, an approach which he obviously thinks is the best.[54]

Theoretically, Talbi sees no way around a multitude of approaches to the Qur'an, nor does he see this as a problem. Again, for him this *ikhtilaf* is natural and good. It has, however, in the past led to unpleasant (even bloody) competitions and conflicts, while in the present, too, "... all the modern movements such as the *Wahhabiyya,* which made its way to power in Saudi Arabia by the sword, the *Salafiyya,* the *Tamamiyya,* the *Islamist extremists and non-extremists,* the *Reformists* and also even the *Secularists,* these are only (based on) different readings of *one text,* Qur'an or *Sunna*".[55] The real problem, says Talbi, occurs, then, when we move from the theoretical plane, to the practical political and social reality, where conflicts take place. For although Talbi personally applauds diversity of views and even the inevitable tensions which accompany them, he does see today a dangerous polarisation within the Muslim world between totalitarianism and anarchy, with people whose particular views, of whatever stripe, on one side or another, have become for them, as it were, divine (*lahuti*).[56] So what is the solution? Talbi here proposes a movement from tolerance of one for the other, *tasamuh,* which is the "lowest level" of liberalness, (*samaha*), to "mutual respect based on the right of the other to disagree ..." (*al-ihtiram al-mutabadal*).[57] This, says Talbi, is in reality the *ijtihad* which the jurists of Islam talked about.

This *ijtihad,* which Talbi defines as the legal *ijtihad* whose gates were closed by the jurists many centuries ago, would legitimate the individualistic interpretations of Qur'an and faith, while placing them in some formal framework which would provide guidelines and boundaries for *ijtihad* in a new consensus (*ijma'*): "a new consensus consonant with the spirit of our age".[58] This consensus would be derived from the creation of a certain (new) intellectual principle (*al-qa'ida al-ma'rifiyya*). All this would occur in the ideal *umma* which Talbi defines as "the community of moderation" (*ummat al-wasat*).[59] This community would allow for free expression of Qur'an interpretations in a way which would presumably preclude the extremism of each person and group considering their own interpretations "divine" and even "... creating terrorist groups".[60] The extremes of totalitarianism and anarchy, both of which represent a societal inability to channel and to direct the natural diversity of Qur'anic (and other) interpretations, would thereby be prevented.

So far, Talbi has spoken much about the principle of "Qur'anic free speech" in the *ikhtilaf* of religious expression, and in "pluralism", and even in "mutual self-respect". But he has skirted the issue of the ways of understanding Qur'an and religion in general and his own approach to the Qur'anic text in particular. It is perhaps incomplete to say, in effect, as Talbi has done, that diversity of views and approaches is a good thing and even natural, without discussing critically some of those views and approaches, even showing some preference for one or more of them over the others. Talbi does do this, in his own way, partly by implication and in part explicitly. By implication, he has already told us that a flexible, non-dogmatic approach is best; he has also criticised those who believe their own interpretations to be somehow divine (*lahuti*). Farther than this he has not gone. But in elucidating his own way of interpreting the Qur'an Talbi will in fact show us what he considers to be the "best" approach to the text.

Talbi first – and briefly – alludes to his interpretative method in Qur'anic studies with a reference in particular to an article he published on the interpretation of verses 34–35 in *surat al-Nisa'* (the Chapter "Women" in the Qur'an). This article, titled "The Issue of Disciplining Women Through Corporal Punishment", is Talbi's attempt to understand these verses which, he says, "... have been taken by some as an excuse to debase and physically to mistreat women, and by others to attack Islam" (presumably for evincing such "illiberal" attitudes towards women).[61] In this article and elsewhere, says Talbi, he used an "historical reading" (*qira'a ta'rikhiyya*). This means that, "We try to understand the text and to read it according to the (historical) circumstances of its revelation".[62] Thus, in the case at hand (3:34), the historical context would enable us to see the particular situation to which God addressed His words, and this would, presumably, help to curb those who would extract universal principles from Qur'anic verses which can be demonstrated to have had limited local and historical applications. In this context, Talbi admonishes Muslims to return to the text itself in making commentaries, in order not to universalise the commentary with claims that it is itself God's word. Only the Qur'anic text is God's word, and it is what unites Muslims, along with their common religious practices of worship and piety. *All* interpretations of the Qur'an, then, are tentative and provisional. They are the word of human beings, not God. For "... only God speaks in the name of Islam, and His Messenger conveys it."[63] Any human being who would arrogate to himself the right to speak in the name of Islam, or to put himself in the place of God, in this way, would thereby "... have fallen into idolatry (*shirk*)".[64] The Qur'anic text (*al-nass al-Qur'ani*) is again for Talbi the saviour in this situation; for even "... when there are differences in interpretation, the text brings us together".[65]

Talbi's insistence on the necessity of *ijtihad,* as discussed above, and the primacy of the Qur'anic text as opposed to interpretations of the text, in some respects puts him in the mainstream of modern Sunni thinking on these issues. This "Protestant" trend in modern Islamic thought has been a major theme in the Sunni Arab world, although it has meant very different things to different people. For Talbi it means the freedom – nay, the necessity – for Muslims to devise their own interpretations of the Qur'an, and in that way to get back to the text itself, the only, true form of God's word and Islamic truth.[66] As a corollary, however, Talbi preaches a cautionary message concerning those same interpretations and commentaries, one's own as well as those of others: lest we believe the interpretations are themselves God's word, as so many have believed, especially in our day with the rise in the trend of "every Muslim having his own Islam". But one must ask, again, is there not an internal contradiction in Talbi's argument here? For what will prevent people naturally from thinking their interpretations are the best and only ones, particularly if they are encouraged to exercise *ijtihad*? Talbi has no direct answer to this question, except to exhort others to make a true "moderate community" (*ummat al-wasat*). But he does certainly have an implicit answer: that his own "historical method" is the one mode of textual interpretation which could never result in the misplaced "authoritative conclusions" which some people draw from their own interpretative approaches. This is because the historical method, in treating the text *in context*, is presumably immune to the extrapolation of universal precepts from specific situations. Thus, except for the large universal ethical principles, which are *general* to begin with, and which the Qur'an presents in that way, in Talbi's view everything else in the text is "situational" and "local". This is clear in Talbi's further extended discussion of religion and politics in this chapter, where, among other things, he argues for a "relativistic" Islamic system of values. This system rests on the universal ethical principles in the Qur'an such as justice (*'adl*), with the more specific elements being "relativised".

Human life and history may then be seen and treated as dynamic and evolutionary, even in religious affairs and behaviour. With the universal moral precepts in the Qur'an serving as a framework, the nitty gritty of Qur'anic ethical obligations for Muslims might then be seen in their *sitz im lieben*. They could be subject to change as a result of changing historical conditions. Thus in discussing the Qur'anic admonition to uphold the good and to reject the bad, for Talbi the question really is: "Is what was considered 'bad' (*munkar*) in the first century of the Hijra in Medina or Cordova 'bad' today for a Muslim living in New York or London? And likewise in the matter of the 'good'".[67] More abstractly: Are ethics fixed or do they change and evolve through the events of time and place? The answer, for Talbi, is clear: If one is talking about the (for Talbi) behavioural details, then evolution and change do and must occur. "Upholding the good and rejecting the bad", the traditional Islamic admonition, has meaning here only in the most general moral sense. In criticising contemporary political Islamic trends which extrapolate from historical behavioural details of the early Islamic period, creating universal behavioural principles from these which emphasise the "bad" to be rejected, rather than the good to be upheld, Talbi says: "We agree that there are here fixed moral values such as justice, peace, abjuring hostility, equality, righteousness, sincerity, etc. But is the length of the beard or the mode of dress a fixed moral behavioural obligation?"[68] Talbi's answer is, of course, a resounding "No". Such things may change with time – indeed it is normal and desirable that they do so. Those Muslims who wish to take their behavioural religious obligations from what they believe to have been the exemplary (and binding) practices of the Prophet and other prominent Muslims of that early period are in Talbi's view wrong. Thus: "Whenever we wish to take this (moral) standard from the time of the *rasul* and the Followers (*al-Tabi'un*) we are thereby obliged to reject everything not found in that time and to consider as 'good' only what was so considered in that time … The moral standard, consequently, becomes one taken from an environment other than our own today. In establishing this standard as authoritative we are in fact attempting to stop the movement of history and the dynamic of development, and we are always and forever enjoining a certain social life (based) on the standard of the past."[69] The consequence of this, says Talbi, is "that many of the people today try in their dress, in their costume, and in their general outward appearance to live a life which in their belief and imagination is similar to the life in the time of the Muslim

Forefathers."[70] But this, says Talbi, is impossible and inevitably fails. It also leads to and is an integral part of the Islamist movements which at their most extreme want not only to impose this dubious "external standard" on their fellows, but they also as well want sometimes to "excommunicate" them through pronouncing *takfir*.[71] The implications of this for the Muslim community are very grave indeed. Talbi's proffered solution here is again to see the details of tradition in historical and political context, realising that changes will occur from time to time, and that this is necessary and desirable. This approach is Talbi's exegetical method discussed above and here transposed in the key of religious observance. If Qur'anic verses must be seen and interpreted in their contexts of revelation (*asbab al-nuzul*) so too must the detailed religious observances of Muslims be seen in theirs; and so too must the Qur'anic verses and extra-Qur'anic traditions connected with the minutiae of observance also be seen in context. Only the large (ethical) principles remain constant. And these have great meaning for Talbi's theory of inter-religious relations as well for his other (internal) Islamic concerns.

The sort of general ethical values found in the Qur'an are for Talbi universal and constant, not only – or even primarily – because they are *revealed,* or politically enjoined, but even more so because they are *innate in human nature.* "We confront here", says Talbi, "a universal ethical value which goes with man as man; it is an ethical value before it is political, although politics often tries – more or less successfully – to underpin ethics. This is, then, a spiritual, ethical principle *in the heart of every man.*"[72] Thus: "… Man loves Justice and the Good, *insofar as he is pure man.*"[73] This truth is part of Islam, for, says Talbi, "… When we use the language of Islam, (it is said) that is by virtue of innate (human) nature."[74] This innate nature (*fitra*) precedes revelation and itself makes the inculcation of the revelatory values possible. For, "… man by virtue of (his) innate nature loves Good and Justice, and he hates evil and injustice. Whenever he does wrong, he knows it is evil".[75] In this way, says Talbi, the Qur'anic admonition to uphold the good and reject the bad is itself a general ethical value "*by virtue of the innate human nature*".[76] This is because "man distinguishes between the virtuous and the abomination *through the innate human nature,* in every existing place. Thus when the Qur'an speaks to man and admonishes him to do good and to reject the bad *it is simply reaffirming this fundamental spiritual value which is innate in every man*".[77] Nobody would disagree with this, says Talbi, but many would dispute the means by which it might be put into practice. This observation is again, from yet another perspective, Talbi's conception of the unity of spiritual, metaphysical truth and the multiplicity of its many forms of mundane expression.

"For Dialogue Between All Religions" is subsection two (*al-fasl al-thani*) of chapter three of *Families of God.* Chapter three is titled *Some Important Questions Concerning Civilisation.* For Talbi, the issue of relations between religions is the main "question concerning civilisation".[78] Talbi, as a "disciple" of the German Catholic theologian Hans Küng, believes with Küng that "there is no peace between the nations without peace between the religions".[79] Inter-religious (and intra-religious) relations for both men are the necessary condition for world peace, as, in their view, religious prejudices, intolerance, and hatred constitute a significant part – if not the whole – of modern civil and international conflicts. For Talbi, Islam's internal situation of a growing militancy and politicisation of religion requires the pluralism (*al-ta'addudiyyah*) and mutual respect (*al-ihtiram al-mutabadil*) which are in like manner so much needed in the larger sphere, among the great religions. In his view, as we have already seen, these are two sides of the same coin, and indeed, if Muslims cannot institute these principles and practices (which in Talbi's opinion are in fact an integral part of true Islam) *within the umma,* then they would be unable to do so in relations with other religions.

For both Küng and Talbi the only "proper" attitude of one religion (or sect) towards others is that all are equal paths to God, even if believers consider their own truth to be "superior". These two positions may indeed coexist in one individual as part of a proper strategy in the conduct of relations with "the other". In his discussion of dialogue between all the religions Talbi touches on three main issues: internal Islamic dialogue, dialogue between all the religions and Islam's mission in our time. In all of this discussion, Talbi has shifted perspective from the theories and principles of Islamic religion and of inter-religious relations to the concept of "dialogue" between religions, in theory and in practice.

Thus *al-ta'addudiyya* and *al-ikhtilaf* as theoretical principles and natural features of human life in the way Talbi previously used them now become implicit foundations of the principle and practice of *dialogue* (*al-hiwar*). Further dialogue within Islam and between Muslims is imperative, says Talbi, not only because of their intrinsic desirability and the natural human inclination towards expression of diverse opinion, but also because *Islam's basic nature impels Muslims in this direction.* In answer to a question about his view of the pride often shown by Muslims in the absence of a "Priesthood" (*Kahnut*) or centralised religious authority in Islam, Talbi, among other things, asserts that this feature is indeed positive, for it reflects the essential Islamic propensity to internal debate. Although sometimes that propensity has been stifled by *taqlid* and even "consensus of fanaticism" and "rejection of the other" which have unfortunately been all too common in Islam, Islam's *essence* is pluralistic. Islam is internally open to all points of view on issues of religious thought, provided all parties begin from a belief in and appeal to its revealed sources. This provides a curb on any tendencies towards relativism (unacceptable to Talbi) and the consequent loss of identity. Thus: "Glory to God who did not obligate us to any petrified (religious) form; nor did our Prophet or God's words so commit us. For we were vouchsafed the freedom to conceive any form we wish which we see as useful and consonant with our times".[80] For Talbi this is an "absolute freedom" (*al-hurriyya al-mutlaqa*).[81] Internal dialogue is therefore built into Islam as is the associated (identical) principle of dialogue between all the religions.

In answer to a question concerning the Islamic religious-legal legitimacy (*mashru'iyya*) of inter-religious dialogue, Talbi, citing his own participation in Muslim-Christian dialogue, says, "I am determined in the pursuit of dialogue, whatever the difficulties, troubles and misunderstanding".[82] Talbi says this is basic to his belief and his thought, and it is derived in his mind from the individual freedom which he believes to be intrinsic in the human condition. This is the freedom of one to pursue and to hold one's own truth and it involves the freedom also to pursue dialogue with the other. Indeed, for Talbi it means as a basic intellectual and moral principle that he must respect every individual "whatever his community, whatever his position, whatever his religion."[83] Against this background, says Talbi, one must understand his own frequent participation in Muslim-Christian dialogue as part of a more general interfaith goal: "the attempt to create an atmosphere of mutual understanding and interchange among the three religions, which have their origins in Abraham, and through him extricating ourselves from the atmosphere of polemics and conflict. And that is because of my belief that the responsibilities of believers (of the three monotheistic religions) in this new world are great".[84] The "human weight" of these three religious communities is very great indeed "... For half of humanity at least adheres to Islam, Christianity or Judaism".[85] Thus if these faiths, derived from the same prophetic source and having certain similar features, cannot be in harmonious relations and live without mutual rancour, what hope can there be for others?

But as a source-based traditional thinker Talbi cannot base his faith in dialogue and its *Shari'a* legitimacy solely *on his own thinking*; that is not God's word, and Talbi, though a believer in the individual's right to full freedom of expression, is not a relativist. The Qur'an, God's word, must provide a foundation for his conception. Thus: "We find the religious-legal legitimacy of dialogue *in the Qur'an*".[86] And in quoting from another of his own works: "Dialogue for Islam constitutes a reversion to an Islamic religious-legal tradition. Indeed, everything in the Revelation calls for dialogue and nothing in it rejects dialogue."[87] In order to be convinced of that, he says, we need only consider two Qur'anic verses: "Call for the path of your Lord with wisdom and fine exhortation, and argue with them in the best way. Indeed your Lord knows best who has strayed from His path. And He knows also the rightly-guided" (16:125).[88] And: "Argue with the People of the Book only with the best argument; but do not argue at all with the bad amongst them. And say, We believe in what has been revealed to us and in what has been revealed to you. Our God and your God are one" (29:46).[89]

The first cited verse, Qur'an 16:125, is an admonition to hold debate and discussion with others, especially the *Ahl al-Kitab,* on a basis of frankness and sensitivity, while conveying one's own religious position. And the notion that only God knows who is obedient to and who has strayed from His laws is, in Talbi's view, an admonition to God's creatures not to judge one another.

The second verse, Qur'an 29:46, may again be seen as an admonition to civilised discussion with the *Ahl al-Kitab,* with the assertion that Islam believes in the revelations to *Ahl al-Kitab* as well as in its own, and that all three faiths share the belief in God's oneness. For Talbi, these two verses in themselves provide the religious-legal legitimation which he was asked about, though later he adduces other verses which he interprets in the same way, and which I shall discuss. But in addition to the specific religious legitimation of dialogue which Talbi finds in the Qur'an, he also sees this elsewhere in the Islamic tradition: "Just as we find the legality of dialogue in our religion, so also do we find it in our history, our culture, and our civilisation, which are of world-renown."[90] There was dialogue between Muslims and Christians, for example, says Talbi, "… in the palaces of the Caliphs".[91] And this was already reflected in the medieval Islamic writings on communities and sects.

The religious foundation in the Qur'an is, however, still the basic legitimation of dialogue for Talbi and the reason why "… We are unable to separate Islam from the religions of the *Ahl al-Kitab* whom the Qur'an addresses with great earnestness in many places".[92] Talbi sees this Qur'anic feature of almost constant talking to and querying the *Ahl al-Kitab* as a divine Islamic injunction to dialogue. And in his mind it makes any conceptual (or real) separation of Islam from its "co-religions", Judaism and Christianity, unthinkable. These constitute a "bloc of faiths" which of necessity are intextricably bound together in their common derivation from their father, Abraham, and in their linked revelations from the One God. Talking to one another, then, for Talbi is not only divinely enjoined, but it is in the nature of things that this should occur. However, as much of the Qur'an's discussion of and querying the *Ahl al-Kitab* is by way of challenging their behaviour and beliefs, as well as promoting "inter-religious dialogue", the issue of the relative status of the three faiths with respect to one another must also be considered, particularly the Qur'an's intention in this matter. As we have seen, Talbi seems to believe in the possibility of spiritual equality while at the same time believers would somehow also reserve the right to attribute to their own faith a certain superiority. Talbi wants to remove the negative components of the exclusivity which seems to be part of the mentality of the bloc of monotheistic faiths, while leaving in place a "clean exclusivity" which would allow believers to consider their religion to be one amongst equals and, at the same time, *without seeming contradiction,* to be "better" in some ways than the others. This notion must be defined clearly in Qur'anic terms, as it is integrally related to the Qur'anic admonition to dialogue. Indeed, the dialogic component which Talbi sees as being a central feature of the Qur'anic worldview and ethical/legal injunction may be fully understood only with elucidation of the Qur'an's view on the intertwined issue of the hierarchy (if there be one) of religions.

Talbi sees the relationship between the Islamic revelation and those of Judaism and Christianity in the Qur'anic framework of spiritual supercession. Thus in the series of the three revelations, the second and third, Christianity and Islam, were sent as *successors* to what had come before. The exact meaning of "succession", however, must be elucidated. Is it supercession? One opinion in the Muslim community has indeed been that the latter supercedes the former in a sense which imputes superiority to the latter. And in the case of Islam its presumed superiority to its predecessors is based, among other things, on Islam's claims of the corrupted nature of the previous revelations (*tahrif*) and the corrupted behaviour of their adherents. In this view, the prophet Muhammad's status as "seal of the prophets", as he is called in the Qur'an,[93] would mean Islam's superiority as well as its finality. But in Talbi's view the Qur'an's meaning here would be somewhat different: "Islam *completes* the revelations which preceded it, through the mission of the seal of the prophets and messengers".[94] Talbi understands the verb *khatama* to indicate the role of *completion* or *fulfilment* of the preceding revelations by Islam's prophet, the *seal* of the prophets. For Talbi, the particular completion or fulfilment brought by the Muslim *khatm* seal of the prophets, or indeed by Jesus in his role with respect to Judaism, does not in any way imply the banishing of the older faith(s) or even its (their) relegation to secondary status. Thus: "Just as Jesus, the last prophet of the Banu Isra'il, did not nullify (Judaism) but rather only completed what had come before, likewise Muhammad did not at all eradicate what had preceded him and was brought by the previous messengers, but he only completed, emended, and fulfilled (it)."[95] This in Talbi's view is the Qur'anic (and New Testament) position on the issue of supercession. He cites Jesus in Matthew 5:17, "Do not think I have come to refute the Law or the prophets, I have not come to refute. I have, rather, come to complete", as a New Testament proof-text for his claims. From the Qur'an, obviously most important for him, Talbi cites from verses in two *suras*, 5:48 and 3:3–4. Thus 5:48: "And we have sent down to you the Book with truth, confirming what preceded it as a Book, and guarding over it". Of most interest to Talbi here, of course, are the words "confirming" (*musaddiqan*) and "guarding" (*muhayminan*). These words for him support his thesis concerning the Qur'an's view of itself as being the final part of an integral series of revelations related in such a way that they are indeed inseparable. The final position of the Qur'an in this series makes it the epitome and guardian of all that came before rather than superceding and rendering it totally irrelevant. Talbi singles out in particular the phrase *"muhayminan 'alayhi"*, asserting that the authoritive lexicon *Lisan al-'Arab* corroborates his understanding, where it makes *muhayminan 'alayhi* synonymous with *shahidan 'alayhi,* "guarding over it".[96] From 3: 3–4, Talbi cites the following: "God sent down to you the Book with truth, confirming what came before. And He sent down the Torah and the Evangel previously as guidance to the people; and He sent down the *Furqan*". The *Furqan,* another name for the Qur'an, is here clearly portrayed as the third in a series of three revelations, "confirming what came before". This again supports Talbi's thesis of the interrelationship of all the revelations in the Qur'an's worldview and the consequent imperative of dialogue among them. Thus "... God's revelation forms an uninterrupted sequence which does not admit of any (internal) distinction", says Talbi; and this is "... through the various stages (of revelation) which the seal of the prophets and messengers completes."[97]

For Talbi, then, the Qur'an's position as the final revelation within the group of religions of *Ahl al-Kitab* and its status as "confirmation" and "guardian" of the other two does not mean the relegation of Judaism and Christianity to the realm of outmoded and corrupted predecessor, but, rather, on the contrary, it obliges the Muslims, as hearers of God's final Word in the series, to conduct continuous dialogue with Jews and Christians. For Talbi's understanding of the Islamic revelation in its own terms sees in it a continuous living dialogue with Judaism and Christianity, a dialogue which the Qur'an by virtue of its own practice enjoins Muslims to continue throughout the ages, even (especially) when strong differences exist. Thus from a Qur'anic message of its own finality and completeness in relation to the previous revelations to *Ahl al-Kitab*, Talbi extracts the message of conciliation and unity of outlook and purpose amongst the three monotheistic faiths. Others have seen in the same Qur'anic ideas a message of Islam's superiority over the others and their consequent relegation to a peripheral lower status, living in a continuous polemical relationship with Islam. Even when Muslims (or Jews or Christians) feel that their religion is superior – and again, this is not totally ruled out by Talbi – they are still obliged to see and to treat the others as equals. There is no contradiction here for Talbi, as for him the Qur'an (and the Jewish and Christian revelations, as well) evinces a universalistic ethos which subsumes and contains the everpresent particularisms. Talbi's conception of the divine-human relationship and of the essential human nature (*fitra*), as discussed above, not only make it possible for him to claim this universalism but they make it imperative for him to do so. Thus: "God is not the God of Quraysh or the Arabs, nor is He the God of the children of Israel. He is only the God of humanity, compassionate to all humanity. So is He 'Lord of the worlds, the merciful, the Compassionate', as was revealed in *Surat al-Fatiha* which opens the Qur'an. With Him do we seek refuge. And we seek refuge with 'the Lord of humanity, King of humanity, the God of humanity', in the last *sura,* which closes the Qur'an. Since, then, God is the God of humanity, nobody has the right to monopolise Him: From the first *sura* in the Qur'an to the last, God speaks to humanity, all of humanity".[98] The great irony in this for Talibi, is that notwithstanding the Qur'an's clarity on this point, so many people in the Muslim world see in that text a very different (even) opposite meaning: "Since God speaks to all humanity, how can it be, then, that we do not have dialogue with all humanity?!".[99]

But although Talbi is a universalist in wanting dialogue between *all* religions and peoples, his main concern, as shown above, is the possibility (nay, necessity) of dialogue between Muslims and the People of the Book, who are, "... amongst all the religions, the closest to us."[100] Thus, even when there would appear to be unresolvable religious differences amongst the People of the Book, there is, says Talbi, "... a common position which is basic and joins us, in belief in God, and in the End of Days. And (also) love of the good and of the other equips us in most areas to speak in one language."[101]

Talbi has mainly spoken thus far only in general terms of *basic conceptions* concerning intra-Islamic dialogue and inter-religious dialogue between Islam and other religions, particularly the monotheistic faiths. Where he has gone into more detail, that detail has itself been mainly conceptual; and where textual references are adduced they are, again, used for conceptual clarification and foundation. There is an historical dimension of the inter-religious situation, however, which Talbi addresses and which he integrates with his main conceptual arguements. This is the question of the actual life of the (mainly) Jewish and Christian *dhimmis* in their historical existence within Islamic society. For Talbi this historical record serves as a sort of "confirmation in the field" of the Islamic potential for a new, modern arrangement and dialogue between Islam and the People of the Book. I shall conclude, then, with this discussion and Talbi's related discussion of Islam's mission in the modern world. Talbi addresses the issue of *dhimmi* history in response to a critical question which says:

> "There is no doubt there are moral principles (you have mentioned) which do serve as a model of the dialogue which (in your view), the Qur'an enjoins. But there are here also contrary principles. Thus does history speak about confrontation between Muslims and the minorities, beginning from the very notion of Ahl al-Dhimma in the framework of Islamic society with respect to the allocation of social-religious space to Muslims and non-Muslims. Consequently, Islam's relation with the others is not necessarily simply just one exemplary way which is predominant, as you have so well expanded on that. Here surely are other aspects of no small significance which call for a study of the reasons for the absence of dialogue?!"[102]

Talbi's response to this question is a spirited but realistic defense of the Islamic historical treatment of the (Jewish and Christian) minorities, which allows him also to expound more on his basic theoretical principles. Though not altogether free of historical, conceptual and logical difficulties, Talbi's arguement here does on balance seem genuinely to buttress further his main thesis.

Talbi first challenges the claim that there was historically a confrontation between Islam and its minorities. Indeed, he says, "... The strange thing is that history does not speak about the confrontation between Muslims and the minorities ..."[103] The real conflict was in fact, *intra-Islamic,* "... between different religious positions or between conflicting tribes and races or between various political persuasions. The non-Muslim minorities did not participate in this conflict which I consider to be alien to them, of no concern for them, and which they did not emulate. Indeed, the issue of the *Ahl al-Dhimma* was not at all present in armed conflicts and revolutions on a religious foundation during the Middle Ages. Generally the legal system of the *dhimma* was accepted by those upon whom it was imposed in proportion to its being (at times) more or less tolerant and just".[104] Further, "the division of social-religious space between Muslims and non-Muslims" which was addressed in the question to Talbi does not in his view imply anything wrong in the traditional pre-modern relations between Muslims and the minorities. For at that time, this sort of "division" was not considered objectionable by either side. It was "a natural thing in its time"[105] and as such it "... did not arouse ethical questions, philosophical disturbance or political unease".[106] Indeed, Talbi says, this propensity for humans to identify and classify others and themselves in relation to the others in religious categories is something which in some places still lives today. Talbi gives his own childhood milieu as an example of this, and also says that "... the division of societies according to religious identity was – and remains so for the Jews – something self-evident."[107] The allusion to the Jews' continuing propensity for this idea and arrangement is obviously with reference to the state of Israel and its internal divisions on mainly religious lines.

In Talbi's view, then, the traditional *dhimma* institution was appropriate for its time. We ought not, as he reiterates, "impose the present on the past", in measuring the mediaeval *dhimma* against the criteria of modern liberal democracy. The real question here, says Talbi is: "Did the mediaeval Islamic order provide justice abundantly or not?"[108] His answer, in brief, is that it did. Citing a variety of sources and authorities – most notably the eminent French historian Claude Cahen – Talbi argues that although the pure human principle of the *dhimma* was at times compromised by difficult historical cicumstances, these were anomalies in a larger picture of generally good relations. Justice (*'adl*) *in its historical context* did usually hold sway. For even the worst laws enacted within the *dhimma* context were not consonant with the true meaning of the institution, and in our assessments of that period we must not exaggerate on one side or the other. The periods of trouble were indeed "... limited in time and space".[109] And even they "... certainly did not reach the point of 'social madness' and elimination of non-Muslims, as had happened to the Muslims in Spain and Sicily".[110] Islam in its *dhimma* aspect was for Talbi, then, highly successful – if not superior to other civilisations – as a just social order.

But the *dhimma* institution was for Talbi not the true Islamic programme and institution for the ordering of society. Indeed, he says, it was not really Qur'anic. It did reflect certain basic Islamic principles of toleration and, as said above, it operated reasonably well to the benefit of all, Muslims and non-Muslims. Thus the most authentic Islamic social order with respect to toleration and majority-minority relations was not for Talbi the *dhimma*, but rather its earlier precursor, the "Constitution of Medina". For there is "... no mention of the *dhimma* order in the Qur'an nor in the Constitution which the Messenger (peace be upon him) issued when he entered Medina, and which it is possible for us to consider as the constitution of the first state established in Islam on the pluralistic model. This is because this state received within it Muslims and non-Muslims, and involved non-Muslims in political life."[111] The non-Muslims here were, aside from the indigenous Arabs, mainly the Jewish tribes, within the new Islamic state. Indeed, it was the Muslims' relations with the Jewish tribes in Medina initially, upon Muhammad's entrance to the town, which prompted the appearance of the constitution of this first Islamic state. Talbi thus quotes from the *sira* of Ibn Hisham on the Muslim-Jewish relations reflected in the Constitution of Medina: "The Jews of Banu 'Awf are a community with the Muslims. The Jews have their religion and the Muslims theirs ... the Jews have their own financial obligations and the Muslims theirs. The Jews and Muslims will provide mutual aid against those who fight the people of this Constitution. Between the Jews and Muslims there will be good counsel, kindness and not bad behaviour".[112] But alas, says Talbi, this great "experiment"[113] failed. It failed for "historical reasons"[114] which impelled the Jews to join the opponents of Islam in Medina in opposition to "the people of the Constitution",[115] and "contextual reasons"[116] which "... led to difficult conflicts and to the expulsion of the Jews from Medina ...".[117] But, says Talbi, "... the foundation remains".[118]

For Talbi, the Constitution of Medina, however short-lived the attempt at its implementation, remains as the main Islamic model for the good society in which – among other things – inter-religious relations may flourish. The *dhimma* institution and its history were a poor substitute for that early model. Indeed, the *dhimma* arose out of the failure in implementation of the early "perfect model". And though the *dhimma* constituted a deviation from the goal, it was not at all a bad pre-modern "second-best" arrangement. But it is certainly not an Islamic model for the modern world. That model does exist, however, in the Constitution of Medina, the goal of which is: "... the creation of one society, pluralistic in religion and (personal) identity, on the basis of inclusiveness, justice, and equality. This is a social order identical to the various arrangements of 'Federalism' today".[119] This "Islamic federalism", implicit in the Constitution of Medina, is derived from and based on a set of fundamental values which facilitate interreligious and intercommunal relations within the quintessentially Islamic order: "... freedom of belief, equality in rights and obligations, social solidarity, justice and the admission of pluralism".[120]

Although these values sound remarkably modern, and indeed they are, Talbi is in fact presuming here that his modern formulations of the various aspects of the Constitution of

Medina are true to the ethos and outlook of that ancient Arabian society. With respect to the institution of *dhimma,* while Talbi previously spoke warmly of its assets and advantages, he also spoke quite frankly of its shortcomings, particularly if one measures it against the values and standards of modern liberal democracies. Indeed, with respect to the *dhimma* Talbi reiterated that one ought not fall into the trap here of "... imposing the past on the present". If that is a valid caution with respect to the mainly mediaeval and early modern *dhimma,* then why not the same stricture on the same use of the Constitution of Medina, an even older document and situation? The answer is that for Talbi the *dhimma* was in most ways not comparable to the values and institutions of modern pluralistic societies while the Constitution of Medina, in spite of its greater antiquity, may actually serve as a modern model for the perfect pluralistic society. In Talbi's view, then, there is no danger with the Constitution of Medina in "imposing the present on the past", as present and past here are "the same". The values implicit in the Constitution of Medina, as discussed above, are the very same values which underlie and inform modern liberal pluralistic society. Islam may in this sense be said to have provided a very early version of modern Western liberal society. For Talbi, the promotion of equal inter-religious relations in this sort of social order is Islam's main role and task in the modern world. It would indeed be the fulfillment of Islam's earliest (and frustrated) social and political impulse.

The essential Islamic social ethos here in Talbi's view is love – the brotherly love which permeates society within, between Muslims, and between Muslims and other faiths, and externally between Islamic nations and others and Islamic communities and others. For individual Muslims their proper role is to observe the religious obligations made incumbent upon them in the revelation. This is the *amana* of the Qur'an; this is for Talbi the pious burden of faith and observance which the Qur'an tells us God offered to the heavens and earth which refused it, while man alone agreed to accept it. Social justice and equality and personal goodness and piety are, then, for Mohamed Talbi, the proper expression of Islam and human nature in the modern world.[121]

Mohamed Talbi's theory of "Islamic pluralism" and inter-religious dialogue is a major contribution to the internal Islamic debate on Islam in the modern world. It is also a profound Islamic vision of inter-religious relations in general and of those among the three monotheistic faiths in particular. With respect to "the other", these faiths have traditionally evinced strong theological exclusivist tendencies which were also expressed institutionally, socially and politically. (For obvious reasons Judaism was for centuries less the "perpetrator" of these practical expressions of exclusivity than were the other two faiths, but *theological exclusivity* in Judaism was clearly equally present.) At the same time, the doctrinal, theological component of exclusivity was in all cases ambivalent, opposed as it was in each tradition by counter-trends of "universalistic" doctrine, while in the practical sphere the fate and fortunes of the religious minorities were everywhere dependent as much (or more) on political and material factors as on religious doctrine. The Islamic doctrine and institution of the *dhimma* are a good example here. Talbi points out that in general the institution was "liberal" in interpretation and practice (within a mediaeval hierarchical outlook), but it could also at times be problematic for the minorities, often for reasons of political, economic, military and other material factors. Talbi seeks, however, to go beyond all of this. In his view, the modern world demands it. But unlike many others who have recognised this demand, and sought to meet it in a secular ideology and programme well beyond the boundaries of tradition, Talbi avowedly aims to work from within Islam.

In an era of attenuated institutions and changed societal forms, as well as the general "marginalisation" of the ancient legal and textual traditions, relations among the (three) religions have now been "freed" of their erstwhile "constraints" and exclusivist hierarchical "impediments". Divorced from social structures which implemented principles of "inequality" (no matter how just these may have been) the religions of Abraham may now face one another in a brave new world of equality. But the ancient structures often provided social, legal and intellectual safeguards against excesses in belief and practice. Eruptions of xenophobic exclusivism occurred, as did inter-religious polemics, and the day-to-day life of minorities could sometimes be difficult; but those same structures, laws and principles also, by and large, militated against a generalised fanaticism which would as well be detrimental to the minorities. The modern "freedom" on the ashes of traditional ways has in fact given rise to militant religious/political trends in all the religions, as well as fostering religious "liberalism". In the Islamic case, with the passing of the *dhimma* institution and its traditional social setting and the emigration of most Middle Eastern Jews and many Christians, Islam's relations with the "Abrahamic other" becomes more diffuse and abstract.

It also becomes more overtly political, with the Jews through the Arab-Israel conflict, and with the Christians in the turbulent colonial period and its uncomfortable aftermath. Talbi faces this new world, where the religions of Abraham no longer live according to the traditional institutions which once ordered their relations. His stance towards this situation is positive and optimistic: acknowledging the dangers in the new politicisation of relations and in their more abstract (necessarily stereotypical) quality, Talbi also recognises the opportunities for a true spiritual liberalisation inherent in our new world. Thus in a world where Muslims now often live in "Christian" countries, and where many "Muslim" countries most often generally operate according to "non-Muslim" legislation (and this in particular with respect to their non-Muslims), and where non-Muslims for the most part no longer live in Muslim countries, Talbi is free (to his mind, compelled) to present his new ideas. The wreckage modernity has caused to the world of tradition may thus be seen to have had a positive side as well. This side may, in Talbi's view, be expressed and developed according to Islam's ancient precedents and foundations in appropriate Qur'anic teachings and in the model of the Constitution of Medina.

Notes

1 Talbi writes on this subject in Arabic, French and English. His most comprehensive and systematic works are two books in Arabic (which include references to some of his other writings): *'Iyal Allah: Afkar Jadida fi 'Alaqat al-Muslim bi Nafsihi wa bi al-Akhirin* (*Families of God: New Ideas Concerning the Relation of the Muslim to Himself and Others*). Ceres Editions, Tunis, 1992; *Ummat al-wasat: al-Islam wa Tahaddiyat al-Mu'asara* (*The Community of Moderation: Islam and the Challenges of Modernity*). Ceres Editions, Tunis, 1996. In English, there is a personal essay which exemplifies the pluralist theory: "Unavoidable Dialogue in a Pluralist World: A Personal Account" in *Encounters* 1:1 (1995), pp. 56–59.

2 My emphasis in analysis will be on this integration. For Talbi, as we shall see, Islam in general and its relations with others are virtually totally identified.

3 Referred to here as *'Iyal*.

4 This connection is apparent most specifically in certain concepts which for Talbi exemplify the intersection of the two issues. An example, discussed in great detail later, is Talbi's notion of religious pluralism, *al-ta'addudiyya*. This concept refers both to religious pluralism and to the true essence of Islam which for Talbi are the same.

5 These general features of Talbi's thought have strong resonances of key concepts in the most prominent line of "modernism" in Sunni Arab Islamic thought. Beginning with 'Abdu, and then through Rida, these concepts have evolved through very different meanings with different thinkers. With Talbi, they take on perhaps some of their most "liberal" forms.

6 *'Iyal*, p. 7.

7 *ibid.*
8 This notion is particularly prominent in Ibn 'Arabi's *Fusus al Hikam,* Arabic edition by A. 'Affifi, Cairo, n.d.; English translation by R. Austin, New York. Paulist Press, 1980.
9 *'Iyal,* p. 21.
10 *'Iyal,* p. 23.
11 *'Iyal,* p. 24.
12 *ibid.*
13 *'Iyal,* p. 28 ff.
14 *'Iyal,* p. 25.
15 *'Iyal,* p. 26.
16 *'Iyal,* p. 27.
17 *'Iyal,* p. 28.
18 *ibid.*
19 *ibid.*
20 *ibid.*
21 *ibid.*
22 Characteristic of Talbi's Islamic vision is its dynamic quality. Islam – like all civilisations – is continually moving, evolving. Those who wish to thwart this natural dynamism through adherence to a detailed programme which they claim was the prophet's own and must, therefore, be recapitulated in each generation are wrong in Talbi's view. The constant factors in a religion are for him only its general ethical and theological principles.
23 *'Iyal,* p. 32.
24 *ibid.*
25 *'Iyal,* p. 31.
26 *ibid.*
27 *'Iyal,* p. 31.
28 *ibid.*
29 *'Iyal,* p. 30.
30 The thought of Ibn 'Arabi has often inspired certain types of Muslim modernist thinkers, particularly in the area of interreligious relations and exegesis of the Qur'an. See, For example: Nasir Hamid Abu Zayd's study of Ibn 'Arabi *FalsaFat al-Ta'wil* Cairo, 1994.
31 *'Iyal,* p. 32.
32 *ibid.*
33 *'Iyal,* p. 38.
34 *ibid.*; Qur'an: 16:120.
35 *'Iyal,* p. 38.
36 *'Iyal,* p. 39.
37 *ibid.*
38 *ibid.*
39 *ibid.*
40 *ibid.*
41 *'Iyal,* p. 44.
42 *'Iyal,* p. 45.
43 *ibid.*
44 *'Iyal,* p. 46.
45 *ibid.*
46 The loosening of the authoritative control of knowledge is for Talbi a prerequisite for internal and external pluralism.
47 *'Iyal,* pp. 65–66.
48 *'Iyal,* p. 66.
49 *ibid.*
50 *ibid.*
51 *ibid.*
52 *ibid.*
53 *ibid.*
54 As we shall see, Talbi's approach presupposes the axiomatic correctness of his own exegetical method which itself posits no absolute fixed points of understanding. However, what appears

here as somewhat of an internal contradiction later does seem to transcend its own seeming paradox.

55 *'Iyal*, p. 68.
56 *ibid.*
57 *ibid.*
58 *'Iyal*, p. 70.
59 *ibid.*
60 *'Iyal*, p. 69.
61 *'Iyal*, p. 70.
62 *ibid.*
63 *'Iyal*, p. 71.
64 *ibid.*
65 *ibid.*
66 This Islamic "Protestant" trend has been typical of many Modernist thinkers this century.
67 *'Iyal*, p. 76.
68 *ibid.*
69 *'Iyal*, p. 78.
70 *ibid.*
71 *'Iyal*, pp. 78–84.
72 *'Iyal*, p. 77.
73 *ibid.*
74 *ibid.* Talbi means that the very idea of a universal ethic in man is posited by the Qur'an in the term *fitra.* See: T. Izutsu, *God and Man in the Koran: Semantics of the Koranic Weltanschaung.* Tokyo, 1964, p. 112.
75 *ibid.*
76 *ibid.*
77 *ibid.*
78 *'Iyal*, pp. 152–53.
79 *ibid.*
80 *'Iyal*, pp. 146–49.
81 *ibid.*
82 *'Iyal*, p. 152.
83 *ibid.*
84 *ibid.*
85 *ibid.*
86 *'Iyal*, p. 153.
87 *ibid.*
88 *ibid.*
89 *ibid.*
90 *ibid.*
91 *ibid.*
92 *ibid.*
93 Qur'an, XXXIII:40.
94 *'Iyal*, p. 153.
95 *ibid.*
96 *'Iyal*, p. 154.
97 *ibid.*
98 *ibid.*
99 *ibid.*
100 *ibid.*
101 *ibid.*
102 *'Iyal*, pp. 174–75.
103 *'Iyal*, p. 175.
104 *ibid.*
105 *ibid.*
106 *ibid.*
107 *ibid.*

108 *'Iyal*, p. 176.
109 *ibid.*
110 *ibid.*
111 *ibid.*
112 *'Iyal*, pp. 176–77.
113 *'Iyal*, p. 177.
114 *ibid.*
115 *ibid.*
116 *ibid.*
117 *ibid.*
118 *ibid.*
119 *ibid.*
120 *ibid.*
121 *'Iyal*, p. 182; Qur'an, XXXIII: 72.

16 Christianity and World Religions

The Dialogue with Islam as One Model

Hans Küng

Following many years of arduous research, the panel of the "World Christian Encyclopaedia" (Oxford, 1982) has calculated that there are 274 million Buddhists in the world, of whom albeit but few are in India itself. The number of Hindus is more than twice that, at 583 million. Seven hundred twenty-three million Muslims constitute the second largest group following the Christians, of whom there are approximately 1400 million. This in itself reveals the enormous importance of the Muslim religion, which, in contrast to the mystical religions of Indian origin, must be seen as a prophetic religion together with Judaism and Christianity.

Islam has now grown closer to us than ever before, and that in a wider sense than purely one of geography and mobility. There are increasing numbers of Muslims living among us, whom we have brought into our countries out of economic considerations. We wanted labor forces and were met with people who just like us have a sharply defined faith and who by means of their very presence constitute a challenge to a closed Christian environment.

I do not wish to go into the centuries-old history of conflict and learning as regards Christianity and Islam, nor to outline in depth a single theme such as Islam and the return to, or the secularization of Islam. Neither do I wish to go into the rule of terror of Muslim fanatics in Iran, who have demolished any sympathies toward Islam which many of us may have had. It is precisely in this situation that I feel it important as a theologian to select the difficult theological points and to ask, more by way of example than holistically: How can Christians today come to terms with the claims made by the Muslim faith about itself? In other words, I shall take up questions which will help us to thoroughly examine our altered ecumenical stance toward other world religions in general, with a view to greater broad-mindedness and openness, questions which will perhaps help us to reread our own history of theological thought and faith as reflected in Islam.

No matter from what theological standpoint we regard the claims of Islam, one thing seems certain to me: despite Khomeini, there can be no return to the centuries-old demonizing of Islam, to immunity through defamation. As in the case of other religions, Islam can no longer be ignored by Christian theology, but must instead be reconsidered both politically and theologically as a reality of the one world in which we live and to which we apply our theological efforts.

Christians still regard Islam, to a great extent, as a rigid entity, a closed religious system rather than a living religion which has been constantly changing through the centuries, developing great inner variety and being shared by real people with a wide spectrum of attitudes and feelings. Today there must be a gradual attempt to understand from the inside why the Muslim sees God and the world, service to God and to people, politics, law and art with different eyes, why he experiences these things with feelings different from those of Christians. Keeping present-day Persia in mind, we must first grasp the fact that even today the Islamic religion is not just another branch in the life of a Muslim, that which secularized people like to refer to as the "religious factor" or "sector" alongside other "cultural factors" or "sectors." Life and religion, religion and culture are dynamically interwoven. Islam strives to be an all-embracing outlook, an all-encompassing perspective on life, an all-determining way of life—and so a way to eternal life in the midst of mortality: a way of salvation. Salvation? What can a Christian theologian say to this claim?

Islam—a way of salvation?

I pose this question considering not least the ambivalent attitude of the World Council of Churches, which due to the conflicting standpoints of its member churches, chose even as late of 1977–79 in its "Guidelines for Dialogue with People of Different Religions and Ideologies" not to answer the question of whether there could be salvation outside of the Christian churches, a question which is doubtless these days of great urgency.

The traditional Catholic position, as prepared even in first centuries of the Christian church by Origen, Cyprian and Augustine, is generally well-known: *extra ecclesiam nulla salus!* (No salvation outside of the Church.) Thus for the future as well: *extra ecclesiam nullus propheta!* (No prophet outside of the Church.) The ecumenical Council of Florence of 1442 defined this very clearly:

> The Holy Church of Rome … believes firmly, confesses and proclaims that no one outside of the Catholic church, neither heathen nor Jew nor unbeliever, nor one who is separated from the Church, will share in eternal life, but will perish in the eternal fire which is prepared for the devil and his angels, if this person fails to join it (the Catholic church) before death.[1]

Does that not settle the claim of Islam, at least for Catholics? It seems to have done so for more than 1200 years.

It is true that a Catholic theology of recent decades has tried to gain a "renewed understanding" of that uncompromising "extra-dogma." For the most part this has meant changing the given interpretation, even producing its very opposite. Nevertheless it has, due to its very infallibility, never been openly corrected. In the seventh century, however, Rome had already been forced to do away with the pronouncement of *extra ecclesiam nulla gratia*—no grace outside of the Church[2]—in dealings with the extremist Jansenists. If after all there is grace, *charis*, charisma to be found outside of the Church, could there not be prophecy, unmistakably one of the *charismata* (spiritual gifts) outside of the Church as well?

Today, at any rate, the traditional Catholic position is no longer the official Catholic position. As early as 1952 the Roman congregation of faith paradoxically enough excommunicated the student minister at Harvard, P.L. Feeney, S.J., who, in accord with the church fathers and the Council of Florence, had maintained that all those outside of the visible Catholic church were damned. The Second Vatican Council declared unmistakably in its constitution concerning the Church that

> those who, through no fault of their own, do not know the Gospel of Christ or his Church, but who nevertheless seek God with a sincere heart and, moved by grace, try in their actions to do His will as they know it through the dictations of their conscience—those too may achieve eternal salvation (Art. 16).

Here particular mention is given to those who, due to their very background, have the most in common with Jews and Christians through their faith in the one God and the execution of His will: the Muslims. "But the plan of salvation also includes those who acknowledge the Creator, in the first place amongst whom are the Moslems: These profess to hold the faith of Abraham, and together with us they adore the one, merciful God, mankind's judge in the last day" (Art. 16). Thus, according to Vatican Two, even the Muslims need not "perish in that eternal fire which is prepared for the devil and his angels"; they can "achieve eternal salvation." That means that Islam, too, can be a way of salvation: perhaps not the usual, "ordinary" way, as it were, but possibly an historically exceptional or "extraordinary" way.

Contemporary Catholic theology does in fact differentiate between the "ordinary" (that is, the Christian) way of salvation and the "extraordinary" (that is, the non-Christian) way of salvation. Should this not mean, however, as a condition attached to the possibility, that it is also possible to differentiate between "ordinary" prophets—Christian prophets, in other words, and "extraordinary" prophets—whatever these may be? Over the centuries, Muḥammad has been held to be a false, pseudo prophet, a soothsayer, magician, counterfeit, at best Arab poet. Ought we not to think instead, perhaps, of a genuine, even a true prophet? But then, was Muḥammad really a genuine, indeed, a true prophet?

I cannot go into the generally familiar story of Muḥammad, which is very different from that of Jesus: this Muḥammad, the son of a merchant, who was offered marriage by a rich merchant widow he had met in his work; this typically Arab prophet, proclaiming the message of the one God and his judgment, in contrast to his polytheistic contemporaries in Mecca, who had to emigrate to Medina, about 350 kilometers away, yet was successful in the end in all he did; who conquered Mecca and united the whole Arab peninsula under his rule—prophet and at the same time politician, military commander, and statesman. From the standpoint of Christian theology, only one question is relevant: Was he really a prophet?

Muḥammad—a prophet?

Of course many religions do not have prophets in the strictest sense. Hindus have their *gurus* and *sadhus,* the Chinese their sages, Buddhists their masters, but none of them have, like Jews, Christians and Muslims, prophets. There is no doubt that if anyone in the whole of religious history is termed *the* Prophet, because he claimed to be just that, but in no way more, then it is Muḥammad. And was he? Even the believing Christian, if he stops to survey the situation, cannot disagree that:

- Like the prophets of Israel, Muḥammad did not work from the strength of an office assigned to him by the community (or its authorities), but out of a special personal relationship with God.
- Like the prophets of Israel, Muḥammad was a person of strong will who felt himself fully imbued with a godly calling, fully consumed, exclusively appointed to the task.
- Like the prophets of Israel, Muḥammad spoke to the heart of a religious and social crisis, and with his passionate piety and revolutionary proclamation he opposed the wealthy ruling caste and the tradition it was trying to preserve.
- Like the prophets of Israel, Muḥammad, who mostly called himself the "Warner," sought to be nothing but the verbal instrument of God and to proclaim not his own, but God's word.

- Like the prophets of Israel, Muḥammad untiringly proclaimed the one God who tolerates no other gods besides Himself and who is at the same time the good Creator and merciful Judge.
- Like the prophets of Israel, so Muḥammd required, as a response to this one God, unconditional obedience, submission, "devotion," which is the literal meaning of the word Islam: everything which includes thankfulness to God and generosity toward other people.
- Like the prophets of Israel, Muḥammad combined monotheism with humanism, belief in the one God and his judgment with a call to social justice: thus judgment is combined with redemption, and the threat to the unjust, who go to Hell, with promises to the just, who are gathered into God's paradise.

Whoever reads the Bible—at least the Old Testament—and the Qur'ān parallel will be led to ponder whether the three religions of revelation of Semitic origin—Judaism, Christianity and Islam, and especially the Old Testament and the Qur'ān—could have the same foundation. Is it not one and the same God who speaks so clearly in both? Does not the "Thus says the Lord" of the Old Testament correspond to the "Speak" of the Qur'ān, and the Old Testament's "Go and proclaim" to the Qur'ān's "Stand up and warn?" In truth even the millions of Arabic-speaking Christians have no other word for God than "Allah."

Might it now therefore be purely dogmatic prejudice which recognizes Amos and Hosea, Isaiah and Jeremiah as prophets, but not Muḥammad? Whatever one may have against Muḥammad from the standpoint of Western Christian morality (violence with weapons, polygamy, a sensual lifestyle), it is indisputable:

- that even today there are almost 800 million people in the huge area between Morocco in the west and Bangladesh in the east, between the steppe of central Asia in the north and the island world of Indonesia to the south, who are stamped with the compelling power of a faith which like virtually no other faith has molded those who confess it into a universal type;
- that all those people are linked by a simple confession of faith (there is no God but God, and Muḥammad is His prophet), linked by five basic obligations (confession of faith, prayer, tax for the poor, a month of fasting, pilgrimage); and linked by complete submission to the will of God, whose unchangeable decision is that even suffering is to be accepted;
- that among all these peoples there has remained a sense of fundamental equality of people before God and of an international brotherhood which is basically capable of overcoming race (Arabs and non-Arabs) and even the castes of India.

I am convinced that despite all renewed fears of Islam there is a growing conviction among Christians that, in the light of the fact of Muḥammad in world history, we cannot escape a correction of viewpoint. The "scourge of exclusiveness" arising from dogmatic impatience, which the British universal historian Arnold Toynbee used to condemn, must be abandoned. Regarding the figure of the prophet, it must be admitted:

- that people in Arabia in the seventh century listened to and followed the voice of Muḥammad;
- that in comparison to the very worldly polytheism of the old Arabian tribal religions, the religion of the people was raised to a completely new level, that of a monotheistic high religion;

- that Muslims have received from Muḥammad—or, better still, from the Qur'ān—an endless amount of inspiration, courage and strength for a new religious start: a start towards greater truth and deeper understanding, towards a breakthrough in the revitalizing and renewal of traditional religion. Islam is the great inspirer of life.

In truth Muḥammad was and is for people in the Arabian world and even further afield *the* religious reformer, law-giver and leader: *the* prophet per se. Basically, Muḥammad, who never wanted to be anything more than a human being, is more to those who follow him (*imitatio Mohahmetis*) than a prophet is to us: he is a model for that mode of life which Islam strives to be. And if the Catholic church, according to the declaration concerning non-Christian religions of Vatican Two (1964) (I hope you will allow me to use not only the ritual quotations) regards "Muslims as well with respect, who pray to the only God ... who has spoken to mankind," then the same church must, in my opinion, also respect that one whose name is absent from the same declaration out of embarrassment, although he and he alone led the Muslims to pray to this one God, so that once again through him, Muḥammad, the Prophet, this God "has spoken to mankind." But does not such an acknowledgement have very grave consequences, especially for the message which he proclaimed and which is set down in the Qur'ān?

The Qur'ān—Word of God?

The Qur'ān is more than an oral tradition which can be easily altered. It is a written word, set down once for all time, and therefore cannot be subsequently altered. In this respect it is similar to the Bible. Through having been recorded in writing, the Qur'ān has retained a remarkable constancy despite the changeableness and variety of the history of Islam from century to century, from generation to generation, from person to person. What is written, is written. Despite all the different interpretations and commentaries, despite all the forms taken by Islamic law, the shar'īa, the Qur'ān remains the common denominator, something like the "green thread" of the prophet across all Islamic form, ritual and institutions. He who wishes to know not only what historical Islam is like, but normative Islam as well, even today cannot avoid returning to its origins, the Qur'ān of the seventh century.

Although the Qur'ān in no way predetermined the development of Islam, it most certainly inspired it. It penetrated the whole shar'īa, molding the legal system as much as mysticism, art, and the whole mentality. Commentators came and went, but the Qur'ān remained intact: it is the one great *constant* in Islam amidst all the countless variables. It provided Islam with moral obligation, external dynamism, and religious depth, as well as with specific enduring doctrines and moral principles: the responsibility of the human being before God, social justice, and Muslim solidarity. Thus the Qur'ān is the Holy Book of Islam, inasmuch as it is understood, in its written form, to be not the word of a human, but of God. For Muslims, therefore, God's word is set down in a book. Our question is, however: Is this book really the word of God?

For centuries it was forbidden even to pose this question seriously. Muslims as well as Christians were threatened with excommunication with all its consequences. And who could deny that this question has caused deep political divisions amongst the peoples of the world, from the first Islamic conquests in the seventh century to the Crusades and the capture of Constantinople, to the siege of Vienna and the Persian revolution under Khomeini? Just as naturally, therefore, as Muslims from West Africa to central Asia and Indonesia have answered this question affirmatively and oriented their life and death according to the Qur'ān, so believing Christians all over the world have said "no," and not only they, but later the secular Western scholars of religion as well, who took it for granted that the Qur'ān was not the word of God, but wholly that of Muḥammad.

In 1962 the Canadian scholar of religion, Wilfred Cantwell Smith, became the first to pose this question clearly, threatening as it was for both sides, and to analyze precisely the mode of questioning itself.[3] We cannot but agree with his assertion that the two possible answers, both of which, strangely enough, were offered by intelligent, critical and thoroughly honest people, relied in effect upon an unquestioned, dogmatic pre-conviction. In each case, the opposite interpretation was seen as a lack of faith (the Christian negation of the question in the case of the Muslims) or superstition (the Muslim affirmation for the Christians).

Is it true then, as Smith's Canadian colleague Willard Oxtoby claims to have established as a rule of thumb in the study of religions, that "you get out what you put in?" In other words, is it true that whoever regards the Qur'ān as the word of God from the start will repeatedly see his convictions confirmed in reading it, and vice versa?

But can we allow this contradiction to remain, even though in the long run it can never be satisfactory from an intellectual standpoint? Are there not increasing numbers of Christians and perhaps even Muslims who have become better informed about the faith of others and about their own position, and who are therefore posing self-critical questions? I shall indicate this briefly in relation to both positions:

a) *Self-critical questioning of an exclusively Christian understanding of revelation:* Alongside all the negative statements concerning the erroneous ways, darkness, and guilt of the non-Christian world and all calls to repentance, do we not also find numerous positive statements, according to which God originally manifested Himself to the whole of humanity? Indeed, according to the Old and New Testaments, non-Christians can also know the one true God. These texts themselves interpret this as the revelation of God in creation.

   Considering this Biblical background, can we exclude the possibility that countless people in the distant past and in the present have experienced, and are experiencing, the mystery of God on the basis of the revelation of God in creation, and that all this also involves the grace of God and the faith of human beings? And can we exclude the possibility that certain individuals have also, within the bounds of their religion, been endowed with special insight, entrusted with a special task, a special charisma? And considering all that we have already said, could not this also apply in the case of Muḥammad, the Prophet? *Extra ecclesiam gratia*—grace outside of the Church as well. Be that as it may, if we recognize Muḥammad as a prophet, then in order to be consistent we must also admit that for the Muslim, everything depends on the message of Muḥammad being not just of his own making, not simply his own word, but the Word of God. What, however, is meant by the Word of God and by revelation?

b) *Critical questioning of the Islamic interpretation of the Qur'ān:* Does revelation supposedly fall directly from heaven, to be inspired unmistakably or dictated word for word from God? It must be remembered that not only Muslims believe this, but some Christians as well, naturally in connection with the Bible. Here we have reached the crucial point.

However one wishes to settle the Islamic question of the origin of the Qur'ān, today it is important that the Qur'ān as the word of God be regarded at the same time as the word of the human prophet. This viewpoint is also shared by Muslim scientific reflection (such as the work of the Pakistani Fazlur Rahman). Thus the Qur'ān poses a problem similar to the Bible. In other words, we are faced with the awkward but unavoidable question: if we have historical criticism of the Bible (for the benefit of a contemporary Biblical faith), why not then also have historical criticism of the Qur'ān, and this for the benefit of a Muslim faith appropriate to modern times? Instead of interpreting the Qur'ān as a collection of fixed maxims, rigid doctrines, and immutable statements of law which, despite the very concrete difficulties involved, must be slavishly reproduced and literally interpreted in all points, even as regards punishment regulations, why not perceive the Qur'ān as a great prophetic witness to the one and only powerful and merciful God, the Creator and Perfector, and to his judgment and promise?

However, I cannot go into these hermeneutical questions any further in this article. I would rather turn to questions of content. Before I begin to iterate theological differences, I wish to bring out a few fundamental points of agreement between Islam and Christianity concerning interpretation of faith, whereby the Jews are also to be included. I shall do this along the lines of the Second Vatican Council's declaration on non-Christian religions.

What are the main common elements?

Common points among Muslims, Jews, and Christians can be summarized under four aspects:

a) The basic common point among Muslims, Jews, and Christians consists in the faith in the one and only God, who gives meaning and life to all. The faith in one God is for Islam a principle truth established as early as "Adam." The unity of the human race and equality of all people before God is grounded in the concept of one God. And whatever may be said concerning the Christian doctrine of the Trinity, even this serves not to question a belief in the one and only God, but to explicate it. This means that in confronting heathen polytheism, Judaism, Christianity, and Islam are just as much one as they are in confronting the multitude of modern gods which threaten to enslave people. Judaism and subsequently Christianity overthrew the old gods of the Pantheon long before Islam.
b) Jews, Christians, and Muslims are of one mind in their belief in the God of history: in that God who is not, as the Greeks believed, only the *arche* or the first principle of nature, the foundation of all things, but who acts as Creator of the world and humanity in history, the one God of Abraham who speaks through the prophets and reveals himself to his people, even though again and again his dealings remain an impenetrable secret. In history, God is most certainly transcendent, but at the same time immanent, closer to the human being than his own "artery," to use the plastic imagery of the Qur'ān, which is unfolded in depth in Islamic mysticism.
c) Jews, Christians, and Muslims are of one mind in their belief in the one God who—although he is invisible and organizes and rules over everything—is an approachable partner. He can be spoken to in prayer and meditation, praised in joy and thankfulness, cried to in need and despair: a God before whom the human being can "fall on his knees in awe," "pray and sacrifice," "make music and dance," to quote a well-known, future-oriented word of Martin Heidegger.
d) Finally, Jews, Christians, and Muslims are of one mind in their belief in a merciful, gracious God, a God who cares for people. In the Qur'ān as in the Bible, people are referred to as the "servants of God," which expresses not the enslaving of people under

> a despot but an elementary human creatureliness in response to the one Lord. The Arabic *al-Rahman*, the "merciful one," is etymologically linked to the Hebraic *rahamim*, which, together with *hen* and *hesed* represents the semantic field for the New Testament *charis* and for the English word "grace" (*gnade* in German). According to individual passages in the Bible or in the Qur'ān, God can appear to be a capricious God, yet according to the whole testimony of the Bible and the Qur'ān, God is decidedly a God of grace and mercy.

Together in the world, Judaism, Christianity, and Islam thus represent faith in the one God; all share in the one great monotheistic world movement. Politically, this faith in the one God ought not to be underestimated; it should be brought to people's attention. For instance, just as this faith played a part in the Camp David agreement, it could also be important in further peace efforts in the Middle East. We dare not forget any of this when we approach the difficult theological questions, in particular those pertaining to Jesus of Nazareth, the Christ of the Christians.

Is the Qur'ān's portrayal of Jesus accurate?

It is well-known that at several points the Qur'ān speaks of Jesus of Nazareth, and always in a positive manner. This is astonishing when one considers the centuries-old history of hatred and curses between Christianity and Islam. How can we assess these passages theologically? A closer examination of the "texts of Qur'ān relevant to Christianity," which Claus Schedel has retranslated and expounded under the title *Muḥammad und Jesus,* reveals that all the material concerning Jesus which is to be found in the Qur'ān is integrated in a fully coherent manner into the whole theological conception of the Qur'ān. From whatever tradition this testimony to Jesus may stem—and we shall go into this more closely—the whole is conspicuously permeated with Muḥammad's intense prophetic experience with the one God. For this reason, Muḥammad has no cause whatsoever to contradict Jesus: the preaching of Jesus is that of himself. Both the virgin birth and miracles are acknowledged without envy, with one exception: Jesus may not be made into a god, may not be put alongside the one God as a second. For Islam, that would be the ultimate abomination.

The position of Jesus in the Qur'ān is unambiguous. Dialogue is therefore not effectually aided by contemporary well meaning Christians who read more into the Qur'ān than it contains, claiming that in the Qur'ān Jesus is the "Word" of God. Not, however, Word of God in the sense of the prologue to John's gospel, in which the pre-existent godly *logos* becomes flesh. And as for the virgin birth in the Qur'ān, it is a sign of God's omnipotence, but not exactly for the deity of Jesus. In other words, in the Qur'ān Jesus is a prophet, a greater prophet than Abraham, Noah, and Moses—but certainly no more than a prophet. And just as in the New Testament John the Baptist is the forerunner of Jesus, so in the Qur'ān Jesus is the forerunner of, and undoubtedly the encouraging example for, Muḥammad. According to the Qur'ān Jesus is created directly from God as a second Adam (this is the meaning here of the virgin birth), unlike the Prophet himself. He is, therefore, God's excellent creation.

For this reason, Christians should avoid wanting to make "anonymous Christians" of Muḥammad and Muslims, as some theologians, against the whole of the Muslims' conception of themselves, now and again try to do. This in turn immediately poses the question of whether Muslims ought to make an "anonymous Muslim" out of Christ. If we who represent Christianity concern ourselves with a revaluation of Muḥammad on the basis of Islamic sources, especially the Qur'ān, we hope too that with time there will be more preparedness on the part of Islam to initiate a revaluation of this Jesus of Nazareth on the basis of historical sources that is, the gospels themselves—as is being carried out already by many in Judaism. The portrait of Jesus in the Qur'ān is all too one-sided, too monotone, and for the most part lacking in content, apart from monotheism, the call to repentance, and various accounts of miracles. At any rate it is very different from the portrait of Jesus in history, who not only confirms the law, as the Qur'ān records, but rather counters all legalism with radical love which even extends to his enemies. That is why he was executed, though the Qur'ān fails to recognize this. At this point, substantial differences emerge between Jesus and Muḥammad. It is wrong to ignore these. Nevertheless, the major theological obstacle to an understanding is not to be found here.

What is the central theological difference?

The focal concern of Jesus himself was to overcome legalism by fulfillment of the will of God in love, in view of the coming Kingdom. For the Christian church, however, the focal concern has slowly shifted to a great extent to the person of Jesus and his relationship with God. The debate between Christianity and Islam then remains wholly focused on this question. Up to now the deciding Christian objection to Islam has been that Islam disputes the two related central doctrines of Christianity: the Trinity and the incarnation. Indeed, the Qur'ān addresses Christians as follows:

> People of the Book, do not transgress the bounds of your religion. Speak nothing but the truth about Allah. The Messiah, Jesus the son of Mary, was no more than Allah's apostle and His Word which He cast to Mary: a spirit from Him. So believe in Allah and His apostles and do not say (of Allah, that He is) three (in one). Allah is but one God. Allah forbid that He should have a son! (S. 4:171).

Have we here, in fact, despite our consideration of common factors in our understanding of God and humanity, come to a standstill in the dialogue? Certainly, there is no truth in the assertion of Christian apologists and many scholars of religion that Muslim theologians have always misinterpreted the Christian doctrine of the Trinity (three in one) as a doctrine of tritheism (three gods). (The Qur'ān does contain the misleading tradition, possibly based on certain apocrypha, that the Trinity consists of God the Father, Mary the Mother of God, and Jesus the Son of God.) Muslims simply cannot understand what the Jews as well have always failed to understand: that when there is one Godhead, one divine nature, how it is that the assumption of three persons in one God does not automatically lead to the relinquishing of the faith in one God which Abraham stood for and which Moses, Jesus himself and finally Muḥammad firmly held to. Why distinguish at all between nature and person in God?

It is obvious that the distinctions between one and three made by the Christian doctrine of the Trinity do not satisfy the Muslim. All these concepts of Syrian, Greek and Latin origin are more confusing than enlightening to him, a game of words and concepts. How can the one and only God, asks the Muslim, be a conglomeration of hypostases, persons, processions and relations? Why all the dialectical tricks? Is not God simply God, combined in neither this way nor that?

According to the Qur'ān, "Unbelievers are those who say, 'Allah is one of three' (or 'three-faceted in trinity')." This viewpoint, which was completely unacceptable to Muḥammad, is flatly rejected with the statement, "There is but one God" (S. 5:73).

How are we to assess the central theological differences?

That which applies to the doctrine of the Trinity applies also to Christology. If Christians and Muslims today wish to come to a better understanding, they must return to the origins, taking a stance of critical discernment in relation to all subsequent developments. At the point of origins we—that is, Jews, Christians, and Muslims—are closer to each other.

Scientific investigation of the New Testament has recognized how great a gap there is between the original statements concerning Father, Son, and Spirit and the later dogmatized ecclesiastical doctrine of the Trinity, as well as how the Christological conceptions of the New Testament differ from one another.

While for instance the later, Hellenistically influenced Gospel of John quotes Jesus as speaking of the glory that he had with God before the world began (17:5), which even conservative exegetes do not hold to be the words of the historical Jesus, the first gospel(s) knows nothing of a virgin birth. And while right up to the account of the passion the Gospel of John presents Jesus almost excessively as god-like as he roams the earth, the synoptic gospels still present him as wholly Son of Man, through whom God acts. Exegetes point especially to the monologues in the Acts of the Apostles, in which Luke uses material from an old tradition which has Jesus totally subordinate to God. Clearly Jesus is spoken of as the servant of God, the Messiah, Christ of God, the chosen one of God: God acts through him, God was with him; he was killed according to the plan of God, but God raised him from the dead and made him Lord and Christ, appointing him Son of God. Do not all these statements of Luke, colored as they are by an "adoptive" perspective, still have a certain place within the framework of a strict Jewish or Islamic faith in one God? Yet this was the faith of Christians, of Jewish Christians.

It is an unparalleled shame that, following the destruction of Jerusalem under the Emperor Hadrian in the year 132 and the flight of all Jewish Christians to the east, the growing Church was almost completely uprooted from its Jewish soil. The Church which had originally been populated by Jews had become a Church of Jews and Gentiles, and it then became a Church of (Hellenistic) Gentiles. The Jewish Christians who did not participate in the development of the Hellenistic church with its increasingly excessive Christology were rejected as heretics, as in the case of the Ebionites, who accepted the virgin birth of Jesus according to the church historian Eusebius but rejected the notion of his pre-existence—just as the Qur'ān does.

Our investigation is not aimed at once again attempting to trace Islam back to Judaism or Christianity. We are instead seeking to take Islam seriously in the form of a renewed challenge to Christians, since from the time of John of Damascus Islam has been disclaimed as a "Christian heresy." For Islam reminds Christians of their own Jewish Christian past. Here, it seems, we have a vital example of interdependence and interaction between the different religious movements in humanity, as stressed in particular by W.C. Smith. In his book *Korankunde für Christen,* Paul Schwarzenau is correct in stating that "It is the Jewish element of the Christian message which decidedly shows the Qur'ān to advantage. The disavowed Jewish Christians come to the fore once again."[4] Schwarzenau calls upon a shrewd analysis of the great Protestant exegete Adolf Schlatter, who had as early as 1926 analyzed clearly the connections between Gentile Christianity, Jewish Christianity, and Islam in the book *Die Geschichte der ersten Christenheit:*

> The Jewish church would, however, have died out only in Palestine west of the Jordan. Christian communities with Jewish practice, on the other hand, continued to exist in

> the eastern regions, in the Decapolis, in the Batanaea, among the Nabataeans, at the edge of the Syrian desert and into Arabia, completely cut off from the rest of Christendom and without fellowship with that rest. ... For the Christian, the Jew was simply an enemy, and Greek opinion, which overlooked both the slaying of the generals of Troy and Hadrian and the well-earned fate of the evil and contemptuous Jews, reached the Church as well. Even its leading men, such as Origen and Eusebius, remained astonishingly ignorant concerning the end of Jerusalem and of the church there. In the same way, the information they leave us concerning the Jewish church in its continued existence is scanty. They, the Jewish Christians [*sic*] were heretics because they had not submitted to the law which applied to the rest of Christendom and had therefore been divorced from that rest. None of the leaders of the Imperial church guessed that this Christendom which they held in contempt would ever see the day when it would shake the world and split a large part of the church dominion which they had built up. That day came when Muḥammad took over the property accrued by the Jewish Christians, their awareness of God, their eschatology with its proclamation of the Day of Judgment, their customs and legends, and set up a new apostolate as the one sent from God.[5]

Is Muḥammad then, according to Schlatter, a "Judaeo-Christian apostle" in Arabian dress? That is an astonishing piece of insight, which Schlatter had incidentally substantiated in depth as early as 1918 in an essay entitled "Die Entwicklung des jüdischen Christentums zum Islam."[6] However, even forty years before Schlatter, Adolf von Harnack had perceived the wider effect of Jewish Christianity on Islam, or more precisely of Gnostic Jewish Christianity, and in particular of the Elkesites, who apart from their beliefs stood for strict monotheism and rejected an ecclesiastical teaching of hypostasis and the Son of God. This is documented in Harnack's history of dogmatics.

Considering the present state of research, any direct dependence of Islam proven from source material will continue to remain in dispute, but the analogies are as baffling as ever. Muḥammad rejected high orthodox (monophysitic) Son of God Christology, yet accepted Jesus as the great messenger (*rasūl*) of God, indeed as the Messiah (*masīḥ*) who brought the Gospel. The Jewish scholar Hans-Joachim Schoeps states correctly in his *Theologie und Geschichte des Judenchristentums* (Tübingen, 1949) that

> although it may be impossible to prove the connection beyond a doubt, there is certainly no doubt of the indirect dependence of Muḥammad on sectarian Judaeo-Christianity. Thus the fact that Judaeo-Christianity has disappeared from the Church but been preserved in Islam and extends even to the present day in some of its leading impulses is a paradox of truly great proportions in world history.[7]

Strangely enough, these pieces of historical insight have hardly been known in Christian theology up to now, let alone been taken seriously. There is much to be investigated in this regard, such as the history of Muḥammad's cousin-by-marriage, Waraqa, who as a Christian (hardly of Greek influence) drew Muḥammad's attention early to the relationship between his revelation experiences and those of Moses. Be that as it may, who could overlook the fact that here there are unimagined possibilities for the very necessary trilateral dialogue, the "trialogue," among Jews, Christians, and Muslims? Whatever the decision concerning the question of genetic dependence, in Muḥammad's interpretation of Jesus traditions of Judaeo-Christianity which had been suppressed, repudiated, and forgotten in the Hellenistic church come to the light of history once more; and this Judaeo-Christianity for its part has kept alive central Jewish concerns of early Christianity.

It must be forgotten that in his struggle of resistance against ancient Arabic polytheism, whereby Allāh had all the sons and daughters imaginable, Muḥammad had no choice but to reject the term "Son of God." At the same time, however, Muḥammad took up the story of Jesus as it was being circulated in Arabia at the time and gave it his own meaning. What had happened so often in the Bible now happened in the Qur'ān: an old tradition was not simply handed down, but was interpreted so as to give it relevance in the light of contemporary experience. This was also the case in the New Testament. Just as the Christians used many expressions ("prophecies") of the Old Testament to refer to Jesus, though they had been intended to mean something different, so Muḥammad used a lot of what he heard about Jesus to refer to himself. To Muḥammad, Jesus' greatness was due to the fact that in him and through him as the servant of God, God himself had worked. Thus Muḥammad's "Christology" was not too far removed from that of the Judaeo-Christian church. What are the consequences of all these new findings?

What should we speak of?

We are faced with a problem of extraordinary moment, the consequences of which are not yet visible. Given that the exegetical and historical findings which we have outlined here are accurate and capable of being further clarified, they then constitute a challenge to both sides to stop thinking in terms of alternatives, of Jesus *or* Muḥammad, and despite all limitations and differences to think instead in terms of synthesis, of Jesus *and* Muḥammad. Muḥammad himself acts as a witness to Jesus, not to a Jesus as Hellenistic Gentile Christians could have viewed him, but to a Jesus as viewed by his first disciples, who were Jews like Jesus himself.

In order to avoid misunderstanding from the outset in approaching this question, delicate as it is for both Muslims and Christians, we must take note of the following. As a European Gentile Christian, I can fully understand the Hellenistic development of Christology and can accept the truth of the great Christological councils from Nicaea to Chalcedon: in the light of the New Testament, their major intentions and content can certainly be affirmed. I do not believe that a Christian today could or should naively start all over again and become a Jewish Christian, so to speak. But in an ecumenical context (in relation to Muslims and Jews), I am haunted by one question: how can I make a Muslim (or a Jew) understand why it is that Christians believe in this Jesus as the Christ, the Word, the revelation of God? This being my intention, I have every right to draw attention to that original and thus thoroughly legitimate Christological option which, though pushed aside and concealed, originated in the oldest Judaeo-Christian church community and was handed down through centuries by the scattered Judaeo-Christian church communities from east of the Jordan to Arabia, thus to be finally passed on to Muḥammad. I wonder, too, whether there could be categories already in existence which more readily enable Jews and Muslims to perceive this Jesus as the revelation of God than the Hellenistic teaching of two natures, divine and human, in the one divine person. How then might a Muslim, viewing from such an ecumenical perspective, attempt to see this Jesus, and how might a Christian likewise see Muḥammad?

a) In what way might Muslims view Jesus? I shall summarize my thoughts here very briefly:

Muslims already see Jesus as the great prophet and messenger of the one God, the one especially designated to be the "Servant of God" by God himself, from his birth to his exaltation to God—one who, along with the message he proclaimed, was of lasting importance to Muḥammad. Certainly for Muslims, Muḥammad and the Qur'ān which he set down will remain, as before, the deciding guidelines for faith and conduct, life and death. However, if in the Qur'ān Jesus is termed the "Word" of God and bringer of the "Gospel," ought not Muslims try to gain a broader understanding of this Gospel and take it seriously? Islamic law, often characterized by an oppressiveness, from the perspective of the message and conduct of Jesus, could be seen in a more relative light, for the sake of God and humanity. And the human being, though not liberated from the law itself, would be liberated from legalism—similar to the case of Jewish Christians.

In this way a new and deeper understanding could also be gained of a God who loves and suffers with people, considering the life of Jesus, his death—which is not to be denied—and his new life. Thus the death of Jesus in the name of this very God could offer meaning to suffering and failure, meaningless as these are on the surface.

b) In what way might Christians view Muḥammad? Many Christians clearly look on him as the prophet of importance to many of the peoples of this earth, one who was already blessed with great success in his lifetime.

Certainly for Christians, Jesus Christ and the good news he proclaimed are the deciding standard for faith and conduct, life and death, the definitive Word of God (Hebrews l:lff.). Thus Christ is and remains the deciding regulating factor for Christians, for the sake of God and humanity. However, ought not Christians, given that according to the New Testament tenet they still acknowledge the existence of prophets even after Christ, take this Muḥammad, who draws from the Judaeo-Christian tradition, and his exhortations more seriously? This, in order that:

- the one incomparable God be placed wholly at the center of faith;
- companionship of other gods be out of the question;
- faith and life, orthodoxy and orthopraxis belong together even in politics.

Thus Muḥammad would repeatedly provide a prophetic corrective for Christians in the name of the one and same God: "I am nothing but a distinctive warner" (S. 4).

I wonder: if a Muslim or Jew should be expected to recognize the Hellenist Councils from Nicaea to Chalcedon, what would Jesus of Nazareth, the Jew, have done? The question is of more than limited importance not only to an Arabian Christian, but also to an African, Indian, Indonesian, Chinese, or Japanese Christian.

Finally—and here I shall close—both Islam and Christianity involve a decision of faith which must be made rationally and in responsibility both to oneself and to others. As a Christian I can be sure that, as long as I have chosen this Jesus as the Christ for my life and death, I have also chosen his follower Muḥammad, inasmuch as he appealed to the one and same God and to Jesus.

In the helpful handbook of recommendations commissioned by the Protestant church in Germany entitled *Christen und Muslime im Gespräch* (published by J. Micksch and M. Mildenberger, 1982), attention is rightly drawn, at least briefly, to the possible connection between Islam and Judaeo-Christianity:

> The most important point of all is that Christians and Muslims live in the same world and have to prove their faith. They will not always react in the same way to all the challenges of this world. Yet despite all the differences, both are obliged by their faith to live responsibly before God and to serve the human community. In full respect for

one another, they cannot fail to provide evidence of their faith for each other (German edition pp. 12ff.).

Notes

1 Henricus Denzinger (ed. Adolfus Schönmetzer), *Enchiridion symbolorum*, Editio XXXIV (Freiburg: Verlag Herder KG, 1965), 714 (p. 342).
2 Denzinger, *op cit.* (1295, 1379).
3 Wilfred Cantwell Smith, "Is the Qur'an the Word of God?," in *Questions of Religious Truth* (New York: Charles Scribners Sons, 1967), pp. 37–62.
4 Paul Schwarzenau, *Korankunde für Christen* (Stuttgart: Kreuz-Verlag, 1982), p. 124.
5 Adolf Schlatter, *Die Geschichte der ersten Christenheit* (Stuttgart: Calwer Verlag, 1983; 1st ed. Aufl. Gütersloh, 1926), pp. 376–77 (transl.).
6 Adolf Schlatter, "Die Entwicklung des jüdischen Christentums zum Islam," *Evangelisches Missionsmagazin,* N.S. LXII (1918), 251–64.
7 Hans-Joachim Schoeps, *Theologie und Geschichte des Judenchristentums* (Tübingen: Mohr, 1949), p. 342.

17 The Quest of the Historical Muhammad

F.E. Peters

Writing in 1962 Stephen Neill listed twelve of what he regarded as "positive achievements of New Testament studies" over the past century.[1] As an affirmation of progress in a notoriously difficult field of investigation, they make satisfying and even cheerful reading for the historian. Who was Jesus of Nazareth? What was his message? Why was he put to death? Why did his few followers become, in effect, the nucleus of the powerful and widespread community called Christianity? These were the enormously difficult questions that had begun to be posed in a critical-historical way in the mid-19th century, and some of the answers Bishop Neill discerned, though by no means final, represented ground gained and truths won. Neill's widely read book was revised in 1988, and though his optimism was here and there tempered by what had been said and thought in the twenty-five years since the first edition,[2] there was still good reason to think that historians were by and large on the right track in pursuing what Albert Schweitzer described in 1906 as "the quest of the historical Jesus."[3]

The pages of Neill and his redactor Tom Wright are lustrous with congratulation and hope for the various tribes of New Testament critics and historians, but they make dismaying reading for their Islamicist cousins who were not too long ago instructed by one of their own eminences that "there is nothing of which we can say for certain that it incontestably dates back to the time of the Prophet."[4] Indeed, there is much in both the first and second editions of Neill's work to puzzle, and even discourage, the laborers in a neighboring historical field, where scholars engaged in the "quest of the historical Muhammad" share many of the problems, tools, and therefore, one would have thought, some of the same successes as Neill's enterprising investigators. However, even though a great deal of effort has been invested in research into the life and times of Muhammad, the results do not seem at all comparable to those achieved in research on Jesus, and the reasons are not at all clear. It may be useful, then, to look at some recent and representative examples of "Muhammad research" and attempt to discover why this is the case.[5]

Muhammad would appear, at least in theory, to be a far more apposite subject for historical inquiry than the founder of Christianity. The most abiding and forbidding obstacle to approaching the historical Jesus is undoubtedly the fact that our principal sources, the documents included in the New Testament, were all written on the hither side of Easter; that is, their authors viewed their subject across the absolute conviction that Jesus was the Christ and the Son of God, a conviction later rendered explicit in Christian dogma. There is, however, no Resurrection in the career of Muhammad, no Paschal sunrise to cast its divinizing light on the Prophet of Islam. Muhammad is thus a perfectly appropriate subject of history: a man born of woman (and a man), who lived in a known place in a roughly calculable time, who in the end died the death that is the lot of all mortals, and whose career was reported by authorities who share the contemporary historian's own conviction that the Prophet was nothing more than a man. What is at stake in Islam, then, is not dogma as it is in Christianity, but rather piety; obversely, it is the same sense of impropriety that a pre-1850s Catholic might have felt in the presence of a positivist-historical study of Mary.[6]

With Muslim piety and Christian dogma put aside, as the historian insists they must be, there would seem at first glance to be sufficient historical evidence on Jesus and Muhammad from which to at least attempt, as many have done, to take the measure of both the men and their milieu. Indeed, in the view of one early biographer of Jesus, the available sources are even better for Muhammad than for Jesus, since Islam was "born in full view of history."[7] Within twenty-five years after Ernest Renan wrote those words, his optimism regarding Islamic origins—or perhaps simply his pessimism at getting at the historical Jesus—already stood in need of serious revision. History's view of the birth of Islam, it turned out, was neither full nor particularly clear, and the search after Islamic origins had to begin where the search for Christianity's origins had, standing before the evidence for the life of the founder and its milieu.

The question of milieu is a critical one for the historian. Many of Bishop Neill's underscored gains in New Testament studies have to do with a better understanding of both the Jewish and the Hellenic background out of which Jesus and his movement issued, and it is in that area that arguably the greatest progress has been made—and the greatest number of new hypotheses spawned—in the last quarter century.[8] Moreover, it is here, historians of Muhammad will discover, that the "full view of history" grows exceedingly clouded and that their own inquiry is not going to run on equal stride with the quest after Jesus.

Quite simply, there is no appropriate contemporary and contopological setting against which to read the Qur'an. For early Islam there is no Josephus to provide a contemporary political context, no apocrypha for a spiritual context, and no Scrolls to illuminate a Palestinian "sectarian milieu." There is instead chiefly poetry, great masses of it, whose contemporary authenticity is somewhat suspect but that was, nonetheless, "the main vehicle of Arab history in the pre-Islamic and early Islamic periods,"[9] and that in any event testifies to a quite different culture. The Qur'an, in fact, stands isolated like an immense rock jutting forth from a desolate sea, a stony eminence with few marks on it to suggest how or why it appeared in this watery desert. The nearest landfalls for our bearings are the cultures of the Yemen to the south, Abyssinia across the Red Sea, and the distant Jewish and Christian settlements of Palestine-Syria to the north and Christian Iraq to the northeast.[10] It is the equivalent, perhaps, of attempting to illuminate the Gospels solely from Egyptian papyri and Antiochene inscriptions. The fact is that, despite a great deal of information supplied by later Muslim literary sources, we know pitifully little for sure about the political or economic history of Muhammad's native city of Mecca or of the religious culture from which he came.[11] Moreover, to the extent that we are ignorant of that history and culture, to that same extent we do not understand the man or the movement that followed in his wake.

The surviving evidence for both Jesus and Muhammad lies primarily in literary works rather than in material evidence,[12] and in both instances those works include an important body of "teaching." Jesus' teaching is incorporated into, but is not the entirety of, the Gospels, while Muhammad's constitute a separate work, the Qur'an, both of which have some claim to be regarded as authentic.[13] "Some claim" is not, of course, the same as self-evident, particularly with regard to Jesus, whose words and teachings are embedded in complex Gospel narratives whose purpose is far more than mere reportage. The argument about the reported words of Jesus has been loud and vigorous, and even if many people now seem to be convinced of the authenticity of at least some of what Jesus is alleged to have said, and likely of the very words of its expression, that conviction remains only the first step in a continuing and even more difficult historiographical process centering on Jesus and Muhammad. Granted that there is *something* of these two men in the works said to be about or by them, what precise part, one must then go on to ask, of what is said and done by Jesus in the Gospels is really his own words and deeds? Similarly, what part of what is reportedly said by Muhammad in the Qur'an and in the extra-Qur'anic reports circulated under his name are really his words,[14] and which of the deeds ascribed to the Prophet in the Muslim historical tradition actually occurred? The disparity is immediately apparent. Both the life and message of Jesus are contained in the Gospels, while for the events of the life of Muhammad we must turn to sources outside the Qur'an, what I have just called "the Muslim historical tradition."

At first glance the question of the authenticity of Jesus' sayings would appear to be a relatively simple one since their *final* tradents, the "evangelists," worked, at the furthest remove, no more than forty to eighty years after the death of Jesus—and quite conceivably even closer, perhaps thirty-five to forty years.[15] Moreover, they give every indication of resting, as Luke maintains quite explicitly in the opening of his Gospel (Luke 1:1–4), upon the testimonies, some recollected, some written, of eyewitnesses themselves. The issue appears no less simple with Muhammad, at least as it concerns the Qur'an. Parts of that document were apparently written down during his own lifetime, and the finished work, what is essentially our Qur'an, was finally assembled or "collected" from various sources, some recollected and some written, no more than fifteen years after the Prophet's death.[16]

Why, then, is there such apparent skepticism about retrieving the actual words of Jesus from the Gospels, while there is no similar debate about the Qur'an, which is generally thought to represent what issued from Muhammad's mouth as "teachings" in the interval from A.D. 610 to 632? Indeed, the search for variants in the partial versions extant before the Caliph Uthman's alleged recension in the 640s (what can be called the "sources" behind our text) has not yielded any differences of great significance.[17] This is not to say, of course, that since those pre-Uthmanic clues are fragmentary, large "invented" portions might well have been added to our Qur'an or authentic material deleted. This latter charge has, in fact, been made by certain Shi'ite Muslims who fail to find in the Qur'an any explicit reference to the designation of Ali as the Prophet's successor and so have alleged tampering.[18] However, the argument of the latter is so patently tendentious and the evidence adduced for the fact so exiguous that few have failed to be convinced that what is in our copy of the Qur'an is, in fact, what Muhammad taught, and is expressed in his own words.[19]

Why, then, are there these differences in recollection, the fluctuating memory of what Jesus said and the apparently flawless and total recall of the words of Muhammad? To advance what is at this point simply a preliminary consideration, we may point to the fact that the anonymous tradents of the pre-Uthmanic Qur'an, Muslims all, were convinced from the outset—the outset being their own conversion to this belief—that what they were hearing and noting "on scraps of leather, bone and in their hearts" were not the teachings of a man but the *ipsissima verba Dei* and so they would likely have been scrupulously careful in preserving the actual wording. In the case of Jesus, however, whatever the respect for him as a teacher—a very particular and unique teacher—by the first auditors of his words, the mere recollection of his teaching, its substance and gist, was all that was required for their moral instruction. Certain phrases and images might have lodged in their memories—formulae used in cures, predictions about the destruction of the Temple, the blessing of the bread and wine at his last supper spring readily to mind—but there is little ground for imagining that during his actual lifetime there would have been any motive for his followers to memorize every word that proceeded from the mouth of Jesus of Nazareth.

The four Gospels are not about Jesus of Nazareth, of course, but about Jesus the Christ, and his sayings and teaching were re-collected after the Resurrection from a very different perspective, it is true. However, the initial impression had already been taken, so to speak, and no change in the understanding of what Jesus *meant* could enlarge the memory of what he had actually *said*. Even then, however, in the very different post-Easter light that bathes the entirety of the New Testament, it is not so much the words of Jesus that were illumined as his deeds. The earliest forms of the Christian *kerygma* (in 1 Corinthians 15:3–7/8, for example, or Acts 2:22ff. and 10:36–43) include not Jesus' teachings but the events of his life: his miracles, his death, and his Resurrection, and Paul's scanting of Jesus' words is, of course, notorious.

We have touched here on a basic difference between the Christians' regard of Jesus and the Muslims' regard of Muhammad. For the Christians Jesus was—whether he intended it or not, the historian carefully adds—an "event." His goal was achieved by deeds, his redemptive death and the probative miracle of his Resurrection: "He was declared Son of God by a mighty act in that he rose [or: was raised] from the dead" (Rom. 1:4). Jesus did not reveal; he was himself a revelation, and that fact informs our Gospels, which bear witness to the event. More, the Christian tradents of the words of Jesus who stood behind the canonical Gospels had no idea, as the early Muslims certainly had, that they were transmitting a revelation, nor did the authors of those same Gospels by any means understand, as Muhammad's scribes and secretaries were convinced, that they were writing down Scripture. Indeed, that was the original understanding of the Arabic word, "a recitation," unmistakably for liturgical purposes.[20] However, for a considerable time after the completion of the Gospels, the Christians' "Scripture" continued to be what it always had been for the Jews, including Jesus and his followers, to wit, the Hebrew Bible.

To sum up at this point: the Qur'an is convincingly the words of Muhammad, perhaps even dictated by him after their recitation,[21] while the Gospels not only describe the life of Jesus but contain some arguably authentic sayings or teachings of Jesus. How does that latter argument proceed? A primary version of it is that devised by Form criticism, and Rudolf Bultmann, one of its masters, formulated the criterion of authenticity with elegant brevity:

> We can only count on possessing a genuine similitude of Jesus where, on the one hand, expression is given to the contrast between Jewish morality and piety and the distinctive eschatological temper which characterized the teaching of Jesus, and where, on the other hand, we find no specifically Christian features.[22]

To take the second point first, where the form of Jesus' reported sayings and stories conform to what we know of contemporary Jewish, that is, rabbinic, didactic forms, the likelihood is strong that they are authentic. The obvious example is, of course, the parables, and whether Jesus is judged a skilled or merely a traditional practitioner of the genre, there are enough rabbinic parables in the Gospels to convince the skeptic that here at least he is face to face with a form of Jesus' teaching that could not, or at least was not, invented by some later Christian pietist. Whether those "rabbis" whose works provide one term of the comparison, namely, the authorities quoted in the Mishna (ca. A.D. 200) onward, may in fact be regarded as Jesus' "contemporaries" for purposes of illuminating either the teachings or the events of the Gospels continues to be a vexing question whose answer is more often assumed than discussed, particularly by Form critics.[23]

Most Form critics have turned with Bultmann from this modest piece of ground gained through "rabbinic parallelism" to the other principal criterion of authenticity, that of "dissimilarity," where the credited sayings can be shown to be unique to Jesus to the degree that we do not find parallels in either the early Church or ancient Judaism. To put it more brazenly: when Jesus sounds like a rabbi, that is authentic; when Jesus does not think like a rabbi, that too is authentic. As far as context is concerned, then, originality is a mark of authenticity, and, by way of an aside at this point, very little of Jesus' teaching has been retrieved on the basis of that criterion, not assuredly because he does not often express original notions in the Gospels, but rather because he sounds all too original, in John's Gospel, for example, and Redaction criticism has denied Jesus most of that originality and credited it instead to the first generation of Christians.

What does Muhammad sound like? His contemporaries thought they caught echoes of a number of familiar charismatic types, seers, or poets (Qur'an 52:29–30; 69:41–42), which the Qur'an stoutly denies, or even a rehash of old stories (25:5). Some modern scholars think the first charge has some merit, though by no means for the entirety of the Qur'an.[24] However, once again we are limited by an almost total lack of contextual background. We know little or nothing of the utterances of the "seer" (*kāhin*); the preserved pre-Islamic poets are patently not the demonic (*majnūn*) type to which Muhammad was being compared; and our only contemporary examples of "ancient tales" are precisely those told in the Qur'an.

There is something curious about the Qur'an's stories, a quality that once again underlines our inability to penetrate into the milieu. In 1982 Anthony Harvey raised the issue of the "constraints of history" in connection with the study of the life of Jesus:

> No individual, if he wishes to influence others, is totally free to choose his own style, of action and persuasion: he is subject to constraints imposed by the culture in which he finds himself. If communication is to take place, there must be constraints recognized by both the speaker and his listeners. ... Now Jesus ... succeeded in communicating with his hearers, his followers, and indeed his enemies. To do so he had to speak a language they could understand, perform actions they would find intelligible, and conduct his life and undergo his death in a manner of which they could make some sense.[25]

What was true of Jesus was equally true of Muhammad. He too was bound by the "constraints" of matter and style "recognized by both the speaker and his listeners." Now it is clear from the Qur'an itself that, though there may have been those of his Meccan contemporaries who doubted the supernatural origin of what Muhammad was proclaiming, there was no problem with understanding it, and in understanding it better in many cases than we do today. The Qur'an is filled with biblical stories, for example, most of them told in an extremely elliptical or what has been called "allusive" or "referential" style.[26] Manifestly, Muhammad's audience was not hearing these stories for the first time, as the remark about "rehashing old stories" itself suggests. These stories were current in Mecca then, though we have little idea how current or for how long, and when Muhammad "retold" them in his allusive style in the Qur'an to make some other moral point (God's vengeance for the mistreatment of earlier prophets, to cite one common theme), his listeners might not agree with the point but apparently knew well enough to what he was referring.

We, however, do not know since these stories are "biblical" only in the sense that they take characters or incidents from the Bible as their point of departure. However, their trajectory is haggadic; they are the residue, echo, recollection—we are at a loss precisely what to call it—of what is palpably Jewish *midrashim*, though which they were, or what were their origins, we cannot even guess. We have only one biblical *midrash* current in 7th-century Arabia, and that is the Qur'an itself.

The accusations of Muhammad's contemporaries that he was no more than a "seer" or a "poet" provided an important guidepost for modern attempts at applying Form criticism to the Qur'an. The literary forms employed in the book range, we can observe, from brief oaths and mantic utterances, through parables and apocalyptic fragments, to rather extended narratives to illustrate in homiletic fashion what awaits those who ignore or mistreat prophets.[27] There are, as well, a large and generally unconnected body of halakic dicta that obviously date from the Medina period of the Prophet's life and prescribe norms of action and behavior for a community-in-being. The remainder consists of the warnings and threats (many of them repeated catchphrases) and a good deal of polemic, sometimes in the form of retorts to questions whose source or thrust we do not know.

However, if Form criticism proved valuable as a clue to the transmission and the secondary *Sitz im Leben* of the New Testament, that is, "the situation in the life of the Church in which those traditions were found relevant and so preserved (as it turned out) for posterity,"[28] it can have no such useful purpose in Islam since there is no conviction that the Qu'anic material was in any way being shaped by or for transmission. On our original assumption that Muhammad is the source of the work, what is found in the Qur'an is not being *reported* but simply *recorded*; consequently, modern Form criticism amounts to little more than the *classification* of the various ways in which the Prophet chose to express himself, a procedure that casts no light forward since the Qur'an was regarded by Muslims as "inimitable,"[29] and none backward where there is, as we have noted, only darkness in the religious past of western Arabia—no convenient rabbis, monks, or Arab preachers to whose words or style we might compare the utterances of the Prophet of Islam.

This is not to say that *no* hands have touched the Qur'anic material. An early investigator of the life of Jesus compared the Gospel stories about him to pearls whose string had been broken. The precious stones were reassembled in the sequel by individuals such as the Evangelist Mark, who supplied both the narrative framework and within it the connective links to "restring" them. The Qur'an gives somewhat the same impression of scattered pearls, though these have been reassembled in quite a different, and puzzling, manner. The Qur'an as we now possess it is arranged in 114 units called suras connected in no obvious fashion, each bearing a name and other introductory formulae, of greatly varying length and, more appositely to our present purpose, with little internal unity. There is no narrative framework, of course, and within the unconnected suras there are dislocations, interpolations, abrupt changes of rhyme and parallel versions, a condition that has led both Muslim and non-Muslim scholars alike to conclude that some of the present suras or sections of them may once have been joined to others. By whom were they joined? We do not know, nor can we explain the purpose of such rearrangements.[30]

Nor do we know the aim or the persons who arranged the suras in their present order, which is, roughly (the first sura apart), from the longest to the shortest. They are not, in any event, placed in the order of their revelation, as everyone agrees. However, there the agreement apparently ends. Early Muslim scholars settled on a gross division into

"Meccan" and "Medinan" suras, which were labeled accordingly in copies of the Qur'an, and they even determined the relative sequence of the suras. However, this system rested on premises unacceptable to modern Western scholars,[31] who have attempted to develop their own criteria and their own dating system, which, though it starts with different assumptions, ends with much the same results as those of the early Muslim savants.[32] This distribution of the suras even into limited categories like "Early-," "Middle-," and "Late-Meccan" or "Medinan" is of critical importance to the historian, of course, since it provides the ground for following the evolution of Muhammad's thought and at the same time for connecting passages in the Qur'an with events that the ancient Muslim authorities asserted had occurred in Muhammad's lifetime. The highly composite nature of many of the suras makes any such distributional enterprise highly problematic to begin with, but an even more serious flaw is the fact that the standard Western system accepts as its framework the traditional Muslim substance, sequence, and dating of the events of the life of Muhammad, an acceptance made, as we shall see, "with much more confidence than is justified."[33]

Redaction criticism, one of the most powerful critical tools developed for an understanding of the Gospels, is founded on the premise that the Gospels are not mere transcripts of Jesus' words or an unretouched photograph of his life, but that both the words and the deeds recorded therein have in the first place been illuminated by the witnesses' belief in his Resurrection, the proof that Jesus was Messiah, Lord, and Son of God; and second, as the Redaction critics have pointed out, the Gospels reflect the perceptions of the Christian community when and where they were written down. Can we make the same assertions with respect to Islam? Does any serious scholar now doubt that the materials in the Qur'an and/or the *Sīra,* the standard life of Muhammad originally composed by Ibn Ishaq (d. 767) and preserved in an edition from the hand of Ibn Hisham (d. 833), were shaped by the needs of the early Islamic community? There is probably no doubt, at least as far as the *Sīra* is concerned,[34] particularly since its re-redactor Ibn Hisham openly admitted as much in the introduction to his reediting of his predecessor's work:

> God willing I shall begin this book with Isma'il and mention those of his offspring who were the ancestors of God's apostle one by one with what is known of them, taking no account of Isma'il's other children, for the sake of brevity, confining myself to the prophet's biography and omitting some of the things which Ibn Ishaq has recorded in this book in which there is no mention of the apostle and about which the Qur'an says nothing and which are not relevant to anything in this book or an explanation of it; poems which he quotes that no authority on poetry whom I have met knows of; things which it is disgraceful to discuss; matters which would distress certain people; and such reports as al-Bakka'i told me he could not accept as trustworthy—all these things I have omitted. But God willing I shall give a full account of everything else so far as it is known and a trustworthy tradition is available.[35]

As for redaction activity ín the Qur'an, that would depend on when the materials were assembled. On the Burton hypothesis there is no need to search for community shaping; on the Wansbrough hypothesis there must have been a great deal of shaping indeed, but "the Qur'an as the product of the early Islamic community" is not a proposition that has found a great deal of favor in Islamicist circles. Indeed, there is a notable redactional "flatness" about the Qur'an. As has already been said, there was no Easter for the Muslims—Muhammad died of natural causes in A.D. 632 and by all reports still rests in his tomb in the mosque at Medina—but the enormous and astonishing expansion of Islam, which was unmistakably underway when the Qur'an was collected into its final form sometime about 650, is an Islamic event of similar if not identical redactional magnitude to the Christians' Easter. If the almost miraculous success of the movement he initiated did not change the Muslims' essential regard for Muhammad, who was after all only a man, it could certainly have cast a different light on his version of God's message. However, we find no trace of this in the Qur'an, no signs that its "good news" was "redacted" in the afterglow of an astonishing politico-military authentication of its religious truths.

Why should this be so? It is probably because of the reason already cited, that the Qur'an was regarded not as preaching or "proclamation" but as revelation pure and simple, and thus was not so inviting to redaction and editorial adjustment as the Gospels. Indeed, what was done to the Qur'an in the redactional process appears to have been extremely conservative. The materials were kept, in the words of one modern scholar, "just as they fell,"[36] or assembled in such a mechanical fashion as to exclude redactional bias. Our conviction that either was in fact the case is strengthened when we look to the other source of Muhammad's teachings, the *ḥadīth,* or traditions, which even on the Muslims' view constitute Muhammad's words and not those of God.

The hadith are discrete reports of the words, or less often the deeds, of the Prophet, each generally accompanied by its own chain of tradents: I heard from Z, who heard from Y, who heard from … A, who reported that Muhammad, upon whom be peace, said. … In other words, each hadith is arguing its own authenticity, something the Qur'an and the Gospels do only occasionally.[37] Muslims were alerted, as we are, by this obvious *petitio auctoritatis* in the hadith, and looked closely at those argumentative chains, accepting many and rejecting a great many more. Modern Western scholars may point disarmingly to these earlier Muslim attempts at separating the authentic Prophetic wheat from the chaff of forgery,[38] but they have at their disposal a different heuristic tool in dealing with the hadith, the now familiar Redaction criticism, which, since the late 19th century, they have wielded with enormous and, what should be, at least for the historian, dismaying success. A great many of the prophetic traditions bear on their own bodies what is for the Redaction critic the equivalent of a smoking gun: circumstantial tendentiousness. If certain of the sayings of Jesus in the Gospels show a suspicious, and very un-Jewish, concern for the Gentiles, many hadith report remarks by Muhammad on personalities, parties, and religious and legal issues that could only have arisen as subjects of community concern after his death, and in some instances, long after his death.[39] If the Gospel critic, or some Gospel critics, think it possible to retrieve a good bit of Jesus' words and at least some of his own authentic teaching from the canonical Gospels, there are only very few modern historians who would make the same claim for Muhammad and the hadith.

If the hadith-sayings of Muhammad are suspect—and they are, after all, mostly halakic in content—what of the Prophet's deeds? Have we grounds for a biography? We have none in the Qur'an, it would appear, since its form is that of a discourse, a divine monologue or catechism so to speak, that reveals little or nothing about the life of Muhammad and his contemporaries. Both the life and the work of Jesus are integrated in the Gospels, and, unlike Paul's letters, which are essentially hermeneutical when they come to speak of Jesus,[40] the Gospels treat both the words and deeds of Jesus in the manner of history; that is, they *describe* events and they *reproduce* teachings, and each is done circumstantially enough for the modern historian to form some kind of unified judgment about the veracity of the first and the authenticity of the second.

For Islam, on the other hand, the pursuit of truth and authenticity is infinitely simpler (though not necessarily more satisfying) since there is a very large gap indeed between the sources for Muhammad's life and those for his teachings. On our assumption that the notions in the Qur'an are Muhammad's own—there is very little historical evidence that they are anyone else's—one can indeed approach them with much the same questions as one might bring to Jesus' reported teachings in the Gospels. Are these words or sentiments likely to be authentic in the light of, first, the context in which they were delivered, and second, the manner of their transmission? The reader of the Gospels is immediately predisposed to give an affirmative answer to the first question since, as Stephen Neill expressed it, "When the historian approaches the Gospels, the first thing that strikes him is the extraordinary fidelity with which they have reproduced, not the conditions of their own time, but the conditions of Palestine in the time and during the ministry of Christ."[41] The Qur'an, on the other hand, gives us no such assurance, nor indeed any instruction whatsoever on the context in which its contents were delivered, and no clues as to when, where, or why these particular words were being uttered; it is as little concerned with the events of the life of Muhammad and his contemporaries as Paul was with the narrative life of Jesus. The Holy Book of Islam is text without context, and so this prime document, which has a very strong claim to be authentic, is of almost no use for reconstructing the events of the life of Muhammad.[42]

There is, however, another, somewhat less obvious, facticity that rests between the lines of Islam's sacred book. If the Qur'an is genuinely Muhammad's, as it seems to be, and if, somewhat less certainly, distinctions between "Early-" and "Late-Meccan" and "Early-Medinan" suras of the Qur'an hold firm, then it is possible in the first instance to retrieve a substantial understanding of the type of paganism confronting Muhammad in his native city—the primary religious *Sitz im Leben* of the Meccan suras of the Qur'an—and even to reconstruct to some degree what appears to be an evolution in Muhammad's own thinking about God.

Though later Muslim historians profess to know a good deal on the subject, there exists, as has already been remarked, no physical or contemporary evidence for the worship and beliefs that prevailed at Mecca on the eve of Islam. The Qur'an, however, averts often to those conditions in its earliest suras. They were, after all, directed toward an overwhelmingly pagan audience whose beliefs and religious practices Muhammad was attempting to change and on which he was not likely to have been misinformed. Since the appearance of his *Muhammad in Mecca* in 1953, Montgomery Watt has concentrated much of his subsequent research on this issue, now summed up in his *Muhammad's Mecca: History in the Qur'ān*,[43] and the work has been pushed further, and argued somewhat more rigorously, by Alford Welch.[44] What emerges is not a very detailed picture, but the outlines are clear and distinct.

Muhammad's own beliefs are somewhat less distinct. Welch was not eager to find "evolution" in the ideas of the Prophet,[45] but viewed through the prism of "the historical Muhammad," that is exactly what he discovered. The name "Allah" does not appear in the earliest revelations, as he has pointed out, and Muhammad refers to his God as simply "the Lord." When he does begin to use a proper name, his preference is for *al-Raḥmān*, "the Merciful," a familiar deity from elsewhere in the Fertile Crescent. It can scarcely be argued that "al-Raḥmān" is identical with "Allah"; otherwise, why would he have introduced the unfamiliar "Raḥmān" (17:110, 25:60) for the known and accepted "Allah" except out of personal conviction?

The issue of "al-Rahman" aside, what distinguished Muhammad from his Meccan contemporaries was (1) his belief in the reality of the Resurrection and the Judgment in both flesh and spirit, and (2) his unswerving conviction that the "High God" was not unique but absolute; that the other gods, goddesses, jinn and demons were subject and subservient to Him: Allah's "servants," as he put it (7:194). Muhammad was to go much further than this; as Welch has demonstrated, sometime around the battle of Badr in 624, two years after the Hijra, a fundamental change took place in his thinking: Thereafter, Muhammad was an absolute monotheist. The other gods had completely disappeared and the now unique and transcendental Allah was served only by his invisible host of angels.[46]

This is genuine history, and it is more secure than anything else we know about Muhammad. It is not very "occasional" perhaps—we cannot firmly connect any of these religious changes with external events—and it tells us nothing about the social or economic life of Mecca. Those aspects of his environment will not yield up their secrets to the biographer unless additional context can be supplied from some other source, as Josephus provides the general background for the Gospels, or much as the Evangelists are thought to have done for Jesus himself, where historical narrative and a "sayings" source like the famous "Q" were integrated into a single Gospel narrative. Mark, the earliest of the Gospels, is already an integrated account of sayings and deeds, and everything else we know indicates that Jesus' followers remembered his sayings, his actions, and what happened to him all in the same context. If events showed that certain of his acts, notably his death and Resurrection, were considerably more consequential than his preaching—witness Paul and the earliest creeds—nonetheless, sayings and deeds were never completely disassociated in the Christian tradition.

Though there is no contemporary Josephus to report on 7th-century western Arabia; there are, in fact, just such integrated, Gospel-like sources in Islam. These *sīras* or traditional biographies of the Prophet, of which the oldest preserved specimen is the *sīra* written by Ibn Ishaq (d. 767), as edited by his student Ibn Hisham (d. 833), provide a richly detailed narrative of the events of Muhammad's career into which at least some Qur'anic material and other "teaching" has been incorporated at the appropriate places.[47] The "appropriate places" were the subject of a great deal of speculative attention by Muslim scholars who studied them under the rubric of "the occasions of revelations," that is, the particular set of historical circumstances at Mecca or Medina that elicited a given verse or verses of the Qur'an. The results of this energetic quest are not always convincing. There is very little evidence, for example, that independent sources of information were brought to bear on the enterprise, and the suspicion is strong that medieval Muslim scholars were re-creating the "occasion" by working backwards out of the Qur'anic verses themselves, an exercise at which a modern non-Muslim might be equally adept.[48] If these "occasions of revelation" are strung together in chronological order, a task accomplished by early Muslim scholars by arranging the suras, or part of suras, of the Qur'an in *their* chronological order, and one which we have already seen rests on extremely problematic grounds, then a semblance of a biography of the Prophet can be constructed, one that covers the ground at least from 610 to 632. This is, in fact, what was done, and the standard "Lives" of the Prophet, Ibn Ishaq's for example, rest on that kind of framework, fleshed out by other material about his early life at Mecca and considerably more elaborate descriptions of his later military expeditions at Medina.[49]

Though the earliest extant lives of Muhammad are far more distant from the events they describe than the Gospels are from the life of Jesus,[50] the Muslim authorities, unlike their Christian counterparts, cite their sources, by name and generation by generation, back to the original eyewitnesses contemporary with Muhammad. Hence, it is not unnatural that historical criticism in Islam has concentrated on those chains of transmitting authorities rather than, as is overwhelmingly the case in early Christian documents, on the matter transmitted. As has already been noted, in the 19th century Ignaz Goldziher,[51] and more recently Joseph Schacht,[52] looked more carefully at the accounts themselves and came to the generally accepted conclusion that a great many of the "Prophetic traditions" are forgeries fabricated to settle political scores or to underpin a legal or doctrinal ruling, a situation with no very convincing parallel in the Jesus material.[53] This conclusion was drawn, however, from the analysis of material in reports that are chiefly legal in character, where both the motives and the signs of falsification are often quite obvious; what of the reports of purely historical events of the type that constitute much of the life of Muhammad? The obvious clues to forgery are by no means so obvious here, nor is the motive quite so pressing since it is not the events of Muhammad's life that constitute dogma for the Muslim but the teachings in the Qur'an.[54] However, so great has been the doubt cast on the bona fides of the alleged eyewitnesses and their transmitters in legal matters that there now prevails an almost universal Western skepticism on the reliability of *all* reports advertising themselves, often with quite elaborate testimonial protestations, as going back to Muhammad's time, or even that of his immediate successors.[55]

Though Goldziher and Schacht concentrated chiefly on the legal hadith, the Belgian Jesuit Henri Lammens argued in a number of works that the historical traditions are equally fictitious, and whatever his motives and his style—Maxime Rodinson, a contemporary biographer of Muhammad, characterized Lammens as "filled with a holy contempt for Islam, for its 'delusive glory', for its 'dissembling' and 'lascivious' Prophet"—Lammens's critical attack has never been refuted.[56] One of the most notable of Muhammad's modern biographers, W. Montgomery Watt, found no great difficulty in this, however:

> In the legal sphere there may have been some sheer invention of traditions, it would seem. But in the historical sphere, in so far as the two may be separated, and apart from some exceptional cases, the nearest to such invention in the best early historians appears to be a "tendential shaping" of the material. ... Once the modern student is aware of the tendencies of the historians and their sources, however, it ought to be possible for him to some extent to make allowance for the distortion and to present the data in an unbiased form; and the admission of "tendential shaping" should have as its corollary the acceptance of the general soundness of the material.[57]

While Watt rejected Lammens's criticism of the hadith, he accepted the main lines of the Jesuit's reconstruction, out of the same type of material, of Meccan society and economy, which in turn provided Watt with the foundation of his own interpretation of Muhammad's career.[58] However, Goldziher, Lammens, and Schacht were all doubtless correct. A great deal of the transmitted material concerning early Islam was tendentious—not only the material that was used for legal purposes but the very building blocks out of which the earliest history of Muhammad and the Islamic community was constructed.[59] "The actual historical material [in Ibn Ishaq's *Life* of Muhammad] is extremely scanty. So the allusions to the Qur'an are taken and expanded; and, first and foremost, the already existing dogmatic and juristic *ḥadîth* are collected and chronologically arranged."[60] This opinion was written near the beginning of the century, and long past its midpoint it was concurred in, as we have seen, by one of Muhammad's most recent biographers, Maxime Rodinson.[61]

Whatever the quality of the material with which he was working, Ibn Ishaq generally hewed much closer than the Gospels to the straight historical line; he was much more a biographer than an evangelist. For one thing, he is excused from presenting the teachings of

Muhammad on two grounds. First, according to the Muslim view, there are no "teachings of Muhammad," at least not in any sense in which a Christian would understand that expression as applied to Jesus. There are the enunciations of God, but *they* are in the Qur'an, and if Ibn Ishaq occasionally reproduces the text of the Holy Book, or paraphrases it, it is generally, if we except the summary types noted above,[62] to set out some particular "occasion of revelation," a circumstance in the life of Muhammad that provided the setting for some particular sura.

The recorded life of Jesus is filled with mysteries, most of which derive not from the fact that we have four disparate written testimonies to what happened—any single Gospel would present the historian with the selfsame problems of interpretation—but because the evangelists were recording events and discourse and at the same time attempting a demonstration. The recording is, in fact, rather straightforward, and apart from certain problems of chronology and the incorporation of what appears to be legendary material (in the infancy narratives, for example), fashioning a biography of the "historical Jesus" from the Gospel materials would pose no unfamiliar or entirely insuperable difficulties for the historian of either Greco-Roman antiquity or post-biblical Judaism.

It is the demonstration that causes the historian's problem. The Evangelists were not simply recording; they were arguing. The conclusion to that argument was already fixed in their minds when they began their work, a fact they made no effort to disguise, namely, that their subject was no mere man but the Messiah of Israel and the Son of God;[63] that he was embarked on a series of events governed not by the historian's familiar secondary causality but by God's provident will; that Jesus was both completing the past—and thus "the Scriptures were fulfilled"—and breaking forth into a new and only gradually revealed eschatological future. Indeed, the death, Resurrection, and Ascension of Jesus do not complete the story; there is more: Pentecost at least, and how much more beyond that no one of the New Testament writers was aware. There is in all the material before the historian an open-ended anticipation that reflects disconcertingly backwards on almost every event in Jesus' life.

Many of the same problems confront the student of the life of Muhammad. Ibn Ishaq's biography of the Prophet begins, at least in the Ibn Hisham version we now possess,[64] much the same way that Mark's Gospel does, with a declaration that "this is the book of the biography of the Apostle of God,"[65] and it has, like Matthew and Luke, a brief "infancy narrative."[66] Moreover, there is a consistent, though low-key, attempt to demonstrate the authenticity of the Prophet's calling by the introduction of miracles, a motif that was almost certainly a byproduct of the 8th-century biographers' contact with Jews and, particularly, Christians.[67] This is sometimes imitative or polemical piety, and sometimes, and perhaps at an even earlier stage, a simple desire to entertain,[68] and its manifestations are not difficult to discern. Moreover, though the *sīra* literature is not used to mask special doctrinal pleading—there are no carefully crafted "theologoumena" on this landscape[69]—there are, in their frequent lists, genealogies, and honorifics, abundant signs of the family and clan factionalism that troubled the 1st- and 2nd-century Islamic community.[70] Finally, there are chronological questions. The earliest "biographers" of the Prophet, who were little more than collectors of the "raids" conducted by or under him, took the watershed battle of Badr as their starting point and anchor, and dated major events in Muhammad's life from it. However, for the years from Badr (624) back to the Hijra (622) there is great uncertainty, and for the entire span of the Prophet's life at Mecca there is hardly any chronological data at all.[71] The historians' only relief, perhaps (if relief it is), is that they do not have four differing accounts with which to work—all the earliest surviving versions of Muhammad's life rely heavily on Ibn Ishaq's original *Sīra*—and that in that *Sīra* he is not constrained to grapple with either a prologue in heaven or an eschatological epilogue.

Ibn Ishaq's *Life* is, on the face of it, a coherent and convincing account, and certainly gives historians something with which to work, particularly if they close their eyes to where the material came from. However, as has already been pointed out, the authenticity of the hadith has been gravely undermined, and a medieval biography of Muhammad is little more than an assemblage of hadith. Most modern biographers of the Prophet have been willing to close their eyes, and while conceding the general unreliability of the hadith, they have used these same collections as the basis of their own works which differ from those of their medieval predecessors not so much in source material as in interpretation.[72] This may be a calculated risk based on the plausibility and internal coherence of the material, or it may simply be the counsel of despair. If the hadith are rejected there is nothing notably better to put in their place.[73]

A few modern biographers, however, have attempted something different, to apply the biblical criteria of Form and Redaction criticism to the basic historical assemblage on which our knowledge of the events of the Prophet's life rests, the *Sīra* of Ibn Ishaq. While Watt contented himself with a brief investigation of the "sources of Ibn Ishaq," first Rudolf Sellheim and then, far more thoroughly, John Wansbrough attempted to see the parts in the whole.[74] As Wansbrough explained the procedure, various motifs (the election and call of a prophet, for example) that are common to many religious societies—Judaism, Christianity, and possibly even Arab paganism among them—were adduced as *topoi* as surely in the construction of the "Gospel of Muhammad" as in the parallel lives of Moses and Jesus.[75]

Thus, if we regard the *Life* through Wansbrough's eyes, the "evangelical" materials of Islam were assembled out of standard Jewish and Christian (or other) *topoi* long after the death of Muhammad, and reflect not so much historical data as the political and polemical concerns of the "sectarian milieu" that shaped them. The Islamic "Gospel" was, as a New Testament critic might put it, the product of the Muslim community, and, in its final form, of the 9th-century Muslim community in Iraq, and far removed in time and space from the primary *Sitz im Leben.* There is, unhappily, no documentary hypothesis to explain the content of the frame-like *topoi* of the *Sīra,* no J or E or P or Q; instead, there are only the discredited bits and pieces of the hadith, snippets of anecdotes, each with an "eyewitness" attached to the end of a more or less complete chain of transmitters, and with chain and witness sharing the same degree of likelihood or implausibility. "P" was an editor, "Q" the collector of *logoi,* but A'isha was the child bride of Muhammad and Abu Hurayra was a Companion of the Prophet, a man who had the simultaneous reputation of knowing more hadith than anyone and of being an idle chatterer. Between them they witnessed an enormous number of the tesserae out of which we attempt to reconstruct what happened between 610 and 632.

One effect of Redaction criticism on the study of the life of Jesus has been to direct the emphasis forward from Jesus himself to Paul and the first generation of Christians who shaped the tradition of Jesus. Muhammad died a success and Jesus died a failure; and historians work within those givens. One common position, then, is to maintain that whatever Jesus may have said or done (to put it in its most obviously agnostic terms), Gospel Christianity, whether Mark's early version or John's later one, was the creation of Jesus' followers. In Islam, on the contrary, where historical agnosticism would seem to be equally justified by the sources, the historians' interest remains riveted on Muhammad and what is imagined to have been his own immediate milieu. Muhammad the charismatic, the mystic, the social reformer, and the political genius are all familiar figures in Western scholarship—as familiar as the same qualities are alien to the present portrait of the historical Jesus—and there is no Paul nor a "Johannine community" to distract from the Prophet's central, or rather, unique, role in the fashioning of Islam.

A degree of reductionism has occurred, and it can be read between the lines of Wansbrough's reluctance to indicate a single or even principal sectarian influence operating on the *Sīra*. In the first half of this century, when there was far greater trust in what the later Muslim sources said about pre-Islamic Arabia, and when there prevailed an innocent freedom to extrapolate from almost any Jewish or Christian source, whatever its date or provenance,[76] the formation of Muhammad had not infrequently been reduced to the sum of the Christian, and particularly the Jewish, influences operating on him,[77] but only to account for the presence in the Qur'an of pervasive and detailed references to things Christian and Jewish, and never to explain Muhammad's enormous impact on his environment. Jesus, on the other hand, often appears in current historical appreciations, and overwhelmingly so in Jewish ones,[78] as a rather commonplace but politically naive rabbi who was the victim, the dupe, or the ploy of other forces or other men whose agenda were political rather than spiritual; who was caught up, probably unwittingly, in a movement of national liberation and paid for it with his life.

With Jesus we have some hope of coming to an informed judgment, of speaking with a degree of conviction about "Jesus within Judaism," or "Jesus and the Transformation of Judaism," with its corollary of taking the measure not only of Jesus' "traditionalism" but of his "originality."[79] Judgments of Muhammad's originality, on the other hand, founder on our almost absolute inability to measure him against any local or contemporary criterion. As Michael Cook has put it, "To understand what Muhammad was doing in creating a new religion, it would be necessary to know what religious resources were available to him, and in what form."[80] However, we do not know. We cannot tell whether Muhammad is innovating or simply borrowing because, if the Qur'an is silent on the matter, as it often is, then:

> We are obliged to turn to the theologians of later periods, to the authors of tradition and *fiqh*, who frequently give accounts expressing variant interpretations. Even if these writers are in agreement with each other, often their consensus is still unacceptable to us. Generally, posterity was inclined to trace back to Muhammad all customs and institutions of later Islam. ... Islamic tradition, however, not satisfied with claiming that the greater part of the cult was introduced by Muhammad, wants to date every institution as early as possible so that in many instances the pre-Islamic Arabs appear as precursors of Islam. This tendency is a consequence of the dogma of the religion of Abraham, the basis of Islam, which Muhammad felt it was his mission to preach.[81]

At every turn, then, historians of Muhammad and of early Islam appear betrayed by the sheer unreliability of their sources. The New Testament documents have their *Tendenz*, as all will quickly concede, and much of the "quest of the historical Jesus" has been in reality a search for a means to get around and behind that historical disability. However, most New Testament scholars also share a conviction that somewhere within the documents at their disposal is a grain or nugget, or perhaps even entire veins of historical truth, and that they can be retrieved. This explains the enormous and ingenious assiduity expended on the quest. Historians of Muhammad entertain no such optimism. They confront a community whose interest in preserving revelation was deep and careful, but who came to history, even to the history of the recipient of that revelation, too long after the memory of the events had faded to dim recollections over many generations, had been embroidered rather than remembered, and was invoked only for what is for historians the unholy purpose of polemic. Islam, unhappily for modern historians, had no immediate need of a Gospel and so chose carefully to preserve what it understood were the words of God rather than the deeds of the man who was His Messenger or the history of the place in which he lived.

Is there anything valuable in this Islamic tradition, which Patricia Crone has pessimistically called the "debris of an obliterated past"? It seems that there must be. It is inconceivable that the community should have entirely forgotten what Muhammad actually did or said at Mecca and Medina, or that the tenaciously memoried Arabs should have allowed to perish all remembrance of their Meccan or West Arabian past, no matter how deeply it might now be overcast with myth and special pleading. Some historians think they can see where the gold lies;[82] what is lacking is a method of extracting that priceless ore from the redactional rubble in which it is presently embedded. Those redactional layers may be later and thus thicker and less tractable than those over the figure of the historical Jesus, but just as the redactional editing of the Gospels was addressed and made to yield substantial results, there is no reason why the enterprise within Islam should prompt either resignation or despair. Faced with his own kind of unyielding tradition, the Islamicist has at least two ways of proceeding, as Julius Wellhausen recognized a century ago in his classic *Prolegomenon* on biblical criticism: either to arrange the accounts, in this instance, the hadith, in an internationally coherent order that would then represent the growth of the tradition—thus, for pre-Islamic Mecca, M. J. Kister and, after him, Uri Rubin, Michael Lecker, and others[83]—or else to deduce the evolution of matters at Mecca from a comparison with parallels in other religious cultures, a task that carried the biblical critic Wellhausen into his equally classic study of "the remains of Arab paganism."[84] This latter method is the one pursued most recently by G. R. Hawting,[85] and though terribly hypothetical, it has the advantage of forming hypotheses about the religious phenomena themselves and not merely about the traditions regarding those phenomena.[86]

Both methods are painstakingly slow and yield results that are notably more successful in analyzing Jewish influences and cultic practices than in dealing with Christian ideas, and more convincing when applied to pre-Islamic Mecca than to the Prophet's own life. Moreover, in dealing with Muhammad, where the Qur'an is the historian's chief "document," it is far easier to do as Watt and Rodinson have done and to apply a combination of common sense and some modern heuristic devices to the traditional accounts than to attempt what Griesbach and Wrede did in the 19th century with the Gospels, or Streeter or Bultmann in the 20th. It is easier still simply to give over the "quest of the historical Muhammad" and produce instead *Muhammad, His Life Based on the Earliest Sources* (1983), Martin Lings's uncritical English conflation of the traditional Muslim accounts which is offered without a word of explanation from the author on what he is about, or why, in this curious undertaking. There may be some value in presenting the Prophet of Islam in the same manner one might write a biography of Moses out of Ginzberg's *Legends of the Jews*, but it is not an enterprise likely to summon forth an Albert Schweitzer from the distraught bosom of Orientalism.

Notes

1 Stephen Neill, *The Interpretation of the New Testament, 1861–1961* (London, 1964), pp. 338–40.

2 Stephen Neill and Tom Wright, *The Interpretation of the New Testament, 1861–1986* (New York, 1988), pp. 360–64.

3 I use this latter expression in the sense isolated by Martin Kähler's famous distinction, first made in 1892 (cf. Martin Kähler, *The So-Called Historical Jesus and the Historic Biblical Christ,* trans. Carl E. Braaten [Philadelphia, 1964]), between the "historical Jesus" and the "historic Christ," the latter being the continuous subject of Christian preaching and the object of both Christian faith and Christian piety. Precisely the same distinction is intended when reference is made here to the "historical Muhammad." While the Prophet's person is not the object of Muslims' faith, as Jesus' is for Christians, his prophethood is, and thus both the person and the role of "the historic Prophet," to adapt Kähler's expression to the Islamic situation, have had an enormous and continuous influence on Islamic piety, practice, and beliefs (cf. Annemarie Schimmel, *And Muhammad Is His Messenger: The Veneration of the Prophet in Islamic Piety* [Chapel Hill, N.C., 1985]), none of which is in question here.

4 Maxime Rodinson, *Mohammed,* trans. Anne Carter from the revised French edition of 1968 (London, 1971), p. xi. This was by way of preliminary to writing a 324-page biography of the Prophet!

5 What follows does not pretend to be exhaustive on either Muhammad or the Qur'an, nor does it generally recover—though it occasionally glances at—the ground surveyed by Rudi Paret and Maxime Rodinson down to the early 1960s (Rudi Paret, "Recent European Research on the Life and Work of the Prophet Muhammad," *Journal of the Pakistan Historical Society,* 6 [1958], pp. 81–96; Maxime Rodinson, "A Critical Survey of Modern Studies of Muhammad," first published in *Revue historique,* 229 [1963], pp. 169–220; and translated from French in Merlin Swartz, *Studies on Islam* [New York, 1981], pp. 23–85). The state of Qur'anic studies through the 1970s is reflected in Alford T. Welch, "Kur'ān" in *EI*², vol. V (Leiden, E. J. Brill, 1981), pp. 400–432; and, more recently, in Angelika Neuwirth, "Koran," in Helmut Gätje, ed., *Grundriss der arabischen Philologie,* vol. II; *Literaturwissenschaft* (Berlin, 1987), pp. 96–135.

6 See generally, on what might be called the "irenic approach" to Islam, Andrew Rippin, "Literary Analysis of Qur'an, Tafsir, and Sira: The Methodologies of John Wansbrough," in Richard Martin, ed., *Approaches to Islam in Religious Studies* (Tucson, 1985), p. 159.

7 Ernest Renan, writing in 1851, and cited by Maxime Rodinson in "The Life of Muhammad and the Sociological Problem of the Beginnings of Islam," *Diogenes,* 20 (1957), p. 46.

8 Neill and Wright, *Interpretation,* p. 363.

9 Nabia Abbott, *Studies in Arabic Literary Papyri,* vol. I, *Historical Texts* (Chicago, 1957), p. 18; and compare Frants Buhl, *Das Leben Muhammeds,* translated from the second Danish edition of 1953 by Hans Heinrich Schaeder (rpt. Heidelberg, 1961), pp. 21ff. The pre-Islamic poetry makes its inevitable appearance in modern surveys on the "background sources" on Muhammad (see Rodinson, "Critical Survey," p. 37), but, except for Henri Lammens's work (see nn. 11, 56 below), it is far less in evidence when it comes to actually describing that background.

10 These are all likewise dutifully reported in surveys of the "sources for the life of Muhammad" (see Rodinson, "Critical Survey," pp. 29–39). It is in the north that we come the closest to the environment of Mecca, since both Jewish and Islamic traditions agree that there were Jewish settlements in the northern Hijaz; and, more important, the assertion is confirmed by epigraphical evidence (see Moshe Gil, "The Origin of the Jews of Yathrib," *Jerusalem Studies in Arabic and Islam,* 4 [1984], pp. 203–24). However, the fact remains that there is between the contemporary Greek, Roman, and Sasanian sources about Syria and Arabia and the later Islamic tradition about the same places a "total lack of continuity" (Patricia Crone, *Slaves on Horses: The Evolution of the Islamic Polity* [Cambridge, 1980], p. 11).

11 Compare Henri Lammens, *La Mecque à la Veille de l'Hégire* (Beirut, 1924), where the Arab literary evidence is collected (and perhaps distorted), with Patricia Crone, *Meccan Trade and the Rise of Islam* (Princeton, N.J., 1987), passim; and F. E. Peters, "The Commerce of Mecca before Islam," in Farhad Kazemi and R. D. McChesney, eds., *A Way Prepared. Essays … Richard Bayly Winder* (New York, 1988), pp. 3–26. A more sober approach than that of Lammens to the same pre-Islamic milieu has been taken over the last quarter-century by M. J. Kister of the Hebrew University (see M. J. Kister, *Studies in Jahiliyya and Early Islam* [London, 1980], and n. 83 below). In the face of the complete dearth of Hijaz evidence, Yehuda Nevo and Judith Koren have recently attempted to extrapolate the pre-Islamic Meccan milieu from what appears to have been a collection of pagan shrines still flourishing in the mid-8th century at Sde Boker in the Negev (Yehuda D. Nevo and Judith Koren, "The Origins of the Muslim Descriptions of the Jahili Meccan Sanctuary," *Journal of Near Eastern Studies,* 49 [1990], pp. 23–44). The argument is

seductive, but whether the buildings in question were indeed shrines does not appear to be at all clear,

12 For Muhammad, see Buhl, *Das Leben*, p. 366. While there is some material evidence for the Galilee and Jerusalem of Jesus' day, the latter conveniently summarized in John Wilkinson, *Jerusalem as Jesus Knew It: Archaeology as Evidence* (London, 1978), there has been no archaeological exploration in either Mecca or Medina, nor are the prospects good that there will be (F. E. Peters, *Jerusalem and Mecca: The Typology of the Holy City in the Near East* [New York, 1986], pp. 72–74). The almost total absence of archaeological evidence for early Islam is particularly striking when contrasted with the role that the excavation of sanctuaries and the discovery of legal and liturgical inscriptions have played in controlling the purely literary material that constitutes the "Hebrew Epic."

13 In all that follows I have left aside the question of "revelation" and "inspiration" and taken as my starting point the historian's normal assumption that the religious documents in question, the New Testament and the Qur'an, are entirely and uniquely the products of human agents, whoever those latter may turn out to be.

14 These latter reports are the hadith or Prophetic traditions allegedly reproducing the actual words of Muhammad on a variety of subjects. Their authenticity, which is of crucial importance to the historian, will be taken up in due course; here it need only be noted that while they do not share the cachet of divine inspiration attached by Christians to the entire New Testament, they have for Muslims a high degree of authority. Though that authority may have originated in their promotion, like that of the Mishna and Talmud, to magisterial authority in legal questions, the hadith soon began to enjoy the same status as purely historical documents.

15 If anything, the gap between the events of Jesus' life and their final redaction in the preserved Gospels appears to be growing narrower as time passes (see John A. T. Robinson, *Redating the New Testament* [Philadelphia, 1976]; and Neill and Wright, *Interpretation*, p. 361).

16 Conceivably even fewer, or perhaps many, many more. Though the later Muslim tradition came to agree that the "collection" of the Qur'an took place in the caliphate of Uthman (644–56), some early Muslim authorities dated it to the Caliph Abu Bakr (632–34) and others to Umar (634–44). This early uncertainty about what would appear to be a critical event in Islamic history is by no means atypical, and two modern scholars have rejected the traditional "Uthmanic" consensus out of hand. One (John Burton, *The Collection of the Qur'an* [Cambridge, 1977]) would make the "collection of the Qur'an" the work of the Prophet himself, while the other (John Wansbrough, *Qur'anic Studies: Sources and Methods of Scriptural Interpretation* [Cambridge, 1977]) would postpone it to the 9th century. It is still early in the career of each hypothesis, but neither seems to have been widely embraced.

17 Arthur Jeffery, *Materials for the History of the Text of the Qur'an* (Leiden, 1937); Rudi Paret, "Der Koran als Geschichtsquelle," *Der Islam*, 37 (1961), pp. 24–42, cited from its reprint in Rudi Paret, ed., *Der Koran* (Darmstadt, 1975), pp. 141–42.

18 J. Eliash, "The Shi'ite Qur'an: A Reconsideration of Goldziher's Interpretation," *Arabica*, 16 (1969), pp. 15–24; E. Kohlberg, "Some Notes on the Imamite Attitudes toward the Qur'an," in *Islamic Philosophy and the Classical Tradition: Essays ... Richard Walzer* (Columbia, S.C., 1973), pp. 209–24.

19 As noted, one who has failed to be convinced is John Wansbrough who, in two major studies (Wansbrough, *Qur'anic Studies*, and Wansbrough, *The Sectarian Milieu: Content and Composition in Islamic Salvation History* [Oxford, 1978]) has attempted to demonstrate that (1) the Qur'an was not finally fixed ("collected") until the early 9th century, and (2) it was shaped out of biblical and other materials by redactors influenced by contemporary Judeo-Christian polemic. For a sympathetic appreciation of Wansbrough's work, see Rippin, "Literary Analysis"; and for a Muslim's criticism of both Wansbrough and Rippin, see Fazlur Rahman, "Approaches to Islam in Religious Studies: Review Essay," in Richard Martin, ed., *Approaches to Islam in Religious Studies* (Tucson, 1985), pp. 198–202.

20 William Graham, "Qur'an as Spoken Word: An Islamic Contribution to the Understanding of Scripture," in Richard Martin, ed., *Approaches to Islam in Religious Studies* (Tucson, 1985), p. 31: "Fundamentally, the Qur'an was what its name proclaimed it to be: the recitation given by God for human beings to repeat (cf. Sura 96:1)."

21 This is believed according to the universal Muslim tradition (W. Montgomery Watt, *Bell's Introduction to the Qur'an* [Edinburgh, 1970], pp. 37–38).

22 Rudolf Bultmann, *History of the Synoptic Tradition* (New York, 1963), p. 205.

23 See W. D. Davies's judicious remarks (*Paul and Rabbinic Judaism* [Philadelphia, 1980], p. 3): "While it is clear that Rabbinic sources do preserve traditions of an earlier date than the second century … [i]t must never be overlooked that Judaism had made much history during that period. It follows that we cannot, without extreme caution, use the Rabbinic sources as evidence for first century Judaism." Study of the life of Muhammad suffers, as we shall see (see n. 80), from the selfsame problem.

24 Watt, *Bell's Introduction*, pp. 77–79; compare R. B. Serjeant, "Early Arabic Prose," in A. F. L. Beeston et al., eds., *Arabic Literature to the End of the Umayyad Period* (Cambridge, 1983), pp. 126–27.

25 A. E. Harvey, *Jesus and the Constraints of History* (Philadelphia, 1982), pp. 6ff.

26 Rippin, "Literary Analysis," p. 159, commenting on Wansbrough's delineation of this style (Wansbrough, *Qur'anic Studies*, pp. 40–43, 47–48, 51–52ff.; Wansbrough, *Sectarian Milieu*, pp. 24–25): "The audience of the Qur'an is presumed able to fill in the missing details of the narrative, much as is true of work such as the Talmud, where knowledge of the appropriate biblical citations is assumed or supplied by only a few words." Far more than this is assumed by the Mishna and Talmud, of course. There, the reader is expected to understand the lines of both the issues and the current state of the debate on those issues when the text opens.

27 Watt, *Bell's Introduction*, pp. 77–82, 127–35. All these would fall within what the New Testament Form critics would call "Paränesis" or "Sayings and Parables" (cf. Robert H. Stein, *The Synoptic Problem: An Introduction* [Grand Rapids, Mich., 1987], pp. 168–72), though with far greater variety than the Gospel examples show.

28 Neill and Wright, *Interpretation*, p. 264.

29 See, most recently, Issa Boullata, "The Rhetorical Interpretation of the Qur'an: *I'jāz* and Related Topics," in Andrew Rippin, ed., *Approaches to the History of the Interpretation of the Qur'ān* (Oxford, 1988), pp. 140–41.

30 For Richard Bell's ingenious but unconvincing hypothesis, see Watt, *Bell's Introduction*, pp. 101–7.

31 Namely, that the present suras were the original units of revelation, and that the hadith, and the historical works incorporating them, provide a valid basis for dating the suras (cf. Neuwirth, "Koran," p. 100). These premises, which roughly correspond to standard rabbinic theory about the books of the Bible, would of course, rule out even the possibility of a "documentary hypothesis" for either the Bible or the Qur'an.

32 The standard statement of what has become the Western position is found in the first volume of Theodor Nöldeke's *Geschichte des Qorans* (Göttingen, 1860), revised by Friedrich Schwally in 1909. Others have slightly revised the Nöldeke-Schwally sequence, but it remains the basic sura order used in the West (Neuwirth, "Koran," pp. 117–19).

33 Watt, *Bell's Introduction*, p. 114: "Like all those who have dated the Qur'an, Bell accepted the general chronological framework [and much else besides] of Muhammad's life as this is found in the *Sīra* … and other works." The value judgment is that expressed in Welch, "Kur'ān," p. 417.

34 This was somewhat disingenuously conceded by W. Montgomery Watt (*Muhammad at Mecca* [Oxford, 1953], p. xiii), and, more helpfully, by Rudolf Sellheim ("Prophet, Calif und Geschichte: Die Muhammad Biographie des Ibn Ishaq," *Oriens*, 18–19 [1965–66], pp. 33–91); and Wansbrough (*Qur'anic Studies* and *Sectarian Milieu*), among others.

35 *The Life of Muhammad: A Translation of Ishaq's Sirat Rasul Allah, with Introduction and Notes by Alfred Guillaume* (Oxford, 1955), p. 691.

36 Michael Cook, *Muhammad* (New York, 1983), p. 68.

37 See Qur'an 10:38–39, where, as usual, God is speaking:

> This Qur'an is not such as could ever be invented in despite of God; but it is a confirmation of that which was before it and an exposition of that which is decreed for men—there is no doubt of that—from the Lord of the Worlds. Or do they say he [that is, Muhammad] has invented it? Then say: If so, do you bring a *sūra* like it, and call for help on all you can besides God, if you have any doubts.

For the Gospels, see John 21:24: "It is this same disciple who attests what has here been written. It is in fact he who wrote it, and we know that his testimony is true"; and cf. Luke 1:1–4.

38 Summarily described, from a Muslim point of view, in Muhammad Abdul Rauf, "*Ḥadīth* Literature—I: The Development of the Science of *Ḥadīth*," in A. F. L. Beeston et al., eds., *Arabic*

Literature to the End of the Umayyad Period (Cambridge, 1983), pp. 271–88. However, they may have included, even by their own criteria, far more chaff than has been suspected; compare G. H. A. Juynboll, "On the Origins of Arabic Prose; Reflections on Authenticity," in G. H. A. Juynboll, ed., *Studies on the First Century of Islamic History* (Carbondale, Ill., 1982), pp. 171–72: "Classical Muslim *isnād* criticism has not been as foolproof as orthodox circles, and in their wake many scholars in the West, have always thought."

39 Consider, for example, what might be taken, were it genuine, as a prime example of early Islamic *kerygma,* Muhammad's own "farewell discourse" on the occasion of his last pilgrimage before his death. It is reported in substantially similar versions by three major historians, Ibn Ishaq, Waqidi, and Tabari, but, remarked R. B. Serjeant, a generally conservative critic, "patently signs of political ideas of a later age, coupled with internal and external contradictions, largely discredit the attribution of much of the extant versions to the Prophet" (Serjeant, "Early Arabic Prose," p. 123). For another example, see n. 62.

40 This is not to say that, as Wright put it (Neill and Wright, *Interpretation,* p. 362):

> It is still universally agreed that our picture of the earliest Church must begin with the study of Paul, and in particular of the letters generally agreed to be authentic. … These writings, which almost certainly antedate the earliest written Gospel, remain central for both the theology and history of the period.

Islam lacks a Paul, that is, an authoritative contemporary interpretation of the founder's message. The Islamic sources for early Islam are, like those on the life of Muhammad himself, later by a century and a half. Paul may have done theological mischief in the Christian context by providing an interpretation before the message, but all in all, it is better to have Paul than Tabari, as either a historian or an exegete.

41 Neill and Wright, *Interpretation,* p. 294.

42 Buhl, *Das Leben,* p. 366. Michael Cook succinctly summed up the contemporary historical data provided by the Qur'an:

> Taken on its own, the Qur'an tells us very little about the events of Muhammad's career. It does not narrate these events, but merely refers to them; and in doing so, it has a tendency not to name names. Some do occur in contemporary contexts: four religious communities are named (Jews, Christians, Magians, and the mysterious Sabians), as are three Arabian deities (all female), three humans (of whom Muhammad is one), two ethnic groups (Quraysh and the Romans), and nine places. Of the places, four are mentioned in military connections (Badr, Mecca, Hunayn, Yathrib), and four are connected with the sanctuary (Safa, Marwa, Arafat, while the fourth is "Bakka," said to be an alternative name to Mecca). The final place is Mount Sinai, which seems to be associated with the growing of olives. Leaving aside the ubiquitous Christians and Jews, none of these names occurs very often: Muhammad is named four or five times (once as "Ahmad"), the Sabians twice, Mount Sinai twice, and the rest once each. (Cook, *Muhammad,* pp. 69–70)

43 W. Montgomery Watt, *Muhammad's Mecca: History in the Qur'ān* (Edinburgh, 1988), especially pp. 26–38. Alford T. Welch ("Muhammad's Understanding of Himself: The Koranic Data," in Richard G. Hovannisian and Speros Vryonis, eds., *Islam's Understanding of Itself* [Malibu, Calif, 1983], pp. 15–52) has likewise attempted a biographical sketch of Muhammad's "self-understanding" as revealed by the Qur'an.

44 Alford T. Welch, "Allah and Other Supernatural Beings: The Emergence of the Qur'anic Doctrine of Tawhid," in Alford T. Welch, ed., *Studies in Qur'an and Tafsir,* JAAR Thematic Issue 47, 1979, 1980, pp. 733–58.

45 Welch, "Muhammad's Understanding," p. 16; and compare the significant omission of the personal pronoun in "A thorough analysis of the Qur'anic contexts involving Allah, other deities, and the 'lower' members of the spirit world shows a clear and unmistakable development of ideas or teachings" (Welch, "Allah," p. 734).

46 Ibid., pp. 751–53.

47 On the genre, see M. J. Kister, "The *Sīra* Literature," in A. F. L. Beeston et al., eds., *Arabic Literature to the End of the Umayyad Period* (Cambridge, 1983), pp. 352–67.

48 The consensus opinion—and reservations—are rendered in Welch, "Kur'ān," p. 414. Similar, and stronger, reservations are expressed by Wansbrough (*Qur'anic Studies*, p. 141); Cook (*Muhammad*, p. 70); and Rippin ("Literary Analysis"), who wrote:

> Their [the "occasions of revelation" narratives] actual significance in individual cases of trying to interpret the Qur'an is limited: the anecdotes are adduced, and thus recorded and transmitted, in order to provide a narrative situation in which the interpretation of the Qur'an can be embodied. The material has been recorded within exegesis not for its historical value but for its exegetical value. Yet such basic literary facts about the material are frequently ignored within the study of Islam in the desire to find positive historical results. (p. 153)

49 On Qur'anic exegesis posing as biography, see W. Montgomery Watt, "The Materials Used by Ibn Ishaq," in Bernard Lewis and P. M. Holt, ed., *Historians of the Middle East* (London, 1962), pp. 23–34; and on the "raids of the Prophet," which Watt regards as the "essential foundation for the biography of the Prophet and the history of his times," see ibid., pp. 27–28, and also J. M. B. Jones, "The *Maghāzi* Literature," in A. F. L. Beeston et al., eds., *Arabic Literature to the End of the Umayyad Period* (Cambridge, 1983), pp. 344–51.

50 Alternatively, as Patricia Crone dramatically stated it (*Slaves on Horses*, p. 203n. 10): "Consider the prospect of reconstructing the origins of Christianity on the basis of the writings of Clement or Justin in a recension by Origen."

51 Ignaz Goldziher, "On the Development of the Hadith," in S. M. Stern, ed., *Muslim Studies* (London, 1971), vol. II, pp. 17–254; originally published in 1890.

52 Joseph Schacht, *The Origins of Muhammadan Jurisprudence* (Oxford, 1950).

53 Compare Stein's recent assessment of the materials attributed to Jesus in the Gospels: "The lack of such material [dealing with the most pressing problems facing the earliest Christian communities] in the Gospels witnesses against the idea that the church created large amounts of the gospel materials and in favor of the view that the church tended to transmit the Jesus traditions faithfully." Moreover, citing G. B. Caird, "There is not a shred of evidence that the early church ever concocted sayings of Jesus in order to solve any of its problems" (Stein, *Synoptic Problem*, p. 189).

54 Thus argues W. Montgomery Watt in *The History of al-Tabari*, vol. VI, *Muhammad at Mecca*, trans. and annotated W. Montgomery Watt and M. V. McDonald (Albany, N.Y., 1988), p. xviii.

55 On these latter see the trenchant Form criticism analysis by Albrecht Noth, *Quellenkritische Studien zu Themen, Formen und Tendenzen frühislamischer Geschichtsüberlieferung*, vol. I, *Themen und Formen* (Bonn, 1973).

56 On Henri Lammens's approach, see "Qoran et tradition: Comment fut composée la vie de Mohamet?" *Recherches de Science Religieuse*, 1 (1910), pp. 25–61, and *Fatima et les filles de Mahomet* (Rome, 1912); and compare C. H. Becker, "Grundsätzlichen zur Leben-Muhammadforschung," in *Islamstudien*, 2 vols. (Leipzig, 1924; rpt. Hildesheim, 1967), vol. I, pp. 520–27, and K. S. Salibi, "Islam and Syria in the Writings of Henri Lammens," in Bernard Lewis and P. M. Holt, *Historians of the Middle East* (London, 1962), pp. 330–42; for Rodinson's characterization, see Rodinson, "Critical Survey," p. 26, and compare Buhl, *Das Leben*, p. 367: "H. Lammens ... dessen Belesenheit und Scharfsinn man bewundern muss, der aber doch oft die Objectivität des unparteischen Historikers vermissen lässt."

57 Watt, *Muhammad*, p. xiii, and compare Watt, "Materials," p. 24. Kister's cautiously worded opinion seems similar:

> The development of *Sirah* literature is closely linked with the transmission of the *Ḥadīth* and should be viewed in connection with it. ... Although some accounts about the recording of the utterances, deeds and orders dictated by the Prophet to his companions are dubious and debatable and should be examined with caution (and ultimately rejected), some of them seem to deserve trust. (Kister, "*Sīra* Literature," p. 352)

58 Compare Rodinson, "Critical Survey," p. 42: "Orientalists are tempted to do as the Orientals have tended to do without any great sense of shame, that is, to accept as authentic those traditions that suit their own interpretation of an event and to reject others." Rodinson, who, as we

shall see shortly, had even less faith than Watt in the source material, may have himself done precisely that in his own biography of the Prophet.

59 Crone, *Slaves on Horses*, pp. 14–15:

> Among historians the response to Schacht has varied from defensiveness to deafness, and there is no denying that the implications of his theories are, like those of Noth, both negative and hard to contest. ... That the bulk of the *Sīra* ... consists of second century *ḥadīths* has not been disputed by any historian, and this point may be taken as conceded. But if the surface of the tradition consists of debris from the controversies of the late Umayyad and early Abbasid period, the presumption must be that the layer underneath consists of similar debris from the controversies that preceded them, as Lammens and Becker inferred from Goldziher's theories.

According to Crone, Watt "disposes of Schacht by casuistry," but Shaban, Paret, Guillaume, and Sellheim have likewise been unwilling to deal squarely with the critical issue he has raised (ibid., p. 211, n. 88). Watt's brief rebuttal is in his "The Reliability of Ibn Ishaq's Sources" in *La vie du prophète Mahomet* (Colloque de Strasbourg 1980) (Paris, 1983), pp. 31–43; and Watt and McDonald, *Muhammad*, pp. xvii–xix.

60 Becker, "Grundsätzlichen," p. 521, cited in Watt, "Materials," p. 23.

61 Cited in n. 4 above; compare his similar remarks in n. 58 above and, earlier, Buhl, *Das Leben*, pp. 372–77.

62 The earliest example of such a summary, in both the serial and the absolute chronology, appears in Ibn Ishaq's *Life* (1:336) on the occasion of some Muslims emigrating to Abyssinia in 615, when the ruler there was given a summary presentation of Islamic "good news." This apparently early Muslim "kerygma" has been analyzed in Wansbrough, *Qur'anic Studies*, pp. 38–43, and Wansbrough, *Sectarian Milieu*, pp. 100–101. That author concludes (*Qur'anic Studies*, p. 41) that "the structure of the report suggests a careful rhetorical formulation of Qur'anic material generally supposed to have been revealed after the date of that event," and, even more sweepingly (*Sectarian Milieu*, p. 100), "Save for the Meccan pilgrimage, no item in these lists falls outside the standard monotheist vocabulary, and is thus of little use in the description of origins."

63 From Mark onward—"Here begins the Gospel of Jesus Christ the Son of God"—all the Gospels make a similar declaration at their outset.

64 In Ibn Ishaq's original "world history" version, before Ibn Hisham removed the "extraneous material," the story began with Creation, and Muhammad's prophetic career was preceded by accounts of all the prophets who had gone before. The life of the man was the "seal" of their line (see Abbott, *Studies*, pp. 87–89). This earlier, "discarded" section of Ishaq's work can be to some extent retrieved (Gordon Darnell Newby, *The Making of the Last Prophet: A Reconstruction of the Earliest Biography of Muhammad* [Columbia, S.C., 1989]), and while its remains are revealing of Ibn Ishaq's purpose and the milieu in which the work was finally composed (Abbott, *Studies*, p. 89), they add nothing of substance to the portrait of the historical Muhammad.

65 Ibn Ishaq 3 in Guillaume, *Life of Muhammad*, p. 3.

66 Ibid, pp. 102–7 in Guillaume, *Life of Muhammad*, pp. 69–73; and compare what Ibn Ishaq calls "Reports of Arab Soothsayers, Jewish Rabbis and Christian Monks" about the birth of the Prophet (ibid., pp. 130ff. in Guillaume, *Life of Muhammad*, pp. 90ff.).

67 Sellheim, "Prophet," pp. 38–39, 59–67; Kister, "*Sīra* Literature," pp. 356–57; and, for a more general consideration of "polemic as a history-builder," see Wansbrough, *Sectarian Milieu*, pp. 40–45 and n. 77 below.

68 Kister, "*Sīra* Literature," pp. 356–57, on the early *Sīra* of Wahb ibn Munabbih (d. 728 or 732) and the "popular and entertaining character of the early *Sīra* stories, a blend of miraculous narratives, edifying anecdotes and records of battles in which sometimes ideological and political tendencies can be discerned." (Compare Cook, *Muhammad*, p. 66.)

69 The New Testament critic Joseph Fitzmyer defined a "theologoumenon" as "a theological assertion that does not directly express a matter of faith or an official teaching of the Church, and hence in itself is not normative, but that expresses in language that may prescind from facticity a notion which supports, enhances or is related to a matter of faith" (Joseph A. Fitzmyer, "The Virginal Conception of Jesus in the New Testament," originally published in 1973, rpt. in Joseph A. Fitzmyer, *To Advance the Gospel* [New York, 1981], p. 45).

70 Sellheim, "Prophet," pp. 49–53; Kister, "*Sīra* Literature," pp. 362–63.

71 Wansbrough, *Sectarian Milieu,* p. 35; and compare Noth, *Quellenkritische Studien,* pp. 40–45, 155–58. The reason for the vague "distributional chronology," as Wansbrough called the pre-Hijra system, was certainly not, as Watt has suggested (in Watt and McDonald, *Muhammad,* p. xxi), that "there were fewer outstanding events." The call of the Prophet, the earliest revelation of the Qur'an, and the making of the first converts would all appear to be supremely important, though the Muslim tradition had little certainty, chronological or otherwise, about them (ibid., pp. xxii, xxv–xli), likely because there was either no way or no reason to remember the date.

72 Crone, *Slaves on Horses,* p. 13:

> The inertia of the source material comes across very strongly in modern scholarship on the first two centuries of Islam. The bulk of it has an alarming tendency to degenerate into mere arrangements of the same old canon—Muslim chronicles in modern languages and graced with modern titles. Most of the rest consists of reinterpretation in which the order derives less from the sources than from our own ideas of what life ought to be about—modern preoccupations graced with Muslim facts and footnotes.

73 One attempt to substitute "genuine" eyewitness testimony (if not to Muhammad himself, then to the first appearance of the Islamic movement on the early 7th-century Near East) has been Patricia Crone and Michael Cook's *Hagarism: The Making of the Islamic World* (Cambridge, 1977), and while a brave and provocative book, it has tempted few others to follow its suggestion: "The historicity of the Islamic tradition is ... to some degree problematic: while there are no cogent internal grounds for rejecting it, there are equally no cogent external grounds for accepting it. ... The only way out of the dilemma is thus to step outside the Islamic tradition altogether and start again" (p. 3). What the external testimony to early Islam amounts to (and it is not a great deal) is summarized in Cook, *Muhammad,* pp. 73–76; and the limitations of this approach are underscored in Wansbrough, *Sectarian Milieu,* pp. 115–16.

74 Watt, "Materials"; Sellheim, "Prophet"; Wansbrough, "Qur'anic Studies"; Wansbrough, *Sectarian Milieu.*

75 Wansbrough, "Qur'anic Studies," p, 66.

76 See n. 80 below. Michael Cook (*Muhammad*) reflects the far more modest aims of contemporary searchers after "influences":

> For the most part we are reduced to the crude procedure of comparing Islam with the mainstream traditions of Judaism and Christianity, and trying to determine which elements came from which. The answers are often convincing, but they fail to tell us in what form those elements came to Muhammad, or he to them. (p. 77).

77 This was done as early as Abraham Geiger's *Judaism and Islam* (originally published in Latin in 1832; rpt. from the translation published in 1898 [New York, 1970]); and then later, Charles Cutler Torrey, *The Jewish Foundations of Islam* ([New York, 1933; rpt. New York, 1967]). There have been a number of suggestive portraits of the "Jewish Muhammad," followed by the arguments of Richard Bell, *The Origin of Islam in Its Christian Environment* (London, 1926; rpt. London, 1968), Karl Ahrens, "Christliches im Qoran" (*Zeitschrift der Deutschen Morganlandischen Gesellschaft,* 84 [1930], pp. 15–68, 148–90); and Tor Andrae, *Les origines de l'Islam et le Christianisme* (Paris, 1955), for a "Christian Muhammad."

78 The political hypothesis, first argued by Eisler and Brandon, took this more recent form in Hyam Maccoby, *The Mythmaker: Paul and the Invention of Christianity* (New York, 1987):

> Though all these [just cited Jewish] writers have their individual approaches, it is characteristic of the school as a whole to use the Talmud to show that Jesus' life and teaching are entirely understandable in terms of the Judaism of his time, particularly rabbinical or Pharisaic Judaism. The corollary is that, since Jesus did not conflict with Judaism, his death took place for political reasons, later camouflaged as religious by the Christian Church in its anxiety to cover up the fact that Jesus was a rebel against Rome. (pp. 208–9).

Cf. Ernst Bammel, "The Revolutionary Theory from Reimarus to Brandon," in Ernst Bammel and C. D. F. Moule, eds., *Jesus and the Politics of His Day* (New York, 1984), pp. 11–68.

79 Harvey, *Jesus,* p. 6, was cited in n. 25 above on the "constraints of history." However, he went on to add:

> This is not to say, of course, that he [Jesus] must have been totally subject to these constraints. Like any truly creative person, he could doubtless bend them to his purpose. ... But had he not worked within them, he would have seemed a mere freak, a person too unrelated to the normal rhythm of society to have anything meaningful to say.

80 Cook, *Muhammad,* p. 77. Moreover, it is here that the Islamicist, like the New Testament scholar (see n. 23), runs into the problem of the usefulness of the "rabbinic sources": to what extent can the Mishna, the Talmud, and the Midrashim (many of these latter sources being, in fact, post-Islamic and so possibly influenced by, rather than influencing, early Islam) be used to illuminate the pre-Islamic milieu of Mecca? Geiger, Torrey (*Jewish Foundations,* p. 34), and, notoriously, Abraham Katsh, *Judaism in Islam: Biblical and Talmudic Backgrounds of the Koran and Its Commentaries. Surahs II and III* (New York, 1954), invoked them almost as if Muhammad had a personal yeshiva library at his disposal, or, as Torrey thought, even a rabbinic teacher (*Jewish Foundations,* pp. 40–42).

81 Arent Jan Wensinck, *Muhammad and the Jews of Medina,* with the excursus, *Muhammad's Constitution of Medina* by Julius Wellhausen, trans. and ed. Wolfgang Behn (Freiburg, 1975), p. 73.

82 Paret, *Der Koran*; Watt, "Materials," p. 28; Watt and McDonald, *Muhammad,* pp. xxi–xxv; Sellheim, "Prophet," pp. 73–77; Kister, "*Sīra* Literature," pp. 352–53.

83 Kister and his students have painstakingly compared variants in early, and largely unpublished, Muslim traditions on various topics—thus, for example, his analysis of a rather mysterious pre-revelation religious practice of Muhammad called *taḥannuth* ("Al-Tahannuth: An Inquiry into the Meaning of a Term," *Bulletin of the School of Oriental and African Studies,* 31 (1968), pp. 223–36)—and attempted to construct the original understanding behind them, on the assumption that the "original" tradition derived, to some degree, from a historical "fact." They did not, however, directly address the critical question of the authenticity of any of the hadith materials with which they are so scrupulously dealing, though Kister for one, as we have seen (n. 68 above), was well aware of the historiographical problems posed by the inauthenticity of the hadith.

84 Julius Wellhausen, *Reste arabischen Heidentums,* 2nd ed. (Berlin, 1897).

85 G. R. Hawting, "The Origins of the Islamic Sanctuary at Mecca," in G. H. A. Juynboll, ed., *Studies on the First Century of Islamic History* (Carbondale, Ill., 1982), pp. 25–47.

86 It is instructive of the two methods to compare Hawting, "Origins," with Uri Rubin, "The Ka'ba, Aspects of Its Ritual, Functions, and Position in Pre-Islamic and Early Islamic Times," *Jerusalem Studies in Arabic and Islam,* 8 (1986), pp. 97–131, both of which deal with the pre-Islamic sanctuary at Mecca.

18 Jesus and Mary as Poetical Images in Rūmī's Verse

Annemarie Schimmel

Poets in Islamic lands, and especially in the Persianate world, used to derive their imagery largely from the Qur'an, and from Qur'anic narratives about the prophets. These appear in the entire corpus of classical poetry, be it lyrical or epic, panegyric or mystical, although they are often strangely transformed.[1] One also finds allusions to Christian themes such as the scene well-known in classical Arabic poetry of drinking bouts in monasteries and the image of a seductive hair style called a "cross" which inspired love poets. But these themes do not concern us here.

Among the Qur'anic prophets, Jesus, the last messenger before Muhammad, plays a special role. Mentioned several times in the Qur'an, along with his virgin mother, he is generally referred to as 'Īsā ibn Maryam, and also called *masīḥ,* "Messiah, Christ." Sometimes he appears as *rūḥ Allāh,* "God's spirit," and now and then as *nabī,* "prophet." Poets made reference not only to the Qur'anic narratives about this messenger, miraculously conceived as a proof of God's omnipotence and able to cure the sick and quicken the dead; they were also aware of the legends that had grown around his personality. The picture poets draw of Jesus is full of love, even though some poetical images may sound strange to a Christian reader.

From early days onward Jesus appears as the ideal ascetic.[2] Sufi lore knows many stories about him as a paragon of meekness and love of God, an idea based on the Qur'anic statement (S. 57:27) that there is kindness and mercy in the hearts of those who follow the Gospel, Jesus' special book. In this context it is important to remember that the rare references from the Gospel are usually allusions to the Sermon on the Mount. Stories from the Apocrypha were taken over very early. One story that seemed to have been very dear to Mawlānā Rūmī[3] concerns the answer Jesus gave to someone who asked him: "What is the heaviest thing in the world?" He answered: "God's wrath." Asked how to find rescue from this Divine wrath he replied: "Suppress your own wrath and oppress your own anger."

The way of Jesus, as often shown in Muslim literature, is that of abstinence and asceticism—however, as the Prophet said, "there is no monkery, *rahbāniyya,* in Islam." Thus in a famous passage of *Fīhi mā fīhi* (chap. 17) Rūmī dwells upon the necessity of marriage as a means of spiritual purification by "putting up with the absurdities of women." This, he claims, is the way of Muhammad and of the strong; those who cannot carry such a burden are advised to go to the desert and follow the way of Jesus by living far away from the world to achieve at least something of the spiritual path.

Although Jesus was the paragon of asceticism, he was seen by Rūmī as not at all sinister and dour looking but rather always smiling, contrary to his cousin John who never laughed: "The smiling was from confidence, and the frowning was from fear" (D 12885). The different behavior of the two prophets is explained in *Fīhi mā fīhi* (chap. 11):

> Jesus, upon whom be peace, laughed much; John, upon whom be peace, wept much. John said to Jesus: "You have become exceedingly secure against the subtle deceits, that you laugh so much." Jesus replied: "You have become all too unmindful of the subtle, secret and wonderful graces and kindness of God that you weep so much." One of God's friends was present when that happened. He asked God: "Which of them has the higher station?" God answered: "He who thinks better of Me"—that is to say: "I am with my servant's thought about Me. Every servant has an image and an idea of Me. Whatever picture he forms of Me, there I am."

Therefore allusions to the "sugarlike smile" of Jesus occur frequently in Rūmī's verse, and he admonishes his listeners to learn from Jesus how to laugh at the grief and worries caused by lust, male and female (D 21021)—that is, to be beyond worldly attachment.

Out of the most important quality of Jesus, the love of God, emerges his love of all creatures. Overlooking ugliness, he sees beauty in everything created by God, for as his soul was beautiful he could discover beauty everywhere. The most famous story in this respect, elaborated not by Rūmī but by both Niẓāmī and 'Aṭṭār, is that of Jesus and his disciples passing by a dead dog. While the disciples complained about the stench and the appalling view of the carcass, Jesus pointed to the shining white teeth of the dead creature. This story found its way even into German literature and is quoted by Goethe in his *West-Östlicher Divan.*[4]

Jesus' ascetic life is highlighted in the allusions to Matthew 8:20, that the Son of Man has no place to put his head. He is the homeless wanderer, as Rūmī dramatically tells in *Fīhi mā fīhi* (chap. 11): when Jesus tried to find shelter in a jackal's den he was driven out by a revelation because his presence disturbed the jackal's whelps. This story (making use of a pun between the Arabic words *āwā,* "jackal," and *ma'wā,* "shelter") is used to instruct the reader that it is preferable to have a spiritual Beloved, a Divine Lord who drives His lover into the wilderness in constant quest for Him, than to live comfortably without knowing the yearning for God. Stories that Jesus did not build a house or own anything that would make life more comfortable were elaborated by Rūmī's predecessors Sanā'ī and especially 'Aṭṭār. Did he not use only half a brick as a pillow to rest his head? But when Satan told him, says 'Aṭṭār, that even this broken brick proved that he had not yet severed his bonds with the world, he threw it away.[5]

One understands well why the saying "The world is a bridge; pass over it but do not stay on it" was attributed to Jesus; it has been quoted frequently by the Sufis and is written in fine calligraphy over the gate of Akbar's palace city Fathpur Sikri. Rūmī therefore tells his audience, "Become a Jesus—if you have no house, let it be so!" (D 20645) Such stories and images are often connected with Jesus' dwelling place in the fourth heaven. Rūmī claims, "I am not bound to a house, for like Jesus, my dwelling place is in the fourth heaven" (D 18388).

One of the miracles mentioned only in the Tradition (*ḥadīth*) is that Jesus could walk on water (as he did, according to the Gospels, on Lake Gennesaret). Early Sufi texts ascribe to the Prophet Muhammad the remark: "If my brother Jesus had had more *yaqīn,* [absolute certainty], he would have walked in the air."[6] This story, well-known among the Sufis, inspired Rūmī to some allusions where he puns on the name of Mary, Maryam, and *yam,* "ocean" (33481). Jesus is not only the perfect ascetic but also the man of prayer: "He went to the fourth heaven on the wings of prayer" (D 2559), said Rūmī, and a sincere prayer will be answered (as Sanā'ī had already stated) by Jesus' saying "Amen" from the fourth heaven.[7] In profane literature, then, the term "the prayer of Jesus" can be used as a symbol for something extremely protective and helpful.

It would be a special task to follow the way allusions to the Gospels appear in Sufi poetry, suffice it to mention that Sanā'ī has an impressive rendering of Christ's saying that one should rather pluck out one's eye than look at something prohibited,[8] advice apparently well-known even in medieval Indo-Muslim circles.

But how did the mystical poets, in the first place Rūmī, elaborate the data given in the Qur'an about Jesus? His creation through the breath of God was administered by Gabriel and has served time and again to point out God's omnipotence.

> He makes appear a child without father,
> He makes the child speak in the cradle,

says 'Aṭṭār in the *Pāndnāma.* This figure of speech is commonplace in hymns of praise. For while Mary had vowed a fast which included silence (S. 3:41), her son spoke in the cradle to defend her innocence (S. 19:31): "Lo, I am God's servant. God has given me the book and made me a prophet. Blessed be He who made me wherever I be, and He has enjoined me to pray, and to give alms, as long as I live, and likewise to cherish my mother." The silence of Mary and the speech of the child is a favorite topic with the poets, so much so that writers could use it in their chains of oath formulas, like Waṭwaṭ who swears, "By the faith in the questions of Jesus in the cradle."[9] Rūmī, like other poets, uses this image in spring poems when

> the once deposed narcissus becomes the overseer of the kingdom
> and the buds, like Jesus, are intelligent and can recite (D 18166).

Or, in another example:

> The wind seeking and running, the waters washing their hands—
> We [are] talking in a way like Christ while the dust is silent like Mary (D 17351)

This mysterious talk of Jesus is the soul's talk: for is not the human soul bound in the body like Jesus in the cradle? (D 16689).

Much later, after Jesus had proved his role as prophet and servant of God by talking in the cradle, he made a table prepared come down from heaven: "For them it was a feast, a meal, and a proof of his mission" (S. 5:111 f.). This table (after which S. 5 received its name) is connected with Jesus' statement that he never told his followers to take him and his mother as two deities. The mysterious table is a sign of Divine grace, comparable to the manna and quails that were given to the children of Israel in the desert:

> From the lovely desert of Moses and from the table of Jesus—
> What kind of dainties and food and sweets is this, O God! (D 1052)

But Rūmī knows well that people will not be satisfied with this divinely sent table, as they had complained when Moses miraculously produced food in the desert (M 1:83). (The miracles of Moses and Jesus often appear as parallels in poetry.)

The table of grace, the spiritual food, is generally mentioned by Rūmī in poems that praise fasting, for

> It is the rule of Your kindness to give a table from heaven
> to those who fast like Christ. (D 19904)

According to the Qur'an (S. 3:43; 5:110) Jesus could fashion little clay birds into which he breathed to make them alive "with God's permission": Rūmī therefore sees himself as a clay bird that learns to fly when the beloved breathes into him (D 14962).

In the same verses of the Qur'an Jesus is mentioned as quickening the dead, and it is this quality of his that is very often alluded to in poetry. For it makes him the ideal symbol of the spiritual leader who quickens the dead souls, as well as of the Beloved who is able to revive those who have been slain on the path of love and longing. In this connection the name of Lazarus, 'Āzar, is often mentioned by poets, including by Khāqānī (who had a thorough knowledge of Christian traditions). Rūmī may claim to see even the dead dancing in their shrouds at the return of the longed-for beloved: "Is this the blowing of the trumpet or a second Jesus?" (D 21736). For Jesus is not only the one who can breathe new life into an individual. He is also the one who will appear to inaugurate a happy time of forty years after killing the *dajjāl* before the resurrection and Last Judgment begin; he is "a sign of the Hour" (S. 43:61). Thus, poets fond of personifying abstractions (and this is one of Rūmī's stylistic peculiarities) can say that Jesus (= the beloved) "will kill the *dajjāl* 'Grief' when he returns" (D 4789).

The beloved is, for Rūmī, "the prophet of the sick" (D 19646); he is so powerful that he can give life to a thousand Jesuses (D 12666). Other loving exaggerations of this kind are not lacking in his verse. Sometimes, however, it is not the beloved but Love itself that is equated with Jesus, for Love revives the dead and heals the sick:

> As Love is the Jesus of the age and seeks someone dead—
> Die completely before its beauty, like me, and don't fear! (D 12918)

The idea that Jesus quickens the dead often takes a turn which may sound frivolous to the Christian reader but is used thousands of times in Persian and Persianate poetry from the earliest days. The life-bestowing breath of Christ is the equivalent of a kiss. This is logical, for from antiquity the exchange of kisses was considered an exchange of souls, the soul being contained in the breath. One of the best known examples of this imagery is Rūmī's oft-imitated verse:

> When someone asks you: "How did Christ quicken the dead?"
> Then give me a kiss in his presence: "Thus!" (D 19180)

Expanding the idea that Jesus' breath grants new life, not only a kiss but almost everything enjoyable can be compared to it. Thus in Rūmī's verse the sound of the harp or other musical instruments has "the quality of Jesus's breath" (D 26636), that is, gives new life to the soul. This, however, seems to be restricted to his imagery as his compositions were generally triggered by music.

The most common usage, on the other hand, is the combination of Jesus and spring or the spring breeze (D 22658). For spring is the time when the "martyrs," the plants which appear dead, slain by winter's cruelty, resurface from their shrouds (D 21172)—an elegant elaboration of the Qur'anic proof of resurrection. One of the oldest Persian lyricists, Abū 'Alī Marvazī, had used the combination of Christ and spring;[10] as did many other writers through the centuries, including Anvarī and Sa'dī.

In many cases, though rarely in Rūmī's verse, Jesus and his breath are combined with Khiḍr, who grants the seeker the Water of Life: both of them could symbolize the beloved and his kiss. The same imagery has been applied in panegyric poetry as well. As early as in the days of Maḥmūd of Ghazna, Farrūkhī compared his patron to Jesus, just as later Khāqānī praises the ruler who, being the "Jesus of the age," has quickened the country's dead body—that is, has reestablished its prosperity. Later poets, especially in India, sometimes twisted this very theme ironically, asking whether in their day there was any difference between the shop of Christ and that of a vet.[11]

Besides as reviver of the dead, Jesus appears even more frequently as the great physician who heals all ailments and grants sight by means of his *fusun,* his incantation, to those born blind (cf. S. 4:100). But his healing breath is a sign of God's creative breath:

> Sometimes He breathes and makes a Jesus son of Mary
> So that the one with a breath like Jesus becomes a witness to His breath. (D 30659)

For it was the pre-eternal Divine grace that was active in his miracles as in those of other prophets.

In his quality as physician Jesus is usually called *ṭabīb,* and Rūmī claims, "We are skilled physicians for we are disciples of Christ" (D 15549). It is only the beloved's Christ-like breath that can heal those who have fallen ill from longing (D 1766). Since Christ can heal the blind-born, *akmah,* his name appears sometimes in connection with *surma* or *kuḥl,* the collyrium or antimony used to brighten the eye and to strengthen the eyesight.

> I was an eye full of pain, so I grasped Jesus (D 16624)
> Why should the eye weep all the time when it has found collyrium from the prophet
> Christ? (D 31682)

Thus asks Rūmī, who also tells a lovely story about an ascetic who was blamed by worldly people because of his uninterrupted weeping. He is admonished,

> Do not grieve about your eyes when Jesus is yours—
> Don't seek the life of the *body* from your Jesus. (M 2: 449 ff.)

For even if the bodily eyes are lost, the eyes of the spirit will be opened.

But in order to be blessed by such a transformation one must look at Jesus and not at his donkey (D 12254), that is, seek a spiritual cure and not a material one. Once such a healing process has been performed, Rūmī calls those who have experienced it to enter the cosmic dance:

> The blind and the deaf in this world who were healed by the son of Mary,
> are called by him to enter the mystical dance. (D 2100)

The same idea of transformation leads Rūmī to call Jesus the Great Alchemy that produced spiritual changes in man, "who transforms your copper into gold" (D 25598).

Jesus can heal almost every ailment, but there is one illness even he is unable to cure by means of his miracle-working breath. That is foolishness. Rūmī elaborates this idea in an entertaining story in the *Mathnavī* (M 3: 2570 ff.): Jesus was seen running as if he were fleeing from wild lions, withdrawing to a mountaintop to retreat from the world. The reason for his behavior, as he explains, it is that there are too many fools around him and these are the only people whom even he cannot cure.

The main difference between Qur'anic and biblical christology is found in the negation by the Qur'an of Jesus' crucifixion. Sūra 4:155–57 states that "they did not kill him and did not crucify him but We lifted him up and made someone to look like him." Persian writers sometimes connect the word *tarsa,* "Christian" and its other meaning "afraid"; Rūmī uses this expression to denote *guman,* "doubtful thought," because the true believer does not think that Christ has been crucified (D 7642). And the four-pointed cross becomes a symbol of the four elements of which the world is made:

> Far be the portico of joy from fire and water and dust and wind!
> The composition of the true confessors of Unity be as far away from those four simple elements as from the cross! (D 7215)

It is the Christians who have invented such things, and Mawlānā has told in great detail in the first book of the *Mathnavī* how a Jewish vizier helped his king to uproot the Christians by disguising himself as a zealous Christian hermit. Before committing suicide, he distributed his "will" to his twelve closest Christian friends. But as each document contradicted the other, the followers of the twelve leaders began to fight among themselves and were extinguished, with the exception of those who studied the Gospels intensely and found the name of *Aḥmad* (= the most praised one, *perikletos*)—that is, the *paraklet*—and became as it were Muslims *avant la lettre.* A similar criticism of "Jewish rancor" appears once more in the end of the *Mathnavī* (6: 3267–70): A treacherous vizier wanted to cheat Jesus and went out in the hope of becoming the leader of the people who followed Christ, but because he looked like Jesus it was he who was crucified in Jesus' place.

The place to which Jesus was uplifted is, according tó tradition, the fourth heaven. Thus he becomes a symbol of the spiritual ascension of the soul:

> You draw the Jesus "Soul" from dust (*tharā*) beyond the Pleiads (*thurayyā*)—
> Without above and below you draw him every moment to the Highest Lord. (D 35788)

For this reason it is said:

> The soul that belongs to the Divine Throne goes toward Jesus;
> The soul that belongs to Pharaoh goes toward Qārūn. (D 8677)

For Jesus, symbol of the spiritual part of man, is sometimes contrasted in poetry with Qārūn, the biblical Korah, who hoarded immense treasures and was swallowed by the earth due to their weight. Sanā'ī seems to have been the first poet to allude to Jesus and Qārūn together in one verse;[12] the comparison then became commonplace.

The poets often mentioned Christ's heavenly abode: living in this lofty place, "What has he to do with grieving about heat or cold?" (D 11661). And even more: "What has Jesus, dwelling in the fourth heaven, to do with the church?" (D 1283). Astrologically speaking, the fourth heaven is the place of the sun. For this reason Rūmī could mention Jesus even more in this connection than other writers would, because it enabled him to allude to the miracles of his spiritual beloved Shamsaddīn, the "Sun" of Tabrīz: through him, the representative of Muhammad, the power and glory of earlier prophets manifests itself.

It may seem strange that Jesus, the Spirit of God, appears not in the immediate presence of the Divine Throne but only in the fourth heaven, even though this is the central sphere because of the sun. Whatever the reason for the tradition (which may have developed from an aversion to the Christian formula of Jesus "sitting at God's right hand"), the Sufis found an explanation: although Jesus was perfect in his asceticism, he still carried a comb and a cup with him. Seeing someone combing his hair with his fingers, he threw away the comb and, discovering that one could drink water from the fountain by using the palm of one's hand, he parted with the cup. And yet, it was discovered that he had a needle in his garment, and for a spiritual being like him, "a needle will become a veil like the treasure of Qārūn" (D 27085). Rūmī had taken over the story of the needle from Sanā'ī who, as it seems, had used it for the first time in mystical Persian poetry:

> Had he not carried that needle with him,
> He would have arrived just beneath the Throne of God.[13]

The source for Sanā'ī is probably al-Ghazālī's *Iḥyā' 'ulūm al-dīn.* Somewhat later, 'Aṭṭār alluded to it in his Persian epics, as did Ibn al-Jawzī in his Arabic prose work. Poets of the sixteenth and seventeenth centuries speak of the needle and the long thread, a thread which is "extended hope," *ṭūl al-amal,* a quality disliked by the Sufis. As for the meaning of the original story, Jāmī, following Rūmī, explains that such a needle "is like a thorn in the foot of the *himmat* [spiritual high ambition] of Jesus"[14]—the more spiritualized one becomes the more dangerous is even the smallest attachment to anything that is part of "the world."

Less mystical poets, however, would compare the beloved's slender waist to the needle of Jesus, or claim that their bodies were much more worn out than his needle while (and because) the beloved's lips are finer than the *rishta-i Maryam,* the extremely fine thread Mary spun. These images, used in Khāqānī's poetry, sound quite exaggerated to a modern Western reader, who might enjoy better a verse by Ghanī Kashmīrī stating that even Jesus' breath can work only if there is an innate capacity to receive it—even he will not be able to make the needle's blind eye able to see.[15]

The fourth heaven, place of high spirituality, is often contrasted in poetry with the world of matter, as symbolized by Jesus' donkey. One knows that

> Jesus used to ride on a donkey out of modesty—
> Otherwise, how would the morning breeze ride on a donkey's back? (D 35585)

In Rūmī's work the combination of Jesus and donkey occurs so frequently that one wonders what the reason might be. It seems impossible to assume that a dim remembrance of early Christian days had survived, when in the time of Emperor Severus around A.D. 200, a picture of a crucified donkey was drawn in the Palatin to ridicule and shock the Christian community in Rome. In any case, the donkey had a bad reputation as an extremely stubborn and, more than that, sensual creature (works like Apuleius's *Golden Ass* come to mind, and Rūmī's *Maihnavī* contains some coarse and even obscene donkey stories). Sanā'ī had used the Jesus-donkey contrast to point to the contrast of soul and matter:[16] the soul should not sleep in the mud like a donkey, as Rūmī says (D 31107). Again, the "donkey in the mud" image is found frequently in both Sanā'ī's and 'Aṭṭār's verse. They repeat with slight variations the idea that the loving soul goes to heaven like Jesus and one need no longer care for the dead ass (D 1090)—that is, man's material part.

> Jesus son of Mary went to heaven, and his donkey remained here—
> I remained on earth, and my heart went up. (D 19085)

In a considerable number of stories and verses Rūmī tells of the loss of a donkey and interpreting them one finds that to lose the donkey is, in the end, not really a loss (D 14608) but rather a gain because after losing the material mount the soul can fly to heaven (D 20053). Those who serve the "donkey," the world of matter, do not understand anything of mysteries; therefore one should not cast so many delicate words of the Jesus "Soul" into the ass's heart and ear (D 18523) or offer the dainties of Jesus, such as selflessness and spiritual intoxication (D 31341), to the donkey in his stable; in short, one should not cast pearls before swine. For, as Sanā'ī says:

> How could the donkey know Jesus's worth?
> How could the deaf know David's melodies?[17]

Rūmī, however, thinks that kindly Jesus would probably not withhold candy from the donkey, even though the stupid creature is more interested in straw (M 6:152).

It is amazing to see what foul language Rūmī uses when emphasizing the contrast between spirit and matter. Could one speak of Christ and at the same time smell a donkey's urine or dung (D 26025)? And, "Far be the ass's arse from the cradle of Jesus!" (D 11698). For

> The lip that has kissed the ass's arse—
> how could it find the sweet kiss of Christ? (D 1070)

There is no end to such remarks in Rūmī's *Dīvān*—remarks which at times bring a blush to the translator who tries to render his poetry into another language.

Yet, despite all his aversion to "material donkeys," Rūmī never gives up hope—Love can transform even an ass:

> When the donkey drinks the wine of Jesus,
> at some point he will sprout wings. ... (D 10730)

The Jesus-donkey combination remained alive in Persian poetry throughout the centuries until Ghanī Kashmīrī in seventeenth-century India says in an amusing turn of the image: "Anyone who talks about Jesus in front of the beloved's life-bestowing lips, is a donkey!"[18]

Jesus, spirit from the Divine Spirit, stands beyond the multiple sects and creeds. He is, as Rūmī states (M 1: 500), *yakrang*, "unicolored"; he adheres to the one truth and thus comes to represent those who have taken the *ṣibghat Allāh* (S. 2:132), the "coloring" or "baptism" of God by which all the various colors of this world are washed off so that the saint or prophet appears in the radiant white garb of Divine Light This idea had already been expressed by Sanā'ī, who admonishes his reader:

> Take away this seven-colored gown from your hand,
> Take a unicolored robe like Jesus

> So that you may walk on the water like Jesus
> And travel with sun and moon![19]

As Jesus is frequently called "Son of Mary" it is natural that his virgin mother should play an important role in Persianate poetry. Was she not, as the *Musnad* of Ibn Ḥanbal states, one of the four best women that ever lived on earth? The poets loved Mary (a love still visible, for example, in the visits of pious Turks at Mary's alleged tomb near Ephesus), and Mawlānā Rūmī is no exception. However he seems to be the only major poet to have devoted a full chapter (of his *Mathnavī,* M 2: 3602–13) to the story how Yaḥyā, John the Baptist, bowed in worship before Christ while still in his mother's womb.

The Qur'anic statements about Mary begin with her birth and her mother's vow. Zacharias, her relative, was made her guardian, and whenever he came to bring her food in the inner chamber where she lived she had already received food from the Unseen and had seen the fruits of Paradise. (The term *miḥrāb,* used in the Qur'an for this chamber, inspired the pious to write this story, or at least its beginning, around *miḥrābs* in mosques all over the world.) Rūmī quotes this story and the prayer of Zacharias through which his old, barren wife became pregnant in *Fihi mā fihi* (chap. 44) as proof of God's omnipotence, which is displayed at such occasions. Mary had vowed her virginity to God and the Qur'an describes how Gabriel, the Holy Spirit, presented himself to her as "a man without fault" (S. 19:17). Rūmī dwells upon the story of the annunciation in the third book of the *Mathnavī* (M 3: 1700 ff.) and tells it with such tenderness that it almost sounds as if it were taken from a medieval Christian book of devotions. It happened during her bath that the spiritual form came to her to blow into the shirt which she had taken off—hence later poetical allusions to the "breath in her sleeve."

Mary could easily become a symbol of the pure soul (D 18042) or the heart made pregnant by the Divine spirit (D 5475), and Rūmī once equates the gift that came to her from the Unseen with the *amāna,* the entrusted good mentioned in S. 33:72. But he knew that one thing is required to make the "Heart"—Mary pregnant with Jesus, and that is pain, grief, and sorrow:

> The thought, touched by grief as though that were Gabriel,
> becomes pregnant with two hundred Jesuses. (D 24406)

And, even more beautiful:

> If the treasure "Grief for Him" is in your heart, that heart becomes "light upon light" (S. 24:35)
> like the lovely Mary who has Jesus in her womb. (D 5490)

Phrases of this kind appear in Rūmī's verse rather often but images alluding to Mary's virginity and pregnancy can be found in less spiritual connections as well. This is the case especially when poets speak of their novel "virgin" thought which then results in the eloquent child Jesus and his sweet words.

Even an untutored reader may perhaps understand that, as Khāqānī says, the lips of the beloved seem to give birth to a Jesus in such a way that a Mary seems to be hidden in the friend's mouth;[20] but when an eighteenth-century poetaster in India compares the wine bottle to Mary who carries in her womb the fragrant Jesus, the life-bestowing wine, one may not exactly relish the image.

At the end of her pregnancy Mary was overcome by birth pangs and, as the Qur'an tells, went to a dried-up date palm which she grasped, and the tree showered fruits upon her. It is this kind of fruit that called out to Mary: "Eat, drink and be in good mood!" (S. 19:25), that the faithful should eat (D 1213). The giving of fruit by the barren tree parallels the miracle of Zacharias's barren wife giving birth to John (D 35797): in all these events it is the breath of God that acts (D 13058). For Rūmī it is once more the question of "pain" that is central in his allusions to the dry palm tree (M 2: 93). Had Mary not felt the pangs of labor she would never have received such a sweet gift. Just like Mary's virginity and pregnancy, the miracle of the dates was also alluded to by poets to point to their creativity: "The word is a witness to the virgin, that is, my thought as the date palm is for Mary's miracle,"[21] and it did not take long for authors to compare the reed pen that produced sweet words to the dry date palm that yielded sweet fruit.[22]

That Mary took a vow of silence led to her son's defense of her and thus, her silence and his eloquence are often juxtaposed:

> Sometimes, like Jesus, we have become all tongue;
> Sometimes, like Mary, we have a silent heart. (D 17402)

Likewise her fasting, which is "a preparation of Divine Love" (D 32065) is seen in relation to the table of Jesus (D 26303).

One of the loveliest usages of the image of Mary is her connection with the garden. Although the Qur'an states that she and her son were given a quiet place with springs (S. 23:52), it seems unlikely that this remark contributed much to the garden imagery. It was the experience of the revival, the miraculous new birth of greenery in spring that inspired the poets to use such a combination, which goes back to the earliest days of Persian poetry. Kisā'ī wrote, "It seems that the midnight breeze became Gabriel so that the roots and dry trees became Mary!"[23] Rūmī has taken over this idea with a rather daring extension:

> The wind seems to be Gabriel and the trees Mary:
> Look at the hand-play, like that of husband and wife! (D 21030)

The result of such a play between wind and trees is the birth of the Jesus "Rose" (D 10589), again not a novel image. Long before Rūmī, Abū 'Alī Marvazī had sung:

> The Mary "Bud," in whose womb the rose "Jesus" is found
> comes with her face opened like the paradisiacal virgins![24]

Such an image reminds the Christian reader of one of the old Christmas carols, which begins in German "Es ist ein Ros entsprungen."

Persian poets have also compared the cloud that becomes pregnant from the wind to Mary,[25] and in seventeenth-century India the monsoon cloud that brings sweet fruits[26] appears in a similar comparison. Other authors might invent more mundane images; Rūmī, however, loved to speak mainly of Mary and the garden in spring. In swinging rhythms he sings of all the branches which look

> as if they were Marys, pregnant by the angel's breath;
> They are all houris, born from amidst the dark dust. (D 30260)

Mary, the lovely branch which, touched by the sweet breeze, gave birth to the Jesus-like rose—that was a theme dear to many writers. But Rūmī emphasizes one aspect of Mary in particular: he repeats time and again that only pain and suffering made Mary, the pure soul, experience spiritual pregnancy and helped her to receive the sweet fruits when pain seemed unbearable. Alluding to the "birth of Jesus in the soul" in several verses of his *Dīvān,* he has fully elaborated the idea in *Fīhi mā fīhi* (chap. V):

> It is pain that guides a person in every enterprise ... It was not until the pain of labor appeared in Mary that she made for the tree ... Those pangs brought her to the tree, and the tree which was withered became fruitful. ...
> The body is like Mary. Everyone of us has a Jesus within him, but until the pangs manifest in us our Jesus is not born. If the pangs never come, then Jesus rejoins his origin by the same secret path by which he came, leaving us bereft and without portion of him.

Thus, the birth of Christ in the soul was expressed by a Muslim mystic in Anatolia half a century before Eckhart in Germany spoke of this central experience of the mystic in Christianity.

Notes

1. See, e.g., Asin Palacious, "Logia et agrapha Domini Jesu," in *Patrologia orientalis* 13 (1919): 335–431, 19 (1926): 532–624; Michael Hayek, *Le Christ de l'Islam* (Paris: Éd. du Seuil, 1959); Roger Arnaldez, *Jesus fils de Marie, prophète de l'Islam* (Paris: Desclée, 1980); Abdal Jalil, *Marie et l'Islam* (Paris: Beauchesne, 1950); Olaf Schumann, *Der Christus der Muslime* (Gutersloh: Gerd Mohn, 1975); James Robson, "Stories of Jesus and Mary," *The Muslim World* 40 (1960): 235–42; W. N. Wyham, "Jesus in the Poetry of Iran," *The Muslim World* 42 (1960): 104–11.
2. S. Tor Andrae, *In the Garden of Myrtles,* trans. Birgitta Sharpe (Albany: State University of New York Press, 1988).
3. M 4: 113–15; *Fīhi mā Fīhi,* ed. Badī'uzzmān Furūzanfār (Tehran: Tehran University Press, 1328sh/1959); English trans. Arthur J. Arberry, *Discourses of Rūmī* (London: London University Press, 1961), chap. 64.
4. Johann Wolfgang von Goethe, *West-Ostlicher Divan,* hrsg. Ernst Beutler (Leipzig: Dietrich, 1943), "Noten und Abhandlungen: Allgemeines" (S. 192).
5. Sanā'ī *Ḥadīqat al-Ḥaqīqat wa Ṭarīqat al-Sharī'at,* ed. Mudarris Razavī (Tehran, Tahuri, 1329sh/1959), p. 317; Farīduddīn 'Aṭṭār, *Muṣībatnāma,* ed. N. Wisal (Tehran, Zawwar, 1338sh/1959), chap. 36/10. For references to Jesus in 'Aṭṭār's epics, see Hellmut Ritter, *Das Meer ser Seele* (Leiden: E.J. Brill, 1957), index s.v. Jesus.
6. Abū Naṣr as-Sarrāj, *Kitāb al-Luma' fi'l-Taṣawwuf* ed. Reynold Alleyne Nicholson (London: Luzac; Leiden: E.J. Brill, 1914), p. 155.
7. Sanā'ī, *Ḥadīqa,* p. 635.
8. Ibid., p. 353ff.
9. Rashīduddīn Waṭwaṭ, *Dīvān,* ed. Sa'īd Nafīsī (Tehran: Barani, 1339sh/1960), p. 26.
10. 'Awfī, *Lubāb al-Albāb,* ed. Edward G. Browne and Mohammad Qazwini (London-Leiden: Luzac and Brill, 1903, 1906), 2: 340.
11. Ṭālib-i Āmulī, quoted in S. M. Ikram, *Armaghan-i Pak* (Karachi: Government of Pakistan Press, 1953), p. 279.
12. Sanā'ī, *Ḥadīqa,* p. 443.
13. Ibid., p. 392.
14. 'Abdurraḥmān Jāmī, *Dīvan-i Kāmil,* ed. Hāshim Riẓā (Tehran: Payruz, 134sh/1962), p. 199, nr. 172.

15. Muḥammad Aṣlaḥ, *Tadhkirat-i Shu'arā-i Kashmīr*, ed. Sayyid Ḥusāmuddīn Rahsdī, 5 vols. (Karachi: Iqbal Academy, 1969–70), 2: 999.
16. Sanā'ī, *Ḥadīqa*, p. 304.
17. Sanā'ī, *Mathnavīha*, ed. Mudarris Razavī (Tehran: University Press, 1343sh/1965), "Sayr al-'ibād ilā 'l-ma'ād," line 13.
18. S.M. Ikram, *Armaghan-i Pak*, p. 241.
19. Sanā'ī, *Ḥadīqa*, p. 132.
20. Khāqānī Shirvanī, *Dīvan*, ed. Zia'uddīn Sajjāḍī (Tehran: Zawwar, 1338sh/1959), ghazal p. 564.
21. Khāqānī Shirvanī, *Dīvan*, p. 24.
22. Jāmī, *Dīvan-i Kamīl*, p. 227 nr. 247.
23. 'Awfī, *Lubāb al-Albāb*, 2: 46.
24. Ibid., 2: 341.
25. Ibid., 2: 111.
26. Naziri, *Dīvan*, ed. Mazāhir Muṣaffā (Tehran: Amir Kabir, 1330sh/1961), ghazal nr. 48.

19 Extracts from *The Muslim Jesus: Sayings and Stories in Islamic Literature*

Tarif Khalidi

107

Jesus said, "The heart of a believer cannot really support the love of both this world and the next, just as a single vessel cannot really support both water and fire."

Abu Bakr ibn Abi al-Dunya (d. 281/894), *Kitab Dhamm al-Dunya*, in *Mawsu'at Rasa'il*, 2:44, excerpt no. 76. Cf. al-Ghazali, *Ihya'*, 3:200 (Asin, p. 369, no. 35; Mansur, no. 120; Robson, p. 65).

It may be worth noting that in the Gnostic Gospel of Philip it is asserted that soul and spirit "are constituted of water and fire"; see Bentley Layton, *The Gnostic Scriptures*, p. 341, excerpt 58. But this is only a stylistic parallel, since the clearly Gnostic elements in the Muslim gospel are few. There is also some superficial resemblance to Matthew 6:24, and the unattributed saying, which immediately follows this one in Ibn Abi al-Dunya, is in fact a paraphrase of Matthew.

108

A man once accompanied Jesus, saying to him, "I want to be with you and be your companion." They set forth and reached the bank of a river, where they sat down to eat. They had with them three loaves. They ate two loaves, and a third remained. Jesus then rose and went to the river to drink. When he returned, he did not find the third loaf, so he asked the man: "Who took the loaf?" "I do not know," the man replied.

Jesus set forth once more with the man, and he saw a doe with two of her young. Jesus called one of the two, and it came to him. Jesus then slaughtered it, roasted some of it, and ate with his companion. Then he said to the young deer, "Rise, by God's leave." The deer rose and left. Jesus then turned to his companion and said, "I ask you in the name of Him who showed you this miracle, who took the loaf?" "I do not know," the man replied.

The two of them then came to a body of water in a valley. Jesus took the man by the hand and they walked upon the water. When they had crossed over, Jesus said to him, "I ask you in the name of Him who showed you this miracle, who took the loaf?" "I do not know," the man replied.

They then came to a waterless desert and sat down upon the ground. Jesus began to gather some earth and sand, and then said, "Turn to gold, by God's leave," and it did so. Jesus divided the gold into three portions and said, "A third for me, a third for you, and a third for whoever took the loaf." The man said, "It was I who took the loaf." Jesus said, "The gold is all yours."

Jesus then left him. Two men came upon him in the desert with the gold, and wanted to rob and kill him. He said to them, "Let us divide it into three portions among us, and send one of you to town to buy us some food to eat." One of them was sent off, and then said to himself, "Why should I divide the gold with those two? Rather, I shall poison the food and have the gold to myself." He went off and did so.

Meanwhile, the two who stayed behind said to each other, "Why should we give him a third of the gold? Instead, let us kill him when he returns and divide the money between the two of us." When he returned, they killed him, ate the food, and died. The gold remained in the desert with the three men dead beside it. Jesus passed by, found them in that condition, and said to his companions, "This is the world. Beware of it."

Abu Bakr ibn Abi al-Dunya (d. 281/894), *Kitab Dhamm al-Dunya,* in *Mawsu'at Rasa'il,* 2:49, excerpt no. 87. Cf. al-Ghazali, *Ihya'*, 3:267 (Asin, pp. 383–84, no. 54; Mansur, no. 136; Robson, pp. 97–99); al-Makki, *Qut,* 1:255 (Asin, pp. 387–88, no. 54 quater; Mansur, no. 26); al-Turtushi, *Siraj,* pp. 79–80; Ibn 'Asakir, *Sirat,* p. 95, no. 82; al-Abshihi, *al-Mustatraf,* 2:263–64 (Asin, p. 385, no. 54 bis and pp. 386–87, no. 54 ter; slight variation).

A moral fable of perennial interest in many cultures. In the original Arabic, this fable is immediately followed by another, narrated by al-Hasan al-Basri from Muhammad. It is introduced with the words: "You and I and the world are like a group of people lost in a desert and on the point of death." This group then meets a man who guides them to greenery and water. When the man calls on them to move once again to greenery and water unlike what they have had, most disobey him, preferring what they have already enjoyed. The man and his few faithful followers then depart. Those who remain are attacked by enemies and killed or taken captive.

109

Jesus said, "Truly I say to you, just as a sick man looks at food and does not enjoy it because he is in pain, so a lover of this world does not enjoy worship or appreciate its delights because of his love for this world. Truly I say to you, if a beast of burden is left unridden and undisciplined, it grows headstrong and changes its character. So also if the heart is not softened by mention of death and the strain of worship, it grows hard and callous. Truly I say to you, if a water skin is not torn or withered, it may hold honey. So also if the heart is not torn by desires, defiled by avarice, or hardened by luxury, it can be a vessel of wisdom."

Abu Bakr ibn Abi al-Dunya (d. 281/894), *Kitab Dhamm al-Dunya,* in *Mawsu'at Rasa'il,* 2:52, excerpt no. 90. Cf. al-Ghazali, *Ihya'*, 3:211 (Asin, p. 377, no. 47; Mansur, no. 129; Robson, pp. 68–69).

In the Islamic literature on prophecy and prophets, Jesus came to be known as the prophet of the heart. This saying is an early example of his teaching on the heart. The wisdom referred to at the end is *hikmah,* a Qur'anic term denoting the understanding that accompanies faith and makes it possible.

110

Jesus was asked, "Why do you not acquire a house to shelter you?" He replied, "Let us be satisfied with the ruins of those who came before us."

Abu Bakr ibn Abi al-Dunya (d. 281/894), *Kitab Dhamm al-Dunya,* in *Mawsu'at Rasa'il,* 2:68, excerpt no. 129. Cf. al-Ghazali, *Ihya'*, 3:200 (Asin, p. 369, no. 36; Mansur, no. 121; Robson, p. 65).

See Saying 60, above.

111

Jesus said, "The world existed and I was not in it, and it shall exist and I shall not be in it. All I have are my days which I am now living. If I sin in them, I am indeed a sinner."

Abu Bakr ibn Abi al-Dunya (d. 281/894), *Kitab Dhamm al-Dunya,* in *Mawsu'at Rasa'il,* 2:105, excerpt no. 216. Cf. Ibn 'Asakir, *Sirat,* p. 182, no. 213 (variant).

This saying may serve to emphasize the human nature of Jesus by denying his eternity on the one hand and suggesting the possibility of his sinfulness on the other.

112

Jesus said, "It is a mark of the ascetics in this world that they shun the company of any companion who does not desire what they desire."

Abu Bakr ibn Abi al-Dunya (d. 281/894), *Kitab Dhamm al-Dunya,* in *Mawsu'at Rasa'il,* 2:109, excerpt no. 225.

This austere shunning of anyone not desiring what the ascetic desires is more typical of early Muslim ascetics than of the Jesus of the Gospels.

113

Jesus passed by a village and found its people lying dead in its yards and alleys. He turned to his disciples and said, "These men died from divine anger, for otherwise they would have buried one another." "Spirit of God," they said, "would that we could learn what happened to them." Jesus asked God Almighty, and God revealed that he should call upon them when night fell and they would answer him. So when night fell, Jesus walked onto high ground and called out, "O men of the village!" "At your command, Spirit of God," answered one of them. Jesus asked, "What is your state and what is your story?" The man replied, "We went to sleep in good health and woke up to find ourselves in the pit." "How so?" Jesus asked. The man replied, "Because of our love of the world and our subservience to sinners." "How was your love of the world?" Jesus asked. "As the child loves its mother," said the man. "When she approached we were happy, and when she departed we became sad and wept for her." Jesus asked, "Why did your fellow villagers not answer me?" "Because they are fettered with fetters of fire and guarded by harsh and mighty angels," the man replied. "Then how is it that it was you who answered me from among them?" Jesus asked. "Because I was with them but not of them," the man replied. "When the calamity struck them, I too was struck down. I am now suspended on the edge of the precipice of hell, and I do not know whether I shall escape from it or be plunged into it." Then Jesus said to his disciples, "In truth, the eating of barley bread with uncrushed salt, the wearing of haircloth, and going to sleep on dunghills is more than enough if one desires to be safe and secure in this world."

Abu Bakr ibn Abi al-Dunya (d. 281/894), *Kitab Dhamm al-Dunya,* in *Mawsu'at Rasa'il,* 2:128–29, excerpt no. 282. Cf. Ibn Babuya, *'Ilal,* 2:151–52; al-Ghazali, *Ihya'*, 3:201 (Asin, pp. 371–72, no. 39; Mansur, no. 123; Robson, pp. 95–96).

A resurrection fable where Jesus interrogates one of the dead. The expression "harsh and mighty angels" is from Qur'an 66:6. This is also an early description of hell. The fable ends with an admonition we have already encountered; see Sayings 42 and 67, above.

114

Jesus said, "You work for a petty world and you ignore the great afterlife, and upon you all death shall pass."

Abu Bakr ibn Abi al-Dunya (d. 281/894), *Kitab Dhamm al-Dunya,* in *Mawsu'at Rasa'il,* 2:129–30, excerpt no. 286.

The image of a "petty" world contrasted with a "great" afterlife occurs also in à saying attributed to an early Muslim ascetic. See the excerpt immediately following this one in Ibn Abi al-Dunya (no. 287).

115

Jesus said, "He who seeks worldly things is like the man who drinks sea water: the more he drinks the more thirsty he becomes, until it kills him."

Abu Bakr ibn Abi al-Dunya (d. 281/894), *Kitab Dhamm al-Dunya,* in *Mawsu'at Rasa'il,* 2:146, excerpt no. 342. Cf. Ibn Hamdun, *Al-Tadhkira,* 1:249, no. 638; al-Ghazali, *Ihya'*, 3:212 (Asin, p. 378, no. 48; Mansur, no. 130; Robson, p. 69); Ibn 'Asakir, *Sirat,* p. 147, no. 150.

The bitter taste of sea water is mentioned twice in the Qur'an: at 25:53 and 35:12. The saying was also found in Syriac literature; see E. A. Wallis Budge, *The Laughable Stories Collected by Mar Gregory John Bar-Hebraeus* (London: Luzac, 1897), p. 28, no. 110, where it is attributed to an Indian sage.

116

Jesus said, "O Disciples, be ascetics in this world and you will pass through it without anxiety."

Abu Bakr ibn Abi al-Dunya (d. 281/894), *Kitab Dhamm al-Dunya,* in *Mawsu'at Rasa'il,* 2:146, excerpt no. 344.

117

Jesus said, "Woe to you, evil scholars! For the sake of a despicable world and a calamitous desire, you squander the kingdom of paradise and forget the terror of the Day of Judgment."

Abu Bakr ibn Abi al-Dunya (d. 281/894), *Kitab Dhamm al-Dunya,* in *Mawsu'at Rasa'il,* 2:158, excerpt no. 377.

See Sayings 92 and 94, above.

118

It is related that Jesus looked at Satan and said, "Here is the pillar of the world. It is to the world that he went out, and it is the world that he demanded. I do not share anything of it with him, not even a stone to place beneath my head. Nor will I laugh much in it until I have left it."

Abu Bakr ibn Abi al-Dunya (d. 281/894), *Kitab Dhamm al-Dunya,* in *Mawsu'at Rasa'il,* 2:168, excerpt no. 409.

The word *urkun,* translated here as "pillar," is intriguing. The classical dictionaries derive it from the root *rkn* and state that it means a ruler or grandee. But they often equate it with the word *dihqan,* the ancient Persian countryside potentate who continued well into the Islamic period. Hence, doubt remains as to whether it is really of Arabic origin. It is tempting to identify it with the archon or archons of Gnostic gospels, the so-called world rulers of whom the devil was one. The image of the stone beneath the head is repeated in the saying that follows.

119

Satan passed by while Jesus was reclining his head upon a stone. "So, then, Jesus, you have been satisfied with a stone in this world!" Jesus removed the stone from beneath his head, threw it at him, and said, "Take this stone, and the world with it! I have no need of either."

Abu Bakr ibn Abi al-Dunya (d. 281/894), *Kitab Dhamm al-Dunya,* in *Mawsu'at Rasa'il,* 2:168, excerpt no. 410. Cf. Miskawayh, *al-Hikma al-Khalida,* 129 (an "idler" instead of Satan); al-Ghazali, *Ihya'*, 4:11 (variant) (Asin, pp. 392–93, no. 63; Mansur, no. 145; Robson, p. 70); Ibn 'Asakir, *Sirat,* p. 127, no. 112.

In this charming story, Jesus is jeered at by Satan for having finally succumbed to a worldly comfort. For other references to stones, see Sayings 47 and 71, above.

120

Jesus was asked, "Teach us one act through which God may come to love us." He answered, "Hate the world and God will love you."

Abu Bakr ibn Abi al-Dunya (d. 281/894), *Kitab Dhamm al-Dunya,* in *Mawsu'at Rasa'il,* 2:170, excerpt no. 415. Cf. al-Ghazali, *Ihya'*, 3:201 (Asin, p. 373, no. 41; Mansur, no. 125; Robson, p. 67).

There are echoes here of John 15:18–19. The commandment to hate the world is also quite common among the sayings of the Egyptian desert fathers; see, e.g., Ward, *The Sayings of the Desert Fathers,* p. 8, no. 33.

121

Jesus said, "O disciples, be satisfied with what is vile in this world while your faith remains whole and sound, just as the people of this world are satisfied with what is vile in religion while their world remains whole and sound."

Abu Bakr ibn Abi al-Dunya (d. 281/894), *Kitab Dhamm al-Dunya,* in *Mawsu'at Rasa'il,* 2:179, excerpt no. 449.

A graceful turn of phrase, in the spirit of Adab.

122

Jesus said, "God likes His servant to learn a craft whereby he can become independent of people, and God hates a servant who acquires religious knowledge and then adopts it as a craft."

Abu Bakr ibn Abi al-Dunya (d. 281/894), *Kitab Islah al-Mal,* in *Mawsu'at Rasa'il,* 2:95, excerpt no. 316.

For the need to earn a livelihood, see the resurrection story in Saying 247, below. Religious knowledge, in contrast, imposes awesome moral responsibilities, as seen in many sayings above.

123

Among the revelations of God to Jesus is the following: "It is only right and proper for the servants of God to display humility before God when God displays His bounty to them."

Abu Bakr ibn Abi al-Dunya (d. 281/894), *Kitab al-Shukr lillah,* in *Mawsu'at Rasa'il,* 3:53–54, excerpt no. 127. Cf. al-Ghazali, *Ihya'*, 3:332 (Asin, p. 391, no. 58; Mansur, no. 140; Robson, p. 78).

The speaker here is the Negus of Ethiopia, who, according to Muslim tradition, granted hospitality to a group of very early Muslims fleeing Meccan persecution. The Muslims found him one day sitting on the ground. In explanation, he told them that he had just received news of a Muslim victory and was duly grateful to God. He then recited to them this saying of Jesus. The Negus is often depicted in Muslim sources as a pious Christian king who nevertheless recognized the truth of Muhammad's mission, thus becoming a type or model of sincerity of faith. That God's favors will be multiplied if man gives thanks for them echoes Qur'an 14:7.

124

John the son of Zachariah met Jesus the son of Mary, John smiling of face and welcoming while Jesus was frowning and gloomy. Jesus said to John, "You smile as if you feel secure." John said to Jesus, "You frown as if you are in despair." God revealed, "What John does is dearer to Us."

Abu Bakr ibn Abi al-Dunya (d. 281/894), *Kitab al-Ikhwan,* p. 190 (no. 136). Cf. Ibn 'Abd Rabbihi, *al-'Iqd,* 6:380 (Asin, p. 544, no. 120; Mansur, no. 21; Robson, p. 108); idem, 6:380–81 (Asin, p. 544, no. 121; Mansur, no. 22; Robson, pp. 108–9); Abu Hayyan, *al-Basa'ir wa al-Dhakha'ir,* 7:197 (no. 379); idem, *Risala fi al-Sadaqa wa al-Sadiq,* p. 105; Ibn 'Aqil, *Kitab al-Funun,* 2:635–36; Ibn 'Asakir, *Sirat,* p. 200, no. 246; al-Damiri, *Hayat,* 2:205 (Mansur, no. 233).

This encounter between Jesus and John is perhaps meant as a veiled criticism of excessive asceticism which borders on despair. To a Muslim audience, the saying would be interpreted as a reminder of God's infinite mercy. The words of God at the end imply that in some respects Jesus is less meritorious than John. The story itself recalls the well-known Greek anecdote about the encounter between the philosophers Democritus and Heraclitus; cf. Montaigne, *Essays* (Harmondsworth: Penguin, 1960), p. 432. The same attitudes are reported of two celebrated early Muslim figures, al-Hasan al-Basri and Ibn Sirin (d. 110/728); see Ibn Sa'd, *Tabaqat,* 7:162.

125

They asked Jesus, "Show us an act by which we may enter paradise." Jesus said, "Do not speak at all." They said, "We cannot do this." Jesus replied, "Then speak only good."

Abu Bakr ibn Abi al-Dunya (d. 281/894), *Kitab al-Samt wa Adab al-Lisan,* p. 215 (no. 46). Cf. Miskawayh, *al-Hikma,* p. 123; al-Ghazali, *Ihya'*, 3:107; Ibn 'Asakir, *Sirat,* p. 158, no. 172 (Mansur, no. 110).

The virtue of silence is a common theme in the wisdom literature of the Near East. This saying is taken from a work of Ibn Abi'l Dunya devoted entirely to this subject. Similar sayings are also ascribed to Muhammad; see, e.g., Ibn al-Mubarak, *Kitab al-Zuhd,* p. 125, no. 368.

Bibliography of Arabic Sources

Al-Abi, Abū Sa'd Mansur b. al-Husayn (d. 421/1030). *Nathr al-Durr.* Ed. Muhammad 'Ali Qarna et al. Cairo: al-Hay'a al-Misriyya al-'Amma, 1981–1991.

Al-Abshihi, Baha' al-Din Muhammad b. Ahmad (d. 892/1487). *Al-Mustatraf fi kulli Fannin Mustazraf.* Cairo: al-Matba'a al-'Amira al-'Uthmaniyya, A.H. 1306.

Abū al-Faraj al-Baghdadi, Qudama b. Ja'far (d. 337/948). *Kitab Naqd al-Nathr* [attributed]. Ed. Taha Husayn and 'Abd al-Hamid al-'Abbadi. Cairo: Dar al-Kurub al-Misriyya, 1933.

Abū Hayyan al-Tawhidi, 'Ali b. Muhammad al-Baghdadi (d. after 400/1010). *Risala fi al-Sadaqa wa al-Sadiq.* Istanbul: Matba'at al-Jawa'ib, A.H. 1301.

—— *Al-Imta' wa al-Mu'anusa.* Ed. Ahmad Amin and Ahmad al Zayn. Cairo: Lajnat al-Ta'lif wa al-Tarjama wa al-Nashr, 1942.

—— *Al-Basa'ir wa al-Dhakha'ir.* Vols. 1–3, ed. Ibrahim al-Kaylani. Damascus: Maktabat Atlas, 1965–1977.

—— *Al-Basa'ir wa al-Dhakha'ir.* Vol. 7, ed. Wadad al-Qadi. Libya: al-Dar al-'Arabiyya li-l-Kitab, 1978.

Abū Nu'aym al-Isbahani, Ahmad b. 'Abdallah (d. 430/1038). *Hilyat al-Awliya' wa Tabaqat al-Asfiya'.* Cairo: Matba'at al-Sa'ada, 1932–1938.

Abū Rifa'a ai-Fasawi, 'Umara b. Wathima al-Farisi (d. 289/902). *Les Légendes prophétiques dans l'Islam.* Ed. Raif G. Khuri. Wiesbaden: Harrassovitz, 1978.

Abū Talib al-Makki, Muhammad b. 'Ali (d. 386/996). *Qut al-Qulub fi Mu'amalat al-Mahbub.* Cairo: al-Matba'a al-Maymaniyya, A.M. 1310.

Al-'Amiri, Abū al-Hasan Muhammad b. Yusuf al-Naysabūri (d. 381/992). *Al-Sa'ada wa al-Is'ad.* Ed. Mujtaba Minowi. Wiesbaden: Franz Steiner, 1957–1958.

Al-Antaki, Dawud b. 'Umar al-Darir (d. 1008/1599). *Tazyin al-Aswaq bi-Tafsil Ashwaq al-'Ushshaq.* Ed. Muhammad al-Tanji. Beirut: 'Alam al-Kutub, 1993.

Al-Baladhuri, Ahmad b. Yahya (d. 279/892) *Ansab al-Ashraf.* Vol. 2, ed. M. B. al-Mahmudi. Beirut: Mu'assasat al-A'zami, 1974.

Al-Balawi, Abū al-Hajjaj Yusuf b. Muhammad (d. 604/1207). *Kitab Alif Ba'.* Cairo; Jam'iyyat al-Ma'arif, A.H. 1287.

Al-Damiri, Kamal al-Din Muhammad b. Musa (d. 808/1405). *Hayat al-Hayawan al-Kubra*. Cairo: al-Matba'a al-Maymaniyya, A.M. 1305.

Al-Ghazali, Abū Hamid Muhammad b. Muhammad (d. 505/1111). *Al-Tibr al-Masbuk fi Nasihat al-Muluk*. Cairo: Matba'at al-Adab wa al-Mu'ayyad, A.H. 1317.

—— *Minhaj al-'Abidin*. Cairo: al-Matba'a al-Husayniyya, A.H. 1322.

—— *Ihya' 'Ulum al-Din*. Cairo; Mustafa al-Babi al-Halabi, 1939.

—— *Ayyuha al-Walad*. Ed. 'Ali al-Qaradaghi. Beirut: Dar al-Basha'ir al-Islamiyya, 1985.

—— *Mukashafat al-Qulub al-Muqarrib ila Hadrat 'Allam al-Ghuyub*. Cairo: Matba'at Muhammad 'Atif, n.d.

Al-Hakim al-Tirmidhi, Abū 'Abdallah Muhammad b. 'Ali (d. 285/898). *Al-Salat wa Maqasidiha*. Ed. Husni Zaydan. Cairo: Dar al-Kitab al-'Arabi, 1965.

Ibn 'Abd al-Barr al-Qurtubi, Abū 'Umar Yusuf (d. 463/1071). *Jami' Bayan al-'Ilm wa Fadlihi*. Medina: al-Maktaba al-'Ilmiyya, n.d.

—— *Mukhtasar Jami 'Bayan al-'Ilm wa Fadlihi*. Cairo: Matba'at al-Mawsu'at, A.H. 1320.

—— *Bahjat al-Majalis*. Ed. M. M. al-Khawli. Cairo: Dar al-Katib al-'Arabi, n.d.

Ibn 'Abd al-Hakam, 'Abd al-Rahman b. 'Abdallah al-Misri (d. 257/870). *Futuh Misr wa Akhbaruha*. Ed. Charles Torrey. Leiden: E. J. Brill, 1920.

Ibn 'Abd Rabbihi, Ahmad b. Muhammad al-Qurtubi (d. 328/940). *Al-'Iqd al-Farid*. Cairo: Lajnat al-Ta'lif wa al-Tarjama wa al-Nashr, 1940–1953.

Ibn Abi al-Dunya, Abū Bakr 'Abdallah b. Muhammad (d. 281/894). *Kitab al-Ashraf*. Ed. Walid Qassab. Doha/Qatar: Dar al-Thaqafa, 1993.

—— *Al-Ikhwan*. Ed. Mustafa 'Ata. Beirut: Dar al-Kutub al-'Ilmiyya, 1988.

—— *Kitab al-Samt wa Adab al-Lisan*. Ed. Najm Khalaf. Beirut: Dar al-Gharb al-Islami, 1986.

—— *Mawsu'at Rasa'il Ibn Abi al-Dunya*. Ed. Mustafa 'Ata. Beirut: Mu'assasat al-Kutub al-Thaqafiyya, 1993.

Ibn Abi al-Hadid, 'Abd al-Hamid b. Hibatullah (d. 655/1257). *Shahr Nahj al-Balagha*. Ed. M. A. F. Ibrahim. Cairo: 'Isa al-Babi al-Halabi, 1959–1964.

Ibn 'Aqil, Abū al-Wafa' 'Ali al-Baghdadi (d. 513/1119). *Kitab al-Funun*. Ed. George Maqdisi. Beirut: Dar al-Mashriq, 1970.

Ibn 'Arabi, Abū 'Abdallah Muhyi al-Din Muhammad b. 'Ali (d. 638/(240). *Al-Futuhat al-Makkiyya*. Cairo, A.H. 1305.

—— *Muhadarat al-Abrar wa Musamarat al-Akhyar fi al-Adabiyyat wa al-Nawadir wa al-Akhbar*. Cairo: Matba'at al-Sa'ada, 1906.

Ibn 'Asakir, Abū al-Qasim 'Ali b. al-Hasan (d. 571/1175). *Tarikh Madinat Dimashq*. Vol. 1, ed. Salah al-Din al-Munajjid. Damascus: al-Majma' al-'Ilmi al-'Arabi, 1954.

—— *Sirat al-Sayyid al-Masih*. Ed. Sulayman Murad. 'Amman: Dar al-Shuruq, 1996.

Ibn Babūya al-Qummi, Abū Ja'far Muhammad b. 'Ali (d. 381/99). *'Ilal al-Shara'i'*. Ed. Fadlallah Tabataba'i. Tehran, A.H. 1377.

Ibn Hamdun, Abū al-Ma'ali Muhammad b. al-Hasan (d. 562/1166). *Al-Tadhkira al-Hamduniyya*. Ed. Ihsan 'Abbas. Beirut: Ma'had al-Inma' al-'Arabi, 1983.

Ibn Hanbal, Abū 'Abdallah Ahmad b. Muhammad al-Shaybani (d. 241/855). *Kitab al-Zuhd*. Ed. Muhammad Zaghlul. Beirut: Dar al-Kitab al-'Arabi, 1988.

—— *Kitab al-Wara'*. Ed. Muhammad Zaghlul. Beirut: Dar al-Kitab al-'Arabi, 1988.

Ibn al-Hanbali, Abū al-Faraj 'Abd al-Rahman b. Najm (d. 634/1236). *Al-Istis'ad bi-man Laqaytuhu min Salihi al-'Ibad fi al-Bilad*, in *Shadharat min Kutubin Mafquda*, ed. Ihsan 'Abbas. Beirut: Dar al-Gharb al-Islami, 1988, pp. 175–205.

Ibn Hisham, 'Abd al-Malik (d. 218/833). *Kitab al-Tijan fi Muluk Himyar*. Ed. F. Krenkow. Hyderabad, India: Da'irat al-Ma'arif, 1928.

—— *Al-Sira al-Nabawiyya*. Ed. M. al-Saqqa et al. Cairo: Mustafa al-Babi al-Halabi, 1936.

Ibn al-Jawzi, Abū al-Faraj 'Abd al-Rahman b. 'Ali (d. 597/1201). *Al-Adhkiya'*. Ed. Usama al-Rifa'i. Damascus: Maktabat al-Ghazali, 1976.

—— *Dhamm al-Hawa*. Ed. Mustafa 'Abd al-Wahid. Cairo: Dar al-Kutub al-Haditha, 1962.

Ibn Maja, Muhammad b. Yazid (d. 274/887). *Al-Sunan*. Ed. M. F. 'Abd al-Baqi. Cairo: Dar Ihya' al-Kutub al-'Arabiyya, 1952.

Ibn al-Mubarak, ʿAbdallah al-Marwazi (d. 181/797). *Kitab al-Zuhd wa al-Raqaʾiq*. Ed. Habib al-Rahman al-Aʿzami. Beirut: Dar al-Kutub al-ʿIlmiyya, n.d.

Ibn Munabbih, Hammam (d. 131/748). *Sahifat Hammam b. Munabbih*. Ed. Muhammad Hamidullah. Damascus: al-Majmaʿ al-ʿIlmi al-ʿArabi, 1953.

Ibn Qudama al-Maqdisi, Abū Muhammad ʿAbdallah b. Ahmad (d. 620/1223). *Kitab al-Tawwabin*. Ed. George Maqdisi. Damascus: al-Maʿhad al-Faransi li-l-Dirasat al-ʿArabiyya, 1961.

Ibn Qutayba, Abū Muhammad ʿAbdallah b. Muslim (d. 271/884). *Kitab ʿUyun al-Akhbar*. Cairo: Dar al-Kutub al-Misriyya, 1925–1930.

Ibn al-Qutiyya, Abū Bakr Muhammad b. ʿUmar al-Qurtubi (d. 367/977). *Tarikh Iftitah al-Andalus*. Ed. Ibrahim al-Abyari. Cairo: Dar al-Kitab al-Misri and Dar al-Kitab al-Lubnani, 1989.

Ibn Saʿd, Muhammad (d. 230/845). *Al-Tabaqat al-Kubra*. Beirut: Dar Sadir, n.d.

Ibn al-Salah, Abū ʿArar ʿUthman b. ʿAbd al-Rahman (d. 643/1245). *Fatawa wa Masaʾil Ibn al-Salah*. Ed. ʿAbd al-Muʿti Qalʿaji. Beirut: Dar al-Maʿrifa, 1986.

Ibn al-Sariyy, Hannad (d. 243/857). *Kitab al-Zuhd*. Ed. ʿAbd al-Rahman al-Firyawaʾi. Kuwait: Dar al-Khulafaʾ li-l Kitab al-Islami, 1985.

Ibn Sida, Abū al-Hasan ʿAli b. Ismaʿil al-Andalusi (d. 458/1066). *Kitab al-Mukhassas*. Bulaq: al-Matbaʿa al-Kubra al-Amiriyya, A.H. 1316.

Ibn Wasil, Jamal al-Din Muhammad b. Salim (d. 697/1298). *Mufarrij al-Kurub fi Akhbar Bani Ayyub*. Ed. Jamal al-Din al-Shayyal. Cairo: Jamiʿat Fuʾad al-Awwal, 1953.

Ikhwan al-Safaʾ (d. fourth/tenth century). *Rasaʾil Ikhwan al-Safaʾ wa Khillan al-Wafaʾ*. Ed. Khayr al-Din al-Zirikli. Cairo: al-Matbaʿa al-ʿArabiyya, 1928.

Al-Jahiz, Abū ʿUthman ʿAmi b. Bahr (d. 255/868). *Al-Bayan wa al-Tabyin*. Ed. ʿAbd al-Salam Harun. Cairo: Matbaʿat Lajnat al-Taʾlif wa al-Tarjama wa al-Nashr, 1949.

—— *Kitab Kitman al-Sirr wa Hifz al-Lisan*, in *Rasaʾil al-Jahiz*. Ed. ʿAbd al-Salam Harun. Beirut: Dar al-Jil, 1991. Vol. 1, pp. 139–172.

—— *Al-Mahasin wa al-Addad*. Cairo: Matbaʿat al-Furuh, A.H. 1332.

Al-Kalabadhi, Abū Bakr Muhammad b. Ishaq (d. 380/990). *Al-Taʿarruf li-Madhhab Ahl al-Tasawwuf*. Ed. Arthur John Arberry. Cairo: Matbaʿat al-Saʿada, 1933.

Al-Kulayni, Abū Jaʿfar Muhammad b. Yaʿqub (d. 329/941). *Al-Usul min al-Kafi*. Ed. ʿAli Akbar al-Ghaffari. Beirut: Dar al-Adwaʾ, 1985.

Majlisi, Mulla Muhammad Baqir (d. 1110/1698). *Bihar al-Anwar*. Tehran: Dar al-Kutub al-Islamiyya, n.d. (1957?).

Al-Mawardi, Abū al-Hasan ʿAli b. Muhammad al-Basri (d. 450/1058). *al-Ahkam al-Sultaniyya*. Cairo: Matbaʿat al-Watan, A.H. 1298.

—— *Adab al-Dunya wa al-Din*. Ed. Mustafa al-Saqqa. Cairo: Mustafa al-Babi al-Halabi, 1955.

Miskawayh, Abū ʿAli Ahmad b. Muhammad (d. 421/1030). *Al-Hikma al-Khalida*. Ed. ʿAbd al-Rahman Badawi. Cairo: Maktabat al-Nahda al-Misriyya, 1952.

Al-Mubarrad, Abū al-ʿAbbas Muhammad b. Yazid (d. 285/898). *Al-Fadil*. Ed. ʿAbd al-ʿAziz al-Maymani. Cairo: Dar al-Kutub al-Misriyya, 1956.

—— *Al-Kamil*. Ed, M. Abūʾl Fadl Ibrahim and A. Shahata. Cairo: Dar Nahdat Misr, n.d. (1970?).

Al-Mubashshir b. Fatik, Abūʾl Wafaʾ (wrote 445/1053). *Mukhtar al-Hikam wa Mahasin al-Kalim*. Ed. ʿAbd al-Rahman Badawi. Beirut: al-Muʾassasa al-ʿArabiyya liʾl Dirasat waʾl Nashr, 1980.

Muslim b. al-Hajjaj (d. 261/875) *Sahih Muslim*. Beirut: Dar al-Maʿrifa, 1972.

Al-Qurashi, Abū Zayd Muhammad b. Abiʾl Khattab (d. circa 171/787). *Jamharat Ashʿar al-ʿArab*. Beirut: Dar Beirut, 1984.

Al-Qushayri, Abū al-Qasim (d. 465/1073). *Al-Risala al-Qushayriyya fi ʿIlm al-Tasawwuf*. Cairo: Mustafa al-Babi al-Halabi, A.H. 1318 (A.D. 1900).

Al-Raghib al-Isfahani, Abū al-Qasim al-Husayn b. Muhammad (d. early fifth/early eleventh century). *Muhadarat al-Udabaʾ*. Beirut: Maktabat al-Hayat, n.d.

Al-Samarqandi, Abū al-Layth Nasr b. Muhammad (d. 373/983). *Tanbih al-Ghafilin*. Cairo: al-Matbaʿa al-Yusufiyya, n.d.

Al-Siraʿrani, ʿAbd al-Wahhab b. Ahmad al-Misri (d. 973/1565). *Al-Tabaqat al-Kubra*. Cairo, 1286.

—— *Lata'if al-Minan wa al-Akhlaq*. Cairo: Dar al-Tiba'a, A.H. 1288.
Sibt Ibn al-Jawzi, Shams al-Din Yusuf b. Quzughli (d. 654/1256). *Mir'at al-Zaman*. Hyderabad, India: Da'irat al-Ma'arif al-'Uthmaniyya, n.d.
Al-Suhrawardi, Shihab al-Din 'Umar (d. 632/1234), *'Awarif al-Ma'arif*, in the margins of Ghazali, *Ihya' 'Ulum al-Din*. Cairo: Al-Matba'a al-Maymaniyya, A.H. 1306.
Al-Tabari, Muhammad b. Jarir (d. 310/923) *Tafsir al-Qur'an*. Cairo: al-Matba'a al-Maymaniyya, 1903.
Al-Turtushi, Muhammad b. al-Walid b. Abi Randaqa (d. 520/1126). *Siraj al-Muluk*. Ed. J. al-Bayati. London: Riyad al-Rayyis, 1990.
Al-Waqidi, Muhammad b. 'Umar (d. 207/823). *Al-Maghazi*. Ed. J. Marsden Jones. London: Oxford University Press, 1966.
Warram b. Abi Firas, Abū al-Husayn (d. 606/1208). *Majmu'at Warram; Tanbih al-Kkawatir wa Nuzhat al-Nawazir*. Ed. Muhammad Akhundi, Tehran, Dar al-Kutub al-Sultaniyya, n.d.
Al-Zabidi, Muhammad Murtada b. Muhammad al-Husayni (d. 1205/1791). *Ithaf al-Sada al-Muttaqin bi-Sharh Asrar Ihya' 'Ulum al-Din*. Cairo: al-Matba'a al-Maymaniyya, A.H. 1311.
Al-Zamakhshari, Mahmud b. 'Umar (d. 538/1144). *Rabi' al-Abrar*. Ed. Salim al-Nu'aymi. Baghdad: Matba'at al-'Ani, n.d.
Al-Zubayr b. Bakkar (d. 256/870) *Jamharat Nasal, Quraysh*. Vol. 1. Ed. M. M. Shakir. Cairo, 1962.

Bibliography of English Sources

Bentley, Layton. *The Gnostic Scriptures*, Anchor Bible Reference Library. New York: Doubleday, 1995.
Ward, Benedicta. *Sayings of the Desert Fathers*. Spencer, Massachusetts: Cistercian Publications, 1987.

20 The Praiseworthy Amity of Christians

Jane Dammen McAuliffe

The most striking example of Qur'ānic praise of Christians occurs in *sūrat al-mā'idah* (5):82–83. These verses figure prominently in virtually all attempts to base Muslim-Christian rapprochement upon specific Qur'ānic texts. The passage itself constitutes an exegetical challenge of considerable proportions. Within the verses one finds a configuration of seven categories: the Jews, the idolaters (*mushrikūn*), 'those who believe', the Christians, priests and monks (*qissīsūn wa-ruhbān*), those who hear what was sent down upon Muḥammad and weep, and, finally, those who bear witness (*shāhidūn*). Obviously, issues of identification will occupy a considerable portion of the exegetical effort expended on this pericope, as will the desire to ascertain the circumstances surrounding this revelation (*asbāb al-nuzūl*). One possible translation *of sūrat al-mā'idah* (5):82–83 is as follows:

> You will find the people most intensely hostile to the believers are the Jews and the idolaters. You will surely find those closest in friendship to those who believe to be those who say "We are Christians." That is because among them are priests and monks and because they are not arrogant. (82)
>
> When they heard what was sent down to the Messenger their eyes overflowed with tears because of what they recognized as the truth. They say, "Our Lord, we believe, so write us with those who testify (*shāhidūn*)." (83)

Those Persons Who Elicit Praise

Al-Ṭabarī begins his discussion of 5:82 with a rapid survey of the principal groups mentioned. He then proceeds to evaluate the various views proposed about the occasion for this revelation. The first of two competing theories advanced is one that associates the verse with the contact made between Muḥammad and the Abyssinian king, the Najāshī.[1] Different scenarios for this are sketched, but the first one presented by al-Ṭabarī on the authority of Sa'īd b. Jubayr runs as follows: the Najāshī sent a delegation of his Christian subjects to the Prophet who recited from the Qur'ān for them. As they listened, they were overcome and immediately declared themselves Muslims. Upon their return to the Najāshī, they told him all they had learned and he, too, entered Islam and remained a believer until his death.[2] Subsequent *ḥadīths* included in al-Ṭabarī's commentary flesh out this brief sketch.

One such from Mujāhid adds the fact that this Christian delegation formed part of the group that returned with Ja'far b. Abī Ṭālib from Abyssinia. Another, more lengthy *ḥadīth* from Ibn 'Abbās fills in the background with an account of what occurred during the first Muslim emigration to Abyssinia. A synopsis of this *ḥadīth*, highlighting the main characters and events, will doubtless be useful in understanding both this and subsequent commentaries: Muḥammad, fearing the escalating persecution of his followers in Mecca, sent a group headed by Ja'far b. Abī Ṭālib, Ibn Mas'ūd, and 'Uthmān b. Maẓūn to seek the protection of the Najāshī, the king of Abyssinia.[3] When the Prophet's Meccan opponents, here tagged as the 'idolaters (*mushrikūn*)', discovered this scheme they quickly dispatched their own delegation, led by 'Amr b. al-'Āṣ.[4] This group reached the Najāshī first. They addressed the king saying: "There is a man from among us who declares the minds and thoughts of the Quraysh to be stupid. He claims to be a prophet! He has sent a group (*raht*) to you in order to alienate you from your people. We wanted to come and inform you about them."[5]

The Najāshī was not immediately persuaded and remained willing to give the Muslim deputation a hearing. When they finally arrived, the king questioned them about Muḥammad's thoughts on Jesus and Mary. The group's spokesman made this response: "He [Muḥammad] says that Jesus is the servant (*'abd*) of God and the word (*kalimah*) of God, which God cast into Mary, and His spirit (*rūḥ*). About Mary he says that she is the virgin (*al-'adhrā' al-batūl*)."[6] The Najāshī responded to this statement with an illustrative command: "Pick up," he said, "a twig from the ground: between what your leader said about Jesus and Mary and what I believe there is not more than a twig's worth of difference."[7] Frustrated in their plans, the *mushrikūn* rivals left in disgust.

Among the group that later returned to the Prophet, according to a *ḥadīth* from al-Suddī, were a number of Abyssinian priests and monks. These were the ones who were so struck by the Qur'ānic verses that Muḥammad recited to them that they immediately converted. They then went back to the Najāshī and convinced him of the validity of this new religion so that he too converted and started back with them to Muḥammad. The *ḥadīth* closes with the statement that the king died on this trip and when the news reached Muḥammad, he prayed for him.[8]

Quite different is the second major interpretive theory advanced to identify these *Christians*. This one is far less specific or colorful. Rather it views the phrase *those who say "We are Christians"* as a general reference to those who in an earlier time believed in Jesus and followed his teaching. "However when God sent His Prophet, Muḥammad, they acknowledged him as a true prophet and believed in him, recognizing that what he brought was the truth."[9]

Al-Ṭabarī balances these two theories with a third that acknowledges the insufficiency of available information, a recognition to be found not infrequently in his commentary. He grounds himself in a very literal reading of the text, from which he seems loath to extrapolate. All that can be asserted, according to the exegete, is that God described a people who say "*We are Christians*" and whom the Prophet would find friendliest to the believers. "But," al-Ṭabarī emphatically asserts, "He did not name them for us."[10] It may be that the Najāshī and those around him were meant or perhaps the pre-Islamic followers of Jesus were intended. This exegete maintains that the text offers no real support for either option.

Two of these possible referents are accepted by al-Ṭūsī as well. The first, garnered from accounts of al-Suddī and Mujāhid, comprises the Abyssinian king and his followers who became Muslims, especially those who returned from Abyssinia with Ja'far b. Abī Ṭālib. The alternative proposed by Qatādah is "a people of the *ahl al-kitāb* who lived in accord with the truth as strict adherents of the law of Jesus (*mutamassikūn bi-sharī'ati 'Īsā*). When Muḥammad came, they believed in him."[11]

While al-Ṭabarī's only comment on the phrase *the Jews and the idolaters* (*al-mushrikūn*) is to explain the latter term as "the worshipers of idols (*al-awthān*) who take idols as gods to be worshiped rather than God," al-Ṭūsī explores the connection between the two terms. He attributes the association to political connivance between the two groups: "The Jews aided the *mushrikūn* against the believers despite the fact that the believers had faith in the prophethood of Moses and the Torah which he brought." The fact that the Muslim belief in Moses and the Torah has not resulted in Jewish congeniality clearly puzzles al-Ṭūsī. The dissonance he perceives is expressed in the following comment: "It would be more appropriate for them [the Jews] to be closest to those who agree with them by believing in their prophet and their scripture. Instead they helped the *mushrikūn* out of a grudge against the Prophet (*ḥasadan lil-nabī*)."[12]

This exegete then returns to the question of identifying *those who say "We are Christians,"* examining it now in light of the Jewish-*mushrikūn* alliance. He cites the view of al-Zajjāj and al-Jubbā'ī that "perhaps it means *al-naṣārā* [Christians in general] because they were much less helpful to the idolaters."[13] However he immediately neutralizes this possibility with a counter-quotation from Ibn 'Abbās: "Whoever claims that it is about the Christians in general certainly lies. They [the ones to whom the phrase refers] are only the forty Christians whose eyes overflowed when the Prophet recited the Qur'ān to them, thirty-eight from Abyssinia and two from Syria. They hurried to become Muslims (*sāra'ū ilā al-islām*) while the Jews did not."[14]

Then, at the very end of his commentary on this verse, al-Ṭūsī allies himself with one of the two major interpretations that seek to identify the groups mentioned in the verse. His affiliation with the specific rather than general identification is clearly stated: "God made an announcement about those Jews who were the Prophet's neighbors (*mujāwirū al-nabī*) and the friendship of the Najāshī and his followers who became Muslims."[15] Apparently almost as an afterthought, al-Ṭūsī then connects these two groupings with the two major emigrations in the early history of Islam: "There was an emigration (*hijrah*) to Medina where the Jews lived, and to Abyssinia where the Najāshī and his followers lived, so an announcement was made about the hostility (*'adāwah*) of the former and the friendship (*mawaddah*) of the latter."[16]

Given the divine descriptives of friendliness (in this verse) and weeping at hearing the Qur'ān read (in the next verse), al-Zamakhsharī finds the episode involving the Najāshī and his followers the only meaningful referent for *those who say "We are Christians."* Without attribution, al-Zamakhsharī sketches the scene played out in the Najāshī's audience chamber between the two delegations from Mecca. Responding to the ruler's query about Qur'ānic mention of Mary, Ja'far recited selected portions of the *sūrah* that bears her name, *sūrah Maryam* (19), and of *sūrah Ṭā' Hā'* (20). The ruler recognized the truth and wept, as did the cohort of seventy whom he sent to the Prophet.[17]

Any notion that all Christians are intended by the divine praise recorded in this verse is forthrightly rejected by Abū al-Futūḥ Rāzī. His reason for such rejection is clear: "Christians (*tarsāyān*) are no less hostile to the Muslims than [are] the Jews."[18] Although he follows al-Ṭūsī in citing the identification proposed by Qatādah, Abū al-Futūḥ Rāzī clearly favors association of this verse with the emigration to Abyssinia.[19] This commentator recounts the story in considerably more detail than have previous commentators. He includes material about Muḥammad's proposal of marriage to Umm Ḥabībah, the daughter of Abū Sufyān, who, with her husband, had been among the immigrants to Abyssinia.[20] He also mentions the profession of faith in Muḥammad made by one of the Najāshī's slave girls. The Prophet's joy at the return of the immigrants, which coincided with the conquest of the Jewish oasis, Khaybar, in 7/628, is also recounted.[21]

This narrative of the Najāshī story differs from al-Ṭabarī's telling in the details of the Najāshī's conversion. According to Abū al-Futūḥ Rāzī, the Najāshī wrote to the Prophet a profession of faith and sent it by the hand of his son. In it he said: "I have come to believe in you and sworn allegiance to you (*man bi-tū īmān āvardam va tū-rā bay'at kardam*)." As his son crossed the sea to deliver this message to Muḥammad, the boat he was in foundered and sank.[22] He and part of his delegation of ascetics and pious worshipers (*zuhhād va 'ubbād*) were drowned. The rest of the party finally reached Medina where they were presented to the Prophet in the company of a group of men from Syria, including Baḥīrā, the Christian monk who is said to have recognized the youthful Muḥammad as the last of the prophets.[23] The numbers and composition of this combined delegation is in dispute. Abū al-Futūḥ Rāzī cites several variants ranging from 40 to 80, and including men from Abyssinia, Byzantium, Syria, and the 'Yemenite district of Najrān.[24]

Ibn al-Jawzī repeats al-Ṭūsī's definition *mushrikūn* and the charge that "the Jews helped the *mushrikūn* out of a grudge against the Prophet." He then poses the question about the phrase *those who say "We are Christians"* quite precisely: "Is this a generalization about all Christians or is it specific?" If the phrase means particular Christians then one of two groups could be intended. On the authority of Ibn 'Abbās and Ibn Jubayr the first possibility is, of course, the Christian king of Abyssinia and his followers who subsequently became Muslims. The second possible specification repeats al-Ṭūsī's and Abū al-Futūḥ Rāzī's use of an identification proposed by Qatādah: "they are a group of Christians who were strict adherents of the law of Jesus (*mutamassikūn bi-sharī'at i 'Īsā*)."[25] If the phrase is to be taken in a general sense, then Ibn al-Jawzī quotes, as did al-Ṭūsī, the rationale offered by al-Zajjāj, that the Christians were less helpful to the *mushrikūn* than were the Jews. As noted above, this position had been strongly contradicted by Abū al-Futūḥ Rāzī.

Fakhr al-Dīn al-Rāzī begins his commentary on this verse by reinforcing the divine castigation of the Jews. He, too, sees in the close placement of the words *the Jews* and *the idolaters* a measure of the degree of Jewish belligerence. He repeats the Prophetic *ḥadīth* that brands all Jews as potential Muslim-killers and quotes those who speak of a generalized Jewish hostility. "Jewish teaching requires them to inflict evil (*īṣāl al-sharr*) by any means on those who oppose them in religion. If they can do so by killing, then they choose that way. Otherwise they act by forcible seizure of property or robbery or any sort of cheating, deception, and trickery."[26]

The Christians, on the other hand, are characterized as milder-mannered (*alyan 'arīkatan*). Fakhr al-Dīn al-Rāzī contrasts their ethics with those of the Jews by saying that "in their religion causing harm is forbidden (*al-īdhā' fī dīnihim ḥarām*)."[27] Yet he is certainly unwilling to view all Christians in so flattering a light. Fakhr al-Dīn al-Rāzī cites Ibn 'Abbās, Sa'īd b. Jubayr, 'Aṭā', and al-Suddī as referents for the association of this verse with the Najāshī and his associates. It is the only specification that he proposes. He immediately follows it with the caution that certainly the verse does not mean all Christians (*jamī' al-naṣārā*), given the visible evidence of their animosity toward Muslims (*ẓuhūr 'adāwatihim lil-muslimīn*).[28]

On the other hand, he does raise a question about the text that previous exegetes have not addressed in quite this fashion. He queries the purpose for which this verse was included in divine revelation, and finds his answer in the tension that developed between Muḥammad and his nascent Islamic community, on the one hand, and the Jewish groups with whom they came in contact. Fakhr al-Dīn al-Rāzī understands the verse as an instance of divine clarification for Muḥammad, meant "to alleviate the Jewish problem for the Messenger (*takhfīf amr al-yahūd 'alā al-rasūl*)."[29] To highlight this explanation he paraphrases the divine word: "I swear that you will find the Jews and *mushrikūn* the people most hostile to the believers. I have already made plain to you that this recalcitrance and disobedience (*al-tamarrud wa-al-maʿṣiyah*) is a long-standing habit with them. So put them out of your mind and pay no attention to their deception and treachery."[30]

While Ibn Kathīr, too, associates the verse with the Najāshī, he does so in a more discriminating fashion, noting both historical and source-critical discrepancies. On the grounds that the verse was revealed in Medina, he questions the plausibility of its being occasioned by an episode, that of Jaʿfar with the Najāshī, that took place before the *hijrah* to Medina.[31] Ibn Kathīr also notes the position of those, such as Saʿīd b. Jubayr and al-Suddī, who find the revelatory context to be the delegation that the Najāshī sent to Muḥammad.[32] Here, however, he takes issue with al-Suddī's assertion that the Najāshī, persuaded by the testimony of the returning delegation, himself goes to join the Prophet and dies on the way. Ibn Kathīr dismisses this as a view idiosyncratic to Suddī (*min afrād al-Suddī*) and counters it with the more generally accepted historical tradition that the Najāshī died in Abyssinia.[33] Although the increasingly general identifications of ʿAṭāʾ b. Abī Rabāḥ and then Qatādah are repeated, Ibn Kathīr concludes his survey of possible attributions with the position taken by al-Ṭabarī: "Ibn Jarīr's [i.e., al-Ṭabarī's] decision is that this verse was sent down to describe various groups of this sort (*fī ṣifah aqwām bi-hādhihi al-mathābah*) whether they be from Abyssinia or elsewhere."[34]

Kāshānī is adamant in his rejection of such a broad understanding. Expanding Abū al-Futūḥ Rāzī's position he states: "The number of Christians who kill Muslims, devastate countries, and destroy mosques is no less than the number of Jews."[35] Thus the only possible identification for *those who say* "*We are Christians*" would be the Abyssinians and their king. He, too, relates in considerable detail the story of the *hijrah* to Abyssinia and of the hospitality accorded the immigrants. While his account corresponds closely to that found in Abū al-Futūḥ Rāzī's commentary, certain embellishments are unique to it.

Kāshānī describes a fight that broke out among the Quraysh delegation while en route to the Najāshī's court. ʿAmr b. al-ʿĀṣ was thrown overboard when he repulsed another man's drunken advances to his wife. He was able to swim to the front of the boat and hoist himself aboard but the whole incident is used to illustrate the sinful and contentious nature of the Quraysh group.[36] When this embassy appeared before the Najāshī they were bested by the debating skills of Jaʿfar b. Abī Ṭālib, in a debate that Kāshānī recounts in some detail. Muḥammad's proposal to Umm Ḥabībah, the return of Jaʿfar b. Abī Ṭālib, and the death of the king's son are all described. Also included is mention of the monk Baḥīrā as a member of the combined delegations that appeared before the Prophet. In almost every particular, Kāshānī accords with Abū al-Futūḥ Rāzī's account, but adds considerably more detail to the narrative.

Rashīd Riḍā takes as his first task the clarification of the terms here translated as 'hostility (*ʿadāwah*)' and 'friendship (*mawaddah*)'.[37] He next questions to whom this verse was directed, whether it be Muḥammad or a wider audience, such as all who might eventually hear the words. No immediate response is given because the answer to this is closely tied to the identification of the primary categories.

Here again the issue is whether that identification should be particular or general. Rashīd Riḍā begins by exploring the first option, which is especially compelling if the verse is considered to have been addressed chiefly to the Prophet. Briefly put, the referents would then be the Jews living in the Ḥijāz, the Arabic *mushrikūn*, and the Christians of Abyssinia who were alive during the time of Muḥammad.[38] This last group is praised for their friendliness "to the emigrants (*muhājirūn*) whom the Prophet sent at the beginning of Islam from Mecca to Abyssinia because he was afraid that the Meccan *mushrikūn*, who were causing them great trouble, would lure them from their religion."[39] Rashīd Riḍā also notes that this tripartite identification is the most commonly held view in the exegetical tradition.

But this commentator's interest in early Christian-Muslim contact does not stop with the Islamic *hijrah* to Abyssinia. He also brings into consideration the story of Muḥammad's missions to foreign rulers. The traditional accounts of this missionary activity record some interesting aspects of the Christian reaction to Islam. The first that Rashīd Riḍā mentions is the approach made to Heraclius, "the king of Byzantium (*Rūm*) in Syria." He is credited with an unsuccessful effort to persuade his subjects to accept Islam. Their refusal to do so is attributed to their persistence in following uncritically their old ways (*li-jumūdihim 'alā al-taqlīd*) and to their inability to comprehend the true nature of the new religion (*'adam fiqhihim ḥaqīqat al-dīn al-jadīd*).[40]

The Muqawqis, the Coptic ruler of Egypt, is reputed to have been more successful and is praised for having sent a handsome offering to Muḥammad. As a historical footnote Rashīd Riḍā adds that "when Egypt and Syria were conquered and their two peoples recognized the superiority of Islam, they entered the religion of God in droves, the Copts being the quicker in accepting it."[41] Of particular interest is the debate he recounts between the Muqawqis and the Prophet's messenger, Ḥāṭib b. Abī Balta'ah. When Ḥāṭib urges the Muqawqis to turn to Islam, the latter's first response is that he will not forsake his own religion unless shown something better. Ḥāṭib's rejoinder makes reference to the oft-repeated chronological analogy that Islamic theology draws between first the Jewish and Christian religions and then the Christian and Muslim religions: "There is no difference between Moses' foretelling (*bishārah*) of Jesus and Jesus' foretelling of Muḥammad; our inviting you to the Qur'ān is exactly like your inviting the people of the Torah to the Gospel." He then proceeds to explain that every prophet comes unexpectedly to his people, yet it is their duty to submit to his revelation. Ḥāṭib concludes his argument by saying "we are not prohibiting the religion of the Messiah for you; rather we are ordering you to it."[42] What this means – as Rashīd Riḍā hastens to clarify – is that Islam is the essence of Christianity itself (*al-islām 'aynuhu*). The Muqawqis promises to consider the summons, assuring the Prophet's messenger that he suspects Muḥammad of no deviousness or sorcery. Rather he finds associated with him the sign of prophethood (*āyat al-nubūwah*), which consists in bringing forth hidden meanings and announcing what has been concealed.[43]

The description of the Prophet's mission to Oman brings to the fore certain figures previously mentioned. The first to appear is 'Amr b. al-'Āṣ, who was the Muslims' adversary in the court of the Najāshī of Abyssinia. He has since offered allegiance to Muḥammad and been sent as the Prophet's emissary to the ruler of Oman, Jayfar b. Julandā. He first approaches the king's brother, 'Abbād b. Julandā, who is reputed to be more accessible and more discerning. As a way of convincing this noble, he describes his own conversion and that of the Najāshī. His curiosity piqued, 'Abbād b. Julandā questions him initially about the reaction of the Abyssinian people and then about the response of the bishops and monks (*al-asāqifah wa-al-ruhbān*).[44] When 'Amr reports that they have all become Muslim, ᶜAbbād accuses him of lying. 'Amr protests that lying is not permitted in Islam and then goes on to tell him about how the Najāshī, once he was a Muslim, refused to continue paying tribute to Heraclius, the Christian king of Byzantium. When Heraclius was faced with the Najāshī's defection, his response was a model of tolerance: "A man's preference and choice in religion is personal (*li-nafsihi*), what can I do to him? By God, were I not so anxious to hold on to my kingdom, I would do what he did."[45] When 'Abbād is then told the obligations and prohibitions that Islam imposes, his reply is reminiscent of Heraclius's words: "How fortunate is the one who is called to it [Islam]!"[46]

Rashīd Riḍā uses the accounts of these missionary deputations as well as the story of the *hijrah* to Abyssinia as evidence of the fact that Christians in the areas surrounding the Ḥijāz were particularly open to Islam and friendly to the Muslims. Those who did not actually accept Islam were held back by rulers jealous of their power. The commentator does remark that Islam did not spread in Abyssinia after the Najāshī's death nor was Muslim law instituted there as it was in Egypt and Syria. However he adds that this is a matter for historical research and not germane to the commentary on this verse.[47]

In this analysis of the views supporting a particular identification of the Christians, Rashīd Riḍā mentions the opinion of those who hold that geography determines amicability. That is, the more distant Christians could afford to be friendlier to the Muslims than the Jews and *mushrikūn* of Mecca and Medina. Those summoned to Islam from afar were less concerned about the consequences that their hostile response to the summons might provoke than those to whom that call was addressed orally. "Therefore the Jews in Syria and Spain were favorably disposed to the Muslims at the beginning and wanted to help them against the Christians of Byzantium and the Goths (*Qūṭ*)."[48] The hostility that eventually developed between the Muslims and these two groups of distant Christians, continues this commentator, was far more intense than that displayed by early-seventh-century Jews and *mushrikūn*. But, he adds, many instances of Muslim-Christian opposition and Muslim-Jewish opposition have nothing to do with religious matters but are rooted in struggles for earthly domination. Contemporary examples come immediately to mind: "This can be confirmed by the irritating effect that Christian propaganda has on contemporary Muslims, and by the outrage and enmity (*al-baghy wa-al-ʿudwān*) existing between Islamic and Christian nations which is nonexistent between Muslims and Jews."[49] A similar state of animosity is found between the Muslims and *mushrikūn* of India because their interests and advantages conflict there (*li-taʿāruḍ maṣ-āliḥihim wa-manāfiʿihim fīhā*).[50]

Thus Rashīd Riḍā's vision of his own contemporary situation appears to run counter to that of nascent Islam, with the descending order of hostility being Christians – *mushrikūn* – Jews, rather than the reverse. Rashīd Riḍā points out that recent warfare among the Christian Balkan states and between other Christian nations of Europe, such as England and Germany, confirms the fact that much international strife has no basis at all in religious matters. As a consequence, he feels, any particular identification of those groups mentioned in this verse is inappropriate and counter to the true meaning of the verse. The Qur'ān is not making a circumscribed but a general statement: "The real reason for the hostility of those who are hostile, and for the friendliness of those who are friendly, is the mental attitude (*al-ḥālah al-rūḥīyah*) which is the result of their religious and customary traditions (*taqālīduhum al-dīnīyah wa-al-ʿādīyah*) and their moral and social upbringing (*tarbiyatuhum al-adabīyah wa-al-ijtimāʿīyah*)."[51] He notes that while this verse does offer a rudimentary explanation for Christian friendship, it gives no explanation for the hostility exhibited by the Jews and the *mushrikūn*.

Although explanations are forthcoming elsewhere in the Qur'ān, Rashīd Riḍā ventures his own analysis. This amounts to little more than a list of unfortunate characteristics shared by the Jews and the *mushrikūn*: unbelief, insolence, injustice, love of preeminence (*ḥubb al-ʿulūw*), racial solidarity (*al-ʿaṣabīyah al-jinsīyah*), ethnic protectiveness (*al-ḥimāyah al-qawmīyah*), egoism, cruelty, and weakness of sympathetic and compassionate feeling (*ḍuʿfʿāṭifat al-ḥanān wa-al-raḥmah*).[52] Despite these shared characteristics, this exegete finds the *mushrikūn* less culpable than the Jews. Although they were religiously ignorant, they were more generous and altruistic, far more liberal in thinking and more independent.[53] He reiterates some of the Qur'ānic accusations against the Jews and dismisses any effort to rehabilitate their image based on their siding with the believers in the Holy Land, Syria, and Spain. This, he insists, was solely for financial and strategic motives: "They act solely for their own benefit."[54]

Ṭabāṭabā'ī takes the initial approach of contextual analysis and sees this verse as crowning the fifth *sūrah*'s treatment of the *ahl al-kitāb*. Earlier verses have detailed the errors of the *ahl al-kitāb*, both moral and doctrinal, so the revelation concludes with a more general statement about the various religious groups, relating them to the Muslims and their religion. The *mushrikūn* are included "so that the discussion of the impact of Islam on non-Muslims, relative to how near or far they are from accepting it, should be complete."[55]

In commenting upon the matter of the greater Christian amicability, this exegete takes issue with one stream of traditional exegesis on this verse. To think that the divine commendation is based on the response of a particular group of Christians does violence to the logic of the text.[56] "If the coming to believe of a group had authenticated it, then the Jews and *mushrikūn* would have to be reckoned like the Christians and credited with the same attributes, since a group of Jews became Muslims … and a number of *mushrikūn* from Arabia became Muslims; in fact, today they are the generality of Muslims."[57] The very specification of the Christians, then, is proof of their greater receptivity to Islam and more positive response to the Prophet.

Without actually using the term *dhimmah*, which is commonly used by Muslim authors to designate the legal status of the *ahl al-kitāb*, Ṭabāṭabā'ī describes the options available to the various groups of newly subject people at the dawn of Islamic history.[58] The Christians could choose between staying in their religion and paying a tax, the *jizyah*, or accepting Islam and fighting in its name. For the *mushrikūn* there was no choice other than accepting the Islamic summons. (Ṭabātaba'ī does not explain that the obvious reason for this is that the *mushrikūn*, as their designation indicates, were not considered monotheists by the Muslims, as were the Jews and Christians.) The fact that they had no choice makes their numerically greater conversion rate to Islam no particular factor in their favor. That many Christians, who did have a choice, chose to become Muslims is a strong argument for this divine commendation.[59]

To complete his argument, Ṭabāṭabā'ī must then ask why another group of the *ahl al-kitāb*, the Jews, are not accorded equal praise. After all, they, too, have the option of remaining in their religion and paying the *jizyah* or converting to Islam. What, then, differentiates them from the Christians? Ṭabāṭabā'ī finds his answer in those perennial accusations of arrogance (*nakhwah*) and racial solidarity. He adds to this the sins of treachery and scheming and claims that they "wait for disaster to befall the Muslims."[60]

Ṭabāṭabā'ī finds historical confirmation of this greater Christian receptivity to the message of Islam. The greater number of Jews and *mushrikūn* who became Muslims in the first years of Islam – due in large part to their geographical proximity – has given way to "Christian numerical superiority in acceptance of the Islamic summons (*da'wah*) during past centuries."[61] So self-evident does this exegete find the argument for Christian receptiveness that his commentary on *you will find the people most intensely hostile to the believers are the Jews* consists of nothing more than citing two Qur'ānic passages (*sūrat al-mā'idah* [5]:62 and 80) that describe Jewish perfidy.

Reasons for Christian Amicability

Several themes raised in the modern commentaries of Rashīd Riḍā and Ṭabāṭabā'ī were anticipated in that part of the earlier exegetical tradition that sought to clarify and develop the basis for the contrast of the Jews and Christians in *sūrat al-mā'idah* (5):82. Such a concern moves beyond an interest in purely historical specification. Rather it seeks to understand the religio-cultural structures that buttress the varying relations among religious groups. The focus for such an investigation is to be found in the pivotal sentence *that is because among them are priests (qissīsīn) and monks (ruhbān) and because they are not arrogant.* Al-Ṭabarī does not, of course, ignore the need to determine historical context for these two categories. After a word study of the terms themselves, he proposes two possible referents for the individuals so designated.

The first theory is that the *priests and monks* are Jesus' disciples, those who answered when he summoned them and lived according to his law (*wa-ittaba'ūhu 'alā sharī'atihi*). The single supporting *ḥadīth* from Ibn 'Abbās cited by this exegete is interesting for the terminology it uses: "They were sailors (*nawātī*) on the sea, i.e., mariners (*mallāḥūn*). Jesus, son of Mary, walked by them and called them to submission (*da'āhum ilā al-islām*), so they responded to him."[62]

The second interpretation returns to the Abyssinian interlude described above, by identifying the *priests and monks* with the delegation that the Najāshī sent to Muḥammad. The *ḥadīths* brought in support of this view on the authority of Abū Ṣāliḥ al-Miṣrī (d. 223/838) and Sa'īd b. Jubayr offer bits of information, sometimes contradictory. The number of delegates ranges from fifty to seventy. They are described as hermits (*ṣāḥib ṣawma'ah*) and wool wearers (*'alayhim thiyāb al-ṣūf*) in one *ḥadīth*, while in another they are given the more general appellation of 'the elite (*khiyār*)'.[63]

Al-Ṭabarī, however, probes beyond these two identification theories to a more comprehensive concern. He moves from attempting to decide who exactly are these *priests and monks* to pointing out the explanatory nature of this whole phrase. It is because of the very presence of such individuals among the people who call themselves Christians – whoever they may be – that there is such friendliness with the believers. This divinely commended amicability on the part of the Christians is due to the presence among them of "a people diligent in worship (*ahl ijtihād fī al-'ibādāt*), living monastically in cells and hermitages (*tarahhub fī al-diyārāt wa-al-ṣawāmi'*). They are not far from the believers because they assent to the truth when they recognize it, and they are not too proud to accept it when they see it clearly."[64] He then proceeds to refer to them as "people of a religion (*ahl dīnin*)" vastly different from "the Jews who habitually killed prophets and messengers, stubbornly opposed God's commands and prohibitions, and altered the revelation that He sent down in His books."[65] By implication, then, it is the very lack of a faithful remnant among the Jews that exacerbates their hostility to the Muslims and prevents the development of the concord that exists between Christians – at least a certain group of them – and Muslims.

Al-Ṭūsī's principal concern is also the logical connection between this phrase and what precedes it. He, too, reads *that is because among them are priests and monks and because they are not arrogant* as an explanation for the discrepancy between Muslim-Christian and Muslim-Jewish relations. It is a problem of inhibiting pride: "The Christians who believe are not too proud to follow the truth and submit to it (*ittibā' al-ḥaqq wa-al-inqiyād lahu*), as are the Jews and idol worshipers (*'ubbād al-awthān*)."[66]

Al-Zamakhsharī confronts the basic issue of foundational perspective directly when he summarizes this verse by pitting Jewish recalcitrance (*ṣu'ūbah*) against Christian tractability (*līn*) and the ease with which the latter repent and incline toward submission to God (*suhūlat ir'awā'ihim wa-maylihim ilā al-islām*).[67] The association of the Jews with the *mushrikūn* is a gauge of the intensity of their hostility to the believers. Furthermore this commentator is another who finds significance in the relative placement of the terms *al-yahūd* and *alladhīna ashrakū*. The fact that the Jews are mentioned before the *mushrikūn* in this verse demonstrates the longer duration of Jewish hostility to the believers.[68] As a supporting verse he draws upon *sūrat al-baqarah* (2):96: "You will find them [the Jews] the most avid (*aḥraṣ*) of people for life [more so than] those who are idolaters (*alladhīna ashrakū*)." Al-Zamakhsharī adds his own rejoinder to this commentary-verging-on-anti-Jewish-polemic with the words: "By God, they are really like that and worse!" To cap it off he quotes a Prophetic *ḥadīth:* "No two Jews can be alone with a Muslim except with intent to kill."[69] By contrast, Christian pliability is to be explained in terms of the presence of priests and monks (*qissīsūn wa-ruhbān*). The synonyms al-Zamakhsharī has selected for these two words are 'people of learning (*'ulamā'*)' and 'pious devotees (*'ubbād*)'. He describes them as humble and submissive, devoid of arrogance and, as such, quite the opposite of the Jews.[70] However, his understanding of this phrase is not restricted by the designation of these two groups. Rather he finds in this reference a general laudation of learning, of which the Christian priests and monks are but a particular instance.

Semantic association of the term *qissīsūn* with connotations of 'learning' is continued by Abū al-Futūḥ Rāzī who also includes Ibn Zayd's gloss of the term as 'ascetics (*zuhhād*)'. He, however, adds to the developing tradition a curious bit of etymological lore on the authority of 'Urwah b. al-Zubayr (d. 94/712). This begins with the statement that "the Christians ruined the Gospel by alteration and substitution (*tarsāyān injīl ẓāyiʿ kardand va ānrā taghyīr va tabdīl kardand*)."[71] There were five men involved: four of them altered and made substitutions in the Gospel. These four were Lūqās, Marqūs, Baljīs, and Mīmnūs. "The one who remained steadfast in the truth was [named] Qissīs. Therefore, anyone who imitated him by remaining truthful was called *qissīs*."[72] As further explanation for the term, Abū al-Futūḥ Rāzī quotes a *ḥadīth* from Salmān al-Fārisī in which the Prophet recites this verse to him and substitutes 'righteous men (*siddīqīn*)' for *qissīsīn.*

The final segment of this sentence, *and because they are not arrogant*, is then understood to be intimately connected with these two foregoing categories, expressing a further praiseworthy qualification possessed by such individuals. Once again, it is the notion of priests and monks functioning as a kind of leaven or 'saving remnant' among the main body of Christians that comes strongly to the fore.[73]

According to Ibn al-Jawzī, who is here quoting al-Zajjāj, *qissīsūn* means 'leaders of the Christians (*ru'asā' al-naṣārā*)'; on the authority of Abū 'Alī Muḥammad al-Quṭrub (d. 206/821) the word comes from the Syriac where it means 'a learned man (*'ālim*)'. As for *ruhbān*, while no etymology is given, the synonyms *'ubbād* ('worshipers') and *arbāb al-ṣawāmiʿ* ('cell people') are proffered.[74] After these etymological considerations, Ibn al-Jawzī raises an interesting question, one that broadens the range of exegetical discussion on this verse. He asks "why the Christians are being praised *because among them are priests and monks* when that is no part of our law (*wa-laysa dhālika min amr sharīʿatinā*)?"[75] The question, of course, refers to the oft-mentioned prohibition against "monkery" in Islam. The answer this exegete proposes clearly distinguishes the difference between these two religious traditions in the matter of monasticism: "Monasticism (*rahbānīyah*) was well-regarded (*mustaḥsan*) in their [the Christians'] religion."[76] However, divine praise is not being offered for communal celibacy as such, but for learning and erudition. The Christians are praised, in Ibn al-Jawzī's paraphrase of the Qur'ānic citation, because "among them were men learned in what Jesus had enjoined about Muḥammad (*'ulama' bimā awṣā bihi 'Īsā min amr Muḥammad*)."[77] This commentator thus maintains the chronological discrimination between what is expected of Christians before and after the advent of Muḥammad, but does so with greater specification. This makes the critical word in the following statement the conjunction "until": Christians "are being praised for adhering to the religion of Jesus *until* they act upon what their scripture enjoins upon them with respect to Muḥammad."[78]

Should any ignoramus, continues Ibn al-Jawzī, find in this verse praise for the Christians in general, he would be completely wrong. It is praise only for those among them who believe (*man āmana*), that is, who become Muslims. Lest there be any lingering doubt about pervasive Christian defectiveness this commentator contrasts Jewish and Christian doctrine (*maqālah*) to the grave detriment of the latter: "There is no doubt that Christian doctrine is more repugnant (*aqbaḥ*) than Jewish."[79] The only redeeming feature attributable to the Christians is the presence among them of men of learning whose scholarly ability has not been corrupted by arrogance. Verification of this is found in the Qur'ānic description *they are not arrogant* (*lā yastakbirūna*), which Ibn al-Jawzī explains as not being too proud to follow the truth.[80]

Rather than immediately involving himself in a philological analysis of the terms *qissīsūn* and *ruhbān*, as other commentators have, Fakhr al-Dīn al-Rāzī uses the phrase as the basis for a continued analysis of Jewish-Christian differences. This time he finds a contrast not between Jewish belligerence and Christian tractability, but between Jewish greed for worldly things and Christian renunciation of them. It is this latter polarity between avidity and renunciation that generates the resultant belligerent or compliant behavior. Fakhr al-Dīn al-Rāzī locates proof for this accusation of Jewish greed, as did al-Zamakhsharī, in *sūrat al-baqarah* (2):96. Greed (*ḥirṣ*), says this exegete, is the root and source of discord, because "the man who is greedy for worldly things discards his religious duty in pursuit of worldly pleasures. He has the audacity to do any forbidden or abominable deed in the search for temporal goods. Naturally his hostility increases towards anyone who gains wealth and fame."[81]

The obverse of this stark picture of Jewish moral deformation is Fakhr al-Dīn al-Rāzī's idealistic depiction of Christian rectitude. He maintains that unlike the Jews (who are greedy for the world's goods), the Christians are a people who renounce temporal satisfactions (*mu'riḍūn 'an al-dunyā*) and who turn to divine worship (*muqbilūn 'alā al-'ibādah*). As a result their behavior is devoid of self-aggrandizement, arrogance, and haughtiness; their inner virtue is reflected in outward action. Anyone whose eyes are diverted from worldly gain "does not envy people or hold grudges against them or quarrel with them; rather his is a nature open to the truth and prepared for compliant submission to it."[82]

Having said this, Fakhr al-Dīn al-Rāzī hastens to add a strong corrective to his complimentary portrayal of Christianity. The issue he raises is that of the nature of Christian unbelief: "The unbelief (*kufr*) of the Christians is cruder (*aghlaẓ*) than that of the Jews because the Christians dispute about matters theological-metaphysical and prophetical (*yunāzi'ūna fī ilāhīyāt wa-fī al-nubūwāt*) while the Jews debate only about the latter."[83] Yet the Christian lack of worldly greed and inclination toward the Hereafter (*mayl ilā al-ākhirah*) partially redeems them in God's eyes, as the divine honor accorded them in this verse attests. Again, in contrast stands the divine denunciation of the Jews "whose belief is not as coarse as that of the Christians" but whose condemnation is occasioned by "their greed for worldly things."[84]

Fakhr al-Dīn al-Rāzī concludes his commentary on 5:82 with the postponed word study of *qissīsūn* and *ruhbān*. He closely follows the philological exegesis of Ibn al-Jawzī here, explicitly acknowledging the attribution to Quṭrub but not to al-Zajjāj. Then Fakhr al-Dīn al-Rāzī quotes on the authority of 'Urwah b. al-Zubayr a condensed form of the curious bit of etymological lore first found in Abū al-Futūḥ Rāzī: "The Christians fabricated the Gospel (*ṣana'at al-naṣārā al-injīl*) and introduced extraneous material. But one of their learned men remained steadfast in the truth and his name was Qissīs. So whoever lives according to his guidance and religion is a *qissīs*.[85]

The questions of how to reconcile this phrase with the Qur'ānic rejection of monasticism found in *sūrat al-ḥadīd* (57):27 and the Prophet's denunciation of it is answered by Fakhr al-Dīn al-Rāzī again in terms of Christian-Jewish contrast. The point, he insists, is not that monasticism is praiseworthy in general. Rather it is something to be praised "in comparison with the Jewish way of harshness and ruthlessness (*al-qasāwah wa-al-ghilẓah*)."[86]

When Ibn Kathīr starts to probe the interreligious dynamics to which this verse testifies he intensifies the initial condemnation of the Jews by remarking upon the pervasive obstinacy and denial (*'inād wa-juḥūd*) of the Jews and their defamation of the truth (*mubāhatah lil-ḥaqq*). These serious moral deficiencies are the cause of their killing previous prophets – a Qur'ānic charge repeated here by Ibn Kathīr. They are thus the cause of Jewish attempts on the life of Muḥammad: "They poisoned him and used sorcery against (*sammūhu wa-saḥarūhu*) and incited the like-minded *mushrikūn* against him."[87] Ibn Kathīr reinforces this accusatory exegesis by quoting two versions of the oft-mentioned Prophetic *ḥadīth* about general Jewish hostility to Muslims, both on the authority of Abū Hurayrah but one of which he characterizes as very uncommon.

When dealing with the phrase that refers to Christians, this commentator speaks of Christians as a whole and first proposes a sort of Christian self-definition: "Those who claim (*za'amū*) to be Christians based on following the Messiah and living according to the ways of his Gospel (*maḥājj injīlihi*)."[88] They are friendly both to Islam and its people, in the sense that this friendship is "in their hearts since kindliness and compassion (*al-riqqah wa-al-ra'fah*) are part of the religion of the Messiah."[89] Qur'ānic support for this description is found in *sūrat al-ḥadīd* (57):27: "We put compassion and mercy in the hearts of those who followed him [Jesus]."[90] Ibn Kathīr even goes beyond the Qur'ān to Christian scriptural sources. He observes that in "their book," the Gospel, the following dictum occurs: "Whoever strikes you on your right cheek, turn to him your left cheek."[91] This is clearly an almost verbatim citation of Matthew 5:39 (cf. Luke 6:29) from which Ibn Kathīr draws the conclusion that fighting is unlawful in Christianity (*wa-laysa al-qitāl mashrū' fī millatihim*).[92]

This exegete expands the usual definition offered for *qissīsūn* to include not only 'learned men (*'ulamā'*)' but also 'preachers (*khuṭabā'*)'. For *ruhbān* he cites the single synonym of 'worshiper (*'ābid*)'. Ibn Kathīr then moves beyond these etymological considerations to introduce several versions of a *ḥadīth*, earlier noted in Abū al-Futūḥ Rāzī, which is traced back to Salmān al-Fārisī. It begins with the explanation that *qissīsūn* live in churches and ruins (*al-biya' wa-al-khirab*). (In another version this is given as hermit cells [*al-ṣawāmi'*] and ruins.)[93] Then Salmān records that when he recited to the Prophet *that is because among them are priests and monks* Muḥammad glossed the Qur'ānic phrase by adding "that is because among them are sincere and righteous men (*ṣiddīqīn*) and monks."[94] Ibn Kathīr concludes by recasting the terms of this verse's final phrase to create a laudatory catalogue of Christian attributes: among them are to be found knowledge (*'ilm*), veneration (*'ibādah*), and humility (*tawāḍu'*); they can be described as complying with truth (*inqiyād lil-ḥaqq*), adhering to it (*ittibā'uhu*), and acting with equity (*al-inṣāf*).[95]

In commenting upon this verse's opening phrase, Kāshānī spends rather more time detailing the vices of the Jews than did Abū al-Futūḥ Rāzī. The now-familiar catalogue of accusations includes "the multiplication of their unbelief (*taẓā'uf-i kufr-i īshān*)," "being slaves to their passions (*in-himāk-i īshān dar ittibā'-i-havā*)," and "obstinately refuting prophets (*tamarrud-i īshān bar takẕīb-i anbiyā'*)."[96] The *mushrikūn* are treated as equivalent to the Jews in these offenses, and even the *ḥadīth* on the authority of Abū Hurayrah that portrays the Jews as an ever-present threat is applied to them also.

By contrast the phrase referring to the Christians occasions a listing of the virtues that may be found in this group. Christians are praised for "their soft and tender hearts, for their little interest in worldly things (*qillat-i ḥirṣ-i īshān bar dunyā*) and their great diligence in knowledge and action (*kasrat-i ihtimām-i īshān bi-ʿilm va ʿamal*)."[97] Since the *mushrikūn* do not share these qualities, an alliance between them and the Christians could not develop. Kāshāni understands the *that* in *that is because among them are priests and monks* to refer to the nearness of friendship (*qurb-i mawaddat*). He offers as a translation for *qissīsūn* 'truth-speaking sages (*dānāyān-i rāstgū*)'; that given for *ruhbān* is 'cell-dwelling worshipers (*ʿābidān-i ṣawmaʿa-nishīn*)'.[98] Chief of the Christian virtues, as attested to by the last phrase of this verse, is an absence of arrogance. Being open to the reception of truth, when it is heard and understood, is the meaning Kāshānī assigns to *they are not arrogant.* Once again praise of Christians is contrasted with condemnation of the Jews, who, Kāshānī insists, boast that they will always remain Jews.[99]

Rashīd Riḍā continues the tradition of finding an explanation for Christian amicability in the sentence *that is because among them are priests and monks and because they are not arrogant.* For this exegete the *qissīsūn* are the teachers, the ones responsible for religious education, while the *ruhbān* are concerned with world-renouncing and worshiping God.[100] Their willingness to submit to the truth is eased by their religion's insistence on humility (*al-tawāḍuʿ*), self-abasement (*al-tadhallul*), and the acceptance of any authority (*qabūl kulli sulṭatin*).[101] "Of particular note," says Rashīd Riḍā, echoing Ibn Kathīr, "is the admonition to love the enemy and to turn the left cheek to anyone who strikes the right cheek."[102] Although these exhortations were directed to all Christians, they were more seriously heeded by the priests and monks, who act as a spiritual leaven within the whole community. It is their edifying presence, then, that accounts for greater Christian amicability.

The Jewish-Christian antithesis highlighted by the phrase *and because they are not arrogant* is given further explanation. Rashīd Riḍā locates the source of Christian tractability in the greater ease with which the authority of an adversary is accepted (*qabūl sulṭat al-mukhālif lahum*).[103] They have long acquaintance with the acceptance of submission to such authority and with showing themselves publicly and privately content with it. "The Jews, on the other hand, may publicly exhibit satisfaction under compulsion but secretly they conceal treachery and they delude with great cunning."[104]

Having followed the traditional exegetical schema of commenting on each phrase of the verse, Rashīd Riḍā then moves back for a macroscopic view and discusses some matters to which the verse as a whole gives rise. The first of these he prefaces with the remark that though "these are general descriptions of the two groups, they do not suffice to explain individual characters."[105] Thus, among the Jews there are good people and bad, and the Qur'ān makes this distinction in *sūrat al-aʿrāf* (7):159. Yet this commentator feels called upon to draw attention once more to Jewish racial exclusivity "upon which all its [Judaism's] statutes and stipulations are built."[106] He bases the historical explanation for this exclusivity within Israel's growth as a monotheistic community (*ummah muwaḥḥidah*) among idolatrous nations (*umam wathanīyah*). The exodus from Egypt and entrance into the Holy Land (*al-arḍ al-muqaddasah*) was overlaid with divine admonitions to avoid all contact with that land's original inhabitants.[107]

Rashīd Riḍā seeks to still the objections of those who doubt whether the Jewish religion can be at all connected with God. Given such wicked behavior among the Jews, how could one say that their religion is from God? The commentator responds that "the answer to this doubt is easy for Muslims; it can be explained by the fact that this *sharī'ah* [that of the Jews] was temporary, not permanent."[108] It was a stage in the development of monotheism. Prophets would repeatedly exhort their people to reform. The Psalms of David (*zabūr Dāwūd*) and the Wisdom of Solomon (*ḥikam Sulaymān*) reflect these prophetic concerns, reaffirming spiritual values and cautioning against excessive materialism.[109]

Then came the greatest reformer of Israel (*muṣliḥ isrā'īl al-a'ẓam*), Jesus the Messiah. Rashīd Riḍā expresses the extent of Jesus' reformation by juxtaposing Jewish defects with Christian virtues: "The Jews' extreme materialism was countered with extreme spirituality, their extreme selfishness with extreme altruism, which the Christians call self-denial (*inkār al-dhāt*), and their exaggerated inflexibility about the literal meanings of the law with careful attention to observing the law's intent."[110] Jesus directed his followers away from concern with temporal power and wealth and the enjoyment of earthly happiness. Rather he enjoined them to love their enemies and not to seek retaliation. "All that was a preparation for God's completing His religion by sending the Seal of the prophets and messengers, Muḥammad."[111] It was only with Muḥammad's arrival that God's religion achieved a proper balance. This prophet's reformation "combined for mankind those things beneficial to soul and body and enjoined both just action (*'adl*) and gratuitous charity (*iḥsān*), not just the latter."[112]

Of course, Rashīd Riḍā continues, few among the Jews took the Messianic reformation to heart and most were openly hostile to Jesus. Comparable was the reception accorded to the reformation initiated by Muḥammad. The most receptive and quickest to believe were the group of *qissīsūn* and *ruhbān*. This commentator equates them with the reference in *sūrat al-a'rāf* (7):157 to "those who follow the Messenger, the *ummī* Prophet [whom they find written with them in the Torah and the Gospel]." Such individuals follow the Prophet whom they find foretold in the Torah and Gospel and he, by rightly guiding them, "relieves them of their burden and the fetters which bind." Identifying this weight and these shackles brings Rashīd Riḍā again to the element of balance which Islam introduced: "That 'burden' and those 'fetters' were none other than the severity (*shiddah*) of the Torah's prescriptions about food and drink and the civil and criminal statutes (*al-aḥkām al-madanīyah wa-al-jinā'īyah*), and the severity of the Gospel's precepts about asceticism (*al-zuhd*), self-abasement (*idhlāl al-nafs*), and self-deprivation (*ḥirmānuhā*)."[113]

Rashīd Riḍā then raises the issue of subsequent historical confirmation for this verse by remarking upon "the large number of Christians who embraced Islam in every age and the small number of Jews who did so."[114] Obstacles to Christian conversion to Islam in the present day are attributed to a number of factors. He parcels out the blame between Muslim and Christian defects. On the Islamic side Rashīd Riḍā lists such things as the general 'weakness (*ḍu'f*)' of Muslims in this time, "their turning away from the guidance of the Qur'ān, and their neglecting to proselytize for Islam (*ihmāluhum al-da'wah ilā al-islām*) and to present it in its correct form so as to disclose the corruption of their governments (*fasād ḥukūmātihim*) together with the impotence of their [the governments'] administrative officials in political/diplomatic affairs (*'ajz rijālihā fī al-siyāsāt*), and their not keeping up with other nations in learning and culture (*takhallufuhum 'an mujārāt al-uman fī al-'ilm wa-al-haḍārah*)".[115] The most immediate obstacle to increased Christian conversion to Islam, according to Rashīd Riḍā, is the political disputes between Christian and Islamic nations. Were it not for these, "then the friendship between the two groups would be fuller and there would be a more general diffusion of Islam among them, because Islam is an amelioration of Christianity (*li-anna al-islām iṣlāḥ fī al-naṣrānīyah*) just as Christianity is an enhancement of Judaism."[116] Rashīd Riḍā then finds in the logic of this development another reason for Jewish-Muslim enmity. In instances of Jewish-Christian dispute, Muslims should take the Christian side, because Christianity is a closer stage to the perfection of religion, Islam.[117]

One historical event this commentator feels compelled to deal with is the Crusades, a war "whose fire the Christians ignited in the name of religion."[118] Nothing like it ever occurred between the Muslims and Jews or *mushrikūn*. Rashīd Riḍā deals with this problem from two perspectives. The first is that of the medieval Christian misunderstanding of Islam. Plainly stated, the Christians simply did not realize that Islam was an improvement on their religion. Christians had only the most distorted image of Islam, "an image [of something] pagan, wild and ugly – the most repulsive defacement."[119] This exegete even locates the source of this falsification "in the writing, letters and speeches which Peter the Monk (*Biṭrus al-rāhib*) and his like produced."[120] In fact, insists Rashīd Riḍā, so intimidating was the misrepresentation that had the Muslims themselves been summoned to fight a people so described they would have fled.

The second line of response that he takes on the problem of the Crusades contrasts the Gospel message of peace and love with the nationalistic thrust for power and temporal dominion. The Christian teaching never triumphed over European belligerence and aggressiveness: "These characteristics had already reached full maturity in the era of Byzantine sovereignty and were the reason for the annihilation of paganism in all of Europe as well as being the cause of the Crusades and the attempt to eliminate the Muslims from the Holy Land or the whole Eastern world."[121]

Lest the impression remain that Christian aggression is directed principally against Muslims, Rashīd Riḍā mentions the bitter wars that have been fought between various Christian groups themselves. These he attributes to differing religious beliefs and practice (*ikhtilāf al-madhāhib*) or nationalistic contention. Both derive from Satan (*shayṭān*), not from the Spirit of God (a Qur'ānic expression used in relation to Jesus), "even though it is reported that he said: 'I have not come to bring peace on earth, I have come only to bring the sword.'"[122] This quotation from Matthew 10:34, presented without explanation, of course undercuts the statement it was ostensibly intended to support.

Unlike the doctrinal disputes at the base of some intra-Christian wars, Muslim-Christian conflict is not commonly founded on religion, but occurs beyond the guidance range of each religion. "No one but an ignorant man or a fool connects it to the nature of the two religions."[123] Yet the call to religion has certainly been used as a goad to incite nations to war. Rashīd Riḍā makes this point well in a statement that resounds with an ironical prophetic ring: "The deceptive political *imāms* of the two groups continue to use religion as a trick to deceive the masses into supporting their politics to a degree that is criminal both to the religion and its people."[124]

Taking another tack, this exegete now moves from historical to doctrinal objections. Could it not be said, he ponders, that Judaism is closer to Islam than Christianity because it is a monotheistic religion (*diyānah tawḥīd*) while Christianity is trinitarian (*diyānah tathlīth*)? After all, affirming the oneness of God (*tawḥīd*) is the essence of God's religion and the perfection of all religious teaching. "God pardons every sin except that of associating other gods with Him (*al-shirk*)."[125] Rashīd Riḍā responds to this query by denying the importance of the doctrine of the Trinity within Christianity (an unusual line of argument in Islam): "The doctrine of the Trinity which belongs to Christianity (*dākhil fī al-masīḥīyah*) is so unfathomable and incomprehensible that it has no effect on the souls of its people which would distance them from Islam; in fact it might be one of the reasons for accepting the summons to Islam."[126] With that, the exegete returns to his theme of the enduring friendship between

Muslims and Christians, a friendship never achieved with the Jews and *mushrikūn*, a friendship "which has not weakened in any country except through administrative intrigue and the nationalistic strivings of those in power (*'aṣabīyah ahl al-riyāsah*)."[127]

In a curiously placed epilogue Rashīd Riḍā provides a word study of *qissīsūn* and *ruhbān* and comments upon the Christian institution of monasticism. A 'monk (*rāhib*)' is one who separates himself from the world by living in a monastery or hermitage in order to engage in divine worship. "He deprives himself of the enjoyment of wife and child and the delights of food and fine adornment."[128] A 'priest (*qissīs*)' is a religious leader "who is superior to the deacon (*al-shammās*) but inferior to the bishop (*al-usquf*)."[129] The *qissīsūn* are men learned in their religious traditions and scriptures, pastors of their people and authorized to deliver legal opinions (*ru'āt wa-muftūn*). The words *ruhbān* and *qissīsūn* are used in this verse to mean 'worshipers' and 'scholars'.[130] Rashīd Riḍā's consideration of monasticism as a religious institution is brief. He characterizes it as an innovation (*bid'ah*) in Christianity that had some influence on increasing Christian friendship for Muslims but is of no great importance.

Ṭabāṭabā'ī's etymological reflections are brief but include mention of the fact that the the root meaning of *RHB*, from which *rāhib* (pl. *ruhbān*) is notionally derived, is 'to fear'. Based on this consideration, Ṭabāṭabā'ī defines monasticism as "exaggerated devotional piety deriving from excessive fear (*ghulūw fī taḥammul al-ta'abbud min farṭ al-rahbah*)."[131] He is consonant with most of the exegetical tradition in treating the concluding phrase of the verse as an explanation for Christian-Muslim friendship. Among the Christians there are three characteristics that both the Jews and the *mushrikūn* lack: the presence of priests, the presence of monks, and the absence of arrogance.[132]

The mention of arrogance provides Ṭabāṭabā'ī the opportunity for an exhortatory digression on the need for eliminating bad attitudes in order to move from knowledge of the good to right action. "Attaining the truth does not suffice to prepare one to act in accordance with it;" the individual must first "pluck from himself the attitude that is holding him back from it (*al-hay'ah al-māni'ah 'anhu*)."[133] The obstructive attitude to which Ṭabāṭabā'ī is referring is "haughty disdain for the truth because of racial pride and so forth (*al-istikbār 'an al-ḥaqq bi-'aṣabīyah wa-mā yushābihuhā*)."[134] He realizes that such attitudes do not develop in a vacuum but are greatly influenced by one's society and culture. Right thinking flourishes with societal reinforcement as do right actions in an environment "in which it would be embarrassing for the individual to neglect them."[135]

The prerequisites, then, for a society's reception of the truth are the presence in that society of learned men who know and teach it, as well as the presence of men who act in accordance with it, so that people can see that it is both possible and right to do so. The people themselves must be accustomed to surrendering to the truth (*al-khuḍū' lil-ḥaqq*) and must lack haughty disdain for it (*'adam al-istikbār 'anhu*).[136]

These prerequisites have been met by the Christians, as the final sentence of this verse manifests. Ṭabāṭabā'ī paraphrases this sentence in a way that makes completely clear how the Christians have satisfied the conditions he sets: "Among them are learned men who keep reminding them of the importance of truth and the things that must be known about religion, by word; among them are ascetics (*zuhhād*) who keep reminding them of the greatness of their Lord and the significance of their earthly and heavenly fortune, by deed; and among them there is no sense of being too proud to accept the truth."[137] The exegete then catalogues the deficiencies of the Jews and *mushrikūn* that prevent them from fulfilling these divinely instituted requirements. The Jews, in spite of their learned rabbis (*aḥbār*), are disqualified because "the vice of obduracy and presumed superiority does not induce them to be ready to receive the truth."[138] The *mushrikūn* are found wanting on all three counts: not only are they bereft of learned men and of ascetics, but they too are guilty of the vice of arrogance.

Tears and Testimony

The following verse, 5:83, is taken by most commentators as a continuation and specification of this Qur'ānic commendation of Christians. As such it shares, for the most part, the same 'occasion of revelation', that combination of incidents involving the Christian Abyssinian king and his subjects. Ibn al-Jawzī succinctly presents the two principal scenarios. In the first, on the authority of Ibn 'Abbās, it is the emigrants from Mecca to Abyssinia who recite the Qur'ān aloud in the court of the Najāshī. The *qissīsūn* and *ruhbān* who were present heard this recitation and wept, for they recognized the truth in those utterances. The second depiction, from Sa'īd b. Jubayr, features a delegation sent by the Najāshī to Muḥammad. When the Prophet recited the Qur'ān, this group, which also contained priests and monks, wept in recognition of the truth and entered Islam.[139]

While Ibn al-Jawzī shows no preference for either of these two scenarios, Ibn Kathīr indicates a clear inclination for the second. Although he includes a *ḥadīth* from 'Abdallāh b. al-Zubayr that locates the source of this revelation in the Najāshī and his followers, he pays far more attention to one from Ibn 'Abbās that describes the Abyssinian delegation to Muḥammad. The account includes speculation by Muḥammad about the constancy of these new converts. The Prophet queries them: "Perhaps when you return to your country, you will return to your religion (*intaqaltum ilā dīnikum*)?" They respond, saying, "We will not turn from our religion (*lan nantaqila 'an dīninā*)."[140]

Ibn Kathīr then draws upon other Qur'ānic citations to specify further the identity of this group: "These sorts of Christians are the ones mentioned in *sūrah Āl 'Imrān* (3):199 and *sūrat al-qaṣaṣ* (28):52–53 [quoted in Ibn Kathīr's text]."[141] In conclusion he ties this verse to two that follow it, 5:85 and 5:86. The first decrees the rewards to be gained by the blessed "on account of their belief (*īmānuhum*), their attesting to the truth (*taṣdīquhum*), and their confessing the truth (*i'tirāfuhum bi-al-ḥaqq*)."[142] That triad of laudable activities neatly parallels the three steps of the conversion process recorded in 5:83. In the first stage *they recognized … the truth*, that is, they came to belief. In the second stage they announced this belief by saying "*Our Lord, we believe.*" In the third stage they asked to be placed in the category of those who witness to the faith, the *shāhidūn*. The second verse to which Ibn Kathīr alludes, 5:86, consigns those who reject belief to hellfire (*al-jaḥīm*).[143]

While Kāshānī locates 5:83 within the same cluster of incidents as have Ibn al-Jawzī and Ibn Kathīr, he does so in a novel way. In the narratives upon which he draws, revelation is prompted not by piety but by provocation. In the first briefly sketched situation, Kāshānī depicts Jewish taunting of the companions of Ja'far because they so quickly became believers: "Although they have been summoning us [to Islam] for a long time," the Jews are quoted as saying, "we do not accept."[144] The second, even briefer, suggestion is that the verse was revealed because the people of Abyssinia chided the Najāshī for believing in someone whom he had never seen (i.e., Muḥammad).

A citation by Abū al-Futūḥ Rāzī marks the only significant exception to this pattern of association. Drawing from 'Amr b. Murrah he states: "In the time of Abū Bakr, a group arrived from the Yemen and said 'Recite something from the Qur'ān for us.' The Qur'ān was recited for them and they wept." Struck by this response, Abū Bakr remarks that "at first, we, too, were like this. When we heard the Qur'ān, we wept. But now our hearts have hardened."[145]

The weeping and tear-filled eyes to which this verse attests are explained by the phrase here translated as *because of what they recognized as the truth*. Al-Ṭabarī glosses this succinctly as "because of their recognition that what had been recited to them from the Book of God, which was sent down to the Messenger of God, was true," an understanding consonant with the above translation. Al-Zamakhsharī, however, stresses the partitive nature of the Arabic preposition in the expression *as the truth* (*min al-ḥaqqi*), insisting that those involved "recognized [only] part of the truth (*annahum 'arafū ba'ḍ al-ḥaqq*)." To underscore this he appends this exclamation: "Imagine what it will be like when they have understood all [the truth], read the Qur'ān and become fully acquainted with the *sunnah*!"[146] Fakhr al-Dīn al-Rāzī, Kāshānī, and Rashīd Riḍā subsequently share this understanding and repeat a version of al-Zamakhsharī's exclamation.[147]

An issue that preoccupies virtually all of the commentators on this verse is the precise specification of *those who testify* (*al-shāhidūn*). Once again Ibn al-Jawzī proves to be a useful source of reference. He offers five choices for this phrase, one of his own and four from other exegetes. His own preference is for a broad definition, "those who testify to the truth." The four interpretations that he offers from earlier authorities are presented with no elaboration or explanation. The first two, both traced ultimately to Ibn 'Abbās, are (1) Muḥammad and his community and (2) the Companions of Muḥammad. The third, on the authority of al-Ḥasan al-Baṣrī, is "those who testify to the faith (*bi-al-īmān*)," while the fourth, from al-Zajjāj, makes the phrase coextensive with "the prophets and the believers."[148]

Such breadth does not accurately mirror the spectrum of exegetical reflection on this phrase. Most commentators, such as al-Ṭabarī, al-Ṭūsī, Abū al-Futūḥ Rāzī, Ibn Kathīr, and Kāshānī, restrict the scope to the community of Muḥammad.[149] Fakhr al-Dīn al-Rāzī, on the other hand, permits a more inclusive reading. He presents the more restricted meaning as one option, basing it – as have other commentators – on a Qur'ānic parallel in *sūrat al-baqarah* (2):143: "We have made you a community of the middle (*ummatan wasaṭan*) so that you may be witnesses (*shuhadā'*) for people." He is willing to consider, however, a much broader second reading, one that expands the definition of al-Zajjāj. *Those who testify* (*shāhidūn*) is rephrased as: "all those among Your prophets and mankind's believers who witness that there is no God but You."[150] Such a definition would apparently cover not only Muslims but all professing monotheists. As such it could include both Christians and Jews as well as any others who acknowledge that there is but one God.

While Ṭabāṭabā'ī does not comment upon this question, Rashīd Riḍā continues the tradition of a more restrictive understanding of *shāhidūn*. He does, however, combine with this something of the sequential nature of the conversion process first noted by Ibn Kathīr. Thus Rashīd Riḍā notes that although recognition of the truth is an essential element of faith, it is incomplete without verbal acknowledgment. The second phrase of this verse, *They say*, "*Our Lord, we believe, so write us with those who testify*," is important. Rashīd Riḍā maintains that such a faith statement was possible only because of preparatory revelation and teaching about the nature of the final stage of religious evolution; those who wept "can say that only because they would know from their scriptures, or from what had been reported to them on the authority of their ancestors, that it is the followers of the last prophet – the one in whom God brings religion to perfection – who are witnesses to mankind."[151] Therefore asking to be "written among the witnesses" is equivalent to inclusion within the community of Muḥammad. In fact, for Rashīd Riḍā, the term *shāhidūn* is the most noble descriptive that can be applied to the community (*ummah*).

Conclusion

Structurally, the first of these two verses is constituted as a declaration buttressed by reasons and justifications. The statement that Christians are *closest in friendship* to the Muslims reinforces the pervasive sense of group configuration and identification that permeates the exegesis of all the verses thus far examined. The unequivocal certitude of this declaration poses an urgent exegetical problem for the commentators. Several hasten to assert that the range of signification, the numbers of Christians to whom such praise is actually or potentially applicable, is indeed limited. An interesting division develops on this issue between the classical Sunnī and Shīʿī exegetes. Some of the former, such as al-Ṭabarī and Ibn Kathīr, are unwilling to condone a narrow reading. Arguing from the lack of divine specification in this verse, they both reject the notion that there is any explicit warrant for restricting the range of relevance to a particular group of Christians. In opposition to such latitude stand the Shīʿī scholars, al-Ṭūsī, Abū al-Futūḥ Rāzī, and Kāshānī. Each candidly contends that the verse does not intend *all* Christians. Each goes beyond the implicit limitation of positing a particular *sabab al-nuzūl* to insist squarely upon such restriction of signification. The modern commentator, Ṭabāṭabāʾī, represents the only break in this Shīʿī exegetical front.

Yet the stance taken by such Sunnī commentators as al-Ṭabarī and Ibn Kathīr makes no positive argument for unrestricted or universal applicability to all Christians. The degree of detail lavished on the episodes that center upon the Najāshī inevitably focuses attention upon a historically and geographically limited group of Christians. Nor are even these allowed to occupy center stage for long. Frequently the narratives express less interest in highlighting the Abyssinian Christians than the Muslim emigrants from Mecca. It is the fortitude and persistence of the latter that garner the most praise.

Additionally, the opening phrases of this verse group provide a lexical focus for that castigation of the Jews which often accompanies praise of Christians. At no other point in the Qurʾān does the one group stand so sharply contrasted to the other. Fakhr al-Dīn al-Rāzī even cites early Muslim-Jewish tension as a principal purpose for this revelation. Several of the commentators combine harsh denunciation of the Jews with their limited praise of Christians, repeating a pattern uncovered in the analysis of other verses in this study.

The need to understand the Qurʾānic reasons given for Christian-Muslim amicability produces the most persistent praise of Christians and of Christianity found in the exegesis of any of the verses examined for this work. The etymological consideration of *qissīsūn* and *ruhbān* elicits from the commentators sustained reflection upon those qualities in the religion and its adherents which could prompt divine approbation. Once again the description is frequently contrastive, Christian virtues being catalogued in tandem with Jewish vices. The specific points of praise mentioned by the exegetes manifest a closer knowledge of Christianity than has elsewhere been exhibited. Ibn Kathīr's reference to Christian pacifism draws upon a passage in the Gospel of Matthew. Al-Ṭabarī recognizes the seafaring vocation of some of Jesus' disciples. Distinctions are made between ecclesiastical categories represented by the terms *qissīsūn* and *ruhbān*. Yet misinformation about Christianity is certainly not lacking. One etymology for *qissīs* repeated by both Abū al-Futūḥ Rāzī and Fakhr al-Dīn al-Rāzī, which traces the word to a supposed Christian figure named Qissīs, is but the most obvious example.

Nevertheless a continuing chorus of commendation marks the treatment of Christianity in the exegetical history of this verse. Consistently but not exclusively this commendation is directed at two qualities that Christianity is perceived as promoting. These are a veneration of learning and an aptitude for ascetic disciplines. The first, associated with the eccelesiastical category of *qissīsūn*, finds unqualified acclaim among the commentators. The further Qur'ānic compliment, *and because they are not arrogant*, is regularly understood as a right-minded respect for the truth or as an openness to the truth that finds its heart-sought fulfillment in the embrace of Islam.

Praise for asceticism as embodied in the Christian institution of monasticism is somewhat more problematic for the commentators. Muḥammad's proscription of "monkery" casts a long shadow over the acknowledgment of any positive value in Christian asceticism. Ibn al-Jawzī, for one, decides that monks are being praised not for their celibacy but for their scholarship. Fakhr al-Dīn al-Rāzī allows only that Christian renunciation is a general improvement on Jewish avidity and self-aggrandizement. He is particularly anxious to refute any approval of Christian doctrine. While willing to admire the psychological and behavioral consequences of Christian ethical formation, Fakhr al-Dīn al-Rāzī underlines the abysmal crudity of Christian doctrine. Here comparison with the Jews is to the latter's advantage. In the chronology of this exegetical survey, however, that is a short-lived exception. Ibn Kathīr and Rashīd Riḍā replay the dominant theme – albeit in terms consonant with their respective exegetical agendas – commending Christianity as a higher stage of spiritual evolution than Judaism, a stage marked by deeper knowledge, more profound religious devotion, and greater humility. Those three qualities themselves summarize the results of the full exegetical search for the reasons underlying the divine praise that this verse records. They are nicely recast by Ṭabāṭabā'ī using sociological categories and configurations. In his view, a religious group guided by the truth must incorporate learned individuals who can know and convey it, devoted adherents who by their actions can witness to its efficacy and value, and, finally, a pervasive sense of humility and openness among all those who affiliate themselves with the group.

Such an attitude will sometimes manifest itself in fervent tears, as caught in the brief narrative scenario of 5:83. The affective response to revelation received is unabashedly conveyed in these few lines. A psychology of conversion deftly sketched captures the movement from reception to testimony. The commentators wonder, of course, about the moment that might be herein recorded and return to some of the now-familiar incidents, as well as noting other conversion scenes. The fulfillment of those qualities for which the Christians are lauded is that moment of recognition when the Qur'ānic message is apprehended. Yet even here a cautionary note is sounded, a final qualification is laid upon the words recorded. Fakhr al-Dīn al-Rāzī, Kāshānī, and Rashīd Riḍā all emphasize the partitive nature of this moment of recognition. Lest the Christians be applauded unreservedly, that ultimate circumscription prevails.

Notes

1 This episode is recounted in Ibn Isḥāq, *Sīrah*, 1:208–21 (Guillaume, *Life*, 146–53). A narrative summary is offered in Mehmet Aydin, "Rapporti islamo-cristiani all'epoca di Muhammad," *ISC* 5 (1986): 12–15.

2 al-Ṭabarī, *Jāmi' al-bayān*, 10:499.

3 Ja'far b. Abī Ṭālib was Muḥammad's cousin and an older brother of 'Alī. L. Veccia Vaglieri, "Dja'far b. Abī Ṭālib," *EI*[2] 2:372. For Ibn Mas'ūd see Chapter 1, notes 5 and 13. The *Sīrah* (1:243–44) of Ibn Isḥāq recounts the occasion on which the poet 'Uthmān b. Maẓ'ūn renounced the protection of a Meccan opponent of Muḥammad's, al-Walīd b. al-Mughīrah.

4 'Amr b. al-'Āṣ (d. 42/663) is best remembered for his conquest of Egypt and founding of Fusṭāṭ, the forerunner of present-day Cairo. A.J. Wensinck, "'Amr b. al-'Āṣ," *EI*[2] 1:451.

5 al-Ṭabarī, *Jāmiʿ al-bayān,* 10:500.
6 al-Ṭabarī, *Jāmiʿ al-bayān,* 10:500. The closest Qur'ānic equivalent to Ja'far's declaration would be *sūrat al-nisā'* (4):171, which both Muslim and Western scholars date as Medinan, i.e., well after the Abyssinian emigration. On the use of the terms *kalimah* and *rūḥ* in association with Jesus see Thomas O'Shaughnessy, S.J., *The Koranic Concept of the Word of God* (Rome: Pontificio Istituto Biblico, 1948) and *The Development of the Meaning of Spirit in the Koran* (Rome: Pontificium Institutum Orientalium Studiorum, 1953), as well as Henninger, *Spuren,* 32–38.
7 al-Ṭabarī, *Jāmiʿ al-bayān,* 10:500.
8 al-Ṭabarī, *Jāmiʿ al-bayān,* 10:501. Other accounts of the Najāshī's death form a major part of the *asbāb al-nuzūl* for *sūrah Āl ʿImrān* (3):199, which was discussed in Chapter 5.
9 al-Ṭabarī, *Jāmiʿ al-bayān,* 10:501.
10 al-Ṭabarī, *Jāmiʿ al-bayān,* 10:501. Ahmad von Denffer presents only this episode (of the delegation sent by the Najāshī to Muḥammad) as the *sabab al-nuzūl* of the verse, adding that only such a carefully specified group of Christians is intended in this verse and, therefore, that "this verse, when seen in its historical context, does not seem to be meant as a general statement characterizing Christians as such as being nearest to Muslims." *Christians in the Qur'ān and the Sunna,* 13.
11 al-Ṭūsī, *al-Tibyān,* 3:614.
12 al-Ṭūsī, *al-Tibyān,* 3:614.
13 al-Ṭūsī, *al-Tibyān,* 3:614.
14 al-Ṭūsī, *al-Tibyān,* 3:614–15.
15 al-Ṭūsī, *al-Tibyān,* 3:616.
16 al-Ṭūsī, *al-Tibyān,* 3:616.
17 al-Zamakhsharī, *al-Kashshāf,* 1:669. The passages recited were 19:1–33 and 20:1–8.
18 Abū al-Futūḥ Rāzī, *Rawḥ al-jinān,* 4:303.
19 Abū al-Futūḥ Rāzī, *Rawḥ al-jinān,* 4:305–6. The *ḥadīth* from Qatādah is appended, almost as an afterthought, to Abū al-Futūḥ Razī's lengthy description of the Abyssinian episode.
20 Abu al-Futūḥ Rāzī, *Rawḥ al-jinān,* 4:304. Abū Sufyān was among the most prominent of Muḥammad's Meccan opponents. He eventually submitted to the Prophet and one of his sons, Muʿāwiyah, became the first Umayyad caliph. On the relations between Muḥammad and Abū Sufyān, particularly the legal issues surrounding the Prophet's marriage to Umm Ḥabībah, see M. J. Kister, "O God, Tighten Thy Grip on Muḍar … : Some Socio-economic and Religious Aspects of an early Ḥadīth," *JESHO* 24 (1981): 258–67.
21 Abū al-Futūḥ Rāzī, *Rawḥ al-jinān,* 4:304–5. L. Veccia Vaglieri, "Khaybar," *EI*[2] 4: 1137–43. For the relations of this incident to the development of *jizyah* legislation, see Albrecht Noth, "Minderheiten als Vertragspartner im Disput mit dem islamischen Gesetz," in *Studien zur Geschichte und Kultur des vorderen Orients: Festschrift für Bertold Spuler zum siebzigsten Geburtstag,* ed. by Hans R. Roemer and A. Noth (Leiden: E. J. Brill, 1981), 289–309. Gordon Newby provides information on the life of Ḥijāzī Jews with specific reference to Khaybar, *A History,* 49–77.
22 Abū al-Futūḥ Rāzī, *Rawḥ al-jinān,* 4:305. The episode of the shipwreck to which Abū al-Futūḥ Rāzī's account refers may be found in al-Ṭabarī's *Ta'rīkh al-rusul wa-al-mulūk,* ed. by M.J. de Goeje (1879–1901; reprint, Leiden: E.J. Brill, 1964), 1:1569 (Guillaume, *Life,* 657–58).
23 Abū al-Futūḥ Rāzī, *Rawḥ al-jinān,* 4:305.
24 Abū al-Futūḥ Rāzī, *Rawḥ al-jinān,* 4:305. The specifics of this enumeration are: (1) in Abū al-Futūḥ Rāzī's narrative the number is seventy, with sixty-two from Abyssinia and eight from Syria; (2) on the authority of Muqātil and al-Kalbī, the number is forty, with thirty-two from Abyssinia and eight from Byzantium; (3) 'Aṭā' gives the figure of eighty, forty being of the Banū al-Ḥārith b. Kaʿb from Najrān, thirty-two from Abyssinia, and eight from Byzantium.
25 Ibn al-Jawzī, *Zād al-masīr,* 2:408.
26 Fakhr al-Dīn al-Rāzī, *al-Tafsīr al-kabīr,* 12:66.
27 Fakhr al-Dīn al-Rāzī, *al-Tafsīr al-kabīr;* 12:66. The Christian promotion of such virtues as 'turning the other cheek' or forgiving one's enemies has often provoked puzzlement or ridicule from Muslim writers. A clear example may be found in the *al-Raddʿalā al-naṣārā* of 'Amr b. Baḥr al-Jāḥiẓ (d. 255/868–69), who mocks the Christians for "their ideas on forgiveness, their aimless spiritual wandering, their censure on meat-eating and their predilection for cereals." His derision is further prompted by their "preaching abstinence from marriage and reproduction" and their "venerating their leaders and praising their patriarchs and metropolitans, their bishops and monks, for practicing celibacy." These translations of al-Jāḥiẓ's are from an unpublished paper by

G.M. Wickens entitled "Anti-Christian Polemic in Islam." Portions of al-Jāḥiẓ's essay have been translated by Joshua Finkel, "A Risāla of al-Jāḥiẓ," *JAOS* 47 (1927):311–34.

28 Fakhr al-Dīn al-Rāzī, *al-Tafsīr al-kabīr*, 12:66.

29 Fakhr al-Dīn al-Rāzī, *al-Tafsīr al-kabīr*, 12:66.

30 Fakhr al-Dīn al-Rāzī, *al-Tafsīr al-kabīr*, 12:66.

31 Ibn Kathīr, *Tafsīr al-Qur'ān al-'aẓīm*, 2:85. John Wansbrough has analyzed Ja'far b. Abi Ṭalib's speech before the Najāshī and decided that "the structure of the report suggests a careful rhetorical formulation of Quranic material generally supposed to have been revealed after the date of that event." *Quranic Studies*, 41.

32 Ibn Kathīr, *Tafsīr al-al-Qur'ān al-'aẓīm*, 2:85. While Ibn Kathīr repeats some of the enumerations given for this delegation, he does so without specific attributions.

33 Ibn Kathīr, *Tafsīr al-Qur'ān al-'aẓīm*, 2:85.

34 Ibn Kathīr, *Tafsīr al-Qur'ān al-'aẓīm*, 2:85.

35 Kāshānī, *Minhaj al-ṣādiqīn*, 3:291.

36 Kāshānī, *Minhaj al-ṣādiqīn*, 3:292.

37 Rashīd Riḍā, *Tafsīr al-Manār*, 7:2. For *'adāwah* Rashīd Riḍā offers as a synonym *bughḍ* (hatred) as it is expressed in word and deed. Likewise *mawaddah* is equated with *maḥabbah*, not absolutely but as manifested in speech and behavior.

38 Rashīd Riḍā, *Tafsīr al-Manār*, 7:3.

39 Rashīd Riḍā, *Tafsīr al-Manār*, 7:3.

40 Rashīd Riḍā, *Tafsīr al-Manār*, 7:3. The disavowal of *taqlīd* is an important note in the thought of both Muḥammad 'Abduh and Muḥammad Rashīd Riḍā. For a classical-period repudiation of this form of traditionalism see J.R.T.M. Peters's work on the Mu'tazilī Abū al-Ḥasan 'Abd al-Jabbār (d. 415/1025), *God's Created Speech* (Leiden: E.J. Brill, 1976), 43–45. For Rashīd Riḍā's conjunction of the terms *jumūd* and *taqlīd* see Hourani, *Liberal Age*, 235.

41 Rashīd Riḍā, *Tafsīr al-Manār*, 7:3. A. Grohmann reviews the scholarship that denies the historicity of this incident in "al-Muḳawḳas," *EI*[1] 6:712–25.

42 Rashīd Riḍā, *Tafsīr al-Manār*, 7:4.

43 Rashīd Riḍā, *Tafsīr al-Manār*, 7:4.

44 Rashīd Riḍā, *Tafsīr al-Manār*, 7:4.

45 Rashīd Riḍā, *Tafsīr al-Manār*, 7:4.

46 Rashīd Riḍā, *Tafsīr al-Manār*, 7:5. Accounts of these deputations to various rulers may be found in Ibn Isḥāq, *Sīrah*, 1:971–72 (Guillaume, *Life*, 652–59.) Guillaume's presentation of this incorporates material from al-Ṭabarī's *Ta'rīkh*.

47 Rashīd Riḍā, *Tafsīr al-Manār*, 7:5.

48 Rashīd Riḍā, *Tafsīr al-Manār*, 7:5. J. Sadan draws attention to this same geographical argument in the *al-Radd 'alā al-naṣārā* of al-Jāḥiẓ. "Some Literary Problems," 354, note 5.

49 Rashīd Riḍā, *Tafsīr al-Manār*, 7:6. Rashīd Riḍā's remarks predate the partition of Palestine and establishment of the state of Israel.

50 Rashīd Riḍā, *Tafsīr al-Manār*, 7:6.

51 Rashīd Riḍā, *Tafsīr al-Manār*, 7:6.

52 Rashīd Riḍā, *Tafsīr al-Manār*, 7:6. The translation of *qawmīyah* as 'ethnic' has been chosen in light of Bernard Lewis's remarks about the use of the cognate, *kavmiyet*, by Turkish-educated writers in the early years of this century "to denote identity and solidarity based on ethnic affinity." "On Modern Arabic Political Terms" in his *Islam in History* (London: Alcove Press, 1973), 285. For Rashīd Riḍā's application of *al-'aṣabīyah al-jinsīyah* to the *ahl al-kitāb* as a whole, see Chapter 6.

53 Rashīd Riḍā, *Tafsīr al-Manār*, 7:6.

54 Rashīd Riḍā, *Tafsīr al-Manār*, 7:7.

55 Ṭabāṭabā'ī, *al-Mīzān*, 6:79.

56 Ṭabāṭabā'ī repeats this in his comments on the *ḥadīth* material to which he makes reference for this verse, insisting that "the evident meaning (*ẓāhir*) of the verse is general not specific." *al-Mīzān*, 6:85.

57 Ṭabāṭabā'ī, *al-Mīzān*, 6:79–80. The author was apparently unaware of the vast demographic shift that has taken place in the Muslim world with the largest Muslim populations now to be found in south and southeast Asia.

58 See Claude Cahen, "Dhimma," *EI*[2] 2:227–31. A standard source is Antoine Fattal, *Le statut légal des non-musulmans en pays d'islam* (Beirut: Imprimerie Catholique, 1958). The Islamic legal

regulations pertinent to *dhimmīs* are presented in Adel Khoury, *Toleranz im Islam* (Munich: Kaiser, 1980) while a selection of translated legal and historical material has been collected by Bat Ye'or (pseud.), *The Dhimmi: Jews and Christians Under Islam*, trans. by David Maisel et al. (Rutherford, N.J.: Fairleigh Dickinson University Press, 1985). An earlier French edition carries the more polemical title *Le Dhimmi: Profil de l'opprimé en Orient et en Afrique du Nord depuis la conquête arabe* (Paris: Éditions Anthropos, 1980). Berthold Spuler presents a historical overview in "L'Islam et les minorités," in *Die Islamische Welt zwischen Mittelalter und Neuzeit: Festschrift für Hans Robert Roemer zum 65. Geburtstag* (Beirut: Orient-Institut der Deutschen Morgenländischen Gesellschaft, 1979), 609–19. For a recent historical study of the early classical period see André Ferré, "Chrétiens de Syrie et de Mésopotamie aux deux premiers siècles de l'Islam," *Islamo* 14 (1988): 71–106.

59 Ṭabāṭabā'ī, *al-Mīzān*, 6:80.

60 Ṭabāṭabā'ī, *al-Mīzān*, 6:80.

61 Ṭabāṭabā'ī, *al-Mīzān*, 6:80.

62 al-Ṭabarī, *Jāmiʿ al-bayān*, 10:504. The term that puzzles al-Ṭabarī, *nawātī* (*sing. nūti*), and for which he offers the synonym *mallāḥīn*, is defined by Lane as "sailor upon the sea." He adds that according to Abū Naṣr Ismāʿīl al-Jawharī (d. 397/1006) it is derived from a Syriac word, while others (unnamed) consider it an Arabicized form of the Greek *nautēs*. *Arabic-English Lexicon*, 8:2863. Ibn Manẓūr mentions only a Syriac etymology. He quotes this same *ḥadīth* from Ibn ʿAbbās but in connection with 5:83 not 5:82. *Lisān at-ʿarab*, 3:101.

63 al-Ṭabarī, *Jāmiʿ al-bayān*, 10:505. In a final *ḥadīth* from Saʿīd b. Jubayr the *qissīsūn* and *ruhbān* are identified as "messengers from the Najāshī who brought word of his submission (*islāmuhu*) and the submission of his people (*islām qawmihi*)" and further equated with those referred to in *sūrat al-qaṣaṣ* (28):52–54, which will be discussed in Chapter 8.

64 al-Ṭabarī, *Jamiʿ al-bayān*, 10:505. The basic study of the Qur'ānic understanding of monasticism, which examines the three relevant loci (*sūrat al-mā'idah* [5]:82–86, *sūrat al-tawbah* [9]:29–35, and *sūrat al-ḥadīd* [57]:27), is that by Edmund Beck, *Das christliche Mönchtum im Koran* (Helsinki: Societas Orientalis Fennica, 1946).

65 al-Ṭabarī, *Jamiʿ al-bayān*, 10:506.

66 al-Ṭūsī, *al-Tibyān*, 3:616. In his note on the phrase *dhālika bi-anna minhum qissīsīna wa-ruhbānan wa-annahum lā-yastakbirūna*, Rudi Paret remarks that *istakbara* is found frequently in the Qur'ān and "er bedeutet in der Regel nicht Stolz gegen Menschen, sondern Hochmut in religiösem Sinn, nämlich mangelnde Ehrfurcht vor Gott und der göttlichen Offenbarung." *Kommentar und Konkordanz*, 128.

67 al-Zamakhsharī, *al-Kashshāf*, 1:668.

68 al-Zamakhsharī, *al-Kashshāf*, 1:668.

69 al-Zamakhsharī, *al-Kashshāf*, 1:668. The editor quotes a variant of this *ḥadīth* in which the word "Jew" is in the singular.

70 al-Zamakhshari, *al-Kashshāf*, 1:668. Tor Andrae argues that the tenor of Muḥammad's religious experience, "the deep earnestness, the keen expectation of future life, the contrition and trembling before the Day of Judgment, fear as an actual proof of piety, the warning against the carelessness which forgets responsibility and retribution," show a close relationship to "the basic mood of *Christian ascetic piety* [Andrae's italics]." *Mohammed: The Man and His Faith* (*Mohammed, sein Leben und sein Glaube*), trans. by Theophil Menzel (1936; reprint of revised edition, New York: Harper and Brothers, 1960), 83. This judgment is developed at length in Andrae's *Les Origines de l'Islam et le Christianisme*.

71 Abū al-Futūḥ Rāzī, *Rawḥ al-jinān*, 4:306.

72 Abū al-Futūḥ Rāzī, *Rawḥ al-jinān*, 4:306. The synonym that Abū al-Futūḥ Rāzī gives for *ruhbān* is the expected *ʿubbād* (devotees) while the root meaning noted for *RHB* is *khawf* (fear). Al-Ṣadūq Abū Jaʿfar Muḥammad b. Bābawayh's (d. 381/991) *Kitāb al-tawḥīd offers* another Shīʿī account of Gospel origins: after the *injīl* of Jesus was lost, Luke, Mark, John, and Matthew reproduced it from memory. David Thomas has translated the relevant portion of Ibn Bābawayh in "Two Muslim-Christian Debates from the Early Shīʿite Tradition," *JSS* 33 (1988): 74.

73 Abū al-Futūḥ Rāzī, *Rawḥ al-jinān*, 4:307.

74 Ibn al-Jāwzī, *Zād al-masīr*, 2:408. Abraham Geiger, drawing as well upon Syriac etymologies, concludes that "*ruhbān* does not really mean the ordinary monks ... but the clergy; whereas *qissīs* stands for the presbyter, the elder. ..." *Judaism and Islam* (*Was hat Mohammed aus dem Judenthume*

aufgenommen?), trans. by F.M. Young (1898; reprint with Prolegomenon by Moshe Pearlman, New York: Ktav, 1970), 36.

75 Ibn al-Jawzī, *Zād al-masīr*, 2:408. In contrasting this verse's praise of priests and monks with the denunciation of rabbis and monks (*aḥbār wa-ruhbān*) in *sūrat al-tawbah* (9):31, Kenneth Cragg remarks that "it is hard to resist the impression that Muḥammad's attitude changed, when he discovered that his claims failed to receive the hospitable welcome he had first expected from the people of the earlier Book." *The Call of the Minaret*, 1st ed., 261. Geoffrey Parrinder finds a possible reference to "saint cults" in the phrase found in 9:31, "they take their scholars and monks (*aḥbār wa-ruhbān*) as lords apart from God." He then adds that "it is well known that legends and devotions grew up around the lives of some of the Christian martyrs and ascetics." *Jesus in the Qur'ān*, 157.

76 Ibn al-Jawzī, *Zād al-masīr*, 2:409. Louis Massignon counters those who would understand the *ḥadīth* "*lā rahbānīyah fī al-islām*" as a complete disavowal of celibacy with the reminder that temporary celibacy is one of the *ḥajj* requirements. *Essai sur les origines du lexique technique de la mystique musulmane*, 2nd ed. (Paris: Librairie Philosophique G. Vrin, 1968), 1:147. The Qur'ānic conception of monasticism is briefly contrasted with its variety of Christian forms in the chapter entitled "L'antinomie de la 'rahbaniyya' en Islam" in Jean-Paul Gabus, Ali Merad, and Youakim Moubarac, *Islam et Christianisme en dialogue* (Paris: Les Éditions du Cerf, 1982), 161–69.

77 Ibn al-Jawzī, *Zād al-masīr*, 2:409.

78 Ibn al-Jawzī, *Zād al-masīr*, 2:409.

79 Ibn al-Jawzī, *Zād al-masīr*, 2:409.

80 Ibn al-Jawzī, *Zād al-masīr*, 2:409. The central place of 'arrogance (*istikbār*)' within the semantic field of *kufr* is analyzed by Izutsu, *Ethico-Religious*, 142–52.

81 Fakhr al-Dīn al-Rāzī, *al-Tafsīr al-kabīr*, 12:66.

82 Fakhr al-Dīn al-Rāzī, *al-Tafsīr al-kabīr*, 12:66.

83 Fakhr al-Dīn al-Rāzī, *al-Tafsīr al-kabīr*, 12:67. For a more extended discussion of Fakhr al-Dīn al-Rāzī's various religious categories see the section on "Qur'ānic parallels" in Chapter 3.

84 Fakhr al-Dīn al-Rāzī, *al-Tafsīr al-kabīr*, 12:67. Rudi Paret highlights this reason for Jewish/ Christian contrast in his remarks on 5:82. *Muhammed und der Koran: Geschichte und Verkündigung des arabischen Propheten*, 5th revised ed. (Stuttgart: W. Kohlhammer, 1980), 141.

85 Fakhr al-Dīn al-Rāzī, *al-Tafsīr al-kabīr*, 12:67.

86 Fakhr al-Dīn al-Rāzī, *al-Tafsīr al-kabīr*, 12:67. Fakhr al-Dīñ al-Rāzī here repeats the famous *ḥadīth* that is usually translated as "There shall be no monkery in-Islam" (*lā rahbānīyah fī al-islām*). For contrastive purposes, it is interesting to note the view found in the *tafsīr* often attributed to Ibn al-'Arabī. For this exegete the Jews represent a fairly primitive stage of spiritual development, for "they are veiled from the [divine] essence and attributes, having nothing but the *tawḥīd* of actions." Thus does he explain their affinity for the *mushrikūn*, "those who are absolutely veiled," completely beyond the range of God's self-revelation. In like manner is Christian-Muslim rapport understood. Since the Christians "have emerged from the veil of the [divine] attributes and nothing but the veil of the [divine] essence covers them, their relationship with the believers (*mu'minūn*) is stronger." This, says Ibn al-'Arabī, is what the idea of friendship connotes. Unlike other commentators, he does not go on to explore the nature of Muslim-Jewish hostility. Rather he emphasizes the Jewish-*mushrikūn* affinity which the density of their 'veils' ensures. (This final statement is based on reading the sentence *wa-al-mushrikūna al-yahūdu ashaddu 'adāwatan li-qūwati ḥijābihim* with a *wa* inserted between the first two nouns.) Ibn al-'Arabī, *Tafsīr al-Qur'ān al-karīm*, 1:340.

87 Ibn Kathīr, *Tafsīr al-Qur'ān al-'aẓīm*, 2:85.

88 Ibn Kathīr, *Tafsīr al-Qur'ān al-'aẓīm*, 2:86.

89 Ibn Kathīr, *Tafsīr al-Qur'ān al-'aẓīm*, 2:86. For Ibn Taymīyah the friendliness of Christians will not necessarily save them from punishment or merit eternal reward for them. His response to the arguments of Paul of Antioch also stresses the importance of reading 5:82 and 83 in tandem. T. Michel, *A Muslim Theologian's Response*, 243–46, and P. Khoury, *Paul d'Antioche*, 66–67 of Arabic text.

90 This verse will be the subject of Chapter 9.

91 Ibn Kathīr, *Tafsīr al-Qur'ān al-'aẓīm*, 2:86.

92 Ibn Kathīr, *Tafsīr al-Qur'ān al-'aẓīm*, 2:86.

93 Ibn Kathīr, *Tafsīr al-Qur'ān al-'aẓīm*, 2:86. The story of Salmān al-Fārisī forms one of the *asbāb al-nuzūl* for 2:62, which is treated in Chapter 3.

94 Ibn Kathīr, *Tafsīr al-Qur'ān al-'aẓīm*, 2:86. Arthur Jeffery finds *ṣiddīqīn* instead of *qissīsīn* in the codex of Ubayy b. Ka'b, *Materials*, 129.
95 Ibn Kathīr, *Tafsīr al-Qur'ān al-'aẓīm*, 2:86.
96 Kāshānī, *Minhaj al-ṣādiqīn*, 3:291.
97 Kāshānī, *Minhaj al-ṣādiqīn*, 3:291.
98 Kāshānī, *Minhaj al-ṣādiqīn*, 3:291.
99 Kāshānī, *Minhaj al-ṣādiqīn*, 3:291.
100 Rashīd Riḍā, *Tafsīr al-Manār*, 7:7. Although he does not divide these functions between the two groups, Beck takes a similar position by speaking of an "inner" and an "outer" basis for the Qur'ānic presentation of Muslim-Christian affinity. The inner basis would be that spiritual state which is characterized by the lack of religious arrogance, while the outer is the educational function of biblical exegesis correctly performed and thus conducive to the reception of God's final revelation. *Das christliche Mönchtum*, 5–7.
101 Rashīd Riḍā, *Tafsīr al-Manār*, 7:7.
102 Rashīd Riḍā, *Tafsīr al-Manār*, 7:7.
103 Rashīd Riḍā, *Tafsīr al-Manār*, 7:7. Jomier has drawn attention to the difference between Christian and Islamic understandings of *istikbār*. In commenting upon *lā-yastakbirūna* he states: "L'orgueil, dans le Coran, ne s'applique point d'abord à ce sentiment que les auteurs spirituels chrétiens essaient de pourchasser partout où ils le trouvent, cet orgueil 'qui se glisse même dans les oeuvres bonnes pour les faire périr', comme l'écrivait saint Augustin dans la *Règle* qui porte son nom. L'orgueil, dans le Coran, est avant tout une attitude d'âme qui pousse à refuser l'Islam. N'être point orgueilleux signifie que l'on est prêt à se faire musulman." *Le commentaire coranique du Manār*, 303.
104 Rashīd Riḍā, *Tafsīr al-Manār*, 7:7. H. Zafrani draws upon a number of sources, including documents from the Cairo Geniza, to sketch some of the legal ramifications encountered by Jews under Muslim hegemony. "Les relations judéo-musulmanes dans la littérature juridique," in *Les relations entre juifs et musulmans en Afrique du Nord: actes du colloque international de l'Institut d'histoire des pays d'Outre-Mer* (Paris: Éditions du Centre national de la recherche scientifique, 1980), 32–48.
105 Rashīd Riḍā, *Tafsīr al-Manār*, 7:7.
106 Rashīd Riḍā, *Tafsīr al-Manār*, 7:7.
107 Rashīd Riḍā, *Tafsīr al-Manār*, 7:7.
108 Rashīd Riḍā, *Tafsīr al-Manār*, 7:8.
109 Rashīd Riḍā, *Tafsīr al-Manār*, 7:8.
110 Rashīd Riḍā, *Tafsīr al-Manār*, 7:8.
111 Rashīd Riḍā, *Tafsīr al-Manār*, 7:8.
112 Rashīd Riḍā, *Tafsīr al-Manār*, 7:8.
113 Rashīd Riḍā, *Tafsīr al-Manār*, 7:9
114 Rashīd Riḍā, *Tafsīr al-Manār*, 7:9. Richard Bulliet has used the quantitative analysis of data drawn from Muslim biographical dictionaries to graph the rates of conversion in selected areas of the medieval Islamic world. *Conversion to Islam in the Medieval Period* (Cambridge, Mass.: Harvard University Press, 1979).
115 Rashīd Riḍā, *Tafsīr al-Manār*, 7:9.
116 Rashīd Riḍā, *Tafsīr al-Manār*, 7:9.
117 Another argument Rashīd Riḍā offers for the closer proximity of Christianity to Islam is presented in Chapter 3.
118 Rashīd Riḍā, *Tafsīr al-Manār*, 7:10.
119 Rashīd Riḍā, *Tafsīr al-Manār*, 7:10. The most comprehensive study to date of medieval Christian attitudes toward Islam is that of Norman Daniel, *Islam and the West: The Making of an Image* (Edinburgh: The University Press, I960).
120 Rashīd Riḍā, *Tafsīr al-Manār*, 7:10. James Kritzeck published a study of this "major source of informed European Christian knowledge of Islam" (p. viii), including an interpretive translation of this *Summa totius haeresis Saracenorum*, entitled *Peter the Venerable and Islam* (Princeton: Princeton University Press, 1964). For a summary and critique of Kritzeck's work see Cutler, *The Jew as Ally of the Muslim*, 22–51.
121 Rashīd Riḍā, *Tafsīr al-Manār*, 7:10. Rashīd Riḍā's explanation of Muslim-Christian enmity as a failure of each side to act according to the best principles of its religion has captured the attention of Father Maurice Borrmans. He finds in the document *Nostra aetate* of the Second Vatican

Council an echo of such sentiments: "Si, au cours des siècles, de nombreuses dissensions et inimitiés se sont élevées entre Chrétiens et Musulmans, le Concile les exhorte tous à oublier le passé, à s'efforcer sincèrement à la compréhension mutuelle, et à garder et promouvoir en commun, pour tous les hommes, la justice sociale, les valeurs morales, la paix et la liberté." "Le Commentaire du Manâr à propos du verset coranique sur l'amitié des musulmans pour les chrétiens (5, 82)," *Islam* 1 (1975): 72.

122 Rashīd Riḍā, *Tafsīr al-Manār*, 7:10.
123 Rashīd Riḍā, *Tafsīr al-Manār*, 7:10–11.
124 Rashīd Riḍā, *Tafsīr al-Manār*, 7:11.
125 Rashīd Riḍā, *Tafsīr al-Manār*, 7:11.
126 Rashīd Riḍā, *Tafsīr al-Manār*, 7:11.
127 Rashīd Riḍā, *Tafsīr al-Manār*, 7:11.
128 Rashīd Riḍā, *Tafsīr al-Manār*, 7:11.
129 Rashīd Riḍā, *Tafsīr al-Manār*, 7:11.
130 Rashīd Riḍā, *Tafsīr al-Manār*, 7:11.
131 Ṭabāṭabā'ī, *al-Mīzān*, 6:80.
132 Ṭabāṭabā'ī, *al-Mīzān*, 6:80–81.
133 Ṭabāṭabā'ī, *al-Mīzān*, 6:81.
134 Ṭabāṭabā'ī, *al-Mīzān*, 6:81.
135 Ṭabāṭabā'ī, *al-Mīzān*, 6:81.
136 Ṭabāṭabā'ī, *al-Mīzān*, 6:81.
137 Ṭabāṭabā'ī, *al-Mīzān*, 6:81–82.
138 Ṭabāṭabā'ī, *al-Mīzān*, 6:82.
139 Ibn al-Jawzī, *Zād al-masīr*, 2:409. Cf. al-Ṭabarī, *Jāmi' al-bayān*, 10:508–9. One *ḥadīth* cited by al-Ṭabarī on the authority of al-Suddī parallels that from Sa'īd b. Jubayr. While the remaining *ḥadīths* that al-Ṭabarī mentions do not specify the incident, they all maintain the connection of this verse with the Najāshī.
140 Ibn Kathīr, *Tafsīr al-Qur'ān al-'aẓīm*, 2:86. The wording of this exchange is admittedly ambiguous and depends for its meaning on understanding the first use of *dīn* as a reference to Christianity and the second as a reference to Islam.
141 Ibn Kathīr, *Tafsīr al-Qur'ān al-'aẓīm*, 2:86. The verses mentioned are discussed in Chapter 5 (3:199) and Chapter 8 (28:52–53).
142 Ibn Kathīr, *Tafsīr al-Qur'ān al-'aẓīm*, 2:86.
143 Ibn Kathīr, *Tafsīr al-Qur'ān al-'aẓīm*, 2:87.
144 Kāshānī, *Minhaj al-ṣādiqīn*, 3:294.
145 Abū al-Futūḥ Rāzī, *Rawḥ al-jinān*, 4:307.
146 al-Zamakhsharī, *al-Kashshāf*, 1:670.
147 Fakhr al-Dīn al-Rāzī, *al-Tafsīr al-kabīr*, 12:68; Kāshání, *Minhaj al-ṣādiqīn*, 3:294; Rashīd Riḍā, *Tafsīr al-Manār*, 7:12.
148 Ibn al-Jawzī, *Zād al-masīr*, 2:409. The term *shāhidūn* is semantically related to the word *shahādah*, commonly defined as the basic faith confession for Muslims, the first of the 'five pillars' of Islamic orthopraxis. M.J. Kister discusses a line of tradition that accepts an attenuated form of the *shahādah*, one that does not include testifying to the prophethood of Muḥammad, as sufficient to guarantee the legal and economic rights of a Muslim. "… *illā bi-ḥaqqihi* …: A Study of an Early Ḥadīth," *JSAI* 5 (1984): 33–52.
149 Al-Ṭabarī, *Jāmi' al-bayān*, 10:509–11; al-Ṭūsī, *al-Tibyān*, 4:3–4; al-Zamakhsharī, *al-Kashshāf*, 1:670; Abū al-Futūḥ Rāzī, *Rawḥ al-jinān*, 4:307; Ibn Kathīr, *Tafsīr al-Qur'ān al-'aẓīm*, 2:86; Kāshānī, *Minhaj al-ṣādiqīn*, 3:294. Al-Ṭabarī cites *ḥadīths* on the authority of Ibn 'Abbās in several versions and Ibn Jurayj in support of this restricted connotation. However his own rephrasing goes considerably beyond this: the *shāhidūn* are "those who bear witness on behalf of Your [God's] prophets on the Day of Resurrection that they had communicated Your messages to their communities." *Jāmi' al-bayān*, 5:110. This is a far broader definition of the term because it includes not only those who attest to the veracity of Muḥammad but also all who responded rightly to former prophets sent by God. However, in his concluding remarks on this phrase al-Ṭabarī agrees that in the present context the correct meaning of *shāhidūn* is those who testify to the truth of what God has sent down on Muḥammad in the Qur'ān. These are the people eligible for divine reward and recompense. Al-Zamakhsharī continues this eschatological emphasis

when he defines the *shāhidūn* as the community of Muḥammad "who will testify against all [other] peoples (*'ala sā'ir al-umam*) on the Day of Resurrection." *al-Kashshāf*, 1:670.

150 Fakhr al-Dīn al-Rāzī, *al-Tafsīr al-kabīr*, 13:68.

151 Rashīd Riḍā, *Tafsīr al-Manār*, 7:12. J, Chelhod contrasts the increasing use of the reference *Allāh* and the decreasing use of *rabb* (Lord) in the chronology of Qur'ānic revelation and suggests that attention to this phenomenon may be one contribution to the efforts to date particular passages. "Note sur l'emploi du mot *rabb* dans le Coran," *Arabica* 5 (1958): 159–67. Daniel Gimaret notes that in its more than 1000 Qur'ānic occurrences, the term *rabb* is always found in pronominal or nominal constructions. He also remarks upon the fact that, despite its Qur'ānic frequency, it is not to be found in the most well-known list of the divine names (*al-asmā'al-ḥusnā*). *Les noms divins en Islam* (Paris: Éditions du Cerf, 1988), 318–19.

21 Rachel, Mary, and Fatima

Susan Sered

The Jewish matriarch Rachel, the Christian Virgin Mary, and the Islamic Fatima al-Zahra are female saints whose cults are located within monotheistic, male-dominated religious traditions.[1] Each of these saints is either the only or the most important female cultic figure within her own tradition. Comparison of the stories and cults of Rachel, Mary, and Fatima reveals two sets of issues. First, on every level of analysis the three figures differ from one another in substantive ways: these saints are associated with dissimilar myths, imagery, and theological notions. Second, all three saints are addressed in rather similar rites for similar purposes. In the ritual sphere three different myth-types within three different theological and cultural frameworks are transformed into intercessors who epitomize and specialize in concrete, human problems.

A number of studies of Mary have appeared during the past half century, yet she has usually been viewed in the context of ancient goddesses rather than of female saints (Bachoffen 1967; Briffault 1927; Harding 1971; Kinsley 1989; Neumann 1963; Walker 1983).[2] There have been no major cross-cultural studies of cults of female saints (for studies focusing on the internal life of the female saint rather than on cult, see Ramanujan 1984; Watkins 1983; Weinstein and Bell 1982) and Rachel and Fatima have accordingly received almost no attention in the religious studies or social science literature (on Fatima see Lammens 1912; Massignon 1955; Veccia Vaglieri 1965; on Rachel see Lipshitz 1967). While saints are situated somewhere in between the divine and human realms, it is my contention that studies of goddesses are of limited value in helping us understand the phenomenon of female saints. Saints' stories may encompass elements of earlier goddess mythologies, yet saints, unlike goddesses, are mortal beings perceived as possessing neither the ability to create nor to destroy. Furthermore, the active cults of the three saints described in this article developed many centuries after local goddess cults disappeared, making a historical connection difficult to prove. Instead, as I shall argue below, cults of female saints may be better understood in terms of their structural significance within particular cultural contexts.

The Saints

Rachel

Rachel is presented in the scriptural narrative in contexts of interpersonal relationships. Genesis 29:23–26 relates that Laban tricked Jacob into marrying Leah instead of his beloved Rachel. Expanding upon this brief story, later *midrashim* describe how Jacob and Rachel, suspecting that Laban would try to trick Jacob, arranged secret signals for Rachel to give Jacob during the wedding ceremony (*Lamentations Rabba,* Opening 24). At the last minute, however, Rachel took pity on her sister and told Leah the signals. Later that night Rachel hid beneath Jacob and Leah's wedding bed and spoke instead of Leah so that Jacob would not recognize by Leah's voice that he had married the wrong sister. Her self-sacrificing acts thus saved her sister from both public and private humiliation.

According to the biblical story Rachel was barren for many years (Genesis 30 and 35), and then died in childbirth on the road to Ephrat (Genesis 47:6). Jewish tradition stresses that because of Rachel's infertility she is especially compassionate and understanding of other women who suffer from the same affliction. To this day women visit her tomb to seek her assistance in matters related to pregnancy and the female life cycle (Sered 1986).

In Jeremiah 31:15–16 Rachel is portrayed as weeping for her children as they are led into exile in Babylonia. God then comforts her, promising that the exiles will indeed return from captivity. The midrash (*Pesikta Rabbati,* 3) sees Rachel as actually rising from her grave to weep, and interprets God's promise as Rachel's reward for her generosity to Leah. Rachel's special relationship to God is expanded to indicate that because of Rachel's merit God can deny nothing that she asks. Her tears are seen as particularly potent in enlisting God's aid for her children. Individual Jews in need of healing, livelihood, and fertility, and the Jewish people collectively in need of a homeland, appealed to Rachel in order to secure divine aid.

> "And she [Rachel] was buried there" … Why? It was known and expected by Jacob that the Temple would eventually be destroyed and his children exiled, and that they would go and ask the Patriarchs to pray for them. But their [the Patriarchs'] prayers would not be effective. Then, while on the road [from Jerusalem into exile] they would come to Rachel's Tomb and hug it. And she would stand up and ask mercy from the Holy One Blessed Be He. She would say to Him, "Master of the World, listen to me crying [and have mercy] for my children or give me my compensation." Right away, the Holy One Blessed Be He would listen to the voice of Rachel. [*Pesikta Rabbati* 83]

One would perhaps question my choosing Rachel as the central female saint in Jewish tradition. In Patai's (1978) controversial book *The Hebrew Goddess* Rachel is barely mentioned; Lilith, the Shekhina, and the Sabbath Queen appearing as more important figures. However, for Jews living today, particularly in Israel, Rachel is the only female figure who is truly potent. Significantly, there are no other shrines in Israel dedicated to female Jewish saints.

Mary

Mary is scarcely mentioned in the New Testament. The fullest description of Mary's conceiving Jesus appears in Luke 1 where an angel announces to Mary that she will bear a child, and then Mary, in a hymn known as the Magnificat, praises God. In Luke 2 Mary gives birth to Jesus in a manger. The story of Jesus's birth is told in a more abbreviated form in Matthew and Mark. Matthew 2:13–14 tells of the flight of the Holy Family into Egypt to escape Herod's decree to kill male babies. In John 19 Mary stands at the foot of the cross, and in Acts 1:14 Mary prays with the Apostles.[3]

As compared to the scanty references to Mary in Scripture, in the early centuries of the Christian era many fascinating Marian legends developed. These stories were recorded in various apocryphal gospels. According to the accounts in *Pseudo-Matthew* and *Protoevangelium of James* Mary's mother, St. Anne, was an old woman who had been barren for many years when an angel told her that she would have a child. Anne dedicated Mary to God and at the age of three Mary ran up the Temple steps. As a child, Mary was fed heavenly food by angels and she performed many miracles. When she reached puberty the high priest chose Joseph to be her husband and they lived together chastely. Mary gave birth to Jesus and miraculously remained a virgin even postpartum.

Other gospels, notably the *Transitus* or *Passing Away of Mary,* deal with her death. Jesus told Mary that she would die, and in preparation for her death she magically summoned the Apostles to her bedside. The most interesting element in this story is that Mary did not really die, but was assumed to heaven. Like Jesus, her body was placed in a cave and three days later disappeared. In later centuries, August 15, the day on which Mary is believed to have been assumed, became a major festival. Many other incidents in Mary's life have also served as the reason or model for feasts, festivals, and holy days.

From the time of the Reformation, Mary has been a more important figure for Catholics than for Protestants. Current Catholic Mariology stresses her role in redemption. While this theme can be traced back at least to the 3rd-century writings of Irenaeus in which Mary is described as the second Eve bringing salvation to the world (*Dem.,* 33), it is among modern theologians that this notion has particularly flourished. Pope Pius XII in 1956 wrote, "in bringing about the work of human redemption, the Most Blessed Virgin Mary was, by will of God, so indissolubly associated with Christ, that our salvation proceeded from the love and sufferings of Jesus Christ intimately joined with the love and sorrows of His Mother" (quoted in *New Catholic Encyclopedia* 1967:IX, 360). Mary's redemptive role is twofold. First, she consented to the coming of the Savior into the world and later accepted the fruits of her Son's redemptive act when, at Calvary, she officially represented the members of the Mystical Body. Further, she has a direct share in what is called the subjective redemption; that is, the dispensation of graces. According to one writer, Christ's merits and intercession will be of no avail without Mary's cooperating intercession, and so, every grace is conjointly obtained by her (Scheeben 1948:264).

Fatima

In texts concerning Fatima, as in writings about Rachel and Mary, there is a vast discrepancy between her biography as it appears in early Islamic sources, and the embellishments and legends added by later admirers. The basic story is as follows: Fatima al-Zahra (The Shining One) was the daughter of Muhammad and Khadidja, who died shortly after giving birth. Fatima married Ali, one of Muhammad's earliest followers and a cousin of the Prophet, but as Ali was poor their married life was both a struggle against poverty and filled with disputes. Ali is said to have acted so harshly toward Fatima that she complained to her father about his treatment (for other versions of this story see Kohlberg 1978:349). Ali is said to have considered marrying two more women, a plan that Muhammad rejected, saying that whoever hurts Fatima hurts him. Fatima bore two sons (Hassan and Hussayn), two daughters, and one stillborn son.

According to Shi'ite tradition, throughout her married life she maintained close contact with her father, and is often remembered tending his wounds following the battle of Uhud. Muhammad, to indicate his special regard for Fatima, embraced Fatima, Ali, and their two sons in his cloak, calling them "The People of the House." During Muhammad's final illness Fatima grieved for him and he comforted her by telling her that she would be the first member of the family to join him in the next world.

After Muhammad's death Abu Bakr, a follower of Muhammad who claimed the right to succeed the Prophet, demanded that Ali pay homage to him. In the Shi'ite account Fatima bravely proclaimed that Ali, not Abu Bakr, should be Muhammad's successor. Shortly afterward, she fell ill and died. The exact location of her grave is not known. Fatima is clearly a more important figure for Shi'ite than for Sunnite Muslims.[4]

The two pervasive Shi'ite images of Fatima are as the Eternal Weeper and as the Judge at the End of Days. According to Ayoub (1978:40) Fatima is depicted in Shi'ite sources as a bitter woman who spent her last days mourning the death of her father; her suffering and death are the first tragedy of Islam. Fatima also wept at other occasions: at the deaths of Hamza, Muhammad's uncle who was killed in battle and his body cannibalized, and of Dja'far, Muhammad's cousin and Ali's brother who met a bloody end in battle on the Byzantine frontier (Ayoub 1978:45–46; Juynboll 1983:103). The cosmic significance of her crying is rooted in her crying for her two sons, Hassan and Hussayn, who, according to Shi'ite sources, were murdered while fighting against the Umayyads. According to tradition, Fatima weeps eternally, and her tears in Paradise kindle God's wrath. Shi'ite Muslims believe that they share in Fatima's sufferings, and that the tears of the faithful on earth are a way both of taking part in her sorrows and of consoling her (Ayoub 1978:144).

Fatima is closely connected with the notion of redemption in her dual role of Mistress of the House of Sorrows (in this world) and Mistress of the Day of Judgment. Her sufferings will be rewarded and she and her sons and faithful followers will be vindicated (Ayoub 1978:19). As Fatima endured the greatest sufferings on earth, so on the Day of Resurrection she will enjoy great rewards. On that day Fatima will hold her son's blood-stained shirt in her hand and judge mankind. God will act according to her decisions, and her sole criteria in judging will be whether one loved her descendants or was their enemy. Of the many bloody descriptions of her vengeance, one that stands out is a scenario in which all of mankind is gathered in the desert. All the women will hold on to the fringes of Fatima's garment and they will speed across a narrow bridge. Enemies of her children will fall off into hell, and those who wept for her children will be carried into heaven; Muhammad will perform the same task for the men (Donaldson 1938:77). The Shi'ites interpret the name Fatima (which is derived from the root *ftm*, "to wean") as meaning that God "weaned" (= freed) her and all who love her from the fires of hell (Veccia Vaglieri 1965:847).

Comparisons

Mythological and Theological Considerations

Mary, like Isis, mourns the death of her dying and soon to be resurrected divine son. Rachel, on the other hand, is a purely mortal mother who dies giving birth and whose soul continues to haunt the earth searching for her human children (for other examples of this myth, see Gaster 1969). Thus while Mary more closely resembles the ancient goddesses who mourn their dead divine sons, Rachel embodies a different myth, that of a human mother dying in childbirth and eternally seeking her live children. The essence of Mary's power is that she is alive. The essence of Rachel's power is that she is dead. Mary today is above all worshiped at those places where she appeared on earth. Rachel is worshiped at her grave.

Because Mary is chosen by God to be Christ's mother, she becomes the universal mother. Rachel, beginning as the mother of a newborn human infant, is chosen by God to die and so becomes the universal mother. Fatima also mourns her son, but even as a mourner she is more closely connected to myths of the Judge at the End of Days. The type of myth that most resembles Fatima's story is, for example, the Zoroastrian myth which describes the beautiful/hideous women who accompany good/bad souls from the place of judgment (Hinnells 1973:62). Another mythological type to whom Fatima possibly may be related is Anat, the vengeful sister of Baal who slew his enemies and waded in blood up to her knees (Cassuto 1971:87–89 [Tablet V AB remnant of column ii and beginning of column iii]).

As we saw earlier, only Mary has a necessary role in the scheme of redemption. Fatima plays a more active role at the End of Days than does Mary, but there is no suggestion in Islam that redemption would be impossible without her. According to the Islamic view of redemption as the fulfillment of human life through suffering, Fatima, as the greatest sufferer on earth, will enjoy the greatest rewards on the day of resurrection (Ayoub 1978:23–25). However, this concept differs from the Catholic notion of Mary's consent and intercession as necessary for redemption. While Rachel, as the symbol of the return to Zion, is associated with the historical redemption signified by the return from the Babylonian Captivity, she is not directly connected with cosmic redemption. However, in kabbalistic writings where she is identified with the *Shekhina* (the female aspect of God), she must be reunited with the (male) Holy One Blessed Be He in order to bring about *tikkun olam* or "the mending of the world" (Scholem 1972:149–50). Fatima, unlike the benevolent Mary and Rachel, is thought to appear wrathful at the End of Days, demanding vengeance for her murdered children.

All three of these saints function within religious traditions that posit a faraway male god, yet each is portrayed in a different type of relationship to that god. In one fascinating midrash God promises Rachel that the next world will be good for her children, but she demands that this world shall also be good for them. "And our mother Rachel refused those comforts [that the next world will be good] and demanded that her children will also enjoy this world" (*Sefer Tiul b'Pardes,* Tanina, chapter 200, paragraph 3). When Rachel bargains with God for the return of her children (*Yalkut Reuveni,* VaYetze, 128) her role is simultaneously complementary to and in opposition to the male God. If the children of Israel do not return to their Land, there can be no eternal covenant. Yet Rachel has to negotiate, threaten, and cajole God to remember that covenant. Mary's relationship to the male God is quite different. The essence of the cult of Mary is that she is eternally alive—her body ascended to Heaven, unharmed and undecayed, while the central Christological image is of a man, wounded and dying. As Ashe has pointed out, Christians tend to perceive Christ as being too dead (Ashe 1978:123). The very alive Mary is necessary for redemption; as a living life-giver she mitigates the death imagery of God incarnate crucified. Fatima's relationship to the male deity is again very different. For Shi'ite Muslims *baraka* or divine blessing is made available to humans primarily through descendants of the Prophet. Fatima is the one through whom, in a biological sense, baraka is channeled from God to man. Another aspect of Fatima's relationship to the male deity is in the eschatological realm: she is the female ancestor of the *mahdi* (loosely translated as messiah) and will assist God judge souls at the End of Days.

Finally, while each saint is associated with one or several of the most central theological issues within her tradition, the actual content of the issues is diverse: Mary is necessary in explaining how God can become man, Rachel is concerned with exile and convenant, and Fatima is primarily interested in the End of Days.

Key Imagery

Suffering is a central image for all three women. But while Rachel herself suffers, and Mary suffers by seeing her son suffer, Fatima's entire life is perceived as a metaphor for suffering. Mary and Fatima are both referred to as "virgin." For Mary the paradox of being a virgin mother is addressed head on and solved by asserting that she conceived by the Holy Spirit and even remained physiologically a virgin postpartum (see, for example, *The Protoevangelium of James*). Fatima is called "virgin" although she bore five children, but the physiological intricacies of this have not received much attention.[5] Rachel, infertile for many years, is never called "virgin," although as Callaway (1986) notes there may be a connection between virginity and infertility in Hebrew literature. Mary and Fatima are seen as having been born free of sin, and to both are attributed childhood miracles. Rachel's birth and childhood are completely and totally mortal.

Mary and Joseph (or Mary and Jesus) as well as Rachel and Jacob function as couples in societies where the nuclear family is a significant cultural unit. Fatima, as Wolf (1969:287–301) correctly points out, is the point of intersection between two agnatic lines, Muhammad's and Ali's. Mary and Fatima receive their theological significance primarily because of their relationships with men: Fatima is the daughter of the Prophet and Mary is the mother of the Savior. Rachel, however, receives moral praise chiefly as Leah's sister and it is in the merit of her relationship to her sister that the children of Israel receive the divine promise of the return to Zion.

Rachel and Mary are both frequently called "Mother"; Rachel's most widely used appellation in Yiddish is *Muter Ruchel* and in Hebrew she is called *Rachel Imeinu* (Our Mother Rachel). Fatima in fact gave birth to more children than either Mary or Rachel, but she is not usually addressed as "Mother." In the popular imagination Rachel is most commonly pictured as rising from her solitary grave and crying. On the other hand, the Mater Dolorosa is only one of Mary's numerous personae. Mary is frequently portrayed as holding the baby Jesus to her breast, whereas Rachel died in childbirth and Fatima, according to Islamic tradition, did not even suckle Hussayn. Instead, Muhammad nursed him via his tongue or his finger (Ayoub 1978:75–76). Both Fatima and Rachel are seen as the biological mothers of their respective followers. Most Jews today are descendants of the tribes of Judah and Benjamin, Rachel's son. Mary, on the other hand, left no biological descendants—instead, she is the spiritual "mother of us all."

Rachel, unlike Fatima and Mary, is consistently portrayed as loving and kind. In many midrashim Rachel is seen as pleading with God on behalf of the Jewish people, and her bargaining tool is her having controlled her anger when Jacob married Leah (*Yalkut Reuveni*, VaYetse). Marian legends abound with instances of Mary aiding poor widows and lost travelers (see Ashe 1978; Warner 1976). Deliege, for example, argues that for lower caste Christians in India,

> In a supernatural world inhabited by coarse, cruel and bloodthirsty people, the Virgin Mary stands out through her kindness and love. She is the only divinity which does not hit out. She rights wrongs caused by others and cures a range of illnesses. [1986:75]

Yet, in other cultural contexts both Carroll (1986:63ff.) and Harrington (1988) have discovered nonbenevolent Marian images. While there are legends of Fatima helping those in need, in many legends she appears angry or punishing. For example, on one occasion she is said to have closed up a well leading to Mecca because a man walked through it and saw her washing clothes (Masse 1938:236), and in another anecdote she is credited with punishing a mule and so causing all mules to become sterile (Davis 1982:108).

Mary, as the Virgin Mother of God, is essentially inimitable, whereas Rachel and Fatima are more realistic models. While women can strive to be faithful, modest, generous, or wise, to be a virgin mother is an impossible goal for mortal women. In a different sense, though, Mary is the most positive model of the three. Fatima and Rachel suffered in life, died young, and weep in eternity; Mary is rarely portrayed as a victim. Especially during the past two decades (with the influence of the modern feminist movement) the Church has made some effort to describe Mary not only "as a mother exclusively concerned with her own Divine son, but rather as a woman whose action helped to strengthen the apostolic community's faith in Christ" (Pope Paul VI, *Devotion to the Blessed Virgin*, Section 37, page 27, in Warner 1976:338). An odd twist is that Rachel is the only one of the three saints to experience all of the female physiological processes. Both Fatima and Mary are said to have not menstruated and to have been exempt from pain in childbirth. Rachel, conversely, suffered disproportionately from female ailments throughout her life.[6]

The following poem written by Sir Muhammad Iqba (a modern Muslim poet and thinker, quoted in Smith 1963:165–66) about Fatima could fit certain Marian traditions (substituting the word "son" for "husband"), but could not possibly suit the Rachel of Jewish tradition:

> The chaste Fatima is the harvest of the field of submission,
> The chaste Fatima is a perfect model for mothers.
> So touched was her heart for the poor,
> That she sold her own wrap …
> She who might command the spirits of heaven and hell
> Merged her own will in the will of her husband.
> Her upbringing was in courtesy and forbearance;
> And murmuring the Qur'an, she ground corn.

Pictures of Mary adorn Catholic churches and shrines all over the world, while the Jewish prohibition against images has prevented the artistic development of a cult of Rachel (her tomb, however, is a common theme in Jewish art). Portraiture of Muhammad and the Saints is avoided, especially by Sunnite Muslims. Shi'ites do have more artistic representations of religious scenes, but Fatima rarely, if ever, appears even in Shi'ite art. In one of the very few pictures of Fatima that I have been able to find (a miniature from late 16th-century Turkey) she is shown heavily veiled and none of her features are visible. As Crone (1980:64) concludes, "Christian art … was granted recognition by a series of concessions. … In Islam, by contrast, such concessions to practice were staunchly refused." One can only guess to what extent the presence or absence of visual representation of the saints affects and affected the ways in which people "see" saints, yet it is reasonable to suggest that the power of an image that appears in millions of churches, shrines, and private homes must be great.

As a result of Mary's physical assumption into Heaven, she is able to appear on earth. The most famous recent Marian appearance was of course in Lourdes. Rachel's body is in her tomb, so she is really present only there, and rarely appears in visions. Fatima also seldom appears in visions.[7]

Only Mary has a formalized role in the public liturgy of her Church. All three saints are associated with shrines, albeit of varying numbers and importance (see Burton 1906:11, 41–42; Sered 1989). Fatima has a world-famous symbol, the ubiquitous *hamsa* or "hand of Fatima" which is used in many parts of the Islamic world to guard against evil spirits or the evil eye. Mary has a color, blue, associated with her cult. Red string is associated with Rachel's tomb (as a charm for pregnancy and easy delivery). Mary in the festival-rich Catholic tradition has numerous holidays and feast days connected both with biographical events and with appearances after her death. Islam in general has few official festivals (Lazarus-Yafet 1981:47) and there are a number of rather minor holidays associated with Fatima. Rachel has the anniversary of her death and the Eve of the New Moon, days on which some Israeli Jews visit her tomb.[8]

Cultic Considerations

> In the merit of Our Mother Rachel we will all be healthy and whole. [written by a pilgrim in the Rachel's Tomb *Daybook*, 19/7/44]

> The shrine at Lourdes drew nearly three and half million pilgrims in 1971, of whom three hundred and ninety-four thousand were sick and travelled there in specially equipped hospital trains ... millions of beads run through millions of fervent fingers daily in quest of earthly miracle. [Warner 1976:309]

> Persian women would make feast offerings to Fatima in order to be healthy, free of debt, or to go on pilgrimage. [Masse 1938:302]

The arena in which there seem to be the most meaningful similarities among the three saints is that of cultic activity. Each saint has a different story and each has a different role in the mythological and theological framework, yet all three are turned to by individuals—particularly, but not only, women—seeking assistance with problems of health, personal happiness, and fertility. Rachel, Mary, and Fatima are all intermediaries/intercessors within male-oriented religious traditions.

The experiences in the lives of the female saints that have earned cultic attention are not connected to extraordinary spiritual pursuits or powers; Rachel, Mary, and Fatima are not considered holy because of asceticism, contemplation, miracle-working (while alive), or vast learning. On the contrary, the striking features in the biographies of the three saints are the common human situations confronted by each: death of parents and children, marital love and discord, difficulty conceiving and bearing children, conflict with siblings and parents. These are situations that both resonate with the actual life experiences of most human beings, and touch upon grave theological and existential issues.

The role of intermediary/intercessor is multifaceted and the female saint is far more than a messenger-girl: she in fact mediates between two realms of discourse. In all three religious cultures God is conceived as infinite, while human needs naturally remain immediate. The critical expertise of the female saint is that she translates personal matters into universal symbols, at the same time that she transforms cosmology and theology and mythology and rules and rites into personal matters. The female saint is both expert at conveying human needs in a form that is consistent with divine discourse, and expert at conveying cosmic messages in a form that speaks to human needs. Rachel, Mary, and Fatima, in myth and in ritual, mediate not only between petitioners and petitioned; they also mediate between the concrete and the abstract, the personal and the universal, the immediate and the infinite. By embodying both realms of meaning, the saints function as intermediaries between the individual and the cosmos. These saints are important not only at the level of so-called "magical" interventions; these saints, through their life stories, help individuals make sense out of the real, human problems with which we all are confronted in the course of our lives. All three saints are known as the one who truly understands human needs.

The model that I have presented here is not a simple matter of ignorant "folk" diluting or perverting the symbols and concepts of the great tradition. The complex processes which resulted in the cults of Rachel, Mary, and Fatima should be seen as a dialectic: the impetus for the cult comes simultaneously from the writings of the great tradition,[9] the needs and hopes of human beings, and the interaction between the two. Significantly, in all three instances popular devotion exceeds the limits set by strict ecclesiastic law for praying through/to saints, yet the religious authorities have chosen to "channel" popular enthusiasm, rather than quash it (Turner and Turner 1978:192).

Linking individuals' lives to theology and cult is a concern of all religious systems, and a female-saint-intercessor is not the only means of doing so; pilgrimage, icons, amulets, and other sorts of ritual activity may all fill similar functions. Yet it is suggestive that Protestant Christians, Sunnite Muslims, and "enlightened" Jews, groups who do not find meaning in and so do not emphasize the notion of intercessor, also do not elaborate cosmologies that have important roles for female figures. And conversely, in those traditions that do allow room for intercessors (Catholicism, Shi'ite Islam, Hassidic and North African Judaism), female saints occupy extremely powerful positions. I do not claim that female saints are the only solution for linking great tradition doctrines and symbols to little tradition beliefs and needs—I am rather suggesting that female saints seem to be particularly good at it.

Saints, Great Goddesses, and Family Structure—A Critique

Few social scientists have explored in detail the myths and cults of female saints, and scholarly literature dealing with Mary has been dominated by psychological (and particularly psychoanalytic) approaches. Writers in the Jungian tradition, treating Mary as one more manifestation of the Great Goddess, have tended to gloss over even the most glaring differences among the various female figures (Jung 1970). Carroll, dissatisfied with the Jungian approach, proposes that

> Fervent devotion to the Mary cult on the part of males is a practice that allows males characterized by a strong but strongly repressed sexual desire for the mother to dissipate in an acceptable manner the excess sexual energy that is built up as a result of this desire. ... Identifying strongly with the Virgin Mary allows women to experience vicariously the fulfillment of their desire for sexual contact with, and a baby from, their fathers. [1986:56, 59]

The basis of Carroll's argument is that these psychological conditions arise most strongly in the "father-ineffective family."

This sort of schema, however, ignores the formative effect that religion may have on society. Carroll defines a causative chain that proceeds from social conditions to psychological characteristics to mythology and cult. While Mary (and Rachel and Fatima) may indeed be described in certain ways because human mothers really act in those ways, we need to at least raise the possibility that real women behave as they do because the religious system both implicitly and explicitly encourages them to do so (see Russell 1987 for further critique of Carroll's study; also cf. McGilvray 1988; Preston 1982:327).

For example, in Jewish, Catholic, and Shi'ite traditions women are taught to identify with female saints, and all three saints are held up as prototypes of perfect womanhood.

Fatima in particular has been effectively used in the writings of modern Iranian Muslims as a role model for the good, pure, modest, Muslim woman (Hermansen 1983:87–96). Mary and Fatima have often been described as examples of submission and "women's place." "The gentle Fatimah ... typifies the woman whose life is spent, and whose personality is fulfilled, in service to her family" (Waddy 1980:49). And, "In my day, Mary was a stick to beat smart girls with. Her example was held up constantly, an example of silence, of subordination, of the pleasure of taking the back seat" (Gordon 1982:11).

Furthermore, it is crucial to bear in mind that all three cults described in this article have existed within a wide range of cultural settings. Mary, Rachel, and Fatima are associated with religious traditions that developed over many centuries in a variety of Asian, African, American, and European societies characterized by a multitude of kinship structures and intrafamilial dynamics. The psychological approaches favored by many modern scholars tend to back away from examining the broad cultural conditions that could explain how three such different myth-types were transformed into similar cultic figures within diverse social settings. Reading first Jung and then Carroll, we are left asking why, on the one hand, the three saints look so different, and why, on the other hand, their cults are so similar.

Women Saints in Patriarchal Cultures

Regarding each of the three saints it is said that God cannot deny anything that she asks, yet none is portrayed as using that power to threaten the patriarchal status quo. Instead, the requests made to and by each have to do with health, fertility, happiness, prosperity, and a future salvation that is clearly granted by the male deity. Within the context of patriarchal culture where by definition men, real or mythical, dominate the public realm (Reiter 1975; Rosaldo 1974), female saints tend to excel at domestic matters.

Rachel, Mary, and Fatima share a similar structural role within the various patriarchal traditions in which their cults have developed. Despite their different myths and imagery, all are associated with the private rather than the public realm, with positions of subordination rather than dominance, with relationships rather than rules. In short, they resemble mortal women in patriarchal cultures.

But mortal women, like female saints, are not totally powerless. Women, excluded from formal or public power, may amass power within the private domain (Rosaldo 1974). In 1974 Ortner asked whether women are to men as nature is to culture. Her conclusion, as I understand it, is not that women are more "nature" than are men, but rather that within patriarchal cultures women tend to be defined as associated with nature. A close look at the ethnographic record suggests that the "woman-nature" complex does not merely refer to dirt, vegetables, blood, and animals, but also to individual, affective relationships (as opposed to institutionalized, society-wide associations). This, then, is the same structural slot that I have described for the female saints; Rachel, Mary, and Fatima are experts at dealing with immediate, personal, and interpersonal problems. It is around this expertise that their cults have flourished.

Rachel, Mary, and Fatima embody different myths; they are described using different imagery; their liturgical and theological statuses vary considerably. However, all three mediate between transcendent male gods and natural human needs. The same cultural conditions—male dominance and the association of women with nature—which shape the lives of mortal women have shaped the cults of the three saints. Maneuvering within cultural contexts that, while diverse in many critical ways, share the key characteristics of deep-rooted gender inequality, these female saints are specialists at understanding and sometimes ameliorating the sufferings of individuals.

Notes

1 While I believe that the male dominance of the Jewish, Christian, and Islamic traditions is self-evident (male deity, male religious leaders, ideology of female subordination or pollution), the reader interested in feminist analysis of these religions can look at Ruether (1974) and al-Hibr (1982).
2 Most of these studies emphasize the ways in which Mary is similar to goddesses rather than the ways in which she differs. My choice of analyzing Mary within the context of saints seems obvious in light of the fact that in the New Testament Mary is associated with Rachel (Matthew 2:17–18) and in Islamic tradition Fatima is sometimes called "The Great Mary" (Veccia Vaglieri 1965:848).
3 The other biblical references to Mary are: Galatians 4:4 (Jesus was born of a woman); Mark 6:3 (Mary is Jesus's mother); Mark 3:31ff., Matthew 12:46ff., Luke 8:19ff. (Jesus says that his real family is those who do the will of God); John 2:3–5 (wedding at Cana—Mary asks Jesus for more wine).
4 Aisha, Muhammad's favorite wife and known for her active involvement in politics after the Prophet's death, is more important for Sunnite Muslims (on Aisha see Abbott 1973). It is interesting to note that while Mary and Fatima both became rallying points for defining certain subgroups within the larger traditions (Fatima is the ancestor and symbol of Shi'ite Muslims and veneration of Mary is clearly a dividing line between Catholics and Protestants) Rachel never became the favorite saint of any particular group.
5 Engelsman (1979:128–29) points out that "virgin" is an ancient title for goddesses meaning "independent" rather than "hymen intact." One traditional Islamic explanation for Fatima's title "virgin" is that it indicates that no woman comparable with her ever existed (Veccia Vaglieri 1965:848).
6 For two conflicting traditions concerning Fatima see Veccia Vaglieri (1965:847) and Ayoub (1978:75).
7 For two Rachelian visions see *Sefer HaYashar*, 92, and Lipshitz (1967:234). One of the few recorded examples concerning Fatima can be found in Masse (1938:236).
8 In general, Rachel's cult is far more limited in geographical distribution than the cults of the other two saints.
9 All three saints were particularly popular among mystics of the late Middle Ages. Probably the great impetus to Mariology came from the writings of such mystics as St. Bernard; Rachel as the Shekhina is a kabbalistic notion; and Fatima is particularly important for Sufis (Schimmel 1975). I thank R. J. Zvi Werblowsky for pointing this out to me.

References

Abbott, Nabia 1973[1942] Aisha the Beloved of Mohammed. New York: Arno Press.
al-Hibr, Azizah, ed. 1982 Women's Studies International Forum Special Issue on Women and Islam, 5.
Ashe, Gregory 1978 Miracles. London: Routledge & Kegan Paul.
Ayoub, Mahmoud 1978 Redemptive Suffering in Islam. Hague: Mouton.
Bachoffen, J. J. 1967 Myth, Religion and Mother Right. Princeton, N.J.: Princeton University Press.
Briffault, Robert 1927 The Mothers (3 volumes). New York: Macmillan.
Burton, Richard F. 1906 Personal Narrative of a Pilgrimage to Al-Madinah and Meccah. London: George Bell and Sons.
Callaway, Mary 1986 Sing, O Barren One: A Study in Comparative Midrash. Atlanta: Scholars Press.
Carroll, Michael P. 1986 The Cult of the Virgin Mary. Princeton, N.J.: Princeton University Press.
Cassuto, U. 1971 The Goddess Anath. Jerusalem: Magnes Press.
Crone, Patricia 1980 Islam, Judeo-Christianity and Byzantine Iconoclasm. Jerusalem Studies in Arabic and Islam 2:59–96.

Davis, Susan S. 1982 Patience and Power: Women's Lives in a Moroccan Village. Cambridge, Mass.: Schenkman Publishing.
Deliege, Robert 1986 Arockyai Mary, gardienne du village chez les Parayars de l'Inde du Sud. Social Compass 33:75–89.
Donaldson, Bess Allen 1938 The Wild Rue—A Study of Muhammadan Magic and Folklore in Iran. London: Luzac and Co.
Engelsman, Joan Chamberlain 1979 The Feminine Dimension of The Divine. Philadelphia: Westminster Press.
Gaster, Theodor 1969 Myth, Legend, and Custom in the Old Testament. New York: Harper & Row.
Gordon, Mary 1982 Coming to Terms with Mary. Commonweal 109:11.
Harding, M. Esther 1971 Woman's Mysteries: Ancient and Modern. New York: Harper & Row.
Harrington, Patricia 1988 Mother of Death, Mother of Rebirth: The Mexican Virgin of Guadalupe. Journal of the American Academy of Religion 56(l):25–50.
Hermansen, Marcia K. 1983 Fatimeh as a Role Model in the Works of Ali Shari'ati. *In* Women and Revolution in Iran. Guity Nashat, ed. Pp. 87–96. Boulder, Colo.: Westview Press.
Hinnells, John 1973 Persian Mythology. London: Hamlyn Publishing Group Ltd.
Jung, Carl G. 1970 Four Archetypes: Mother, Rebirth, Spirit, Trickster. Princeton, N.J.: Princeton University Press.
Juynboll, G. H. A. 1983 Muslim Tradition. Cambridge: Cambridge University Press.
Kinsley, David 1989 The Goddesses' Mirror. Albany: State University of New York Press.
Kohlberg, E. 1978 Abu Turab. Bulletin of the School of Oriental and Africa Studies 41(2):347–52.
Lammens, Henri 1912 Fatima et les Filles des Mahomet. Rome: Scripta Pontificii Instituti Biblici.
Lazarus-Yafet, Hava 1981 Some Religious Aspects of Islam. Leiden: E. J. Brill.
Lipshitz, Arie 1967 Yesod 'LKRI' Ohel Rachel Imeinu. Jerusalem: Published by the author, [in Hebrew]
Masse, Henri 1938 Croyances et Coutumes Persanes. Paris: G. P. Maisonneuve Editeur.
Massignon, Louis 1955 La Mubahala de Medine et L'Hyperdulie de Fatime. Paris: Libraire Orientale et Americaine.
McGilvray, Dennis B. 1988 Sex, Repression, and Sanskritization in Sri Lanka. Ethos 16:99–127.
Neumann, Erich 1963 The Great Mother: An Analysis of the Archetype. Princeton, N.J.: Princeton University Press.
New Catholic Encyclopedia 1967 New York: McGraw-Hill.
Ortner, Sherry 1974 Is Female to Male as Nature Is to Culture? *In* Women, Culture, and Society. Michelle Zimbalist Rosaldo and Louise Lamphere, eds. Pp. 67–87. Stanford, Calif.: Stanford University Press.
Patai, Raphael 1978 The Hebrew Goddess. New York: Avon Books.
Preston, James J., ed. 1982 Mother Worship: Theme and Variations. Chapel Hill: University of North Carolina Press.
Ramanujan, A. K. 1984 On Women Saints. *In* The Divine Consort—Radha and the Goddesses of India. John S. Hawley and Donna M. Wulff, eds. Pp. 316–67. Delhi: Motilal Banarsidass.
Reiter, Rayna, ed. 1975 Towards an Anthropology of Women. New York: Monthly Review Press.
Rosaldo, Michelle Zimbalist 1974 Women, Culture, and Society: A Theoretical Overview. *In* Women, Culture, and Society. Michelle Zimbalist Rosaldo and Louise Lamphere, eds. Pp. 17–42. Stanford, Calif.: Stanford University Press.
Ruether, Rosemary, ed. 1974 Religion and Sexism: Images of Women in the Jewish and Christian Traditions. New York: Simon & Schuster.
Russell, Jeffrey Burton 1987 Book Review of 'The Cult of the Virgin Mary: Psychological Origins.' Journal of the American Academy of Religion 55(3):593–97.
Scheeben, M. J. 1948 Mariology. St. Louis: B. Herder.
Schimmel, Annemarie 1975 Mystical Dimensions of Islam. Chapel Hill: University of North Carolina Press.
Scholem, Gershom 1972 On the Kabbalah and Its Symbolism. New York: Schocken Books.

Sered, Susan Starr 1986 Rachel's Tomb and the Milk Grotto of the Virgin Mary: Two Women's Shrines in Bethlehem. Journal of Feminist Studies in Religion 2(2):7–22.

——1989 Rachel's Tomb: Societal Liminality and the Revitalization of a Shrine. Religion 19:27–40.

Smith, Wilfred Cantwell 1963 Modern Islam in India: A Social Analysis. Kashmir Bazar, Lahone: Sh. Muhammad Ashraf.

Turner, Victor, and Edith Turner 1978 Image and Pilgrimage in Christian Culture. New York: Columbia University Press.

Veccia Vaglieri, L. 1965 Fatima. *In* Encyclopedia of Islam, New Edition. B. Lewis, Ch. Pellat, J. Schacht et al., eds. Vol. II, pp. 841–50. Leiden: E. J. Brill.

Waddy, Chris 1980 Women in Muslim History. London: Longman.

Walker, Barbara 1983 The Women's Encyclopedia of Myths and Secrets. New York: Harper & Row.

Warner, Marina 1976 Alone of All Her Sex, The Myth and The Cult of The Virgin Mary. New York: Pocket Books.

Watkins, Renee Neu 1983 Two Women Visionaries and Death: Catherine of Siena and Julian of Norwich. Numen 30(2): 174–98.

Weinstein, Donald, and Rudolph M. Bell 1982 Saints and Society: The Two Worlds of Western Christendom 1000–1700. Chicago: University of Chicago Press.

Wolf, Eric R. 1969 Society and Symbols in Latin Europe and in the Islamic Near East. Anthropological Quarterly 42(3):287–301.

22 "No God in Common"

American Evangelical Discourse on Islam after 9/11

Richard Cimino

Introduction

While the number of Muslims in the U.S. is in dispute, their very presence in the U.S., like the earlier presence of Jews, challenges older establishments and ways of doing things. A Diversity Survey conducted by Robert Wuthnow found that 48% of the public claimed to have had at least some personal contact with Muslims, and eight percent have attended a Muslim mosque. Wuthnow noted that these figures are considerably larger than the percentages of Americans in the 1970s who experimented with Eastern new religions. "In short, there is a kind of cultural awareness, undoubtedly forged as much by television and motion pictures and by international travel and cultural mixing as by recent trends in immigration, which far exceeds and transcends the actual numbers of Muslim, Hindu, or Buddhist adherents" (Wuthnow 2003). A growing symbolic influence of Muslims in American society could be seen in the appointment of a Muslim chaplain to the Senate and even in the fact that a Muslim led the benediction during the Republican Convention in 2000.

But it took September 11, 2001 (referred to throughout this article as 9/11) to bring these changes home to many other Americans and to evangelicals in particular. In the years following the terrorist attacks, evangelical Protestants have shown themselves to be among the most caustic critics and antagonists of Islam in the U.S. In 2002, evangelist Franklin Graham called Islam a "very wicked and evil religion," while Pat Robertson and Jerry Falwell criticized Islam as essentially violent and sympathetic to terrorism. In a similar manner, Southern Baptist leader Jerry Vines created headlines by preaching that Mohammed was a "demon-possessed pedophile" (Plowman 2002). These comments were ridiculed and criticized by more liberal Christians and other religious and political leaders. The Bush administration on several occasions distanced itself from these anti-Islamic statements, maintaining its public stance that Islam is a religion of peace.

But the public statements revealed a pattern of anti-Islamic polemics that is found in much of the literature of evangelicals and charismatic Christians in the period after 9/11. This article examines the recent anti-Islamic polemics in the light of the evangelicals' encounter with the new pluralism that has developed within American society during the past decade. I also attempt to relate these polemics to evangelical statements and writings about syncretism and relativism that have appeared since 9/11. These concerns have led evangelicals to reassert and sharpen the differences between the teachings of Christianity and Islam.

There is considerable disagreement in the sociological literature as to the effects of interreligious conflict and pluralism among evangelicals. Hunter (1987) argues that the conflict associated with religious and cultural pluralism erodes evangelical identity, leading either to an isolationist stance or to a gradual bargaining away of essential teachings and practices.

In contrast, Smith (1998:115) asserts that "conflict with ideological and subcultural competitors that religious groups may confront in a pluralistic society ... can strengthen religious beliefs and practices." The present article is not so much about actual conflicts between evangelicals and Muslims as about how American evangelicals are reasserting their differences with Islam as a way of battling what they see as the more pervasive cultural forces of relativism and syncretism. In such a conflict with modern American society, I argue that such anti-Islamic polemics function to strengthen the subcultural identity of evangelicals. Throughout this article, I use the term "evangelical" in the broad sense to include both non-charismatic and charismatic conservative Protestants who adhere to the three basic tenets of this movement: stressing a personal relationship with Christ, the authority and inspiration of the Bible, and the importance of evangelizing others (Marsden 1991). When specifically referring to charismatics and fundamentalists, I will use those terms.

Recent surveys have found that American evangelicals are more likely than other Americans to be opposed to Islam and to believe there is little common ground between the two faiths. In a Pew Survey shortly after 9/11, 62% of evangelicals said they believed their religion to be very different from Islam, as compared to 44% of non-evangelicals who held this view (Pew 2001). A Beliefnet/Ethics and Public Policy survey in 2003 found that 77% of evangelical leaders had an overall unfavorable view of Islam. Seventy percent also agreed that Islam is a "religion of violence." Yet 93% said it was either "very important" (52%) or "of some importance" (41%) to "welcome Muslims into the American community." Seventy nine percent said it was very important to "protect the rights of Muslims" (Beliefnet, EPPC 2003). This seeming contradiction between condemning Islam while accepting Muslims in the U.S. suggests that much of the anti-Islamic rhetoric is based on issues of religion and values rather than on racial and ethnic prejudice. Another study by Pew in July of 2003 found that most Americans continue to rate Muslim-Americans favorably, though the percentage is inching downward. A declining number of Americans say that their own religion has a lot in common with Islam: 22% in 2003, compared with 27% in 2002 and 31% shortly after the terrorist attacks in the fall of 2001. White evangelical Christians and political conservatives hold more negative views of Muslims and are more likely than other Americans to say that Islam encourages violence among its followers (Pew 2003, Islam Online 2004).

The Diversity Survey conducted in 2003 found that 47% of respondents agreed that the word "fanatical" applied to the religion of Islam, and 40% said the word "violent" described the religion. Nearly one quarter (23%) said they favored making it illegal for Muslim groups to meet in the U.S. for worship (Wuthnow 2003). Aside from survey research, however, there has been little qualitative research about evangelical attitudes on Islam. A recent content analysis (Hoover 2004) of the two primary evangelical magazines, *Christianity Today* and the newsweekly *World,* does reveal the growth of anti-Islamic attitudes after 9/11, at least among a segment of evangelicals. *Christianity Today* magazine, representing more moderate or "mainstream" evangelicals, was found to downplay the idea of inevitable conflict between Islam and the West in its coverage in the two years after 9/11. Articles about evangelizing Muslims and religious persecution of missionaries were the most prominent kinds of articles in the magazine during this period. In contrast, *World,* which more closely reflects the positions of the Christian Right, adopted a harder line, stressing the violent nature of much of Islam and criticizing news coverage that the magazine viewed as favorably biased toward the religion (Hoover 2004).

The present article finds that the evangelical stance toward Islam is even more complex and diverse. I divide the evangelical positions on Islam, as reflected in their literature, into four categories: apologetic, prophetic, charismatic-spiritual warfare, and contextualist.

Method

In this article, evangelical anti-Islamic discourse is examined through a content analysis of popular evangelical literature from the ten year period before September 11, 2001, and in the three years following that event. The 10-year span prior to 9/11 was chosen in order to have a large enough sample to analyze (there were very few evangelical books written on Islam before 2001). The impact of 9/11 on evangelical attitudes on Islam is most evident in the apologetic books; the anti-Islamic themes in the prophetic and charismatic literature had already emerged a decade earlier, although popularized and intensified after the terrorist attacks.

The books selected for analysis in this study were taken from the online listings and catalog of the Family Christian Bookstores, one of the largest evangelical Christian bookstore chains in the U.S. An attempt was made to collect all of the evangelical books on Islam that have been published and distributed to these bookstores. Family Christian Bookstores tends to exclude scholarly evangelical publishers and books, although I located several of such titles and have included them in the analysis and comparisons. This article thus analyzes a total of 18 books, 13 of which were written or reissued after 9/11. According to criteria discussed at the beginning of this article, each book was analyzed for its discourse on the nature of Islam (which is related to the question of whether the religion is inherently violent), and for its explanation of the relationship of Islam to Christianity and Judaism (which is related to the question of whether Muslims worship the same God as Jews and Christians).

In addition to these issues, the prophetic and the spiritual warfare-charismatic books were analyzed using more specific criteria, including the role of Islam in the end times and the concept of "spiritual warfare" in the critique of Islam. Finally, a content analysis of the conservative evangelical newsweekly *World* was conducted between the years of 1996–2002 to explore the context of anti-Islamic discourse and how it is related to concerns over interfaith involvement and pluralism.

Evangelical Apologetic Literature on Islam Before and After 9/11

Within the evangelical apologetic movement one finds a distinctively anti-Islamic thrust. The idea that evangelical Christianity can be reasonably defended against critics and rival philosophies or worldviews has long been a staple of the movement, with hundreds of books comparing Christianity with rival thought systems – from Mormonism to the New Age – to show where they are in error. Until the late 1980s and early 1990s, the literature on Islam was very sparse and those books that did treat the religion included little on the new Islamic resurgence expressed in the rise of the Ayatollah Khomeini. Since apologetic books are usually aimed at the ordinary layperson in their everyday encounters with those of other faiths, the need for this literature was not especially pressing prior to Islam's greater visibility and growth in the 1990s.

One of the most popular of these apologetic books was *Answering Islam* by Norman Geisler and Abdul Saleeb (1993). The book is still used by many evangelical seminaries and colleges in their apologetics courses, though the more recent anti-Islam apologists have criticized it. The book is a straightforward polemic against Islam, distinguishing Islamic from Christian doctrine. Islam's disavowal of the Trinity, the incarnation of Christ, and the sufficiency of the Bible as God's word, as well as its teachings on the importance of performing good works in attaining salvation are all critiqued from a standard evangelical perspective. Although written well after the growth of Islamic fundamentalism and the religion's general resurgence in much of the world, there is surprisingly little involving terrorism, violence, jihad or Islamic militancy in general. Most importantly for the purposes of this article, Geisler and Saleeb state that the God that Muslims address and worship as "Allah" is the same God of the Old and New Testaments that Jews and Christians invoke. Of course, the authors hold that the Islamic view of God as taught in the Quar'an is seriously distorted and marred by non-biblical sources, but they do give, if grudgingly, a place to Muslims in the monotheistic family of Jews and Christians. This is not to say that all other pre-9/11 apologetic literature takes a moderate approach toward Islam. One of the books that foreshadows many elements of the more recent post-9/11 literature is *Islam Revealed* (1988) by Anis Shorrosh. But while this book sees armed Jihad and violence as central to Islam, it also views Muslims as fellow monotheists along with Christians and Jews, a view that stands in contrast to the post-9/11 literature.

It should also be noted that those with a more fundamentalist orientation (for whom apologetics assume a more central role in their faith) have long expressed negative views concerning Islam. Apologists such as Dave Hunt and Robert Morey virulently attack Islam on their web sites, with the latter using the imagery and language of the Crusades to battle the Islamic threat (Hunt 2003; Morey 2003). Popular radio broadcaster and prophecy teacher John Ankenberg's booklet *The Facts On Islam* (1991) is a fiery expose of the religion, touching on the familiar nerve points of Islam's essential violence and evil nature. It is not only fundamentalists and evangelicals that hold anti-Islamic views: fairly similar positions can be found in the conservative wings of Roman Catholicism and Eastern Orthodoxy (Spencer 2002, Trifkovic 2002).

The books and articles that were published – or re-issued – after September 11 share a number of similar characteristics. Like the Shorrosh book, they are often written by ex-Muslims who converted to Christianity (usually after a period of living in the West). The books are usually publicized as revealing the "real truth" about Islam that has been hidden or obscured by the media and other elite segments of American society. But the two principal themes that distinguish these books from that of the pre-9/11 literature is the dual emphasis on Islam's inherently violent nature, a fact revealed by the September 11 attacks, and, most importantly, the assertion that Muslims worship a false god distinctly different than the God of Christianity and Judaism. One of the most popular of these books is *Unveiling Islam,* written by ex-Muslims Erg and Emir Caner (2002), which was the source Vines cited when he made the remark about Muhammad. The book is reported to have sold over 100,000 copies and seeks to dispel the position of Geisler and Saleeb that Allah is the same God (Jehovah) that Christians and Jews worship, arguing that Muhammad himself viewed followers of Moses and Christ as "children of Satan, not separated brethren." The Caners also assert that violent jihad and armed conflict is an "essential and indispensable tenet" of Islam. "The [September 11] terrorists were not some fringe group that changed the Koran to suit political ends. They knew the Koran quite well and followed the teachings of jihad to the letter." This polemic against Islam is not only directed at Muslims; a good part of the book also takes aim at liberal American society itself. Thus, the Caners write that establishing the difference between the true God of Christianity and the false God of Islam is "neither popular nor welcome [in a] politically correct, politically charged, postmodern culture. ... But [it] is essential to an effective witness." A concern about syncretism, which is the blending of faiths, and relativism, holding that no one particular faith is right or wrong, frames much of the Caners' and the other polemicists' arguments, a point that will be returned to later in this article (see also Schmidt 2004: 232–58).

Throughout much of the post-9/11 evangelical literature, there is a rethinking of formerly held views in the light of new realities. A vivid example of this is found in the book *Secrets of the Koran* by popular evangelical missionary Don Richardson (Richardson 2003, Staub 2003), who is most well-known for his book *Peace Child.* The book is an account of his missionary experience in Indonesia where he developed what he calls the "redemptive analogy" thesis. This is the idea that each culture has some story, ritual, or tradition that be used to teach or illustrate the Christian gospel message. After 9/11, Richardson studied the Koran to see if the redemptive analogy could be used to build bridges to Islam but came to the conclusion that it would not work. He writes that Islam has so redefined biblical teachings and concepts (such as heaven, Christ, and God) that it is impossible to find common ground. In an interview, Richardson says that the Koran and Islam are essentially violent, claiming that if Mohammed was alive today he would support Osama bin Laden rather than moderates because he wanted to create a theocracy on earth. Even in the more moderate popular book *Answering Islam,* the updated post 9/11 edition (2002: 328) leaves its strictly theological approach behind to include a section on "Islam on Violence." Geisler and Saleeb also write that there is a "religious foundation for violence deeply embedded within the very world-view of Islam. ... Such violence [goes] to the very roots of Islam, as found in the [Koran] and the actions and teachings of the prophet of Islam himself." In another co-authored work with evangelical theologian R.C. Sproul, Saleeb reiterates the view that the violence present among contemporary Muslims and in Islamic societies has its roots in the Koran (Sproul and Saleeb 2003:83–100).

It should be added that these writers attempt to avoid the charge of anti-Islamic prejudice by stating that most Muslims in the U.S. are not violent and that one should not engage in stereotyping. For instance, in his new book *Islam and the Jews,* Mark Gabriel (2003), an Egyptian and former Muslim professor, writes that most American Muslims are "ordinary Muslims," meaning that they do not really practice Islam as laid down in the Koran and are Muslim because of their culture and tradition. It is the "committed" and "fanatical" Muslims who are most likely to support or engage in terrorism, according to Gabriel.

Islam as a Player in the End-Times

Another area where evangelical anti-Islamic polemics have flourished in recent years is in the biblical prophecy movement. This movement gathers together pre-millennial evangelicals and fundamentalists, who interpret the Bible as providing a blueprint of the end-times and the return of Christ. An important part of the premillennial prophecy is the strategic role that Israel will play in gathering together the Jews of the world and rebuilding the temple, thereby hastening the return of Christ to earth. The significant place given to Israel in such prophetic scenarios has influenced a significant segment of the evangelical and fundamentalist communities to become steadfast friends and supporters of Israel. The tilt toward Israel, at least in contemporary times, implies a critical and at times adversarial view toward the Islamic Palestinian community, which occupies much of the historical biblical territory. But it is actually only in the last decade that Islam has assumed a central role in biblical prophecy.

In his book *The Last of the Giants* (1991) charismatic missions strategist and futurist George Otis, Jr. writes that since the fall of communism Islam has become the main protagonist in the invasion of Israel from neighboring countries to the north – the "most important end-time events" allegedly prophesied in the Bible. The "standard assumption" in early prophetic literature was that this invasion would be communist-led or inspired, but it had always been a puzzle why communists would be in alliance with the Arab nations to the north of Israel. The fall of communism solved that problem, leaving Islam (especially now that the religion is active and growing in former Soviet republics) as the main antagonist in prophetic end-time scenarios. Otis goes on to speculate that an ultimate "jihad" will be waged against Israel by the Islamic nations. While these nations will be defeated, there will emerge a miracle-working false prophet known as the anti-Christ, who Otis identifies as the "Mahdi," a messiah-like figure in Shi'ite Islam. The rise of the Mahdi will signal the beginning of the war of Armageddon, the last battle that will usher in the final return of Christ.

The close connection made between Islam and the unfolding of biblical prophecy is evident in other evangelical prophetic works, though not always to the extent found in Otis' writings. Since 9/11 there have been several prophetic works that are based almost completely on the central role of Islam in end-time events. Hal Lindsey, author of the 1970s bestseller *The Late Great Planet Earth,* recently wrote *The Everlasting Hatred: The Roots of Jihad* (2002:10), where he chronicles the ancient enmity between Muslims and Jews that is leading up to the end-times, and adds that "Islam represents the single greatest threat to the continued survival of the planet." In Mark Hitchcock's *The Coming Islamic Invasion of Israel* (2002), the "final jihad" between Israel and the Islamic nations takes center stage. *War On Terror: Unfolding Bible Prophecy* (Jeffrey 2002) has a photo of the burning World Trade Center on its cover and focuses more on how terrorism itself – from the Taliban and Al Queda to even Sadaam Hussein in Iraq (in restoring the biblical empire of Babylon) – ushers in the end-times.

Charismatic-Spiritual Warfare Literature and the Demonization of Islam

The next grouping of charismatic and Pentecostal anti-Islam books and articles are somewhat similar to the apologetic books, but they are even more extreme, and tend literally to demonize the religion. In this literature, there is an emphasis on what Pentecostals and charismatics call "spiritual warfare" – that is, battling demonic influence through the use of deliverance practices (similar to exorcism) and performing "signs and wonders" or miracles to demonstrate the power of God over such forces. This perspective has been evident in the decade before 9/11, though it has gained a much larger following since 2001. The spiritual warfare perspective animates much of Reza Safa's (1996) popular book *Inside Islam,* which was updated and reissued after 9/11. Safa touches on all of the familiar themes listed above – that Islam is inherently violent and that there is a wide chasm between the God of the Bible and Allah – but he also introduces some new elements. He writes that Allah is not only a false god distinct from the true God of the Bible, but that he is actually a pre-Islamic pagan deity who is identified with worship of the moon. The association of the occult with Allah and Muslim worship and practices is prominent in most of the charismatic and Pentecostal literature. Safa, a convert from a "radical Shi'ite" background, writes that Islam is more than a religious and a political system; it is a "spiritual force, an antichrist spirit manifested to oppose the work and the plan of God." Islam opposes God's plan by hindering an "end-time revival" of the world (especially since Muslim countries are closed to

Christian missionaries) as well as by opposing the Jewish people and taking over "their God-given land." Safa concludes that only way to conquer Islam is through taking authority over this spiritual force through prayer and fasting.

Spiritual warfare teachings have become entrenched in charismatic churches and teaching centers, and this anti-Islamic polemic seems to be spreading through these same networks. Setting much of the tone is C. Peter Wagner, a former Fuller seminary professor who trains pastors and missionaries in prophetic and spiritual warfare teachings through a school operated in his name and through his organization, Global Harvest Ministries. In a recent issue of his newsletter, he writes that "one billion Muslims worship a high-ranking demon who has gone by the name of 'Allah' since long before Mohammed was born," and that the "deeper dimension of the war on terrorism is not Taliban vs. America, but Allah vs. God the Father" (Wagner 2002:4–5).

To understand why Islam is so enmeshed in spiritual warfare teachings among charismatics, it is necessary to return to a source that many of the above authors and leaders cite: George Otis Jr.'s book, *The Last of the Giants* (1991). Aside from its prophetic teachings, the book sought to devise a new map and strategy for world evangelization. A new map was necessary because "As the spiritual balance of power in the world shifted steadily away from Marxist-atheism in the 1980s, it became increasingly clear that a new order of powerful competitors was vying for preeminence." Otis identifies Islam as the most serious challenge, since Muslims make up much of the 95% of the world's non-Christians who reside in what is called the "10/40 window" – a missionary term meaning the geographical region between the tenth and fortieth latitudes, including North Africa, the Middle East, as well as parts of India, China and Central Asia. Otis sees the 10/40 Window as the "primary spiritual battle ground of the 1990s and beyond" and identifies two of the region's "powerful strongholds"—Iran and Iraq. This tendency to view demonic and even Satanic forces as influencing a territory, a group of people, a government, or an institution was conceptualized by C. Peter Wagner as a way to locate and then expel influences that may block the reception of Christianity by an unreached population in a new region. The anti-Islamic polemic in the charismatic literature is closely connected to global competition for influence and dominance between Christianity and Islam. This is most closely seen in a country such as Nigeria, where Pentecostals have demonized Islam in a similar manner to that of their American counterparts, although they face the actual threat of the imposition of Islamic Sharia law.

The Contextualist Approach

It would be inaccurate, however, to view the anti-Islamic polemical literature as representing the whole evangelical community. For instance, the trend of missions among Muslims has moved away from confrontation and condemnation of Islam as a false religion that must be totally forsaken by the potential convert to one of contextualization. This approach teaches that the missionary must meet the Muslims on their own ground and that their culture and religious sensibility should be affirmed, even if ultimately "fulfilled" through the Christian gospel. For instance, such missionaries would speak of God as Allah and use Islamic prayer and worship practices (which, it should be added, Muslim critics view as deceitful). There have been recent evangelical books that argue against viewing Islam as an essentially violent and evil religion, but they are in the minority and often exist outside the mainstream of the evangelical apologetic movement (Poston and Ellis 2000; George 2002; Mallouhi 2002). Evangelical missionaries have been among those most critical of these anti-Islamic views. In January, 2003, a group of missionaries from the Southern Baptist Convention sent a letter to its church leaders pleading for a cessation of anti-Islamic statements which only hamper mission work among Muslims, not to mention threatening the safety of missionaries themselves (Buettner 2003). Lynn Green, the director of Youth With A Mission, called on Western Christians to refrain from "collectively demonizing" Muslims after 9/11 (Dixon 2002). The leadership of the National Association of Evangelicals joined with an influential conservative think tank, the Institute on Religion and Democracy (IRD), in issuing a joint statement of guidelines to calm the evangelical-Islamic tensions and initiate dialog. The guidelines condemn stereotyping Islam and Muslims and even affirm that both groups share a concept of "natural law" or "common grace" in morality and theology (Guidelines for Christian-Muslim Dialogue 2003).

The Threat of Syncretism and Relativism

The different forms of anti-Islam outlined above reveal new patterns of competition and confrontation with Islam both as a global force and as a presence in the United States. The fact that these anti-Islamic polemics are frequently stronger among American evangelicals than among missionaries, or among Arab and Middle Eastern Christians who have extensive contact with Muslims, suggests that this phenomenon has as much to do with conflicts and changes within evangelicalism as it does with interfaith relationships. The fear and criticism of religious relativism and syncretism in an increasingly religiously pluralistic society is common in most of the books and articles analyzed in this article. While the concern with pluralism is most evident in the apologetic literature, the message of the charismatic and prophetic literature also reflects the theme that the true nature of Islam is obscured in a "politically correct" and godless society, as well as in that society's treatment of the global competition between Islam and Christianity.

One can understand the linkage this literature often makes between Islam and violence, especially since surveys show that other Americans have increasingly come to a similar position since 9/11. But the evangelical tendency to draw a sharp line between Christians and Muslims, including the denial of their belief in the same God, requires more exploration. *Christian News,* a conservative Lutheran newspaper, strongly praised the Caners' *Unveiling Islam,* and recommends it both to leaders of the Lutheran Church-Missouri Synod "and the Roman Catholic Pope who assert that Jews, Muslims, etc., all believe in the same God" (Reising 2003). The reference to the Lutheran Church-Missouri Synod is important because this church body has been embroiled over a controversy involving interfaith relations. One of its leaders, David Benke of New York, participated in an interfaith prayer service with Muslims and other non-Christian groups at Yankee Stadium a few days after 9/11 and was immediately disciplined by the synod for engaging in syncretism and promoting a false unity with non-Christian religions.[2] The incident has served as a case study for evangelicals on the growth of relativism and syncretism in the churches; even the moderate *Christianity Today* magazine took an editorial position favoring, with some qualifications, the synod position. The evangelical concern was that many of the services held, and of the public religious voices heard in the media—even the response of political leaders after 9/11 stating that Islam is a religion of peace—were close to promoting the view that Christianity is no different from other faiths and that all religions should be viewed as equal.

The relationship between the negative critique of Islam discussed above, and the alarm over religious pluralism and relativism, is evident in the coverage of the conservative evangelical news weekly *World,* which is one of the evangelical magazines which is the most critical of Islam. In analyzing *World's* coverage of Islam, one finds that before 9/11, references to Islam were generally sparse. From 1996 to 1999, for instance, there were a total of 25 references to Islam in articles, mainly having to do with the persecution and restrictions against Christians in Islamic nations. As one might expect, that number increased dramatically in 2001, and in 2002 alone, there were 91 references to Islam (usually full articles). What is more significant is how these articles frequently address Islam within the framework of a critique of pluralism and syncretism in American religion and society. This is most starkly seen in a controversial editorial appearing just after September 11 in *World* which laid much of the blame for the attacks on the "gods of nominalism, materialism, secularism and pluralism" (Belz 2001: 5).

The magazine later gave its annual "Daniel of the Year Award" (named after the Old Testament prophet who faced a lions' den) to Franklin Graham for "telling the hard truths, about Islam" as well as for standing up for Christian convictions in the face of a religiously and culturally relativistic society. "In a world of religious relativism, the very suggestion that any one belief might be superior to another is precisely the kind of heresy that will get a preacher tossed to the lions of political correctness," stated the article (Jones 2002: 1–6). In *World's* editorials, Marvin Olasky frequently stated that Muslims and Christians do not worship the same God and that the violent tendencies of militant Islam are deeply embedded in the Qu'aran (Olasky 2002). But he often placed these views within a broader critique of the American media as being biased against conservative Christians but tolerant and uncritical of Islam and other non-Christian faiths (Olasky 2001, 2003).

Discussion

September 11 and the events surrounding it rendered Islam and pluralism in general an increasingly visible and immediate presence among evangelicals that demanded a response. It was only after September 11 that interfaith worship and prayer became a pressing reality and concern in most communities. The media and government efforts to portray Islam as a peaceful religion and to draw parallels between this faith and others became almost a civic necessity after the terrorist attacks. National Muslim groups such as the American Muslim Council and the Council on American-Islamic Relations, together with liberal Christian groups, attempted to popularize such terms and concepts as "Judeo-Christian-Islamic" or "Abrahamic" (referring to Abraham) and to include Islam as an American religion in partnership with Christianity and Judaism. The change in terminology was considered of symbolic importance for Muslims trying to find their role in the U.S. after September 11 and the Iraq war, yet the strongest opposition came from evangelical groups and leaders.

Opponents viewed these developments as a new threat to maintaining the boundaries of evangelical identity. Pluralism means that those holding specific truth claims are regularly confronted with rival truth claims, running the risk that all faiths could be relativized or that different elements of each faith could be sampled and borrowed by uncommitted consumers. Doctrines and practices that have served as boundary markers in maintaining the distinction between theological conservatives and liberals, such as biblical inerrancy and creationism, have given way to new concerns about the blurring of lines between Christianity and other faiths. Recent charges and disciplinary measures against theologians by evangelical seminaries and theological associations suggest that such issues as universalism (that one may be saved without faith in Christ), syncretism (as demonstrated in the Benke case), and relativism represent the new battlegrounds over heresy as well as the prime boundary markers for evangelical identity in today's pluralistic society (Hunter 1987; Olson 2003).

Of course, Islam is also opposed to relativism and syncretism. On this point, the conservative evangelical polemics are addressed not so much toward American Muslims, but rather toward secularists and religious liberals who are accused of using religious pluralism to dismantle normative and biblical values and establish relativism in American society. What has been called the "third disestablishment," where religious pluralism and personal autonomy in belief replaces a collective Protestant ethic or "American way of life," is most keenly felt by these conservative evangelicals. This is particularly true for those of a Reformed or Calvinist background, as is shown in publications such as *World* magazine, where the vision of a "Christian America" still retains a strong hold (Hammond 1992; Casanova 1994). Just as the inclusion of Jews and Catholics into this once-Protestant system generated earlier conflict, the entrance of Muslims into the public sphere is a new source of dissonance for conservative Protestants. But the new pluralism is not necessarily a weakening and destabilizing factor in terms of maintaining evangelical identity, even though such a scenario is regularly cited to sustain these polemics. As Smith (1998: 107) argues, a "sacred canopy" of unified, shared meaning on religion is not necessary to ensure a faith's survival. "In the pluralistic, modern world, people don't need macro-encompassing sacred cosmoses to maintain their religious beliefs. They only need 'sacred umbrellas,' small, portable, accessible relational worlds—religious reference groups – 'under' which their beliefs can make complete sense." In fact, finding and maintaining "enemies" to the faith tend to have the "unwitting result of maintaining unity and internal cohesion." The subcultural theory is especially helpful in this case because the conflict is not solely about one large group (evangelicals) battling against a minority religious group (Muslims), but rather concerns how evangelicals are redefining themselves in relation to the perceived dominant cultural and religious forces in a pluralistic society.

In conclusion, further research is needed to determine whether the strengthening of evangelical subcultural identity in a pluralistic setting is necessarily correlated with interfaith tensions and conflict. The case can be (and has been) made that Muslims share a consensus on several moral/social issues with their conservative Protestant counterparts. In the mid-1990s, there were several calls from Muslim and evangelical leaders and activists to bring both groups together to work on family and other conservative moral issues (*The Minaret* 1997). But any such coalitions have been difficult to sustain because many of these same Protestants retain a vision of a Christian (or at least Judeo-Christian) America accompanied by a concern to reinforce the boundaries of their faith in an increasingly pluralistic society.

Appendix

Books and publications surveyed through content analysis

Ankenberg, John, and John Weldon. 1991. *The Facts On Islam.* Eugene, OR: Harvest House.
Caner, Ergun Mehmet, and Emir Caner. 2002. *Unveiling Islam.* Grand Rapids, MI: Kregel Publications.
Gabriel, Mark A. 2003. *Islam and the Jews* Lake Mary, FL: Charisma House.
Geisler, Norman L., and Abdul Saleeb. 1993. *Answering Islam.* Grand Rapids, MI: Baker Book House. 2002. *Answering Islam.* Grand Rapids, MI: Baker Book House
George, Timothy. 2002. *Is the Father of Jesus the God of Muhammed?* Grand Rapids, MI: Zondervan.

Hitchcock, Mark. 2002. *The Coming Islamic Invasion of Israel.* Sisters, OR: Multnomah Publishers.
Jeffrey, Grant. 2003. *War On Terror: Unfolding Biblical Prophesy.* Toronto: Frontier Research Publications.
Lindsey, Hal. 2003. *The Everlasting Hatred.* Murrieta, CA: Oracle House Publishing.
Mallouhi, Christine. 2002. *Waging Peace On Islam.* Downers Grove, IL: InterVarsity Press.
Poston, Larry A., and Carl F. Ellis, Jr. 2000. *The Changing Face of Islam in America.* Camp Hill, PA: Christian Publications Co.
Otis, George. 1991. *The Last of the Giants: Lifting the Veil on Islam and the End Times.* Grand Rapids, MI: Chosen Books.
Richardson, Don. 2003. *Secrets Of The Koran,* Ventura, CA: Gospel Light Publications.
Safa, Reza. 1996. *Inside Islam.* Lake Mary, FL: Charisma House.
Schmidt, Alvin. 2004. *The Great Divide: The Failure of Islam and the Triumph of the West.* Boston, MA: Regina Orthodox Press.
Shorrosh, Anis. 1988. *Islam Revealed.* Nashville, TN: Thomas Nelson Publishers.
Spencer, Robert. 2002. *Islam Unveiled.* San Francisco, CA: Encounter Books.
Sproul, RC., and Abdul Saleeb. 2003. *The Dark Side of Islam.* Wheaton, IL: Crossway Books.
Trifkovic, Serge. 2002. *The Sword of the Prophet.* Boston, MA: Regina Orthodox Press.
World magazine, 1996–2002 issues online at http://www.worldmag.com.

Notes

1 A charismatic missions group taking a more liberal position than other agencies (as seen in their close cooperation with Roman Catholics).
2 He was, however, later cleared by the denomination.

References

Ankenberg, John, and John Weldon. 1991. *The Facts On Islam.* Eugene, OR: Harvest House.
Belz, Joel. 2001. "Editorial." *World,* September 22, 2001.
Buettner, Michael. 2003. "Missionaries: Anti-Islamic Statements Put Us At Risk," *Associated Press,* January 19, 2003.
Caner, Ergun Mehmet, and Emir Caner. 2002. *Unveiling Islam.* Grand Rapids, MI: Kregel Publications.
Casanova, Jose. 1994. *Public Religions In the Modern World.* Chicago: University of Chicago Press.
Dixon, Tomas. 2002. "Youth With A Mission Calls for Reconciliation." *Charisma,* September, 2002.
Ethics and Public Policy Center/Beliefnet, "Evangelical Views of Islam," http://www.beliefnet.com/story/124/story_12447.html.
Gabriel, Mark A. 2003. *Islam and the Jews.* Lake Mary, FL: Charisma House.
Geisler, Norman L., and Abdul Saleeb. 1993. *Answering Islam.* Grand Rapids, MI: Baker Book House. 2002. *Answering Islam.* Grand Rapids, MI: Baker Book House.
George, Timothy. 2002. *Is the Father of Jesus the God of Muhammed?* Grand Rapids, MI: Zondervan.
Guidelines for Christian-Muslim Dialogue. 2003. National Association of Evangelicals and the Institute for Religion and Democracy, May 7, 2003. http://www.ird-reneworg/News/News.cfm?ID=631&c=4.
Hammond, Phillip. 1992. *Religion and Personal Autonomy.* Columbia, SC: Univ. of South Carolina Press.
Hitchcock, Mark. 2002. *The Coming Islamic Invasion of Israel.* Sisters, OR: Multnomah Publishers.
Hoover, Dennis R. 2004. "Is Evangelicalism Itching for a Civilization Fight?" *The Brandywine Review of Faith & International Affairs* Spring, 2004, pp.11–16.
Hunt, Dave. 2003. *The Berean Call* web site, http://www.thebereancall.org, accessed November 24, 2003.
Hunter, James Davison. 1987. *Evangelicalism: The Emerging Generation.* Chicago: University of Chicago Press.
IslamOnline, "44% of Americans Back Limits On Muslims' Rights: Poll," December 18, 2004, http://www.islamonline.net/English/News/2004–12/18/article03.shtml.
Jeffrey, Grant. 2003. *War On Terror: Unfolding Biblical Prophesy.* Toronto: Frontier Research Publications.
Jones, Bob. 2002. "Speaking Frankly." *World,* December 17, 2002, http://www.worldmag.com/world/issue/12–07–02/cover_l.asp.

Lindsey, Hal. 2002. *The Everlasting Hatred.* Murrieta, CA: Oracle House Publishing.

Mallouhi, Christine. 2002. *Waging Peace On Islam.* Downers Grove, IL: InterVarsity Press.

Marsden, George. 1991. *Understanding Fundamentalism and Evangelicalism.* Grand Rapids, MI: Eerdmans.

Morey, Robert. 2003. Faith Defenders web site: http://www.faithdefenders.org, accessed November 23, 2003.

Olasky, Marvin. 2001. "Islamic Worldview And How It Differs From Christianity." *World,* October 27, 2001, http://www.worldmag.com/world/issue/10-27-01/cover_3.asp

2002. "The Big Chill," *World,* October 26, 2002, http://www.worldmagcom/world/issue/10-26-02/opening_2,asp

2003. "Coverage of Islam." *World,* March 9, 2003, http://wwwworldmag.com/world/issue/03-09-03/cover_3.asp.

Olson, Roger, E. 2003a. "Tensions in Evangelical Theology." *Dialog,* Spring, 2003, 76–85.

2003b. "The Opposing Armies of God." *Ethics and Public Policy Newsletter,* Winter, 2003, pp. 1–2.

Pew Research Center. 2001. "Post-9/11 Attitudes." Pew Forum on Religion and Public Life, December 6, 2001, http://www.pewforum.org.

2003. "Survey on American Attitudes Toward Islam." Pew Forum on Religion and Public Life, July, 2003, http://www/pewforum.org.

Plowman, Edward. 2002. "A Little More Conversation." *World,* November 30, 2002, http://www.worldmag.com/world/issue/11-30-02/national_l.asp.

Poston, Larry A., and Carl F. Ellis, Jr. 2000. *The Changing Face of Islam in America.* Camp Hill, PA: Christian Publications Co.

Otis, George. 1991. *The Last of the Giants: Lifting the Veil on Islam and the End Times.* Grand Rapids, MI: Chosen Books.

Reising, Richard F. 2003. "Unveiling Islam." *Christian News,* March 24, 2003, pp. 1, 15.

Richardson, Don. 2003. *Secrets Of The Koran.* Ventura, CA: Gospel Light Publications.

Safa, Reza. 1996. *Inside Islam.* Lake Mary, FL: Charisma House.

Schmidt, Alvin. 2004. *The Great Divide: The Failure of Islam and the Triumph of the West.* Boston, MA: Regina Orthodox Press.

Shorrosh, Anis. 1988. *Islam Revealed.* Nashville, TN: Thomas Nelson Publishers.

Smith, Christian. 1998. *American Evangelicalism: Embattled and Thriving.* Chicago: University of Chicago Press.

Spencer, Robert. 2002. *Islam Unveiled.* San Francisco: Encounter Books.

Sproul, RC., and Abdul Saleeb. 2003. *The Dark Side of Islam.* Wheaton, IL: Crossway Books.

Staub, Dick. 2003. "Why Don Richardson Says there's No 'Peace Child' for Islam." *Christianity Today,* February 11, 2003, 1–4, http://www.christianitytoday.com/global/pf.cgi7/ct/2003/106/22.0.html

The Minaret, "A Closer Look at the Christian Coalition." June, 1997, 24–29.

Trifkovic, Serge. 2002. *The Sword of the Prophet.* Boston: Regina Orthodox Press.

Wagner, C. Peter. 2002. "Allah 'A' and Allah 'B'." *Global Prayer News,* April-June, 2002, http://lyris.strategicprayer.net/cgi-bin/lyris.pl?sub=67908&id=203515133

World magazine, 1996–2002 issues online at http://www.worldmag.com.

Wuthnow, Robert. 2003. "The Challenge of Diversity." Unpublished Presidential Address given at the conference of the Society for the Scientific Study of Religion, Norfolk, Virginia, October 25, 2003.

23 *Aw qāla: 'Li-jārihi'*

Some observations on brotherhood and neighborly love in Islamic tradition

Oddbjørn Leirvik

When, in October 2007, 136 Muslim leaders and intellectuals published their open letter to the world's Christian leaders, *A common word between us and you* (ACW), they proposed the double commandment of love as a common frame of reference for future dialogue and cooperation between Muslims and Christians. As for neighborly love, their biblical reference was the commandment to love your neighbor as yourself.[1] Regarding love of the neighbor in Islam, their primary reference was to a hadith which comes in two different versions, in *Ṣaḥīḥ al-Bukhārī* and *Ṣaḥīḥ Muslim*.[2] In ACW, the two versions are quoted as follows: 'None of you has faith until you love for your brother what you love for yourself.'[3] And: 'None of you has faith until you love for your neighbour what you love for yourself.'[4]

Brother or neighbor?

As one can see, in citing the injunction to love for the other what you love for yourself, the hadith refers alternatively to 'brother' and 'neighbor' (in *Ṣaḥīḥ al-Bukhārī* and *Ṣaḥīḥ Muslim* respectively). With regard to *isnād*, all the variants are reported on the authority of Anas ibn Mālik, allegedly the last Companion of the Prophet to die in Basra (Juynboll 2007, 131)[5] – but with differing chains of transmitters, including and not including Shub'a ibn al-Ḥajjāj, who seems to have opted for 'brother'.

Al-Bukhārī seems not to be in doubt regarding the exact wording and renders the hadith using 'brother'.[6] In *Ṣaḥīḥ Muslim*, alternative versions that give preference to 'neighbor' and 'brother' are quoted side by side. In Abdul Hamid Siddiqui's translation, the first one runs as follows:

> It is arrested [sic] on the authority of Anas b. Malik that the Prophet (may peace and blessings be upon him) observed: one amongst you believes (truly) till one likes for his brother (*akh*) or for his neighbour (*aw qāla: 'Li-jārihi'* [or he said: 'for his neighbor']) that which he loves for himself.[7]

The ensuing hadith in *Ṣaḥīḥ Muslim* renders the alternatives in the reverse order:

> It is narrated on the authority of Anas that the Prophet (may peace and blessings be upon him) observed: By Him in whose Hand is my life, no, [sic] bondsman (truly) believes till he likes for his neighbour (*jār*), or he (the Holy Prophet) said: for his brother (*aw qāla: 'Li-akhīhi'*), whatever he likes for himself.[8]

In some documents from the ACW process, the two versions are confused[9] and no attempt appears to have been made in the context of ACW to examine the potential tension between the notions of 'brother' or 'neighbor' (for instance, in terms of group solidarity versus universal obligations).

Communal solidarity versus universal obligation?

In light of other contemporary discourses, which emphasize Islamic brotherhood over faith-transcending community, it is nevertheless tempting to ask whether the cited alternatives (*akh* or *jār*) may be used to express different understandings of the range of moral obligation in Islam. Could the injunction to love your 'brother' be taken as referring to intra-Muslim solidarity and protection, whereas the admonition to love your neighbor as yourself would be understood to have more universal implications?

The authors of *A common word* clearly read both versions of the hadith in a universalistic perspective. The same is true of contemporary reform thinkers, such as Abdullahi Ahmad an-Na'im, who, in his outline of a legal reformation in Islam, reads the occurrence of the Golden Rule in different religions as a reflection of 'the universal principle of reciprocity' (an-Na'im 1990, 1, 162–65). An-Na'im does not give his attention to differing versions of the hadith in question but concentrates on warning against imposing communal (or gender-based) restrictions on the Golden Rule in whatever version it may be found in the world religions. He realizes that the Golden Rule can actually be read in a more narrowing, communalist sense:

> The problem with using the principles of reciprocity in this context is the tendency of cultural, and particularly religious, traditions to restrict the application of the principle to other members of its cultural or religious tradition, if not to a certain group within the given tradition. (Ibid., 163)

More specifically, and as a concrete background to his efforts at reinterpreting the Islamic sources so as to reconcile them with modern human rights standards, an-Na'im notes that classical Shari'a 'denies women and non-Muslims the same degree of honor and human dignity it guarantees to Muslim men' (ibid.).

With regard to communal restrictions, this is actually how al-Bukhārī's version of the hadith is interpreted in two commonly-used English translations of his *Ṣaḥīḥ*, both published in their present form in 1993. In the translation by M. Muhsin Khan, the hadith in question is rendered as follows: 'None of you will have faith till he wishes for his (Muslim) brother what he likes for himself.'[10] The same narrowing parenthesis is inserted in Mahmoud Matraji's translation: 'No one of you will become faithful till he wishes for his (Mulim [sic]) brother what he likes for himself' (Bukhārī 1993, 1:15).

As for Mahmoud Matraji's translation of *Ṣaḥīḥ Muslim*, there is no corresponding parenthesis in his rendering of the alternative versions cited above: 'No one amongst you believes (truly) till one likes for his brother or for his neighbour what he loves for himself.' However, the heading of this hadith in Muslim unequivocally defines brother as a brother in Islam: 'It belongs to the qualities of faith that one should like the same good thing for one's brother in Islam as one likes for oneself' (*min khiṣāl al-īmān an yuḥibba li-akhīhi al-muslim mā yuḥibbuh li-nafsihi min al-khayr*) (Muslim 1993, 1a: 37).[11]

Semantics and conceptual history

In the following, I will examine the notion of 'neighborhood' and its relation to 'brotherhood' in Hadith, but I will first consider qur'ānic uses of *akh* and *jār*, in light of classical *tafsīr* and (in the latter part of the article) modern commentaries. (In this article, unless otherwise stated, the term 'brotherhood' refers to the status of being a brother, not to a brotherly organization, and 'neighborhood' refers to the status of being a neighbor, not to a locality).

From a *semantic* perspective, it should be noted that *jār*, the common Arabic word for neighbor, belongs to a rather interesting field of meaning. The root meaning of the stem *j-w-r* might seem to connote injustice and oppression, as reflected in the noun *jawr* (Wehr 1979). Since nouns related to the third and sixth forms of the verbal stem may also have meanings related to proximity and neighborhood (*jār*, *jiwār*), one might speculate whether the stem itself reflects the fact that proximity in settlement may often be quite troublesome and morally challenging. As emphasized in the classical dictionary *Lisān al-ʿarab*, the verbal stem can also (in its fourth and tenth forms) be used as an admonition to protect one's neighbor (Ibn Manẓūr 1955, 154–56). It can be argued that the ambivalence between foreigners both being a potential threat and having a right to protection (as guests) actually lies at the very root of *jiwār* and its Semitic cognates such as the Hebrew *gēr* (Lecerf 2010).

Neighborly ambivalence seems thus to belong to the very etymology of *jār*, just as the word *akh* resonates with age-old tension between ties of kinship and communities of conviction.

I would suggest, however, that the *conceptual history* of the notions in question is more important than sheer semantics. According to the German historian, Reinhart Koselleck, and his method of *Begriffsgeschichte* (conceptual history), every concept is associated with a word, but not every word is a concept. Different from a mere word, concepts 'possess a substantial claim to generality and always have many meanings …' (Koselleck 1985, 83). But words also resonate with historical context and Koselleck's method may in fact be regarded as a way of connecting lexicography to social history, by literary investigation and socio-philosophical reflection. Koselleck emphasizes the role of the context in the shaping of a word into a concept: '… a word becomes a concept when the plenitude of a politicosocial context of meaning and experience in and for which a word is used can be condensed into one word' (ibid., 84).

Regarding the hadiths in question, their possible meaning in the ninth-century social and political context of al-Bukhārī and Muslim is a complex historical issue, which cannot be further investigated in this article. Thus, in light of Koselleck's understanding of *Begriffsgeschichte* as a meeting point between philology and social history, the following investigation will only scratch the surface of the conceptual histories of *akh* and *jār*.

As for the modern context, is hard to guess what might have been the contextual impetus behind M. Muhsin Khan and Mahmoud Matraji's insertion of a narrowing parenthesis ('Muslim') when rendering the word brother in Bukhārī's version of the hadith. Did they want to correct popular usages in the Arab and Muslim world in which the notion of 'brother' (in tune with the generous usage in ACW) may be used to express heartfelt affection, irrespective of religious belonging? Or did the translators just link up with an established, interpretative tradition that takes for granted that *akh* in the canonical scriptures refers to a Muslim brother?

There *are* clearly traditional reasons for taking brother as a reference to religious community. In al-Nawawī's (1234–78) famous explanation to *Ṣaḥīḥ Muslim*, he comments on the difference between Muslim's and al-Bukhārī's renderings of the hadith. He notes that Muslim (differently from al-Bukhārī and others) was 'in doubt' as to the exact wording, but al-Nawawī does not discuss any further the difference between obligations towards a brother and a neighbor. He does, however, seem to take 'brother' in the sense of a Muslim brother, citing the hadith specialist Shaykh Abū 'Amr bin al-Ṣalāḥ (1181–1245) who – in tune with the traditional heading in *Saḥīḥ Muslim* – reads the hadith as 'until he likes for his brother in Islam' (*li-akhīhi fi-l-islām*).[12]

Kinship, brotherhood and neighborhood in the Qur'an

Before exploring references to brothers and neighbors in Hadith, some observations regarding the notions of *akh* and *jār* in the Qur'an will be in order.

The Qur'an contains numerous references to the bonds of kinship and pays due attention to kinship-related matters such as marriage and inheritance. However, in much the same way as in the Jesus movement (Moxnes 2003), the first Muslim community in Medina redefined the relation between family solidarity and obedience to God, also offering a new form of 'household' (eventually, a new *umma*) for those who, in the name of a higher obligation, broke with the ties of kinship. In this context, a special practice of 'brothering' (*mu'ākhāt*) in pairs immigrants from Mecca and 'helpers' in Medina was actually introduced (Watt 2010).

In Q 9.23f, those who believe are admonished not to take for protectors 'your fathers and your brothers if they love infidelity above faith'. This does not mean that the category of physical kinship is neglected. Out of 82 occurrences of *akh* in the Qur'an, 68 refer to physical brotherhood. But as *Sūrat Yūsuf* indicates (with its 18 occurrences of *akh*), brotherhood may be a trial and hindrance rather than a blessing and help for those who seek the will of God.

In the Meccan revelations, as the conflict between Muhammad and his kinsfolk escalates, one may sense that kinship and brotherhood has already become a critical issue, but 52 out of 68 Meccan occurrences still refer to physical brotherhood. In the Medinan revelations, when a new community is formed, the situation – and hence the usage – is different. More often than not in Medina, *akh* now refers to symbolic brotherhood – as in Q 3.103: 'For ye were enemies and He joined your hearts in love, so that by His grace, ye became brethren.' All those who now repent become 'your brethren in faith' (Q 9.11), so that all believers constitute now 'a single brotherhood' (*innamā al-mu'minūn ikhwatun*, Q 49.10). In this sense, brotherhood in the Medinan revelations comes close to the notion of *umma*, as reflected in some translations into English: 'And verily this brotherhood (*umma*) is a single brotherhood' (*ummatan wāḥidatan*, Q 23.52).

In this context, a demarcation line is drawn not only against pagan kinsfolk but also against 'misbelieving' Jews and Christians. Thus in Q 59.11, the 'hypocrites' in Medina are cited as having declared their solidarity with 'their misbelieving brethren' (*li-ikhwānihim alladhīna kafarū*) among the People of the Book: 'If ye are expelled, we too will go out with you. ...'

This means that, in the Qur'an, the notion of brotherhood in Islam is shaped not only in contradistinction to ties of kinship (as in the Meccan phase), but also (gradually in Medina) in critical consciousness of competing religious allegiances. With regard to religious ties, it is well known that the so-called Medinan constitution (as later described in the *Sīra*) invited the Jews to form 'one community (*umma*) with the believers', although the Jews and the Muslims would nevertheless have their distinctive religions (*dīn*; Guillaume 1996, 233). As things evolved, however, with growing suspicion between Muslims and Jews in Medina, the notion of *umma* gradually acquired the meaning of Muslim brotherhood – supplanting even qur'anic usage which in many places presupposes 'a plurality of ummas' (Gibb and Kramers 1991, 603).[13] This is probably how the evolving meaning of *akh*, in the direction of religiously defined brotherhood, should also be seen.

As for the notion of neighbor, apart from a metaphorical usage in Q 5.48, the only occurrence of the term *jār* in the Qur'an is Q 4.36 (from Medina):

> Serve Allah, and join not any partners with Him; and do good to parents, kinsfolk [*bi-dhī al-qurbā;* cf. 2.83], orphans, those in need, neighbours who are near [*al-jār dhī al-qurbā*], neighbours who are strangers [*wa-al-jār al-junubī*], the companion by your side [*al-ṣāḥib bi-al-janb*], the wayfarer (ye meet), and what your right hands possess: For Allah loveth not the arrogant, the vainglorious.

Strangely enough, *A common word* does not mention this verse. To illustrate 'Love of the neighbour in Islam', it quotes instead (in addition to the hadiths cited above) Q 2.177 and 3.92. Since our task in this article is to investigate the conceptual history of the notion of *jār*, we will nevertheless focus on Q 4.36 in what follows.

Classical *tafsīr* discussions: close in kinship or religion?

In classical *tafsīr*, the discussion of this verse focused on how to understand the relation between the two categories of neighbors here mentioned: Is it simply a matter of neighbors who are kinsfolk or not, or does the latter category (*al-jār al-junubī*) also imply other distinctions, such as religious allegiance?

This question was already discussed in the *tafsīr* attributed to the Prophet's Companion Ibn 'Abbās (d. 687), but is only accessible in much later editions, such as the fifteenth collection *Tanwīr al-miqbās* (Ibn 'Abbās 2008). Here, 'the neighbor who is near' (*al-jār dhī al-qurbā*) is taken to be a neighbor who is also kin, whereas the other category (*al-jār al-junubī*) would then refer to neighbors who are not kinsfolk. Altogether, the explanation implies that there are three types of neighbors, all with different rights: 'the neighbour who also happens to be your relative has three rights over you: the right of kinship, the right of Islam and the right of being a neighbour' (ibid., commentary on 4.36). As one can see, religious difference appears here as a distinctive category in addition to physical kinship and local proximity. It is not further explained, however, what the different sets of rights might imply in concrete terms.

As a contextual background to the tripartite definition of being a neighbor, it should be remembered that the coming of Islam created ruptures not only in the family structure but also in neighborhood relations. As Tarif Khalidi notes,

> ... the *Maghazi* [books of war] depict what was all too often a war of cousins and neighbors, of clans who were one's allies before the days of Islam but were now divided by religion. Indeed, one could read the *Maghazi* as an Arabian civil war. (Khalidi 2009. 91)

From this perspective, the tripartite definition of what constitutes a neighbor implied in *Tanwīr al-miqbās* – i.e., proximity in locality, kinship or religion – could be taken as an attempt to redefine and graduate moral obligations in the light of new social divisions.

The tripartite division is also found in other major works of *tafsīr*. For instance, in al-Ṭabarsī's *Majma'al-bayān* (a Shī'ite commentary from the twelfth century[14]), it is related that the Prophet said:

> There are three [types of] neighbors: the neighbor with three rights: the right of neighborhood (*jiwār*), the right of kinship (*qarāba*) and the right of Islam; the neighbor

> with two rights: the right of neighborhood (*jiwār*) and the right of Islam; and the neighbor with [only] the right of neighborhood, namely the idolator from among the People of the Book. (Ṭabarsī 1959, 3–4:45; my translation)

As one can see, al-Ṭabarsī defines the 'neighbor only' category as a relation to unbelievers. In support of this interpretation, he cites scholars who point to the fact that the category of kinship has already been mentioned in the first part of this qur'anic verse: 'do good to parents and kinsfolk (*bi-dhī al-qurbā*)'. Ergo the dichotomy in the next part of the verse (between *al-jār dhū al-qurbā* and *al-jār al-junubī*) must refer to some other distinction where kinship is not a factor (ibid.).

In the interpretation seemingly favored by al-Ṭabarsī, religious difference in fact stands out as the most pointed one. It appears, however, that this view has been controversial in the history of classical *tafsīr*. In the comprehensive ninth-century *tafsīr* attributed to the Persian historian al-Ṭabarī (838–923), the discussion of Q 4.36 also concentrates on the relation between kinship and religious brotherhood (Ṭabarī 1955–, 332–40).

But al-Ṭabarī's perspective is different from that of al-Ṭabarsī. He notes initially that the interpreters disagree in their understanding of this verse but proceeds by citing a majority of scholars (including Ibn 'Abbās) who without any doubt identify the first category of neighborhood (*al-jār dhī al-qurbā*) with kinship. He then notes that some scholars take it in another sense, namely as proximity in religion, i.e. Islam. But according to al-Ṭabarī, this interpretation is at odds with normal usage among the Arabs – 'in whose tongue the Qur'an was revealed' (ibid., 337). In conclusion: 'That the neighbor is near (*dhū al-qurbā*) means that he is close kin (*qarīb al-raḥim*), not that he is close in terms of religion' (ibid., my translation).

Logically then, the other category (*al-jār al-junubī*) would be a neighbor who is not kin (*qarāba*), or as Ibn 'Abbās has it, is of a foreign tribe (*min qawm junub*). Al-Ṭabarī cites a number of authorities in support of this view, before taking issue with those who see foreignness as religious difference and identify the neighbor who is a stranger as an idolater, a Jew or a Christian. In al-Ṭabarī's conclusion, 'the meaning of *junub* in this case is a distant stranger, be he Muslim or idolater, Jew or Christian' (ibid., 339). Again, he argues that this interpretation (which concentrates on difference in kinship, not in religion) is closer to normal Arabic usage.

Moreover, in another *tafsīr* from the ninth century, namely the Sufi-oriented *Tafsīr al-Tustarī* attributed to Sahl ibn 'Abd Allāh al-Tustarī (d. 896), the only distinctions drawn are those between kinship and geographical proximity. As for the outward meaning, says al-Tustarī, 'the neighbour who is a stranger is the one who is not related to you and is foreign' (Tustarī 2009, commentary on Q 4.36). But al-Tustarī, as a Sufi commentator, adds an inner meaning: 'the neighbour who is near refers to the heart (*qalb*), and the neighbour who is a stranger is the self in its natural state (*nafs ṭabīʿī*)'.

Al-Ṭabarī's view that the two categories of neighborhood in Q 4.36 primarily refer to whether or not there exists a relation of kinship (that is, not to religion) is followed in other major works of *tafsīr* such as the fifteenth-century one-volume commentary *Tafsīr al-Jalālayn*,[15] which briefly states that the two categories of neighbors refer to kinship and physical proximity. Religion is thus not an issue (Maḥallī and Suyūṭī 2008, commentary on Q 4.36).

In view of these divergences among the commentators, the commentary on Q 4.36 in the *tafsīr* of Ibn Kathīr (1301–73) is also interesting. Ibn Kathīr starts out by recalling Ibn 'Abbās' interpretation that the two kinds of neighborhood refer to whether or not a relation of kinship exists. He then adds (on the authority of Mujāhid) that the neighbor who is a stranger might just as well be a companion on a journey as a settled neighbor (Ibn Kathīr 2002, commentary on Q 4.36). Without mentioning the following idea cited in *Tanwīr al-miqbās* of three types of neighborhood, one of them characterized by proximity in religion, Ibn Kathīr simply goes on to quote several well-known hadiths that concretize responsibilities towards the neighbor – irrespective of which category he might belong to (ibid.).

In conclusion, *tafsīr* interpretations differ between those that imply that the range of one's obligations towards the neighbor may vary according to religious fellowship, and those that see no difference in this regard. As a background to modern interpretations, no clear development in any direction can be traced and a fuller investigation of different *tafsīr* interpretations of Q 4.36 would have to delve deeper into the historical context of each particular work and its general inclination with regard to interreligious relations.

Brotherhood and neighborly love in Hadith

Proceeding now to different hadiths that speak of brotherhood and neighborly obligations, it should be noted that the notion of 'Hadith' itself should not be mistaken for a uniform body of canonical utterances. Views on the authenticity of individual hadiths and the canonical bearing of the different Hadith collections (or of Hadith in general) vary widely, even within Sunni Islam. The most important question is probably how and for which purposes particular hadiths are being invoked – to support this or that position in any given discussion about the right interpretation of Islam.

This said, the Hadith collections abound with admonitions to care for a needy neighbor and with advice on good neighborliness in general. Religious difference is generally not a theme. However, a hadith reported by Abu Dāwūd in *Kitāb al-adab* explicitly identifies the neighbor as a Jew:

> Mujahid said that Abdullah ibn Amr slaughtered a sheep and said: Have you presented a gift from it to my neighbour, the Jew, for I heard the Apostle of Allah (pbuh) say: Gabriel kept on commending the neighbour to me so that I thought he would make an heir?[16]

This particular hadith is interesting for two reasons. (1) It presents the duty of neighborhood as reaching so far as to approximate responsibilities towards one's own kinsfolk ('so that I thought he would make an heir'). (2) This maximum expression of the duty of neighborliness is exemplified by one's duty not towards a brother in Islam, but towards a neighbor who happens to be a Jew. It should be noted, however, that the Hadith collections also contain a number of Prophetic sayings that are not particularly friendly in relation to neighboring Jews.[17]

Whereas the mention of religious difference in connection with neighborhood seems to be unique to this particular hadith, the comparison of neighborly duties with family ties – as illustrated by the theme of inheritance – is also found in *Ṣaḥīḥ al-Bukhārī*[18] and *Ṣaḥīḥ Muslim*.[19] In al-Bukhārī, it is also stated – without any reservation regarding kinship or religious difference – that 'the neighbour has more right than anyone else because of his nearness'.[20] Although difference in religion is not a theme in this hadith, it is interesting to note that in the immediate context of *Kitāb al-salam* ('The book of prepayment'), the Prophet's readiness to mortgage even his iron armor in prepayment of some foodstuff bought from a Jew, is emphasized.[21]

A recurring feature of hadiths pertaining to neighborhood is their concreteness in delineating the duties of a true believer. It has to do with such issues as sharing food, generous irrigation, and neighborly rights of preemption in connection with real estate transactions. The regulating principle is 'the need of one's neighbor'.[22] In some hadiths, the rights towards the neighbor are also compared with those towards a guest. In negative terms, Muslim's 'Book of faith' has a separate subheading concerning the prohibition to harm the neighbor: 'He will not enter paradise whose neighbor is not secure from his wrongful conduct.'[23] Committing illegal sexual intercourse with the wife of one's neighbor is singled out as a particularly grave transgression.[24]

As for brotherhood in Hadith, the duties towards an *akh* (whether he is kin or a brother in Islam) do not seem be qualitatively different from those towards a neighbor, although it could be argued that, in some hadiths, Muslim solidarity is emphasized in a special way:

> Do not hate one another, and do not be jealous of one another, and do not desert each other, and O, Allah's worshipers! Be brothers. Lo! It is not permissible for any Muslim to desert (not talk to) his brother (Muslim) for more than three days.[25]

As in the case of the Golden Rule, here too the translator M. Muhsin Khan takes brother in the sense of Muslim brother. There are probably good semantic reasons for this, since both in the Qur'an and in Hadith *akh* seems to connote either physical kinship or brotherhood in Islam.

There are also hadiths that literally address Muslims as brothers in arms, as in the following saying reported by al-Bukhārī in his 'Book of afflictions':

> None of you should point out towards his Muslim brother with a weapon, for he does not know, Satan may tempt him to hit him and thus he would fall into a pit of fire (Hell).[26]

Although 'Muslim' is again added by the translator, the immediate context indicates that his addition is reasonable (cf. the heading of this section: 'Whoever takes up arms against us, is not from us').

On the other hand, it should also be noted that some hadiths emphasize that all God's prophets are 'brothers in faith, having different mothers', with special emphasis of Muhammad's proximity to Jesus.[27] Brotherhood between Muhammad and Jesus does not, however, necessarily imply brotherhood between Muslims and Christians.

Brotherhood and neighborhood in modern usage (including modern commentaries)

The question of religious difference as a possible criterion of differentiation between various types of neighborhood remains an issue in some modern commentaries on the Qur'an ('Abduh, Asad), but seems in fact more often to be bracketed (Quṭb, Maududi, Yūsuf 'Alī). In fact, 'Abduh and Islamist and modernist commentaries all seem to agree (explicitly or implicitly) that difference in faith does not take anything away from the moral obligation to do good towards your neighbor. The evidence might be different if modern commentators of the neo-traditional Salafi tendency were also examined (cf. Duderija 2010).

The neighbor in modern commentaries

The reform movement associated with Muḥammad 'Abduh (1849–1905) has inspired both Islamist and more liberal reformers in the twentieth century. Muḥammad 'Abduh and Rashīd Riḍā's *Tafsīr al-Manār* was initiated by 'Abduh's commentaries on Suras 1–4, which were printed in the periodical *Al-Manār* from 1900 onwards, continued by Riḍā after 'Abduh's death in 1905, and completed in 1927. In the several pages dedicated to Q 4.36 ('Abduh and Riḍā 1928 – 1948, 5:90–93), 'Abduh offers a detailed discussion of the implied notions of neighborhood. He notes that the *mufassirūn* differ in their interpretation of this verse and that some of them include difference in religion when explaining what is meant by 'the neighbor who is a stranger'. In this connection, he also cites the tradition that operates with three types of neighborhood, one of them including fellowship in Islam. 'Abduh characterizes this as a weak hadith and counters it by another hadith, mentioned above, which underlines the obligation to share food with 'my neighbour, the Jew'.[28] Although this hadith is actually found in Abū Dāwūd's *Sunan* (cf. above), 'Abduh refers to it as a *ṣaḥīḥ* hadith reported by al-Bukhārī (ibid., 5:92). In the following, 'Abduh explicitly speaks of one's duty to do good towards the neighbor as a general or absolute injunction (*min al-waṣāyā al-muṭlaqa*) which includes 'Muslim as well as non-Muslim neighbors'. He also mentions that the virtue of good neighborliness is actually a pre-Islamic virtue among the Arabs, which Islam further expanded.

Sayyid Quṭb's (1906–66) *In the Shade of the Qur'ān* is a widely read commentary on the Qur'an whose readership extends far beyond those who adhere(d) to his confrontational type of Islamism, which was characterized, among other things, by his aversion towards the perceived moral deviations of the West and his strong critique of Judaism and Christianity. The general heading of his commentary on Q 4.36–43 is 'Unfailing kindness' but he begins by noting that the passage's exposition of some main features of the new Islamic life adds 'a clear warning against the scheming of former religions, particularly the Jews in Madinah. Evil is ingrained in their characters' (Quṭb n.d., 120f.). As for verse 36, Quṭb seems not to exclude either Jews or other non-Muslims from the 'certain groups of one's immediate family and of the human family at large' towards whom kind treatment is required.

In his elaborations on various degrees of moral obligation, Quṭb discusses varying categories of social need but pays no attention to religious difference.[29] With regard to kinship, his take on this category is to underline – 'coherently with the Islamic view of social organization' – family values as the anchoring point of any form of compassionate care and social security (ibid., 123).

As for Islamist movements on the Indian sub-continent, among the most influential is Jamaat-e-islami, founded by Syed Abul A'ala Maududi (1903–79). In the Islamic Foundation's English edition of *Tafhim al-Qur'an* (*Towards understanding the Qur'an*), religious differences are not discussed in connection with Q 4.36. The relevant part of the verse is translated as follows: 'to the neighbour who is of kin and to the neighbour who is a stranger.' Maududi offers no further explanation of this part of the verse and concentrates instead on the following sequence. His commentary shows that 'the companion by your side (*janb*)' is taken in a very inclusive sense: 'for instance, either the person who walks beside one on the way to the market or who sits beside one while buying things from the same shop or one's fellow traveler' (Maududi n.d.).

Turning to reformers of a more liberal inclination, the convert Muhammad Asad (1900–92) offers an interesting example of how Q 4.36 might be read by a modernist with a universalistic perspective on ethics. In his commentary *The message of the Qur'ān*, Asad rules out kinship as a relevant category when trying to understand the distinction between neighbors near and far. Like many scholars (cf. al-Ṭabarsī above), Asad notes that the category of kinship (parents, kinsfolk) is dealt with in the first part of the verse. The two categories of neighborhood must therefore refer to something else. According to Asad, *al-jār dhū al-qurbā* should be translated 'your own people'. The distinction between the neighbor who is near and the neighbor who is a stranger thus refers to 'whether he belongs to your own or to another community'. Asad does not explain exactly what he means by 'community'. But from his commentary, it is clear that faith is at least implied:

> The Prophet often stressed a believer's moral obligation towards his neighbours, whatever their faith [in Spanish: 'de todo creyente']; and his attitude has been summed up in his words, 'Whoever believes in God and the Last Day, let him do good unto his neighbour. …' (Asad 2007)[30]

In the case of Asad, then, his stress on community and faith does *not* mean that one has lesser obligations towards a neighbor who belongs to a different (faith) community. On the contrary, Asad stresses the faith-transcending universality of moral obligation in Islam.

The last example to be cited is *The meaning of the holy Qur'ān*, the work of 'Abdullah Yūsuf 'Alī (1872–1953), which, like Asad's *The message of the Qur'ān,* offers a translation of the Qur'an with explanatory footnotes.[31] Yūsuf 'Alī mentions neither kinship nor religious belonging when explaining the various degrees of proximity implied by Q 4.36. He sees neighbors who are near as those who are near 'in local situation as well as intimate relationships', whereas neighbors who are strangers 'includes those whom we do not know or who live away from us or in a different sphere altogether'. He gives a similar explanation to the ensuing pair of 'the companion by your side' and 'the wayfarer you meet', implying that the duties towards the latter (who 'may be a casual acquaintance on your travels') represent the widest range of moral obligation.

Summing up, neither Quṭb, Maududi nor Yūsuf 'Alī pays any attention to religious difference when commenting on Q 4.36. Whether this should be taken as neglect or as (implicit) inclusiveness, must be considered in light of the general tenor of their commentaries. 'Abduh and Asad, on the other hand, are critically aware of religious differences but state emphatically that such differences do not take anything away from one's obligation towards the neighbor.

The relation between brotherhood and neighborhood in contemporary usage

As for the notion of brotherhood, the prominence of the Muslim Brotherhood (*al-ikwān al-muslimūn*) has of course heavily influenced present-day usage of the term, which associates brotherhood in Islam with religiously-based group solidarity – and with Islamism. In late twentieth-century discourses, the notion of Muslim brotherhood has also become embedded in various types of Muslim identity politics that emphasize religious belonging over against any other identity marker. Thus in the demonstrations in Oslo against Israel's offensive in Gaza in 2009, many young activists explained their rage and solidarity by proclaiming that 'All Muslims are brethren'.[32] Correspondingly, when in 2010 taxi drivers in Oslo mobilized their protest against another caricature of the Prophet, text-messages called on 'Muslim brothers and sisters' to demonstrate, in a discursive framework dominated by the dichotomy of 'you' and 'us'.[33]

On islamonline.net, the influential website associated with Yūsuf al-Qaraḍāwī, 'Rights of brotherhood in Islam' are explained by 'A group of Islamic researchers' in a posting from 2004.[34] Here, brotherhood is dealt with entirely as a matter of intra-Muslim affection and solidarity. Indifferent Muslims are chastised for spending time in cafes and hotels 'at the times that their brothers are being slaughtered at some other parts of the globe'. In this connection, the hadith about loving for one's brother what one loves for oneself is also cited – with the clear implication that brother means Muslim brother. In a 2002 fatwa by al-Qaraḍāwī himself about 'the true concept of brotherhood', the dominant perspective is also intra-Muslim, although with emphasis on the more universal virtue of class-transcending equality.[35]

As for the notion of neighborly love in present-day usage, another article on islamonline.net explains what it means to show 'kindness to a non-Muslim neighbor'.[36] Emphasizing the tolerant aspect of Islam – 'especially with people of other faiths' – the author, El-Sayed M. Amin, states unequivocally that 'it makes no difference whether the neighbors are Muslim or non-Muslim'. However, Amin goes on to quote the tradition cited above about three different categories of neighbors: a relative, a Muslim and a non-Muslim. This classical distinction implies of course some additional obligations towards one's family and one's fellow Muslims, in comparison with what you owe one who is a 'neighbor only'. Notwithstanding such implications (which are not further developed), the author encourages searching for common ground if a non-Muslim neighbor brings up issues pertaining to religion, while nevertheless reminding the reader that opportunities to invite one's neighbor to Islamic events should not be missed. But 'you can also visit the church where your neighbors pray if they invite you to do that'.

With regard to neighborly obligations, a book by the contemporary Saudi author Muhammad Ali al-Hashimi entitled *The ideal Muslimah* may be cited as a striking example of how care for one's neighbor may also be thoroughly gendered. Two chapters in this book deal with 'The Muslim woman and her neighbours' and 'The Muslim woman and her friends and sisters in Islam'. Commenting on Q 4.36, al-Hashimi emphasizes that 'everyone whose home neighbours yours has the rights of a neighbour over you, even if you are not connected by kinship of religion' (al-Hashimi 1994, ch. 8).

Al-Hashimi proceeds to cite a host of hadiths relevant to the understanding of neighborly relations. The alternative versions of the Golden Rule (brother/neighbor) are noted but not elaborated upon. Noting that Islam wants to spread mutual love and affection among neighbors, faith-transcending obligations are once more emphasized. Under the heading 'She treats her neighbours well even if they are not Muslim', al-Hashimi states:

> The true Muslim woman does not restrict her good treatment only to neighbours who are related to her or who are Muslims, but she extends it to non-Muslim neighbours too, in accordance with the tolerant teachings of Islam which encourage kindness towards all people, regardless of their race or religion, so long as they do not commit any acts of hostility or aggression towards Muslims. (Ibid.)

In the next chapter, the Muslim woman's particular obligations towards her 'friends and sisters in Islam' are unfolded – in some more detail than in the case of neighborly duties.

The examples cited above give an impression of how the notions of brotherhood and neighborhood are currently dealt with on influential Islamic websites. Although extra obligations towards fellow Muslims are often implied (typically, with reference to the notion of brother- or sisterhood), reflections on neighborly love seem regularly to have a more universal outlook, although the potential tension between universal obligations and brotherly (Muslim) solidarity is not explained.

Interreligious perspectives

In circles committed to interreligious dialogue, other types of discourses seem to evolve, expanding the notion of brother- and sisterhood across religious divides. For instance, in connection with *A common word*, Archbishop Rowan Williams addresses his response to 'Muslim brothers and sisters everywhere' (Williams 2008). In conferences held in the context of *A common word*, similar interfaith extensions of brother- and sisterhood have also been heard from the Muslim side. Such ecumenical extensions of the notion of brotherhood might in fact correspond to widespread popular usages in which (as noted above) any good friend can be called a brother or sister, irrespective of faith.

Different usages can also be combined in creative ways. In an interreligious meeting in an Oslo mosque in March 2010, held in connection with the launching of a Norwegian translation of Maududi's translation of the Qur'an, the Muslim host addressed the audience with the following words: 'Brothers and sisters in Islam, brothers and sisters in humanity.'[37]

Similar tensions between inclusive and exclusive notions of brotherhood can also be identified in the Christian tradition. Whereas in the New Testament the notion of brotherhood refers mainly to intra-Christian solidarity, the word neighbor (*plēsíon*) pulls more clearly in a faith-transcending direction. In Rowan Williams' abovementioned response to *A common word*, 'love of our neighbour' in the Christian perspective is illustrated by reference to (1) the commandment to love one's enemy in Matthew 5 and Luke 6 and (2) the parable of the good Samaritan in Luke 10.25–37. The selection of references serves to illustrate a pivotal point in the Archbishop's reasoning, namely the faith-transcending nature of neighborly love:

> Commentary on this parable frequently points to the way in which Jesus challenges the assumptions of the question; instead of defining a necessarily limited group of people who might fit the category of 'neighbours' to whom love should be shown, he speaks of the need to prove ourselves neighbours by compassion to whoever is before us in need or pain, whether or not they are akin to us, approved by us, safe for us to be with or whatever else. Such neighbourliness will mean crossing religious and ethnic divisions and transcending ancient enmities. (Williams 2008)

Another feature of the New Testament's treatment of the commandment to love one's neighbor as oneself is the way it functions as a summary of the entire Torah (cf. Romans 13.9–10 and Galatians 5.14). The same is true of the Golden Rule as formulated in the Sermon on the Mount: 'Therefore, whatever you want men to do to you, do also to them, for this is the Law and the Prophets' (Matthew 7.12). In comparison, hadiths about neighborly love tend to be much more concrete, almost casuistic in their admonishment.

As for the Golden Rule in Hadith, we have noted a potential tension between brotherhood and neighborly love, as reflected in the double rendering of the Golden Rule in *Ṣaḥīḥ Muslim* and in differing *tafsīr* interpretations of the various types of neighborhood implied in Q 4.36. Tensions between brotherhood and neighborly love – and their ethical implications – can clearly be found in the New Testament too. Brothers in a metaphorical sense refer mostly to 'the faithful brethren in Christ' (Colossians 1.2). As illustrated in 1 John 4.21, this also affects the understanding of love (*agapē*): 'And this commandment we have from

Him: that he who loves God *must* love his brother also'. Intra-Christian solidarity is also called for by use of other family-related metaphors: 'Do good to everyone, especially to those who belong to the family of believers' (*oikeíous tēs pisteōs*, Galatians 6.10).

It could be argued, then, that the tension between religious group solidarity and universal obligations arises as a *common* theme from the classical Islamic and Christian sources.

Gender perspectives

Further dialogue about and research into the notions of brotherhood and neighborly love in Islamic and Christian tradition will also have to deal critically with gendered aspects of the ethical and identity-related questions at hand.

The notion of brotherhood is of course gendered in itself. Metaphorical use of the New Testament notion of *adelphós* (brother) abounds, on a par with the qur'anic notion of *akh*. Being semantically linked with *filadelphía* (love between siblings, cf. Romans 12.10), it could be argued that the plural form *adelphoi* refers in fact to siblinghood rather than brotherhood (Aasgaard 2004). The male form constitutes, however, the dominant norm and references to sister (*adelphē*) in the metaphorical sense are comparatively few in the New Testament (cf. Romans 16.1 and seven other places).

In the Qur'an, there are no references to sister (*ukht*) in the metaphorical sense. The expression '(brothers and) sisters in Islam' thus illustrates a modern need to balance the male notion of brotherhood with more gender-inclusive usages. In further exploring the notion of brotherhood in Islam, critical gender analysis would also have to examine the extent to which this notion (as found in the classical sources and in later usage) implies a limitation on the equality in moral obligation and legal rights normally associated with the Golden Rule in its modern interpretation. As an-Na'im has observed in his discussion of the Golden Rule, classical Shari'a does discriminate against women in this respect (an-Na'im 1990, 175–77).

As we have seen, the Islamic version of the Golden Rule refers alternatively to 'brother' and (as in Christian tradition) 'neighbor'. Just as a neighbor may be either male (*jār*) or female (*jāra*), neighborly duties in Hadith refer both to traditionally male spheres (real estate and irrigation affairs; males' relation to others' wives) and to female domains (sharing food, etc.). In a modern context – as reflected in *The ideal Muslimah* – neighborly love seems in fact to be further gendered, reflecting perhaps a feminized interpretation of good neighborliness with emphasis on empathy and care.

The most pressing issue, however, is whether Shari'a-based inequality between men and women in terms of rights is at all compatible with a universalistic interpretation of the Golden Rule (cf. an-Na'im). With regard to the hadith in question, the critical point in any given interpretation would be whether 'wishing for this brother the same as he wishes for himself' is taken as a reference to *male* reciprocity only, within the framework of the religious community, or as a gender neutral and universal obligation. That obviously depends more on the eye of the beholder than on the actual wording of the hadith itself – although the words in question may carry a heavy weight of patriarchal reasoning.

Conclusion: texts and contexts

In further research into the notions of brotherhood and neighborhood in Islam, varying views on the interreligious and gender implications of these notions should be examined in the light of changing contexts. The exposition above has focused on texts rather than contexts. Contextual aspects are hinted at but not explored in any depth. For example, the present study has not answered the question begged by the alternative versions in *Ṣaḥīḥ Muslim* of what might have been the contextual impetus behind the double rendering of the Golden Rule. That question remains to be explored. One might ask, for instance, whether people of different religious belongings lived more separately in the ninth century when the Hadith collections were put together, than at the time of the qur'anic revelation, when even members of the same household might have had different religious affiliations. One might also wonder whether, in the ninth century, moral obligations had generally come to be seen in the light of Shari'a-regulations, as is possibly reflected in *tafsīr* distinctions between moral obligations towards Muslim and non-Muslim neighbors.

Too much focus on texts might also blur the way in which kinship remains a dominant category with regard to moral formation and imposed obligation. The notion of brotherhood in fact borrows the strong sense of affection and solidarity normally associated with family relationships.[38] Although the notions of brotherhood in both Islam and Christianity initially implied a radical breach with established family ties, social anthropological research reveals that in many religious cultures family and kinship retain their status as a primary (and highly affective) frame of reference for moral obligation.

The notions of kinship, brotherhood and neighborhood – and the implicit tension between them – thus capture some of the most pressing issues in modern ethics and moral identity formation today: the relation between family values, religious brotherhood and faith-transcending solidarity.

Notes

1. The biblical references are Matthew 22.38–40, Mark 12.31 and Leviticus 19.17–18 (ACW 2007, part II).
2. Samir Khalil's allegation (see section II in his response the ACW website: http://www.acommonword.com/index.php?page=responses&item=14) that ACW simply borrows Christian language seems to overlook the fact that the root-meaning of both *plēsíon* (in the New Testament) and *jār* (in numerous hadiths and in Q 4.36) is physical-geographical proximity, with the possibility for *both* notions to be expanded semantically.
3. Cf. Bukhārī n.d., book 2 (*Kitāb al-īmān*), number 12. Unless otherwise stated, Hadith references in this article refer to the numbering found in the web versions of al-Bukhārī and Muslim published by the Center for Jewish-Muslim Engagement, University of Southern California.
4. Cf. Muslim n.d., book 1 (*Kitāb al-īmān*), number 72.
5. Juynboll raises some doubt regarding the probability that Anas, who is said to have died in 712, could actually have been a companion of the Prophet (Juynboll 2007, 131). Tarif Khalidi, in his *Images of Muhammad*, seems not to harbor such doubts (Khalidi 2009, 51f).
6. Al-Bukhārī's *isnād* runs as follows: Anas via Qatāda, Shub'a, Yaḥyā and Musaddad.
7. Muslim n.d., book 1, number 72. On the authority of Anas ibn Mālik, via Qatāda, Shu'ba, Muḥammad ibn Ja'far, Ibn Bashshār, Muḥammad ibn al-Muthannā. Shu'ba has also transmitted another hadith modeled on a similar formula: 'No one is a true believer until he loves me more than his son, his father or all the people together' (Juynboll 2007, 479f). In Muslim, two versions of this hadith are quoted just before the two variants of the Golden Rule. According to Juynboll, Shu'ba (the third authority in this chain) is frequently the common link 'in traditions which represent a rather late stage in legal discussions that hark back to ancient times' (Juynboll 2007, 479f).
8. Muslim n.d., book 1, number 73 – on the authority of Anas, via Qatāda (but excluding Shub'a), Ḥusayn al-Mu'allim, Yaḥyā ibn Sa'īd and Zuhayr ibn Harb.
9. For instance, in the 'Final Declaration' from the First Seminar of the Catholic-Muslim Forum (Rome, 4–6 November 2008) the version that reads 'neighbour' is erroneously attributed to al-Bukhārī (Catholic-Muslim Forum 2008, point 1).

10. Bukhārī n.d., book 2 (*Kitāb al-īmān*), number 12.
11. Note also that the heading qualifies 'whatever one likes' as 'the good' (*al-khayr*). With reference to al-Bukhārī, Ghassan Abdul-Jabbar notes that he uses chapter titles to guide the reader to his understanding of the hadith in question (Abdul-Jabbar 2007, 24). The same would apply to Muslim.
12. In addition, an-Nawawī underlines that what one likes for oneself (and hence for one's brother) must be within the realm of 'the good' (*al-khayr*, cf. the heading of this hadith in Muslim), and not transgress the confines of Islamic law (Nawawī n.d., 64).
13. See Q 5.48: 'If Allah had so willed, He would have made you a single *umma* …' (cf. 42.8). Compare the use of the term *umma* with reference to Jews and Christians in Q 5.66 and 3.133 and cf. Asma Afsaruddin's discussion of inclusivist vs. exclusivist interpretations in Afsaruddin (2009).
14. Abū 'Alī al-Faḍl ibn al-Ḥasan al-Ṭabarsī died in 1153.
15. By Jalāl al-Dīn al-Maḥallī (d. 1459) and Jalāl al-Dīn al-Suyūṭī.
16. Abū Dāwūd n.d., book 41 (*Kitāb al-adab*, in the section *Ḥaqq al-jiwār*), number 5133. For the Arabic original, see http://hadith.al-islam.com/Display/Display.asp?Doc=4&Rec=6405 (accessed 16 May 2010).
17. See 'Excerpts from the Canonical Hadith Collections', in Bostom (2008, 229–34). Interestingly, these excerpts (which are compiled in order to illustrate 'Islamic Antisemitism') do not include the more friendly hadith quoted above. The story (much cited among present-day Muslims) about Muhammad showing care and compassion for a Jewish woman who used to throw garbage in his path, is not found in the canonical Hadith collections.
18. Bukhārī n.d., book 73 (*Kitāb al-adab*), number 43–44.
19. Muslim n.d., book 32 (*Kitāb al-birr wa-al-ṣalāḥ wa-al-adab*), numbers 6354 and 6356.
20. Bukhārī n.d., book 35 (*Kitāb al-salam*), number 459.
21. Ibid., number 453–54.
22. Muslim n.d., book 22 (*Kitāb al-aḍāḥī*), number 4833.
23. Ibid., book 001 (*Kitāb al-īmān*), number 0074. Cf. Bukhārī n.d., book 73, number 45, 47f., 158, and book 76, number 482.
24. Bukhārī n.d., book 60 (*Kitāb tafsīr al-Qur'ān*), numbers 4 and 284 as well as five other occurrences. Cf. Muslim n.d., book 1, number 156–57.
25. Bukhārī n.d., book 73 (*Kitāb al-adab*), number 99 (cf. 100). Cf. Muslim n.d., book 32, number 6205.
26. Bukhārī n.d., book 55 (*Kitāb al-fitan*), number 193.
27. Muslim n.d., book 30, number 5836. Cf. Bukhārī, book 55 (*Kitāb al-anbiyā'*), number 51–52.
28. Abū Dāwūd n.d., book 41 (*Kitāb al-adab*), number 5133.
29. When the orphans and the needy are mentioned before the neighbor, this means (says Quṭb) that 'these are given precedence over one's neighbours because their need may be more pressing and they must be looked after more immediately. Kindness is then urged towards a neighbour who may be a relation [relative?], and so to any other neighbour. Both takes precedence over friends [*al-ṣāḥib bi-al-janb*], because a neighbour always remains next to us' (Qutb n.d, 124).
30. Mohammed Knut Bernström's translation (Asad 1998) takes Asad a step further by simply translating 'community' as 'of same belief or not' (in Swedish: 'av samma tro eller inte').
31. Yūsuf 'Alī' s translation and commentary was first published in 1934 and has long been one of the most commonly used English versions of the Qur'an.
32. 'Alle muslimer er brødre, og det som skjer på Gaza setter sinnene våre i kok …'. *Aftenposten*, 17 Januar 2009. http://www.aftenposten.no/nyheter/iriks/article2872660.ece (accessed 16 May 2010).
33. 'Drosjesjåføren Muhammed demonstrerer mot trykking av karikaturer …'. *Morgenbladet*, 12 February 2010.
34. Rights of brotherhood in Islam. http://www.islamonline.net/servlet/Satellite?pagename=IslamOnline-English-Ask_Scholar/FatwaE/FatwaE&cid=1119503544842 (accessed 16 May 2010).
35. What is the true concept of brotherhood in Islam? http://www.islamonline.net/servlet/Satellite?pagename=IslamOnline-English-Ask_Scholar/FatwaE/FatwaE&cid=1119503545426 (accessed 16 May 2010).
36. Kindness to a non-Muslim neighbor, http://www.islamawareness.net/Neighbours/kindness.html (accessed 16 May 2010).
37. Islamic Cultural Centre, 14 March 2010.

38. Cf. Reidar Aasgaard's observations regarding Paul's use of the notion of brotherhood/siblingship: 'Paul emphasized notions of harmony among Christian siblings: they were to display the unity expected of members of a family and of siblings. In particular, the emotional element was central: Christians were to harbour positive and strong emotions towards one another' (Aasgaard 2004, 307).

References

A common word between us and you (ACW). 2007. http://www.acommonword.com/index.php71angen&page=option l.

Aasgaard, Reidar. 2004. *'My beloved brothers and sisters!' Christian siblingship in Paul.* London: T&T Clark.

'Abduh, Muḥammad, and Rashīd Riḍā. 1928–48. *Tafsīr al-Qur'ān al-ḥakīm al-shahīr bi-al-Manār.* 12 vols. Cairo: Maṭba'at al-Manār.

Abdul-Jabbar, Ghassan. 2007. *Bukhari.* London: I.B. Tauris/Oxford Centre for Islamic Studies.

Abū Dāwūd. n.d. *Sunan Abī Dāwūd.* http://hadith.al-islam.com/Display/ffier.asp?Doc=4&n=0.

Afsaruddin, Asma. 2009. The hermeneutics of inter-faith relations: retrieving moderation and pluralism as universal principles in qur'anic exegisis. *Journal of Religious Ethics* 37, no. 2: 331–54.

al-Hashimi, Muhammad Ali. 1994. The ideal Muslimah: the true Islamic personality of the Muslim woman as defined in the Qur'an and Sunnah. http://www.kalamullah.com/Books/The%20Ideal%20Muslimah.pdf.

an-Na'im, Abdullahi Ahmed. 1990. *Toward an Islamic reformation: civil liberties, human rights, and international law.* New York: Syracuse University Press.

Asad, Muhammad. 1998. *Koranens budskap.* Trans. Mohammed Knut Bernström. Stockholm: Proprius förlag.

Asad, Muhammad. 2007. *The message of the Quran translated and explained by Muhammad Asad.* http://aurthursclassicnovels.com/koran/koran-asad10.html.

Bostom, Andrew G., ed. 2008. *The legacy of Islamic antisemitism: from sacred texts to solemn history.* New York: Prometheus Books.

Bukhārī, al-, 1993. *Sahih al-Boukhari.* Trans. M. Matraji. 9 vols. Beirut: Dar el Fiker.

Bukhārī, al-, n.d. *Sahih al-Bukhari.* Trans. M. Muhsin Khan. http://www.usc.edu/dept/MSA/fundamentals/hadithsunnah/bukhari/.

Catholic–Muslim Forum. 2008. *Final declaration: first seminar of the Catholic–Muslim Forum,* http://acommonword.com/en/attachments/108_FinalFinalCommunique.pdf.

Duderija, Adis. 2010. Constructing the religious self and the other: neo-traditional Salafi. *manhaj. Islam and Christian–Muslim Relations* 21, no. 1: 75–93.

Gibb, H.A.R., and J.H. Kramers, eds. 1991. *Shorter encyclopaedia of Islam.* Leiden: Brill.

Guillaume, A. 1996. *The life of Muhammad. A translation of Ibn Ishaq's Sirat Rasul Allah.* Karachi: Oxford University Press.

Ibn 'Abbās. 2008. *Tanwīr al-miqbās min tafsīr Ibn 'Abbās.* Amman: Royal Aal al-Bayt Institute for Islamic Thought, http://www.altafsir.com/Ibn-Abbas.asp.

Ibn Kathīr. 2002. *Tafsīr Ibn Kathīr.* http://tafsir.com.

Ibn Manẓūr. 1955. *Lisān al-'arab.* 4. Beirut: Dār Ṣādir.

Juynboll, G.H.A. 2007. *Encyclopedia of canonical Ḥadīth.* Leiden: Brill.

Khalidi, Tarif. 2009. *Images of Muhammad: narratives of the Prophet in Islam across the centuries.* New York: Doubleday.

Koselleck, Reinhart. 1985. *Futures past: on the semantics of historical time.* Trans. K. Tribe. Cambridge, MA: Massachusetts Institute of Technology Press.

Lecerf, J. 2010. art. D̲jiwār. In *EI2.*

Maḥallī, Jalāl al-Dīn al-, and Jalāl al-Dīn al-Suyūṭī. 2008. *Tafsīr al-Jalālayn.* Amman: Royal Aal al-Bayt Institute for Islamic Thought, http://www.altafsir.com/Al-Jalalayn.asp.

Maududi, Sayyid Abul Ala. n.d. *Towards understanding the Qur'an (Tafhim al-Qur'an).* Leicester, UK: Islamic Foundation, http://www.islamicstudies.info/tafheem.php.

Moxnes, Halvor. 2003. *Putting Jesus in his place: a radical vision of household and kingdom.* Louisville, KY: Westminster John Knox Press.

Muslim, Imam. 1993. *Sahih Muslim.* Trans. M. Matraji. 8 vols. Beirut: Dar el Fiker.

Muslim, Imam. n.d. *Sahih Muslim.* Trans. Abdul Hamid Siddiqui. http://www.usc.edu/dept/MSA/fundamentals/hadithsunnah/muslim/.

Nawawi, al-, n.d. *Ṣaḥīḥ Muslim bi-sharḥ al-Nawawī.* http://hadith.al-islam.com/Display/Display.aspDoc=l&Rec=165.

Qutb, Sayyid. n.d. *In the shade of the Qur'an.* Trans. Adil Salahi. http://www.kalamullah.com/shade-of-the-quran.html.

Ṭabarī, al-. 1955–, *Tafsīr al-Ṭabarī.* 8. Cairo: Dār al-Ma'ārif.

Ṭabarsī, Abū 'Àlī al-Faḍl ibn al-Ḥasan al-. 1959. *Majma' al-bayān fi tafsīr al-Qur'ān.* 10 vols. Beirut: Dār Iḥyā' al-Turāth al-'Arabī.

Tustarī, Sahl al-. 2009. *Tafsīr al-Tustarī.* Amman: Royal Aal al-Bayt Institute for Islamic Thought.

Watt, W. Montgomery. 2010. art. Mu'ākhāt. In *EI2.*

Wehr, Hans. 1979. *Arabic–English dictionary: the Hans Wehr dictionary of modern written Arabic,* ed. J.M. Cowan. 4th ed. Ithaca, NY: Spoken Language Services.

Williams, Rowan. 2008. *A common word for the common good,* http://www.archbishopofcanterbury.org/media/word/2/j/A_Common_Word_for_the_Common_Good.doc.

Index